P9-BZZ-583

Printing Technology

Second Edition

J. Michael Adams/David D. Faux

State University of New York at Oswego

With Contributions by
Lloyd J. Rieber

Breton Publishers
North Scituate, Massachusetts

Breton Publishers
A Division of Wadsworth, Inc.

Library of Congress Cataloging in Publication Data

Adams, J. Michael.
Printing technology.

Bibliography: p.
Includes index.
1. Printing, Practical. I. Faux, David D.
II. Rieber, Lloyd. III. Title.
Z244.A515 1982 686.2'24 81–18070
ISBN 0–534–01016–4 AACR2

Printed in the United States of America

4 5 6 7 8 9 — 86 85 84

PRINTING TECHNOLOGY, 2nd Edition was prepared for publication by the following people: Lloyd J. Rieber, special projects editor; Jacqueline Dormitzer, copy editor; Trisha Hanlon, interior text designer; Joseph Landry, cover designer. Barbara Gracia, Woodstock Publishers' Services, supervised production. The sponsoring editor was Edward L. Francis. Cover photograph courtesy of M.A.N.–Wood Industries, Inc. Reprinted by permission. Chapter opening photographs: Chapter 2 courtesy of Halliday Lithograph and Jay's Publisher's Services; Chapter 3 by Trisha Hanlon; Chapter 4 courtesy of Compugraphic Corporation; Chapters 5, 6, and 22 by Trisha Hanlon courtesy of Jay's Publisher's Services; Chapter 8 courtesy of Louis Dovner; Chapters 9, 10, 11, 12, 13, 20, and 21 by Trisha Hanlon courtesy of Halliday Lithograph; and Chapter 15 courtesy of Advance Process Supply Company. The book was set in Palatino by Modern Graphics Inc.; printing and binding was by Halliday Lithograph.

To our wives, Mignon and Jeanne,
for their continued support,
encouragement, and love.

Foreword

In a society that depends on mass communication, the techniques and printing processes of the graphic arts industry are particularly important. Michael Adams and David Faux's book is a comprehensive presentation of the technology and art of graphics communication.

The authors have designed this book to be a fine introduction to the technical information and skills necessary for a career in the graphic arts. The book describes how the industry functions from the idea to the printed page, beginning with layout techniques and including both the concepts and the skills needed to complete the various tasks. It follows the contemporary thinking in the industry concerning the overlapping functions of the major processes in the graphic arts. The content reflects the changes in the industry: emphasis on craft, skill, and mechanical process has broadened into manufacturing to include chemistry, optics, electronics, and physics. Numerous illustrations and photographs amplify the text material and clarify the various processes.

The authors have included information about the organization of the industry, its career opportunities, and its business functions.

The book is a survey of graphic arts and not an in-depth study of one narrow aspect. Workers in this industry and others seeking a career in graphic arts will find the contents helpful in acquiring expertise or initial exposure to printing technology.

I have worked closely with the authors during all stages of this book's development and highly recommend the text. It is accurate, up to date, and comprehensive. I hope each reader enjoys this book as I have.

Frederick D. Kagy
Illinois State University

Preface

With renewed exuberance we are pleased to present this second edition of *Printing Technology*. We appreciate the kind support of many high school, junior college, and university educators who have used the first edition and ensured the degree of popularity that led to this second edition. The book has been used at nearly every level of graphic arts education—in public, private, and industrial training—and has found wide national and international acceptance.

Several thoughts have occurred to us as we finish this second edition. The first is a realization of the significance of this field called printing. It is both an endeavor that spans every aspect of human existence and a tool that helps to meet almost every human need. The field is changing. It is rapidly becoming more of a technology than a craft. Advances in electronics and information processing have altered every area and presage even greater changes to come. This new edition attempts to include many of these changes but, at the same time, retains the basic language and approach that printing students have found so appealing. There are new anecdotes, new illustrations, expanded chapters, and updated information. Chapter 5, on layout and paste-up, has been expanded. Chapter 20, on paper and ink, has been restructured, and new material on ink has been added. Chapter 19, on gravure printing, has been added as a totally new chapter.

It is not possible to complete a work of this size without the assistance of many people. We would like to recognize the contributions that our families have made to the completion of a project that grew much larger than originally envisioned and took away time that they deserved. Special mention should be made of Ms. Mignon Adams for her accurate proofreading and critiquing of every single page of every draft of the manuscript, of Ms. Jeanne Faux for proofreading the early chapters, and of Mrs. Cloe Faux for her timely support.

Dr. Fred Kagy has been the principal reviewer for this work, and remains a valued colleague and friend. Without his dedicated assistance, this book would never have been possible.

In addition to the individuals mentioned in the preface to the first edition, several others need to be thanked for their more recent assistance. Bob Decker processed and printed all the new photographs. Warren Daum, vice president and executive director of the Gravure Technical Association; Steve Berg, Arcata Graphics; and William Yardley, manager, and David McFarlane, Jr., president of the Morrill Press, all assisted with the new chapter on gravure. Jim Lentz, a loyal colleague and friend, supported this author-team at the State University of New York.

Of special note are the legion efforts of Lloyd Rieber to edit and assist in the reorganization of the entire book. He is an exceptionally skilled wordwright who knows the printing field and has the ability to translate his understandings to structures that heighten student learning. It was his hand that guided the thread of continuity through all the restructuring of this work. He devoted literally hundreds of hours to checking the usability of every line and suggesting improvements. We are deeply in his debt.

For those of you who are using this edition as your first introduction to printing, we wish you well. We hope you will find the book informative, exciting, and motivating. Both of us recall our first introduction to this marvelous field of printing. Francis J. Kafka, Professor Emeritus, Millersville State University, and Frederick Kagy, Professor, Illinois State University, were our first guides. We are only two of their former students whom they influenced and assisted, both as students and as colleagues.

J. Michael Adams
David Faux

Contents

Chapter One

A Beginning

Anecdote to Chapter One

The father of printing in the Western world is generally considered to be Johann Gensfleisch zum Gutenberg, who was born in the city of Mainz, Germany, in 1397. The wealth of the Gutenberg family freed Johann for a life of leisure and pleasure, during which he developed an interest in technology—primarily seal making and goldsmithing. In 1438 he started a business of producing religious mirrors in Strasbourg. By that time he was considered a master craftsman in metalworking.

There is evidence that by 1444 he had returned to Mainz to set up a printing shop. As a goldsmith he had cut letters and symbols in precious metals or in reverse in wax to form a mold to cast jewelry. The idea of casting individual letters for printing would not be a difficult transition. He designed a hand-casting device that could hold a matrix. The matrix was a die formed in the shape of a letter. The character was first cut by hand in reverse on a piece of hard metal. The hard metal character was then punched into a soft copper mold to form a matrix.

Johann Gutenberg—The father of printing

Gutenberg next needed a suitable metal to cast in the mold. He first experimented with pewter hardened with large quantities of antimony, but the material shrank when it cooled and pulled away from the matrix. The letters formed were imperfect. His experience with lead in mirror manufacturing finally encouraged him to try a combination of lead, tin, and antimony. Gutenberg's original formula (5% tin, 12% antimony, and 83% lead) remains nearly unchanged to this day. Characters can be perfectly cast with this alloy because it expands when it cools and forms an exact duplicate of the matrix outline. Using his system, two workers could cast and dress (trim away excess material) twenty-five pieces of type an hour.

Gutenberg's most notable work, his forty-two–line Bible (a Bible with forty-two lines to the page), was begun in 1452 and completed by 1455. Each page contained around 2,800 characters. Two pages were printed at the same time, so 5,600 pieces of type were needed to make each two-page printing. It was the common practice for the next two pages to be composed during the press run, so at least 11,200 letters were needed even to begin printing. Working a normal workday (twelve hours), two craftsmen took more than thirty-seven workdays to prepare the initial type. At this rate of speed, over three years were needed to complete just 200 copies.

Much of the language of modern printing comes to us from the craft of hot type composition, developed by Johann Gutenberg and his workers more than 500 years ago. Terms such as "form," "leading," "uppercase," "lowercase," "type size," "impression," and "makeready" originated with the relief process. All printers today owe a debt to the hundreds of early craftsmen who followed Gutenberg in the tradition of hand-set type and gave us both a language and an art.

Objectives for Chapter One

After completing this chapter you will be able to:

- Recognize that the purpose of all technology is to help meet human needs.
- Recognize that people communicate using only their five senses.
- Understand that printing is a permanent, graphic, visual medium of human communication.
- Remember the cycle of the printing industry—to begin with a human need, to printing management, to production, to distribution and back to yet another human need.
- Remember and be able to define the six steps in all printing—image design, image assembly, image conversion, image carrier preparation, image transfer and finishing.

Introduction

Technology has become a common word in this society's vocabulary. Technology is often discussed as if it were some living being that had only recently burst upon the scene; yet it is as old as the first hand tool used by prehistoric people (such as in the biblical story of Sampson and the jawbone of an ass). We tend to view technology as some physical object that can be pointed to or even visited, like a tourist attraction. But technology is not a physical object or living being. It is a group of ideas created and controlled by people to meet human needs. **Technology** is any concept (or group of concepts) that extends or amplifies the ability to meet a human need.

It is easy to confuse the tools of a technology with the technology itself. For example, a potter sitting at a wheel with a mound of clay is part of a technology. The clay is the **medium** or material of the technology. The potter's wheel is a **tool** used to produce the result of the technology. But the concept of shaping or controlling the material with the tool is the technology itself.

It is difficult to neatly categorize all technologies. Some technologies, such as metal technology and wood technology, center around a material to be shaped. Others extend a human sense. We have designed elaborate tools, such as records, magnetic tapes, and stereo systems, to store or amplify sounds for our sense of hearing. The technology of transportation does not relate to a specific material or to a human sense, yet it is concerned with a very real human need. Technologies can also evolve from abstract ideas, although they are rarely labeled technologies. A good example is a written language. Pencils, pens, and typewriters are the tools of this technology, but the technology itself is based on the concept of a symbol or code that transfers sounds into visual images.

The point of this discussion is that the label "technology" can often be misleading and confusing. It is not really possible to classify and separate one technology from another. All technologies are interrelated and depend on or are a part of many others. This book is concerned with the complex technology of the reproduction of visual images that meet the human need to communicate ideas. As the title implies, there are several technologies involved with the communication of visual ideas. However, they are all interrelated and are concerned with making the human communication process as efficient as possible.

The Process of Communication

We have a tremendous potential to receive and send information. If we imagine each individual as an information sender/receiver, we can form a model of how communication takes place.

We are constantly sending and receiving bits of information, often without even being

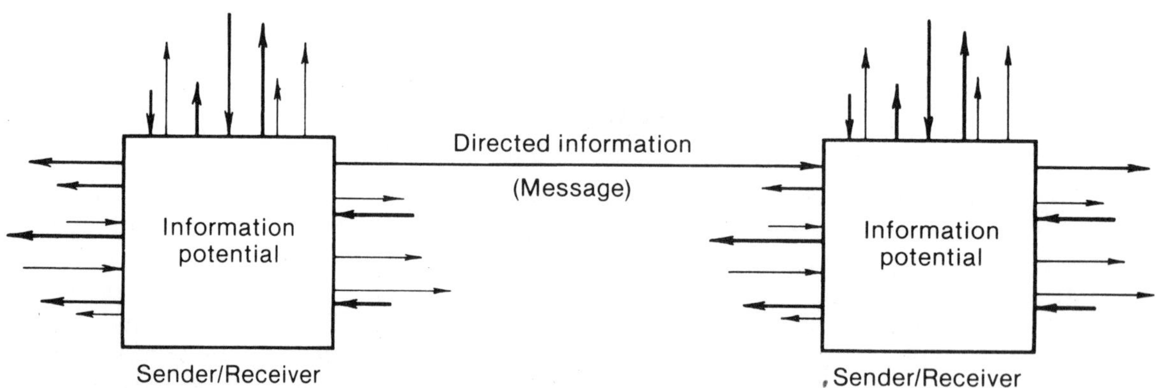

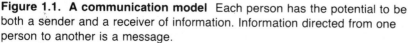

Figure 1.1. A communication model Each person has the potential to be both a sender and a receiver of information. Information directed from one person to another is a message.

conscious of the process. The way we look, act, smell, or carry a book sends information about us to other individuals. How others look, act, smell, or carry a book sends information about them to us. We also receive data from objects—the stove is hot, the floor is dirty, the steak needs salt—without conscious effort.

When we consciously select a bit of information from our information storehouse and direct it to some other individual, it becomes a message (figure 1.1). The primary concern of this book is the efficiency of sending a special form of directed message: a printed message. First let's consider how we might direct a message outward from ourselves.

Channels of Human Communication

The boss picks up a telephone and says, "Watson, come here, I want you"; a composer plays a song for a loved one; we thunderously applaud a skillful theatrical performance. All these actions are designed to communicate a particular idea through communication that can be heard. For centuries ideas and traditions have been carried by "word of mouth." Until recently, this method was considered the only efficient way to send a message.

You are receiving a message through your eyes as you read these lines. An actor might wear a costume, walk with a limp, or gesture in some way to communicate visually an idea about the role he is playing. The visual channel of communication is a busy one and is not limited to the printed word. It has been estimated that each individual sends and receives thousands of different visual messages every day. Printing technology, the concern of this book, is one of the media of the visual channel of communication.

Our mass marketing system has coaxed us to buy perfumes, deodorants, mouth washes, aftershave lotions, toothpaste, and scented hair spray—all designed to help us send a pleasing message to someone else's nose. Our sense of smell is not as powerful as that of some other animals, but we do receive important messages—such as "something is burning," "that steak smells good," or "that must have been a skunk"—through that channel.

Eskimoes rub noses, grandparents hug, and business executives close contracts with a firm handshake. People can pat, scratch, rub, swing a fist, or embrace to communicate a message. The sense of touch can be a very specific information carrier.

Taste is a subtle sense for humans. We do not often send taste messages, although Aunt Mabel might send Christmas greetings with a delicious fruitcake. Taste is more often used as a receiving channel or to judge food likes and dislikes. Given two piles of finely ground white powders—one salt, the other sugar—taste is the most efficient method of telling which is which.

Sight, sound, smell, taste, and touch are the five channels that we use to send and receive messages. If people worked as efficiently as diagrams in communicating messages, the communication process would be no problem. In reality we don't operate that way, and there are problems.

Some Problems of Human Communication

Human communication does not take place in a vacuum. It occurs in an environment, or setting, filled with "noise" that can distort

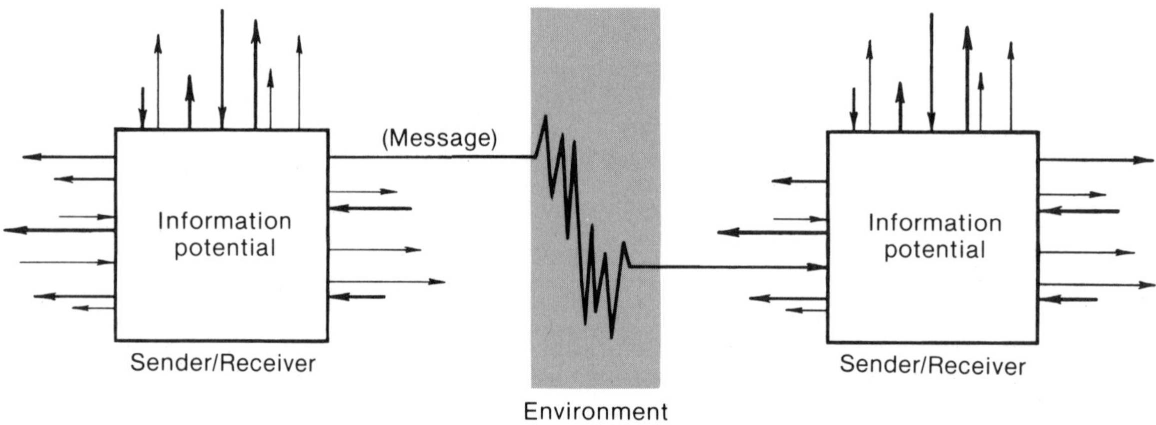

Figure 1.2. A communication model with a distorted message

and affect the meaning of a message (figure 1.2). For example, it is extremely difficult for humans to taste underwater. Our sense of smell cannot distinguish between more than three different smells in a row. It is almost impossible to find a needle in a haystack. We cannot see in the dark. The sound of a diesel engine interferes with conversation. The environment can be physical or emotional, but in either form it can interfere with our sending or receiving a message.

There are some basic problems with communication channels themselves. Bees dance, and so do humans. But bees can give out more information in a single motion than we could possibly do in an hour of frenzied pantomime. We cannot communicate a complex mathematical notion by smell, and we cannot taste an abstract idea. Some messages are simply better sent by one channel than another.

As senders and receivers of messages, we also have many built-in problems. We all have different experiences and therefore possess different bits of information—the message I send might not be the message you receive. If I say "PI," depending on your past experience your mouth might water at the thought of a plate of hot apple pie, you might ponder the true value of the mathematical pi (3.141592+), or if you are a printer you might realize that pi is a pile of foundry type of different sizes, series, and styles. If we have had similar experiences, you can intelligently make a decision to accept or reject my offer of some "PI."

There are also biological sender/receiver problems that can interfere with a message. Blindness blocks visual messages; deafness blocks verbal information; and any degree short of total blindness or total deafness can interfere with receiving the correct message.

It is the sender's responsibility to make sure that the message arrives intact to the receiver. As senders, we are always considering the efficiency of the channel, the environment, and the limitations of the sender/receiver; but we are seldom aware of such concerns.

Visual Communication

Media of Visual Communication

We have very briefly examined the basic channels and problems of human communication. The purpose of this discussion is somehow to classify visual communication so that we can begin to work with it. One view is that visual communication has two purposes: to send visual messages to our contemporaries (those living at the same time we are) and to send or store visual messages for our descendants (those not yet born). These can serve as a classification for all visual media: a medium is either temporary or permanent in format.

Temporary Visual Media. Human body movement is a temporary visual medium. Human actions communicate messages to living human beings. We can wave a greeting, smile with pleasure, move our head to mean "yes" or "no," or weep with sorrow. The subtleties of human motion have even evolved into art forms (dance and the theater). Lack of motion can also communicate an idea such as sorrow, solitude, illness, or death. Messages are sent between ships at sea by blinking lights. Using a special code, soldiers and boy scouts wave flags to send messages. Stop lights signal us to pass or yield. All these are temporary visual messages.

Human movement is not a technology, but the concepts behind blinking lights, waving flags, and stop signals are. The device called television is the result of an idea: television amplifies and extends the visual sense and is therefore a technology. Its purpose is to transmit auditory and visual information to our contemporaries, so it is a medium of temporary visual communication.

Permanent Visual Media. Closely linked with the idea of television is the storage of images on videotape. Early television programs were recorded by a method called "kinescope," but the images were of such poor quality that many are lost and will never be viewed again. Because videotape can store quality visual images that our descendants will be able to receive, it is a medium of permanent visual communication. Movies, photography, and printing are all permanent visual media that can carry messages to our descendants long after our death.

Societies and their languages have evolved and vanished during human history. Even though we cannot reproduce the sounds of lost languages, we can understand our forebears' ideas because they stored visual information in symbol systems that we can read.

Graphic Media. Temporary and permanent visual images can be further subdivided into graphic and nongraphic. **Graphic images** are images formed from lines. The lines might be constructed by an artist working at a drawing table or by a stonecutter chiseling words into granite. The lines may be so large that one line may cover an entire page or so small that you need a magnifying glass to see them. All major printing processes work only with lines. Photography is classified as a graphic medium. Blinking lights, waving flags, and human motion are all nongraphic images.

Development of Graphic Symbols

Graphic visual messages are possible because lines can be made that have meanings to humans. We see lines every day and think nothing of it. We are so bombarded by lines, from words on a subway wall to drawings in books, that we rarely realize their significance.

As early as 35,000 BC people were drawing messages on cave walls (figure 1.3). These were probably intended to be temporary messages, but they became permanent. They were simple drawings—merely lines—but they carried meaning to the people of that period: "This is a mammoth," "Oh, what a feast we had," or "We hunted a great hairy beast."

Development of Pictographs. Drawings that carry meaning by attempting to look like real objects are called **pictographs** (figure 1.4a). Pictographs have a one-to-one relationship with reality. To symbolize one ox (called *aleph*), draw one symbol. To represent five oxen, draw five symbols. It is difficult to use pictographs to communicate complex ideas, such as "I have six oxen—one brown, four white, and one white and brown. All have four legs, except one that was born with five." It is impossible to symbolize abstract ideas, such as love or hate, with a pictographic system.

About 1200 BC, in a small country called Phoenicia (now a part of Syria), a group of traders began to realize the limitations of the pictographic system. They attempted to simplify the picture notations in their account books by streamlining their symbols. But however they drew the lines, *aleph* still symbolized one ox and *beth* still stood for one house (figure 1.4b). The system was too cumbersome.

Development of Ideographs. The next step was to have drawings symbolize ideas. These drawings are called **ideographs.** With this system *aleph* became the symbol for food and *beth* represented a dwelling or shelter (figure

Figure 1.3. An early message Pictured is a cave drawing (message) made by prehistoric people in the Altamira caves in Spain.
Courtesy of Spanish National Tourist Office, New York.

1.4c). **Ideographs** are simple drawings that symbolize ideas or concepts rather than concrete objects. They are a vast improvement over pictographs because complex or abstract ideas can be easily represented, but ideographs are still clumsy. The sheer number of symbols can be overwhelming. The Japanese and Chinese both still use ideographic symbol systems that contain over ten thousand different characters. It could take a lifetime to understand such a system.

Development of Phonetic Symbols. By 900 BC the Phoenicians had made another change. Instead of symbolizing the actual ox or food, the picture came to represent a sound. Whenever the readers saw the symbol, they could make the sound. When the symbols were placed together, words could be repeated. This idea of representing sounds by symbols is known to us as a **phonetic symbol system** and is the basis for most modern written languages. The Phoenicians developed nineteen such symbols, but they were traders and were not concerned with recording all words used in everyday conversation. We form verbal symbols by combining consonants and vowels. The Phoenician system contained no vowels and was of little use in recording everyday speech.

By 403 BC the Greeks had officially adopted the Phoenician system, after adding five vowels and changing the names of the letters (figure 1.5). *Aleph* became *alpha* and *beth* became *beta,* which form our term *alphabet.*

About a hundred years later, the early Roman empire borrowed the Greek alphabet and refined it to meet their needs. They accepted thirteen letters outright, revised eight, and added *F* and *Q,* which gave them twenty-three—all that was necessary to write Latin. The Roman system stood firm for nearly

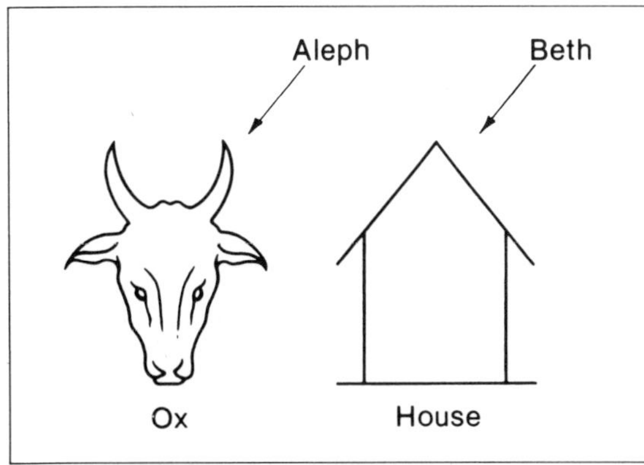

(a)

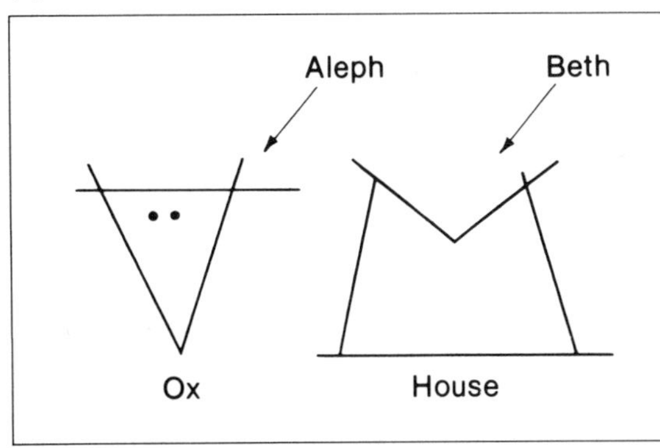

(b)

Aleph
Beth
Food
Shelter

(c)

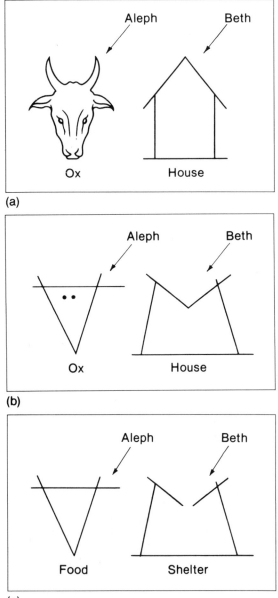

Figure 1.4. The development of ideographs
Pictographs shown here in (a) and (b) were drawn to represent real objects. They were gradually simplified to represent general ideas and became known as ideographs (c).

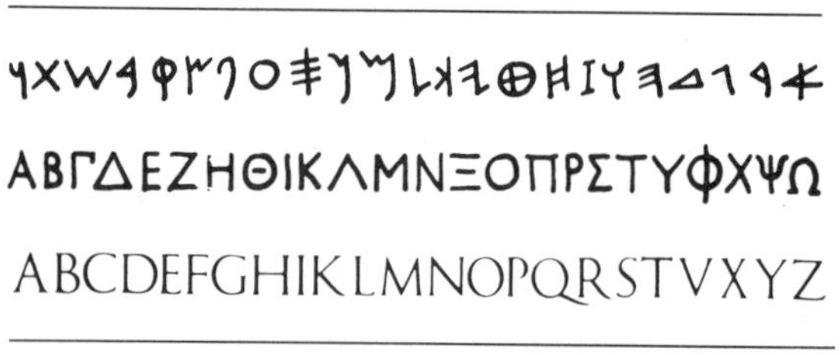

ΑΒΓΔΕΖΗΘΙΚΛΜΝΞΟΠΡΣΤΥΦΧΨΩ

ABCDEFGHIKLMNOPQRSTVXYZ

Figure 1.5. The development of our alphabet Illustrated from top to bottom are the Phoenician alphabet (900 BC), the Greek alphabet (403 BC), and the Roman alphabet (300 BC).

twelve centuries. About one thousand years ago the letter *U* was added as a rounded *V*, and two *V*s were put together to form *W*. Five hundred years later the letter *J* was added to give us a total of twenty-six letters that form our contemporary Latin alphabet.

There were still some problems to be worked out. Early Greek and Roman writing was done by scribes—all with different "penmanship." Some wrote from left to right, some from right to left. Combine these differences with the lack of punctuation marks or spaces between words or sentences, and the whole thing could be quite a mess.

It wasn't until movable metal type was introduced in the mid-fifteenth century that any true standard of punctuation or sentence structure was achieved. It took the printing arts to stabilize the phonetic symbol system as we know it today. Slight changes have been made—we have dropped the long *s* from our type cases—but the basic composition of our alphabet has remained the same from the time of Gutenberg.

Printing Technology

Printing Processes

All printing processes reproduce lines, either lines that form drawings or lines that form phonetic symbols or letters. **Printing** is a permanent, graphic, visual communication medium. It includes all the ideas, methods, and devices used to manipulate or reproduce graphic visual messages. Although most people generally think of printing as ink on paper, printing is not limited to any particular materials or inks. The embossing process uses no ink at all; and all shapes and sizes of metals, wood, and plastics are common receivers of printed messages.

Printers use the following four main techniques, called **printing processes,** to reproduce graphic images:

- Relief printing,
- Intaglio printing,
- Screen printing,
- Lithographic printing.

The **relief printing** process is also referred to by other terms, such as hot type, foundry type, flexography, hand-set type, and letterpress printing, to name a few. Whatever the label, the process describes all methods of transferring an image from a raised surface (figure 1.6a, p. 12).

Intaglio printing is the reverse of the relief concept. An **intaglio** image is transferred from a sunken surface (figure 1.6b). The term "intaglio" refers to such subprocesses as etching, engraving, gravure, and collotype.

Screen printing transfers an image by allowing ink to pass through an opening or stencil (figure 1.6c). The screen process is sometimes called silk screen printing, mitography, or serigraphy.

Lithography as it is known today is a relatively new process, dating from around 1798. A lithographic image is transferred from a flat surface by using chemistry. Certain areas on the surface are chemically treated to accept ink, and other areas are left untreated so they will repel ink. When a material such as paper contacts the flat surface, the chemically treated (ink receptive) areas transfer an image to the paper (figure 1.6d). This process is sometimes called planography, offset lithography, offset, or photo offset lithography.

Although there are several older processes (such as collography, which prints from a fragile gelatin emulsion), and also new processes (such as electrostatic printing, which forms images by electromagnetic projection), the four major printing processes still form the main structure of the printing industry.

Printing is a technology; it expands and satisfies the human need to communicate. The printed material can be temporary, such as newspapers, magazines, advertisements, or packaging materials. These materials are intended to be consumed and then never used as a communication tool again. Or the printed material can be permanent, such as books, metal plaques sent to distant planets, or microfilm. But when compared to the fleeting images on a cathode ray tube or to blinking lights between ships at sea, printing must be classified as a permanent visual medium.

The tools of printing technology can also be used for other technologies. Photo-fabrication is a growing segment of the metal-working industry. Printed circuits are used to control many mechanical devices. Photography is used extensively in nearly all types of research.

Printing technology has long been a powerful tool for social change. Edward George Bulwer-Lytton wrote, "The pen is mightier than the sword." But his statement assumes the distribution of the ideas that the pen recorded. Without printing, few would read the ideas, and the pen would become a rather weak weapon.

Printers have long been the most influential individuals in the community. Early colonial printers helped to shape our country by reproducing, recording, and distributing the ideas and events of the period. Benjamin Franklin, himself an early American patriot, was proudest of his role as a printer. After being active in the Revolution, a signer of the Declaration of Independence, a member of the First and Second Continental Congresses, founder of the first American library, an author, an inventor, a publisher, and ambassador to France, he made sure his epitaph read "B. Franklin, Printer."

Printing Cycle

Since the time of Franklin, the basic cycle of the printing industry has not changed much from the following procedures:

1. Identifying a need,
2. Creating an image design,
3. Reproducing the image design,
4. Distributing the printed message.

The contemporary industry begins the printing cycle with an identified need. The need might be as simple as the reproduction of a form or as sophisticated as a poster intended to change human attitudes about pollution. It could be as ordinary as a package designed to convince a consumer to buy one brand of cereal rather than another. Whatever the need, however, the idea, the intended receiver, the environment, and all other communication problems are considered, and a graphic image design evolves. Special agencies are often set up whose sole purpose is to sell ideas and coordinate the design between the printing management and the printing customer.

The function of printing management is to be responsible for reproducing the image design. The most efficient printing process (relief, intaglio, screen, or lithography) must

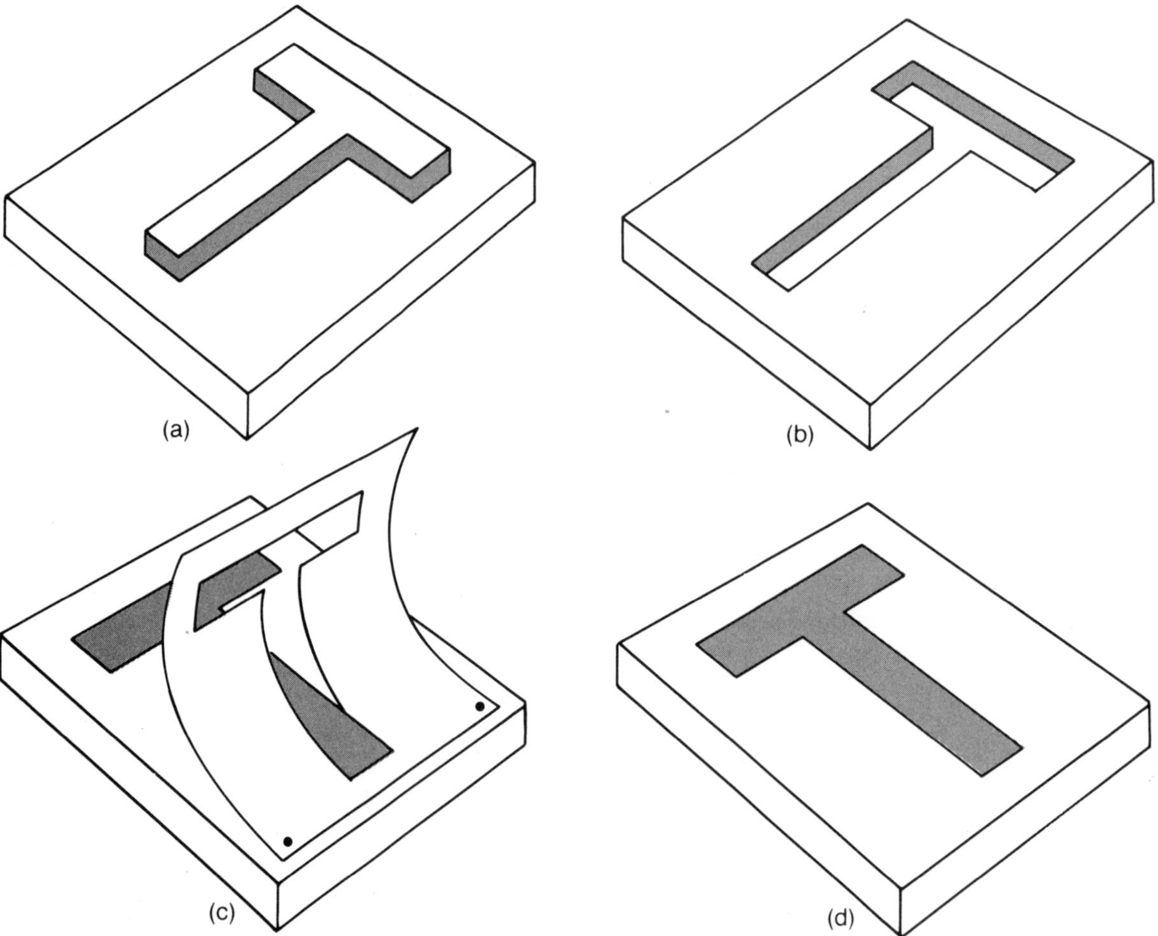

Figure 1.6. Four main printing processes Relief printing transfers an image from a raised surface (a). Intaglio printing transfers an image from a sunken surface (b). Screen printing transfers an image through a stencil (c). Lithographic printing transfers an image chemically from a flat surface (d).

be identified. Such variables as the type of material to be used, length of run, number and types of colors, time requirements, desired quality, and customer's cost limitations must all be considered. An estimate must be made for each job. A profit must be made, and yet the estimate must be low enough to attract work in a very competitive market. If the customer approves the estimate, management must schedule the job, arrange for all materials, ensure quality control, and keep track of all phases of production so the job is finished on schedule.

The production phase of the cycle is often the only phase the customer, consumer, and printing student ever see. A large part of this book is concerned with production procedures, but it must be realized that the production process is only one part of the cycle.

The final test of the cycle is the method of distributing the printed message. Without an audience for the graphic images created by the artist and printer, the whole cycle is useless. The distribution system of printed materials is so complex and diverse that it cannot be classified. Printing is mailed; handed out on busy streets; sold by newsboys on street corners; and shipped to department stores, corner drugstores, and local newsstands. It is passed out in highway tollbooths, filed in offices, pasted on billboards, carried on placards, or even thumbtacked to poster boards. The purpose of all this activity is to place printed matter into the hands of consumers. When consumers receive the messages, the ideas represented are either accepted or rejected, new needs are generated, and the cycle begins again.

Organization of Printing Processes

The printing industry has long consisted of shops identified with a particular process, such as relief or lithography. Craftsmen were trained and then bound by union or guild structure to that particular process. Printing educators have recently suggested a new view of printing education. There is a sequence of steps, they say, that all printers follow, regardless of the method of reproduction. This sequence consists of the following:

- Image design,
- Image assembly,
- Image conversion,
- Image carrier preparation,
- Image transfer.

The image is designed to meet a need. Thumbnail sketches (rough layouts) and final layouts are made, and variables such as type style, visual position, type size, balance, and harmony are all considered—independent of any particular process. This is the **image design** step.

After the customer approves the design, the image must be assembled into a final form. Whether the printing technique selected uses individual pieces of hand-set type or images generated by a computer, the image design is always carefully followed during **image assembly,** and there is the same concern for quality.

All printing processes now rely to some degree on photography. Images are often converted to transparent film and then photographically recorded on an image carrier during the **image conversion** and **image carrier preparation** steps. The carriers—that is, relief, intaglio, screen, or lithographic—may operate differently, but all must be prepared with the same general considerations.

The image must be transferred to the receiver material. Printing presses for each of the four processes are used during the **image transfer** step. The last step is to combine the printed material into a final finished form so that it can be delivered to the customer.

This book is designed to reflect a technology. The three printing processes of relief, screen, and lithography are examined in detail. The intaglio process is only briefly discussed because the complexity of carrier preparation and image transfer for intaglio printing are beyond the scope of this work.

For years printing educators have realized that the printing industry is much larger than any particular printing process. The printing industry reflects a technology. A technology cannot be learned by examining tools or materials. A technology is mastered by understanding the concepts.

Key Terms

technology
graphic
printing processes
relief
intaglio
screen printing
lithography
image design
image assembly
image conversion
image carrier preparation
image transfer

Questions for Review

1. What are the five channels that human beings use to communicate with each other?
2. What is the difference between a permanent visual medium and a temporary visual medium?
3. What is a pictograph?
4. What is an ideograph?
5. What is a phonetic symbol?
6. What are the four main printing processes?
7. What is the sequence of steps that all printers follow regardless of the printing process they are using?

Chapter Two

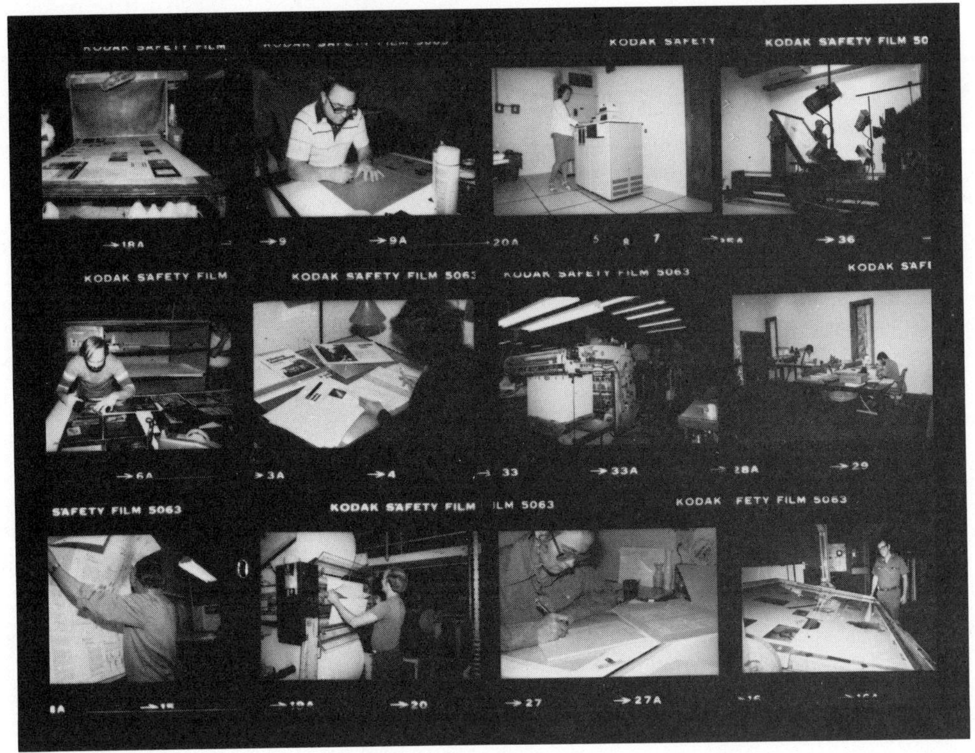

Careers in the Printing Industry

Anecdote to Chapter Two

Benjamin Franklin is famous for many reasons. He invented the Franklin stove, bifocal glasses, the lightning rod, and even swim fins. He founded the first public library in America, the first volunteer fire department, the first street-cleaning department, and the University of Pennsylvania. Ben was also the postmaster for all the colonies, signer of both the Declaration of Independence and the U.S. Constitution, and ambassador to France. Of all his accomplishments, he was proudest of his occupation of printer.

Ben began his apprenticeship at the age of twelve in his older brother's print shop. By the time he was twenty-two, he owned his own business and was publishing the popular newspaper *Pennsylvania Gazette.* Franklin often used the press to communicate his sometimes revolutionary ideas. He drew and published the first American newspaper cartoon in the *Gazette* in 1754. The cartoon showed a snake cut into pieces; each piece represented a separate colony. The point was that our country was in pieces and we needed to unite.

Franklin's Political Cartoon

One of Franklin's most famous publications was *Poor Richard's Almanac.* In Ben's time most families owned only two books: the Bible and an almanac. *Poor Richard's* contained the usual information that an almanac should have, such as predictions about the weather, lists of holidays, charts showing the cycles of the moon, and even instructions on what days to plant crops. Franklin, however, made *Poor Richard's* famous by writing clever sayings that were intended to guide people on how to live. Many of these American proverbs, written by a printer, are still in use today—for example:

- Beware of little expenses; a small leak will sink a great ship.

- If you want to know the value of money, go and try to borrow some.

- Early to bed and early to rise makes a man healthy, wealthy, and wise.

- Lost time is never found again.

Objectives for Chapter Two

After completing this chapter you will be able to:

- Recognize the importance of printing technology in everyone's daily life.
- Understand the structure and purpose of each level of typical printing companies.
- Remember and be able to describe the kinds of services provided by the printing industry—commercial printing, special-purpose printing, quick printing, in-plant printing, publishing, package printing, trade shops and related industries.
- Understand the different ways to enter, train, and advance in the graphic arts industry.

Introduction

Printing is a mammoth industry. The printer's skills often extend into other industries and lose their identity. This can be frustrating to an individual trying to make a career decision. It is sometimes difficult for students to see the tremendous number of job possibilities that emerge as a result of studying printing. It will be valuable to examine some broad areas that give an overview of the industry. This will help the reader gain an appreciation of the number of potential jobs that use these skills. The following three broad areas can be examined to help give a broad overview of the industry:

- The industrial structure,
- Organization of printing services,
- The industry and career development.

The Industrial Structure

Economic Importance

Economists use several measures to gauge the importance of an industry in a society's economy. The "gross national product" (GNP) is a figure that represents the overall annual flow of goods and services in an economy. In the United States, the printing industry is ranked among the top ten contributors to this country's GNP. "Value added" is a measure of the difference between the cost of raw materials and the final market price of a product.

The higher the value-added figure, the more valuable the skills that went into the manufacturing of the product. Again printing ranks among the top ten. In addition, the graphic arts industry is among the top five U.S. industries in terms of the number of individual shops, and among the top ten when the number of people employed is counted.

Size of Companies

The printing industry is dominated by small-to-medium-sized companies that employ one to twenty-five people. The Kodak *Graphic Arts Industry Manpower Study* conducted in 1971 and 1972 found that almost half the nation's printing companies were made up of one to nine workers. The other half was fairly evenly divided between businesses with ten to twenty-five employees and those with more than twenty-five. There are "giants" in the industry that employ many hundreds of workers, but they account for a very small proportion (perhaps as small as 5%) of all the companies involved with the printing trade.

Structure of Companies

The structure of any individual printing company depends on many things, such as size, location, physical facilities, type of product, financing method (corporation, partnership, etc.), or management style. In fact, it is probably safe to assume that no two printing organizations are structured exactly alike. Figure 2.1 shows a possible structure for a small-to-medium-sized company made up of ten to twenty-five employees. In smaller organizations one individual might serve several functions. In larger concerns many workers might be assigned one area.

Board of Directors. The board of directors represents the financial control of the company. The board might be the actual owners or it might be an elected body, as in the case of large corporations. In either case, the board defines the scope and purpose of the company and deals with the problems such as arranging for financing in the case of expansion. The president is generally a member of the board of directors and acts as the board's representative to carry out its policies.

Management. The president delegates top-level management of day-to-day operation to the general manager. The office manager directs such important tasks as correspondence, record keeping, accounting, payroll, and customer billing. The sales manager directs the most important part of the company; without something to print, the rest of the organization stands idle. Sales representatives make contacts with customers who require printing and with skilled estimators who calculate costs. The production manager is responsible for directing the materials, printers, and equipment so that a fine-quality printing job will be produced.

Production. The production phase is generally divided into two categories:

- Production planning,
- Manufacturing.

One aspect of planning production control is scheduling work efficiently within the limitations of time, equipment, and human skills. People in charge of purchasing, inventory control, and receiving and storage are responsible for the advance ordering of all supplies. Accurate material handling ensures that supplies are delivered to the correct station (camera, press, etc.) as needed and that the

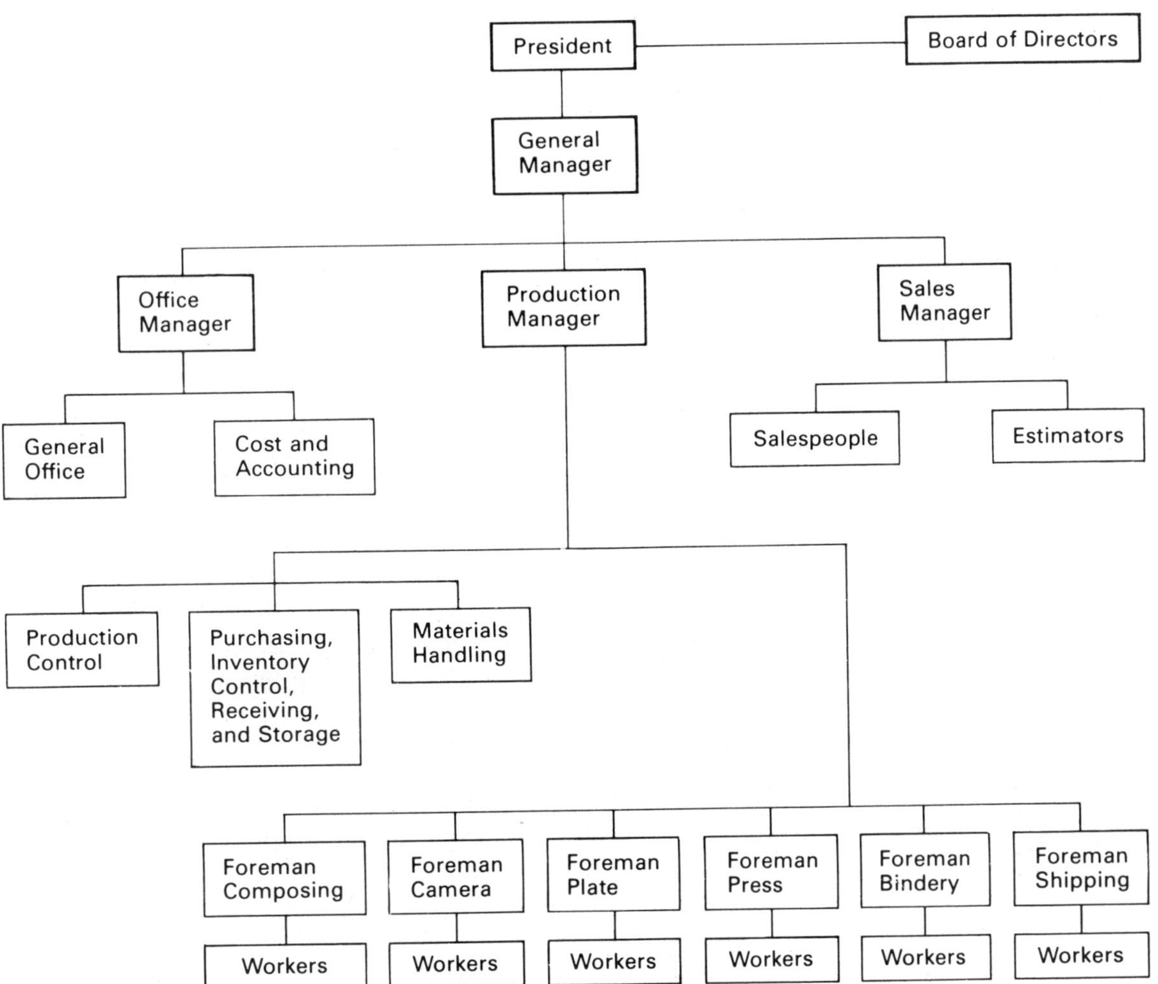

Figure 2.1. Typical organizational structure of a small-to-medium-sized (ten to twenty-five employees) printing company

finished product is removed from the last station. Production stations of composition, camera, plate making, press, bindery, and shipping must be directed by skilled supervisors who work to meet the schedules set up by production control. The actual production must be carried out by individuals who are highly skilled in the printing trades.

Although a worker's skill is not directly related to any form of organization or managerial control, it is important that employees understand the basic structure of the industry. The efficiency of the organization directly influences continued employment. Many managerial positions in the printing industry are filled by individuals who have moved up the ranks from the trade level.

Organization of Printing Services

There are several ways to categorize individual printing companies and their services. One way, as discussed in chapter 1, is to classify them by the four major printing processes: relief, intaglio, screen printing, and lithography. Although this view of the industry is not the most accurate one, it does reflect a traditional view of how printing shops are organized.

A more accurate reflection of contemporary industrial organization is to categorize printing businesses according to the kinds of services they provide. With this view in mind, we can categorize all printing services in the following way:

- Commercial,
- Special purpose,
- Quick service,
- In-plant,
- Publishing,
- Packaging,
- Trade shops,
- Related industries.

Commercial Printing

The term **commercial printing** refers to a shop that is willing to take on nearly any sort of printing job. Commercial printers are usually not bothered by sheet size, number of ink colors, length of run, or even binding requirements. Typical products produced in the same shop might include small business cards, letterhead stationery, posters, and even large four-color glossy advertising sheets to be mailed.

Special Purpose Printing

Special purpose printing is defined by the limited number of jobs performed by each company. One company might decide to print only labels. It would purchase special equipment and accept orders for only one type of product. However, the company would make labels to any size, shape, number of colors, length of run, or purpose. Another printer might want to specialize in business forms, such as order forms, estimate blanks, filing sheets, school note paper, or duplicate sales slips. Forms printing is an important area of the industry in terms of size and yearly sales. Yet another example of special purpose printing is called "legal" printing. It is concerned with reproducing such pieces as insurance policies, property titles, and loan contracts. Legal printing is an expensive process because it requires accurate proofreading for a perfect product.

Quick Printing

A rather recent but fast-growing category of printing services is called **quick printing.** Quick printing is defined by rapid service, small organizational size, and the limited format of the printed product. Most quick print companies have only one to five employees and are community-based concerns that serve a limited geographic region. Most quick printers offer "while you wait" service. The key to quick printing is in the production organization. Almost all quick printers use the lithographic process, set their presses for a standard sheet size, and are equipped with some form of automatic direct image platemaking system. Equipment manufacturers are currently marketing "systems" with a platemaker "in line" with a press, collator, and binder. With the systems approach the customer can enter the plant with original copy (such as a typed form or a line drawing) and in a matter of minutes leave with any number of medium-quality, standard size reproductions (figure 2.2).

In-plant Printing

Probably the largest service area in the printing industry today is **in-plant printing.** It is defined as any printing operation that is owned by and serves the needs of a single company or corporation. A business might manufacture a variety of products that must each be packaged with an instruction sheet. The management might decide that it is more convenient to set up their own shop to print the instruction sheets themselves than to send the job to a commercial printer. The company would then also be able to produce in-house forms, such as letterhead stationery or time cards.

Publishing

Another category of printing services that we use nearly every day is **publishing.** Within this group are the thousands of companies that serve local needs by producing a daily or weekly newspaper and the even larger group that produces periodicals, such as *Time* and *Newsweek,* that sell to a national market. Consider also the group of businesses that produce and market books. The publisher of this book is a private company that produces textbooks. It is important to understand that printers don't usually make decisions to publish a book or magazine. Printers are rarely the publisher. Publishers, however, require the skills of the printer to manufacture their products.

Package Printing

Hundreds of different containers we use every day are produced by **package printing.** The idea of impact buying (buying a product on the visual appeal of the package) has skyrocketed the demand for high-quality multicolor packages that attract the consumer's attention. Package printers decorate and form hundreds of millions of folded paperboard boxes, flexible packaging, and corrugated boxes each year. Packaging, however, is not restricted to paper containers. Think of all the steel and aluminum soft drink and beer containers sold every day. These packages are produced by a special process called "metal decorating." Millions of printed plastic bags are used every day in grocery stores and companies that distribute or package food. Thin plastic is printed by a process called flexography.

Trade Shops

Some shops provide services only to other printers. These are called **trade shops.** Not all commercial, special function, in-plant, publishing, or packaging companies can afford to own and operate all the equipment necessary to meet their total production requirements. For example, some printers may find it far more economical to contract with another company to produce all their composition needs. Another company might decide not to buy bindery equipment because only a small percentage of their work requires folding, collating, or binding. When they receive a contract that requires binding, they send it to a trade shop that specializes in this function.

Related Industries

The last category of services in the printing industry is called **related industries.** The raw materials of the printer are such things as ink, paper, plates, chemicals, and many other supplies. Printers also use special purpose equipment, such as presses, paper cutters, platemakers, cameras, and light tables, to produce their product. Companies that provide services to printers by either producing or providing these supplies and equipment are called related industries. Other businesses, such as consulting firms and advertising agencies that prepare designs for reproduction, might also perform a service, but they do not make a physical product.

Viewing the printing industry as made up of commercial, special purpose, quick service, in-plant, publishing, package printing, trade shops, and related industries is only one way to look at a broad industry. The industry does not stand alone; it is carried by people. There is a need for skilled people power. The way in which these individuals are trained and advanced is discussed in the next section.

Figure 2.2. Quick print production equipment Quick print production is usually done with a "systems" approach and with equipment that automates much of the time-consuming labor.
Courtesy of Multigraphics Division, Addressograph-Multigraph Corporation.

Entering a Career in the Graphic Arts Industry

There are no fixed paths to entering the printing industry, but a few general observations can be made.

Entering Upper-Level Graphic Arts Management

Managerial levels—specifically upper-level positions (see figure 2.1)—usually, but not always, require a bachelor's degree. There are several schools that offer degrees with an extensive specialization in printing technology. Two examples are Rochester Institute of Technology (RIT) in Rochester, New York, and Illinois State University in Normal, Illinois. Printing specialization, however, is not an absolute requirement. Individuals with experience in such areas as art, journalism, engineering, chemistry, physics, research, data processing and computers, sales, marketing, and management are also employed in printing companies.

Entering Lower-Level Graphic Arts Management

Lower-level management, such as section foremen or production control people, and skilled crafts people enter the industry by a variety of routes. There are trade high schools, such as the New York School of Printing, designed to provide high school graduates with skills necessary for direct entrance into the industry. Other secondary school programs offer short vocational or industrial arts classes combined with a cooperative work experience (where the student spends part of a day in a local printing company and part of the day in school). There are also technical printing programs offered in two-year community colleges that lead to an associate degree.

Craft-Level Entry

Two ideas influence craft-level entrance into the industry. They are called closed and open shops. A closed shop requires union membership for a craftsperson to keep his or her job. An open shop does not have such a requirement. In an open shop, individuals can belong to a union, but they don't have to in order to keep their job.

Union Membership. There are several craft unions in the United States that represent the printing trades. Some are narrow and reflect only one specific type of skill, such as press operators. Others are very broad and extend across many craft lines. There is an increasing movement to join all these organizations into a single unit, such as the AFL-CIO, which combines both specific skill unions like the American Federation of Labor with broad-based unions like the Congress of Industrial Organizations. One advantage of union membership is a national negotiating power for wages and benefits. In closed shops trainees enter the industry through on-the-job training and a structured apprenticeship program.

Nonunion Organizations. Even though nonunion open shop workers are not represented in national-level collective bargaining, there are organizations that provide services such as retirement benefits and health insurance to nonunion printers. The advantage of open shop work is that the wage level is not necessarily linked to time on the job. Open shops emphasize previous skills and on-the-job training. There is a national nonunion certification called the Master Craftsman Program, coordinated through the Printing Industries of America (PIA).

Career Advancement

Advancement in the printing industry is based on performance. The most skillful managers and workers gradually assume more responsibility through practice and additional training. A great many organizations provide continuing updating and training to the printing professions. Two examples are the Graphic Arts Technical Foundation (GATF) in Pittsburgh, Pennsylvania, and the Education and Technical Center of the Graphic Arts in Rochester, New York (associated with RIT).

The Graphic Arts Technical Foundation is a nonprofit organization designed to meet the research, technical and educational needs of its members. It is supported by printers, suppliers, manufacturers, graphic arts educators and students. GATF is involved in solving industrial problems, conducting applied research, publishing the results of its work in the form of books and audio visual aids, and conducting workshops.

Many other types of printing organization serve both professional and social needs. There are several management organizations, a number of fellowship groups, and even student clubs. The printing industry is made up of a vast group of people all devoted to the goal of fulfilling the graphic communication needs of a technical world.

Key Terms

commercial printing
special purpose printing
quick printing
in-plant printing
publishing
package printing
trade shops
related industries
closed shop
open shop

Questions for Review

1. What is the purpose of the board of directors of a printing company?
2. What is the task of the production manager in a printing company?
3. What is one job of the production planning department in a printing company?
4. What kind of printing services do trade shops provide for the printing industry?
5. What is the difference between a closed shop and an open shop in the printing industry?

Chapter Three

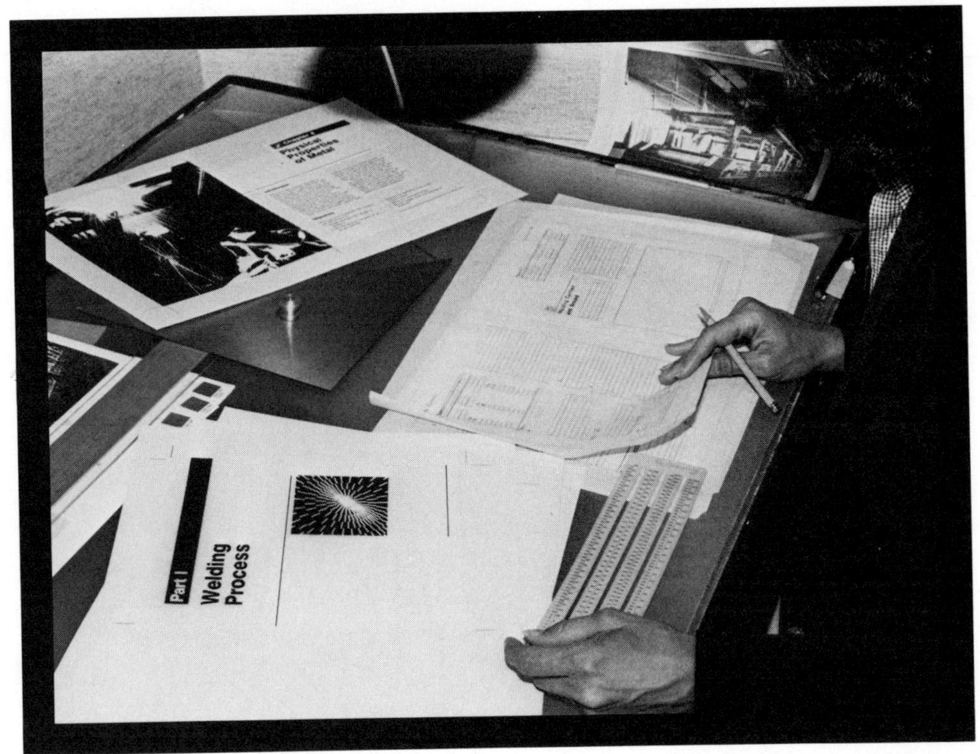

Designing for Printing Production

Anecdote to Chapter Three

On March 9, 1972, an unmanned U.S. rocket—*Pioneer 10*—began a two-year, half-billion-mile journey to the planet Jupiter and beyond. It was our first effort to leave this solar system. Along for the ride were a robot and a six-by-nine-inch gold-plated aluminum plaque attached to the rocket's antenna supports. The plaque carried a message for any extraterrestrial creatures that might encounter it. The message explained the robot's purpose and who its builders were.

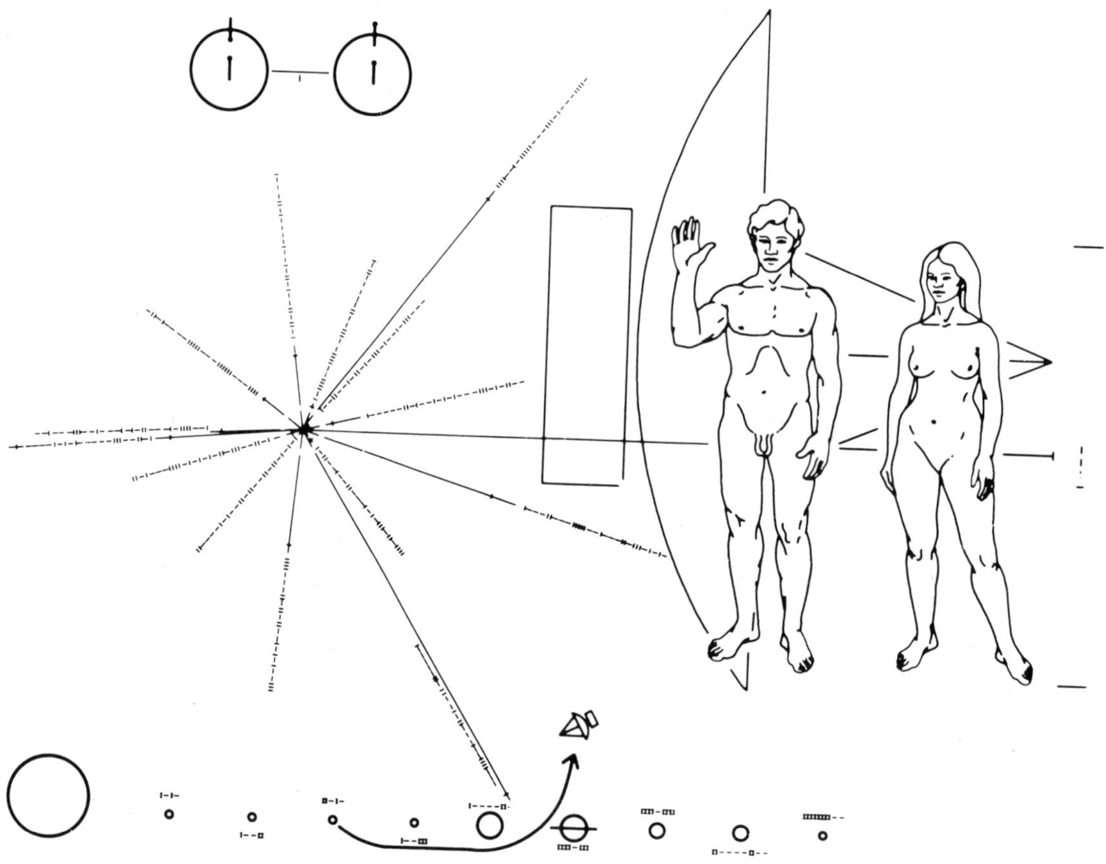

Graphic message carried on Pioneer 10.
Courtesy of NASA.

Once the decision had been made to send a message with the rocket, the problem was what to say and how to say it. If there were other creatures like us in the universe, what language would they speak—English, Russian, French? What experiences could we share with creatures that were not from Earth?

The solution was to use lines to draw the basic shape of a man and a woman standing in front of a scale outline of *Pioneer 10.* That could communicate what sort of animal we are and show our size. A code was then devised that used the wavelength of radiation given off by a hydrogen atom (the most common element in the universe). The code described where the rocket came from and how far our sun is from the center of the galaxy.

Traveling at a speed of seven miles a second, it should take *Pioneer 10* more than eighty thousand years to reach the nearest star. The chances that the message will collide with an inhabited planet are slim. But that small grouping of lines and symbols stands as our first attempt to communicate with and confirm the existence of humanity to the rest of the universe.

Objectives for Chapter Three

After completing this chapter you will be able to:

- Realize that measures of good design often change over time.
- Identify the common parts of a typeface.
- Understand the different factors that control alphabet design.
- Identify different type styles, families, and series.
- Recognize and to explain the design considerations of balance, dominance, proportion, and unity.
- Remember some important design limitations including imposition, gripper margin, bleeds, surprints and reverses, screen tints, dealing with photographs, and image placement.
- Understand that design dictates production methods and determines, to a great extent, printing costs.
- List and explain the design steps used to produce a printed product.

Introduction

To many individuals **design** is a very threatening and frightening word. It is often associated with drawing ability and unfortunately, most students leave art classes convinced they cannot draw. Design is often taught as a set of rules, just like a paint-by-numbers set—fill in the lines and you have created a masterpiece.

What is good or bad design is a subjective, changing thing. Consider the many style changes in the usually male ornament called a necktie. Within a few decades, fashion has moved from ties so wide they could be mistaken for dinner napkins tucked into the collar, to narrow, barely visible cords, then back to sizes of mammoth proportions. A tie looks "right" according to the fashions of the year—one from previous years might look funny. It is often equally difficult to define good or bad design in other areas.

If acceptable design is so subjective a thing, then it seems strange that there is indeed "good" and "bad" design. The function of the design process is to meet a human need. If a design meets that need, it must be called good. If it fails, it is bad. The important question is how can the novice designer or printer begin to learn the difference? Good design is not created by memorizing and then rigorously following a set of rules. The rules can change so frequently and easily. The key is that even though there might be no strict rules, there is a language of design that artists use to describe the characteristics of any work.

It is important to understand that the ability to create well-designed images for printing reproduction is not necessarily related to freehand drawing ability, although freehand drawing will always be a useful skill. The generation or creation of images is distinctly different from the layout and design of those images. If the language of design is learned and the tools of printing reproduction are mastered, good design will follow through practice.

A printer once took a design to a customer who complained that the layout needed more "oomph," the color didn't have enough "pizzaz," and the whole thing just didn't "zow" him. This chapter is concerned with design as a human process. It will examine design characteristics with a bit more definition than "oomph," "pizzaz," or "zow"; but it will not present them as constraints, only as a means of communication. It will also consider the role of the artist-printer and explain the limitations and advantages of the printing processes.

Alphabet Design—the Basic Design Tool

Symbol Characteristics

Graphic designers work with the placement of images and the manipulation of white or open space. The most basic group of images is the twenty-six symbols of our Latin alphabet. Just as each individual person possesses a different and distinctive handwriting style, printers can reproduce the alphabet in many different **typefaces.** There are, in fact, so many typefaces or alphabet designs that it is often difficult for the novice to recognize differences or to select a useful design from an ever-growing list.

No matter how the characters are structured, every typeface is made up of common parts (figure 3.1). Early alphabets contained

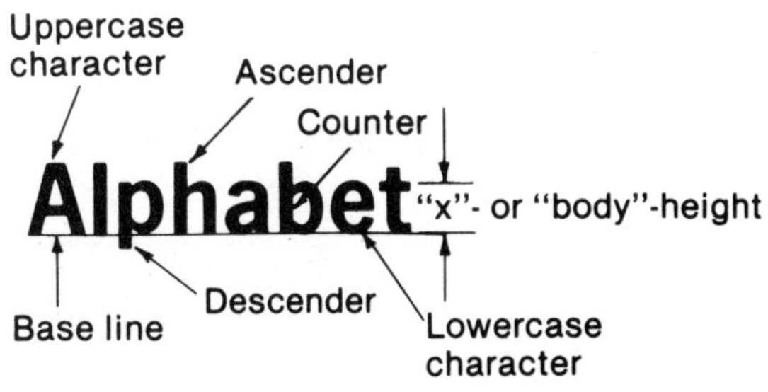

Figure 3.1. Parts of a typeface

Figure 3.2. Recognizing words by their ascenders Cover the top line and ask someone to read the bottom. Then reverse the procedure. Which was easier?

characters of only one design, but ours is made up of characters of the following two designs:

- **Uppercase** (capital) symbols,
- **Lowercase** symbols.

Both upper- and lowercase letters are formed along a common base line. The **x-height,** or **body-height,** of a typeface is the distance from the base line to the top of a lowercase letter *x*. It is the x-height that influences the visual impression of the type size on the printed page. Any part of a letter that extends below the base line is called a **descender.** Any part that extends above the base line is called an **ascender.** It is interesting that accurate word recognition depends on the visual impact of the ascenders and descenders above and below the dimensions of the x-height (figure 3.2).

Given these common characteristics, only the following three variables affect the design of any alphabet:

- Stroke,
- Stress,
- Serif.

Stroke defines the thickness of the line that forms the individual letter (figure 3.3). The thickness might be perfectly uniform throughout the character, as with the popular typeface Helvetica, or the character might be formed with widely contrasting line weights, such as with Bodoni. **Stress** describes the distribution of visual "heaviness" or "slant" of the character. It is easy to visualize the stress of a letter as the angle of a line that passes through its center (figure 3.4). Most handwriting has a heavy slant or stress to the right. **Serifs** are the small strokes that project out from the top or bottom of the main letter strokes (figure 3.5). Serifs can be simple square lines placed at right angles to each main stroke; they can vary in thickness; they can be stressed; they can form a **fillet** (an internal curve) between the serif stroke and main stroke; or they can be rounded instead of squared. It is important to keep in mind that all typeface design (the design of alphabets) is nothing more than the manipulation of a character's stroke, stress, or serif.

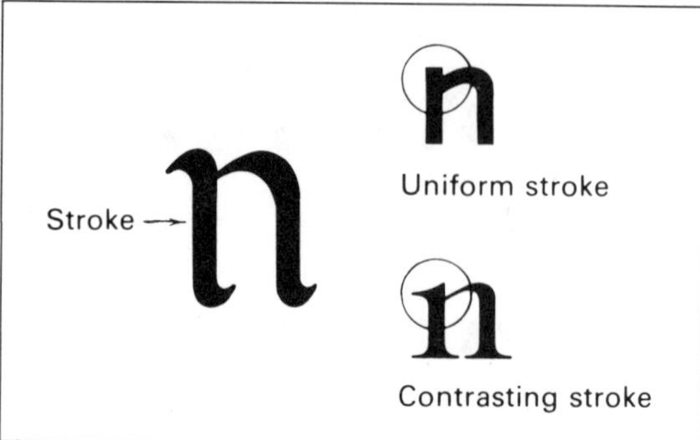

Figure 3.3. Stroke The stroke or thickness of typeface designs varies among designs.

Figure 3.4. Stress The stress of a character is sometimes called the slant.

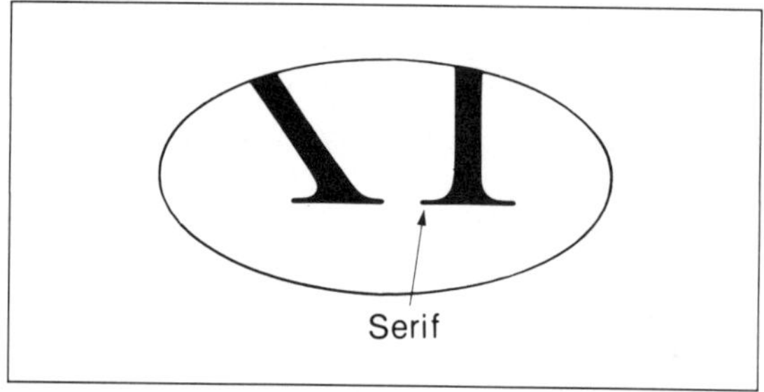

Figure 3.5. Serifs Serifs are often the distinguishing feature between similar typefaces.

Alphabet Styles

With a good understanding of these symbol characteristics, it is possible to categorize all alphabet variations into the following six groupings called **typeface styles:**

- Roman,
- Sans serif,
- Square serif,
- Text,
- Script,
- Occasional.

Typeface style is a label applied to all designs with a common stroke, stress, and serif.

Roman. The body of this book is set in Palatino, a Roman typeface. The Roman design is based on the characteristics of letterforms cut into granite by early Roman stone masons. Iron chisels were used to cut horizontal and vertical lines. Where strokes did not intersect, the tool left a ragged appearance at the end of a line. A cut made with the tool straightened the unevenness. The cut was called a serif. Today we define any design that has the main characteristics of stroke variation and serifs as a **Roman** typeface.

There are three subcategories of the Roman design—oldstyle, transitional, and modern (figure 3.6). An "oldstyle Roman" has little stroke contrast. There is usually a slight rounding of the serif base, and fillets fill in the area between main and serif strokes. A "modern Roman" character is formed from massive strokes contrasted with almost hairline portions. There is generally no rounding or filleting of the serif. Between the two is the "transitional Roman," with greater stroke contrast than oldstyle but a significantly less than modern face. Transitional serifs are not scooped at the base but have massive fillets.

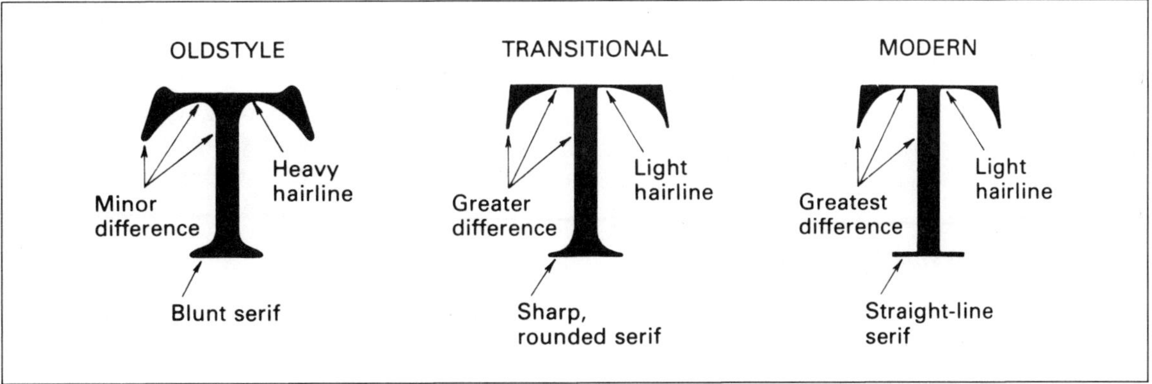

Figure 3.6. Roman designs Roman designs can be oldstyle, transitional, or modern.

A Roman alphabet is an efficient design to read. Most books, magazines, and newspapers are set in a Roman face. Oldstyle Roman designs communicate a feeling of strength, and modern forms give an impression of classical, fragile elegance. All Roman designs are dignified and project confidence.

Sans Serif. **Sans serif** means literally "without serifs" (figure 3.7). Sans serif characters are formed from uniform strokes, with perfectly vertical letter stress. Sans serif faces are very popular and communicate a contemporary feeling. However, the design is tiring to read as body composition in a book or article and projects an impersonal attitude. It is effective for title headings when contrasted with a Roman composition.

Square Serif. **Square serif** alphabets are generally formed from uniform strokes, including serif dimensions (figure 3.8). Sometimes the label "Egyptian" is applied to the same characteristics. Square serif faces are easily recognizable and are often used in publications designed for young, inexperienced readers.

Sans Serif Style

Franklin Gothic

Sans Serif Style

Helvetica

Figure 3.7. Examples of sans serif design typefaces

Square Serif Style

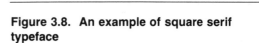

Playbill

Figure 3.8. An example of square serif typeface

Text Style

Old English

Figure 3.9. An example of text typeface

Text. **Text** typefaces attempt to recreate the feeling of the era of medieval scribes (figure 3.9). They are generally used in very formal situations, such as wedding invitations. Text characters are difficult to read and become almost illegible when set in all caps (uppercase). Such designs are not often used in contemporary messages.

Script

Figure 3.10. An example of script typeface

Script. **Script** (or cursive) designs give the feeling of free-form handwriting (figure 3.10). Script is gradually replacing text for contemporary communications. As with text, script is not easy to read and should never be set in all uppercase (figure 3.11). A wide range of impressions can be made with script type, from delicate sweeping forms to extremely strong and rugged characterizations.

Figure 3.11. An example of all uppercase script Words of script set in all capital letters are almost unreadable. This word is Diane.

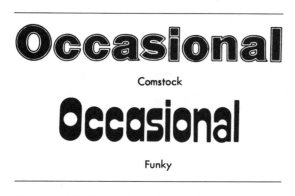

Occasional. The last classification, **occasional,** is really an "other grouping" (figure 3.12). Anything that cannot be classed in one of the first five categories is labeled occasional. Some **typographers** (type designers) use the labels "novelty" or "decorative," but whatever the group is called, there are no design limits. Occasional typefaces are usually created to meet a specific design need. Companies often design and copyright a particular letterform so that consumers will associate it with their product or service.

Occasional

Comstock

Occasional

Funky

Figure 3.12. Examples of occasional typefaces

Families, Series, and Fonts

A **type family** is created by a unique combination of stroke, stress, and serif conceived by a typographic designer. The characteristics of a type family are represented in each letter of the alphabet design. There are thousands of different type families, each identified by a specific title or name and classified under one of the six type styles.

A variation within a type family is called a **series** (figure 3.13). Just as human families are made up of many members—sisters, brothers, cousins, aunts, and so on—that typically carry a family resemblance, type families are composed of many letterform variations that are all based on the main family characteristics. It is possible to manipulate the basic letter design a bit without altering the relationships between stroke, stress, or serif. A basic family design can be made bold, light, condensed, expanded, extra bold, extra light, or italic (or combinations such as "extra bold condensed"). The word that describes the manipulation—for example, bold or italic—is added to the family name—in this case, Century—to distinguish between family members. Each family is not always made up of the same number of series—a family's size depends on the desires of its creator.

Every series of a type family can be reproduced in a wide range of sizes (figure 3.14). A **font** is a collection of all the characters of the alphabet that are of one size and series. Alphabet sizes are measured with the printer's measurement system. In this system six **picas** equal one inch, and twelve **points** equal one pica (figure 3.15). Fonts are classified according to point size.

Printers use this special system to measure almost all printed images. Letter size is almost always described in points. Common letter sizes are 6, 7, 8, 9, 10, 11, 12, 14, 16, 18, 24, 36, 42, 60, and 72 points. Any type size over 72 points is commonly specified in inches.

Space between lines of type is also measured in points. When a customer requests a type page to be set 10 on 12 (10/12), the printer understands that the letters will be 10 points high, with 2 points between each line (12 points − 10 points = 2 points).

Lines of type are specified in picas. Most newspaper columns are 13 picas wide. A 36-

Century Light
Century Light Italic
Century Bold
Century Bold Italic
Century Bold Condensed
Century Bold Extended
Century Textbook
Century Textbook Italic
Century Textbook Bold

Figure 3.13. An example of a type family The family name of this type is Century. Its series variations are combinations of different weights—light, bold, regular—and different stress—roman and italic.

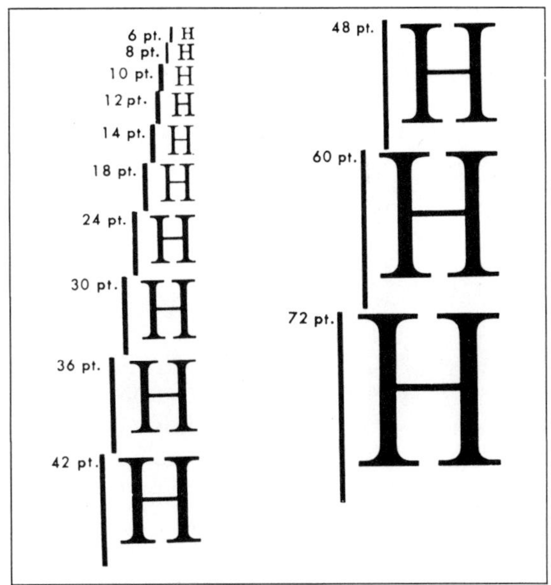

Figure 3.14. Font size Font size is measured in points, shown here from a small letter of 6 points to a display letter of 72 points.
Courtesy of Mackenzie and Harris, Inc., San Francisco.

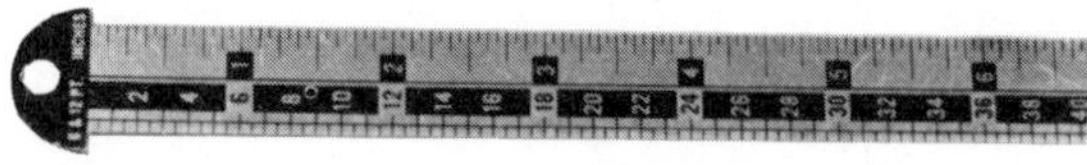

Figure 3.15. Pica-inch ruler The printer's system of measurement is based on pica units of measure. The divisions shown on the bottom scale in this figure are 6 points and 12 points (1 pica).

pica line is 6 inches long, since one inch equals six picas. Column depth is measured in picas from the top of the first line on a page to the bottom of the last line of type.

Alphabet designs are fundamental tools of the graphic artist. Volumes have been published containing nothing more than different families of type. It is not possible in a few pages to do more than introduce a system of organizing type. It is better to begin design with a few families within each style than to try to select forms from the thousands available.

Design Language

Balance

Balance is concerned with the equilibrium of the visual images on a sheet. It is often compared to the idea of a balance scale—the visual weight of images must be equal on each side of a center point, or fulcrum. For graphic design the visual center of a page is not the physical center (sometimes called the mathematical center), but rather the **optical center.** To locate the optical center of any rectangular page, first measure down the length a distance equal to the sheet's width to form a square. Then draw lines from each corner of the square. Where the lines intersect is the optical center of that page (figure 3.16).

The visual weight of an image on the sheet depends on the image's size and density. Solid areas have more visual weight than outlines. Circular forms appear heavier than rectangles.

There are three kinds of balance:

- Formal balance,
- Informal balance,
- Subjective balance.

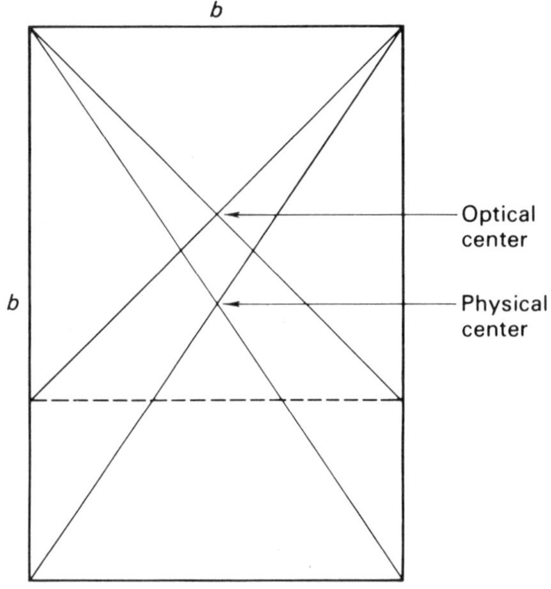

Figure 3.16. Diagram of optical and physical centers The optical center of a page is not the same as the physical center. Note that the optical center is determined by the width of the page.

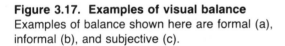

Figure 3.17. Examples of visual balance
Examples of balance shown here are formal (a), informal (b), and subjective (c).

Formal balance (figure 3.17a) places objects of identical weight on each side of a center line. It is used in situations that demand dignity, formality, and strength. **Informal balance** (figure 3.17b) has a freer, more contemporary feeling. Instead of being symmetrically placed, images create a sense of balance by their size, weight, and position. But the idea of a balance point is still used. The third form of balance is called **subjective** (figure 3.17c). In subjective balance, images are combined with bold white space to achieve a sense of balance.

Dominance

Dominance refers to the main purpose of the printed piece—to communicate a message. If jthe message did not dominate the sheet, the reader would have to search for meaning and might well think the whole thing not worth the effort. Remember, it is the sender or designer's responsibility to see that the message reaches the receiver.

Dominance is usually achieved by contrasting the most important parts of the message with the rest of the sheet. Some lines of type can be set larger than others. Boldface, italic, or underlining can help create dominance. Words can be printed in special colors or tints, reversed, or dropped (figure 3.18).

Good control of contrast can also direct the eye to the most important part of the message, even though it might not be the largest part. A prime example is the use of white space around densely set copy.

Proportion

Proportion is concerned with size relationships. Both the sheet size and the size and placement of the images on the sheet are important when proportion is considered. The Greeks evolved what they thought to be the ideal proportion, called the "golden rectangle." It was formed by a sheet two units wide and three units long. Ideal image placement was obtained by dividing the vertical portion of any page into eight equal parts. The third line from the top represented the "line of golden proportions" (figure 3.19). It is interesting that this line falls very close to the optical center of the page that was used as a fulcrum for image balance. The line of golden proportions can be used to achieve good vertical balance, which means good proportion.

Figure 3.18. Examples of a screen tint, a drop, and a reverse

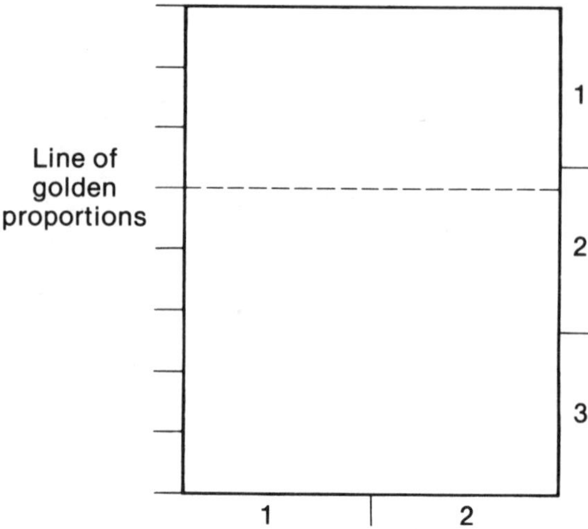

Figure 3.19. Golden rectangle The line of golden proportions is shown on a golden rectangle.

Proportion plays an important part in the selection of margins for pages made up of "body composition" (the type that makes up the major part of a book or other printed piece). The two vertical margins are typically set equal, the head is wider than the sides, and the bottom margin is larger than the other three (figure 3.20).

Unity

The idea of **unity** ties together all the design functions. It is concerned with how the entire piece flows together into a complete message. Several ideas should be considered under this label. One is called theme and deals with the selection of appropriate typefaces for the message being printed. Letterforms create feelings and moods by their characteristics. We enjoy certain books and magazines without being aware of the contribution of the type and page arrangement, which is independent of what the author has to say. Typefaces can be down to earth, businesslike, dignified, humorous, gentle, or harsh (figure 3.21). Type can generate strong emotions, like anger. It can shout an alarm or quietly whisper a warning. For example, when describing large or heavy physical objects, the type should be strong. Roman serifs communicate dignity. Decorative faces can be used for fun. During the late 1800s designers used every conceivable letter design on a printed piece. Each line was competing with every other for attention. Thankfully, that style has gone out of fashion. It is wise for a beginning printer/designer to stay within one type family on any given job.

Images other than letters on the piece should also maintain the idea of unity. It is better to stay with similar shapes than to introduce shapes that are radically different. Different shapes will compete for attention and the ultimate message will be lost. To maintain unity, the same shape is frequently repeated on the sheet in some sort of pleasing pattern. The repetition of the shape reinforces the theme without too much image competition.

Design language can be confusing to a novice designer. The ideas of balance, dominance, proportion, and unity are not constraints. They are merely classifications that allow individuals to work together toward the goal of creating an image that will effectively communicate a message.

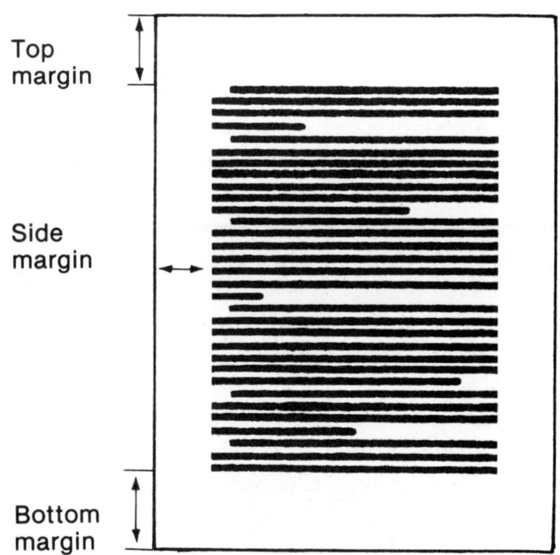

Figure 3.20. Margin proportions Margins must appear proportionally correct on the page. The top margin is usually larger than the side margins, and the bottom margin is usually larger than the top margin.

Some Basic Printing Tricks

Many design considerations depend on the limitations and advantages of the printing processes and equipment that will be discussed in later chapters. These limitations and advantages are really learned only by working with the reproduction of a design. A chapter on design for printing production might be more meaningful, therefore, at the end of this text. Let's try to ease the situation by introducing some basic information that will make the design process more effective and efficient.

Imposition

Imposition refers to the problem of placing the images in positions on the printing plate so they will be in the desired location on the final printed sheet. The designer/printer can lower production costs and so become very popular by the use of efficient imposition.

Sheetwise Imposition. The simplest form of imposition is **sheetwise.** In sheetwise imposition one printing plate is used to print on one side of a sheet as it passes through the printing press. If it is desired to place an image on the reverse (other side), an additional plate is made, the sheets are turned over, and they are passed through the press a second time.

Often the size of the job to be printed is smaller than the press can handle or is so much smaller than the standard press sheet size that printing only one job on each press sheet would be a very inefficient use of equipment. To overcome this problem, several jobs are often "ganged" together, reproduced on a large sheet, and then cut to the final trim size with a paper cutter (figure 3.22). When a press sheet carries only one job, it is called "1-up" imposition. When more than a single job is run on the same sheet, it is called "2-up," "3-up," "4-up," and so on, depending on the number of final jobs run on each press sheet. It makes no difference if the same or different images are printed; the same terms are used.

Signature Imposition. A large single sheet is frequently passed through a printing press and then folded and trimmed to form a portion of a book or magazine. This process is called **signature imposition.** Four-, eight-, twelve-, sixteen-, twenty-four-, and even forty-eight-page signatures are common press

Figure 3.21. Typeface as a design choice A typeface can often help communicate a feeling beyond the meaning of a printed word.
Courtesy of Itek Compositions Systems

runs (figure 3.23). The designer must impose the pages in the proper position so they will be in the correct sequence when folded in the final publication. The last section in this chapter deals with "dummies," which are a check on page placement for signature layout.

Work-and-Turn Imposition. Another common form of imposition is the work-and-turn. **Work-and-turn imposition** employs one printing plate to print on both sides of a single piece of paper (figure 3.24). The sheet is first printed on one side, the pile is turned over, and the sheet is fed through the press again with the same **lead edge** (first edge that enters the press).

Work-and-Tumble Imposition. **Work-and-tumble imposition** also uses one plate; but on the second pass through the press, the pile is tumbled (or flopped) so that the opposite edge enters first (figure 3.25). Both techniques

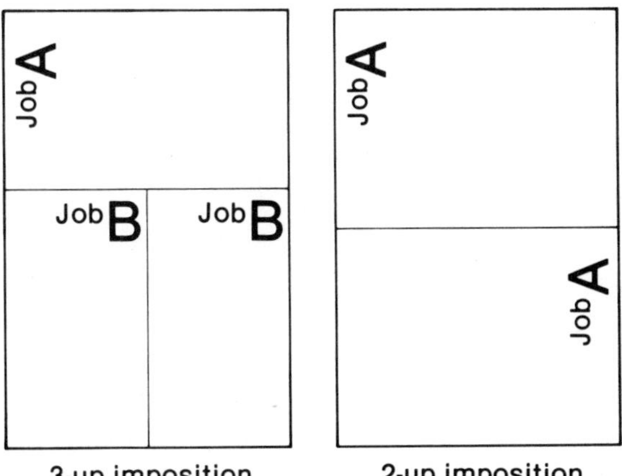

Figure 3.22. Ganged imposition Images or pages are ganged on the press sheet for more efficient use of materials and equipment.

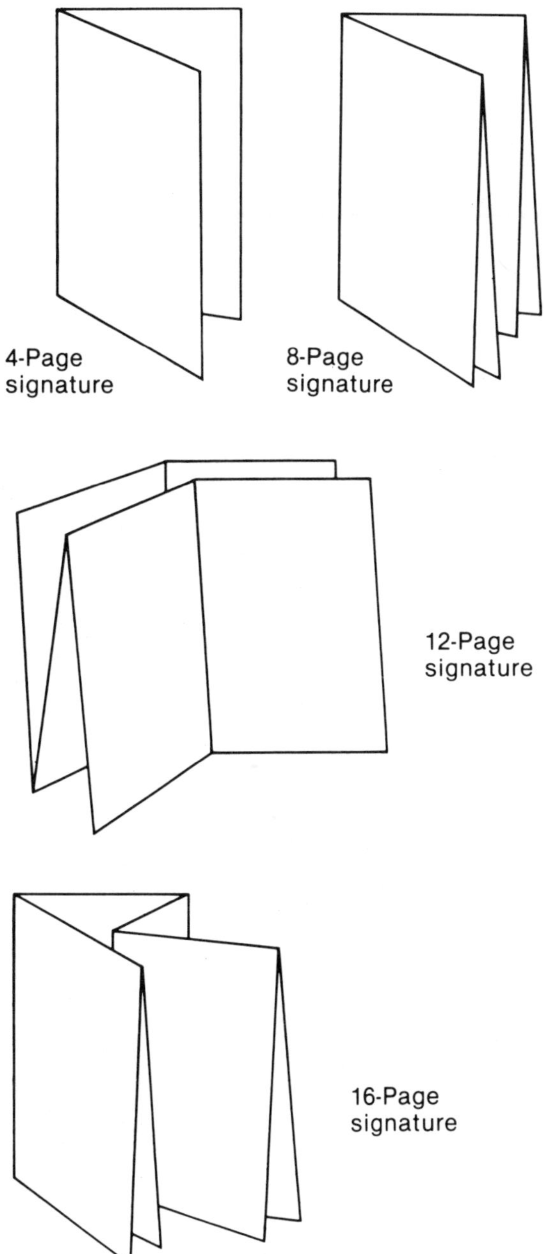

Figure 3.23. Folded signatures A predetermined folded signature of several pages is the result of signature imposition.

are more efficient than sheetwise imposition because only one printing plate is prepared. Work-and-tumble imposition is generally not used where **fit** (critical image position) is desired—such as in multicolor jobs—because the two different lead edges require additional press adjustments.

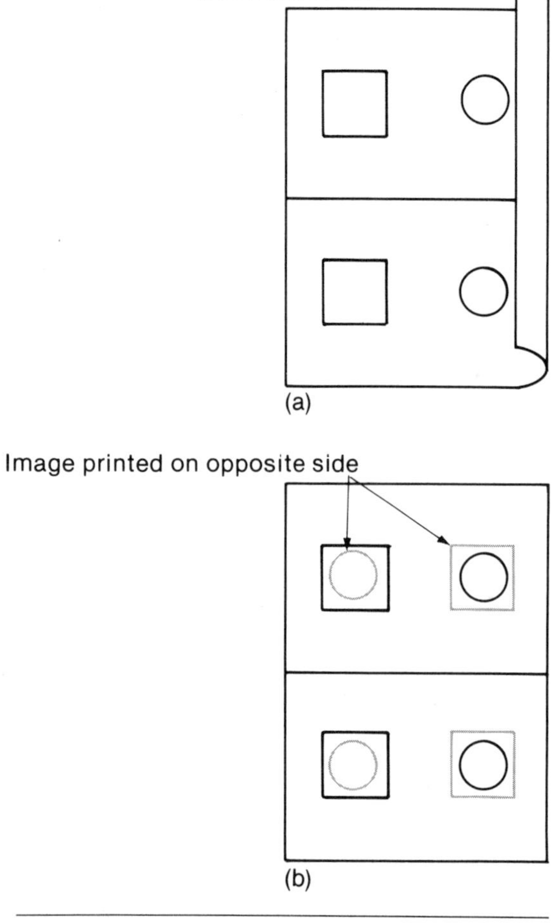

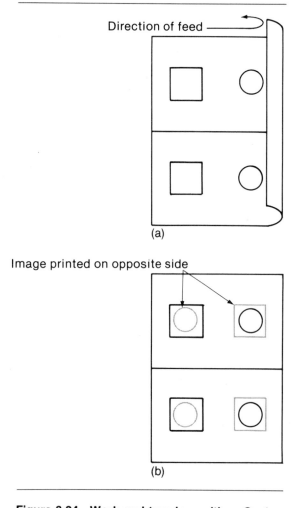

Figure 3.24. Work-and-turn imposition On the first run through the press, the first side of the sheet is printed (a). The back of the sheet is printed on the second run through the press (b).

Bleeds and Grippers

Almost all printing presses employ some sort of automatic paper-handling system. Mechanical fingers, called **grippers,** generally clamp onto the lead edge of the sheet and pull it through the press. The area of the paper that the grippers hold is called the **gripper margin.** The actual size of the gripper margin

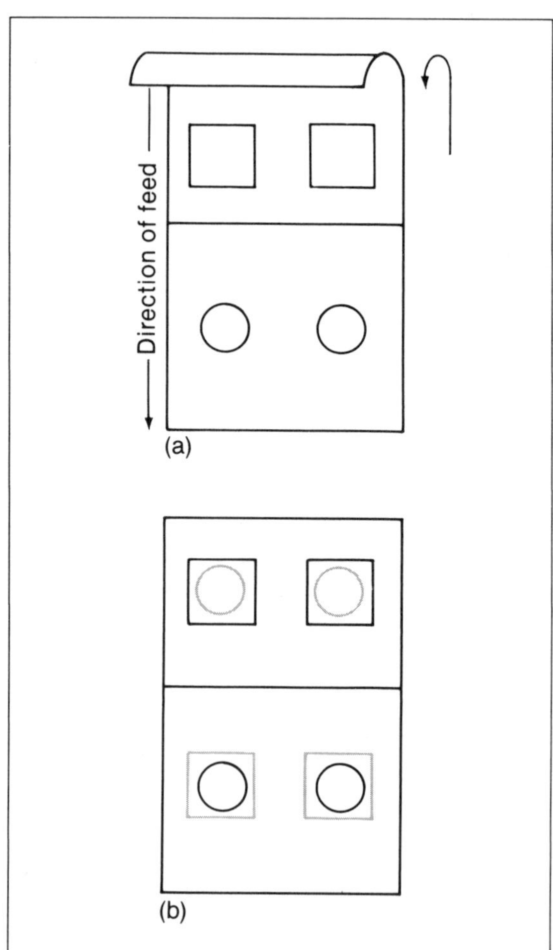

Figure 3.25. Work-and-tumble imposition showing first run (a) and second run (b)

varies from press to press, but it is usually no more than one-half inch. An image cannot be printed in the gripper margin because that area is covered by the metal fingers that pull the paper through the press. If the margins of a sheet are wide, this presents no problems. However, the size of the gripper margin becomes a major concern for some types of imposition, such as multipage or work-and-tumble jobs.

A common printing design is to "bleed" an image off the edge of the page. A **bleed** is a design that extends an image over the edge of the printed sheet. The technique is not difficult, but it often is confusing to novice designers. One approach is to place an image on the printing plate that is slightly larger than the dimensions of the sheet to be printed (figure 3.26). Part of the plate image is lost, but this fact is considered during the layout phase of production. This method is generally used for short runs of 200 or less. An alternative method of creating a bleed image is to use a larger press sheet than is necessary and to trim the paper pile through the image to the final size after it has been printed (figure 3.27). This is the only solution possible when a bleed is desired on the gripper edge of the sheet.

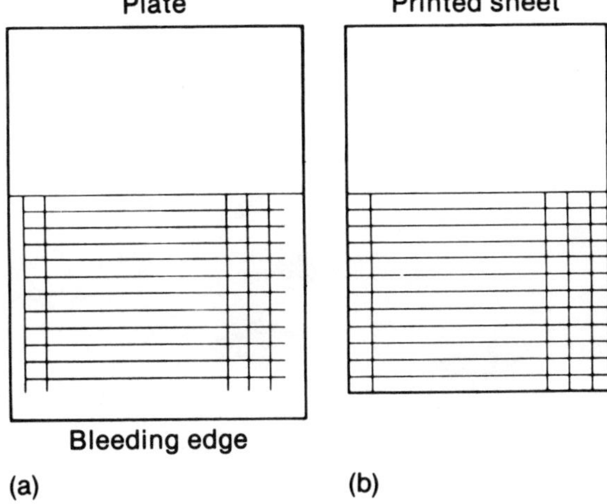

Figure 3.26. Bleed image larger than final printed sheet For short-run jobs an oversized image on the plate (a) can bleed off the edge of the printed sheet (b).

Image Positions on the Printing Plate

Most presses ink printing plates by means of ink rollers. The rollers pick up ink from a reservoir system, pass over the plate to ink the image areas, and then return to the reservoir to re-ink. If the images are placed so that many large areas fall in a line at right angles to the rollers, it is difficult to obtain uniform ink coverage across the plate (figure 3.28). It is important that designs be positioned to balance ink distribution needs (figure 3.29).

Use of Color

With rare exception (such as embossing), all printing is color reproduction because printers count black as a color. When the term "color printing" is used, however, the printer is generally referring to multiple colors on the same sheet. Printers classify color printing in the following three groups:

- Fake color,
- Flat color,
- Process color.

Fake Color. A one-color reproduction printed on a colored sheet is known as **fake color.** Any color of ink or sheet combination could be used, but the sheet must carry only one layer of ink.

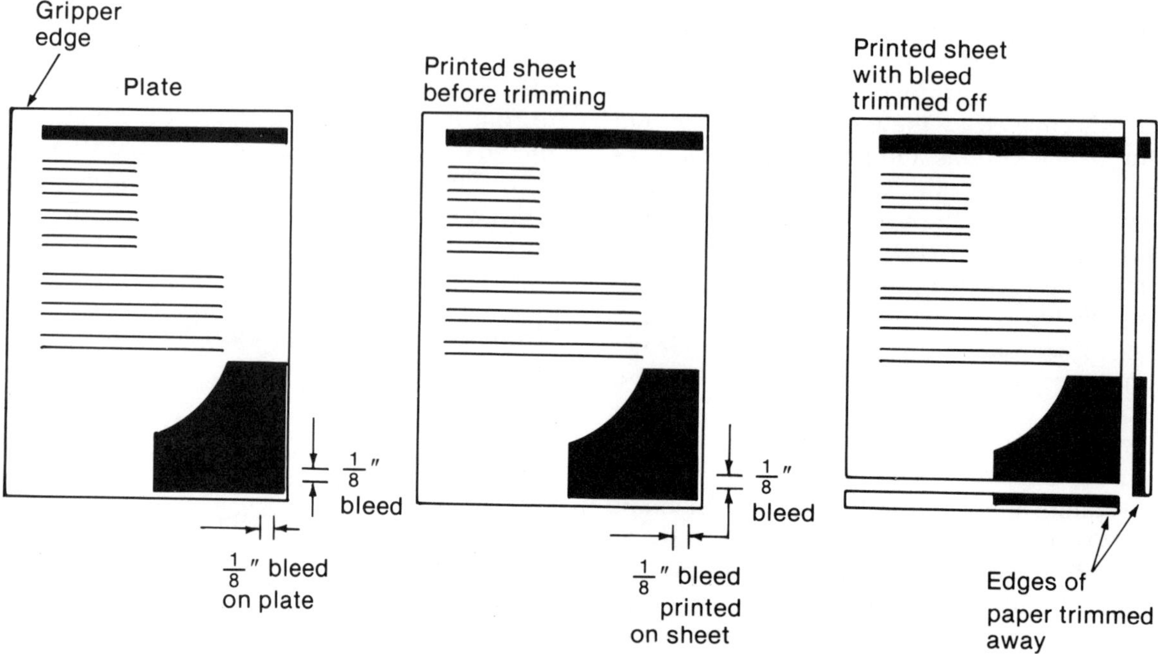

Figure 3.27. Printed sheet dimensions larger than the bleed image
When a bleed is required for long-run jobs, the full image is printed and then trimmed.

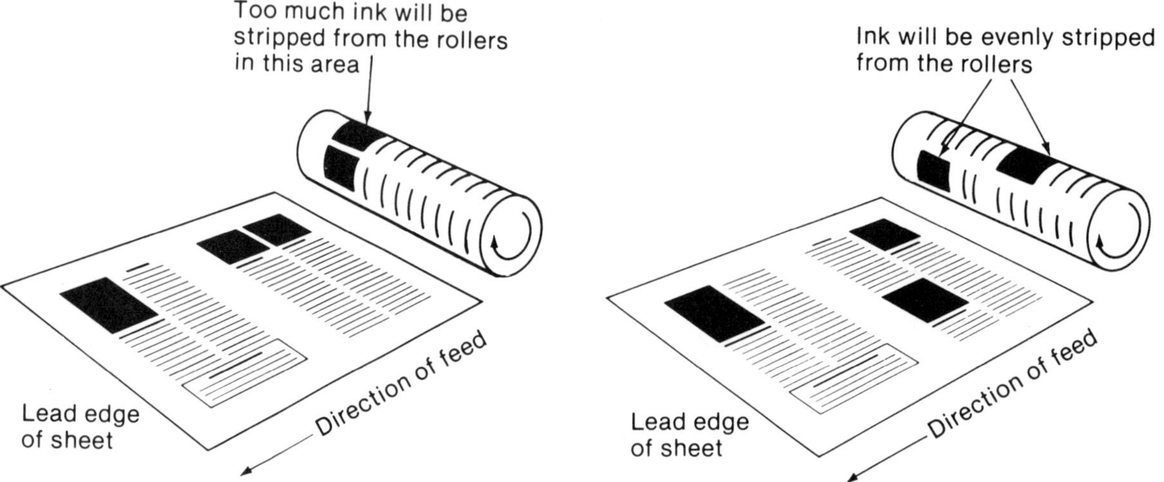

Figure 3.28. Image position that results in poor ink coverage

Figure 3.29. Image position that will improve ink coverage

Flat* (or *Match*) *Color. Inks the printer purchases or mixes for a specific job are called **flat colors.** Flat colors can be specified from a color-matching system or hand mixed to match a color submitted by the designer. A color-matching system generally employs a swatchbook with samples of ink colors printed on both coated and uncoated papers. All colors are numbered, and mixing formulas are included. If the designer specifies a particular swatchbook number, the printer can easily mix the required color. Hand mixing of colors to match a color sample is a more difficult trial-and-error process that relies on luck.

Process Color. The term **process color** refers to the use of four specific colors: cyan (process blue), magenta (process red), yellow, and back (plates B, C, and D pp. 198–200). **Four-color process printing** is used to reproduce images as they would appear in a color photograph (called a continuous-tone print). Chapter 9 deals with the control of these four colors to create the illusion of nearly any color of the visible spectrum on the printed sheet. Flat color can also be printed by using four different inks, but that is not process color.

Color reproduction is more expensive than one-color printing because each additional color represents another printing plate and another pass through the printing press. When designing imposition for a multicolor job, it is best to position pages with the same number and type of colors on the same side of the press sheet.

Tints, Surprints, and Reverses

An interesting technique for creating the illusion of different tones or color hues with a single color is the use of a **screen tint.** Tints break up solid areas into uniform series of dots. The size of the dot is specified as a percentage of the paper area that is covered with ink. A 60% screen tint places dots over 60% of the image area.

Both **surprints** (figure 5.38) and **reverses** (figure 3.18) are images positioned over another design. Surprints are reproduced as solids; reverses, as open areas. Both techniques are often used to set words over a picture or illustration. It is important to consider the density of the background area when deciding whether to use a reverse or a surprint. A surprint will not show up well in a dark background, and a reverse will not show up well in a light background.

Design Considerations

It is easy to become wrapped up in the techniques and language of printing design. It is, however, very important to keep a group of basic questions (design considerations) in mind whenever you are working within the limits of an assignment or job.

Purpose

It is important to remember that design is a response to a need. Avoid thinking "graphically" at first and define the ultimate purpose of the printed piece. Will it sell or simply introduce a product or idea? Will it announce an event? Will it instruct or teach? Should it contain detailed information or should it attract attention? Will it be mailed? Will the piece eventually be posted or filed or discarded? Answers to these questions will determine the format of the sheet, the type of illustrations to use, the amount of color needed (if any), the type of paper, and the finishing and binding techniques.

The customer's expectations of cost must also be considered. The skills of the printer's craft can technically meet nearly any production specification that the designer might identify. However, with increased sophistication comes higher costs. Any job can fluctuate tremendously in price. The final cost will depend on the type of format, method of illustration, paper, and binding.

Format, Illustrations, and Color

Format is determined by the purpose of the piece and the budget. The format could be a folded mailer, booklet, poster, or catalog. It could be printed in one or more colors and have complicated folds, creases, perforations, or die cuts.

How a piece is illustrated will also affect production schedules and cost. The choice is generally between type and line illustrations (illustrations drawn with lines) or type and halftone illustrations (illustrations made photomechanically from continuous-tone photographs). Halftone conversions from continuous-tone prints require a skilled photographer and therefore increase costs. Poor halftones will spoil the product's appearance.

Color adds the potential for more impact, but each pass through a printing press increases the final price. Are duotones, special effects, or multicolor reproductions necessary to the purpose? Is it possible to use colored paper or to add tints of one color to enhance the piece without changing the number of press runs?

Paper

Paper for the job must be selected carefully and is a prime consideration that will influence the appearance and cost of the job. Paper typically accounts for up to half the production costs, so a mistake in selection could mean a tremendous economic loss.

There are some practical considerations when selecting paper. The designer must be sure that the design is compatible with the paper. To be compatible, the paper must have some basic printing characteristics. For example, to be printed on both sides, the paper must be opaque and bulky enough to eliminate show-through. If heavy stock is to be used and a fold is required, grain direction should be considered. If a fold is desired against the grain, the job must be **scored** (or creased by a machine). Paper is available in coated and uncoated surfaces. It also comes in a variety of finishes. Smooth-coated papers will allow the reproduction of fine detail, screen tints, or halftone screens. Rough and textured surfaces will require much coarser screen rulings to reproduce tints or halftones.

Binding

How the job will be assembled and bound is another concern of the designer. If it is a simple sheetwise image, there are obviously no problems. Whenever more than two sheets are used, however, the image placement is affected. Saddle stitching, side stitching, mechanical binding, plastic binding, even perfect or casebound binding will influence how the designer positions the message on the printed sheets.

Many of these considerations and questions are discussed in detail in the following chapters. The skillful graphic designer must have them all firmly in mind before making even the first crude pencil sketch of the job.

Design Steps

The basic task is to bring together all these concerns about design and to produce an image that will communicate the desired message to the intended audience. The steps that graphic artists have traditionally followed to accomplish this task consist of the following:

1. Preparing a set of thumbnail sketches,
2. Preparing rough layouts based on the preliminary thumbnail sketches,
3. Preparing a comprehensive layout,
4. Preparing a final layout or mechanical.

To illustrate this process, let's follow each step on a typical printing assignment.

Assume that we have been contracted to produce an announcement of a local printing association meeting. There will be a dinner followed by a presentation entitled "Role of the Artist." The announcement is to be a self-contained mailer. The text copy and meal information have been provided (figure 3.30). Our task is to design a mailer that will attract attention, communicate the feeling of the title of the presentation, and carry all the necessary information.

Thumbnails

The process begins with a series of **thumbnail sketches** (small, quick pencil renderings that show the arrangement of type, line drawings, and white space). They are in proportion to, but always smaller than, reproduction size. Thumbnails do not necessarily carry the actual wording that will appear on the final product. Penciled lines are frequently used to indicate type placement. A straightedge is rarely used, and the designer concentrates only on the overall visual effect of the printed piece.

Figure 3.31 shows two of the many thumbnails produced for this job. It was decided to prepare a cover that showed an artist at a drawing board, with the title of the presentation carried on the board. Notice that these examples meet the criteria for thumbnails: they are in proportion to, but smaller than, final size; they are quick sketches; and they do not carry all of the message. From the thumbnails the designer selects the one that he or she thinks will best meet the assignment. For this job, figure 3.31b was chosen.

Roughs—A Floor Plan of the Job

A **rough layout** is a detailed expansion of the thumbnail sketch that carries all the necessary printing information. Any printer should be able to produce the final reproduction from the directions on the rough. The rough layout is the same size as the final product, contains the actual wording (if there is a great deal of body composition, the copy is sometimes attached and the rough indicates where it is to be placed), margin specifications, image placement for any line drawings or halftone photographs, and **type specifications** (styles and sizes to be used). In addition, if any special operations, such as folding, trimming, or perforating, are to be performed, they are so indicated. The drawing is done in pencil and may be sketched, but it must be an accurate representation of the final printed sheet.

ThumbNAil
ROUGH
COMPRUSIVE comprehensive
FINAL LAYout

TYPE AND ILLUSTRATION SPECIFICATIONS
for "Role of the Artist" mailer (inside)

1. ROLE OF THE 18 pt. Spartan Book, caps (all capitals)
2. Artist 30 pt. Brush, C & C.L. (caps and lowercase)
3. Body composition Bodoni & Bodoni Bold, 9 pt.

About the speaker: (Bold) Art's formal preparation in advertising design began with a year at Pratt Institute in Brooklyn. He left Pratt to enter the army in 1952. After completing intelligence school at Fort Riley, he went to Germany with the Second Armored Division. Completing his hitch with the army in 1955, he did design drafting for Oneida Products. In 1956 Art entered Mohawk Valley Technical Institute to further his education in the area of design. He received his AAS degree in 1958 at the top of his class. While attending MVTI, Art completed his work experience program at Canterbury Press and was immediately hired by the company. Concentrating mainly in the art area, he also gained experience in single- and multicolor stripping, specification and production scheduling, estimating and full-service sales. He also became involved in the first phototypesetting establishments in Central New York. While at Canterbury Press Art increased his education by receiving a certificate in Commercial Art and Illustration from the Famous Artist School.

In 1966 Art accepted a position as an artist with Concord Studios, Ltd., of Syracuse—a subsidiary of Midstate Printing Corp. His present responsibilities include the design and preparation of commercial brochures and catalogs.

Supported by his charming wife Sheila, he became active in the Syracuse Club in 1966 and has served as rough proofs editor, table host, treasurer, second and first vice president, president, and currently is chairman of the board of governors.

We are pleased to have a talented, local craftsman make a presentation about a controversial and misunderstood area of our business.

Come witness a verbal and visual presentation of the ROLE OF THE ARTIST in the printing industry. (Bold)

4. EXCELLENT LADIES PROGRAM 9 pt. Bodoni Bold
5. at Raphaels Restaurant, (Bold) Tuesday, February 19, 1974
   State Fair Boulevard, Lakeland, New York
6. COCKTAILS 6:30 DINNER 7:30 (Bold)
7. Hot Buffet Dinner—only $5.00 (Bold)—includes tax and gratuity
   Reservations Please: To your key man or Gene Cook (472–7815)
8. Support Graphic Arts Education
   Cover by H. Rose—Student, Oswego State University
9. Halftone of artist
10. Speaker (Bold, C & L.C.)
    ART LANGE (Bold, Caps)
11. 20% background tint

Figure 3.30. Copy for "Role of the Artist" mailer Type and illustration specifications for use by the printer are marked on the copy.

In our example several decisions were made after the thumbnail sketch was produced. It was judged to be most economical to produce the job as a single sheet folded and stapled, with one side, after the fold, left blank for the mailing address. The final trim size was to be 4½ × 6¼ inches. The rough layout for the cover of this job, therefore, was constructed so the image would fill only half of one side of the press sheet (figure 3.32a).

To produce the actual layout, the outline of the paper size to be run through the press was first placed on a clean sheet of white drawing paper. This outline forms the **paper lines.** It was decided to bleed the image off three edges of the sheet, so **trim lines** were drawn to represent where the pile would be cut after the job was printed. The image is generally allowed to bleed into the trim area from 1/16 to ⅛ inch. A line was also drawn to indicate the position for the final fold. The fold line is important for this type of job because it becomes the top image limit for the cover. After all guidelines were positioned, the thumbnail idea was transferred in detail to the rough. The wording was actually placed on the drawing. Although it is not necessary to duplicate the type styles to be used, it is important that the styles and sizes be included. The complexity of this cover warranted the use of numbers to indicate printing instructions on a second sheet (figure 3.32b).

All image positions, whether type or illustrations, should be accurately indicated. In the case of photographs, the image is generally sketched in place, and the original is carried in a work envelope with the rough.

In addition to the rough layout, the graphic designer typically prepared a detailed work sheet for the job (figure 3.33). A work sheet should contain any information not specifically used for detail images on the rough but necessary for the job to be printed.

Comprehensives—A Prediction

In most instances the customer approves the rough, and the design immediately goes into production. In some cases, however, such as in large-account situations or for multicolor runs, the customer expects to see a comprehensive layout. Most printing customers have had little experience interpreting roughs and are unable to visualize the final product from them.

A comprehensive is an artist's rendering that attempts to duplicate the appearance of the final product. It is drawn to final size, it carries no guidelines or printing instructions, display type is hand lettered to resemble the actual type styles and sizes, and any illustrations are drawn in place. Figure 3.34 shows

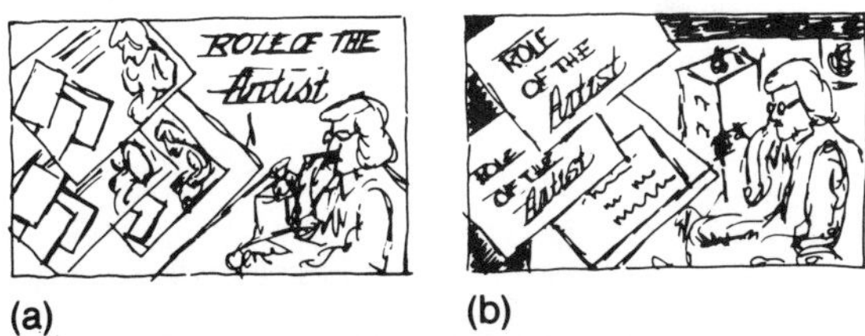

Figure 3.31. Two thumbnail sketches for "Role of the Artist"

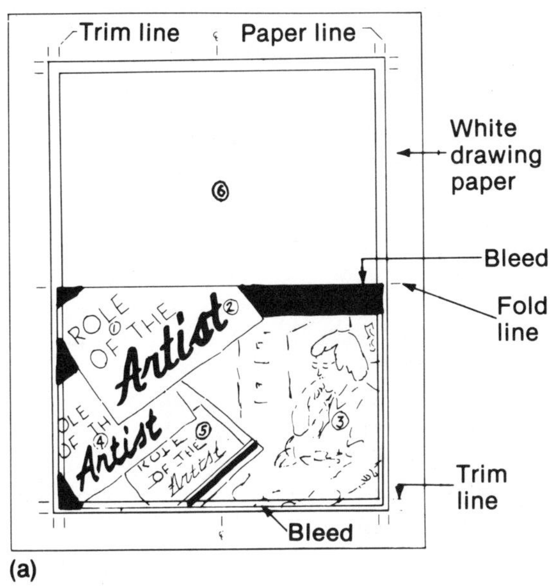

TYPE AND ILLUSTRATION SPECIFICATIONS for "Role of the Artist" mailer

1. Role of the *36 pt. Spartan Book*
2. Artist *60 pt. Brush*
3. Two-tone posterization of artist
4. Lettering to represent rough layout
5. Lettering to represent thumbnail layout
6. Space for the address

(b)

Figure 3.32. The rough layout for "Role of the Artist" mailer

WORK SHEET FOR "Role of the Artist" mailer

1. Type of stock: Warren, Cameo Dull Cover
2. Weight of stock: Cover 80
3. Color of stock: White
4. Finish of stock: C2S (coated two sides)
5. Basic sheet size: 20 × 26
6. Number of basic size sheets needed: 500
7. Process of production: Offset
8. Finish trim size: 5 5/8 × 7 1/2
9. Ink color: Black
10. Length of run: 4,500
11. Imposition: 1-up
12. Finishing techniques: Score for fold
13. Special processing: Trim

Figure 3.33. Job work sheet for "Role of the Artist" mailer The work sheet contains all printing and materials specifications.

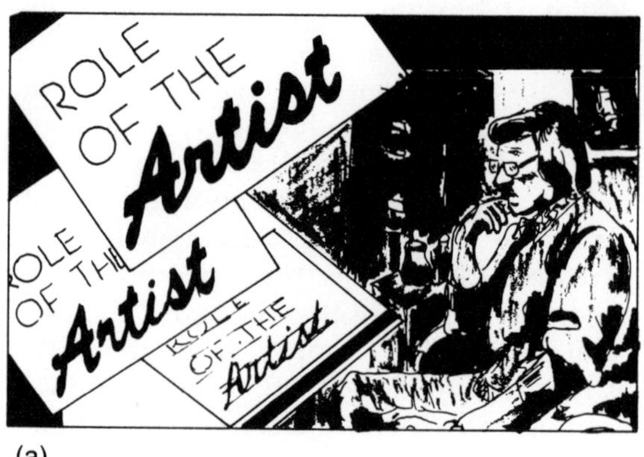

(a)

(b)

Figure 3.34. Comprehensive layouts for "Role of the Artist" mailer The cover layout is illustrated in (a). The text copy comprehensive is illustrated in (b).

the comprehensives for the cover and the text of the printing association's meeting.

In the case of detailed text, or body composition, a soft lead pencil, no. 3B, is used to indicate type position. A razor blade is used to shave the pencil point to the x-height of the type, the line spacing is accurately measured, and the lines are drawn with the chiseled pencil to represent body composition. With this method the customer gets an impression of the type weight on the page, yet the artist does not have to spend the time to hand letter accurately a great deal of copy.

Final Layout

If the job is to be produced by hand-set foundry type or by some form of machine hot type composition method, the image carrier is prepared directly from the rough layout. Chapter 16 deals exclusively with this technique and illustrates the procedures involved.

Figure 3.35. Camera-ready copy for "Role of the Artist" mailer

If the process of reproduction relies on photography as an intermediary step to prepare image carriers, one more layout must be made. A final or **camera-ready** layout (often called a **mechanical**) is made from the detailed information on the rough. Its quality is such that a negative made from the mechanical is used to make the actual printing image. Figure 3.35 shows the camera-ready layout for the sample job. Chapter 5 deals with the process of preparing camera-ready images.

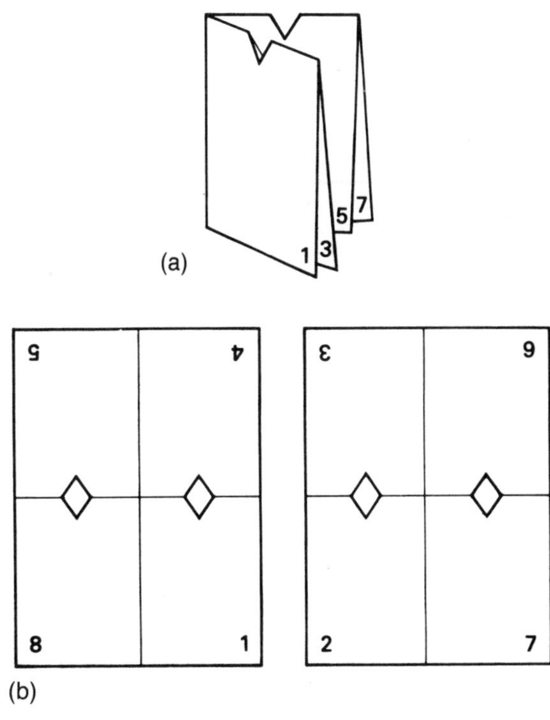

Figure 3.36. Preparing the dummy The press sheet is folded, numbered, and notched at the top of the signature (a). The opened sheet, which is numbered on the front and back, is a guide to correct imposition of the pages (b).

Dummy—A Roadmap

Jobs that are made up of pages formed by folding one or several press sheets can be very confusing in the final layout stage. To simplify the process, a **dummy** is usually prepared. A blank press sheet that is identical in size to the paper that will be used for the job is folded in the order that it will be folded after the final press run. With more than an eight-page job, the sequence of folds is important and will influence page placement.

Without trimming the folded sheet, the printer numbers each page and cuts a notch in the top of the signature. When the dummy is unfolded, the notch indicates the head of each page and the pages appear in their proper order for the final layout. Figure 3.36 illustrates this process.

Key Terms

x-height
descender
ascender
stress
stroke
serif
fillet
type style
sans serif typeface
square serif typeface
text typeface
Roman typeface
script typeface
occasional typeface
type style
type family
type series
type font
pica
point
balance
imposition
dominance
proportion
unity
gripper margin
bleed
fake color
flat color
four-color process printing
screen tint
surprint
reverse
thumbnail
rough layout
comprehensive
camera-ready (mechanical)
dummy

Questions for Review

1. What are the six typeface styles?
2. What is a type family? Give several examples.
3. What is a type series? Give several examples.
4. What is a type font?
5. What does the term "16-up imposition" mean?
6. What is a signature?
7. What is the difference between a surprint and a reverse?
8. What is the purpose of thumbnail sketches?
9. What are the characteristics of a rough layout?
10. When is a comprehensive layout commonly used?
11. What is the purpose of a final or camera-ready layout?

Chapter Four

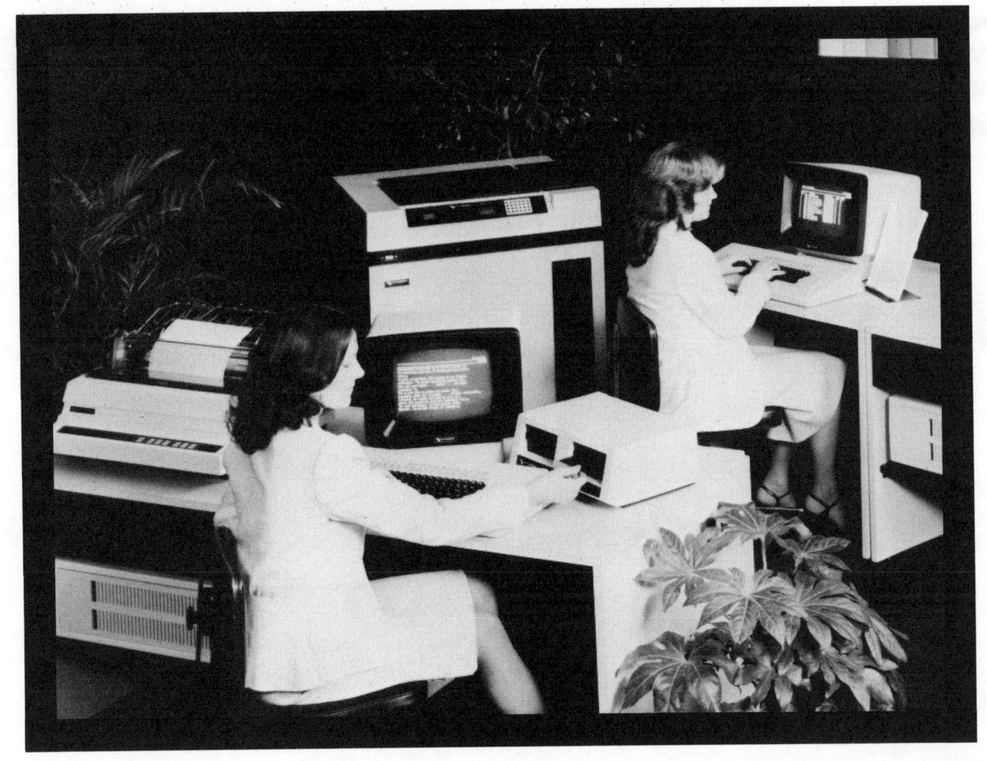

Cold Type Composition

Anecdote to Chapter Four

The introduction of the first successful typewriter—then called a writing machine—in the fall of 1867 began a series of important changes in this country and the world. The typewriter contributed to a revolution in the printing industry. What is such a commonplace printing tool today was feared as a threat to the printers of the 1800s.

Christopher Sholes and several associates built the first successful typewriter in Milwaukee in the summer of 1867. Sholes began as a printer's apprentice and later became a successful editor and publisher. By the time he perfected the first typewriter, he had already invented several other machines that had an impact on the printing industry. One example was an automatic labeling-pasting machine that was the forerunner of the high-speed machines used today to address newspapers, magazines, and envelopes for bulk mailing. Another example of Sholes's work was a numbering machine that could be mounted

An early writing machine
Smithsonian Institution, Photo No. 38–785F.

in a press to automatically number each successive print.

The first writing machine was a cumbersome tool that "typed" under the page, so the writer could not see what had been produced until the sheet was removed from the machine. Only thin tissue paper could be used because the characters, or keys, hit the paper from the back and pushed the sheet against a piece of carbon paper to form the image.

One of the first persons to purchase a commercially manufactured typewriter was the printer-author, Mark Twain (Samuel Clemens). Despite the machine's disadvantages, Twain thought it was a marvelous device, much preferable to handwriting. He managed to reach a typing speed of twelve words per minute.

The writing machine was not well received by all printers when it first began to enjoy acceptance by the business world. Before that time all letters were handwritten. If more than two or three copies were required, as in law offices or the courts, a printer would hand set the job and make copies on a printing press. By the mid-1850s the typewriter was so popular that several type founders cut typefaces for the print shop that duplicated typescript. With such fonts of type, jobs could be run on the press but would look as if they were typewritten, with ribbon marks, imperfect alignment, and inconsistent impression. There was great fear that much of the printer's work would be taken over by an office machine. In 1885 the *Inland Printer* wrote that the time might come when each printing office would have a type writing machine and could execute jobs on it as well as on any other printing apparatus.

This did happen. The typewriter has emerged as one of the greatest friends of today's printers. The development of high-quality machines that can produce strong, consistent images linked with the tool of photography made a perfect printing combination. Today, printers can "set type" on a piece of paper, photograph it, and transfer the image to a printing plate, all without touching a type case. Later developments in computers teamed the typewriter keyboard with a memory storage and then with machine-controlled output by photo or cathode ray tube devices. The typewriter or the typewriter keyboard is now an important part of almost every printing company's composition department.

Objectives for Chapter Four

After completing this chapter you will be able to:

- Explain the difference between hot type and cold type composition.
- Recognize and select appropriate manual image generation techniques.
- Recognize appropriate use of strike-on composition for image generation.
- Use the language of photographic image generation, including both body and display information storage and retrieval systems.

Introduction

Composition is the process of assembling symbols (whether letters or drawings) in their proper printing sequence according to specifications defined on the rough layout during image design. All composition fits into one of the following two broad classifications:

- Hot type composition,
- Cold type composition.

Hot type composition is a term that defines techniques used to form symbols that will be printed by a relief process (figure 4.1). The term **hot type** dates from the use of foundry type cast from molten metal. Today the term is used to describe any method of composition designed for a printing process that carries ink from a raised surface.

Cold type composition is a term that defines techniques used to assemble symbols for photographic reproduction. The photographic images can then be used to generate any form of image carrier for printing production.

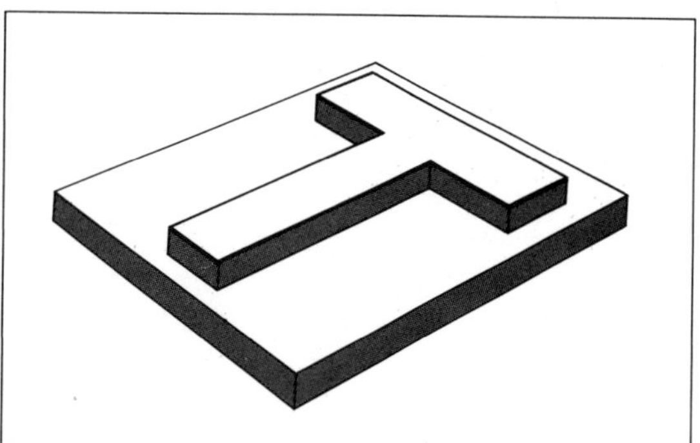

Figure 4.1. Relief symbol Relief printing is the transfer of an image from a raised surface carrier to the printed sheet.

There is some overlap between the two classifications, but all techniques are defined according to the intended use of the assembled images. The typewriter assembles symbols from cast characters that strike a sheet of paper through an inked ribbon. If the image on the page is intended to be photographically reproduced, it is cold type composition. It is also possible to set hot type symbols, such as foundry type, and then make copies or "proofs" on a special press. These copies can then be photographed and used to generate any form of image carrier. This technique would be classified as cold type. It is also possible to prepare cold type images that can be used to generate relief printing plates, as in photoengraving.

The purpose of this chapter is to examine the principal techniques of generating cold type images. There are three basic cold type procedures:

- Manual image generation,
- Strike-on composition,
- Photographic image generation.

Manual Image Generation

Hand Techniques

Images can be created by hand with such instruments as a pen, pencil, or brush. We all understand how to use these devices, but there are some special considerations when drawing for printing production.

The use of any pencil image for cold type composition should be avoided, because graphite does not photograph well. All drawings should be prepared with a pen and black india ink. A variety of devices are designed for hand illustration with ink. Some are as simple as the traditional ruling pen. Others, such as the speedball system, have interchangeable quill points (figure 4.2). Still others, such as a Rapidograph, have ink reservoirs and interchangeable floating points. Whatever pen is used, however, the concerns are the same. The lines should be dense, with sharp, uniform edges. It is better to draw illustrations larger than reproduction size and then photographically reduce them than to draw them small and enlarge them. Reduction always sharpens an image; enlargement decreases line quality.

Paper influences the quality of any drawing. Uncoated papers such as newsprint tend to absorb ink rapidly into the paper fibers and give a ragged edge to any inked line. Coated papers generally have a slick, shiny surface that does not absorb ink. The ink dries by evaporation and produces nearly ideal line quality. Most hand-drawn images are placed on coated stock or are set directly onto special layout illustration board.

Pressure-Sensitive Materials

Several types of material are designed to transfer an image to illustration board or paper by means of adhesion. One type uses a plastic support sheet that carries a dense image on one side and an adhesive layer on the other. Many special-effect tints or images are available in sheet form (figure 4.3). A large piece of this material can be placed over an inked image, the plastic cut to the image outline, and the unwanted materials removed. The plastic-based image will be nearly permanently affixed if it is then burnished (pressed flat) with a roller or blunt instrument. Sheet pressure-sensitive materials should always be cut in the center of any inked image lines (figure 4.4).

Adhesive alphabets can be purchased on large acetate sheets. Individual letters are cut and will adhere to nearly any surface. Letter spacing of characters depends on the illustrator's own visual judgment.

Other forms of adhesive image generation material are available on rolls, like cellophane tape, with an image affixed to the base side. The roll form is typically used to create decorative borders, but tapes of varying widths can be used to generate black lines on any layout (figure 4.5).

Dry transfer is a pressure-sensitive material that carries a carbon-based image on a special transparent sheet (figure 4.6). The image can be transferred by merely rubbing the

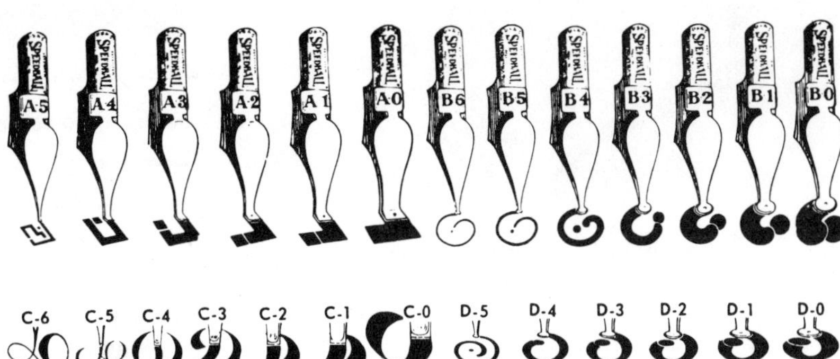

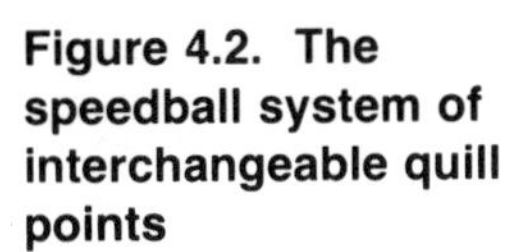

Figure 4.2. The speedball system of interchangeable quill points
Courtesy of Speedball.

Figure 4.3. Pressure-sensitive images and tints These are some examples of special-effect images or tints that are available as pressure-sensitive materials.

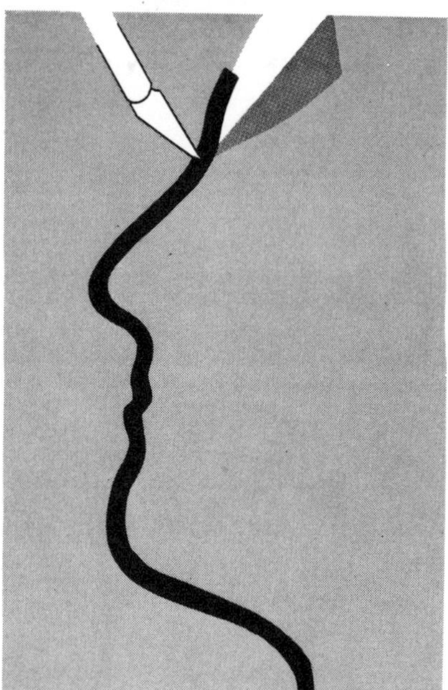

Figure 4.4. Cutting pressure-sensitive materials The proper place to cut pressure-sensitive materials is in the center of the inked image line.

face of the sheet after the symbol design is positioned over the desired spot on the illustration board. A wide variety of alphabet styles and special symbols can be purchased from an ever-increasing number of manufacturers. Dry transfer is widely used as an inexpensive cold type composition method for headlines or large display messages.

Prepared Images

Prepared images are designs produced and sold as a service to small printers who cannot afford to hire full-time artists. The printer pays a small subscription fee, and books of camera-ready drawings are supplied on a monthly basis. With the fee comes certification that the designs are copyright-free to the printer. Most prepared-image services are nationwide organizations that mass produce printed illustrations on coated papers. Figures are usually provided in several different sizes, so enlargements or reductions are not

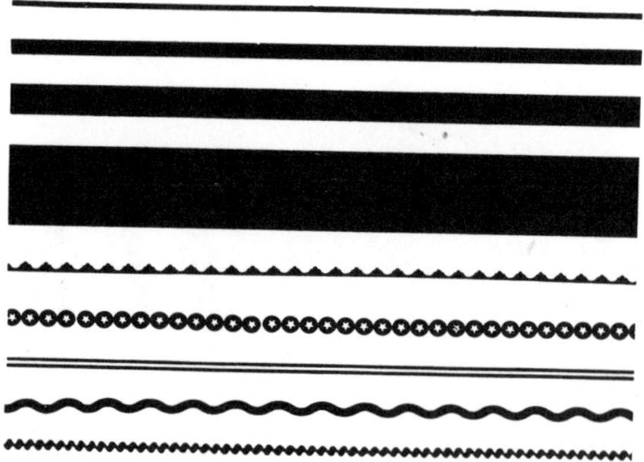

Figure 4.5. Pressure-sensitive tape Examples of pressure-sensitive images that are available on rolls include rules and borders.

necessary. Prepared images on particular themes can also be ordered. Some services even provide camera-ready four-color separations for color printing.

Strike-on Composition

Strike-on Composition Devices

The first practical strike-on composition device—the typewriter—was introduced to America around 1870. Early typewriters were hardly more efficient than writing by hand, but modern electric models produce copy at great speeds and rival hot type for the production of sharp, clear, quality images.

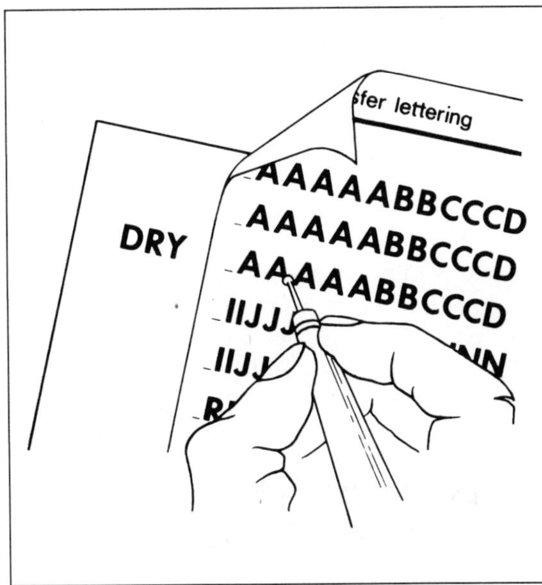

Figure 4.6. Dry transfer images Many typefaces are available in different sizes and series in dry transfer material.

There are several ways to categorize strike-on devices. An important one for printing production is by the type of ribbon used. All typewriters form images by the contact of a raised character through a pigment-carrying ribbon onto some image receiver (usually paper). Ribbons may be cloth or carbon. Cloth ribbons are designed to recirculate. When the ink in the cloth ribbon no longer transfers a quality image to the page, the ribbon is discarded and a new one inserted. Carbon ribbons are formed from a carbon-based pigment adhered to one side of a plastic strip. The ribbon advances each time a character is typed, but it does not recirculate. Carbon ribbons are designed to be used once and then replaced.

The main advantage of a carbon over a cloth ribbon is the quality of the image produced. Because the cloth ribbon recirculates, it is possible for the ink density on the page to vary. It is also common to transfer the design of the ribbon fabric as well as the character outline. The carbon ribbon is used only once, so character density is absolutely consistent. The plastic base prevents any fabric patterns from being formed in the character. Cloth ribbons generally give unacceptable quality for printing reproduction (figure 4.7).

Typewriters can also be classified according to manual or electric operation. On manual devices there is a direct link between the keyboard and the strike-on character. The harder the key is pressed, the harder the character strikes the ribbon. It is difficult for a typist to exert uniform pressure on each key, and the result is typically an uneven appearance of letters on the paper. The keys on an electric typewriter are not physically linked to the character; instead, they direct an electrical impulse that activates a spring mechanism. No matter how hard a key is pressed, the character strikes the ribbon with the same

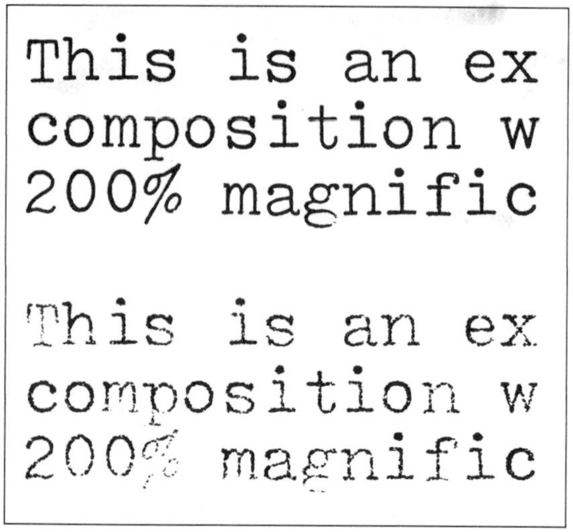

This is an ex
composition w
200% magnific

This is an ex
composition w
200% magnific

Figure 4.7. Comparison of quality between carbon and cloth ribbons Compare the quality of the images produced by carbon ribbon (top) and cloth ribbon (bottom). Both samples are reproduced at 200% magnification.

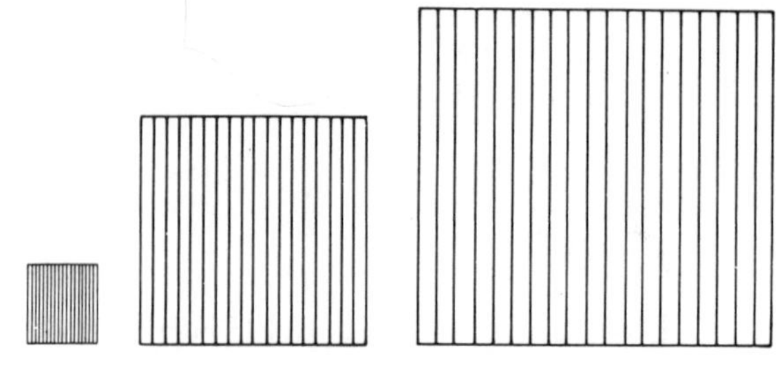

Figure 4.8. Examples of em sizes The em is a variable measure from one type size to another. The em is divided into eighteen uniform segments in the unit system of measure.

amount of pressure. Manual typewriters are considered unacceptable for cold type composition. Most manual machines use only a cloth ribbon and are designed for office or home use.

A third way to categorize strike-on devices is by character width. Most typewriters have a font of symbols of uniform horizontal dimension. If a letter *m* is typed, the machine can be backspaced and a letter *i* can be typed in the same visual space. This design makes for inexpensive machine construction, but it does not give the same visual quality as a line of foundry type. **Proportionally spaced strike-on machines** are more complicated to construct, but they produce characters of differing horizontal sizes, depending on the specific character. A photocopy of a line of foundry type and a line of proportionally spaced strike-on composition should give the same visual quality.

Almost all **strike-on composition** intended for reproduction is formed on electric, proportionally spaced, carbon ribbon typewriters.

Unit Measurement System

All composition systems, whether hot or cold type, are based on some measurement system to specify type sizes and spacing. Cold type composition uses the point and pica system (6 picas = 1 inch, 12 points = 1 pica). However, a variety of specifications are used to determine character width (set width) and spacing. All specifications are based on the unit system of measurement.

In hot type composition of foundry type, word spacing is based on the **em quad.** An em is a unit of measure that changes depending upon the size of type font being used. A 12-point font uses ems that are 12 points on a side, a 36-point font uses ems that are 36 points square.

The unit system for cold type composition systems divides the em into uniform segments—usually eighteen (figure 4.8). Each division is called a unit and can be used to define individual character set width. The smaller the unit size, the more accurate the word and letter spacing for straight composition.

Semiautomatic Strike-on Composition

Semiautomatic machines require the operator to type each line of type twice. The first time determines the quantity of spacing necessary to obtain the required line length. The second typing produces a final camera-ready copy that contains the proper spacing.

Typical of **semiautomatic strike-on composition** is the Varityper composing machine. All models have interchangeable type styles and are designed to use two different fonts (figure 4.9) at the same time. There are over twelve hundred typefaces available, ranging in size from 3½ points to 13 points. The machine has an open carriage, so paper of any size can be used. Special attachments that produce quality ruled lines combined with type material may be added, so the machine is ideal for setting forms and tables. The Varityper has the added feature of being able to control line spacing (or leading) in ½-point increments. The lines may even be set solid.

In actual operation, the typist first sets the desired line length into the machine. The line is then typed, and the required additional space is determined from a "dial pointer system." The operator then tabs to the right and retypes the line. During the second typing, the machine automatically adds the required spacing between words to bring the printed line to the desired length.

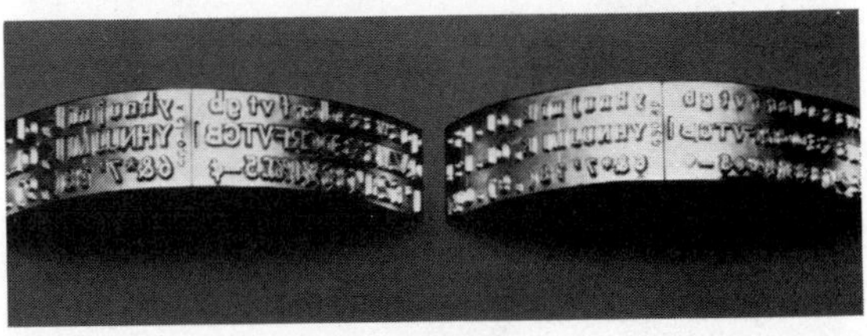

Figure 4.9. The Varityper composing machine and fonts
Courtesy of Addressograph-Multigraph, Varityper Division.

The advantage of any semiautomatic strike-on system is that the operator does not have to have extensive skills or training (such as a Linotype operator must have) in order to produce quality camera-ready composition. However, because each line must be typed a second time, the process is slow and there is twice the chance for a typing error.

Automatic Strike-on Composition

Automatic strike-on machines require the operator to type each line of type only once. A final copy is automatically typed a second

Figure 4.10. The IBM Selectric system and fonts
Courtesy of IBM.

time by the machine according to line length specifications set up by the typist.

One example of **automatic strike-on composition** is the IBM Selectric system (figure 4.10). The Selectric package is made up of a magnetic tape Selectric typewriter (MT/ST) and a magnetic tape Selectric composer (MT/SC). An operator types copy on the Selectric typewriter, and a magnetic tape is produced (some systems produce a paper tape, but the concept of tape control is the same). The typist is not concerned with line length, type size, or leading. An "idiot" tape (a magnetic record of the original manuscript) is generated. If a mistake is made, the operator backspaces, retypes the proper characters, and the tape is automatically corrected. The first typewritten copy becomes a proof before the final camera-ready copy is prepared.

Once the proof sheet is approved, the tape is placed on the tape reader in line with the Selectric composer. The operator places the proper font on the composer and adjusts the settings for required line length and line leading. The tape drive directs the composer at the rate of 150 words per minute for both straight and flush left composition. The machine, however, will not automatically hyphenate. It stops whenever a hyphenation decision needs to be made. The operator must make the decision before the machine will continue to type.

The tape system has clear advantages. With an idiot tape, the printer can store jobs and then reset the copy at any time, in any typeface, and in any length without having to regenerate composition instructions. With magnetic tapes, corrections can be made at any future date without destroying the entire record. Several tapes can be merged to generate a new tape with portions from the original two. The chance for error is diminished with the automatic machine because there is a hard-copy proof of the total job before the machine sets the final copy.

Photographic Image Generation— Body Composition

The bulk of all cold type body composition is photographic in nature. The primary advantage of photo image generation is speed. Hand composition of foundry type can be set by a "quick" (an early term for a skilled compositor) at the average rate of perhaps 1 character per second (CPS). Line-casting hot type machines might average 4 CPS. An expert typist on a good day can generate perhaps 8 CPS (100 words per minute). But the common photocomposing machine for line composition can produce around 150 CPS, and special cathode ray tube machines can produce between 1,000 and 12,000 characters each second.

It is a hopeless task to attempt to examine or even to review the hundreds of different photographic body composition devices. But it is possible to formulate a typical unit and then examine possible variations (figure 4.11). All body composition photographic units have some form of the following systems:

- Input system,
- Information storage system,
- Editing system,
- Computing system,
- Image generation system.

Input Systems

An **input system** is any device that links the human operator with the operation of the composition machine. All current systems

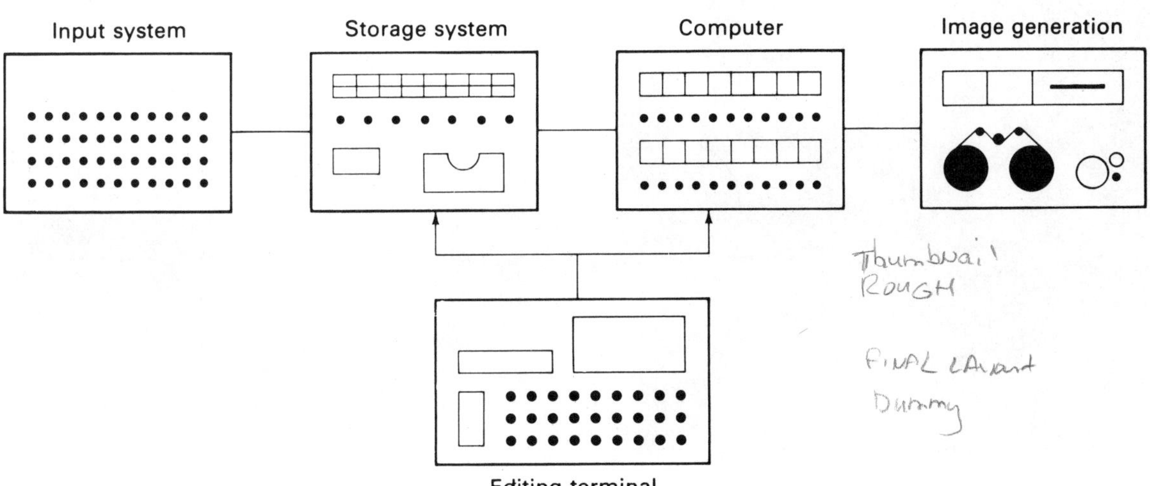

Figure 4.11. A typical body type photographic composition unit

utilize a keyboard that is similar in character distribution to a standard typewriter. Instead of activating a strike-on character, however, each time a key is depressed an electrical impulse is generated that will direct the machine to form that key character. Depending on the machine's level of sophistication, the keyboard function can be classified as "operator controlled" or as an "idiot keyboard."

Operator-Controlled Keyboards. With an **operator-controlled keyboard** (sometimes called a **counting keyboard**) all end-of-line decisions are made as the copy is typed (figure 4.12). The operator must specify type point size, line length, and minimum and maximum word spacing and must have an in-depth understanding of the machine's controls. Most machines subtract the unit width of each character as it is typed from the maximum allowable line length. As the minimum line length is approached, the machine informs the operator that an end-of-line decision must be made. The operator can continue inputting information as close to the maximum line length as possible (with full words or hyphenations) or can decide to end the line at any point. It has been estimated that half of the operator's time is spent making end-of-line decisions under this system.

Idiot Keyboards. **Idiot keyboards** (sometimes called **noncounting keyboards**) require no special operator skills (figure 4.13). The typist must only specify paragraph indentations and mode changes such as changes to a boldface or italic design as the manuscript copy is typed. From an idiot keyboard, the machine can be programmed to make all end-of-line decisions and can be adjusted to any desired line length, type style, or leading size.

Information Storage

On some machines, information from the keyboard is immediately directed to the com-

Figure 4.12. Example of a counting keyboard
Courtesy of Compugraphic Corporation.

Figure 4.13. Example of a noncounting. keyboard
Courtesy of Mergenthaler Linotype Company.

puter control and image formation units. More commonly, the information is stored in some intermediary device, such as a punched paper tape, magnetic tape, floppy disk, or OCR sheet. With high-speed composition machines, a direct link between a human operator and the output device is too slow. It is more efficient to have several typists preparing storage tapes. The completed information records are then placed on a separate unit for output at high speed. In this way, the composition device is rarely standing idle.

Paper Tapes. **Paper tapes** are generally narrow-band (about 1 inch or 2.54 centimeters in width) continuous strips in which holes are punched that correspond to a particular keyboard symbol. The image generation device can then "read" the punches and output the appropriate character. Corrections can be made on the tape by punching a certain code. The output device will automatically delete the undesired symbols.

Magnetic Tapes. **Magnetic tapes** are similar in design to paper tapes, but instead of punched holes, electrical impulses carry the message. One type to emerge in recent years is the small cassette design, which is inexpensive and easy to store and manipulate. Magnetic tapes can be read by machine at a faster rate of speed than paper tapes during the output phase and tend to hold up longer under heavy use. Paper tape can easily tear, and each tape can be used for only one job. Magnetic tapes can be erased by a strong electromagnetic field and can be used and reused to receive different jobs.

Floppy Disks. **Floppy disks** are a special type of magnetic tape. Instead of being wound on a reel, like tape recorder tape, the material comes in sheet form, like a phonograph record. The advantages of the disk over the reel are that the disk can hold much more information, it is less expensive, and the operator can instantly locate pieces of information on a disk surface rather than having to search a reel by rewinding.

OCR System. OCR stands for "optical character recognition." With the **OCR system** a typewriter is used to prepare on paper a visual record of the original copy. Special characters are used that can be interpreted by the machine (figure 4.14). Corrections can be made on the page by use of special symbols that instruct the machine reader to ignore

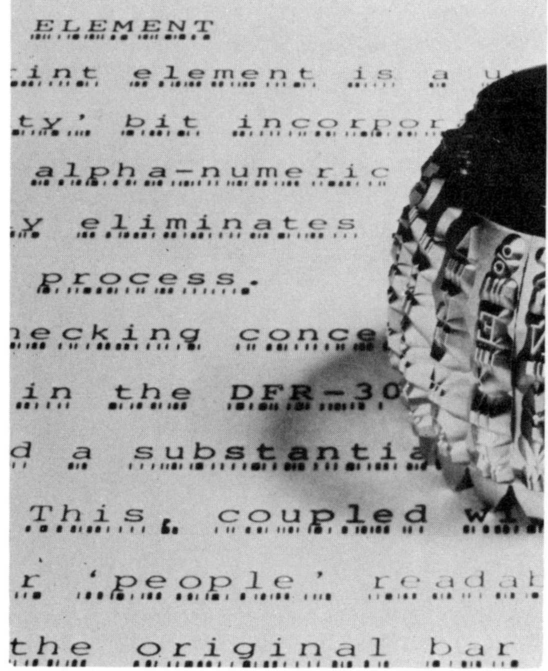

Figure 4.14. Special OCR characters
Courtesy of Addressograph-Multigraph, Varityper Division.

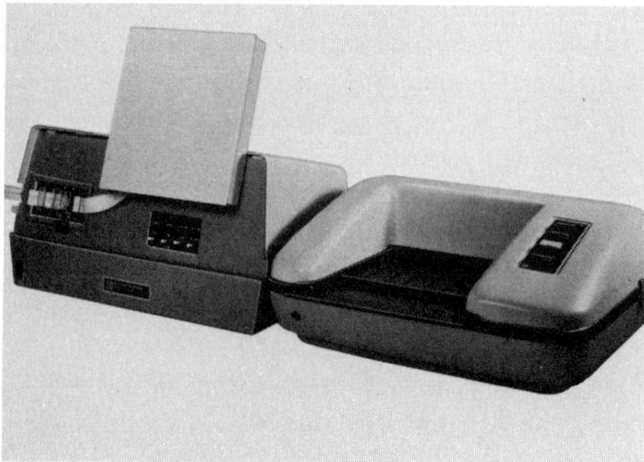

Figure 4.15. An OCR scanning device
Courtesy of Addressograph-Multigraph, Varityper Division.

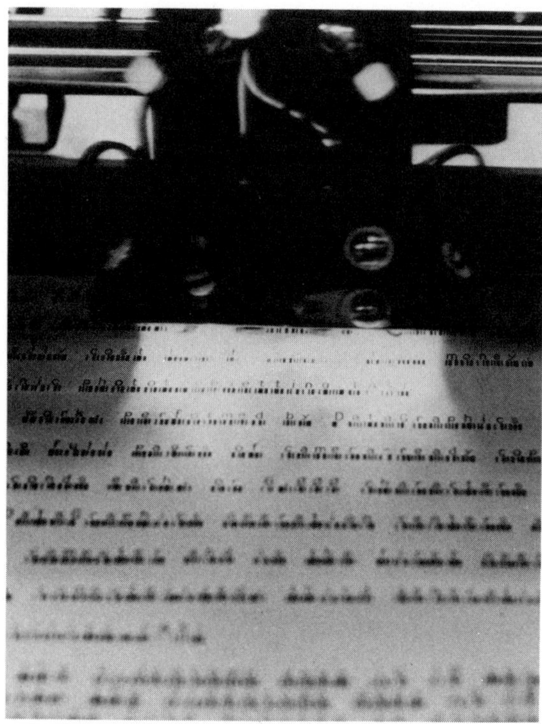

Figure 4.16. Reading OCR characters
Courtesy of Addressograph-Multigraph, Varityper Division.

preceding characters. When the desired copy is prepared, it can be placed on a special optical scanning device that converts the typewritten information to a punched paper tape (figure 4.15). Typical scanners can read nearly 2,500 characters a minute, punch up to 40 characters per second, and will misread no more than 1 out of every 20,000 characters (figure 4.16). Most machines cannot react to light blue or red lines, so the page may be marked with special instructions in those colors without fear of interfering with the read function.

There are several advantages to the OCR system: it is not necessary to have a highly trained operator to control the total system, the hard-copy output allows rapid proofreading before the paper tape is punched, and the sheet can be easily filed for reuse at a later date. Paper tapes, on the other hand, are difficult to store and relocate.

Editing Systems

There are two basic forms of editing systems: operator keyboard editing and tape editing prior to actual machine composition.

Keyboard Editing. The advantage of keyboard editing is that nearly perfect input is produced before the tape is punched. There is usually some form of visual display device on the input unit that the operator can watch as the copy is typed. This system is used on counting keyboards that can store information on a floppy disk or in a small computer. The operator can call up a replay of any part of a job to edit, add information, or proofread. With the recall system, the operator stops the display at any error, makes the correction, and then continues scanning the line. The main disadvantage of keyboard editing is the amount of nonproductive operator time used in the editing process.

Tape Editing. The saving of operator time is the main advantage of the tape-editing approach. When an idiot record is produced with a "blind keyboard" (without a visual display unit), the operator is not concerned with anything except inputting the copy. Special devices are used to read the completed tape and either display the copy on a large video screen or produce hard proofreading copy (figure 4.17). With this system, a trained proofreader can rapidly make corrections by erasing and altering a magnetic tape or by automatically generating a second tape while the keyboard operator is inputting additional copy.

Computer Control

A computer is nothing more than a sophisticated adding machine. It has the ability to store or remember great quantities of information and can operate at very rapid speeds. In phototypesetting, it is the computer that translates keyboard operations into electrical signals that the typesetting unit can understand.

Hyphenless Systems. There are several levels of sophistication with computer control. The simplest is a hyphenless system that makes end-of-line decisions to the nearest complete word and justifies a line by increasing or decreasing word (and sometimes letter) spacing (figure 4.18a). When setting narrow columns, this can produce a poor typographic appearance with "rivers" of visual space down a page.

Discretionary System. With discretionary systems the operator hyphenates every word of three or more syllables with a special symbol that is typed near the end of the line. At the end-of-line decision, the machine can au-

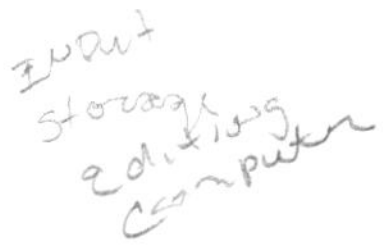

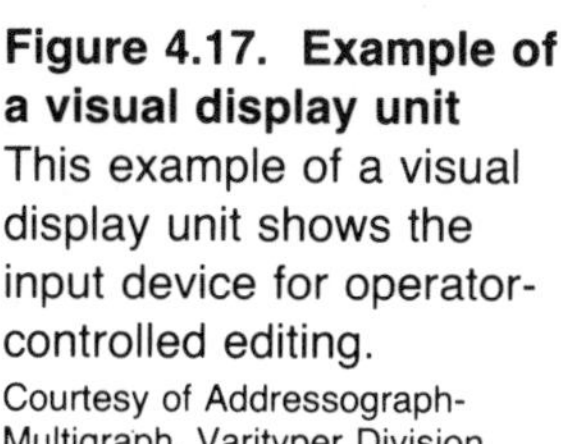

Figure 4.17. Example of a visual display unit
This example of a visual display unit shows the input device for operator-controlled editing.
Courtesy of Addressograph-Multigraph, Varityper Division.

tomatically hyphenate to the nearest syllable and ignore all other hyphenations in the line (figure 4.18b). Although the use of discretionary hyphenation produces a more attractive page, the process is extremely time consuming at the keyboard.

Computer Programmed System. The most complex system is a computer programmed to make end-of-line decisions automatically with a set of detailed hyphenation rules. One of the few disadvantages of this system is that the machine can only follow literal instructions. It cannot tell the difference between two words with different meanings that are spelled the same. It will treat *mi-nute* (small) the same as *min-ute* (a measure of time). To overcome this and other limitations, special exception dictionaries are programmed into the machine to give the machine special instructions for problem words. An operator can program into the exception dictionary any words unique to the vocabulary of the special field being worked with. The last word in each line is compared with every word in the exception list. If the word is located, the appropriate division is made. If the word is not included on the list, it is hyphenated according to the general rules of logic. The automatic hyphenation system is efficient, fast, and produces good typographic composition. But the software (the programming, as compared to hardware, which is the machine itself) is extremely expensive and is therefore limited to only the largest industrial situations.

(a)

The word "technology" has
become a common part of the
vocabulary of this society.
Technology is often discussed as if
it were some mythical beast that
could be coaxed or caged into
submission. We tend to view it as
a physical object or living being
that we can blame for most of our
social ills.

(b)

The word "technology" has become a common part of the vocabulary of this society. Technology is
often discussed as if it were some
mythical beast that could be coaxed or caged into submission. We
tend to view it as a physical object or living being that we can
blame for most of our social ills.

Figure 4.18. Computer justified type In hyphenless end-of-line decisions, the line is finished to the nearest complete word (a). The lines can be further adjusted and the overall appearance of the text improved by using discretionary hyphenation (b).

Image Formation Units

First Generation Phototypesetting. There have been many advances in the way images are actually formed in the phototypesetting processes. The first phototypesetter, commercially introduced in 1946, used the idea of the Linotype casting system. Instead of using a die to cast molten metal, a metal frame carried a small film negative. As a key was hit on the keyboard, a matrix would fall into place in front of a light source. The light would then be projected through the film onto a sheet of photographic paper. The disadvantage was that each character could not be formed until the appropriate negative fell by gravity into the projection position. The process was too slow. The technique of dropping negatives into place and then projecting light through the opening is called the first generation of phototypesetting.

Second Generation of Phototypesetting. The second generation places an entire font of characters on a single carrier and moves each symbol in front of a light source as directed by a computer. One idea is to rotate the font and to flash the lamp as the desired negative outline comes in line (figure 4.19). The negative projection systems typically can compose copy at a rate of 25 to 150 CPS (characters per second). Some models can carry several alphabet designs on the same negative carrier. Others can enlarge, reduce, or make characters oblique (slanted) by movement of the lens element.

Third Generation of Phototypesetting. The third generation of phototypesetting bypasses light projection through a film negative and forms each character by means of a

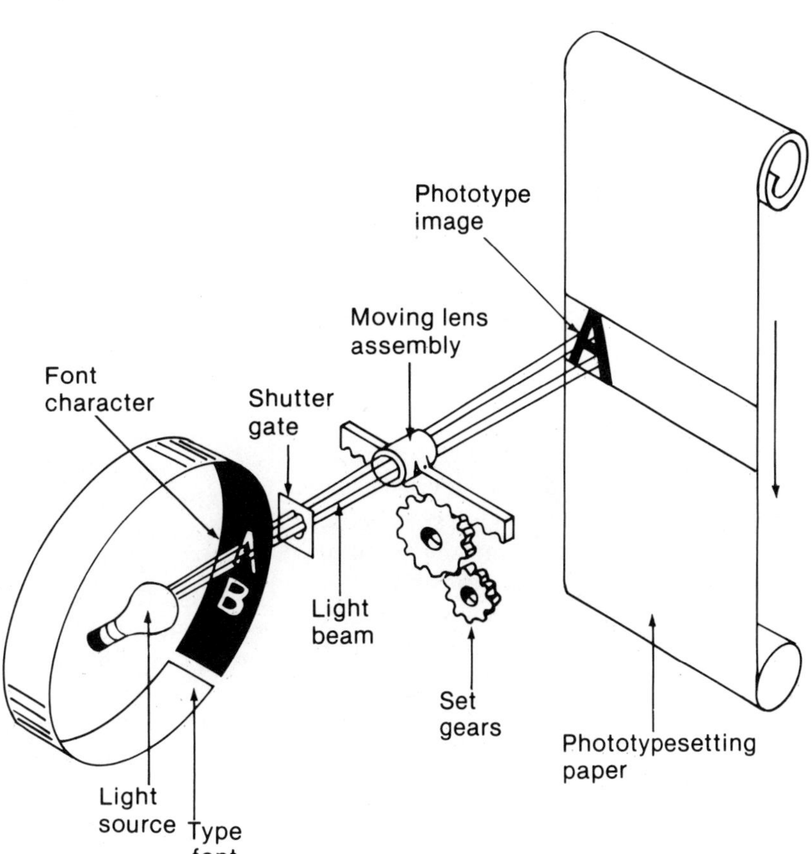

Figure 4.19. Diagram of a rotating font with flashing unit

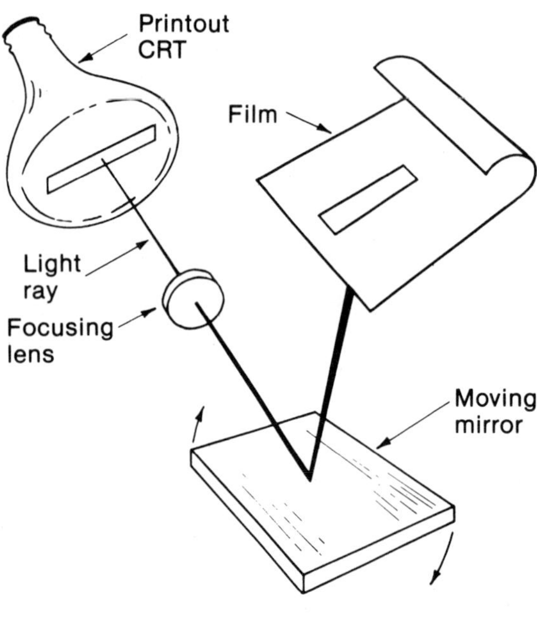

Figure 4.20. A method of transferring CRT images The printout cathode ray tube directs the image through a focusing lens to a moving mirror and onto the film.

computer. The system operates on the idea of image formation on a screen, similar to the way a picture is formed on a television screen. The process is called cathode ray tube (CRT) character generation. Some manufacturers call their process digital composition.

All **CRT character generation** can be classified as either dot or line formation. In the line formation method, a selected character is scanned onto the CRT as a series of individual lines. The number of lines scanned controls the quality of symbol resolution on the film. At standard resolution, characters are formed from 650 successive vertical lines per inch (256 lines per cm); at high resolution, 1,300 lines per inch (512 lines per cm). The standard device can produce sizes from 4 to 30 points, although the machine has an option that gives a maximum size of 72 points.

In dot formation CRT design, the character is stored as electrical impulses in a digital computer. As an information tape calls up a symbol, it is formed on the cathode ray tube as a series of small dots. A lens then focuses the image and projects it onto photographic print paper or film. It is difficult to find any difference of output quality between dot and line formation.

There are two basic techniques for transferring the CRT image to a sheet of photographic paper. In the first, light is focused through a lens from the screen and then bounced from a moving mirror onto the film or paper (figure 4.20). The purpose of the mirror is to direct each character into its proper position as lines of type are composed. A computer controls both image generation and mirror movement.

With the second transfer technique, a series of thousands of pieces of fiber optics material carries the light to the photographic material. The fibers are run from the CRT screen to a glass plate. The film or paper is then moved across the plate as images are formed.

CRT character generation is extremely fast. It is common to compose type at the rate of 4,000 to 5,000 characters per second. Since a type font is not being used to pass light, it is very easy to change size and type style. This quality makes the system valuable for high-quality output jobs such as classified ad pages, telephone books, sophisticated tabular work, or special-purpose production.

One special feature of CRT image generation is the potential to translate continuous-tone images (such as black-and-white photographs) into dots or lines on the cathode ray tube. The original print is fed through a special scanner attachment, and densitrometric readings are converted to electrical impulses that form a duplicate image on the output device. (Density refers to the darkness or lightness of an image; the subject is explained in detail in chapter six.) Unlike halftone photography, the resulting designs are produced from lines or dots of uniform size. With a high number of lines per inch and subsequent reduction onto film, an acceptable duplication can be produced. With this system, both text and illustrations can be projected in final form onto photosensitive paper, film, or even a printing plate.

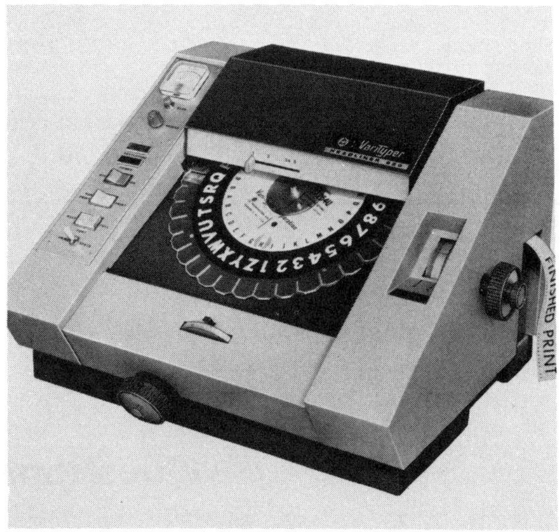

Figure 4.21. An example of an automatic spacing photo display device
Courtesy of Addressograph-Multigraph, Varityper Division.

Photographic Image Generation— Display Composition

Display character generation has usually been defined by the point size of the characters formed. The versatility of body composition machines that allow high-speed assembly of large point size characters makes this definition inadequate. Photographic display machines are more accurately identified by several factors: larger-than-body type size, wide choice of character fonts that can quickly be changed, and the intended use of the composed lines as a headline or body heading.

All photographic display generation devices operate on the basic concept of image formation by light passing through a negative image carrier onto photosensitive paper or film. There is a wide range of display composition machines; but at the most basic level, all devices can be labeled either manual or automatic letter-spacing machines.

Most **manual letter-spacing machines** are designed to be used in a darkroom situation. The advantage of the system is that the operator actually sees what is being composed.

Most **automatic letter-spacing machines** (figure 4.21) can be used outside of a darkroom situation and are designed to develop photosensitive materials automatically (or have a light-trap container that can be used to carry the paper or film from the machine to the darkroom). The operator cannot see the actual results of the composition but rather "programs" the machine automatically to place a uniform quantity of space between each letter.

Key Terms

composition
hot type composition
cold type composition
dry transfer
proportionally spaced composition
strike-on composition
em quad
counting keyboard
non-counting keyboard
paper tape
magnetic tape
floppy disk
OCR system
CRT character generation
phototypesetting

Questions for Review

1. What are the three basic cold type image generation procedures?
2. Why is it better to draw illustrations larger than the desired reproduction size when preparing hand-drawn inked images?
3. Name two types of pressure-sensitive materials.
4. What is the difference between a cloth ribbon and a carbon ribbon for strike-on cold type composition?
5. What does the term "proportionally spaced strike-on machine composition" mean?
6. Describe the basic procedures for preparing copy on a semiautomatic strike-on composition device.
7. What is the advantage of a tape storage system on an automatic composition device?
8. What is the primary advantage of photographic composition?
9. What are the five basic systems that form a typical photograph body composition unit?
10. What is the difference between an operator-controlled keyboard and an idiot keyboard on an input system?
11. What are the two types of character generation on a CRT (cathode ray tube) composition machine?
12. What does OCR mean?
13. What is the difference between body images and display images? How are they defined?

Chapter Five

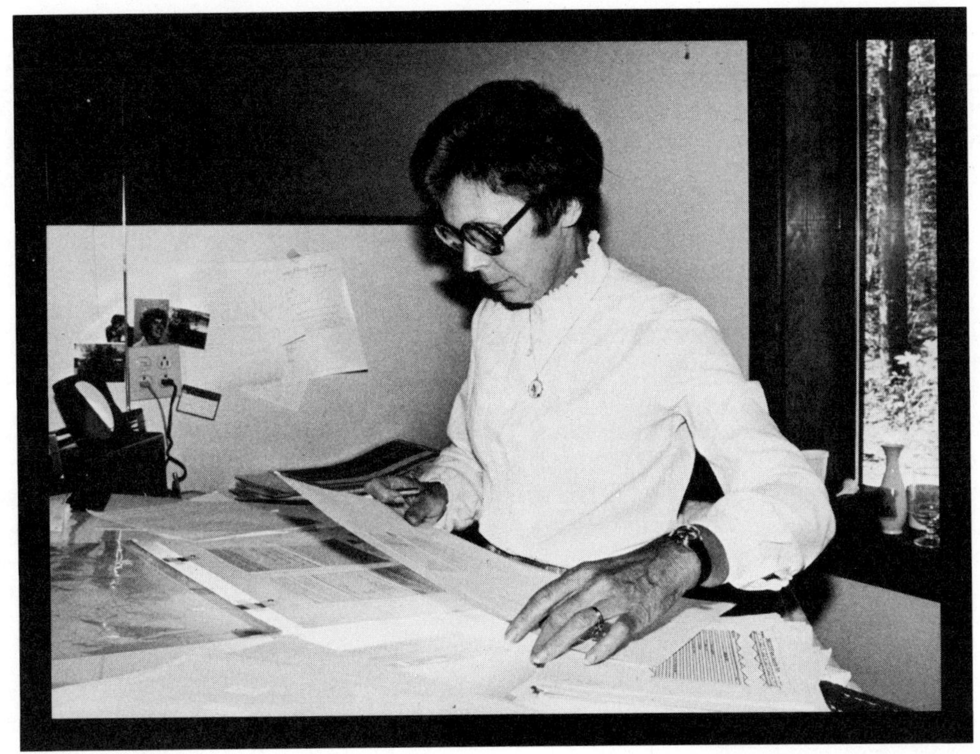

Image Assembly: Layout and Paste-up Techniques

Anecdote to Chapter Five

The practice of paste-up was not widespread until after World War II. The tradition of hot metal type was so firmly entrenched in every printing endeavor that no one bothered much about other ways of creating images. Since World War II, however, the growth of both lithography and gravure as significant industrial processes has pushed the development of alternative methods of setting type. Lithography and gravure are photography-based processes that do not require the raised surface and heavy material of relief printing.

One early practice for applying hot metal to gravure and lithography was to set type by linotype and pull reproduction proofs on a special proof press that produced exceptionally high-quality images. The proofs would be photographed, and plates made. The type would then be melted down and recast into other jobs. This was an expensive process; but even today some printers feel that it is the best method of obtaining ideal word and letter spacing and the sharpest images.

Paste-up artists working at a layout board
Courtesy of Connie Kindred.

The pressure to generate type photographically was so great that one of the first systems was built by the Merganthaler Linotype Company. The system used a gravity-feed design that was identical to the linotype machine. But the electronic revolution made possible controls that rendered obsolete the slow, expensive gravity feed of negatives in metal carriers for composition. The introduction of photocomposition systems created a new job in the printing industry: paste-up artist.

Early paste-up techniques had some problems. One was the type of base used to receive the image. So many fine stable-base materials exist today that we tend to take them for granted. Early paste-up artists soon encountered problems when using paper to carry type or drawings for multicolor work. With a change in temperature, the size of the paper would change, and none of the colors would fit when photographed and run on the press. Some artists used glass to do paste-up. Plate glass tended to be stable but was expensive. It was also dangerous to drop a glass-base paste-up.

With the paste-up artist came a new vocabulary. Cast type was called "hot metal" or "hot type," so it seemed natural to name photographic composition the opposite, or "cold type." Arguments arose over this term. Many thought it was not descriptive enough and suggested as an alternative "flat type." Cold type won the argument, and we still use the term today to describe any composition that is intended to be photographed.

New developments in electronics point to more changes in layout and paste-up. Machines now exist that allow the artist to compose total pages—including rule, line drawings, and windows—on a cathode ray tube. Once set on the screen, the photographic output produces the complete job. Some machines even photographically direct the job onto a plate, thus making the darkroom unnecessary.

The area of paste-up is very young in the printing trades. New roles and more sophisticated techniques are still evolving as the practice matures.

Objectives for Chapter Five

After completing this chapter you will be able to:

- Identify common layout and paste-up tools and materials.
- Use a proportion scale to determine copy size adjustments.
- Identify the three techniques for dealing with photographs on a paste-up.
- Describe the procedure of working from a rough layout.
- Describe the steps for preparing a single-color paste-up, including mounting the board, adding layout lines, and attaching the copy or artwork.
- Describe the procedures for cutting a mask.
- Describe the steps for preparing a multicolor paste-up.
- Describe the steps for preparing a reverse.
- Describe the steps for preparing a surprint.

Introduction

Chapters 3 and 4 dealt with the processes used by designers and printers to create images for graphic reproduction. The different devices and techniques used to generate camera-ready images were discussed in some detail. It is a rare device, however, that can produce all the composition needs for a single job. The final work might be made up of line drawings, body composition, display composition, and photographs, all of which require three or four different techniques or devices to create.

The goal of image assembly is to bring all the different pieces of composition together into a final form that meets job specifications and is of sufficient quality to be

Figure 5.1. Drafting board A drafting board is an acceptable paste-up surface.

Figure 5.2. Glass-top table Some layout artists use a glass surface for paste-up.

photographically reproduced. Printers generally refer to this camera-ready copy as a **final layout,** a **paste-up,** or sometimes a **mechanical.**

Materials for Layout and Paste-up

Surfaces for Layout

There are three basic types of paste-up surface:

- Drafting board,
- Glass-top table,
- Light table.

The least expensive surface is the common **drafting board** (figure 5.1). The surface is usually set at an angle to eliminate light reflection from the paper or board and to reduce back strain for the paste-up artist. Many companies cover the wooden board with thick, coated paper or with a special adhesive-backed plastic. Any surface is acceptable as long as it is flat and smooth and the edges are perfectly straight.

The second common type of paste-up surface is a **glass plate** mounted on an **angled table** (figure 5.2). The main advantage of the glass is that it is hard and will not be damaged when pieces of copy are trimmed with a razor blade or Exacto knife.

The third type of surface is a stripper's **light table** (figure 5.3). Light tables are used during stripping to bring together pieces of transparent film (see chapter 10). A light table is made from a sheet of frosted glass with a light that shines up through the glass from beneath the plate. With a light table it is possible to see through most layout paper. When preprinted layout sheets are used, it is possible to see through the copy to line up images with the printed guidelines.

Paste-up Board

Several different materials are used by the industry for paste-up board. The most stable and expensive material is called **illustration board.** Different manufacturers use their own

Figure 5.3. Light table A light table is also used for paste-up.

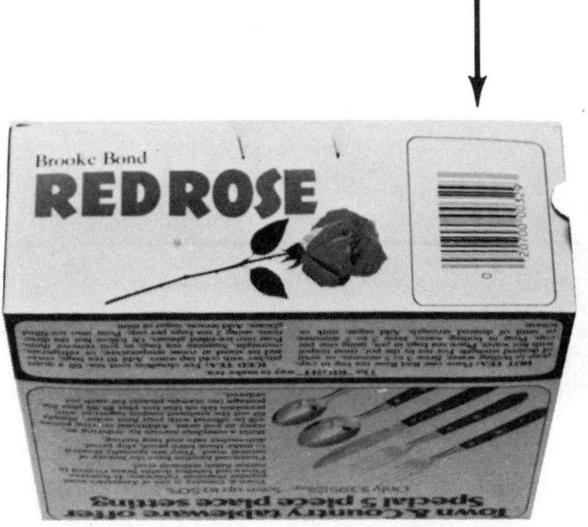

Figure 5.4. Printing the Uniform Product Code (UPC) Printing this code imposes critical size tolerances for the printer because variations in code bar thicknesses will result in inaccurate readings at the cash register.

trade name, but their products all have the same general characteristics. Illustration board is smooth, white, and has a finish that allows for ruling of inked lines without feathering. **Feathering** is the tendency of ink on a rough, porous surface to spread, which is undesirable because it results in uneven weight lines. Illustration board is formed from laminated layers of board stock and paper. It is a thick, strong material that is not easily damaged with handling.

An increasingly common paste-up material is 60- or 70-pound **offset paper** (see chapter 20 for a discussion of paper types). Offset is a paper grade widely used in the printing industry. The pound measure refers to paper weight and is a general description of paper thickness. Sixty- or 70-pound paper is thinner than the stock used for business cards but thicker than most office typing paper.

Companies with jobs that all conform to the same column or page size, such as newspapers, usually print guidelines on offset paper to receive the paste-up. With this technique, the layout artist does not have to redraw guidelines for every paper or job. **Preprinted paste-up sheets** are widely used for this purpose.

Offset paper is popular as a paste-up board material because it is inexpensive and can be used on a light table. Use of preprinted sheets with the light table usually cuts down on labor costs, because paste-ups can be produced very rapidly.

Yet another type of paste-up material is stable-base **mylar** or **acetate** (plastic) **sheets.** Some clear sheeting is used, but the most common type has a frosted surface. The main use of this material is as an overlay to carry images for a second color.

Stable-base means the size of the sheet will not change with moderate changes in temperature. Dimensional stability is very important with jobs involving the register of two

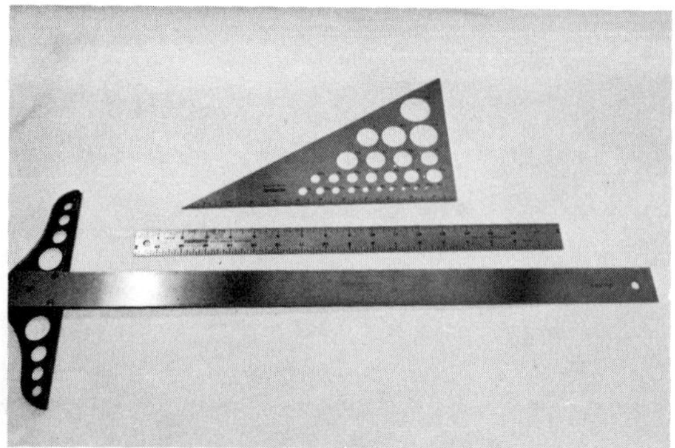

Figure 5.5. Three basic layout and paste-up tools T-squares, triangles, and rulers are available in both plastic and steel and in various lengths.

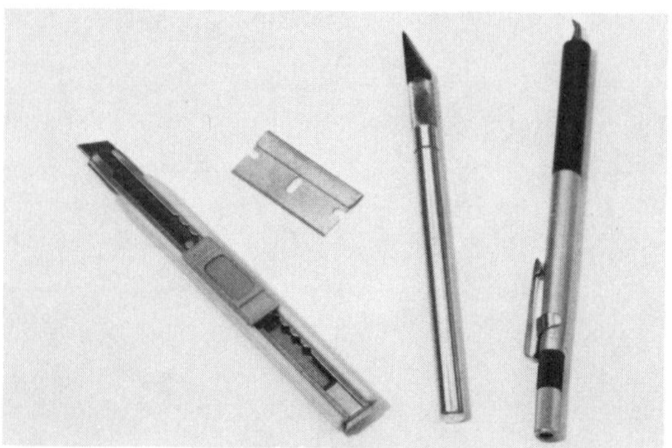

Figure 5.6. Cutting tools Exacto knives (or other stick-type cutters) and single-edged razor blades are commonly used to cut pieces of art. The blades should be replaced often to ensure clean, smooth edges.

or more colors or with work that requires critical size tolerances. The Uniform Product Code is an example of an image that must be held to exact size specifications (figure 5.4, p. 75). Of the three major paste-up materials, illustration board and mylar are the most stable.

Paste-up Tools

Most tools used for layout and paste-up are common artist or drafting equipment. The three most basic are a **T-square, triangle,** and **ruler** (figure 5.5). Both plastic and steel tools are commonly used. Plastic edges are easy to look through when positioning lines of type, but they are easily damaged. This is a special problem when the tools are used for ruling. A nick in the edge of the plastic can ruin a carefully inked line. A plastic edge should never be used as a guide to cut artwork. Steel tools are more expensive than plastic but are nearly indestructable under normal use. Layout rulers are supplied with both English (inch) units and printer's (pica) units.

Several different types of cutting tools are used by the paste-up artist. **Exacto knives** and **single-edged razor blades** are the two most common hand-held cutting tools (figure 5.6). It is always best to hold the blade as low as possible when cutting paper. This technique shears rather than stabs through the paper and so prevents ripping or wrinkling the sheet. Rapid cuts can be made with a small table-model **guillotine cutter** (figure 5.7) or with a proprietary device such as Compugraphic's Easy Trimmer (figure 5.8).

Adhesive tape is used to hold both the board and overlay material in place during paste-up. Designers commonly use masking tape, clear cellophane tape, and white tape. Masking tape is used to secure the board to the working surface. Cellophane tape is used

Figure 5.7. A table-model guillotine cutter

Figure 5.8. Compugraphic's Easy Trimmer

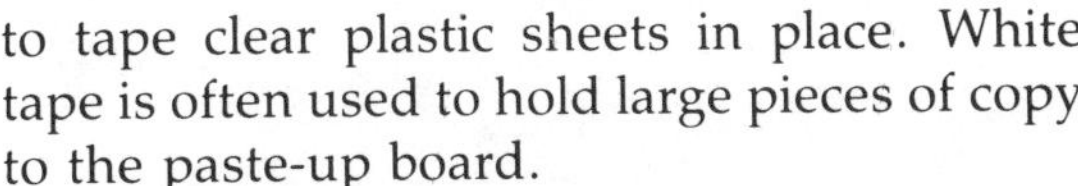

to tape clear plastic sheets in place. White tape is often used to hold large pieces of copy to the paste-up board.

Burnishers are used in the layout room to adhere dry-transfer images or small pieces of pressure-sensitive materials to the paste-up board. Burnishers come in several different shapes (figure 5.9). Ball-pointed tools can be purchased in many styles. Some are even spring loaded, so uniform pressure can be applied to any surface. Straight burnishers are also available, but they are not as popular as the ball type.

Part of the layout artist's job is to add layout and image lines to the paste-up. All guidelines not intended to print are drawn in light-blue (nonrepro) pencil. Light-blue lines on the layout will not be recorded on the film used to make the printing plate. For lines that should be recorded on the film, such as trim or fold marks, special instruments are used (figure 5.10). The most common is a ruling pen with black **india ink.** India ink is especially dense and forms perfect film images. A new tool gaining wide acceptance is called a

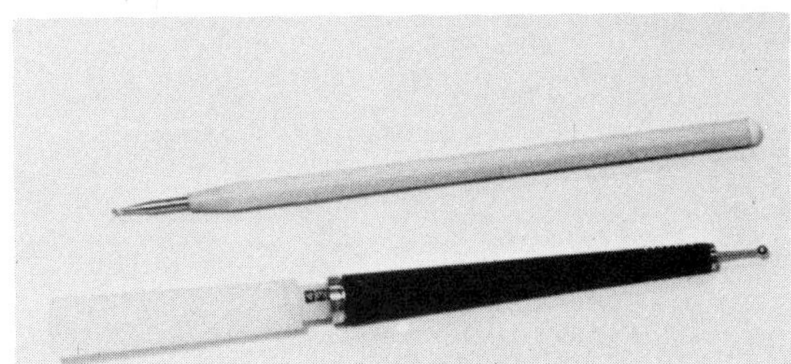

Figure 5.9. Two types of burnishers

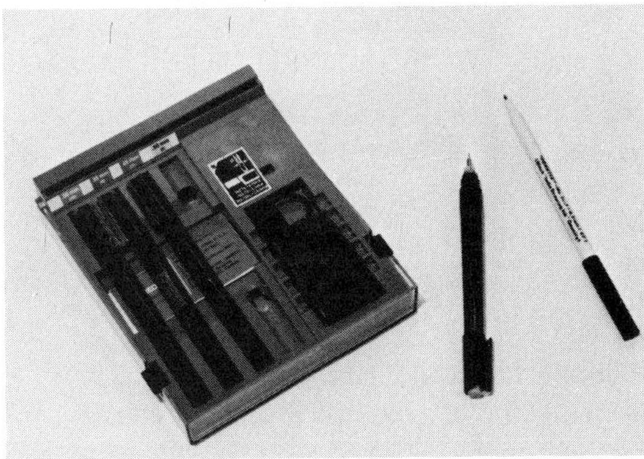

Figure 5.10. Ruling and felt-tip pens Two devices used to create dense black lines on a paste-up are ruling pens (a) and reproduction-quality felt-tip pens (b).

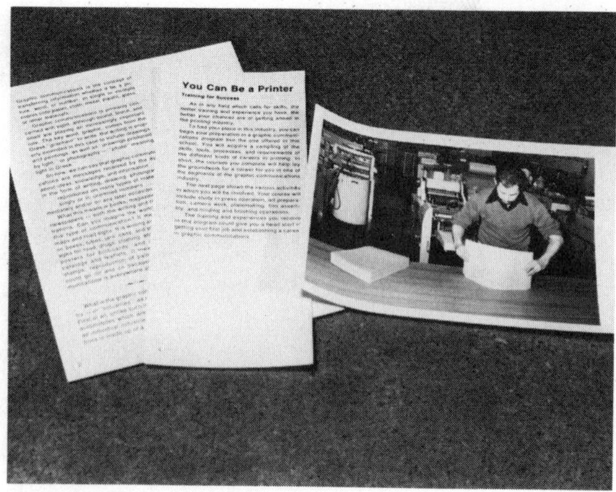

Figure 5.11. Paste-up copy The copy for paste-up is either line work or continuous-tone photographs.

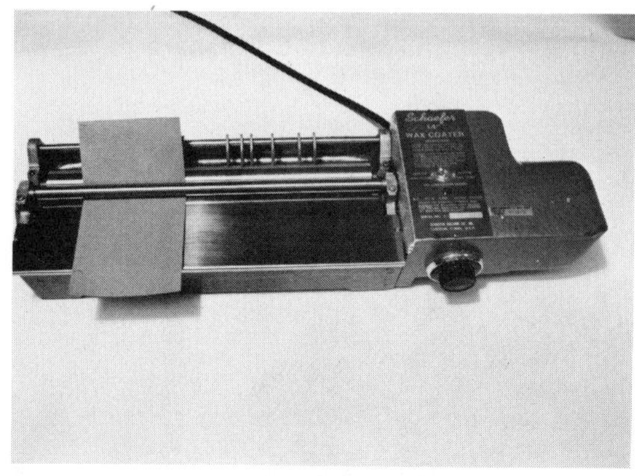

Figure 5.12. A wax coater The drive roller pulls the paper through the wax in the wax coater.
Courtesy of Schafer Machine Company, Inc.

repro-quality (reproduction-quality) **disposable drawing pen.** This inexpensive, felt-tipped instrument is available in a variety of line widths. Most ballpoint or office-grade felt-tip pens are not considered acceptable for paste-up work.

Types of Art

Jobs for paste-up come to the layout room in several forms. Most are black images on an opaque paper base. **Opaque** means that under normal viewing it is not possible to see through the sheet. You can read the words on this page because the paper is opaque. **Line work** (such as type, ink drawings, and clip art) and **continuous-tone photographs** are the two most common sorts of images (figure 5.11). **Clip art** is copyright-free material supplied to printers and designers in forms ready for paste-up.

Jobs sometimes arrive with black or red images on a transparent base. Red reproduces the same way black does for most graphic arts films. **Transparent-based images** can be seen through the backing sheet. These images are typically used for multicolor work.

The term "copy" is commonly used in the layout room. In this situation copy refers to the pieces of art that will be applied to the paste-up.

Adhesives for Paste-up

The main job of the layout artist is to adhere the different pieces of art to the paste-up board in the proper printing positions. Several different adhesives are used to hold the images in place.

A **wax coater** (figure 5.12) is a device designed to place a uniform layer of wax-like material on one side of a sheet of paper. The side to be coated is placed face down on the feeder side of the machine. As the sheet is pushed against the drive rollers, it is drawn through the device, against the wax drum. After coating, the pieces may be laid aside and used at any time. The advantage of using a wax coater is that the adhesive can be pushed in place on the paste-up and then removed to be repositioned any number of times. The adhesive continues to work as long as it remains free of lint or dirt and does not dry out. The wax coating does eventually dry; but its useful life is several weeks, well beyond normal paste-up requirements.

Rubber cement is an inexpensive adhesive that is applied wet to the back of the copy. To use rubber cement, place the copy face down on a sheet of scrap paper and, with a small brush, carefully cover the back of the copy (figure 5.13). Be sure the copy does not shift and no thick areas of cement remain on the sheet. The drying time of rubber cement is short, so immediately place the copy on the illustration board, cement-side down, and position the image with a T-square and triangle.

It is not easy to remove images that have been adhered with rubber cement. The liquid is also messy. The wet cement sometimes creeps out around the edges of the paper. As it dries, it tends to pick up dirt that can form an image on the film when the paste-up is photographed. It is easier to remove excess rubber cement when it is dry than when it is wet. Use a soft eraser to rub away dried bits of cement from the paste-up.

Some companies use **tube** and/or **stick adhesives** to mount copy on the paste-up (figure 5.14). These are available in a variety of forms. Most, however, are applied by coating the back of the paper with a liquid or paste that dries rapidly. Before purchasing, care should be taken to read the product directions and specifications. For example, one popular

Figure 5.13. Using rubber cement Cover the back of the copy with a thin coating of cement. Use a piece of scrap paper under the copy so that the cement can be applied evenly to all edges without getting onto the layout area.

Figure 5.14. Examples of stick and liquid adhesives

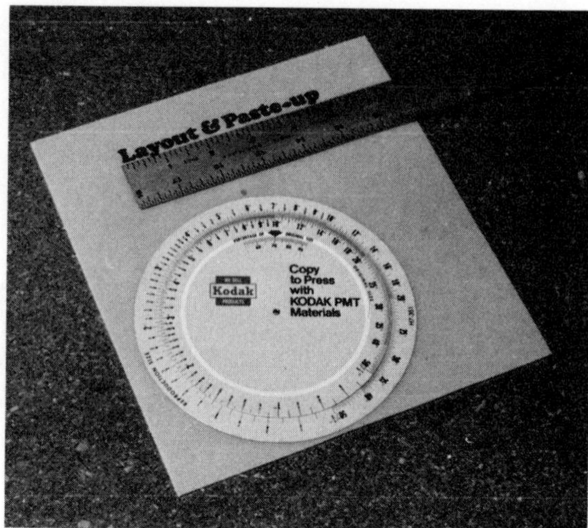

Figure 5.15. Using a proportion scale This job requires a size change from 5 inches to 3½ inches. A 71% reduction is calculated by lining the original width of 5 on the inside scale with the final size of 3½ on the outside scale.

brand specifies that for permanent mounting, the copy should be applied while the solution is wet. If the coating is allowed to dry before mounting, then it can be positioned, removed, and attached again, like a wax coating.

Scaling

It is frequently necessary to enlarge or reduce the size of composition of illustrations to fit a certain space on the paste-up. The industry refers to these photographic conversions as **photostats,** or simply **stats.** Photostats can be prepared on special camera systems that rapidly and easily create positive opaque copies from a positive opaque original. Diffusion transfer is a process that can be used on existing camera equipment in a printer's darkroom to reach the same result. (The technique is discussed in detail in chapter 6.)

A graphic arts **proportion scale** is frequently used to determine actual percentage sizes when it is necessary to reduce type or figures. To use a proportion scale, first measure the existing dimensions (called the original size) of the layout or figure and then determine from your specifications the desired new length. Consider the example in figure 5.15. The line length is 5 inches but must be reduced to fit an area on the copy that is only 3½ inches long. Locate the original size, 5 inches, on the inside scale. Then find the desired final measurement, 3½ inches, on the outside scale. Rotate the wheel until the inside measurement (5) lines up with the outside measurement (3½). With the original and final dimensions in line, read the percentage size difference, 71, at the arrow pointer. A stat must be made at a 71% reduction.

All scaling is based on 100% being considered the original size. If the example in figure 5.15 was copied at 100%, then the stat image would be 5 inches long. A 50% reduction would give an image 2½ inches long. A 200% enlargement would be 10 inches long.

An important concept generally overlooked by new printers is the fact that camera enlargements or reductions alter the size of the copy in two directions, not just in the calculated one. Figure 5.16 illustrates the **diagonal line method** of predicting two-dimensional size changes. Affix to a drawing board the art work to be scaled, tape a sheet of tracing paper in place over the copy, and draw a rectangular box around the edges of the image. Draw a diagonal line from the lower left corner through the upper right corner and continue it across the page. Measure the de-

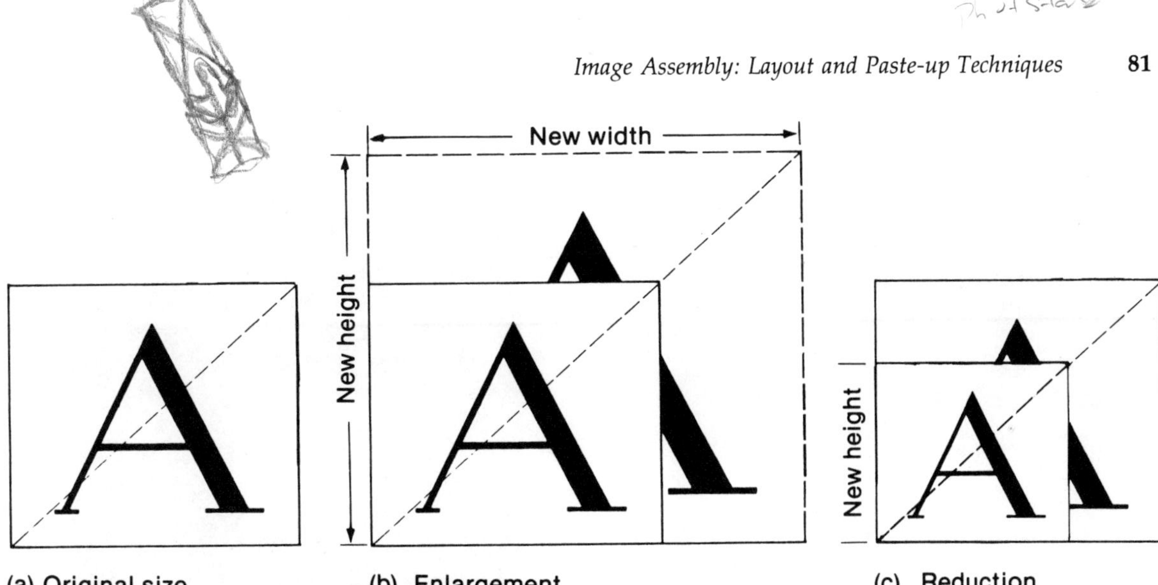

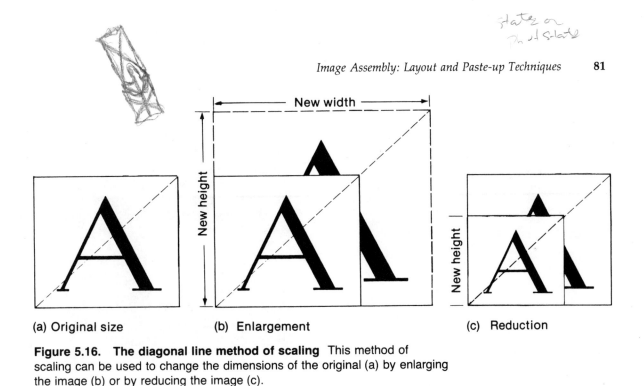

Figure 5.16. The diagonal line method of scaling This method of scaling can be used to change the dimensions of the original (a) by enlarging the image (b) or by reducing the image (c).

sired width along the base of the first rectangle, and from that point draw a vertical line until it intersects the diagonal line. The place where the diagonal and vertical lines meet defines the new height of the scaled copy. The same information can be obtained by reading the proportional scale.

Working with Photographs

Reproducing continuous-tone photographs presents somewhat of a problem to the printer because most printing processes can only reproduce lines. (Chapter 7 deals exclusively with line conversions of photographic prints, called halftones.) It is necessary to allow for the inclusion of such illustrations on the mechanical. There are basically three ways for the printer to handle the problem at this stage:

- By preparing prescreened prints,
- By forming a window on the negative,
- By drawing holding lines.

It is possible for the printer to prepare an opaque halftone that can be pasted directly onto the mechanical and rephotographed with the rest of the job as line copy (figure 5.17). These prescreened prints are sometimes referred to as **veloxes.** Veloxes can be produced by several methods, such as projection through a halftone screen from an enlarger or the diffusion-transfer technique.

The second technique is to place a layer of red or black material in the area where the photograph is to appear in the final reproduction (figure 5.18). Black acetate may be used, but the most common material is transparent red. It is possible to see guidelines

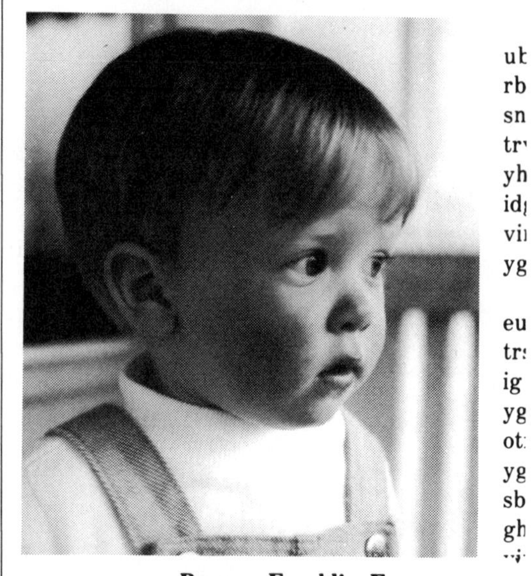

Benson Franklin Faux
Agyrt skk vinoiduyuib gsd nrrb syysvgrf
frdutsnkr yi otivbufr frysukrf otubyubh ubdy
ib ygr osdyr-yu. Ydyskktm s dgrry ig ytsvubh

Figure 5.17. A prescreened print pasted on a mechanical Random letters are used here to visualize copy applied to a typical job.

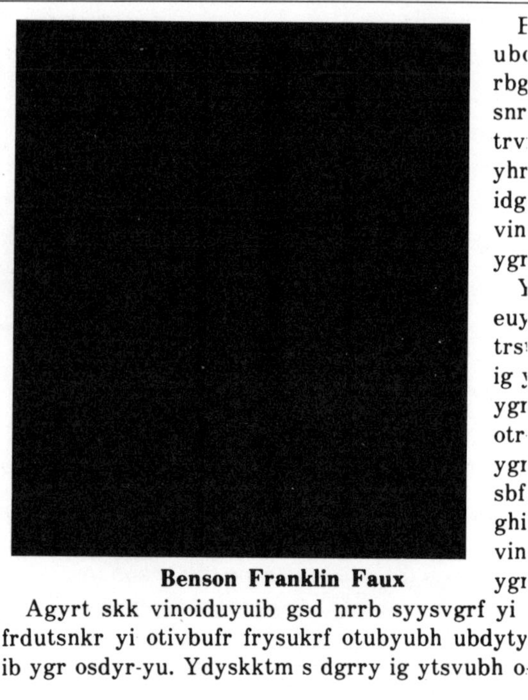

Benson Franklin Faux
Agyrt skk vinoiduyuib gsd nrrb syysvgrf yi
frdutsnkr yi otivbufr frysukrf otubyubh ubdyty
ib ygr osdyr-yu. Ydyskktm s dgrry ig ytsvubh

Figure 5.18. A window on a mechanical When this layout is photographed, the black area will appear on the negative as a clear rectangle into which the halftone negative will be positioned.

through the red material and therefore cut a more accurate rectangle. When photographed, the black or red layer will form a clear area (called a **window**) on the negative. A halftone negative can then be attached under the window prior to making a printing plate.

The last approach to allow for photographs on the mechanical is to draw **holding lines** (figure 5.19). The lines will act as a means of registering a halftone negative when several film images are positioned together on a light table. The holding lines can be simple corner ticks or they can be bold inked lines that will act as a border on the final reproduction.

Working from the Rough

Reviewing Instructions

The first step in beginning any paste-up job is to examine the rough layout. The rough is the detailed guide used to identify and position every piece of art on the paste-up. Recall from chapter 3 that the rough is a sort of

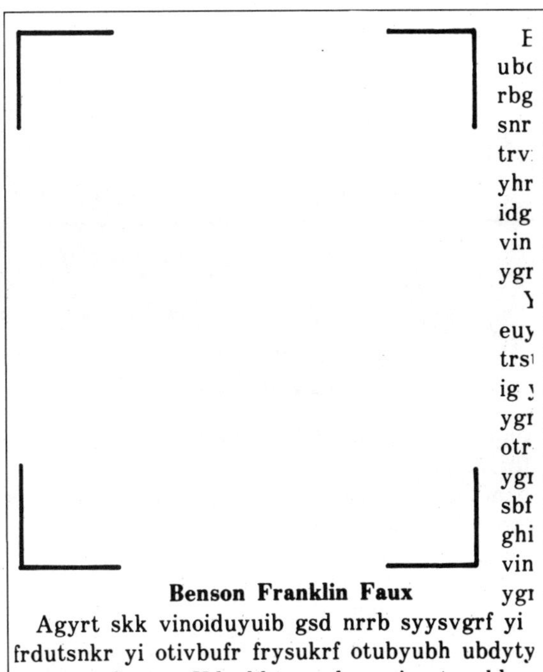

Figure 5.19. Holding lines drawn on a mechanical These lines serve as a guide in the placement of the halftone negative.

"floor plan" that predicts and describes the final product. It should contain all the information necessary to produce the job.

It is important to carefully review every part of the rough before beginning any work. The rough should contain several categories of information. The five most common are the following:

- Type content and specifications (size, style, etc.),
- Product dimensions,
- Image positions for all elements,
- Finishing operations (such as folding, trimming, scoring, or perforating),
- Press specifications (including paper, length of run, imposition, and ink color).

The layout artist must consider every part of the rough in addition to image positions. For example, if a fold and trim is indicated on the job, then lines must be added to the paste-up that can be used in the bindery as guides for the finishing operation. If the layout department forgets to add them, then problems may occur.

The sequence of paste-up operations can vary depending on job requirements. The ability to read a rough and look ahead to anticipate the order of steps is important. This ability is developed with experience.

Checking for Completeness

After reviewing the specifications, it is important to ensure that all necessary pieces are in the job packet. It is frustrating and costly to begin a paste-up and then, when nearing completion, discover that one piece of copy is missing. It is difficult and confusing to remove the job from the layout board, set it aside, and begin another while waiting for the missing copy.

Check the composition against the rough layout. Check that all display and body composition is complete and in camera-ready form. Examine the artwork and review each piece. Measure each piece and determine whether enlargements or reductions are necessary.

Before beginning any work on the paste-up, make sure that everything is ready. Be sure that all instructions are clear and under-

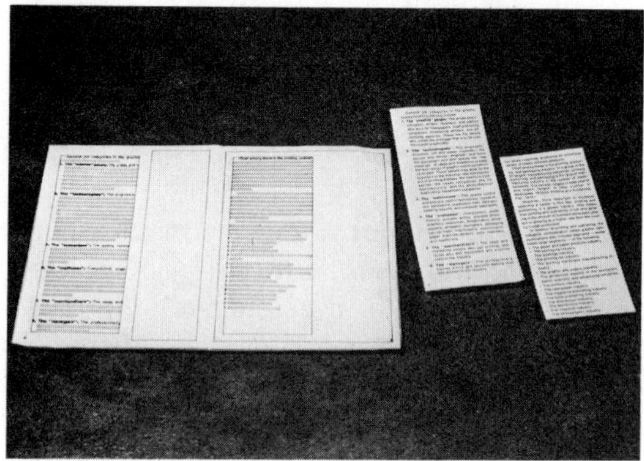

Figure 5.20. Laying out the copy Lay the pieces of copy on the layout table in the order they will appear on the paste-up as determined by your rough layout.

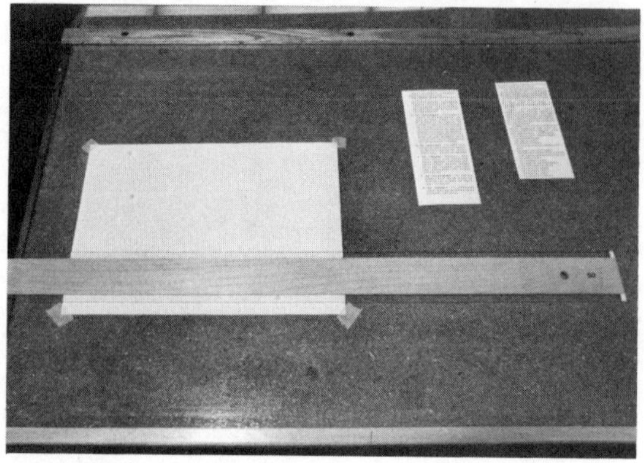

Figure 5.21. Position of the layout board and the head of the T-square This position of the board and the head of the T-square on the left of the table is correct for a right-handed person.

stood. A few minutes' delay at this point prevents problems later on.

Trimming the Copy

The last step before beginning the paste-up is to trim all pieces of copy to a workable size. Use a razor or Exacto knife with a steel ruler to trim each piece within ¼ to ½ inch of the image size. It is better not to use a guillotine paper cutter for this operation, since it is easy to make a mistake and ruin an image.

When cutting copy, it is wiser to always place the ruler over the nonimage area rather than on top of the copy. The back side of the metal might scratch a photograph or the emulsion of photocomposition. It also has a tendency to carry dirt, which can spot the copy. If the amount of trim is too small to support the ruler, then place a piece of scrap paper under the ruler, on top of the image.

When all pieces have been cut to size, place them on the layout table in the positions they will appear on the paste-up (figure 5.20). This technique saves time and prevents confusion. Some layout artists wax coat each piece before trimming. The hot wax does have a tendency to flow over the edge of the paper. If enough wax becomes attached to the edge, then it will pick up dirt when mounted on the board, and will photograph as a line.

Preparing a Single-Color Paste-up

Novice layout artists should begin to develop paste-up skills by working on simple, single-color jobs. Basic layout skills should be developed before attempting multicolor work or single-color jobs that require overlays. The purpose of this section is to review basic paste-up procedures. More sophisticated techniques are discussed in the following sections.

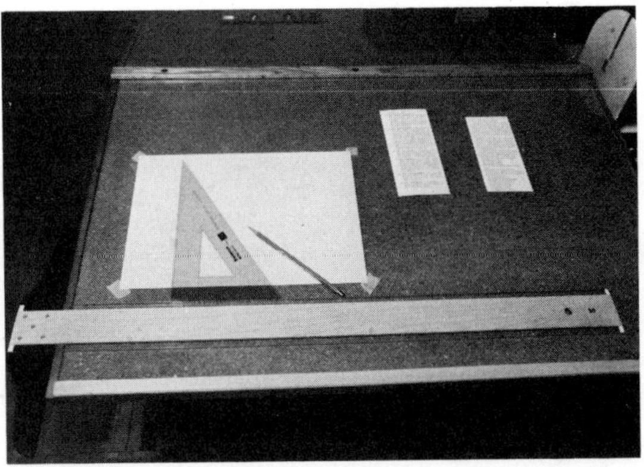

Figure 5.22. Adding layout lines to the board Using a triangle and T-square, draw the dimensions of the press sheet in light-blue pencil so that the rectangle formed is centered on the layout board.

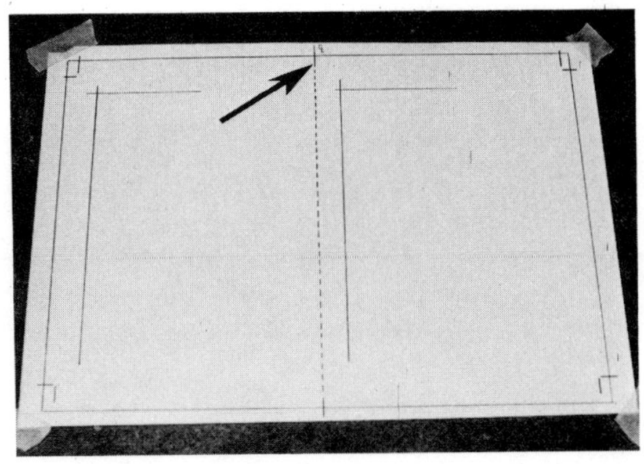

Figure 5.23. Adding fold lines Fold lines are drawn in light-blue pencil, but small black marks are added at the edge of the sheet as guides for the bindery.

Mounting the Board

The first step is to select and mount the paste-up board on the layout table. If preprinted sheets are used, then the selection process is simple. If illustration board, offset paper, or a plastic sheet is used, then the material must be cut to size. Select a piece that is slightly larger than the press paper size. A good approach is to cut the board at least 1 inch larger in each dimension than the press sheet. For example, if the press sheet size is to be 8½ × 11, then cut the paste-up board at least 9½ × 12. Board that is a great deal larger than the job dimensions is cumbersome to work with. A very large board is sometimes impossible to position on the graphic arts camera and is also difficult to store when the job is finished.

Be sure the layout table is clean, without spots of rubber cement or dirt. Position the board near the head of the T-square and to the left side of the layout surface if you are right-handed, and to the right if you are left-handed (figure 5.21). The position of the T-square is important because the blade of a T-square is more stable close to the head than it is out near the end of the blade. This arrangement also allows space to lay the rough and pieces of copy within easy reach. If a preprinted form is used, then position the sheet so the guidelines are in line with the T-square edge.

When the board is in position, secure it to the table with pieces of masking tape at each corner. It is important that the base not shift during paste-up. If the board moves in the middle of the job, then the difficult elements will be crooked and therefore unacceptable to the customer.

Adding Layout Lines

The next step in the paste-up process is to add layout lines to the board (figure 5.22).

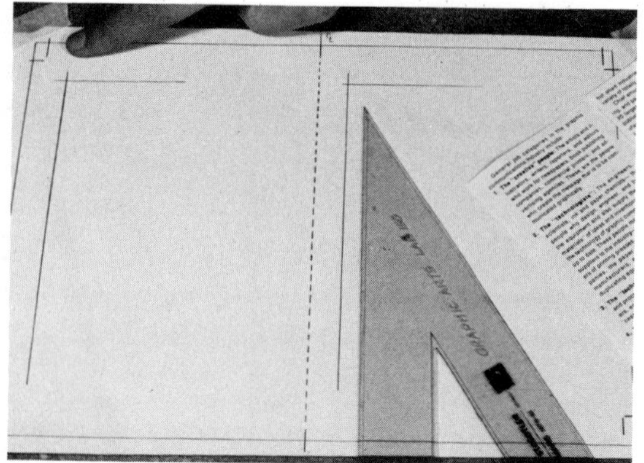

Figure 5.24. Adding trim marks Trim marks must be added if the job is to be cut during the finishing operation.

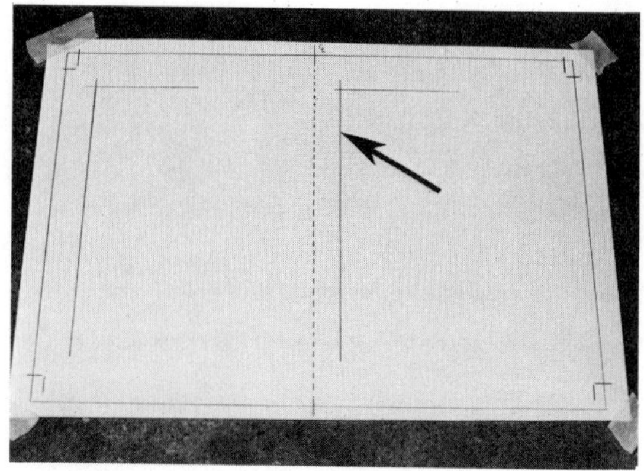

Figure 5.25. Adding image lines Image lines are drawn in light-blue pencil and are used as guides to position the copy.

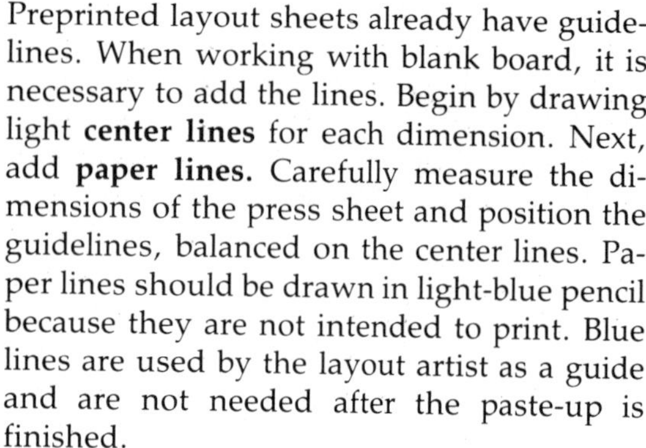

Preprinted layout sheets already have guidelines. When working with blank board, it is necessary to add the lines. Begin by drawing light **center lines** for each dimension. Next, add **paper lines.** Carefully measure the dimensions of the press sheet and position the guidelines, balanced on the center lines. Paper lines should be drawn in light-blue pencil because they are not intended to print. Blue lines are used by the layout artist as a guide and are not needed after the paste-up is finished.

Next, add any **fold lines.** These are also drawn in blue pencil and appear as dashed lines. Small fold lines are sometimes placed on the edge of the paper dimensions as a guide for the bindery room (figure 5.23, p. 85). Use india ink or a repro felt-tip pen to make thin marks on the board. These fold lines will print but are usually lost when the job is finally trimmed.

If the job is to be trimmed, then small black **trim marks** should be placed on the board (figure 5.24). Trim marks are used by the paper cutter to accurately cut the final job to the desired size. Trim marks are cut away during the operation and do not appear on the sheets delivered to the customer. The marks must, however, appear on the press sheet and are therefore added to the paste-up in black.

Image guidelines are added in blue pencil. These lines are used by the layout artist to position pieces of copy. Measure in from the paper lines to define the image margins (sometimes called image extremes) (figure 5.25). Always follow specifications listed on the rough. Then add any special measurements to position the different elements of the job. If a headline is to appear a certain distance from the top of the sheet, then draw a blue line to indicate its position. Do the same for the positions of all pieces of art.

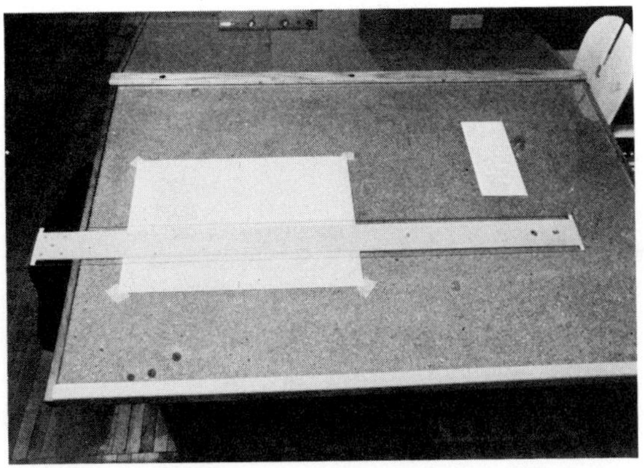

Figure 5.26. Positioning the copy Use the plastic edge of the T-square to position and straighten each piece of copy.

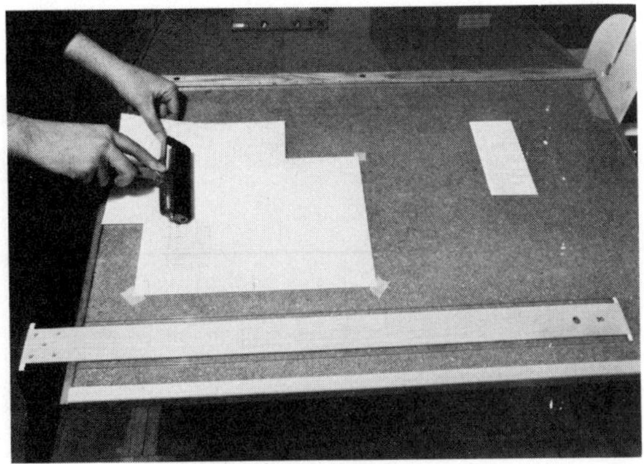

Figure 5.27. Attaching the copy Use a scrap of clean paper over the copy and roll the image that has been adhered to the paste-up board.

Attaching the Art

Begin mounting art at the top of the sheet and work down. Moving the T-square back and forth over the copy can smudge or scratch artwork. By beginning at the top, each piece is positioned and then not touched again. Use the blue image guidelines to position each piece. Use the plastic edge of the T-square to ensure that each piece is straight (figure 5.26). It is also wise to check image position with a triangle to make sure that both horizontal and vertical dimensions are straight and line up perfectly with all other pieces.

Wax-coated sheets are more forgiving than sheets with rubber cement. If the sheet has a wax coating, gently position it and use the point of an Exacto knife to shift it into position. Slight pressure against the T-square will then secure it in place. After checking the vertical edge with a triangle, the sheet can be lifted and repositioned again if necessary.

Some layout artists use a rubber roller to attach the copy firmly to the board. To use this technique, place a piece of clean paper over the image and move the roller firmly against the surface (figure 5.27). The paper keeps the copy clean and ensures that the image will not be scratched during the operation.

The same technique of checking alignment and pressing in place is used for every element on the job. When every piece is positioned, carefully check the placement by referring back to the rough layout. Next, cut a sheet of tracing paper to the same size as the board and tape it in place along one edge so it can be hinged back. Add any directions from the rough that are important for the darkroom or stripping tasks (figure 5.28).

Some layout departments require the addition of a cover sheet to protect the art (figure 5.29). Cut a piece of tissue or cover

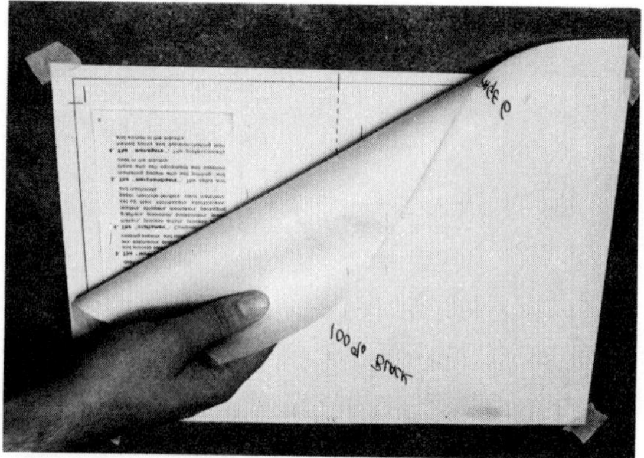

Figure 5.28. Adding directions for shooting the copy A tissue overlay is added to the board and used to specify directions for the camera operator or the stripper.

Figure 5.29. Adding a cover sheet A cover sheet is often used to protect the finished paste-up.

paper to the size of the layout board, but add one inch to the hinge edge. Fold the sheet at the one-inch point and slide it over the board. Tape it on the back side with masking tape.

Cutting Masks

Often a mask must be cut to meet job requirements. A **mask** is material that blacks the passage of light. Most mask material used in layout and stripping is called red masking film. This type of film is not light sensitive, but it does have a thick emulsion that can be cut away with a razor blade or knife, leaving a clear plastic support sheet.

Masks are commonly used to cut halftone windows, to create open areas for screen tints, to drop out areas around a photograph, and to create special overlay images. Most masks are cut to fall in line with a film image. Layout artists, however, are frequently required to cut masks to line up with the artwork.

To prepare a mask, cut a piece of red masking film larger than the image dimensions of the job. Use an Exacto knife or other sharp instrument to cut through the emulsion, but not through the plastic base (figure 5.30). Keep the blade angle low, to make a shear cut. Always cut to the center of any image line (figure 4.4). With this technique, images will overlap and not create an objectionable white line when they don't meet. After the mask sheet is cut, position it over the layout, with the emulsion up, and tape it along one edge so it can be hinged back out of the way (figure 5.31).

After an area has been cut out and positioned, stab the emulsion with the point of the knife. By gently lifting, the outer portion can be lifted away (figure 5.32).

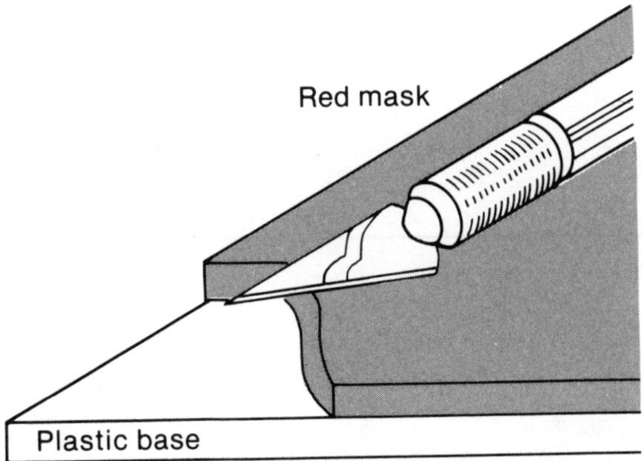

Figure 5.30. Cutting mask material Cut through the red emulsion layer, but not through the plastic support sheet.

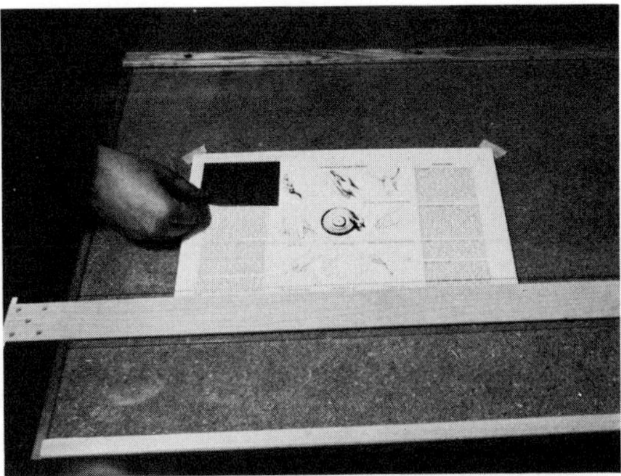

Figure 5.31. Adding masks to the board Cut a piece of red masking film and hinge it in position along one edge on the paste-up board.

Preparing a Multicolor Paste-up

Multicolor jobs are no more complex than single-color work, but they do require a thorough understanding of paste-up procedures.

Begin the job by setting up the board as with single-color work. Draw paper lines, fold lines, and image guidelines in light-blue pencil. Place all image guidelines for both colors on the same paste-up sheet. Add trim or fold marks for the finishing room in black india ink or repro felt-tip pen.

Adding Register Marks

For multicolor work it is necessary to add **register marks** (figure 5.33). Register marks can be purchased commercially on pressure-sensitive tape, as preprinted clip art, or they can be created by drawing with a black layout pen.

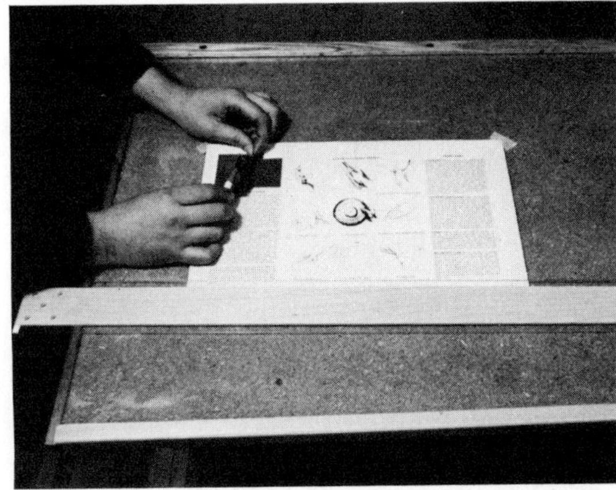

Figure 5.32. Removing excess mask from the board Stab a corner of the masking film and gently lift the excess mask area from around the desired window.

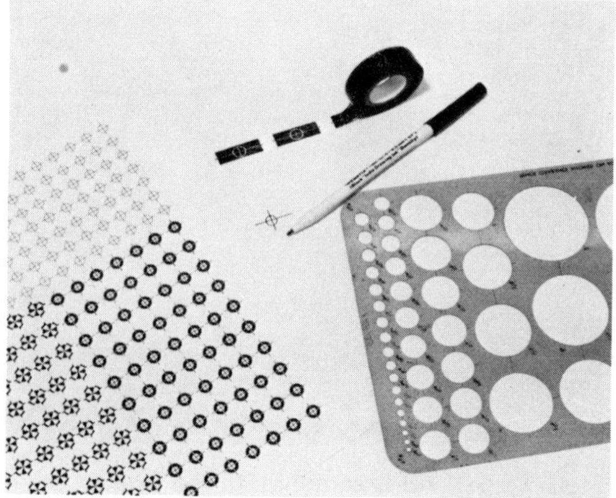

Figure 5.33. Register marks Register marks can be purchased in pressure-sensitive or preprinted form or created by hand with a ruling pen.

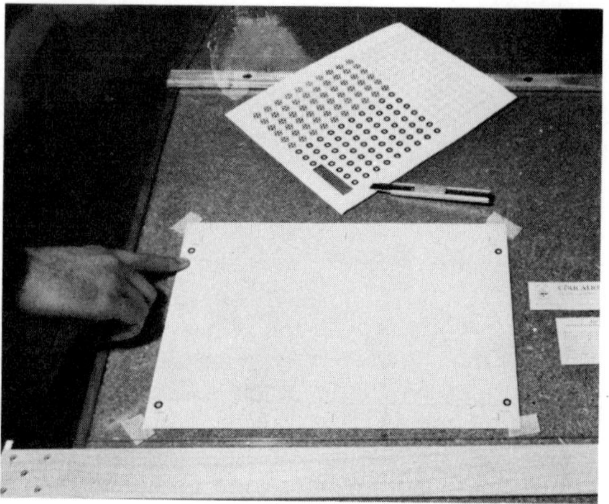

Figure 5.34. Placement of register marks Place register marks in areas of the press sheet that will be cut away in the finishing operation.

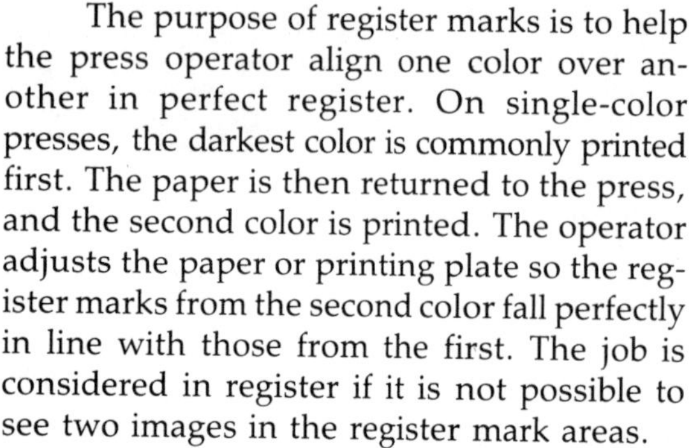

The purpose of register marks is to help the press operator align one color over another in perfect register. On single-color presses, the darkest color is commonly printed first. The paper is then returned to the press, and the second color is printed. The operator adjusts the paper or printing plate so the register marks from the second color fall perfectly in line with those from the first. The job is considered in register if it is not possible to see two images in the register mark areas.

A minimum of three register marks should be placed on the board. Many companies require more, but at least three will ensure good registration. Register marks should always be placed in areas that will be trimmed off after the job is finished (figure 5.34). Some companies prefer to place register marks in the image area and then to remove them from the plate after the first sheets have been checked for register. Always follow shop guidelines in the placement of register marks.

Working with an Overlay

Most two-color jobs involve black and some other color, such as red, green, or blue. Most layout artists always place the images to be printed in black on the illustration board or base sheet. In all cases, the color used for the greatest number of images (or that covers the greatest surface area) will be placed on the board. Position the first set of images by using normal single-color procedures. Check to ensure that all pieces are straight and firmly attached.

The second-color images will be placed on a special **overlay sheet.** Place a piece of clear or frosted plastic over the board. Tape one edge of the sheet in several places to create a hinge (figure 5.35). It should be possible to look through the plastic sheet and see the blue pencil image guidelines for the second set of images.

Mount each piece of copy on the overlay

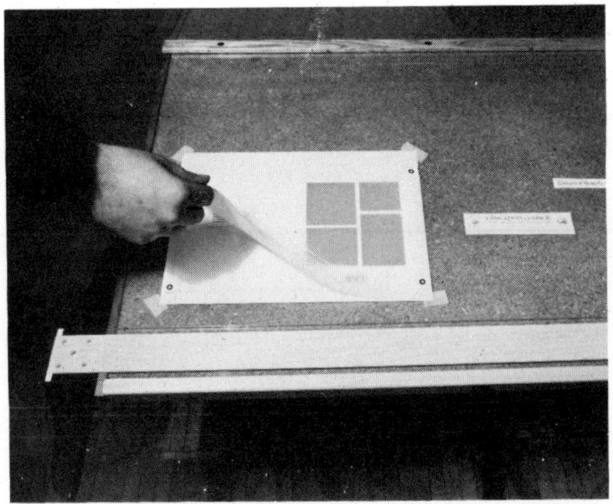

Figure 5.35. Adding the color overlay Hinge a piece of plastic over the board to receive the second set of images. Be sure to cut away the areas over the register marks.

Figure 5.36. Mounting the second color copy Adhere the second set of images to the overlay sheet by using the image guidelines on the first sheet.

as with board material. Use rubber cement, a wax coater, or dry adhesives. Use the guidelines on the board to make sure the new images are in their proper positions and are straight with the first images (figure 5.36).

Most layout artists cut away the overlay in the register mark areas. When the camera room photographs the paste-up, two separate pieces of film will be used. The first will be of the board paste-up, with the overlay hinged back out of the way. Next, the overlay will be hinged back and a white piece of paper placed between the board and overlay. If the register marks can clearly be seen, they will be recorded on both the first and the second pieces of film. Since the marks are identical for both exposures, they will appear in the same position for both color sets. They will then be used to create two printing plates to run on the press.

Again check both the board and the overlay to make sure that all copy is in the correct position, is straight, and is tightly bonded and that the whole area is free from dirt or scratches. After the tissue or cover sheet have been added, the job is ready to be sent to the camera room.

This technique can be used for three- and four-color jobs or for work that uses an overlay for several different screen tints. For each additional color, another overlay is hinged from an edge of the board.

Preparing Reverses and Surprints

Many jobs require the use of reverses or surprints to create a special image or effect. Both techniques can be used for dynamic results and are easy to prepare.

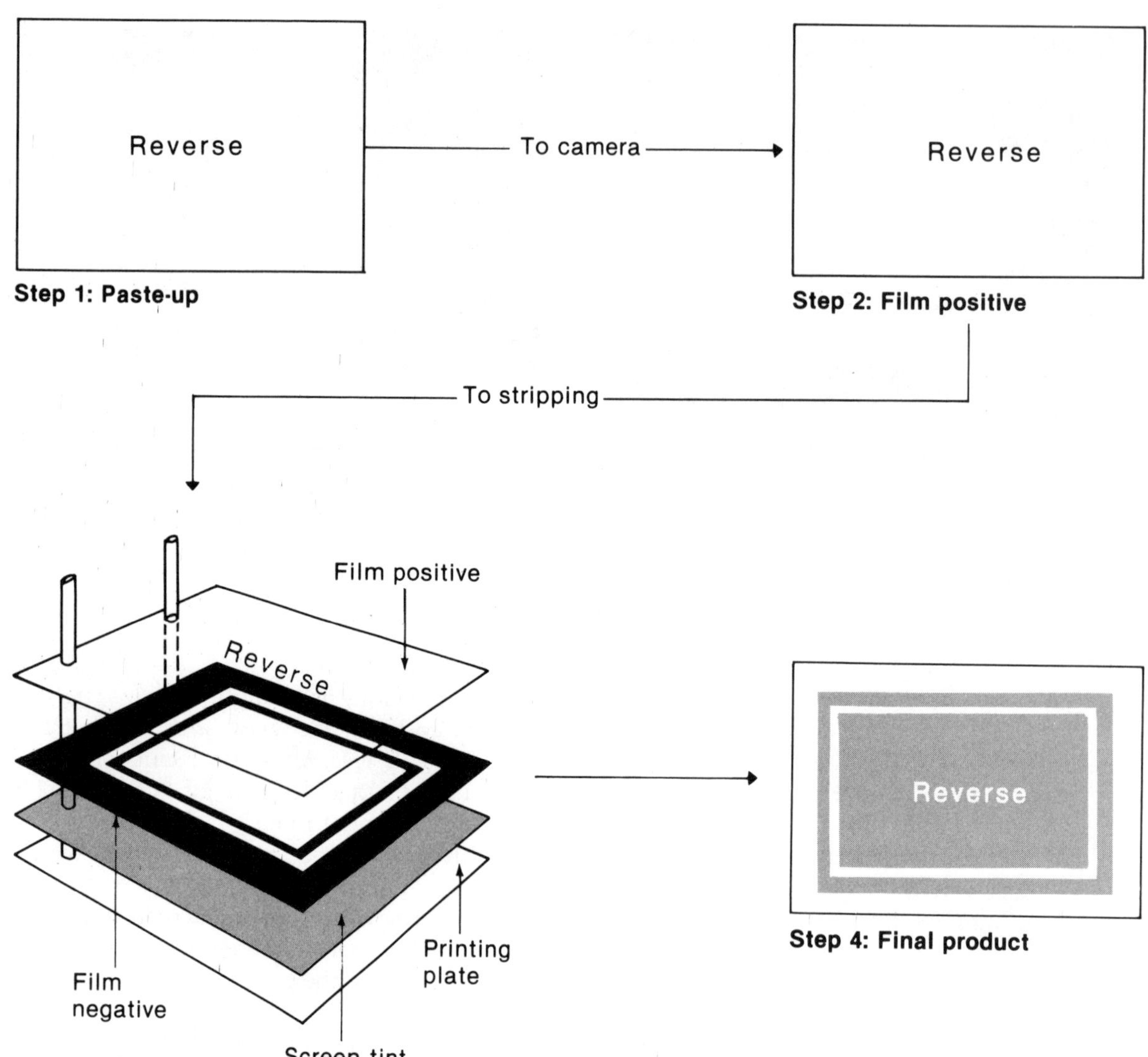

Figure 5.37. Preparing reverse copy for printing A reverse is a recognizable image created by the absence of a printed image. In this example, a screen tint is used with a film negative to create the reverse image.

Reverses

A **reverse** is a recognizable image created by the absence of a printed image (see figure 3.31b). Copy preparation for a reverse involves the following three steps (figure 5.37): (1) Paste-up, (2) film positive, (3) stripping assembly.

First, the desired reverse image is prepared as if it were a normal one-color paste-up. Black or red copy is positioned on the board in the desired printing position. Second, the paste-up is sent to the camera room for a film positive. It is the film positive that blocks the "image" area and creates the desired outline. The third step is managed by the stripper when the pieces of film are assembled prior to plate making. From the directions specified by the layout artist, the film positive will be positioned over another image, usually a film negative. If light is passed through both the positive and the negative to the plate, then a reverse image will be created by the positive.

An alternative method of preparing a reverse is with red masking film. It is possible to cut a design by hand then to use the mask in the stripping operation. The choice of technique depends on the type of image being reversed. If the image can easily be cut by hand, then the masking-film method is acceptable. Reverses that involve type or special designs with complex images commonly use the paste-up technique.

Surprints

A surprint is an image that is printed over another image (see figure 3.31a). Surprints are commonly used to print dark type over a light area of a halftone photograph. The technique used to prepare a surprint is similar to that of preparing a two-color paste-up by using an overlay.

Paste-up with overlay and register marks

Film negative of base

Film negative of overlay

Final printed sheet

Figure 5.38. Preparing surprint copy for printing A surprint is an image that is printed over another image. The two film negatives are separately exposed to the printing plate in a single-color surprint.

The base image (usually a photograph) is mounted on the paste-up board, and the surprint image (usually type) is positioned on the overlay sheet. The camera room prepares separate film images and sends the job to the stripper. Two separate exposures—the first is the base image, and the second is the surprint image—are used to prepare the printing plate. These images are combined to form a single image on the final printed sheet (figure 5.38).

A simpler way of making an overlay is to use dry-transfer letters. The layout artist can carefully burnish the characters directly onto the photograph. Another method is to use a clear plastic overlay sheet to hold the characters. When the job goes to the camera room, it is shot as a single halftone. The first method of using separate exposures, however, is preferred, since it makes for a denser surprint on the final press sheets.

Key Terms

paste-up
mechanical
pre-printed paste-up sheets
t-square
triangle
ruler
opaque
line work
transparent-based images
wax coater
clip art
stats
proportion scale
velox
window
holding lines
center lines
paper lines
trim marks
mask
register marks
overlay sheet

Questions for Review

1. What are the three types of table surface used for paste-up?
2. What are three common paste-up board materials?
3. What is a burnisher?
4. What does the term "opaque" mean?
5. What are the two most common types of image in paste-up?
6. What is the purpose of a wax coater? a proportion scale?
7. Why is a window used on a paste-up?
8. Why is a blue pencil used for paper lines, fold lines, and image guidelines?
9. What is the purpose of trim marks on a paste-up?
10. What is a mask?
11. When are register marks used?
12. What is the purpose of an overlay?
13. What is a reverse? a surprint?

Chapter Six

Line Photography

Anecdote to Chapter Six

Cameras have been produced in all shapes and sizes for purposes from the sublime to the ridiculous. One of the most entertaining periods of photographic history was the brief vogue of "detective cameras." These devices were not intended for police detectives, but rather were designed for amateur photographers who wished to disguise the fact that they were taking a picture. Such cameras were the first attempt at candid or unstaged photography. Cameras were hidden in strange places such as flowers and hats, camouflaged as neckties, and even concealed in walking-stick handles.

Perhaps the strangest detective camera was the gun camera, built around 1882. This camera looked exactly like a gun. It is interesting to speculate how long an individual would stand still if he thought he was being shot at instead of merely having his picture taken.

The gun camera is a part of photographic history, but it is still a common event for a photographer to "shoot a picture."

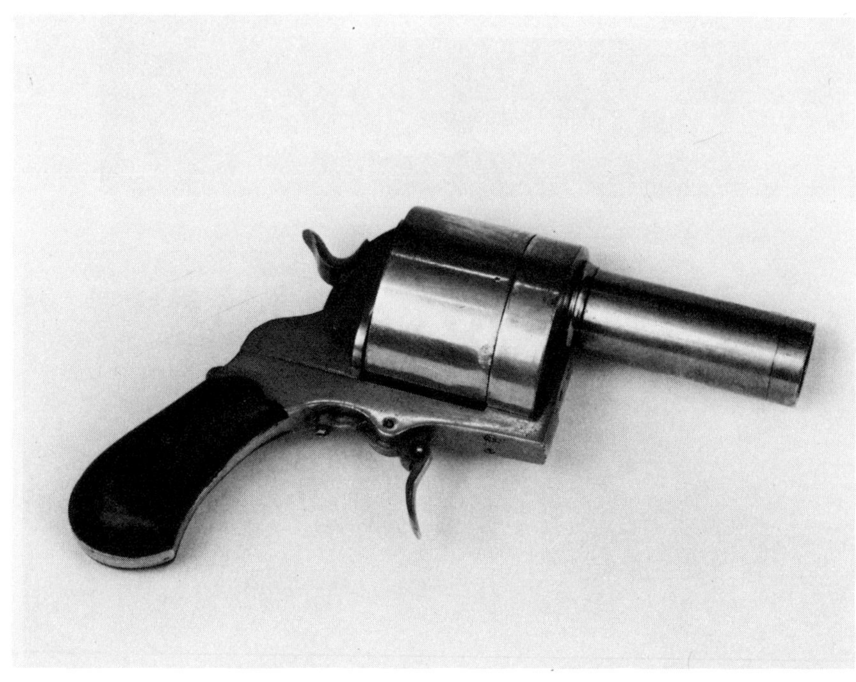

A gun camera

Courtesy of the International Museum of Photography at George Eastman House

Objectives for Chapter Six

After completing this material you will be able to:

- Classify photographic films.
- Identify the basic parts of any camera and recall their names and purposes.
- List the basic line photography tools.
- Define basic exposure.
- Recall the steps in making a basic line exposure on a process camera.
- Identify the variables in photographic chemical processing.
- Recall the steps in chemical processing for line photography.
- Explain the process of making film duplicates.
- Explain the process of making diffusion transfers.

Introduction

When the term *photography* is used, we tend to think first of pictures processed at our corner drug store, school pictures, or perhaps a family portrait. This kind of photography is called "continuous-tone photography" and is an important part of our world. However, the applications of photography are much more far reaching than continuous-tone photography. Infrared photography can predict crop production from photographs taken from airplanes or detect cancer in the human body. X-rays have long been used to assist in setting bones. Photography is used to produce miniature electronic circuits, and photofabrication is a growing part of the metal-working industry.

Printers today also depend on photography as a tool to generate and manipulate graphic images. Images can be composed at extremely high speeds with a variety of optical devices. All image carriers—whether relief, intaglio, screen, or lithography—can be photographically prepared.

The basis of photography is a chemical change caused by the action of light on some light-sensitive material. It is generally agreed that visible light is electromagnetic radiation measured in wavelengths emitted from either a natural source (the sun) or an artificial source (such as an electric lightbulb). When radiation strikes an object, it is either absorbed or reflected. White objects usually reflect light; black objects absorb light. We see colors and shades of gray because objects absorb and reflect varying amounts of this visible radiation. It is reflected radiation that causes a chemical change on a piece of film.

All the major printing processes place a single consistent layer of ink on some receiver, such as paper. This idea cannot be overemphasized. *Printers reproduce only lines.* These lines can be so big that we see them as

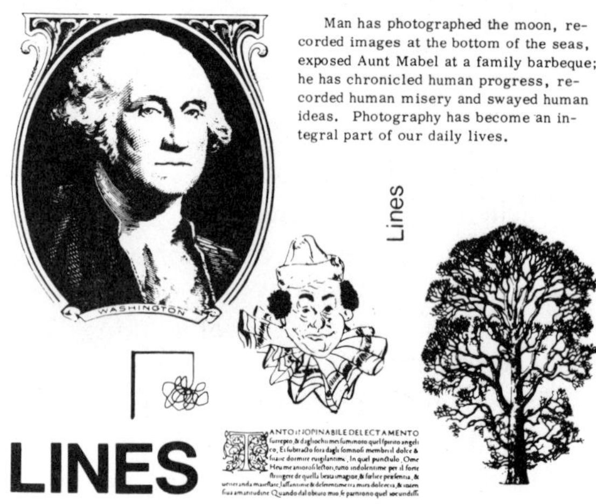

Man has photographed the moon, recorded images at the bottom of the seas, exposed Aunt Mabel at a family barbeque; he has chronicled human progress, recorded human misery and swayed human ideas. Photography has become an integral part of our daily lives.
Lines
WASHINGTON
LINES

Figure 6.1. Examples of line reproduction
This illustration shows some different images that are reproduced by lines.

huge ink areas or so small that we need a magnifying glass to see them, but they all have the same ink density (figure 6.1). The primary concern of this chapter is the production of line images that can be used with the printing processes. This process is called **line photography.**

Except by special techniques, it is not possible to reproduce a **continuous-tone** photograph is this book. An example of this sort of image is a "snapshot" of a member of your family or a friend. These pictures have the characteristic of varying shades of gray, or tones. (Excellent textbooks are available for individuals who wish to become skillful in continuous-tone photography. Such a discussion is beyond the limits of this work.)

A picture reproduced in a book or magazine is not a continuous-tone image. Such a picture is an application of line photography called **halftone photography.** This process breaks the tones of a picture into small, dense dots that trick the eye into seeing what appear to be tones. Chapter 7 deals with this technique.

Photographic Film

All photographic films use some type of light-sensitive material called an **emulsion** to record a visual image. The characteristics of the light-sensitive emulsion as well as the quantity and quality of light reaching that emulsion will determine the sort of visual image recorded on a piece of film. Most film emulsions are formed from a silver halide suspended in a gelatin compound (this is easy to picture as fruit suspended in a bowl of gelatin). The most common film emulsion is silver bromide (AgBr), which reacts rapidly and with predictable results. Silver iodide (AgI) and silver chloride (AgCl) are less common and are almost always used in combination with silver bromide to produce different film characteristics.

Whatever their chemical differences, all films are structured in the same general manner (figure 6.2). Glass was long used as a transparent, extremely stable base material. It is still used in topographic mapping, electronic circuitry, or color work—uses in which perfect registration (image location) is critical and in which the size of the film must not change with humidity, temperature, or age. Graphic arts films are generally made from a cellulose-ester- or polystyrene-based material. The advantage of these materials over glass is that they are flexible and much less expensive. Several patented flexible bases, such as Cronar, have been developed. These materials compete with glass in dimensional stability.

The gelatin compound containing the silver halide emulsion is bonded to the base material by an adhesive lower layer. An additional stability problem is caused by this lamination of two chemically dissimilar materials, each of which is affected differently by the environment and by age.

For many years film was formed from only the base and emulsion material. This type of film had several problems. During exposure the light would pass through the camera lens, strike and expose the emulsion, and then pass on through the base material. Unfortunately, the light would not stop there. It would be reflected from the back of the base material and would again pass through the emulsion, reexposing it (figure 6.3a). To prevent this effect, an **antihalation dye** is now placed over the back of the film base. Instead of being reflected, the light is absorbed and exposes the film only once (figure 6.3b). With flexible base films, the antihalation dye also serves as an anticurl agent. The antihalation dye dissolves during chemical processing.

The second problem with a film made up of only an emulsion and a base was the frailness of the gelatin material in the emulsion. To overcome this problem, the emulsion is now blanketed with a transparent protective layer called **overcoating.** This overcoating protects the gelatin material from fingerprints and adds an antistress factor during handling. The overcoating also dissolves during chemical processing.

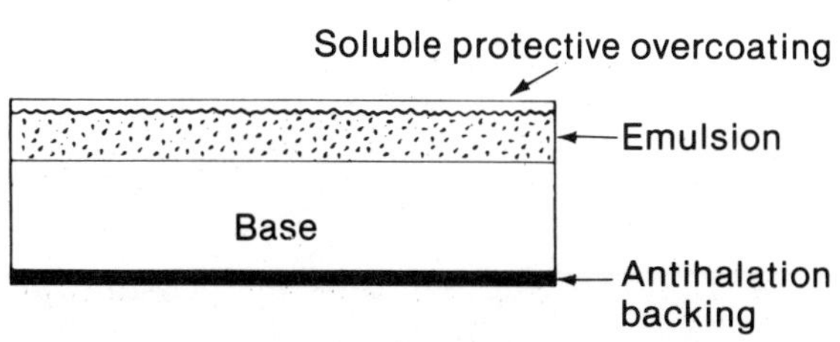

Figure 6.2. A typical film structure

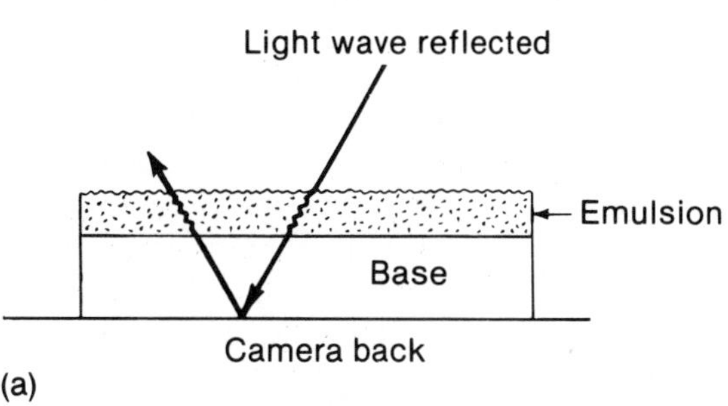

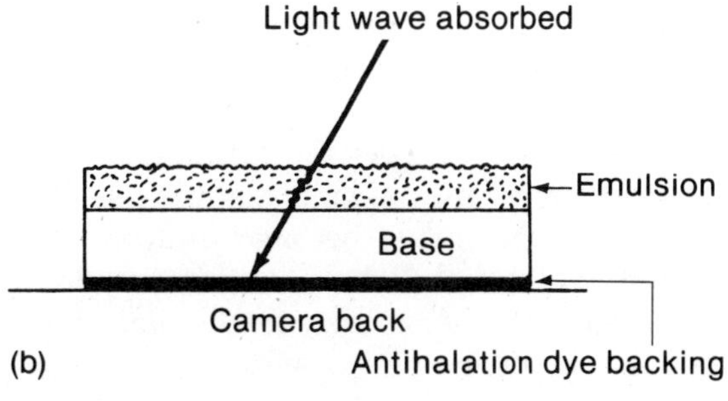

Figure 6.3. Comparison of light rays through two types of film structure Without the antihalation dye layer, light is reflected from the back of the film base and could reexpose the emulsion (a). The antihalation dye absorbs the light rays and prevents the problem of reexposure (b).

Camera Fundamentals

The intent in line photography is to record an accurate reproduction of an image (the copy) on the film emulsion. In order to do this, a device called a **process camera** is used. Cameras vary in type, size, complexity, and cost. Regardless of their differences, all cameras serve three basic functions:

- They provide a place to mount the light-sensitive film,
- They provide a means of focusing an image on the film,
- They provide a system that controls the amount of light that reaches the film emulsion.

It is possible to understand how a process camera works by building a general understanding of how any photographic system operates. Then we can move on to how line photography uses the same approach. All that is required for photography is some light source, a light-tight box to hold the film, a way to focus an image on the film, some way to control the amount of light that reaches the film, and, of course, something to photograph.

Whatever the light source, it should be directed at the object to be photographed. What the film sees is reflected light. If we use artificial light, it is easy to move the light source so that all areas of the object receive the proper amount of light. If we use natural light (the sun), we have to move the object itself to get the proper illumination. In line photography, artificial light is always used to illuminate the image because uniform illumination across the whole image is required.

Photographers refer to the light-tight box that holds the film as a camera. Cameras come in a wide range of shapes and sizes, but they all have the same characteristics and controls. There must be some sort of opening through which to pass and aim the light. This is called a **lens.** It is necessary to be able to move the lens so the reflected light from the object will be sharp and clear on the film—this is called **focusing.** If the image is not in focus, a blurred picture will be produced.

After the image is focused, there must be a way to control the amount of light that passes through the lens. This is important. If not enough light reaches the film, no image will be recorded. If too much light strikes the film, an unacceptable image that does not resemble the original object will be recorded. The two ways to control this passage of light are:

- By controlling the size of the lens opening (**aperture**),
- By controlling the amount of time the lens is open (**shutter speed**).

A simple way to understand the concept of controlling light is to think of a camera lens as a water faucet and of light as the water that passes through the pipe. First, consider the size of the pipe. It seems logical that a 2-inch (5.08 cm) pipe will pass nearly twice the amount of water as a 1-inch (2.54 cm) pipe in the same amount of time. If we run water through the 1-inch pipe for twice as much time as through the 2-inch pipe, the same amount of water should reach each bucket. This example is not exactly accurate in terms of the specific amount of water passed, but it does show the importance of the relationship between time and area.

The light controls for a camera operate in a similar manner. We can, in effect, control the amount of time the lens stays open with the **shutter,** a timing mechanism that accurately measures the amount of time the lens passes light. This amount of time is called shutter speed. it is also possible to vary the size of the "pipe" or lens opening. This control is referred to as the **diaphragm.** The diaphragm controls the aperture, which is the size of the lens opening. This size is based on the f/stop system (figure 6.4).

The **f/stop system** is based on a ratio of opening diameter to the focal length of the camera lens. **Focal length** is the distance from the node, or center, of the lens to the film board when the lens is focused at infinity (maximum reduction for graphic arts cameras) (figure 6.4). If the lens has an 8-inch focal length, a 1-inch opening is assigned the f/stop value of f/8; a ½-inch opening is f/16. Notice in figure 6.4 that the larger the f/stop number, the smaller the aperture opening. For example, changing the f/stop from f/32 to f/22 will double the amount of light that reaches the film. Moving from f/16 to f/22 will halve it. This is because the numbers and openings that designate the f/stop are selected so that adjacent f/stop numbers differ by a factor of two in the amount of light they pass.

Lenses come in all sizes, depending on the size of the camera. However, an f/stop number will always pass the same quantity of light on any size camera or lens.

The aperture and shutter controls work well together. Because each f/stop either doubles or halves the cross-sectional area of the preceding f/stop, the shutter speed can be halved or doubled to correspond with a one-stop diaphragm change. (Remember, when you change the f/stop, you are actually changing the diaphragm.) For example, if the film were being adequately exposed at f/16 for 40 seconds, the same exposure could be made at f/8 for 10 seconds. The same amount of light would hit the film, and the film record would be the same. An understanding of this relationship is a powerful tool for any photographer. A camera operator often seeks to reduce the exposure time to save time and also to save camera lights, which, like any artificial light source, wear out with use.

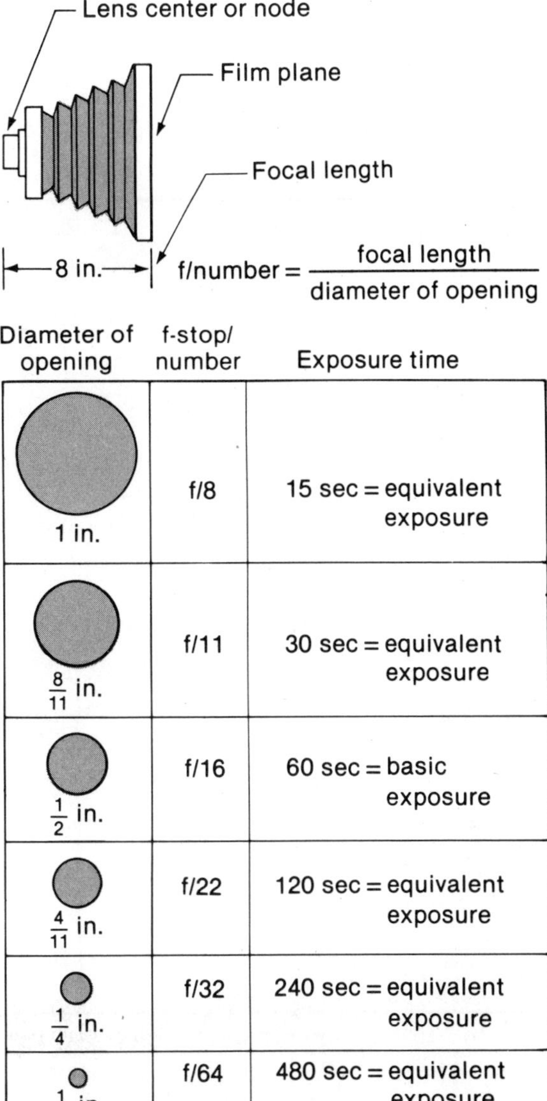

Diameter of opening	f-stop/number	Exposure time
1 in.	f/8	15 sec = equivalent exposure
$\frac{8}{11}$ in.	f/11	30 sec = equivalent exposure
$\frac{1}{2}$ in.	f/16	60 sec = basic exposure
$\frac{4}{11}$ in.	f/22	120 sec = equivalent exposure
$\frac{1}{4}$ in.	f/32	240 sec = equivalent exposure
$\frac{1}{8}$ in.	f/64	480 sec = equivalent exposure

Figure 6.4. Camera f/stops Camera f/stops are the relationship between focal length and lens opening sizes. In this figure the focal length is 8 inches and the lens opening sizes vary from 1 inch to 1/8 inch. The basic exposure time is 60 seconds at f/16. Equivalent exposure times are given for the remaining f/stops.

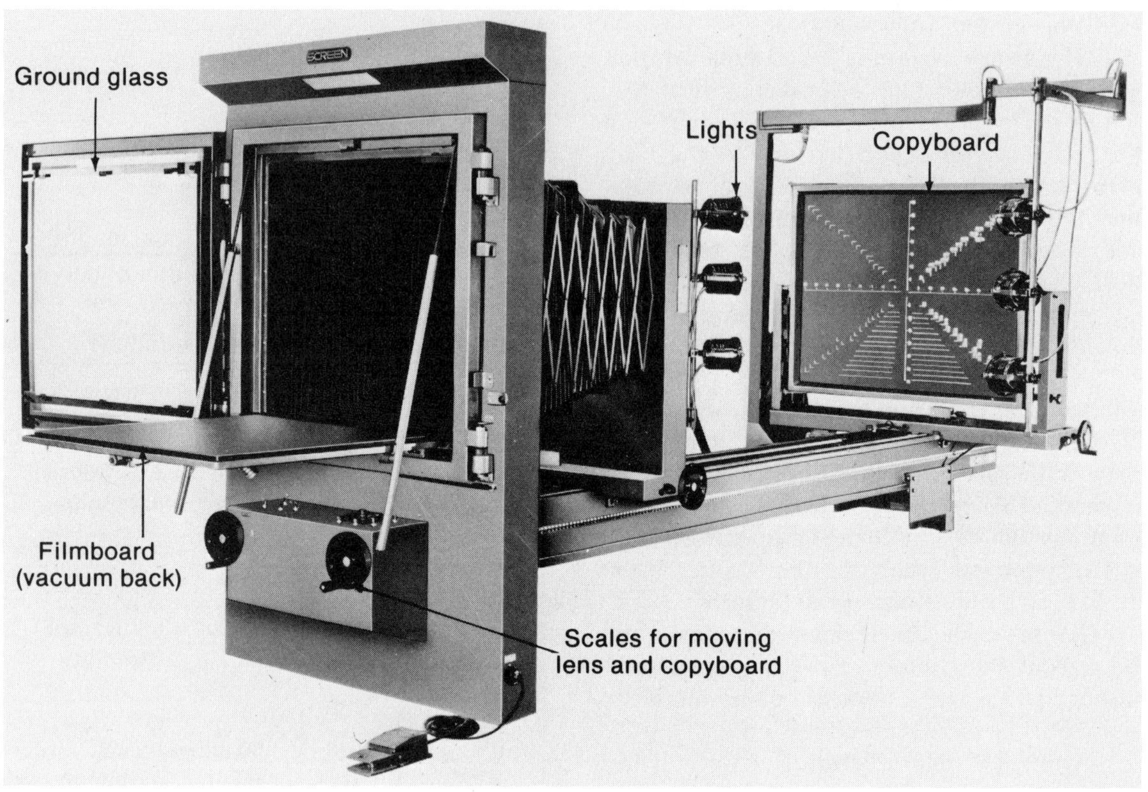

Figure 6.5. A horizontal process camera
Courtesy of nu Arc Company, Inc.

In halftone photography, exposures are predicted by a sort of computer (chapter 7) that is used to select aperture openings and shutter speeds based on the characteristics of the continuous-tone photograph. Sometimes the computer recommends shutter openings that are not available on a particular camera and must be translated into usable f/stops and times. Skilled operators can also use this knowledge to predict new exposure times for difficult originals or problem negatives.

Line Photography Tools

Line photography is also called "process photography," "reproduction photography," or "high-contrast photography." Whatever label is applied, the goals are the same: the photographer must be able to make precision enlargements and reductions and critically control line dimensions. The industry uses a special device called a "process camera" to record images for printing production (figure 6.5).

The process camera is large because it must be able to hold large sheets of film.

Process cameras can be classified according to where they are intended to be used or according to their basic shape. A **galley camera** is designed to operate in normal room light, so the film has to be loaded in a darkroom and then carried in some light-tight container to the camera. A **darkroom camera** is designed to operate in a safelight situation, so the photographer can load the film directly into the camera without leaving the darkroom. A **horizontal process camera** has a long stationary bed, with the film end usually in the darkroom and the lights and lens protruding through a wall into a normally lighted room (figure 6.6). A **vertical process camera** is a self-contained unit that takes up little space in the darkroom itself (figure 6.7). Whatever type is used, all process cameras have the same general controls and characteristics.

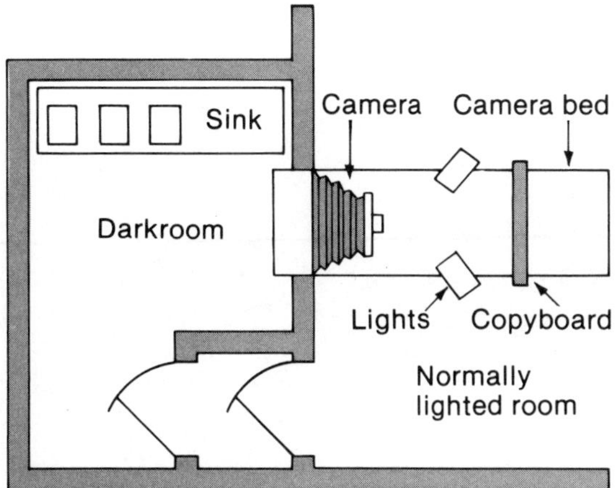

Figure 6.6. A horizontal process camera installed between two rooms The diagram shows a horizontal process camera with the copy end in a normally lighted room and the film end in a darkroom.

A process camera is nothing more than a rather sophisticated light-tight box. The film end of the camera opens to show a **filmboard** (see figure 6.5), which holds the film in place during the exposure. A vacuum back is generally used to hold the film flat and ensure that it will not fall or shift during exposure. The filmboard hinges closed and is perfectly parallel to the copyboard at the opposite end of the camera. The **copyboard** is simply a glass-covered frame that holds the copy or image that is to be photographed (a process camera is not designed to photograph three-dimensional objects). There are generally guidelines on both the film and the copyboard that, if followed, ensure that the image will be recorded in the center of the film.

Process cameras usually have an artificial light source that can direct light at the copyboard. Most light systems are controlled by the camera shutter, which controls the passage of light through the lens. When the shutter is opened, the lights go on. They are automatically shut off when the timer closes the shutter.

The main advantage of the process camera is that it can make enlargements and reductions of the original copy. Size changes are referred to by the percentage size of the original that is to be recorded on the film. A 100% or 1:1 reproduction will expose an image on the film that is the same size as the original copy. A 25% reduction will expose an image that is one-quarter the original size. A 200% enlargement will project an image that is twice the size of the original copy. The percentage of enlargement or reduction is controlled by changing the positions of the camera lens and copyboard. The adjustment is generally made manually by lining up percentage tapes (see figure 6.8, p. 105) or by

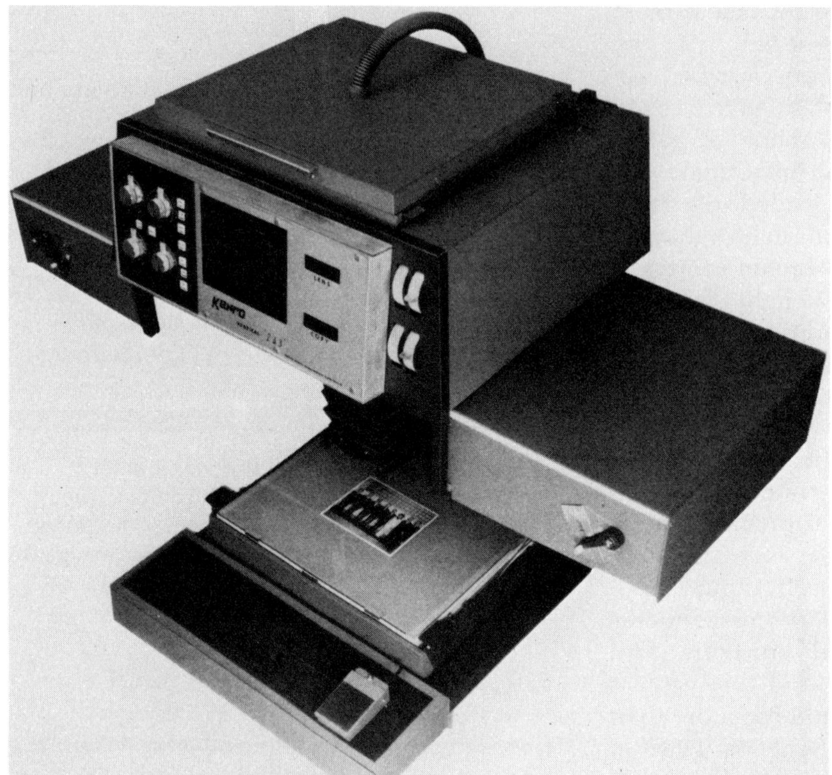

Figure 6.7. A vertical process camera
Courtesy of Kenro Corporation.

following guide numbers provided by the camera manufacturer. Some newer cameras have digital readout devices that set the lens and copyboard automatically.

The amount of light necessary to produce a quality image on the film is calculated at a 100% (or same-size) reproduction called "basic exposure." Whenever the positions of the lens and copyboard are changed, the distance the reflected light must travel to the film is also changed. But whatever the percentage of enlargement or reduction, the quantity of light reaching the film must remain the same as for 100%. Most process cameras have a **variable diaphragm control.** The control changes the f/stop (aperture opening) to correspond to the percentage of enlargement or reduction (see figure 6.14). For example, if a 67% reduction is to be made, the diaphragm control is moved in line with 67%. With this method, the exposure time will always remain the same and only the aperture opening will vary.

A more accurate method of controlling film exposure is with a **light integrator** (figure 6.9, p. 106). A light integrator uses a photoelectric cell that is placed in line with the light passing through the lens. The cell is connected to a device that measures the units of light reaching the film. With an integrated system, the camera operator simply dials in the desired amount of light. The lens will automatically close when that quantity has reached the photoelectric cell. Any variation in copy or light characteristics, such as changes in the voltage in the power source that operates the camera lights, will automatically be accounted for.

Basic Exposure and Camera Operation

Clearly, many considerations are involved in meeting the goal of producing a high-quality photographic image for printing production. As process photographers, our problem is to understand and to control these variables. The task will be easier if all processing conditions are held constant and only the camera exposure is varied. This technique involves the concept of a basic camera exposure.

In general, **basic exposure** is the camera aperture and shutter speed combination that will produce a quality film image of normal line copy with standardized chemical processing. This combination will vary from camera to camera, depending on many variables, such as energy level of the light source, color temperature (see appendix B), processing chemicals, temperature control, rate of agitation, copy characteristics, and type of film. Whenever one of the variables is changed, however slightly, the basic exposure must be recalculated. Once that exposure has been determined, it can be used to accurately predict new times for any change in copy characteristics. The procedures for determining basic camera exposure are simple and are explained in detail in appendix A.

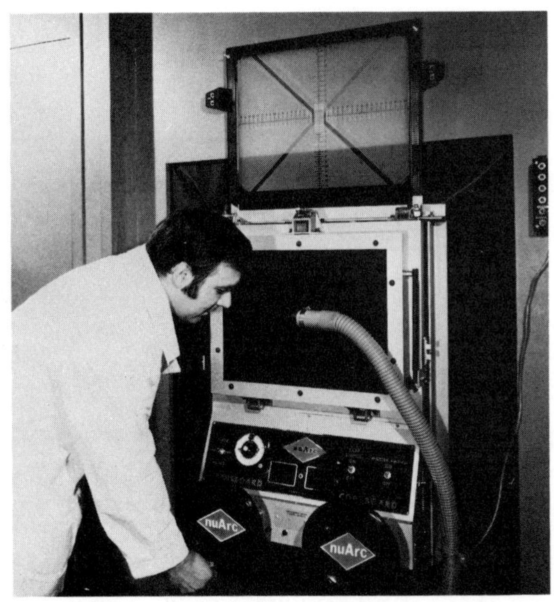

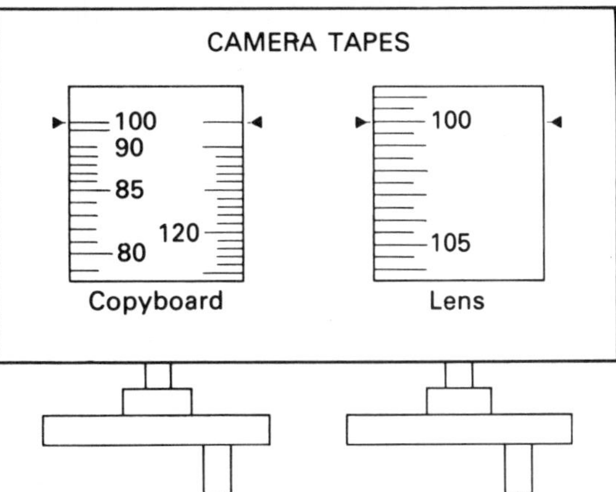

Figure 6.8. Adjusting the distance between the camera lens and the copyboard Before exposing the film, the operator must adjust the camera for the correct size of the final image. This is done by moving the percentage tapes until both are set at the desired reproduction size.

Courtesy of nu Arc Company, Inc.

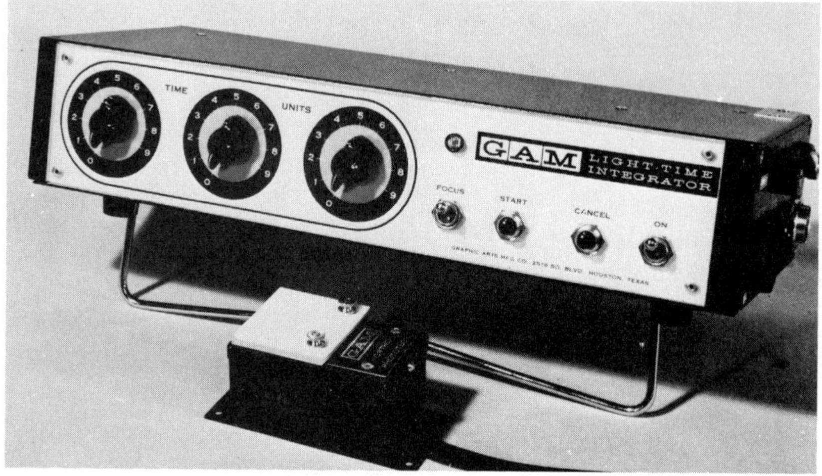

Figure 6.9. A light integrator This machine automatically controls the amount of light used to expose the film in the camera.
Courtesy of Graphic Arts Manufacturing Co.

Let's work through a practical example to show how a typical photographic line conversion is made. Assume that our task is to make a high-contrast negative, such as the copy shown in figure 6.1, so that it can be used to expose a printing plate. In order to meet rough layout specifications, we are told to reduce the original 53%. Our process camera is a horizontal model with a basic exposure of f/16 for 22 seconds. (The explanation that follows can also be applied to a vertical model.)

Mounting the Copy

Begin by mounting the copy in the copyboard. Swing the copyboard to a horizontal position and open the glass cover. Spots of dirt or dust can interfere with image quality, so the glass should be thoroughly cleaned before each use. There is usually some sort of guideline system that will allow the original to be placed nearly perfectly in the center of the board (figure 6.10). The copyboard guidelines are in line with guidelines on the filmboard. Because the camera lens reverses the image, place the copy so that it will be upside down when the copyboard is in a vertical position. This will help if fine focusing is necessary.

A graphic arts **step tablet** or **gray scale** is a tool used by process photographers as an aid in judging the quality of a film image (figure 6.11). With every exposure, the photographer places the gray scale on the copyboard next to the material being photographed (figure 6.12, p. 108). The specific position does not matter, but it is important that the gray scale not cover any line detail, that it receive the same light as the copy, and that it be in a position to be recorded on the film with the copy detail. As the film is processed, both the copy image and the scale will become visible

Figure 6.10. Mounting copy in the copyboard
The copy is centered on the copyboard guidelines and positioned to be upside down when the frame is in the vertical position.
Courtesy of nu Arc Company, Inc.

Figure 6.11. A printer's gray scale

gray. As steps on the scale darken and fill in, they serve as a visual cue that indicates the stage of film development. After washing the film, the image of the gray scale serves as a means of critically judging the film's usability, and if unacceptable, of indicating the method needed to correct the shortcomings.

When the copy and gray scale are in position, close the glass frame and turn on the vacuum pump. Check again for lint or dust in the image area and make sure that the copy has not moved. Swing the copyboard

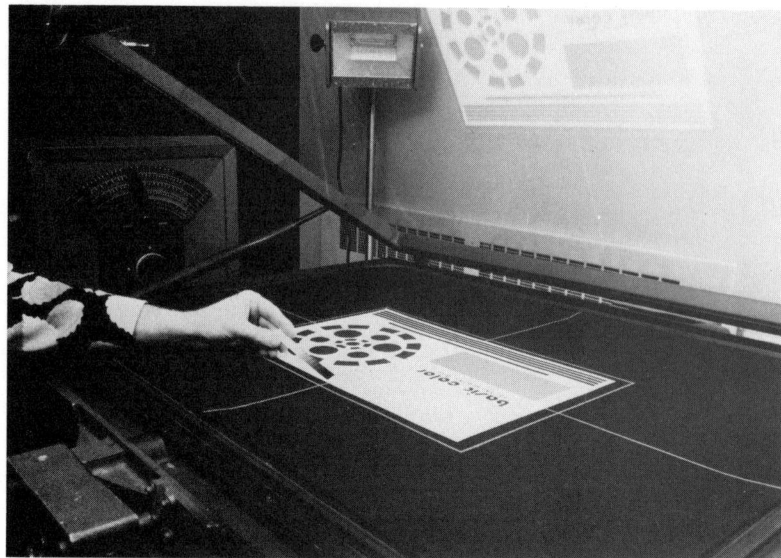

Figure 6.12. Using a gray scale Place a graphic arts gray scale next to the copy, but do not allow it to cover any image area.
Photo by R. Kampas.

into a vertical position so that it is parallel to the filmboard.

Focusing

Enlargement and reduction on our camera are controlled by percentage tapes. By moving the tapes, the relative positions of the lens and copyboard are moved so that the image will be in perfect focus and at the same time will be the required reproduction size. To make our exposure, both tapes are positioned at 53%.

Some cameras have ground glass screens that can be used to check both image position and focus. Swing or place the ground glass into position. When the camera lights are turned on, the reflected image is projected through the lens onto the inside layer of glass. It is then possible to use a magnifying glass to check for focus or to use a ruler to ensure that the final film image will be the desired size.

It might be necessary to adjust the camera lights for even illumination across the image. A general recommendation is to set the lights at a 30° angle from the copyboard frame (figure 6.13). The ground glass image can be used to judge evenness of intensity across the image. Some types of reflection densitometers can be used to make the same, but more precise, measurement.

Setting the Aperture and Shutter Speed

Next, prepare the aperture and timer controls. Set the timer for the basic exposure time, which for our example is a 22-second exposure. Because we are making a 53% reduction, move the variable diaphragm control arm to 53% on the f/16 scale (figure 6.14). This system automatically adjusts the lens opening (aperture) for the proper quantity of light at a 53% reduction.

It is important to understand that when you move the variable diaphragm control along this scale, you are changing the f/stop setting so it corresponds to the basic camera exposure. The f/stop setting for the basic exposure is determined at a 100% (same-size) exposure. In this example, a 53% reduction is being made. When the percentage tapes are set at 53%, the lens and filmboard move farther away from each other (figure 6.15). Because the copyboard or the filmboard is farther away from the light source than at a 100% setting, either a larger lens aperture opening or a longer exposure time will be required to allow the proper amount of light to reach the film. If the exposure time is kept

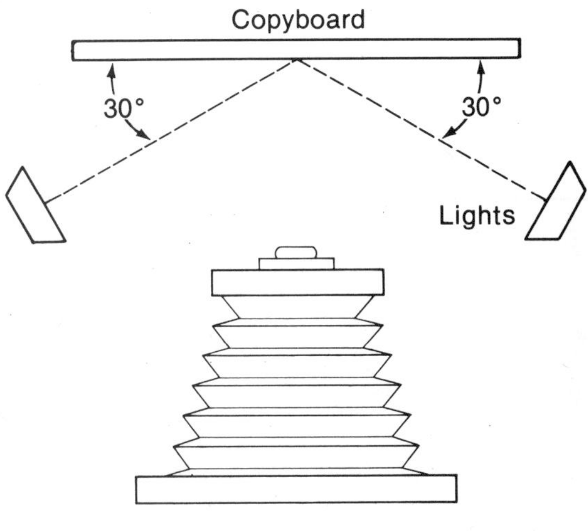

Figure 6.13. Position of camera lights The camera lights are usually positioned at 30° angles from the copyboard.

Figure 6.14. Setting the aperture control Adjust the aperture by moving the diaphragm arm to the reproduction percentage size in line with the f/stop size for the basic exposure.
Courtesy of nu Arc Company, Inc.

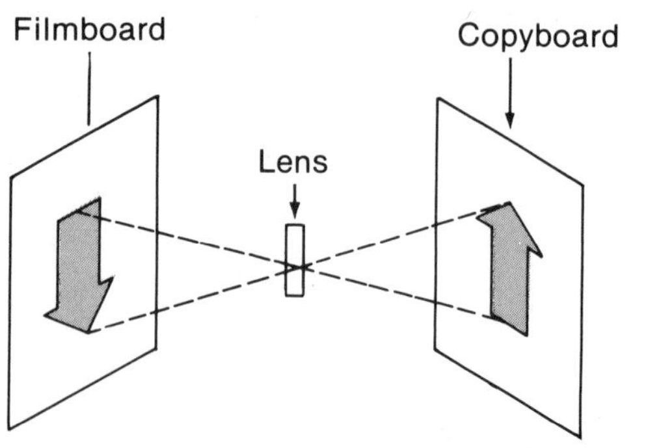

100% Reproduction

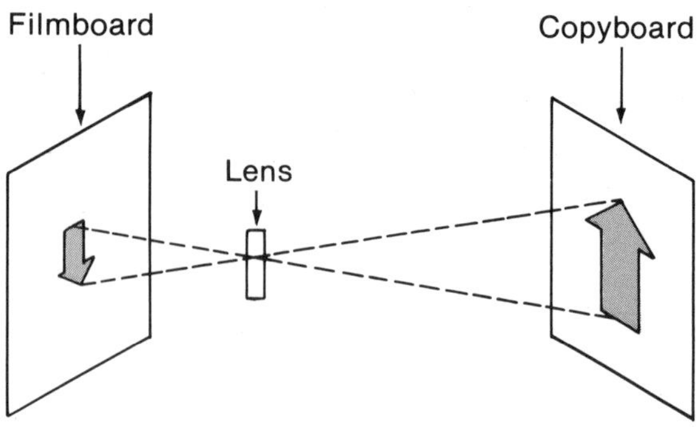

50% Reduction

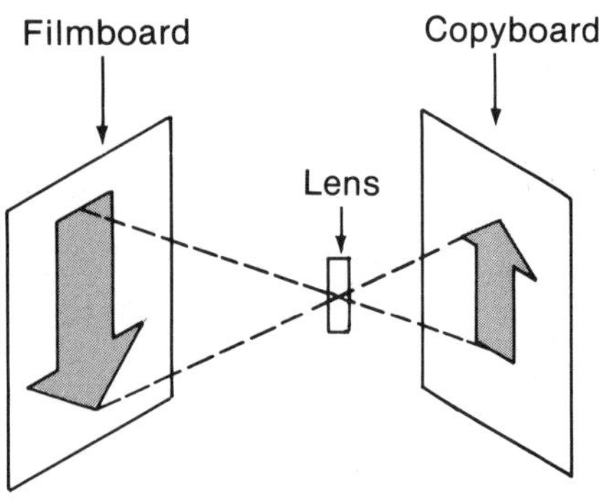

150% Enlargement

Figure 6.15. Adjusting the copyboard for enlargements or reductions The copyboard is moved closer to the filmboard to make an enlargement of the original copy, and it is moved farther away from the filmboard to make a reduction.

the same, then the aperture opening must be increased to provide the extra light. This is what the variable diaphragm control does. If the camera did not have a variable diaphragm control, it would be necessary to calculate the amount of reflected light loss that would result from each change in copyboard position. The process is possible, but it takes time and is tiring. The variable diaphragm control provides a scale with these calculations already made.

Mounting the Film

In most cameras, the film is held in place on the filmboard by a vacuum system. It is necessary to adjust the filmboard so that vacuum pressure will be applied over the entire area of the sheet and will not lose holding power by pulling in air where there is no film. Individual cameras are adjusted differently, but most are designed to accommodate the most common film sizes.

All these first steps of setting up the camera for making a line exposure can be performed in normal room light; the last steps cannot. The process darkroom is normally equipped with a dual lighting system. Use the red light, or **safelight,** when working with high-contrast film. Use the white light for setup only. Some graphic arts films, such as those used for some steps in color separation, cannot be used in any safelight situation and all lights must be turned off. Be sure you know what film material you are using before you open any film container.

With the appropriate illumination in the darkroom, carefully open the film box, remove one sheet of film, and replace the cover. A common error for new photographers is to forget to close the box until after the camera exposure has been made. With some darkroom designs, most of the film in the box has been ruined by that time.

Handle film only by the outside edges. If a wet or even moist finger touches the emulsion, a fingerprint can appear on the developed film and ruin the image's usability.

Center the sheet of film on the guidelines on the filmboard with the emulsion side up (so that it faces the copyboard when the filmboard is closed). There are rare instances when the emulsion side is placed down, but in general the film is always exposed through the emulsion. Even in the red light of the darkroom, it is easy to identify the emulsion side of the film.

There are three basic ways to identify the emulsion side of a piece of film. The easiest is simply to look at the sheet. The darker side is the antihalation dye layer, and the lighter side is the emulsion (figure 6.16). This is easy to remember because the antihalation dye is dark to absorb the light that passes through the film. A second way to identify the emulsion side is by remembering that most films tend to curl into the emulsion side. Be careful, however, because the heat of your hand can cause curling in either direction. The third method of identifying the emulsion side of a piece of film works only for film material that is intended to be used in total or nearly complete darkness. On such film, the manufacturer uses a notching system. Each different type of film has a unique pattern of notches so that the photographer can identify different materials in the dark by using only a fingertip (figure 6.17). The notches also serve to identify the emulsion side. If the sheet is held so that the notches are in the upper right-hand corner, the emulsion is facing the photographer.

Figure 6.16. Identifying the emulsion side by its color The emulsion side, or the lighter side of the film, is placed up on the filmboard.
Photo by R. Kampas.

With the film in place, turn on the vacuum pump and carefully roll the film with a roller to remove any air pockets that might be trapped under the sheet (figure 6.18). Be extremely careful; the emulsion is a very fragile material. As an alternative to this practice, many photographers turn on the vacuum and then roll the film itself into position, thereby eliminating the possibility of air pockets.

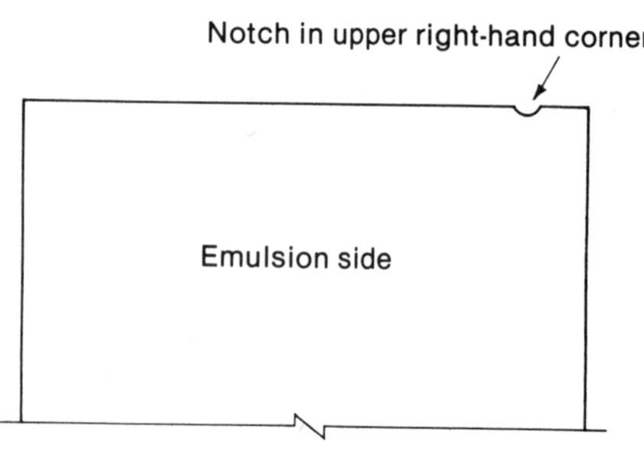

Figure 6.17. Using notches to identify the emulsion side When the film notches are in the upper right-hand corner, the emulsion side is up.

Figure 6.18. Removing air pockets from the film After positioning the film on the filmboard, turn on the vacuum and carefully roll the sheet to remove any trapped air.
Photo by R. Kampas.

Exposing the Film

The last step is to make the actual exposure. Swing the filmboard into position so that it is parallel to the copy and lock the entire frame in place. When you push the timer control button, the camera lights automatically go on and the shutter opens. When the preset exposure time has been reached (for this example, twenty-two seconds), the shutter closes and the lights go off. Open the camera back, turn off the vacuum pressure, and remove the sheet. The film appears no different than it did before the exposure, but it now carries an invisible, or latent, image. Chemical processing is necessary to make the latent image visible and permanent.

Chemical Processing for Line Photography

Processing Chemicals

When light of the proper quantity and quality strikes the light-sensitive silver halide emulsion on the film, a change takes place. It is a subtle change in the chemical structure of the halide crystals, a change that cannot be detected by the human eye. Because this change is invisible, photographers generally call it the result of a **latent image.**

When the image is focused through the camera lens, the light passes to the film and selectively alters portions of the emulsion according to the amount of light reflected from the copy on the copyboard. The white areas of the original copy (generally nonimage) reflect a great deal of light, which changes many halide crystals. The black or pigmented areas (generally the image) absorb most of the light, reflecting little back to the film and thus changing very few halide crystals. This is a very important concept. Photography depends on reflected light from the original copy to record a reverse (or negative) image on a sheet of film (figure 6.19).

Remember, where light is reflected from the original copy, halide crystals are changed. Where light is not reflected from the copy, halide crystals are not changed. Where halide crystals are changed, the film will be black after processing. This will be the film record image of the white areas on the photographed copy. Where halide crystals are not changed, the film will be clear after processing (because the unchanged halide crystals are washed away during processing). The clear areas on the film will be the film record of the dark (image) areas on the copy. This is why a film image is a "negative" of the original copy.

The purpose of chemical processing is to change the latent or invisible image on a sheet of exposed film to a visible and permanent image.

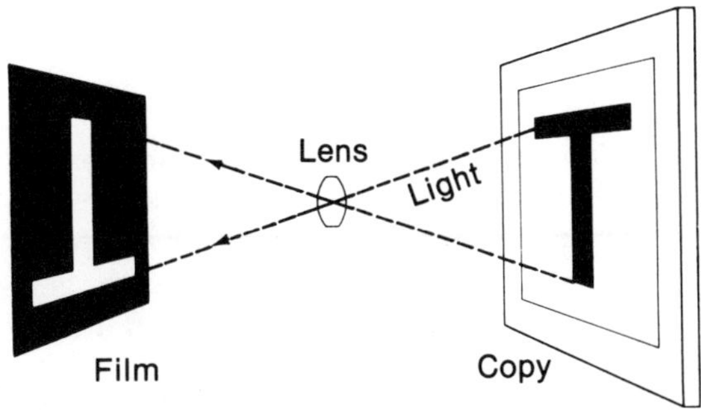

Figure 6.19. Film exposure The light reflected from the nonimage or light portions of the original copy exposes the film and results in a negative image where the reflected light was not absorbed by the film.

Processing Steps

Whatever the type of film, at least three chemical solutions and a water bath will be used during film processing. The steps in film processing are as follows:

1. Developing the film,
2. Stopping the development,
3. Fixing the image,
4. Washing away the chemicals.

Developing the Film. The **developer** is a complex solution designed to make the latent image visible. The solution contains an organic compound, called the developing agent, dissolved in water. The developer changes each exposed silver halide crystal to a grain of black metallic silver (which is why exposed areas of the film turn black during processing.) The change takes place very slowly, so an activator (usually sodium hydroxide) is added to speed things up. An additional problem with the developing agent is that it oxidizes (loses its ability to work when exposed to air). When a developer has turned brown, oxidation has broken down the activity level of the developer and no film can be processed in it. To delay the effects of oxidation a preservative, usually sodium sulfite, is added to the developer solution. The final weakness of the developer is that after all the exposed silver halide crystals have been changed to black metallic silver, the solution begins to work on the unexposed crystals. If the process were to continue, the entire sheet of film would be a solid layer of black silver and would be unusable. This is why the film must be removed from the developer as soon as all the exposed silver halide crystals have changed to black metallic silver.

An unexposed area of film that does not appear clear is "fogged." Fog can be caused by accidental exposure to light or by developer agents. To prevent fog, a restrainer, generally potassium bromide, is added to the developer solution.

Although the actual compounds differ depending on the characteristics of the chemical emulsion of the film, all developers are made up of the following five parts:

- Solvent (water),
- Developing agent,
- Activator,
- Preservative,
- Restrainer.

Table 6.1 shows the formula for a common high-contrast developer.

Developer manufacturers always recommend development procedures for their chemicals. For example, Kodak recommends that Kodalith, a high-contrast film developer, be stored in two separate solutions and mixed in equal parts to form the working solution. Once mixed, oxidation exhausts the activity of the bath in several hours. Manufacturers also recommend the maximum number of square inches of film that should be processed in a quantity of developer solution before new developer should be mixed. Most developer solutions are designed to function at exactly 68°F (20°C). Any temperature fluctuation will decrease the predictability of results.

Stopping the Development. Once the desired level of development has been reached, the developing action must be halted immediately. Plunging the film from the developer (a base) into an acid solution will stop all developer activity. This acid solution is called the **stop-bath** or **short-stop.** It is usually made up of a small quantity of acetic acid combined

Table 6.1. Formula for Kodak Developer, D–72 (A Continuous-Tone Developer)

Function	Ingredient	Quantity	
		English	**Metric**
Solvent	water	64.0 ounces	500.0 ml
Developing agent	Kodak Elon	175.0 grains	3.0 grams
Preservative	sodium sulfite	6.0 ounces	45.0 grams
Developing agent	hydroquinne	1.0 ounce, 260.0 grains	12.0 grams
Activator	sodium carbonate	10.5 ounces	80.0 grams
Restrainer	potassium bromide	115.0 grains	2.0 grams
Solvent	water to make. . . .	1.0 gallon	1.0 liter

with a large amount of water. The stop-bath really serves two functions:

- To halt the development,
- To extend the life of the third solution, the fixer.

Fixing the Image. After development and stop, the image on the piece of film is visible, but not permanent. The silver halide crystals that were not exposed are still present in the emulsion and are visible as cloudy areas in the clear areas of the film. These unexposed crystals are still sensitive to light. The function of the fixing bath is to remove all these unexposed silver crystals and make the film image permanent.

The **fixing bath** is a chemical solution nearly as complex as the developer. As with all photographic chemicals, the main solvent is water. Water does not dissolve unexposed halide crystals, but a compound called **hypo** or sodium thiosulfate does. This is such an important ingredient of the fixing bath that the term "hypo" is often used interchangeably with fixer. Acetic acid, the primary ingredient of the stop-bath, is also added to the fixing bath to neutralize any developer that the film might still carry. However, the acetic acid has a tendency to affect the hypo by turning it into small pieces of sulfur and thus rendering it useless as a fixing agent. To overcome this difficulty, a preservative called sodium sulfite, which combines with the sulfur and changes it back to hypo, is added. During development, the gelatin of the film emulsion swells up because the main solvent is water. To harden the gelatin again, a hardener, such as potassium alum, is added to the fixing bath. If a hardener is used, then a pH of 4 must be maintained. pH is a measure of acidity of a solution. To accomplish this, a buffer, such as boric acid, is used. Table 6.2 (p. 116) illustrates the makeup of a common commercial fixing bath with hardener.

After development and the stop-bath, the unexposed portions of the film negative appear milky white under red safelight conditions. This milk-white color is actually the unexposed silver halide crystals remaining in the clear areas of the film. Fixing time is generally determined by leaving the film in the hypo twice the length of time required to remove these unexposed crystals.

Washing Away the Chemicals. During chemical processing, some of the processing solutions become attached to the film base and emulsion material. If they were allowed to remain, the image could yellow or gradually begin to fade. The fourth step for all photographic processes is to wash away all traces of the processing chemicals. Because water is the main solvent for all the solutions, a simple running-water bath will remove all objectionable chemicals. Depending on the rate of water change, 10 minutes in a strong water flow should be sufficient for films, and 30 to 45 minutes for any other photographic materials.

Controlling Chemical Processing

There are many ways, such as shallow-tray, deep-tank, or automatic processing, to store and work with the chemical baths. Whatever the method, there are three major concerns that the photographer always tries to control:

- Agitation,
- Time,
- Temperature.

Agitation. **Agitation** refers to the flow of the solution back and forth over the film during

Table 6.2. Formula for Kodak Fixing Bath F–5

Function	Ingredient	Quantity	
		English	**Metric**
Solvent	water	2.25 gallons	600.0 ml
Hypo	sodium thiosulfate	7.00 pounds	240.0 grams
Preservative	sodium sulfite	7.00 ounces	15.0 grams
Buffer	boric acid, crystals	3.50 ounces	7.5 grams
Acid	acetic acid (28%)	21.00 ounces	48.0 ml
Hardener	potassium alum	7.00 ounces	15.0 grams
Solvent	water to make . . .	3.50 gallons	1.0 liter

processing. If the film were allowed to sit in the solution, the chemicals immediately in contact with the emulsion would quickly become exhausted. Agitation ensures that new chemicals are continually flowing over the film, giving constant chemical action. The rate of agitation is not important, but the consistency of the motion is. By being consistent, the photographer can duplicate results for every piece of film that is processed.

Consistency is important. If the right and left pages of this book were each made from two different pieces of film, and the piece of film that recorded the right page had been agitated more frequently or rapidly than the piece of film that recorded the left page, the images on the right would appear lighter than the images on the left. This would be true even if both pieces of film were agitated for the same length of time! This is because the film for the right page, being agitated more frequently, would be overdeveloped, and the images would "fill in" (some of the unexposed silver halide crystals in the image areas would start to turn to black metallic silver). All the images on the right page would appear thinner and smaller than all the images on the left page.

Shallow-tray processing is a common processing method in the industry (discussed later in this chapter). Many techniques have been developed to help the photographer with agitation of the tray—even to the point of attaching cams and levers to rock the tray mechanically in two directions at a constant rate. However, the randomness of human motion remains the most ideal—as long as it is consistent. Some photographers even use a metronome to ensure this consistency.

Time and Temperature. Time and temperature are easier to control. The film's manufacturer provides recommended processing times. For example, Kodak recommends that with the shallow-tray method, their Ortho 3 film be developed for 2¾ minutes with 10 seconds in the stop. It should be fixed twice as long as it takes to clear the film. Several different types of darkroom timers are available to assist photographers in controlling processing times. If the temperature of all chemicals is within $\pm \frac{1}{2}°$ of the optimum (68°F or 20°C), the temperature is usually considered "in control" for line photography. Temperature control sinks are generally used to control chemical temperatures.

Automatic Processing. A relatively recent development in chemical control has been the introduction of automatic processing units (figure 6.20). Most machines are designed for dry-to-dry delivery in 8 to 12 minutes. This is a tremendous advantage over tray processing because the photographer never gets wet hands and can be making another exposure in the camera room while a previous sheet of film is being processed.

The most common feeding method is a continuous belt that passes through a developer, a stop-fixer, a washing tank, and a dryer (figure 6.21). With deep-tank chemical storage, there is little problem with oxidation, although long periods of disuse will cause some activity change. Chemical exhaustion as a result of film processing is controlled by the addition of a small quantity of replenisher after each piece of film enters the machine. Replenisher is generally added automatically as a function of the area of the sheet of film being processed. With the use of replenisher, the chemical solutions generally need be removed from the tanks only several times a year for machine maintenance.

Automatic processing can provide accurate time-temperature-agitation control, can free the photographer for increased camera work, and can reduce production costs through fewer makeovers and faster processing. However, automated processing cannot be viewed as a solution for all production problems. It can, in fact, cause more problems than it solves.

There is no single chemical solution that can process all photographic materials a printer might use. After an automated system is installed in the darkroom, the photographer is frequently flooded with requests to develop everything from X-rays to diffusion transfer materials (discussed later), from stabilization paper to snapshots that someone took during lunch hour. If any material that the developer was not designed to process is passed through it, the chemical balance of the machine will change.

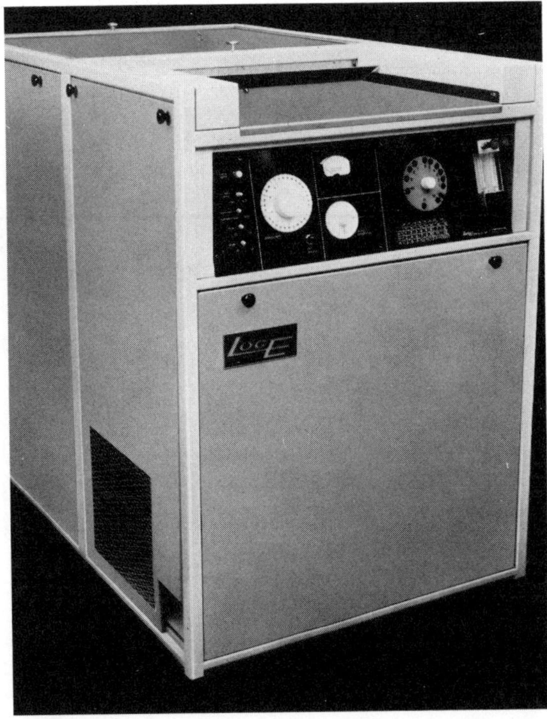

Figure 6.20. An automatic film-processing unit A unit such as this machine provides greater accuracy and control of agitation, time, and temperature than possible by manual processing methods.
Courtesy of Log E/LogEtronics, Inc.

Adding replenisher to the developer to keep the activity level correct is not a simple process. With most machines, huge quantities of replenisher must be added after even an overnight shutdown. **Control strips** (controlled density wedges from the film manufacturer that have been exposed on pieces of

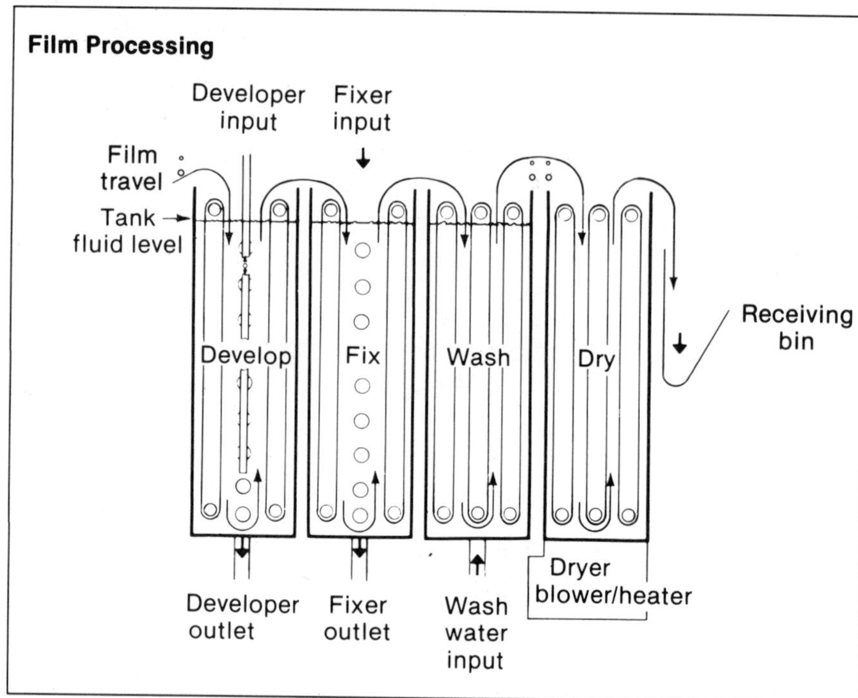

Figure 6.21. Side-view diagram of a typical automatic film processor Rollers move the film from tank to tank.

film of the type the printer is using) are used to measure the activity. Several times a day the photographer must feed a control strip through the machine to check the developer. If the strip is overdeveloped, the activity is too high. If it is underdeveloped, the activity is too low. Too low an activity is corrected simply by manually dialing in replenisher, but too high an activity level is a problem. The general technique for reducing a high activity level is to expose several sheets of film to room light, send them through the machine without replenisher, and then add another control strip. While all this is going on, no productive processing is taking place, film is being wasted, and the average cost of all the day's processing is mounting.

Whatever the method, the problem of controlling chemical processing remains the photographer's primary concern. If the photographer is not aware of all the variables and the ways to control them, high-quality results can be produced only by luck; consistent high-quality results become an impossibility.

Shallow-Tray Chemical Processing

The following steps are necessary for chemical processing with the shallow-tray method (figure 6.22). All these steps, except washing and drying, are carried out under safelight conditions. Before placing the film in the developer, set the timer for the recommended time (usually 2¾ minutes).

1. Place the dry exposed film from the camera into the developer with the emulsion

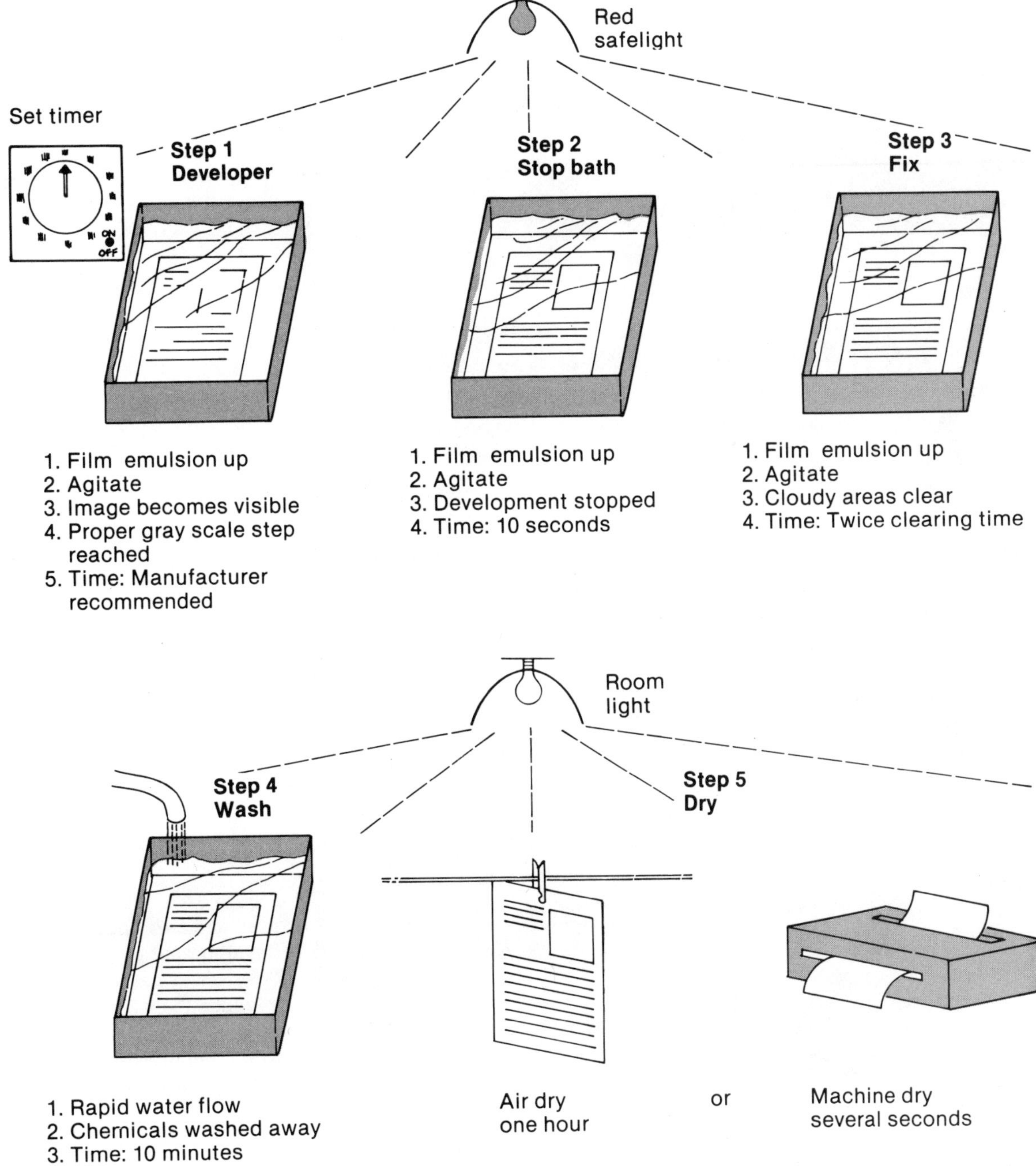

Red safelight
Set timer
ON
OFF
Step 1 Developer
Step 2 Stop bath
Step 3 Fix
1. Film emulsion up
2. Agitate
3. Image becomes visible
4. Proper gray scale step reached
5. Time: Manufacturer recommended
1. Film emulsion up
2. Agitate
3. Development stopped
4. Time: 10 seconds
1. Film emulsion up
2. Agitate
3. Cloudy areas clear
4. Time: Twice clearing time
Room light
Step 4 Wash
Step 5 Dry
1. Rapid water flow
2. Chemicals washed away
3. Time: 10 minutes
Air dry one hour
or
Machine dry several seconds

Figure 6.22. Shallow-tray method of developing film

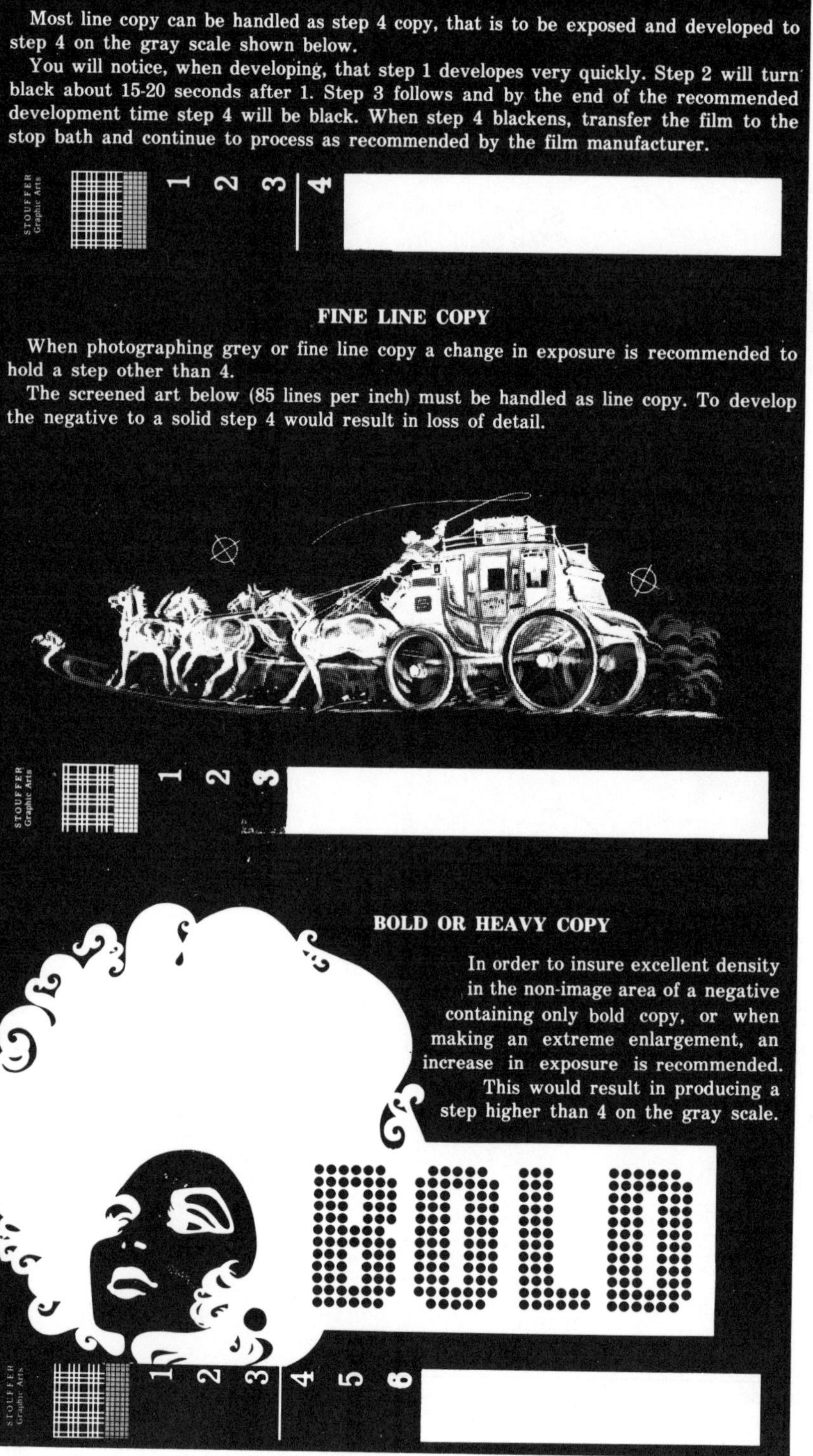

NORMAL COPY
Most line copy can be handled as step 4 copy, that is to be exposed and developed to step 4 on the gray scale shown below.
You will notice, when developing, that step 1 developes very quickly. Step 2 will turn black about 15-20 seconds after 1. Step 3 follows and by the end of the recommended development time step 4 will be black. When step 4 blackens, transfer the film to the stop bath and continue to process as recommended by the film manufacturer.
STOUFFER Graphic Arts
1 2 3 4
FINE LINE COPY
When photographing grey or fine line copy a change in exposure is recommended to hold a step other than 4.
The screened art below (85 lines per inch) must be handled as line copy. To develop the negative to a solid step 4 would result in loss of detail.
STOUFFER Graphic Arts
1 2 3
BOLD OR HEAVY COPY
In order to insure excellent density in the non-image area of a negative containing only bold copy, or when making an extreme enlargement, an increase in exposure is recommended. This would result in producing a step higher than 4 on the gray scale.
BOLD
STOUFFER Graphic Arts
1 2 3 4 5 6

Figure 6.23. Using a gray scale to gauge development of film Gray scales can be used to gauge the stage of development for a piece of film. Different types of copy are developed to different steps. In this example, normal copy is developed to step 4, fine line copy is developed to step 3, and heavy copy is developed to step 6.

side up and the sheet completely covered by the liquid. Place the film emulsion-side up in the developer so that you can inspect the image as it becomes visible. You could see the image even if the film were emulsion-side down in the developer; but because you would be looking through the antihalation backing, the image would appear to be developing more slowly than it is actually doing. Remember to handle the film as little as possible; touch it only along the outside edges. As soon as the film is covered by the developer, turn on the timer and start agitating the film. Keep your agitation as consistent as possible. As the film develops, the latent image will become visible. As soon as you can see the image, look for the image of the gray scale.

By visually inspecting the gray scale on the film as it is processed, it is possible to account for slight variations in the time-temperature-agitation technique of development. For normal line copy, a solid step 4 should usually be obtained on the scale. Extremely fine-line detail should be developed less (steps 2 or 3), and bold lines could be developed much further (steps 5 or 6) (figure 6.23). If for some reason the development time has reached the recommended length and with normal copy the scale shows a solid step 3, then the processing should be extended because optimal results have not yet been obtained. This could happen if the developer was old and almost exhausted. But development should not be extended grossly beyond the recommended time. If the recommended time is 2¾ minutes and a solid step 4 has not been reached after 5 minutes, discard the film and expose a new sheet. You may need either to increase the exposure time because some variable is not in control or to mix new developer.

2. When the correct gray scale step appears on the film, move the film to the stop-bath. To do this, lift the film by one corner out of the developer and let it drain briefly over the developing tray; then place it in the stop-bath. Agitate the film in the stop-bath at the same consistent rate that you agitated it throughout development. Leave the film in the stop-bath for at least 10 seconds.

3. Pick the film up by one corner and let it drain into the stop-bath; then move it to the fixer. Again, the film should be placed in the fixer emulsion-side up. Watch the clear areas on the film as you agitate it in the fixer. Make a mental note of the time that it takes these clear areas to go from cloudy to completely clear. Agitate the film in the fixer for twice the length of time that it takes for the unexposed areas to lose the cloudy appearance. If it takes 20 seconds for the unexposed areas to completely clear, a 40-second fixing bath with constant agitation should be sufficient.

4. When the film has been fixed for the proper amount of time, lift it out of the fixer, let it drain, then put it into a running-water bath. Ten minutes of strong water flow should wash away all chemicals remaining on the film.

5. After the film is washed, either hang it up to air dry or put it through a film dryer. Air drying will usually take up to one hour. Automatic film dryers can reduce this time to less than a minute.

Duplicating Film Materials

There is often a need to produce film positives and duplicate film negatives from previously prepared film materials. Two common methods are used in the industry:

- Camera copying from a back-lighted copyboard,
- Contact printing.

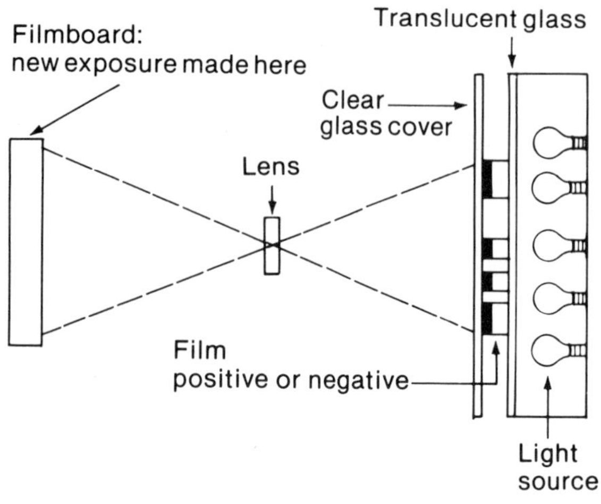

Figure 6.24. Diagram of a back-lighted copyboard A back-lighted copyboard is needed to photograph transparent negative or positive film.

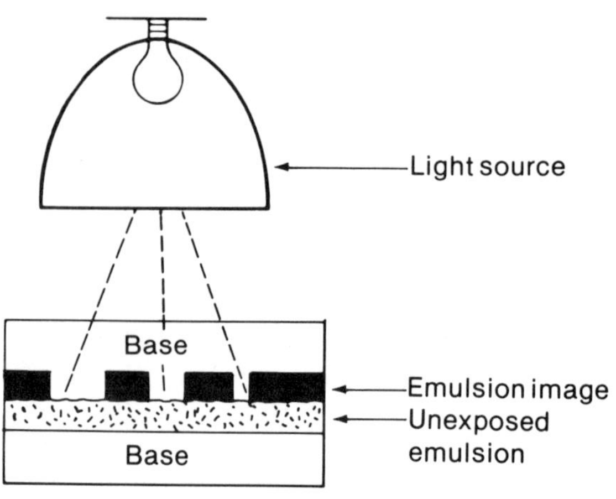

Figure 6.25. Contact printing This diagram shows the proper placement of the film negative against a fresh sheet of film to make a contact exposure. Note that the two pieces of film are placed emulsion to emulsion.

Process cameras can have two types of copyboards. The one we discussed previously was a **solid-back copyboard,** probably covered with black felt cloth. The copy was placed against the felt, and the glass cover held the original copy in place while light was reflected from the image through the camera lens and a film exposure was made. The second type of copyboard is called a **back-lighted copyboard.** With this design, a sheet of semi-opaque or frosted glass is mounted in place of the solid-back board, and the camera lights are placed behind this translucent sheet (figure 6.24). The device is used to photograph transparent film negatives or positives instead of copy placed on illustration board. With the negative or positive in place, light is passed through the film openings, on through the camera lens, and a new exposure is made.

Back-lighted camera copyboards can be used to make film positives from film negatives with normal high-contrast materials. It is also possible to prepare duplicate film negatives with the same copyboard image by using a duplicating film (see appendix B).

Contact printing is the process of exposing a sheet of light-sensitive material by passing light through a previously prepared piece of film. In practice, the emulsion side of a film negative is placed against the emulsion of an unexposed sheet of film, photographic paper, or a printing plate (figure 6.25). The two sheets are then pressed together, usually in a vacuum frame, until there is no air gap between them. A light is projected onto the top sheet, the open areas of the film pass light to the new sheet, and the emulsion areas block the passage of light. Because no gray scale is used with this process, the new sheets must be processed with only time-temperature-agitation control unless a sensitometer is used. However, a contact exposure has a much wider latitude for acceptable development than does a projection exposure, such as from a process camera. With a contact exposure, there is no possibility of light reaching the film from a nonimage area.

Transparent film that has been correctly exposed in a process camera is **right reading** through the base side. In other words, as the printer looks at the film with the base side up, the copy reads from left to right (figure 6.26). This works well for most printing operations. There are, however, several situations, such as photoengraving for relief printing and some printing plates that are exposed through a film positive, that require the film to appear **wrong reading** (the copy does not read from left to right through the base).

Changing a right-reading sheet of film to wrong reading or vice versa is called a **lateral reverse.** It can be accomplished on the camera by reversing the right-reading sheet on the back-lighted camera copyboard. A lateral reverse can also be produced through contact printing by placing the base side of the right-reading film against the emulsion side of the new sheet (figure 6.27). There is a slight spreading of light because of the gap between emulsions, but it is expected and can be diminished by allowing for the spread when preparing the original film negative.

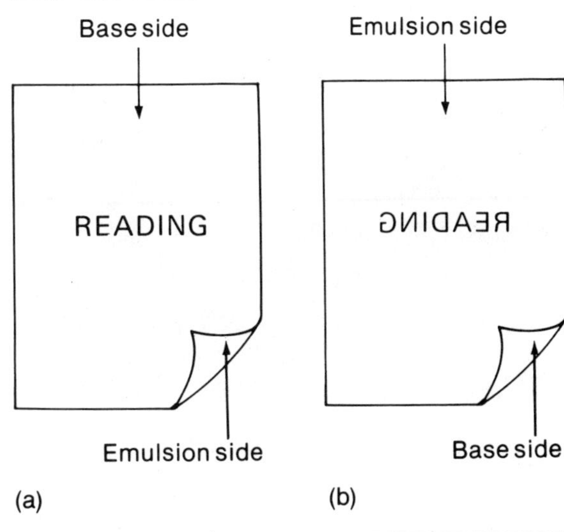

Figure 6.26. Right-reading transparent film Transparent film that has been correctly exposed in a process camera is right reading through the base side (a) and wrong reading through the emulsion side (b).

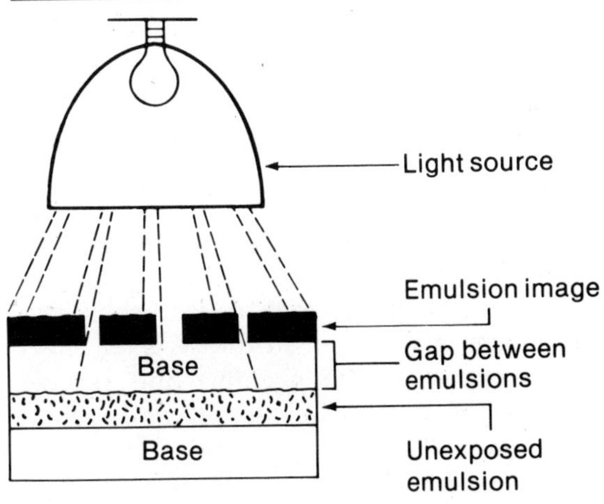

Figure 6.27. Making a lateral reverse This diagram shows the placement of the base side of the exposed film against the emulsion side of an unexposed sheet of film for producing a lateral reverse.

Diffusion Transfer

Diffusion transfer is a photographic process that produces quality opaque positives from positive originals. Diffusion transfer has widespread applications for printing produc-

Figure 6.28. Example of diffusion transfer sheets The sheets that have been through the activator bath can be separated after 30 seconds.

tion in such areas as copy preparation, proofing, and lithographic plate making.

Basically, the concept involves the use of a light-sensitive negative image sheet and a chemically sensitive receiver sheet. The negative sheet is exposed to the camera copy through normal line photography techniques. Wherever light is reflected from the camera copy (the nonimage areas of the copy), an image is recorded on the receiver sheet. Wherever light is absorbed by the camera copy (the black image areas of the copy), no image is recorded on the receiver sheet. After exposure, the negative and receiver sheets are placed in contact and passed through an "activator" solution. The image recorded on the negative sheet from the nonimage areas of the copy acts as a chemical mask and prevents any image from being transferred to the receiver sheet in these areas. Where no image was recorded on the negative sheet (that is, the dark areas of the copy where no light was reflected from the copy to the negative sheet), the activator bath causes an image to be transferred to the receiver sheet. In this way a positive image is produced in the receiver sheet. In other words, wherever chemicals are transferred, an image is formed; where no chemicals are transferred, no image is formed (figure 6.28).

Several characteristics of diffusion transfer material should be mentioned. Because it is a transfer process, the camera exposure results are reversed from a direct line photograph. To increase the density of the image on the receiver sheet, decrease the exposure time. To decrease density, increase the exposure. When processing the materials, place the negative sheet under and before the receiver sheet with the emulsions of the two together. The sandwich is then inserted into a processor, where it is passed between a separator rod through the activator bath and is brought into intimate contact by two pressure rollers. The transfer actually takes place in 5 to 7 seconds, but the sheets should not be separated for at least 30 seconds (figure 6.29). Once the transfer has taken place, the negative sheet cannot be reused and should be discarded. The receiver sheet is still chemically sensitive and can be reused any number of times if multiple images are required, but it must be washed in running water for several minutes to prevent a slight yellowing from age.

Diffusion transfer materials can be used in copy preparation to enlarge or reduce headlines, copyfit text material, clean up soiled original copy, convert color line material to opaque black copy, make reverses, and even prepare prescreened halftones. Diffusion transfer materials can also be used to make reflex proofs (contact proofs from opaque paste-ups), and lithographic printing plates have been developed that will accept a diffusion transfer image.

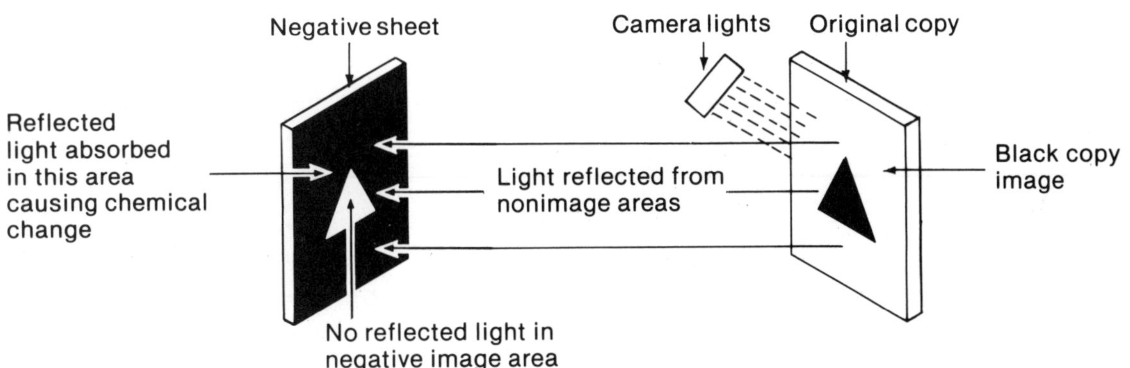

Exposure

Negative sheet

Receiver sheet

Sheets placed in contact

Negative sheet

Receiver sheet

This area acts as chemical mask on receiver sheet

Chemicals activated in this area

Chemical reaction between negative and receiver sheets

Activator

Final positive produced on receiver sheet where chemicals were activated

Final Positive

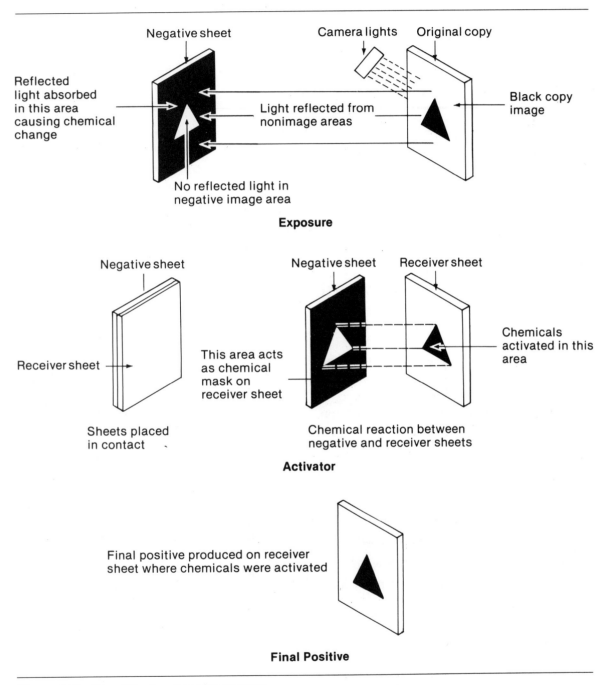

Figure 6.29. The diffusion transfer process

Key Terms

line photography
halftone photography
emulsion
antihalation dye
overcoating
process camera
lens
focusing
aperture
shutter speed
shutter
diaphragm
f/stop system
focal length
filmboard
copyboard
basic exposure
gray scale
safelight
latent image
developer
stop-bath
fixing bath
agitation
right reading
wrong reading
diffusion transfer

Questions for Review

1. What is the basis of photography?
2. What is the common characteristic of all printing processes that forms the primary concern of line photography?
3. What is the purpose of the antihalation backing (or dye) on any piece of film?
4. What is the change in quantity of light passed through the lens when the aperture is changed from f/16 to f/22?
5. What is the difference between a galley camera and a darkroom camera?
6. Why are process cameras so large?
7. What does "basic exposure" mean?
8. What is the purpose of a camera light integrator?
9. Why is it important to clean any dirt or dust from the glass cover of a camera copyboard when making an exposure?
10. What is the purpose of a graphic arts step tablet (sometimes called a gray scale)?
11. What is the purpose of chemical processing for photographic film?
12. What are the three main chemical baths used in photographic chemical processing?
13. What is the purpose of the developer bath in the chemical processing of photographic film?
14. What are the three major concerns that the photographer always tries to control during chemical processing?
15. What is the importance of agitation of photographic chemical baths in film processing?
16. Describe the process of contact printing.
17. What is the difference between a right-reading and a wrong-reading film image?
18. What is the diffusion transfer process?

Chapter Seven

Halftone Photography

Anecdote to Chapter Seven

The first commercial halftone illustration reproduced in a mass circulation publication appeared in the March 4, 1880, issue of the New York *Daily Graphic.* It was a picture of a scene in Shantytown, New York. As the byline advertised, it was a "reproduction direct from nature." Even before the first halftone illustration, however, the New York *Daily Graphic* was a startling venture in both design and manufacture. An editorial from the same period observed that "the boldness of the experiment, when it was proposed to start and maintain in the city of New York a daily illustrated newspaper, was well fitted to take away the breath."

Before halftones, the only way to add illustrations to a printed piece was to include line drawings by artists. It was the day of the "sketch artist" or the "artist on the spot," as many newspapers advertised. The task of providing enough artist's illustrations to fill twelve pages of newspaper was a mammoth undertaking.

The person responsible for the *Daily Graphic*'s success was a young man named Stephen H. Horgan, then twenty-six years old. As early as 1875 Horgan conceived of a method to make gradations in density of a photographic negative into lines. His first commercial halftone was made with a negative screen formed from a series of fine rulings, all slightly out of focus. A print was made by projecting the original photographic negative

The first commercial halftone illustration
Smithsonian Institution, Photo No. 73–5138.

through the negative screen. The result was then treated exactly like a line drawing by the production workers.

Horgan's early work was with a single-line screen. In other words, the gradations from opaque to transparent on the screen ran in parallel lines. The resulting reproduction looked, to many printers, somewhat like the artist's drawings that they had been working with for many years. The single-line ruling was coarse and well suited to reproduction on fast letterpress equipment using inexpensive paper. The single-line illustrations were all right, but every press operator said that only a fool would suggest that a cross-line halftone could be printed without looking like a "puddle of mud."

The "foolish" ideas of people like Stephen Horgan have contributed to the growth and refinement of halftone photography, the subject of this chapter.

Objectives for Chapter Seven

After completing Chapter 7 the student will be able to:

- Explain the difference between density, contrast, and tone.
- Discuss the purpose of a reflection, transmission, and dot area densitometer.
- Discuss the significance of a gray scale in the photomechanical process.
- Explain the difference between a halftone screen and a screen tint.
- Explain how a halftone screen produces dots of varying sizes.
- List standard screen rulings.
- Explain how to determine appropriate highlight and shadow dot sizes.
- Discuss the difference between various types of halftone screens.
- Identify continuous tone copy.
- Identify highlight, midtone, and shadow areas of continuous tone copy.
- Select the proper instrument for measuring highlight and shadow densities.
- Select a method for determining halftone exposures for a graphic arts camera.
- List the data needed to program a Kodak Negative Halftone Computer.
- Discuss the concept of contrast and explain how contrast is controlled in the halftone process.
- Explain the purpose of a main, flash, and bump exposure.
- Identify the characteristics of a quality halftone negative.

Figure 7.1. A high-contrast reproduction of a continuous-tone image We see in this type of print only black and white areas. There are no gray tones reproduced.
Photo by Chris Savas.

Introduction

Much discussion has been devoted in this book to the idea that the major printing processes work exclusively with lines. Lines can have meaning, depending on how they are drawn. High-contrast photography is well suited to line work. A line negative either passes light (in the image area) or blocks the passage of light (in the nonimage area) to a printing plate. If all images that needed to be reproduced were made up only of lines, then simple line exposures would meet all printing needs. There is, however, a large group of images that do not have line characteristics.

A continuous-tone image is not made up of lines. It is formed by a combination of varying shades of gray. The typical photograph is made up of a gradation of tones ranging from "paper white" through grays to the darkest black. Examples of other continuous-tone materials are ink and brush washes, charcoal sketches, watercolor paintings, soft-pencil drawings, and oil paintings. If we attempted to reproduce a continuous-tone print on high-contrast film, we would lose detail (figure 7.1). To reproduce such a print with the use of one of the major printing processes, it is necessary to change it into a special type of line image called a "halftone."

This chapter is divided into three major sections. Section 1 is an introduction to the basic ideas of halftones. Section 2 examines in detail the necessary concepts of halftone procedures. Section 3 discusses methods of evaluating halftone negatives and relates to the materials on densitometry discussed in section 1. It is assumed that not all readers will want to deal with all the information in the last section.

SECTION 1

Density, Contrast, and Tone

In chapter 6 we discussed how to make a line photograph of a high-contrast image. Before proceeding to a discussion of halftone photography, it is necessary to establish a basic understanding of the terms "density," "contrast," and "tone" and of what they mean to the graphic arts photographer.

In the most general terms, **density** describes the ability of a material to absorb or transmit light. It is well known in the construction industry that a house with a white roof is much cooler in the summer than one with a black roof. The white shingles reflect a great deal of light and, consequently, heat. The black shingles absorb the light and store the sun's heat in the house. In the tropics, light-colored clothing is much cooler and more comfortable than dark. Density is not such a strange concept.

In printing production, the density of the copy, film emulsion, and printing plate emulsion are all important. In printing production, a film negative is used either to pass or to absorb light. If properly exposed and processed, the negative should pass light in the image areas and block light in the nonimage areas to expose a light-sensitive printing plate. In other words, the film emulsion must have more density in the nonimage areas than in the image areas. Thus the density of the film emulsion in the nonimage areas directly influences the quality of the printed piece.

While standing over the washing sink examining a wet negative, however, the photographer is hard pressed to make an accurate judgment about the density of the emulsion on the piece of film. The negative could be examined with a magnifying glass on a wet light table. If the copy were grossly over- or underprocessed, the photographer might be able to detect the problem (figure 7.2). However, the film could appear acceptable but still not be giving the best possible results. The photographer has available several tools to ensure that a negative is of truly acceptable quality and will faithfully reproduce the original copy. The gray scale used during development of a line negative, which we discussed in chapter 6, is one such tool. When we watch the gray scale during film development, while waiting for a step 4 to go solid, we are waiting for the film emulsion to reach a specific level of density.

The printer is concerned with both the density of the image on the original copy and the density of the emulsion on a piece of film. The density of the image on the copy is defined by the term "reflectance." The density of the film emulsion is defined by the term "transmittance."

Reflectance is a measure of the percentage of directed light, called **incident light,** that is reflected from an area of the copy. **Transmittance** is a measure of the percentage of directed light that is passed through an area on a piece of film. For example, if 100 units of light are directed from the camera lights to the copy and only 50 units of light are reflected back from an area on the copy to the camera lens, reflectance for that area

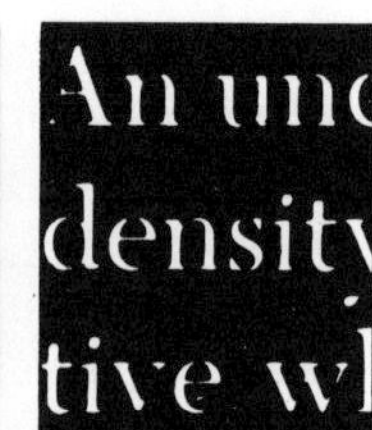

CORRECT EXPOSURE
This segment was exposed correctly. The negative areas are either clearly transparent or densely opaque. Edges are sharp, and detail proportions are true to the original.

UNDEREXPOSURE
This segment was underexposed. Although transparent areas are clear, the dark areas have low density. A positive made from a negative of this type shows thickening of all detail.

OVEREXPOSURE
This segment was overexposed. Although dense areas are opaque, density appears in some areas which should be clear. A positive made from a negative of this type shows loss of fine detail.

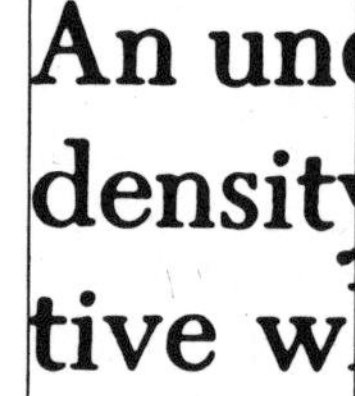

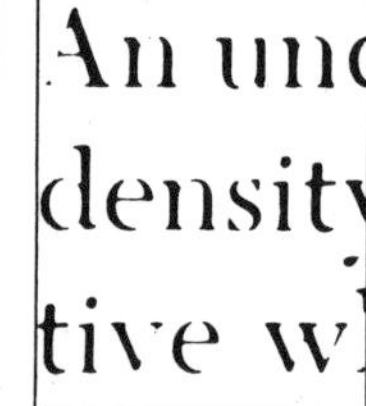

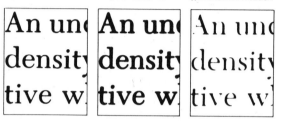

Figure 7.2. Examples of correct exposure, underexposure, and overexposure It is possible to judge underexposure or overexposure by comparing the reproduction with the original copy.

of the copy is 50%. If 100 units of light are directed at an area on a piece of film and only 50 units of light pass through the area of the film, transmittance in that area of the film emulsion is 50%. See figure 7.3.

Up to this point in our discussion of line photography, we have been concerned only with copy that is either all black in the image areas or all white in the nonimage areas. Our object has been to reproduce every area with no density (nonimage area) on the copy as an area of density on the film emulsion, and every area with density (image area) on the copy as an area with no density on the film emulsion. During processing we have examined the gray scale and accepted development of the gray scale image to a solid step 4 as adequate density for the nonimage areas on the film emulsion. This simply means that when the gray scale is solid to a step 4, the nonimage areas on the film are dense enough so that they will not pass light when the negative is used to produce a printing plate.

Copy such as a snapshot is not composed of only white and black areas. Halftone copy is made up of white areas, black areas, and shades of gray. These differing shades from white through grays to black are called **tones.** Different tones have different densities.

Line copy that is either all black or all white is called high-contrast copy, because the two tones of the copy (white and black) are far apart. **Contrast** is simply a measure of how far apart the different tones on a piece of copy are from each other. The two tones on line copy can be said to be discontinuous. There is no continuum of varying tones from white through grays to black. Halftone copy is said to be continuous tone because all (or most) of the tones on such copy are on a continuum from white to black. Each of these tones has a different density on the copy. In fact, it is the differing densities in these tones that give the copy contrast and detail (figure 7.4).

Recall from chapter 6 that in graphic arts photography we use high-contrast film. When exposed and processed, high-contrast film emulsion will have only two tones (areas of density). The emulsion will be either clear and transmit light or black and transmit no light.

Graphic arts film has to be high contrast because printing presses cannot print varying tones. A printing press puts ink density in the image areas and no ink density in the nonimage areas. This is the printer's problem

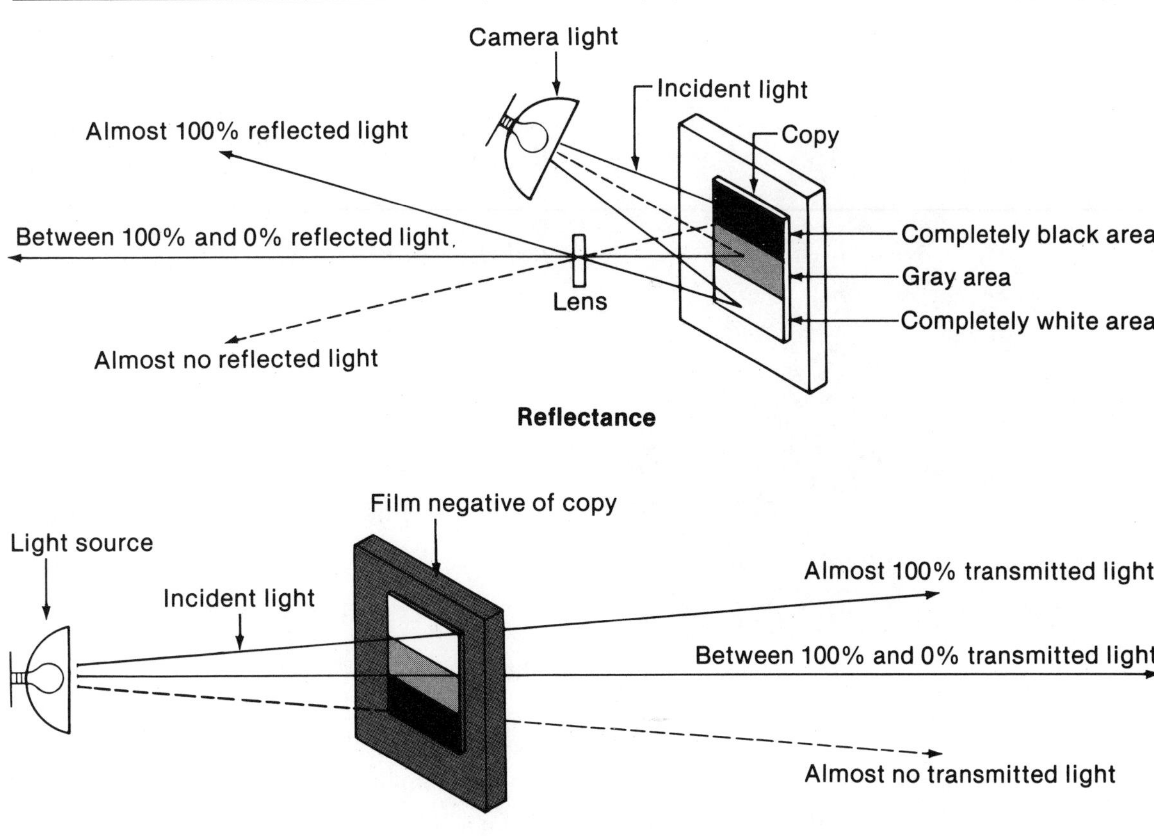

Figure 7.3. The relationship between incident light and reflectance or transmittance From the diagranm we can see that there is an inverse relationship between the light reflected from the original image area and the light transmitted through the negative. That is, from the black area of the image, almost no light is reflected. However, in the corresponding area of the negative almost 100% of the light is transmitted.

when dealing with a continuous-tone photograph: How do you record a continuous-tone image on a high-contrast film? In fact, it cannot be done. What we can do is to break up a high-contrast image into a series of dots of varying shapes and sizes (but all of the same density) and give the illusion of tone variations. The dot patterns are produced by using a special screen that will be discussed later in the chapter.

(a)

(b)

◀ **Figure 7.4. Comparison between a normal contrast picture and a high-contrast picture.** A normal contrast picture (a) shows shades or tones from white through gray to black. A high-contrast picture (b) shows only two colors, white (no ink) and black.

Photograph of Dr. Charly Schindler by Richard W. Foster.

Densitometry

Measurements of density belong to an area called **densitometry.** Transmittance and reflectance can be expressed algebraically as shown below:

$$\text{Reflectance} = R = \frac{I_r}{I_{rw}}$$

where:

R = reflectance,

I_r = intensity of light reflected from a tone,

I_{rw} = intensity of light reflected from white paper.

$$\text{Transmittance} = T = \frac{I_t}{I_i}$$

where:

T = transmittance,

I_t = intensity of transmitted light,

I_i = intensity of incident light.

The dot patterns are produced by using a special screen that will be discussed later in the chapter. But the concept is easy to understand without mathematics. A variety of tools measure transmittance and reflectance, expressed in logarithmic scales.

Table 7.1. Some Common Transmittance and Density Relationships

Transmittance	Density
100%	0.0
10%	1.0
1%	2.0
0.1%	3.0
0.01%	4.0
0.001%	5.0
.	
.	
.	
0.0000001%	9.0
.	
.	
. and so forth	

Logarithms are a way to express large quantities by using small numbers. Logarithmic information is readily available from tables in any mathematics book. As printers, we don't have to be able to manipulate logarithms in order to work with optical density. Densitometric tools read transmittance and provide readings that are already translated to logarithmic numbers.

Table 7.1 shows some common transmittance and density relationships. Although in theory there is no maximum density reading, realistically, for printing, there is no need to measure an optical density much greater than 3.0.

A density reading is nothing more than a logarithmic scale ranging from 0.0 to around 3.0 that equates a numeric value to the relative ability of a material to absorb or transmit light. The higher the density reading, the denser the material. Dark areas on a piece of copy are denser than light areas.

Densitometers

Density is measured by a tool called a densitometer. Densitometers can be grouped in two ways:

- By the materials they are designed to measure (opaque or transparent),
- By the manner in which they measure density (visual or photoelectric).

Visual densitometers operate on the basis of human judgments (figure 7.5). In the device is a set of known density wedges. The printer inserts the material to be measured and visually compares it to the known densities. After identifying a wedge that is identical in density to the test material, the printer records the logarithmic value printed on the wedge.

A **photoelectric densitometer** generally operates on a logarithmic measure of incident

Figure 7.5. A visual densitometer Visual densitometers allow the operator to compare copy, which is placed under the probe, to labeled densities that are seen through the viewing element.

light. A controlled beam is projected onto the material to be tested, and the transmittance or reflectance is measured. Most have a readout device that immediately reports the logarithmic density.

Visual densitometers are the least inexpensive and most rugged of the two types, but they depend too much on the operator's judgment. Most individuals become tired after twenty to thirty visual measurements on continuous-tone black and white material. Color densities are even more difficult to perceive. With the photoelectric densitometer, there is no dependence on the operator's judgment, results are extremely consistent, and most have color heads that will accurately read primary color densities.

The second classification of densitometers is according to the type of materials they are designed to measure: opaque or transparent. Any ink or emulsion on a solid base (such as paper) that is not designed to pass light is called opaque copy. Several examples of opaque materials are drawings, paste-ups, continuous-tone paper prints, or sheets of paper from a printing press. Density of opaque materials is measured by reflected light with a device called a **reflection densitometer** (figure 7.6). This tool directs a narrow controlled beam of light at a 45° angle onto an area of the opaque material. The amount of light reflected back is measured photoelectrically and translated to a logarithmic number. Before any reading is taken, the device is always calibrated to the same reading (usually 0.0, but for some devices 0.10) with the use of a standard white opaque wedge to ensure accurate measurements. The calibration process is called **zeroing.**

Any ink or emulsion that is on a clear base (such as glass) and is designed to pass light is called transparent material. Graphic arts film is an example of a transparent material. The density of transparent material is measured by light passing through the base with a device called a **transmission densitometer** (figure 7.7). A transmission densitometer passes a narrow beam of light at a 90° angle onto an area on the transparent film. The amount of light that passes through the film is measured and then translated to a logarithmic number. Care must be taken when zeroing a transmission densitometer. The base material of all transparent film always has some small amount of density, and the film's fog is always a concern. The device should be zeroed on a clear area on the piece of film being measured.

Gray Scale and Density

It is important to realize that the graphic arts gray scale discussed in chapter 6 is nothing more than a visual description of the loga-

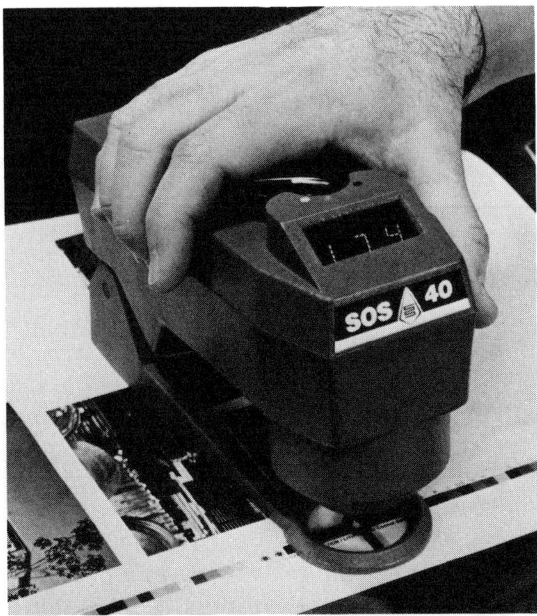

Figure 7.6. A reflection densitometer As the reflection densitometer probe is placed over a specific area of the copy, reflected light is measured. The 1.74 reading on the densitometer indicates that very little light was reflected because the area being measured is very dense.
Courtesy of Cosar Corporation.

Figure 7.7. A transmission densitometer A reading of 1.85 indicates that the probe is measuring a dense area of the negative. Very little light is being transmitted through the film's density.
Courtesy of Cosar Corporation.

rithmic density scale. Each step on the gray scale is an area of a specific measurable density. Scales are commercially available in opaque or transparent forms. The number of steps is arbitrary. Most printers use 10-, 12-, or 21-step gray scales. The opaque scale can be used as a crude sort of visual densitometer, but its best use is as an indicator of film density during and after chemical processing.

Examine the step tablet in figure 7.8. It is actually only an approximation of a 12-step gray scale (an opaque tablet could not be reproduced here because it is made up of different tones), but it can illustrate the usefulness of the tool. Each step represents an increase in density from around 0.00 (no density) to 1.65, evenly divided into twelve steps. Figure 7.8 shows an uncalibrated scale (each step has, printed next to it, the manufacturer's values in increments of 0.15). Uncalibrated scales can be measured with a reflection densitometer.

From the calibrated scale it can be seen that step 4 represents a density of 0.45. If this same scale were placed on the copyboard and photographed, the light reflected by step 4

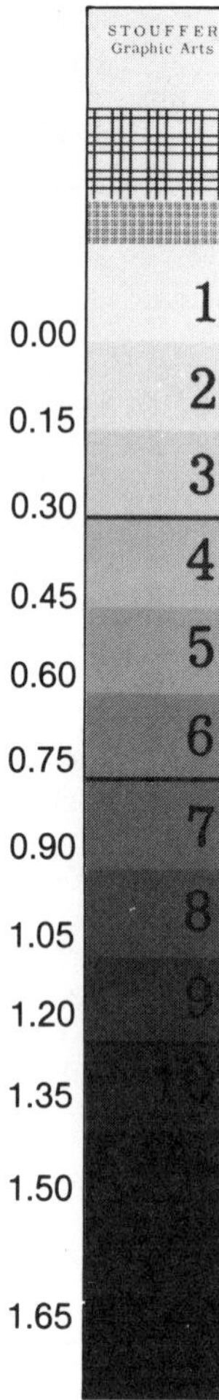

Figure 7.8. A 12-step gray scale This scale is calibrated into 12 steps representing densities from 0.00 to 1.65.

Courtesy of Stouffer Graphic Arts Equipment Co.

would be the same as any part of the copy having a density of 0.45 *and this is the key.*

The white nonimage areas for high-contrast copy such as line copy all have about the same density. This density is 0.45 or less. When determining the basic exposure for line shots on the process camera (see appendix A), we select an exposure time and aperture opening that will cause step 4 on the gray scale to fill in (go solid) at optimum development time (usually 2¾ minutes) and optimum development conditions (usually constant agitation, with fresh developer, at 68°F. or 20°C.). In doing so, we ensure that all white nonimage areas on the copy will record as solid black areas on the film negative when a solid step 4 is reached during film development. Any images on the copy (lines, dots, or even fingerprints and smudges) with greater than 0.45 density (darker than a step 4 on the opaque gray scale) will record as clear areas on the film negative when the film is developed to a solid step 4.

An understanding of the gray scale steps as specific blocks of density is a powerful tool for the graphic arts photographer. With it the photographer can predict the effects that different camera aperture openings or shutter speed changes will have on the density of the film emulsion. Graphic arts photographers have learned that a change of one f/stop number on the camera will produce a 0.30 density shift on the sheet of film. For example, assume that after time-temperature-agitation processing of a line negative, a solid step 2 with a density 0.15 was produced from an exposure of f/16 for 20 seconds. If development of a step 4 (density of 0.45) was desired for normal copy, changing the exposure to f/11 for 20 seconds (or f/16 for 40 seconds) will add 0.30 density to the film (0.15 + 0.30 = 0.45). This one f/stop change in exposure will produce a solid step 4 which is appropriate for normal copy.

This concept of a predictable density shift as a result of exposure can be used in all phases of photography, whether continuous-tone, line photography, halftones, special effects, or color separation.

Extending the concept of a gray scale a bit further is the idea of a device called a sensitometer. A **sensitometer** is an instrument that accurately exposes a gray scale of density from 0.0 to 3.0 in increments of 0.30 or 0.15 density steps. The device has its own calibrated light source and shutter. In practice, an unexposed edge of a sheet of film is inserted under a cover and an exposure is made. If that portion of the film is covered during camera exposure, two separate images will be recorded on the emulsion—a sensitometric step tablet and the reproduced camera image. During processing the step tablet can be checked to judge the stage of development. The advantage of this technique is that if the film is processed to the same step each time, the processing conditions will always be the same and the results on the film will be absolutely consistent. This is not the case for a camera-exposed gray scale because its density is a function of the camera exposure—the smaller the exposure, the longer the development necessary to produce the same density step. The sensitometer is ideal for processing images that require absolutely consistent development, such as halftones or color separations. A sensitometer can also be used to produce control strips for checking the activity level of automatic film processors.

Halftone Screens

Screen Rulings

The most common method of printing a continuous-tone image is to convert the continuous-tone image into line copy by a process called "halftone photography." With this technique, the continuous-tone image is broken up into a series of dots of varying size but of the same density. The dots combine in such a way as to trick the eye into believing that the picture is still continuous-tone (figure 7.9). This trick is accomplished by placing a ruled halftone screen between the copy and the film in a process camera (figure 7.10). On the camera, light is reflected from the white highlight areas of the copy and is absorbed by the black shadow areas. The middle tones (gray areas) absorb light to varying degrees, depending on their density. The reflected light then passes through the openings in the screen and forms dots on the film. The relative size of each dot is controlled by the amount of light that passes through the screen, which is controlled by the amount of light reflected from the different areas on the copy.

It is perhaps easiest to conceive of a halftone screen by picturing crossed solid lines. The openings between the lines pass light; the lines do not. If we were to count the number of parallel lines in an inch of the screen, we would have a simple idea of the size of dot that would be produced with that screen. The more lines per inch, the smaller the average dot produced. This measure is referred to as **screen ruling** and is the method the industry uses to roughly define the dot size a screen will give. Figure 7.11 (p. 141) was produced by using a 65-line screen (there were 65 parallel lines in any given inch in the screen that produced the halftone negative). Figure 7.12 (p. 142) is an example of the same photograph produced by using a 133-line screen. It is apparent that for this book the finer screen ruling produces a more effective picture.

The following variables suggest what screen rulings to use for any particular halftone photograph:

- Normal viewing distance,
- Process of reproduction,
- Type of paper or material being printed.

Figure 7.9. Halftone reproduction A halftone photograph is a series of lines or dots so small that they trick the eye into seeing a continuous effect. Note the dot pattern is visible in the detail enlargement on the left of the halftone.
Photo by Chris Savas.

A halftone photograph appears continuous because at a normal viewing distance the eye cannot detect minute line detail. What is a "normal viewing distance"? It varies with the function of the printed piece. This book is intended to be read at about 14 inches (about 36 centimeters) from your eyes. Therefore, the normal viewing distance for this book is 14 inches. A billboard you might see along a busy highway is designed to be read from approximately 300 yards (about 275 meters). That measure, then, is the normal viewing distance for the billboard. The effective halftone screen ruling for a billboard might range as coarse as 10 lines per inch. Screen rulings range from the huge dot size of a billboard to the fine dots produced from a 300-line screen.

The method and material of reproduction also influence the selection of screen ruling. For example, with current technology, a 300-line halftone is much too fine to be used with screen printing. For other methods, that same ruling is possible, but it becomes a test of sophisticated reproduction control. The ink-absorbing characteristics of papers vary widely. Newsprint rapidly absorbs ink and tends to spread or increase dot size. Clay-based or gloss-coated papers do not absorb or spread ink at all and can "hold" fine detail with little trouble. For most processes and paper characteristics, screen rulings of 85, 100, 120, 133, and 150 lines per inch are the simplest to manipulate and are the most widely used.

Screen Structure

Although a mesh of crossed solid lines is easy to visualize as the structure of a halftone

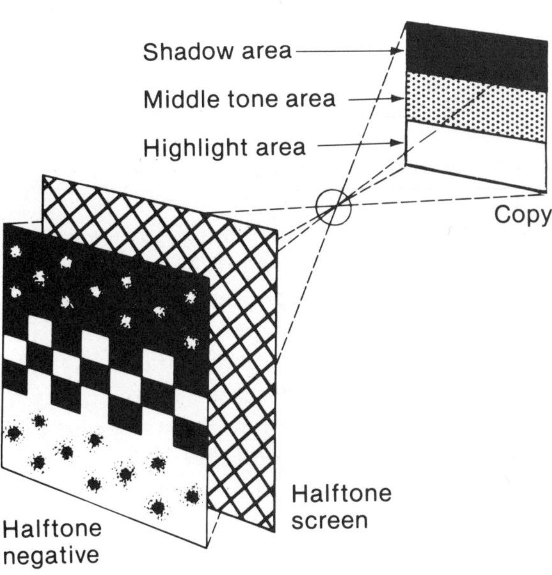

Figure 7.10. Diagram of halftone screen use A halftone screen is placed between the continuous-tone copy and the film when exposing the film to break the continuous-tone image into dots of varying sizes and shapes. White or highlight areas of the copy produce big dots of black on film. Middle tone areas produce intermediate size dots and black or shadow areas produce small dots on the film.

Figure 7.11. Example of a 65-line screen halftone This halftone was reproduced from the original with the use of a 65-line screen.
Photo by Chris Savas.

screen, it is not an accurate idea of how the most commonly used screens are made. The dots formed by the clear openings produced between solid line rulings would all have the same shape and size, but to produce a halftone, we need dots of varying shapes and sizes. There are solid line screens, called **screen tints,** but they are not used to produce halftone photographs. The typical halftone screen is constructed with a photographic emulsion to form a **vignetted screen pattern.** Let's examine the difference between one intersection of two crossed lines on a screen tint and the same area on a vignetted halftone screen. Figure 7.13 (p. 143) is an artist's rendering of what a magnified view of these two areas looks like.

Screen tints have rigidly controlled openings. They are classified according to the amount of light they pass to the piece of film. A 40% screen tint will pass through its open-

Figure 7.12. Example of a 133-line screen halftone This halftone was reproduced with the use of a 133-line screen. Compare the difference between this halftone and figure 7.11.
Photo by Chris Savas.

ings 40% of the light and will block, by solid lines, 60%. Figure 7.14 shows the range of typical screen tints. Some solid line screens are not crossed line. Screens containing such solid line screen patterns are generally referred to as "special effect screen tints." Screen tints and special effect screen tints are not used to produce halftones.

To appear continuous, a halftone must be formed from dots of varying shapes and sizes. Figure 7.13(b) illustrates the vignetted structure that produces these variations. The center portion of the screen opening (the area between the intersection of two lines) is clear, but the density of the emulsion increases as the diameter of the opening grows larger. When reflected light from the copy passes through the screen opening, a dot the size of the clear part of the opening is formed immediately on the film. As the quantity of light reaching the screen increases, more light penetrates the denser portion of the opening and the dot recorded on the film becomes larger. Within any halftone photograph, there is a wide range of individual dot variations. These variations are directly related to the amount of light reflected from the copy and focused through the camera lens onto the halftone screen. The more light that is reflected from the copy, the more light that will penetrate the denser portions of the vignetted dots and the larger the dot recorded on the film. This makes sense if you remember that more light is reflected from the white highlight areas of the copy and less light is reflected from the dark shadow areas. You would want larger dots in the highlight areas on the film negative in order to block more light from reaching the printing plate, thus producing small dots on the plate. These small dots would print as small dots on the final page, thereby providing highlight areas on the printed page that have little density because little ink is printed in them.

Dot Size

To control individual dot variation, it is necessary to identify and measure dot size (the area the dot covers on the printed sheet). Dot size is measured in terms of percentage of ink

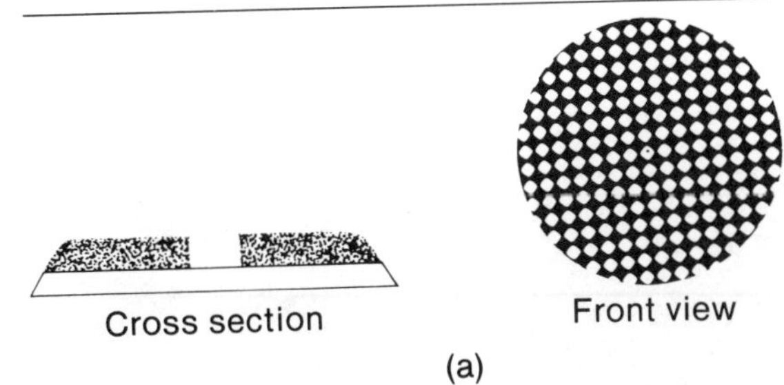

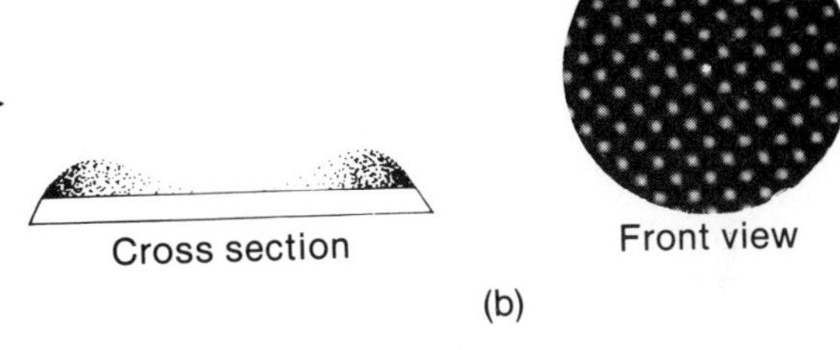

Figure 7.13. Comparison of a solid line screen with a vignetted screen A solid line screen with evenly shaped and sized openings is used to produce an even tone tint. A vignetted screen produces variations in the size and shape of the dots that result in the continuous-tone appearance of halftones.

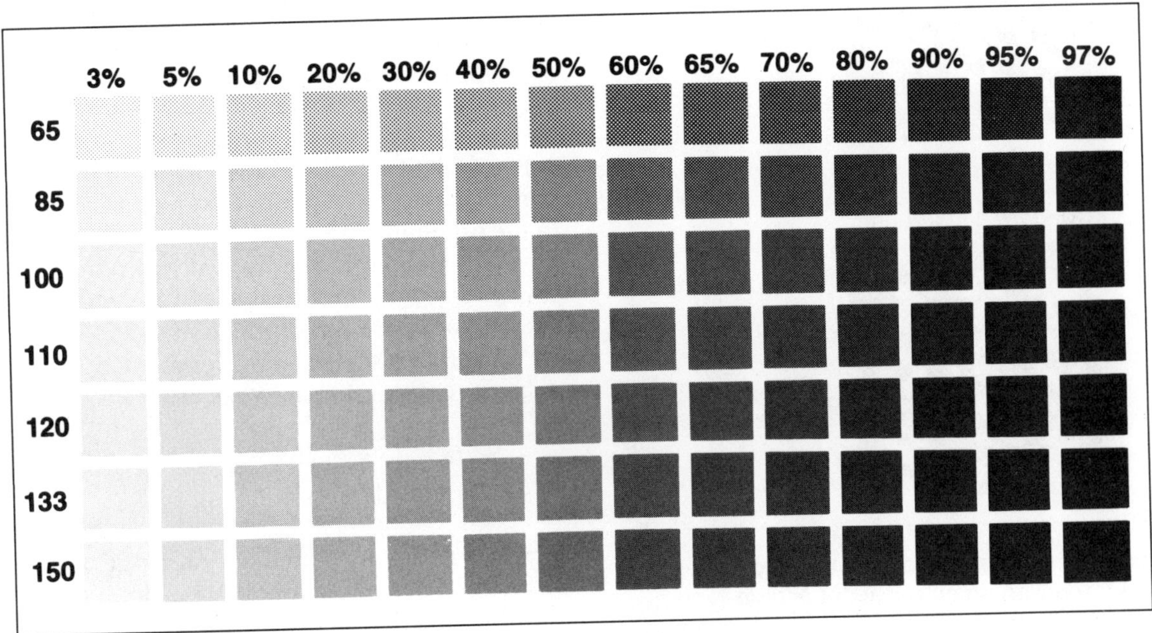

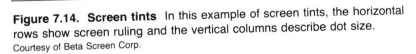

Figure 7.14. Screen tints In this example of screen tints, the horizontal rows show screen ruling and the vertical columns describe dot size.
Courtesy of Beta Screen Corp.

Figure 7.15. Examples of square dot sizes A typical range of dot sizes for a square dot screen is 5% to 95%.

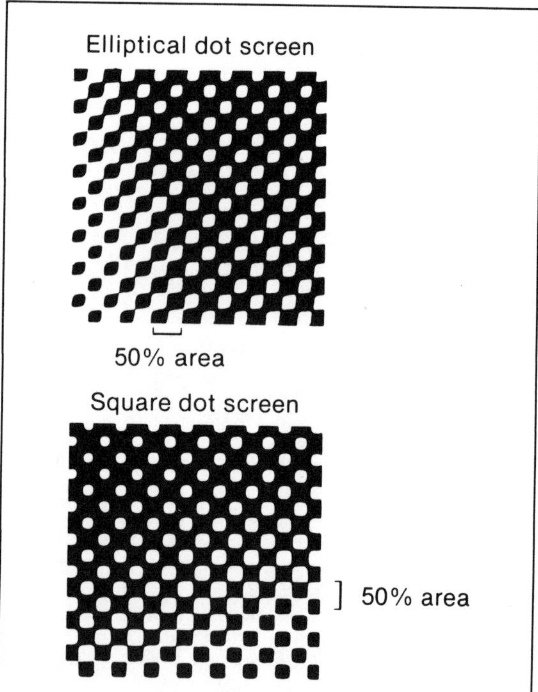

Figure 7.16. Example of a square dot screen compared with an elliptical dot screen The 50% area of the screen has a sudden jump in a square dot screen. The elliptical dot screen has a slower visual shift in the same area.
Courtesy of Eastman Kodak Company.

coverage. Thus a printer will speak of a printed halftone as having a 5% or 10% dot in the highlight area, and a 90% or 95% dot in the shadow area. What is actually meant is that 5% of the highlight area is covered by dots and 95% of the shadow area is covered by dots.

The actual dot size varies according to screen ruling. A 20% dot produced from a 65-line screen would be larger than a 20% dot produced from a 133-line screen. This presents no problems for the printer, however, because a 20% dot produced from a 65-line screen would cover 20% of the printed area with ink. Likewise a 20% dot from a 133-line screen would cover 20% of the printed area with ink. One dot would be smaller than the other, but the percentage of actual ink coverage produced by each would be the same. Comparisons of dot size between different lined screens is made only when printers are selecting the correct screen for a job. Comparisons of dot percentage sizes produced by the same screen, however, are made whenever printers are attempting to assess the results of a halftone they have made, to decide whether they have put the correct-sized dot in the highlight and shadow areas of the negative or whether they are actually printing the correct-sized dot in the highlight and shadow areas of a halftone reproduction.

Halftone screens are designed to produce one of two different types of dot structure:

- Square dots,
- Elliptical dots.

Figure 7.15 illustrates the typical range of dot sizes for a conventional "square dot" structure. Although the square dot screen is the more commonly used one, there are some problems with it. In the area of the 50% dot there is a sudden visual jump in dot size that does not accurately reproduce the original photography (figure 7.16). Figure 7.17 shows the elliptical dot size range that was developed to overcome the square dot limitations. Notice in figure 7.16 that in the 50% area the elliptical dot structure provides a smooth transition to where one dot finally touches another on all four sides (at exactly 50% the elliptical dots touch on two sides). Both the square and the elliptical dots are produced with a halftone screen in exactly the same manner.

Whatever dot structure is used to produce the halftone, there are two ways that printers measure dot area:

- By a visual inspection technique,
- By an optical dot area meter technique.

It is possible with the use of a **linen tester** or magnifying glass to view dots of any ruling size (figure 7.18). By comparing figure 7.16 or 7.17 with a halftone negative, we can approximate dot size. This is done less by comparing the actual size of the dot to the illustration than by comparing the configuration of an area of dots to the illustration. As has been mentioned, the 50% dot is easy to recognize. If a square dot screen was used to reproduce the negative, a 50% dot is found on the negative in an area where the dots just start to touch on all four corners. If an elliptical dot screen was used to produce the negative, the 50% dot is found in an area on the negative where the dots just start to touch on two corners. By viewing the amount of white space around a printed 10% dot, an area on a negative that will produce a 10% dot will become easy to identify.

Visual dot size identification is not as complicated as it may seem. When they are making halftones, graphic arts photographers are mainly concerned with the dots that will

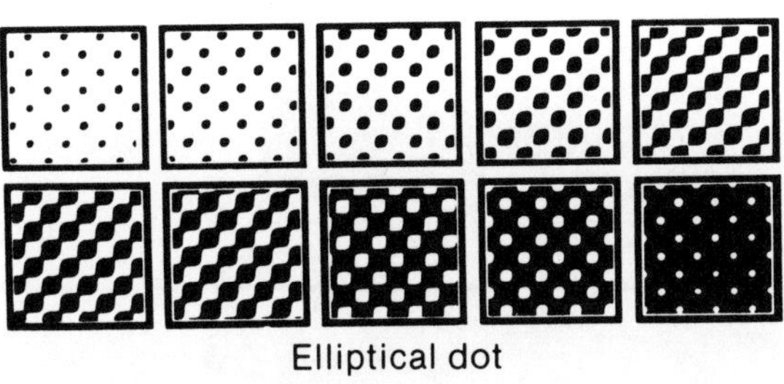

Figure 7.17. Examples of elliptical dot sizes Shown is a typical range of dot sizes (5% to 95%) for an elliptical dot screen.

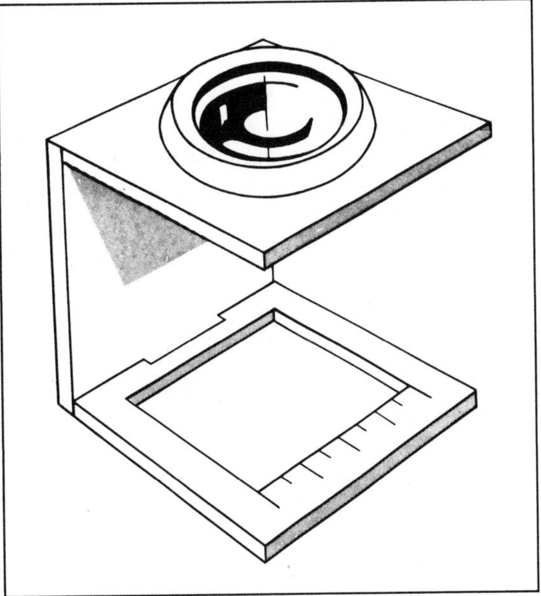

Figure 7.18. A linen tester A linen tester is used to view dot structure.

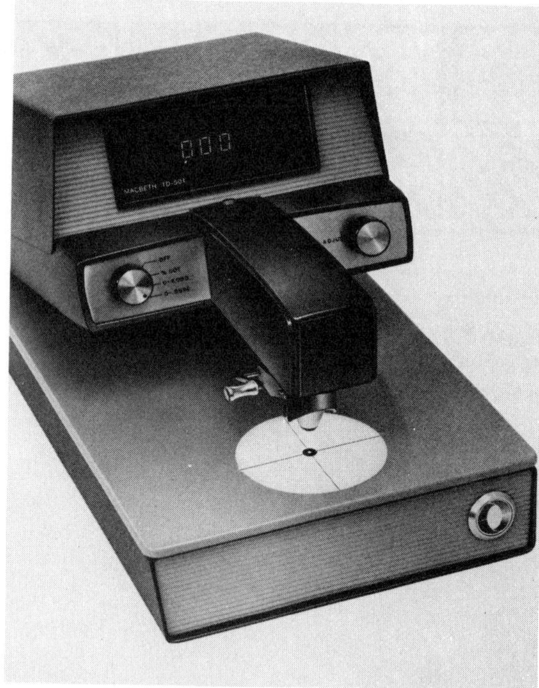

Figure 7.19. Example of a dot area meter This transmission dot area meter measures dot sizes on transparent materials. A reading of 0.10 indicates a 10% dot from the shadow area of a halftone negative. A 10% negative shadow dot produces a 90% shadow dot on the printed sheet. Kollmorgen Corporation, Macbeth Color and Photometry Division.

reproduce the highlight areas of the copy (typically around 5% to 10% dots) and the dots that will reproduce the shadow areas of the copy (typically around 90% to 95% dots). Some practice is required, but an experienced printer can give at least a rough visual estimate of highlight and shadow dot size. However, this becomes somewhat of a subjective problem. Is a dot a 9% or an 11% or perhaps even a 13% dot? As much as a 7% variation in visual judgment among even experienced camera operators is possible. Although we can work with this inaccuracy, a solution is to use a **dot area meter** (figure 7.19). This device "integrates" or averages the amount of light passing through a selected area on a halftone negative and equates that measure to a dot area reading. It is possible to adapt the information from a transmission densitometer for the same function with some slight loss in accuracy (table 7.2).

General Types of Halftone Screens

There are several basic methods for preparing halftone negatives from continuous-tone originals. The earliest technique was a glass ruled screen. Parallel lines were etched on two sheets of glass, which were then cemented together with the sets of lines at right angles to create individual dot-forming openings. In the production of a halftone, the glass screen was placed a predetermined distance from the film in the camera. The camera image was then focused on the screen and finally refocused onto the film. The size of the gap was critical. It was a measure of the ratio of the lens-to-copy and copy-to-screen distance. Halftone negatives produced with such screens were traditionally thought to be of the highest quality. However, the high cost of the screens, the high level of sophistication required to use them, and the recent development of high-quality vignetted contact screens have resulted in a decline in their use.

The simplest method of halftone preparation is the use of "prescreened film," which allows for production of halftone negatives without the use of a halftone screen. A piece of prepared film, simply exposed and processed, gives an acceptable halftone reproduction. The screen is, in a sense, "built

Table 7.2. Conversion from Density Readings to Percent Dot Area

Integrated Halftone Density	Percent Dot Areas	Integrated Halftone Density	Percent Dot Areas
0.00	0	0.36	56
0.01	2	0.38	58
0.02	5	0.40	60
0.03	7	0.42	62
0.04	9	0.44	64
0.05	11	0.46	65
0.06	13	0.48	67
0.07	15	0.50	68
0.08	17	0.54	71
0.09	19	0.58	74
0.10	21	0.62	76
0.11	22	0.66	78
0.12	24	0.70	80
0.13	26	0.74	82
0.14	28	0.78	83
0.15	29	0.82	85
0.16	31	0.86	86
0.17	32	0.90	87
0.18	34	0.95	89
0.19	35	1.00	90
0.20	37	1.10	92
0.22	40	1.20	94
0.24	42	1.30	95
0.26	45	1.40	96
0.28	48	1.50	97
0.30	50	1.70	98
0.32	52	2.00	99
0.34	54		

Use this table to convert integrated halftone densities (halftone densities with fringe area of dots compensated for) into percent dot area.

into" the prepared film. Prescreened film is ideal for simple exposures. Halftone exposures can be produced without a vacuum frame-holding system, and the film can be used in any portable camera (such as a press camera) to make halftones of three-dimensional scenes. However, the control limitations restrict the use of prescreened film. It cannot be used for high-quality halftone reproductions.

Contact halftone screens have revolutionized the industry. They are inexpensive and simple to use, and they require no sophisticated equipment or manipulation. As

Table 7.3. A Classification of Vignetted Contact Screens for Halftone Photography

MAGENTA	
Negative	Camera negatives from positive black and white originals
Positive	Contact positives from continuous-tone separation negatives
Photogravure	Intermediate halftone negatives for the intaglio process
GRAY	
Negative	Halftone negatives from positive color originals (transparency or print)
PMT	Opaque camera positives from black and white positive originals using the diffusion transfer process

we have seen, they form dots using a vignetted structure. All further explanation of the production of halftones will assume the use of a contact screen.

Types of Contact Halftone Screens

There are two basic types of contact screens, classified according to the color of dye used to produce the emulsion. The two colors are magenta and gray. Within both categories are special purpose screens. Table 7.3 outlines these variations and defines the intended use for each. In general, any screen may be used with any sort of copy. However, if a screen is not used for its intended function, special manipulation may be necessary to produce optimum results.

Magenta screens are designed to work with monochromatic (black and white) originals. Filters may be used to change the basic density range of the screen (see section 2). Magenta negative screens are used on a process camera to produce halftone negatives from opaque (paper) positives. Magenta positive screens are designed to make halftone positives in a contact printing frame from continous-tone negative transparencies.

Gray screens are popular for reproducing black and white photographs and are also designed to work with colored continuous-tone originals. Gray screens do not respond to filter control of the basic density range of the screen. Gray negative screens are intended to be used to make negatives from either opaque or transparent copy. Photogravure gray screens have a special structure to produce a "hard dot" for the intaglio printing process. Diffusion-transfer gray screens are designed to make positive opaque halftones from positive opaque originals by using the diffusion-transfer process.

Whatever the type of contact screen used, the basic processing steps are exactly the same.

SECTION 2

Section 1 gave some basic ideas about halftone photography. Now our attention turns to more specific understandings of procedures. This section examines some terminology, shows how exposures can be determined, and provides enough information so that the reader will actually be able to produce an acceptable halftone negative.

Areas of A Continuous-Tone Print

There are three areas that both printers and photographers identify as the most significant measures of the quality of a continuous-tone print (figure 7.20, p. 150):

- Highlight area,
- Shadow area,
- Middle tone area.

The **highlight area** is that portion of the picture that contains detail but has the least amount of density. There is a special kind of highlight, called a "spectral highlight," that has no detail or density. This will be dealt with later in this chapter. The darkest areas of the print are called the **shadow areas.** All the shades of gray between the highlights and shadows are called the **middle tone areas.**

It is possible to compare the density of these three areas of the print with the density of the steps on any graphic arts gray scale. We can also equate these densities with the size of halftone dots on the film negative and on the final printed sheet. For example, in figure 7.20:

1. The highlight detail begins in step 1, or with a density near .05. The highlight dots begin with the smallest reproducible dot (generally about 5%) and extend to about a 20% or 25% dot.
2. The shadow detail ends in step 10, or with a density of about 1.45. The shadow dots extend from about 75% or 80% to the largest reproducible dot (generally about 95%) before a solid black is reached.
3. The middle tone area for this photo is probably from step 3 to step 7 but is not a definite range. Middle tone dots typically range from about a 25% dot to a 75% dot.

Several things need to be emphasized with respect to this comparison. Printers do not typically measure a particular highlight, middle tone, or shadow density. They are primarily concerned with the density extremes (the amount of density from the lightest highlight to the darkest shadow). This measure is called the **copy density range (CDR)** of the photograph. The CDR is equal to the shadow density minus the highlight density. This is an important relationship to remember. The copy density range of figure 7.20 is 1.40 (1.45 minus .05). The typical continuous-tone photograph has a density range of approximately 1.70.

Comparing the dot size and the gray scale tonal area should not be taken to mean that a certain dot size should be formed in any particular part of the gray scale for every halftone negative. Printers are concerned that

Figure 7.20. Areas of a continuous-tone print In this continuous-tone print, the highlight areas correspond to steps 1 and 2 on the gray scale. From the gray scale, we see that the middle range is from 3 to 7. The shadow area ranges from 8 to 11 on the gray scale.
Photo by Chris Savas.

the smallest dot appear in the highlight step and that the largest dot appear in the last shadow step. The placement of all dot sizes between these two extremes controls the contrast of the halftone and depends on the particular photograph being reproduced. There is no rule that states in what step any dot should be placed.

Understanding Halftone Exposures

Two simple exposures are generally used to produce a halftone negative from a vignetted contact screen:

- Main exposure,
- Flash exposure.

They both are relatively straightforward and easy to understand.

The only required exposure is called the **main exposure.** Sometimes referred to as the highlight exposure or detail exposure, it is simply an exposure on film through a contact screen using a process camera. Just as each continuous-tone photograph has a different density range, so does each halftone contact screen. The BDR, or **basic density range,** of a halftone screen is that density range reproduced on the film with one main exposure through the halftone screen. It is the main exposure that controls where the smallest highlight dot will be placed on the gray scale and in the corresponding areas of the negative. Figure 7.21 illustrates three different exposures of the same gray scale. Notice how increasing the exposure moves the highlight dot up the scale, but the basic density range recorded on the gray scales remains the same.

Each gray scale shows discernible dots throughout the range of seven steps. The difference in the three scales is simply the difference in the placement of the highlight dot. In each gray scale, the highlight dot has moved down the gray scale. The main exposure, then, controls the placement of the highlight dot.

The basic density range of a halftone screen could be from 0.15 to 1.05. Assume for a moment that we have a screen with a basic density range of .90. This simply means that our particular screen can record no more than a basic density range of .90 with only a main exposure. If the BDR of the photograph we are shooting is smaller than the BDR of the screen we are using, one main exposure will reproduce the original. But if the BDR of the photograph is larger than that of the screen, there will be problems.

As we have already mentioned, the typical continuous-tone photograph has a density range of 1.70. This difference between copy density range and screen density range is called **excess density.** It must be handled with a secondary exposure.

The **flash exposure** is a nonimage exposure on the film through the contact screen. Light may be flashed through the lens, but a special yellow flashing lamp is typically used. Nearly all the identifiable detail of a continuous-tone photograph is found in the highlight to middle tone areas. A single main exposure will record most of the detail of a typical photograph. However, there is still some detail in the shadow areas and density that affects the contrast of the final product. Most halftone screens are not equipped to record the entire range of shadow density and detail. Because shadows usually absorb more light than they reflect, the film records shadow detail long after any reflected highlight detail has been recorded. The main exposure typically cannot form reproducible shadow dots on the film and still faithfully reproduce the highlight detail. The function of the flash exposure is twofold:

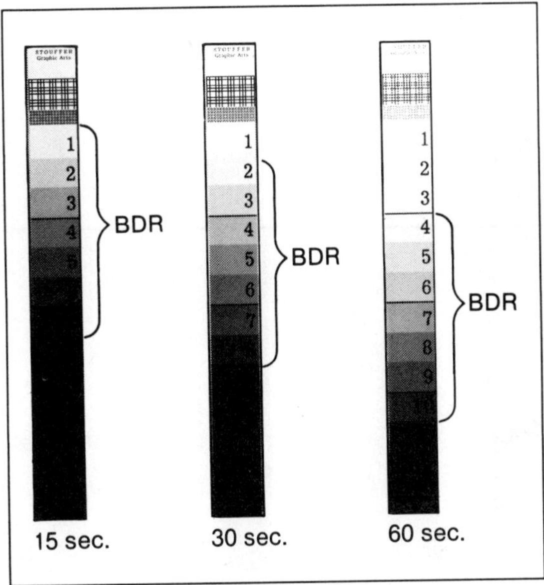

Figure 7.21. Three main exposures of a gray scale Three different main exposures were made of the same gray scale. Notice that the basic density range does not change as the exposure is increased; it just moves down the scale.

- It adds density to the weak shadow dots, bringing them up to a reproducible size.
- It adds uniform exposure to the entire negative, increasing the size of all dots, especially those representing the shadow areas.

The flash exposure is needed to make the final halftone reproduction match as closely as possible the density range of the original print.

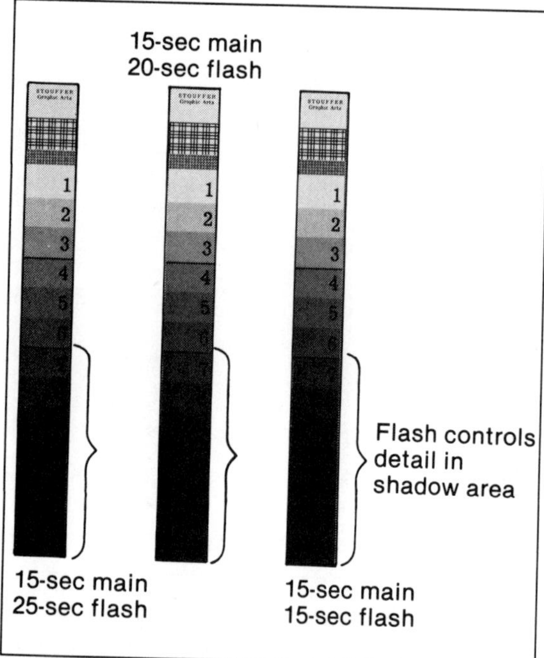

Figure 7.22. Three flash exposures of a gray scale Three different flash exposures of the same gray scale were made with the use of the same main exposure for each. In steps 9 to 7 notice that the shadow dot moves up the scale with increased flash exposure.

This is not difficult to understand if you remember the vignetted dot pattern on the halftone screen. The highlight areas of the copy are going to reflect the most light back to the camera lens. In just a few seconds of main exposure, the reflected light from the highlight areas of the copy will pass through the clear areas in the center of the elliptical dot and produce a dot on the film emulsion. As the main exposure continues, reflected light from the highlight areas will penetrate the denser portions of the vignetted dot, and the highlight dots will grow in size. At the same time, some of the middle tone areas will reflect enough light to penetrate the vignetted dot and they, too, will record an image. However, the shadow areas of the photograph, being dark, absorb most of the camera light and reflect back only a small amount. During the main exposures, this small amount of light reflected from the shadow areas may penetrate only the very center of the vignetted dot, which is clear. The dots produced by the reflected light from the shadow areas during the main exposure are so small that they cannot be printed.

The flash exposure is made directly through the halftone screen and does not rely on reflected light from the copy. Therefore, an equal amount of light is passed through all parts of the screen. The flash exposure increases the size of all the dots recorded during the main exposure, but it has more of an effect on the shadow dots than on the highlight dots. This is because the highlight dots, having been formed from the reflection of the white camera light, are about as large as they can get. Enough light penetrated the vignetted screen dots in the highlight area to almost completely expose the film emulsion in the highlight areas. The yellow flash light will not have much effect in these areas; there just are not many unchanged silver halide crystals left to change. However, the flash exposure greatly affects the shadow area because the shadow area was not affected much during the main exposure. The small dots made in the shadow area during the main exposure are enlarged during the flash exposure. This is why the flash exposure is said to control the placement of the shadow dot.

Figure 7.22 illustrates three different flash exposures of a gray scale, with the use of the same main exposure. Notice that the position of the highlight dot does not signif-

Figure 7.23. A contrast image A print or its reproduction is considered to have contrast when there is very little detail in the highlights and shadows and when there are few intermediate tones.
Photo by Rich Kampas.

icantly change, but the shadow dot moves up the scale as the flash exposure increases. The length of the flash is calculated from the amount of excess density of the print (CDR of print minus BDR of screen). The goal is to print a 95% dot (or largest reproducible dot) in the darkest shadow area containing detail.

Controlling Halftone Contrast

The placement of the middle tone dots in a halftone photograph affects contrast. The term "contrast" is bantered about frequently by both printers and photographers, but what does it really mean? Figure 7.23 is an example of a "contrasty" print. Figure 7.24 shows a normal photograph. Examine each reproduction. Figure 7.23 has fewer visible tones than figure 7.24. Also, figure 7.23 has a greater shadow density with no detail. In other words, a high contrast photograph is usually one with a compressed tonal range and not much detail in the highlights and shadows. It is actually the compression or expansion of tones that defines contrast.

We can control contrast on the final printed sheet when we produce a halftone. By compressing or expanding the tonal range, we shift the middle tone dots up or down the scale. There are two common ways of controlling contrast:

- By using a filter,
- By using a special camera exposure.

When using a magenta contact screen, it is possible to shorten or lengthen a tonal range by using a yellow or magenta filter. The

Figure 7.24. A normal image A normal print or reproduction has highlight detail, shadow detail, and a range of intermediate tones.
Photo by Rich Kampas.

filter is placed in front of the camera lens during the main exposure. What the filter actually does is change the screen's BDR. The following list shows the degree of change of a screen's BDR through the use of this method:

- CC–50M 1.15
- CC–10M 1.35
- NO–FILTER 1.40
- CC–10Y 1.45
- CC–50Y 1.60

(CC = color correcting filter, M = magenta, Y = yellow.)

The most frequently used technique to increase contrast is to use a **bump** or **no-screen exposure.** With this technique, a second image-forming exposure is made on the camera without the contact screen in place. This exposure must be made either before or after the main and flash exposures, but not between the two. The actual exposure time is expressed as a percentage of the main exposure. Figure 7.25 illustrates two different bump exposures of a gray scale, with the use of the same main and flash exposures. The bump compresses the screen range and therefore increases contrast. Figure 7.26 shows how the use of a bump can improve a previously flat image.

Again, this is not difficult to understand if you think about what is actually being recorded on the film during the bump exposure. After the main and flash exposures, the highlight areas on the film are almost completely filled in, and the shadow areas have recorded a printable dot. The bump exposure is made without the halftone screen, with the use of reflected light from the copy that is in the exact location it held during the main exposure. Unlike the flash exposure, the bump exposure is going to affect the highlight areas of the film. These areas have been almost

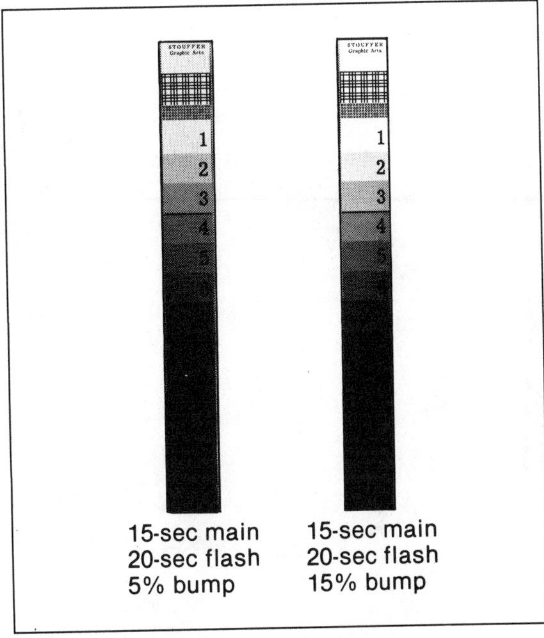

Figure 7.25. Two bump exposures of a gray scale Two different bump exposures of the same gray scale were made with the use of the same main and flash exposures for each. Notice that a 5% bump produces detail from steps one through eight. A 15% bump produces detail from steps two through seven. An increase in bump exposure has eliminated two tones from the gray scale. Instead of eight tones there are now six tones. Contrast has been increased.

(a)

(b)

Figure 7.26. Example of use of a bump to increase contrast Only main and flash exposures were used to produce the print in (a). To increase contrast, a 3% bump exposure was made to produce (b).

Photo by Rich Kampas.

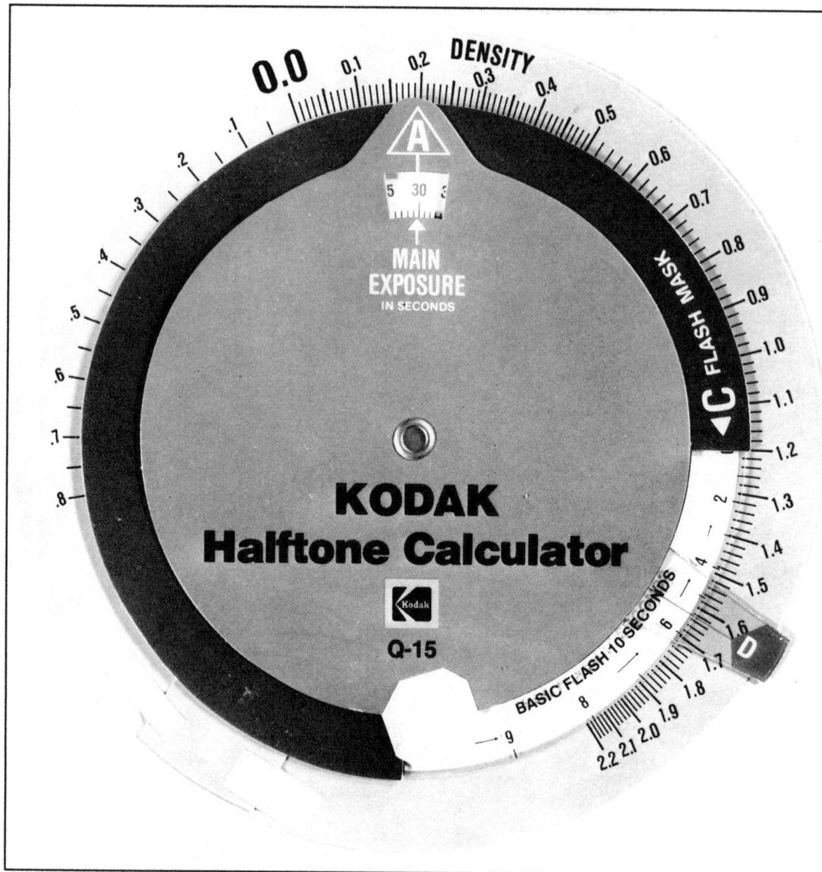

Figure 7.27. The Kodak Halftone Negative Computer, Q–15 This computer indicates precise exposure times for making halftone negatives from photographs, artwork, or other reflection copy.
Courtesy of Eastman Kodak Company.

completely exposed during the main exposure and would require only a small additional exposure to completely fill in. The shadow areas will be relatively unaffected by a small additional amount of exposure.

A bump is a very short exposure. As a small burst of light strikes the copyboard, it is immediately reflected by the extreme highlights and almost completely absorbed by the shadows. The result, when the reflected light passes through the lens to the film, is to close dots in the highlight areas, but dots in the shadow areas are not affected. When the film is processed, the ultimate effect is to compress the tones of the original by reducing the number of density steps between the highlight and shadow areas.

There are several other methods of controlling contrast. They are not typically used, however, because they are neither easily reproducible nor predictable from one trial to another. Changing the rate of agitation during tray development of a halftone negative will affect contrast. Turning a contact screen over and exposing through the base during the main and flash exposures (called **laterally reversing the screen**) will change the contrast. Washing a magenta contact screen will remove dye density and will increase the BDR. (CAUTION: Washing a screen is not recommended unless it is so dirty that it cannot be used. Then carefully follow the manufacturer's directions.) All these manipulations will cause contrast changes, but they are rarely used by the printer.

Calculating Halftone Exposures

It is possible to produce halftone negatives by trial and error. In other words, we can guess at main and flash exposures, produce a halftone, evaluate the results, and then try to compensate for any limitations by manipulating the exposures. If a problem photograph is encountered (such as an especially flat or contrasty print), the rate of waste greatly increases. A much more predictable method is to use some logarithmic method, such as Kodak's halftone negative computer. The halftone negative computer is simply a device that reduces abstract numbers to a graphic scale. The following explanation is for Kodak's computer, Model Q–15 (figure 7.27), but the basic approach is applicable to any other type of calculation. It is necessary to calibrate any halftone negative computer before it can be used. For simplicity, the following explanation assumes the tool has been calibrated for our specific camera and darkroom situation. The detailed procedures for calibration are discussed in appendix C.

1. From the photograph to be reproduced, identify the highlight and shadow areas. Take densitometric readings of each area with either a visual densitometer or a reflection densitometer. It is advisable to take each reading several times. If you come up with different readings in each area, average the readings. Be sure that you take your highlight readings from a highlight area with detail and your shadow readings from the densest shadow area, whether it has detail or not. An area that is completely white has no detail. This area is a **spectral highlight.** A shadow area that is completely black also has no detail. In our printed reproduction, we will want to place small dots to represent the detail in the highlight area and larger dots to represent the detail in the shadow area. Areas on the continuous-tone print that have no detail should have no dots in the printed reproduction. Likewise, areas on the continuous-tone print that are solid black should have no discernible dots in the printed reproduction.

2. Assume, for example, that we identified a highlight density of 0.10 and a shadow density of 1.79. Rotate the large *A* on the inner dial to the highlight density that is 0.10. Then read the main exposure in seconds through the window on the same dial. The main exposure for the example would be 23.5 seconds (figure 7.28).

3. Next move the plastic flash pointer tab, marked D, until the green line matches the 1.79 copy shadow density (figure 7.29). Read the flash exposure on the plastic dial marked in red. At this point it should read 7.5 seconds.

With gray negative screens or autoscreen film, the flash exposure increases the effect of the main exposure, producing overexposed highlight areas. Therefore a com-

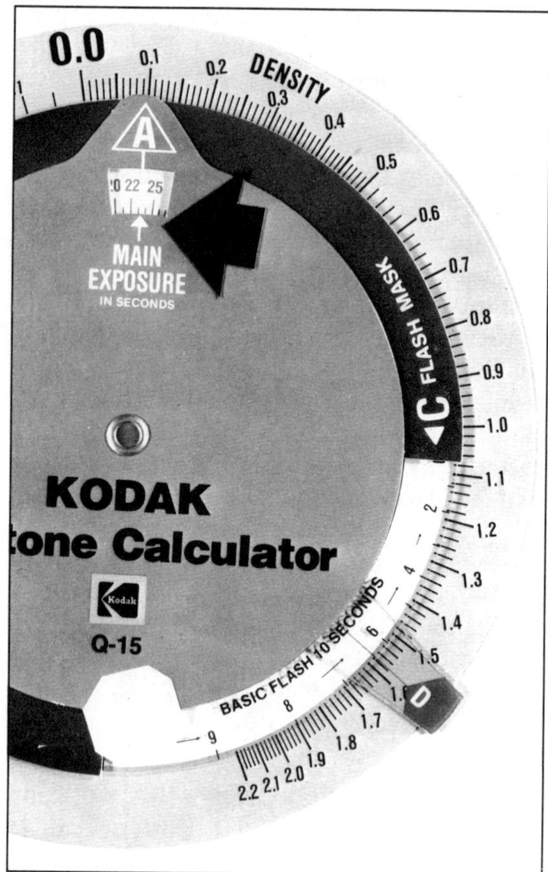

Figure 7.28. Using the computer *A* has been set at the copy highlight density of 0.10. The main exposure is 23.5 seconds.
Courtesy of Eastman Kodak Company.

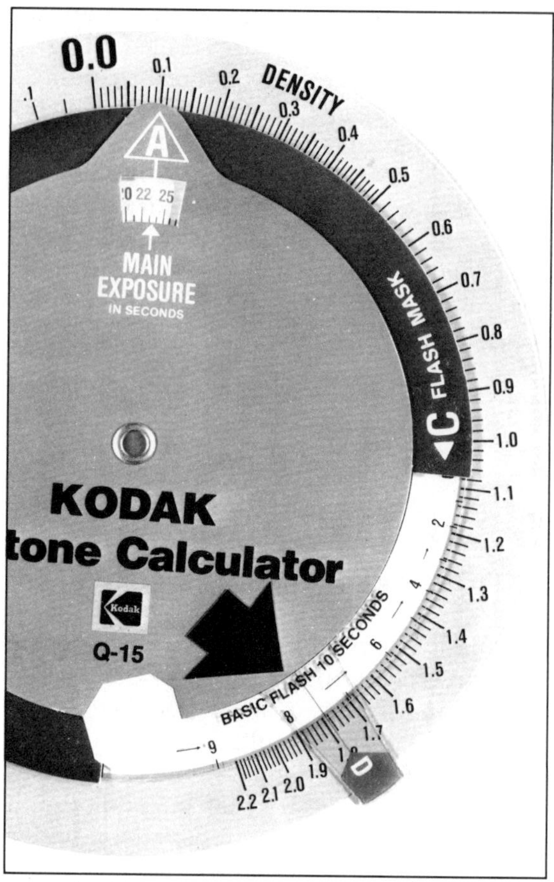

Figure 7.29. Using the computer *D* has been set at 1.79 copy shadow density. The flash quadrant reads 7.5 seconds.
Courtesy of Eastman Kodak Company.

pensation must be made in the main exposure. The Q–15 computer has a system to make this adjustment by moving both dials the length of a small red arrow on the flash scale (see figure 7.27). To use this system, move flash pointer D from the shadow density of 1.79 to the head (figure 7.30) of the nearest arrow. Then, keeping the flash pointer in place, rotate the main exposure wheel counterclockwise the length of the arrow. The new main exposure is now 20.5 seconds (figure 7.31). Finally move pointer D back to the shadow density of 1.79 and read the flash exposure. For this example the flash exposure would be 8 seconds (figure 7.32, p. 160).

4. The halftone computer illustrated in figure 7.27 has an additional procedure for

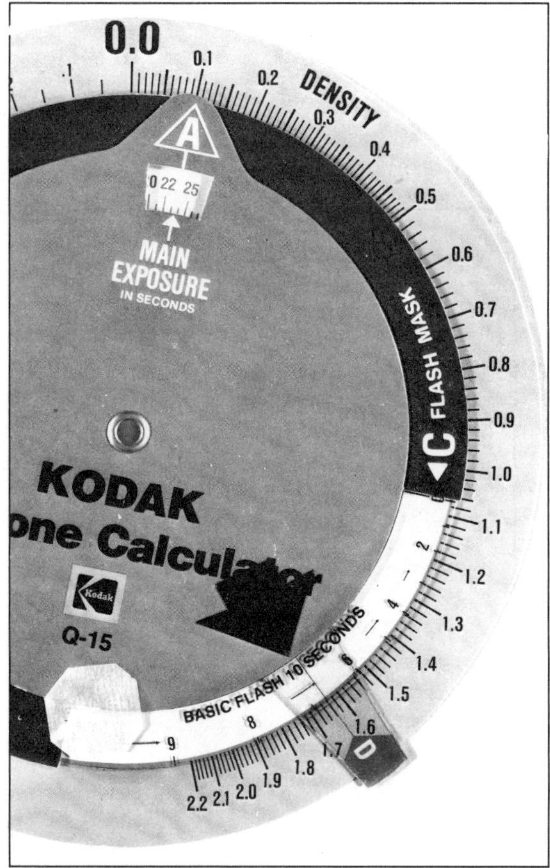

Figure 7.30. Using the computer Flash pointer *D* has been moved from 1.79 to the head of the nearest arrow.
Courtesy of Eastman Kodak Company.

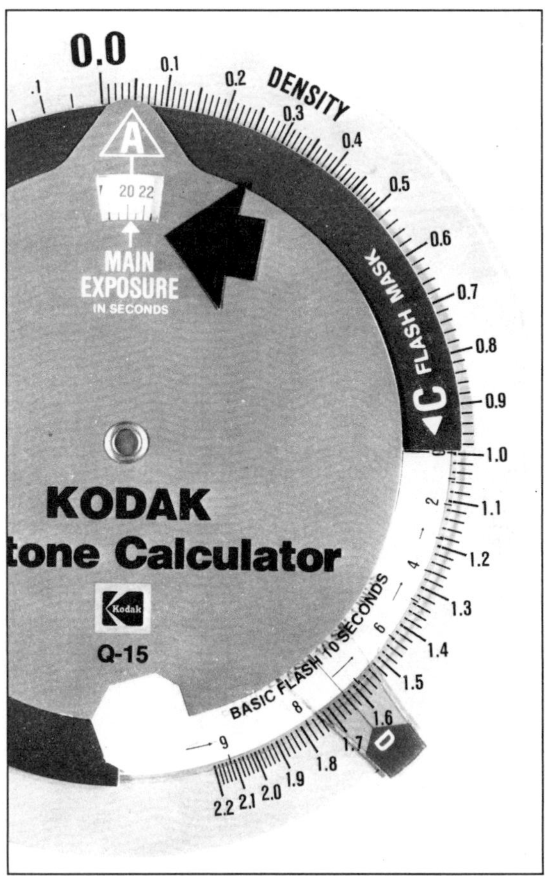

Figure 7.31. Using the computer The main exposure now reads 20.5 seconds. Notice that pointer *D* is now at the tail of the arrow.
Courtesy of Eastman Kodak Company.

calculating a bump or no-screen exposure (refer to appendix C). The bump is calculated by taking a percentage of the original main exposure. A 5% bump is usually used with negative screens and 10% for positive screens.

There is also an interaction between the bump and main exposure times. If a bump is used, the main exposure must be reduced in proportion to the amount the tonal range has been compressed. Once the bump has been calibrated (see appendix C) rotate the 5% mark on the orange dial to the 0.10 highlight density of the copy (figure 7.33). Next, move flash pointer D to the copy shadow density of 1.79 (figure 7.34). Then move pointer D to the head of the nearest arrow (figure 7.35). After rotating the main exposure and flash

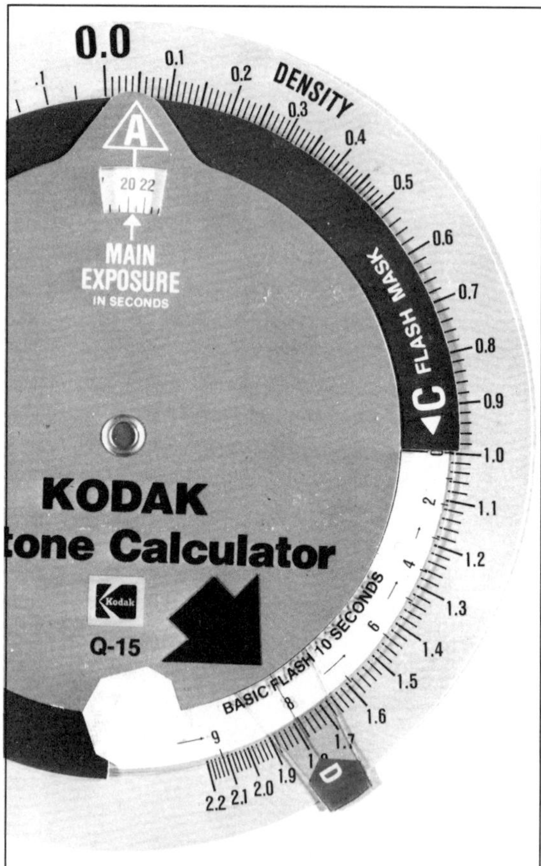

Figure 7.32. **Using the computer** To determine the final flash exposure, pointer *D* has been moved back to the copy shadow density of 1.79. The flash exposure is 8 seconds.
Courtesy of Eastman Kodak Company.

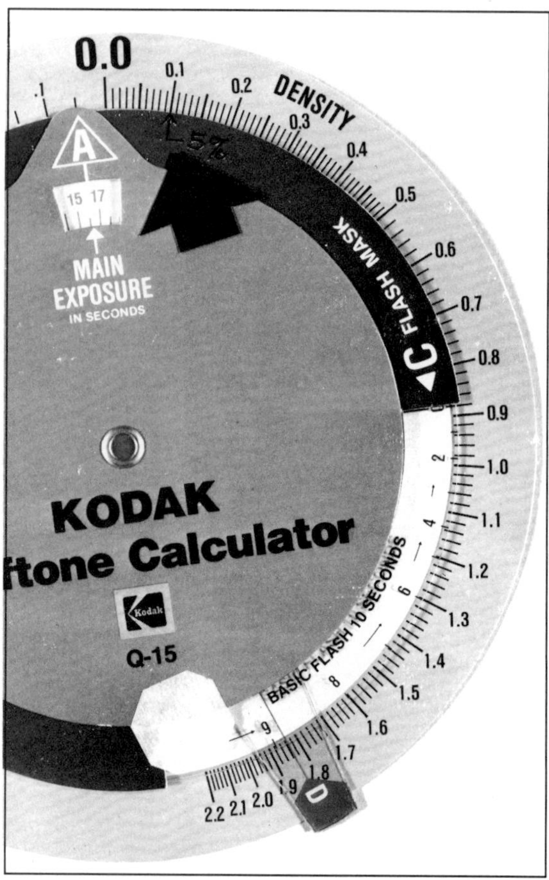

Figure 7.33. **Using the computer** To add a bump exposure, the pre-calibrated *5%* mark on the orange dial has been rotated to 0.10 copy highlight density.
Courtesy of Eastman Kodak Company.

quadrant wheel counterclockwise, the length of the arrow, the main exposure will be reduced from 16 sec. to 14 sec. (figure 7.36). A main exposure of 14 sec. will be used with a 5% bump exposure. Finally, move pointer D back to the shadow density of 1.79 (figure 7.37). Identify the 9 sec. flash exposure. This flash exposure will be used with the main and 5% bump exposure.

In summary the three exposures are as follows: 14 sec. Main, 9 sec. flash, and a 14 sec. no screen exposure using a 1.3 neutral density filter in front of the lens. (Using a 1.3 neutral density filter produces a no screen exposure equal to 5% of the main exposure.) Since 5% of the main exposure is .7 sec., a neutral density filter or filters must be placed in the path of light (in front of the lens). This

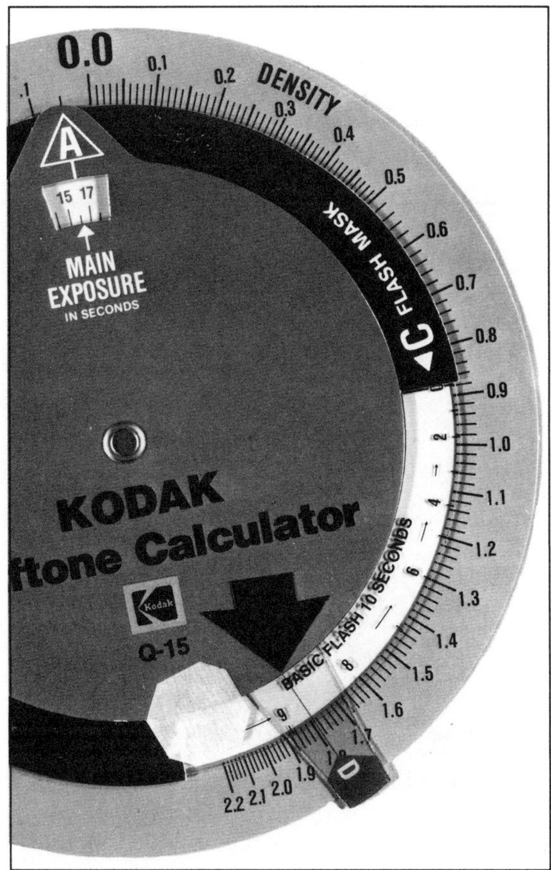

Figure 7.34. Using the computer Flash pointer *D* has been moved to the copy shadow density of 1.79.
Courtesy of Eastman Kodak Company.

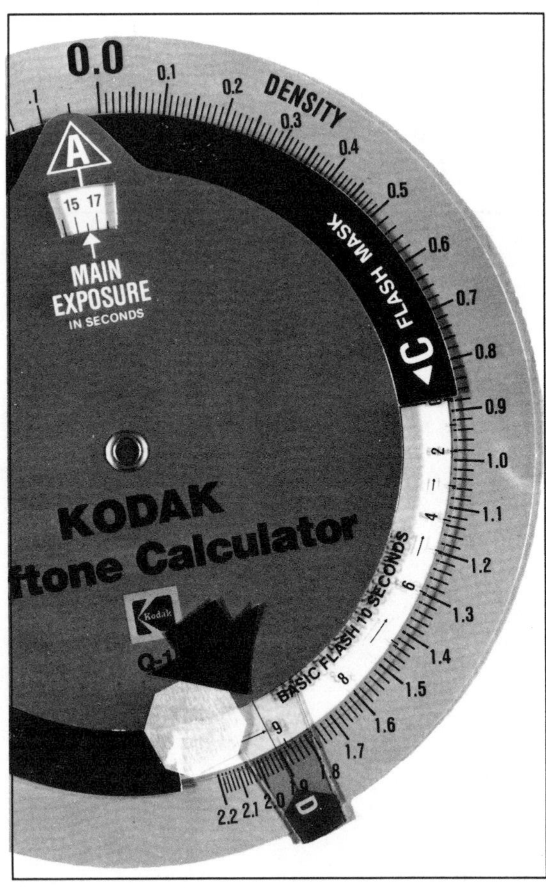

Figure 7.35. Using the computer Flash pointer *D* has been moved to the head of the nearest arrow.
Courtesy of Eastman Kodak Company.

allows longer times, which are necessary, since most inexpensive timers are not capable of repeating a time such as .7 of a second.

There is a significant problem with the use of a bump exposure because the decision of when to use it, and then how much to use, is a subjective one. If 5% is average, when should a 3% or perhaps a 7% bump be used? Keep in mind that as the bump exposure is increased the highlight to middle tone range is compressed or contrast in this area is increased.

A recent advance in the determination of halftone exposures is the **Kodak Q–700 Data Center** (figure 7.38). Magnetic memory cards are used to record test data from shop working conditions. Special data modules store a variety of sets of photographic infor-

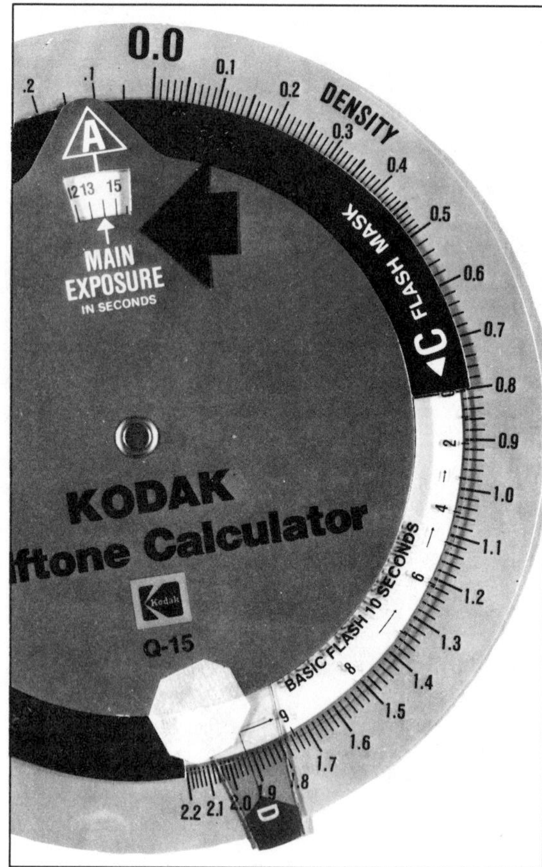

Figure 7.36. Using the computer The main exposure and flash quadrant wheels (taped section) have been rotated counterclockwise the length of the correction arrow.
Courtesy of Eastman Kodak Company.

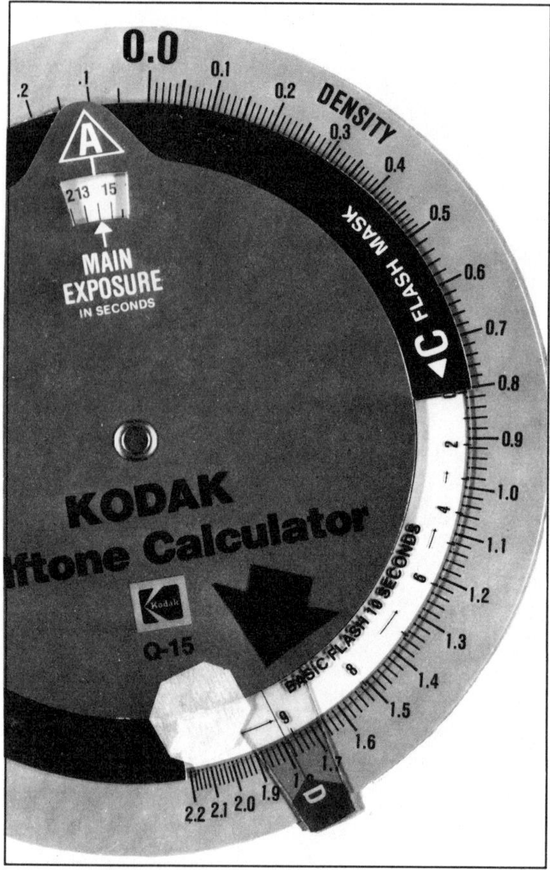

Figure 7.37. Using the computer To obtain the final flash exposure, pointer *D* has been moved back to the copy shadow density of 1.79.
Courtesy of Eastman Kodak Company.

mation. By entering highlight and shadow densities, the Q–700 can predict camera exposures that will give successful results from existing shop variables.

The instrument can be used for many functions other than calculating halftone exposures. The data modules can deliver information on such topics as chemical mixing, conversion from density to dot area, dropping or holding colors, copy scaling, camera exposure adjustments, and filter selection. The Q–700 is a sophisticated system that can greatly assist camera operators who understand photographic variables.

Processing Considerations for Halftone Photography

General film processing was explained in detail in chapter 6. Here we will only emphasize the great importance of being able to repeat exactly every processing step from one negative to the next. With simple line negatives, the extent of development can be judged visually, making it possible to compensate for a slight variation in time, temperature, or agitation and still produce a usable negative. Such visual judgment is difficult when tray processing halftone negatives.

Automatic processors provide the greatest consistency in development. Unfortunately, such processors are not always available. There are several important considerations in tray processing of halftones.

A major problem with shallow-tray development is chemical exhaustion. Once the two parts of the high-contrast developer have been joined, the exhaustion process begins. Even if the mixture is not used, it becomes exhausted in a matter of hours. This is partly a result of solutions being combined and partly a result of the surface of the chemicals coming into contact with room air (aerial oxidation). The developer also becomes exhausted through use because it reacts with the emulsion of the film, and both the developer and the film change chemical structure. Chemical exhaustion radically affects the quality of the final halftone.

The following suggestions diminish the effects of developer exhaustion:

- Don't mix the developer until just before processing the negative.
- Mix a sufficient quantity to cover the negative in the tray completely.
- Don't reuse the same chemicals for additional halftone negatives.
- Discard the developer and mix a fresh batch if another halftone is to be produced.

Figure 7.38. The Kodak Q–700 Data Center This is a multipurpose instrument used to determine various types of photographic information that are valuable to the photographer and printer.
Courtesy of Eastman Kodak Company.

Temperature control is a variable that is often overlooked with halftone processing. Even one degree of difference can result in extreme halftone variation.

The final consideration is the rate of tray agitation. Several techniques discussed in

Figure 7.39. Adding the halftone screen to the film sheet Place the emulsion of the contact screen in contact with the emulsion of the film. Courtesy of nuArc Company, Inc.

chapter 6 are not applicable to halftone work. Still development (a technique that uses no agitation) is perfectly suited for critical development of extremely fine-line detail in a high-contrast negative. But with halftone negatives, the same technique lowers negative contrast and produces a softer, less defined dot. A mechanical tray technique leaves streaks in halftone negatives because currents of chemicals flow in the same paths over the film.

Try to agitate in at least three directions at a consistent rate. The actual speed is not significant, only the fact that the rate is always the same for every piece of film. Watching a sweep second hand on a darkroom timer is helpful. Some photographers even use a metronome to ensure a consistent rate. Another alternative is to use a sensitometer after any camera exposures. By this method it is possible to use visual judgment with tray development of halftones.

Typical Halftone Procedures

Let's tie together the information of this section by following through with the typical procedures for making a halftone negative from a continuous-tone original.

1. With a visual or reflection densitometer, determine the highlight and shadow densities. Be sure to measure the lightest area with detail for the highlights and the densest area (whether there is detail or not) for the shadows. With that information, determine the main and flash exposure times from a halftone computer (see figure 7.27). If a bump exposure is necessary, identify the time with the same tool.

2. Set up the process camera by using the procedures described in chapter 6. Clean the copyboard glass, mount the original photograph and gray scale centered on the guidelines, close the frame (turn on the vacuum system if the camera has one), and move the copyboard so that it is parallel to the film plane. Adjust the diaphragm control to the percentage of enlargement or reduction desired at the f/stop opening that the computer was calibrated for (the photographer generally writes the f/stop on the computer as a reminder). Then move the percentage tapes so that they are balanced at the correct reproduction size. Set the camera timer at the main exposure time. Then adjust the flash timer to the flash exposure time. It is wise to check for even illumination by viewing the image through a ground glass screen. Aim the camera lights if necessary. Adjust the vacuum system on the filmboard to the size of the contact screen, not to the size of the piece of

film. (The contact screen must always be larger than the piece of film that is being used.)

3. To make the halftone exposures, first turn off the normal room lights so the darkroom is under safelight. Remove a sheet of high-contrast film from the storage box (be sure to close the box immediately—this is a good habit to develop) and mount the piece of film on the camera filmboard, emulsion up. If both the copy and the film are centered on the guidelines, there is little chance of ruining a sheet because the image missed the film. Next position the halftone contact screen over the film so that the emulsions of the two pieces are touching (figure 7.39). Turn on the vacuum system and carefully roll out any air pockets that are trapped between the film and the screen. A loss of detail will occur if an air gap between the emulsions is allowed.

Close the camera back and turn on the timer to make the main exposure. When the shutter closes, open the camera back and, without touching the film or screen, make the flash exposure (figure 7.40). If a bump exposure is to be made, reset the camera timer, remove the halftone screen (carefully so the film does not shift), close the camera back, and make the through-the-lens bump exposure.

4. Remove the exposed film from the camera and process it by standard shop procedures. When the film is dry, evaluate the gray scale and image areas for usability. In the most general terms, the negative should carry a 90–95% dot in the same area of the image that was measured on the densitometer for a highlight and a 5–10% dot in the corresponding shadow area. Increasing the main exposure will move the highlight dot farther up the gray scale. Increasing the flash exposure will move the shadow dot farther down the gray scale.

Figure 7.40. Making the flash exposure After making the main exposure, open the camera back, turn on the flashing lamp, and make the flash exposure.
Courtesy of nuArc Company, Inc.

Evaluating the usability of halftone images and making knowledgeable changes to correct defects in the halftones are the most important parts of the photographer's job. The following section takes a closer look at these processes.

SECTION 3

Evaluating Halftone Negatives

The major variables involved in halftone production have now been introduced. The central purpose has been to deal with the basics of the process. The ultimate goal has been, of course, to be able to produce the best possible halftone from any continuous-tone image. We have talked of end-points (highlights and shadows) and suggested that the placement of middle tone dots was an important control of contrast. However, no concrete method of interpreting the true usability of a halftone or of correcting inaccuracies was presented. The interpretation is vital.

It should be obvious that there are some problems with any visual interpretation of a halftone. Most people have difficulty making a judgment of any negative image and sometimes become confused with the difference between shadow and highlight dots. Another problem is that the actual picture is made up of dots that can usually be viewed only through a magnifying glass, and they are of random shape and size.

The solution to these problems is not to deal with the individual dots as they appear in the image itself, but rather to be concerned with their positions on the gray scale that was photographed along with the continuous-tone photograph. The gray scale is simply a numeric measure of density, and each step can easily be equated to a corresponding area of density on the print, so interpretation becomes much easier. The actual technique is to compare the gray scale that was photographed along with the continuous-tone print to the print itself. Assume that when the original highlight and shadow density readings from the continuous-tone print were taken, they were 0.10 for the highlight area and 1.40 for the shadow area. On the gray scale pictured in figure 7.8, 0.10 density lies somewhere between step 1 and step 2; 1.40 density lies in about step 10. (If you do not have a calibrated gray scale, you can calibrate the one you have with a reflection densitometer by simply reading the density in each step.) If your halftone negative (and, consequently, your printed halftone positive) is going to have the same BDR as your continuous-tone original, you would expect to see the gray scale almost completely filled in at step 1 or 2 and almost completely clear at around step 10. Actual dot size in these steps can be determined by looking at them with a magnifying glass. Again, the key is not to look at individual dots, but to look at an area of dots. An area of dots on the negative film image of the gray scale that will produce 10% dots on the printed piece will appear mostly black with a uniform pattern of small, clear openings. An area of dots on the negative film image of the gray scale that will produce 95% dots on the printed piece will appear clear with a uniform pattern of small black dots. If the placement of your shadow and highlight dots on the film image of the gray scale corresponds to the density recordings of the shadow and highlight areas from the original photograph, you can have some confidence that your final printed halftone will accurately represent the continuous-tone original. This should be the case if the halftone negative computer was calibrated and used accurately, and all exposure and processing steps were carried out correctly.

Correcting Defects

What if your dots fall in the wrong place? This is where the concept of a predictable density shift discussed in section 1 of this chapter becomes important. Let's assume for the example above that your highlight dot did not fall in step 2 but instead appeared in step 3. You know that the highlight dot is controlled by the main exposure. If your highlight dot was recorded in step 3, you must have had too long a main exposure. You also know that a change of one f/stop number on the camera will produce a .30 density shift on the film emulsion. You know further that halving or doubling the shutter speed is the same as changing the f/stop one stop up or down. If you were using the calibrated gray scale in figure 7.8, you would see that the density difference between step 3 (where your highlight dot appeared) and step 2 (where you want your highlight dot to appear) is approximately .15 (.32 minus .14 equals .18). This means that you would have to decrease your main exposure by ¼ in order to move the highlight dot from step 3 to step 2. By making this shutter speed adjustment and reshooting the picture with all other conditions (f/stop, flash, chemistry, and processing conditions) equal, you can shift the highlight dot down one stop.

Using the halftone negative computer should eliminate the need of reshooting to produce perfect results. But even the halftone negative computer cannot account for differences in individual processing techniques and conditions. Visual inspection of the gray scale is one method of correcting for improper dot placement. But when you reshoot the photograph, you must vary only the shutter speed and keep all other darkroom conditions constant.

It is worth noting here that a very accurate measure of the dot size on the actual halftone negative can be achieved with a dot area meter or a transmission densitometer. As mentioned in section 1 (figure 7.19), a dot area meter reads the dot coverage in an area of a piece of transparent film material. By measuring the dot area on the halftone negative that corresponds to the areas you identified as the highlight and shadow areas of the continuous-tone positive, you can establish whether you have placed the correct sized dots in the proper location. Measures taken with a dot area meter can be used directly. Measures taken with a transmission densitometer (figure 7.7) must be converted as shown in table 7.1.

Key Terms

density
reflectance
transmittance
tones
screen ruling
screen tints
vignetted screen pattern
dot area meter
copy density range
basic density range
main exposure
excess density

contrast
densitometry
reflection densitometer
transmission densitometer
highlight area
shadow area
middle tone area
flash exposure
bump exposure
spectral highlight

Questions for Review

Section 1

1. Name several examples of continuous-tone images.
2. In general terms, what does the term *density* describe?
3. What does the term *contrast* describe about tones on a piece of photographic film?
4. What is the difference between a transmission densitometer and a reflection densitometer?
5. What does the term *screen ruling* describe?
6. To what does the term *normal viewing distance* refer?
7. What is the difference between a vignetted screen structure and a solid line screen structure?
8. Which will produce a larger dot on the printed page, a 40% or a 60% screen tint?
9. What is the purpose of a dot area meter?
10. Name the two basic types of contact screens.

Section 2

1. What three areas of a continuous-tone photograph are probably the most significant measures of print quality?
2. What is meant by the BDR (basic density range) of a photograph?
3. What two types of halftone exposures are almost always used to reproduce a continuous-tone image?
4. What is the purpose of a bump exposure?
5. What is the major problem when using shallow-tray development to process halftone images?
6. Briefly outline the typical procedures when making a halftone negative from a continuous-tone original.

Chapter Eight

Special Effects Photography

Anecdote to Chapter Eight

Photographers and printers have gone to great lengths to create special photographic effects. One of the early ideas was to create huge illustrations that would dazzle the layman's mind. In 1864 at a photographic exhibition in Vienna, an enlargement of a flea was entered that was more than "a metre" in height. The picture startled those who saw it because they could not imagine how the print was made. Oversized prints of that time were usually made on several pieces of paper joined together. They were usually of such poor quality that elaborate retouching was necessary at the joints.

In 1899, the Chicago and Alton Railroads commissioned the Pullman Train Works to build an elaborate passenger train to celebrate the coming turn of the century. The company also wanted to exhibit a massive photograph of the train at the Paris Exposition the following year. Mr. George R. Lawrence, the company's photographer, was asked to build the largest camera in the world so that the "Alton Limited" could be photographed on one negative.

J.A. Anderson of Chicago, under Lawrence's supervision, spent two and a half months building the camera. When fully ex-

The Mammoth
Smithsonian Institution, Photo No. 72–10645.

tended on four 2-×-6-inch beams, the completed device was almost 20 feet long. It was constructed completely from solid cherry. The heavy rubber bellows took 40 gallons of glue to prepare. A special hinged frame on the back held the 8-×-10-foot glass negative. The two Zeiss lenses used in the camera were specially made. One was wide angle, with a 5½-foot focal length. The other was telescopic, with a 10-foot focal length. The camera with one lens weighed 900 pounds. With the plate holder and plate, it weighed over 1,400 pounds. It was so large that the front lens panel was a hinged door through which the photographer could climb into the device to clean the interior.

In the spring of 1900 the finished camera was placed in a padded van and mounted on a flatcar for a short journey to Brighton Park, where the exposition photo was to be shot. It took fifteen men to set up "The Mammoth," as it was officially named. A special focusing screen was hinged in the back, and the image was "focused" by several men pushing the lens forward or backward on the wooden track.

The exposure took 2½ minutes to make. It took 5 gallons of developer to process the image. Three prints were made from the 5-×-8-foot plate. One was placed on a wall in the train's grand salon. The second was given to the U.S. government as a gift for a new building. The third was sent to the Paris Exposition. The exposition officials found the photograph so remarkable that they required a certified affidavit specifying the details of its manufacture before they would accept it as "the world's largest photograph."

Objectives for Chapter Eight

After completing this chapter you will be able to:

- Outline the procedure for producing a duotone.
- Define the term "moiré pattern."
- Describe how to make a simple line conversion.
- Explain how photoposterizations are classified.
- Outline the procedure for making a three-tone posterization.
- Outline the procedure for making a two-color, three-tone posterization.
- Outline the procedure for making a three-color, four-tone posterization.

Introduction

It should be apparent from chapters 6 and 7 that the nature of photographic materials requires exacting and critical processing controls. This does not mean, however, that all darkroom techniques for printing technology are fixed and allow for no creative individual expression. In the darkroom it is the human element, not the materials, that produces results. A wide variety of problems is continually encountered in an industrial or production situation. The camera operator must be observant and able to creatively apply knowledge and skills to produce optimum results. There is a category of darkroom procedures labeled "creative" because the results require subjective decisions on the part of the photographer. This is not to imply that the processes involve guesswork or trial and error—only that the images can be manipulated to produce a wide range of pleasing and usable results.

Special photographic effects are produced to meet two general goals. The first is to work within material or equipment limitations (or advantages) to produce more economical or effective reproductions. As has been mentioned in chapter 7, printing presses can reproduce only a limited density range. With a "double dot black duotone" it is possible to overprint a second, specially produced halftone in register with the first normal halftone on the printed sheet. The result is to increase the shadow density and therefore enhance the appearance of the final image. Another powerful communication technique is the use of color. However, four-color process reproduction is time consuming, exacting, and expensive (see chapter 9). In many cases the creative use of two colors, as with a "duotone" or a "posterization," can be as effective as four colors (plates B and C, pp. 198–199).

The second goal of any special photographic effect is to be able to generalize an idea or an image rather than to reproduce exactly some specific picture or to create a pleasing visual impression. "Posterizations" can generalize ideas and also produce an attractive image. For example, figure 8.1 is a halftone that shows a man using a microscope. It is a fairly accurate duplication of the original continuous-tone photograph. A posterization of the same picture would evoke the general idea of a person working with some aspect of a craft industry. The same illustration could be reproduced in one or more colors (plates B and C, pp. 198–199).

Of the many special photographic techniques, this chapter will examine only duotones and posterizations. The bibliography provides resource material on more sophisticated or advanced techniques.

Duotones

Understanding Duotones

The duotone process is one method the printer can use to overcome the basic inability of printing presses to reproduce long tonal ranges. The term **duotone** implies the use of two layers of tones to produce one final image. Duotones were once nothing more than the same halftone printed in two colors, one in register over the other. The result was colorful, but it did nothing to change the basic printed halftone density range.

Duotones still involve the use of two halftones, called **printers.** However, the two negatives are made to different specifications. The first halftone, or **light printer,** is produced to carry highlight and upper middle tone detail (see plate A, p. 197). The second, or **dark printer,** is made to carry the lower middle tone and shadow detail. When these two halftones are overprinted, the result is a reproduction with a longer density range than a single halftone can produce. This type of reproduction approaches the actual tonal range of the original photograph.

The duotone color combination is extremely important. Most duotones are produced by using black or some other dark color for the dark printer and a light color, chosen to allow for contrast, for the light printer. The subject of the original photograph should suggest appropriate color combinations. The printer wouldn't choose green to reproduce a beach scene duotone or red as the second color in a picture with a lot of snow.

An effective duotone can also be produced when both halftones are printed in black (a **double dot black duotone**). The result increases the reproduction density range, intensifies the shadow detail, and still holds accurate highlight detail without creating a "flat" reproduction.

There is also a special class of reproductions called **fake duotones,** in which a single halftone is printed over a block of colored tint or even over a solid block of color. However, such duotones do not involve the manipulation and control of the original tonal range of the print and will not be considered in this discussion.

Duotones can be effective if properly used. A two-color duotone will attract more attention than a single-color image, and yet it can be produced less expensively and with less difficulty than can a four-color process print (see chapter 9). A double dot black duotone contains more detail and is a more attractive image than a single black halftone reproduction.

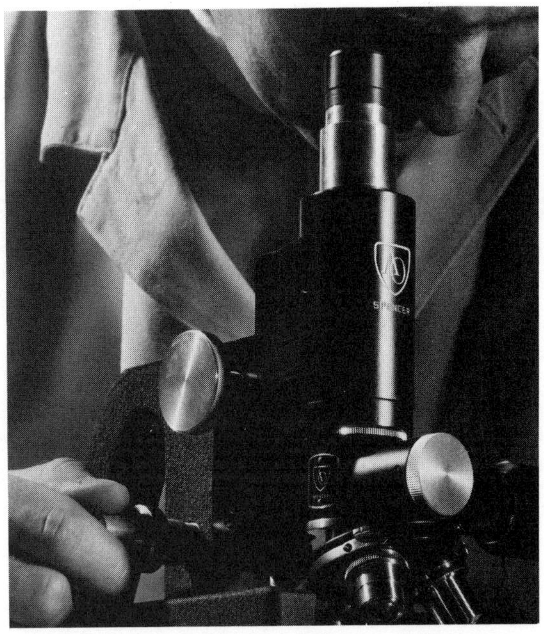

Figure 8.1. A normal halftone conversion This illustration is an example of a normal halftone conversion. Compare it with the posterization made from the same photograph (figure 8.11).

Selecting the Photograph

A duotone can be produced from any black-and-white continuous-tone photograph. However, not all pictures will make effective use of the process. The photograph should have normal contrast and a long tonal range. There should be no large monotone areas,

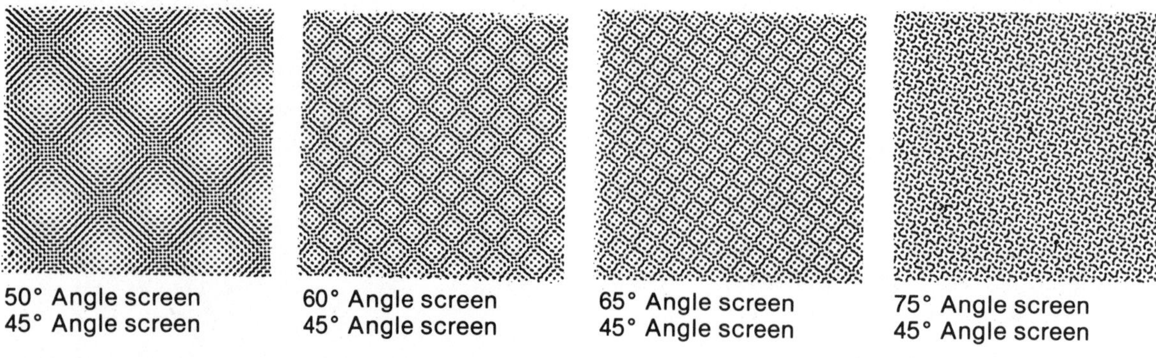

Figure 8.2. Moiré patterns The moiré patterns were formed by a 33-line screen at approximately 20% tone value.
Courtesy of Mead Paper.

and significant image detail should extend from the highlight areas to the shadow areas. The original should be big enough that an extreme enlargement is not required for the final print size. Finally, as with all processes, it is difficult to produce a quality reproduction from an inferior original.

Screen Angles

A complication is introduced whenever two different screen patterns (or dots) are overprinted. If two screens are randomly positioned over each other, an objectional **moiré** (pronounded *more-ray*) **pattern** could form (figure 8.2). The problem is caused by individual dots overlapping at an inappropriate angle. The typical contact screen, whether solid line or vignetted halftone, has a built-in 45° angle. When overprinting two screens, you must angle the second screen pattern 30° from the first, a difference that could be produced by any of the following three methods:

1. Using preangled screens,
2. Changing the angle of the screen,
3. Rotating the angle of the copy.

The most efficient method is to purchase specially preangled screens: a normal 45° screen and another screen angled at 15° or 75°. This method makes more use of available screen area because the screen itself does not have to be angled over the film on the filmboard.

A second possibility would be to actually change the angle of the screen on the vacuum back of the camera (figure 8.3). However, this method can cause vacuum problems, such as a loss of contact between the film and screen. The vacuum openings on most camera backs are designed to hold sheets of film and screens square to the board. When the sheet is angled out of this position, not all the openings are covered and holding power diminishes. This problem can be overcome by using a clear acetate or plastic sheet over the contact screen (figure 8.3).

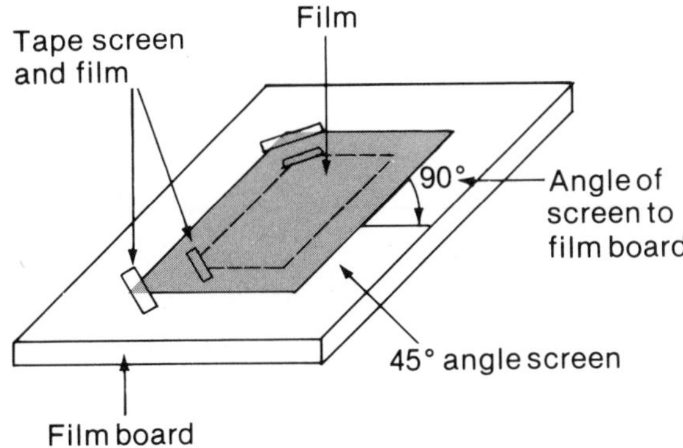

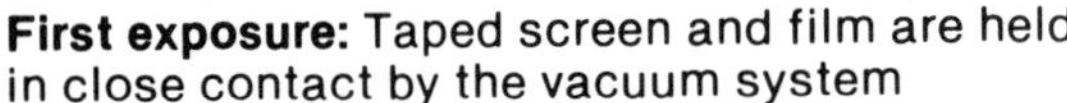
First exposure: Taped screen and film are held in close contact by the vacuum system

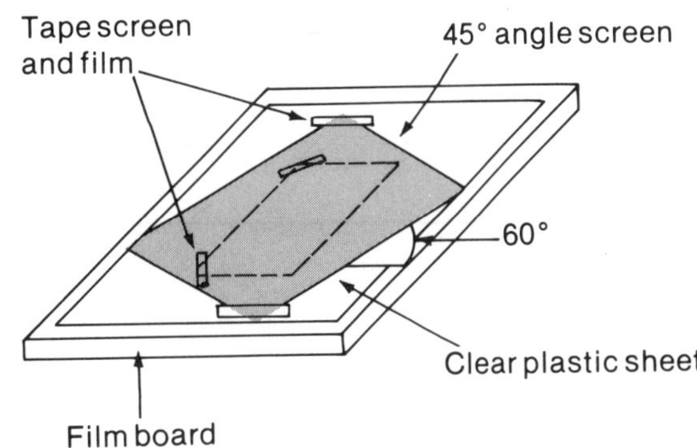

Second exposure: A clear plastic sheet insures holding power by covering vacuum openings missed by the angled screen

Figure 8.3. Angling the screen on the filmboard Working on the filmboard of the camera, the operator moves the screen 30 degrees between exposures. Both film and screen have been taped in position to prevent accidental movement.

The third method to control screen angle of the two printers is to rotate the angle of the copy itself. Figure 8.4a illustrates a simple method that can be used to hold the screen stationary and to shift the angle of the original. A cardboard guide is used to change the angle of the photograph on the copyboard. The first screen exposure is made with the center wheel in line with the 45° mark. For the second screen exposure the wheel is rotated 30° to the 15° or 75° mark. It is important that the contact screen not change position between exposures because a slightly changed screen angle could cause a moiré pattern when the two negatives are printed. For this reason, the edge of the contact screen is usually taped to the filmboard, and the film is slid out and reinserted under it for the second exposure.

Producing the Light Printer

The choice of color combinations and tonal range positions is almost totally subjective, so there are no set rules to direct the printer in making these duotone separations. The following general set of procedures is presented only as a starting point for the printer who has never before attempted the duotone process. With experience, printers develop their own approaches.

In any duotone the light printer carries the most significant detail of the original photograph, thus influencing the appearance of the final product much more than does any other factor. A good starting procedure when making a duotone is to calculate a main exposure as would be done for a normal halftone (see chapter 7). This exposure should

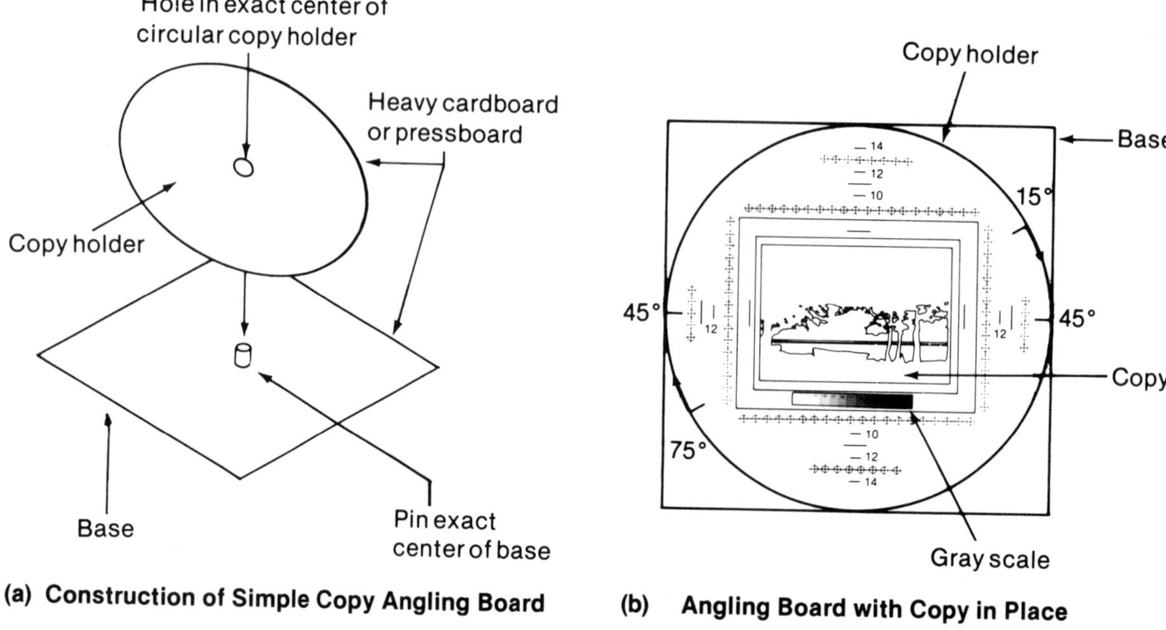

(a) Construction of Simple Copy Angling Board **(b) Angling Board with Copy in Place**

Figure 8.4. Diagram of a simple copy angling board This diagram is an example of a frame made of pressboard with a wheel that can be rotated to the desired angle for each camera exposure.

accurately record the highlight and upper middle tone areas of the continuous-tone print.

The choice of color for this light printer will influence the use of a flash exposure. If a dark color (such as black for a double dot duotone, or even a strong orange) is to be used, a normal flash is called for. It is even possible to increase the flash to build a stronger shadow dot. The important consideration is that no shadow area should reproduce as a solid on the final printed sheet.

If the light printer is to carry a light color, such as yellow or blue, it is desirable to reduce or even drop the flash exposure. This procedure will allow some shadow areas to print solid, which is desirable in this case because the shadows will appear to carry stronger detail when the second color is overprinted and will, thus, create a duotone with a long tonal range.

After the main and flash exposure times have been determined, the camera procedures are simple. The following general procedure assumes the use of the copyboard angling system.

1. Mount the copyboard angling device on the camera copyboard and tape it securely in place. Then tape the photograph in the center of the board; be sure to add register marks and a gray scale (see figure 8.4b). Set

the angle pointer to the 45° position and close the copyboard frame.

2. Set the camera to the desired reproduction size and lock that size in position. It is important that these settings not be touched until both the light and the dark printers have been produced. Any change, however slight, will make accurate registration of the two halftones on the light table or the press impossible.

3. Because the angle of the screen is going to be controlled on the copyboard, you must ensure that the angle of the screen on the filmboard remains constant. You can use a punched tab system (see figure 8.5) or tape one side of the screen to the board (figure 8.6). A clear plastic mask can be put around a halftone screen. This will provide a handling area and a place to punch or tape the screen (figure 8.7). Whatever system you use, you must position the screen for good vacuum control and must not change the screen's position between the light and dark printer exposures. As with any halftone, the screen should be emulsion-side down on the filmboard so that the screen and the film will be emulsion-to-emulsion during the shot.

4. Place a sheet of halftone film emulsion-side up on the vacuum back, place the contact screen in place over the film, and obtain perfect vacuum contact between the two. Turn the copy and film boards into position and expose the light printer using the times you previously determined.

5. You can place the exposed film in an empty film box or develop it immediately. To ensure accurate and reproducible results with tray processing, process the film by the time-temperature-agitation method explained in chapter 6 (see "Controlling Chemical Processing"). Use an automatic processor if one is available.

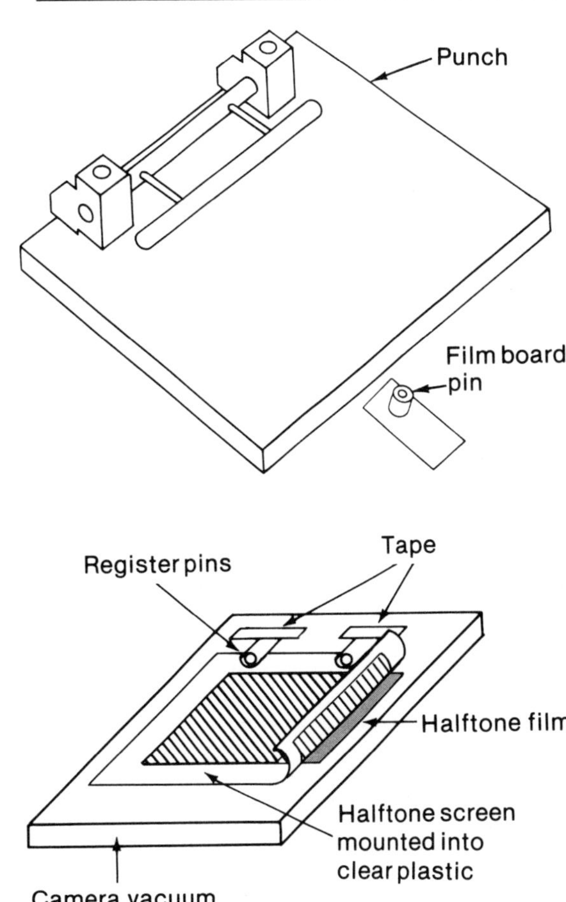

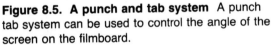

Figure 8.5. A punch and tab system A punch tab system can be used to control the angle of the screen on the filmboard.

Producing the Dark Printer

The dark printer carries the shadow detail of the original photograph and provides a significant increase in contrast and density. Using a normal halftone as this second printer would present problems. Not only would the shadow density be increased, but so would

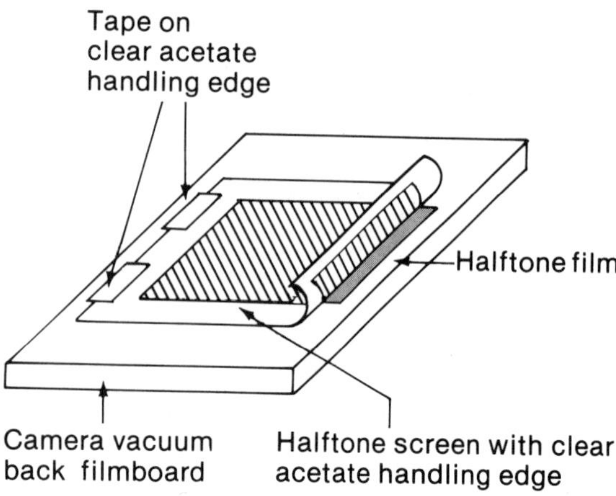

Figure 8.6. Taping the screen to the filmboard Taping the screen will insure that it does not move between exposures.

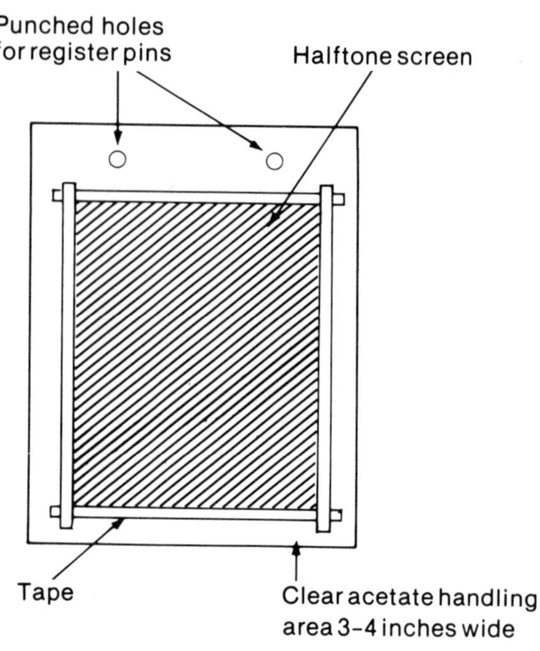

Figure 8.7. A clear acetate sheet put around a halftone screen This use of an acetate sheet will provide a handling area and a place to punch the screen for tab registration.

the highlights and middle tones. The result would be unpleasant and would defeat the purpose of the duotone process, which is to extend the total tonal range of the final print.

In general, the dark printer should carry no highlight detail. Rather, the entire halftone dot structure is shifted down to a higher step on the gray scale to record lower middle tone through shadow detail. One method to accomplish this is to greatly increase the main exposure. A good starting point is to double the amount of light that reaches the film. A simple technique is to open the lens one stop and keep the same exposure time. A suggested starting point for the dark printer flash exposure would be ½ the light printer exposure.

1. Change the copy angle 30° from that of the first exposure. Open the copyboard frame and rotate the angle pointer to 15° or 75°. Be certain that the board, photograph, and register marks do not shift from their taped positions. Only the center dial should move (figure 8.8). It is vital that the camera size settings and the contact screen positions not be changed from those of the first exposure. If any movement has taken place, discard the first negative and repeat the light printer procedure.

2. Place a fresh sheet of halftone film on the filmboard, sliding it under the taped contact screen, and again obtain perfect vacuum contact between the two. Turn the copy and film boards into position and expose, using the exposures determined for the dark printer.

3. After exposure, process the film by using the time-temperature-agitation method explained in chapter 6.

4. When both the light and the dark printers have been developed and fixed, the halftones can be inspected on a wet light table. The gray scale on the light printer should carry a reproducible dot in the highlights, and the dot formation should extend down the scale according to the colors chosen (figure 8.9). The dark printer gray scale should have the first reproducible dot appear at least 3 or 4 steps farther down the scale than the light printer, on a 12-step gray scale.

These procedures are only suggestions designed to introduce the duotone process. The experienced photographer will be able to vary these suggested exposures to obtain the most effective duotone possible from the original photograph.

Any multicolor separations should be proofed before printing plates reach the press. Proofing techniques are discussed in detail in "Multiple-Color Photomechanical Proofing," chapter 10.

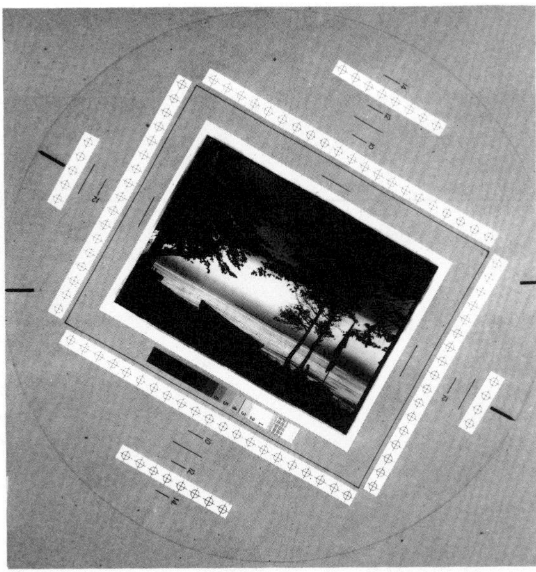

Figure 8.8. Changing the angle of the copyholder When the angle is changed for subsequent exposures, use care to ensure that only the center dial moves and not the frame or photograph.

Photoposterization

During the early days of photography, the sensitivity of most orthochromatic film was so limited that a long range of tones could not be accurately recorded on a single sheet. The solution to this problem was to divide the tonal range of an original into several groups and to deal with each group as a separate exposure on a new piece of film. They were then recombined on the printing plate. The images produced by this method had a poster-like quality, and so the term **posterization** was used. With subsequent film emulsion improvements, this technique was quickly forgotten.

The process has been revived as a simple and economical technique that creates an attention-getting visual effect—or changes a specific photograph into a generalized image. The most elementary posterization is a simple line conversion.

A Simple Line Conversion

A line exposure of a continuous-tone photograph actually is a sort of posterization. It does not accurately represent the photograph and communicates only a general idea or

Light Printer

Dark Printer

Figure 8.9. Examples of light and dark printers The gray scale can be used to identify the areas of the original that have been reproduced for each printer. Here we can see that in the dark printer the first reproducible dot appear at step 4. The dots appear in step 1 in the light printer.

Photo bv Richard Bohall.

impression. Line photography produces a one-color, two-tone conversion (clear paper as one tone and ink as another).

A similar conversion could be produced by placing a solid line screen or special effect screen tint over the film before it is exposed. The resulting image would again record only the highlight detail of the original. Although not a common technique, the conversion would have all the characteristics of a line negative except that the image areas would be broken up into mechanical lines or dots instead of solid ink.

There are two problems with the use of line conversions of continuous-tone originals. Because they contain only two tones, the results from some photographs might be unrecognizable. Also the film exposure determines what tones of the original are recorded. Because not all photographs have the same basic density range and the significant detail is not always located in the same density step, it is difficult to calculate a proper exposure for a line conversion.

Classifying Photoposterizations

Posterizations are classified according to the number of colors and the number of different tones reproduced on the final press sheet. When counting colors, only the number of different ink colors is counted. Although it is possible to print a single ink color on a colored sheet (other than white), the result is still classified as a single-color posterization because there is only one layer of ink on the paper. Figure 8.10 shows a one-color posterization. Plates B and C (pp. 198–199) show two- and three-color posterizations.

The second classification of posterizations is the number of tones contained in the image. Unprinted paper areas (generally assumed to represent the highlight areas of the original) are counted as one tone; solid ink areas (shadows), as another; and any line or tint variation (representing middle tones), as the third. Plates B and C show a three- and four-tone posterization. Notice that in the figures, it is possible to count the distinct tones produced by the different colors. A simple way to remember this is that the number of colors is equal to the number of printed colors, and the number of tones is equal to the number of printed colors plus one (the paper tone).

Any more than two tones generally represent the middle tone area of the photograph and are produced by an additional exposure through a solid line or special effects screen tint. Any variation of the number of tones and colors is possible. The main problem, however, is to produce the tonal separations. The following sections explain and detail the procedures for producing a three- or four-tone posterization.

Understanding Three-Tone Posterizations

Recall that a two-tone conversion (a line photograph) is produced with a single camera exposure. A three-tone conversion or posterization is produced with two camera exposures (figure 8.11). The first exposure records the extreme highlights (as does a normal line photograph). The second records the middle tone area on the same sheet of film.

In the actual production of a normal three-tone posterization, a solid step 4 as a reflection of highlight detail is too far down the scale. That density extends too far into the detail area of most photographs for effec-

Figure 8.10. Example of a one-color posterization

Courtesy of John N. Schaedler, Inc.

tive reproduction. The first exposure should record only the extreme highlights.

It is possible to predict the amount of density that will be recorded from any original at a particular exposure. Recall from chapter 6 that a change in the camera exposure by a factor of two results in a 0.30 density change on the film. In other words, reducing the basic exposure time by one-half will reduce the density of the negative by 0.30. Doubling the basic exposure time will increase the density of the negative by 0.30. With this information, it is possible to control the density of any original recorded as a solid area on the posterization.

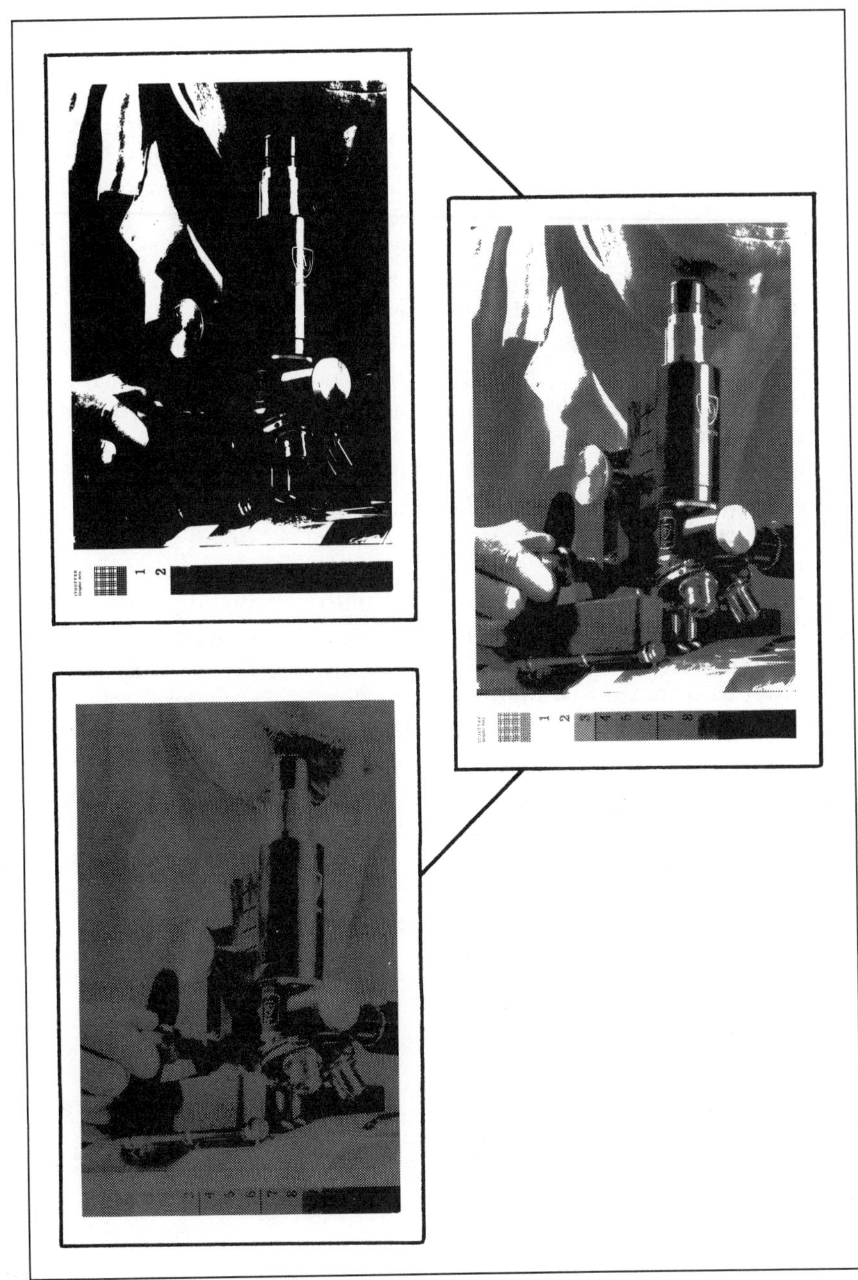

Figure 8.11. Example of a three-tone posterization A three-tone posterization is made by using two camera exposures.

The authors have had great success producing the highlight image for a posterization by merely reducing the basic camera exposure for line film by one-half. As an example, if the basic exposure was f/16 for 20 seconds, the first exposure for our posterization would be f/16 for 10 seconds (or at f/22 for 20 seconds—the results would be the same). In figure 8.12 the basic exposure, with normal processing, produced a solid step 4, or a density of 0.45. When the exposure is decreased by one-half, subtract 0.30 from the density of the last solid step (0.45) to find that any highlight detail with a density of 0.15 or less will be recorded. This density equals a solid step 2 on the gray scale in figure 8.12. This, then, is a first visual cue for shallow-tray processing of the negative.

The three-tone effect is produced with a second camera exposure. A separate image is recorded on the film for the density range that extends from the last highlight record of the first exposure into the middle tone areas of the original. To keep the second film exposure visually separate from the first, a solid line screen is placed over the film before the middle tone exposure is made.

In chapter 7 we discussed the differences between a solid line and a vignetted contact screen. Halftone screens should not be used to produce the second tonal separation. The result would look like a shoddy halftone attempt. Only a solid line screen tint or a special effects screen tint will give the desired results. Recall that screen tints are rated in terms of the amount of light they pass. A 40% tint passes 40% of the light and blocks 60%. Figure 8.13 shows a variety of screens used with the same original image. The choice of which tint or special effects screen to use is a subjective decision.

Because a screen, which will absorb some of the light reflected from the copy, has been placed over the film and because the purpose of the second exposure is to record detail from the middle tone areas, the second exposure should be longer than the first exposure. The authors recommend a second camera exposure four times longer than the first or highlight exposure. Continuing the same example, if the first exposure were f/16 for 10 seconds, the second exposure would be f/16 for 40 seconds (or any combination of f/stop and shutter speed that produces the same quantity of light).

It is also possible to predict the density range of the second exposure. Increasing the quantity of light by four times adds 0.60 den-

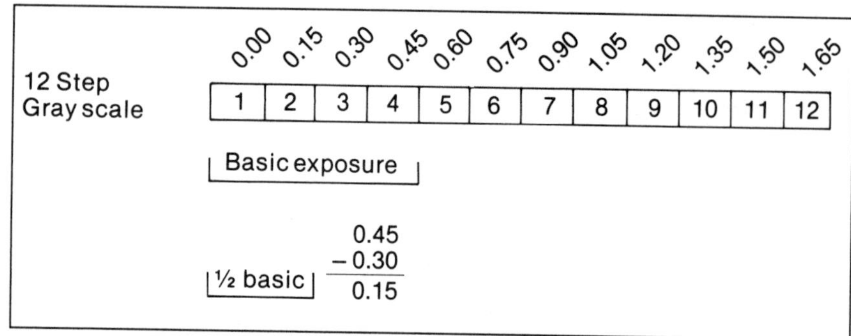

Figure 8.12. Example of calculating the highlight detail based on a ½ basic exposure The computation shown is used to predict the highlight detail that will be recorded from an exposure that is ½ the normal line or basic exposure.

Mahogany

Mezzotint

Circleline

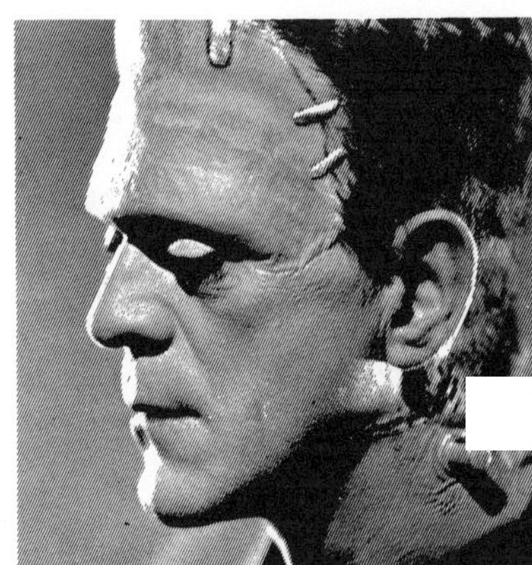

100 Straightline

Wavyline

50 Straightline

Figure 8.13. Examples of special effect tints
Special effect screen tints can be used to create different impressions with the same image.
Courtesy of James Craig, *Production Planning*.

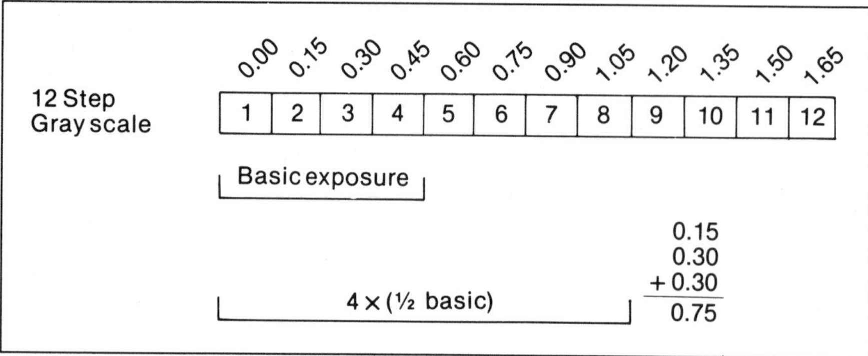

Figure 8.14. Example of calculating the density range of the second exposure The computation is used here to predict the density range of the second exposure.

sity to the film. In figure 8.14 we found that the first exposure would produce detail with a density up to 0.15. Therefore, the second exposure should record detail of the original that has a density of 0.75 or less (or 0.15 + 0.60), which equates to a solid step 6–8 depending on the real density of the gray scale being used. This step then provides a second visual cue for shallow-tray development.

Single-color posterizations can be produced by placing all exposures on a single sheet of film and printing with one press run (see figure 8.11). Multicolor posterizations can be prepared by two methods. The simplest is to print a block of color on the press sheet, then overprint the posterization as a second color (plate D, p. 200). An alternate method for color is to record separate tones on individual sheets of film. Each separation is plated and run as a different color printed in register on the final sheet (plate B & C, p. 198–199). Two methods of producing a three-tone posterization are explained below.

Procedures for Making a Three-Tone Posterization

Method One: Single-Color, Three-Tone (Plate D)

1. Center the copy on the copyboard of the process camera. Position a gray scale next to, but not covering, the copy.

2. Place a sheet of high-contrast film on the camera and make a line exposure sufficient to record the extreme highlights of the photograph. Try an exposure that is half the basic line exposure.

3. Carefully open the camera back and place a solid line screen tint or special effects screen over the film. Be sure not to shift the position of the film. Expose the film a second time to record an image from the middle tone area of the photograph. Try an exposure that is four times the exposure used in step 2 above. For a first attempt use a 40% screen tint.

4. Proces the film as you would normal line film. Use the visual cues explained in the previous section to determine adequate development.

5. Proof or examine the negatives, particularly the gray scale:

1. If it appears that not enough highlight detail was recorded, increase the first exposure.
2. If large clear areas with no detail are produced, decrease the first exposure.

3. If the black area is excessive, increase the second exposure.
4. If there is too little black in the shadow areas, decrease the second exposure.

Method Two: Two-Color, Three-Tone (Plate B)

1. Place a register mark in each corner of the continuous-tone photograph. Center the copy on the copyboard of the process camera. Position a graphic arts gray scale next to, but not covering, the copy.

2. Place a sheet of high-contrast film on the camera and make a line exposure sufficient to record the extreme highlights of the photograph. Try an exposure that is half the basic line exposure.

3. Open the camera back and remove the exposed piece of film. Place it in a light-tight container (such as a film box) and position a new sheet on the camera. Expose the film to record an image from the middle tone area of the photograph. Try an exposure that is four times the exposure used in step 2 above. Do not use a screen tint when making the second exposure.

4. From this point follow steps 4 and 5 of method one.

Key Terms

---

duotone
light printer
dark printer
double dot black duotone
fake duotone
moiré pattern
posterization

Questions for Review

---

1. What are the two general purposes of special photographic effects?
2. What does the term *duotone* imply?
3. What is the purpose of the dark printer in a set of duotone halftone negatives?
4. What is a double dot black duotone?
5. What is a fake duotone?
6. Why is it necessary to change the dot angle between the light and dark duotone printers?
7. How many tones are carried in a simple line conversion photoposterization?
8. How are photoposterizations classified?
9. How many camera exposures are necessary to produce a one-color, three-tone posterization?
10. Doubling the quantity of light that strikes the film adds how much density to the film?

Chapter Nine

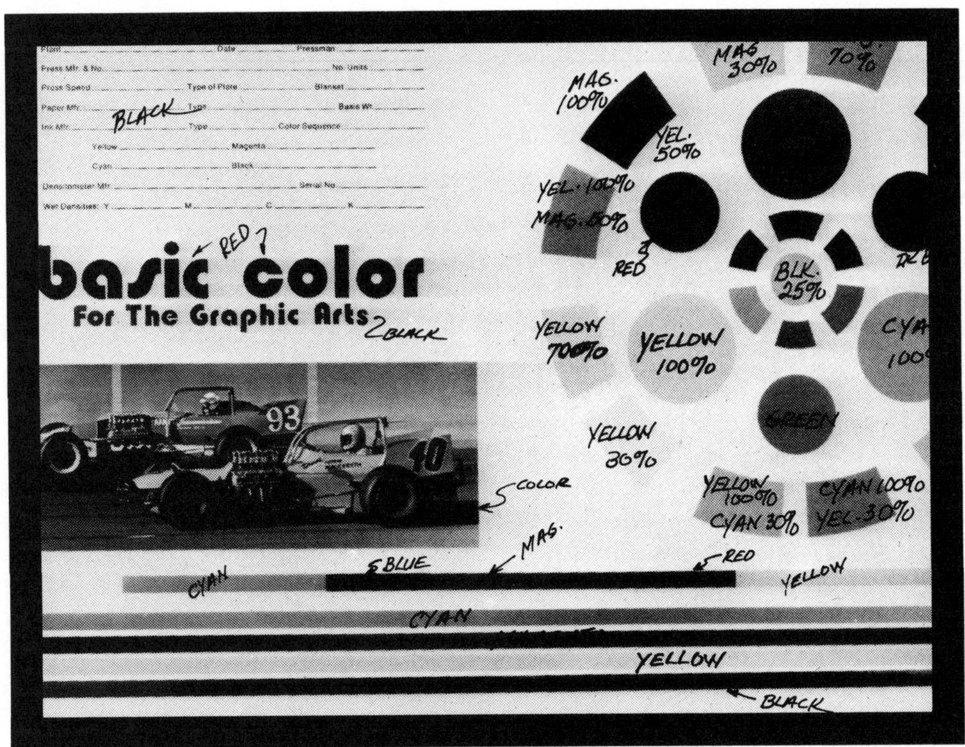

Color Separation Photography

Anecdote to Chapter Nine

In 1862, Louis Ducos du Hauron sent a letter to M. Lelut of the Academie de Medecine et Sciences describing his ideas for a "Physical Solution of the Problem of Reproducing Colors by Photography." Hauron said:

> *The method which I propose is based on the principle that the simple colors are reduced to three—red, yellow, and blue—the combinations of which in different proportions give us the infinite variety of shades we see in nature. One may now say that analysis of the solar spectrum by means of a glass which passes only one color has proved that red exists in all parts of the spectrum, and the like for yellow and blue, and that one is forced to admit that the solar spectrum is formed of three superimposed spectra having their maxima of intensity at different points. Thus one might consider a picture which represents nature as composed of three pictures superimposed, the one red, the second yellow, and the third blue. The result of this would be that if one could obtain separately these three images by photography and then reunite them in one, one would obtain an image of nature with all the tints that it contains.**

It was Hauron's ideas that were, in part, responsible for the later development of successful additive color plates and film.

*Louis W. Sipley, *A Half Century of Color* (New York: Macmillan, 1951), p. 22.

A man named Frederick E. Ives was a journeyman printer who became interested in photography. In 1880 he moved from Ithica, New York, to Philadelphia. From that time on he only did research in color photography and photomechanical printing. He was familiar with Hauron's early ideas and worked to refine them.

By the end of 1881 Ives had received two U.S. patents for a specialized halftone printing process and was beginning to spend most of his energy on color. In 1885, at the Philadelphia "Novelties Exhibition," he exhibited a process of photographing colors and a photomechanical method for reproducing them.

In May of 1892, Ives was invited to present a paper outlining his ideas before the Society of Arts in London. At that time he displayed the Photochromoscope camera he had invented. Using a single exposure, the device recorded a three-color image on three separate plates. The transparent separations could then be viewed through red, green, and blue color filters.

The illustration on page 204 was produced by Ives in 1893 with his tricolor process. It is perhaps the first photomechanically printed color image. It is uncertain whether it was reproduced by using a relief plate or a rotogravure cylinder, but the halftones were certainly made from crossline screens. By the turn of the century, almost all printers and photographers understood the color separation process, and national publications such as the *National Geographic* used full-color picture printing.

Objectives for Chapter Nine

After completing chapter 9 the student will be able to:

- Define process color photography.
- Explain additive color theory.
- Discuss how subtractive colors are related to additive colors.
- Explain how a color filter works.
- Explain the reason for concern about screen angle on process color separation negatives.
- Discuss how four black and white halftones can produce a full color reproduction.
- Briefly describe the purposes of a mask.
- Outline the steps necessary to produce a direct color separation halftone negative.
- Describe the difference between direct and indirect color separation methods.
- Define and give examples of color reflection copy.
- List and describe four systems for producing separation negatives.
- Explain the purpose of dot etching.
- Outline the process of making separation negatives by the contact direct screen method.

Introduction

For centuries printers have attempted to use color on their printed sheets. As recently as the turn of the century, the use of two colors on a single newspaper page would have successfully attracted reader attention. Today the use of color printing in the Sunday comics, the magazine section, and even on a weekly's front page is commonplace. As people become accustomed to color illustrations, their demands increase for more and higher-quality color reproductions.

Today's graphic designers rely heavily on color in the communications process. Color allows consumers to sit comfortably in their homes and view the color and pattern of a new shirt or dress from a mail-order catalog, explore the wilds of Africa, view a Hawaiian sunset, or select the color scheme of a new car.

It is no longer sufficient that a page merely carry several colors. Now the goal is to eliminate printing defects, such as poor fit, inaccurate color balance, or insufficient ink density, and to produce a perfect color reproduction. The technology of color reproduction has evolved to a sophisticated level of interrelated concepts and skills, all of which begin with the process photographer.

Chapter 3 outlined a classification of the types of color printing: flat color, fake color, and process color. This chapter is solely concerned with the photographic preparation of images for process color reproduction.

Basic Concepts

Process Color Photography

Process color photography is not magic, although the novice printer might think so after a number of failures to reach a specified A–B density range on a separation negative. **Process color photography** is nothing more than the skillful manipulation of light, filters, and film. The result of process photography is a set of color separations of a color original. When printed together in three colors and black, the separations combine to form the illusion of many colors and accurately duplicate the original illustration. Although plate M appears to be made up of a broad range of hues (tonal gradations of color), it is actually formed from only four printing plates. Each of these plates carries a halftone image of the colors cyan, magenta, yellow, and black, separated from the original continuous-tone photograph. The first three colors (cyan, magenta, and yellow) are called the **subtractive primary colors** and are all that is necessary to form the illusion of many other colors. Black is added to obtain density in the shadow areas to increase the overall image contrast.

In order to understand this process better it is necessary to examine in detail the nature of light.

Light and Color

Isaac Newton demonstrated the hues of the visible spectrum by passing a beam of light through a glass prism (plate E). He not only produced a rainbow of color but passed the rainbow through a second prism and reconstructed the original beam of light. Newton therefore proved that color is in the light and what we see as white light is really a mixture of all colors.

Through science courses in school, nearly everyone has been exposed to Newton's experiment in one form or another. A popular technique to illustrate his theory is to use three projectors focused on a white screen. By placing a blue gelatin filter on one projector, a green one on the second, and a red one on the third, it is possible to produce white light where all three overlap (figure 9.1 and plate F). These three colors—red, blue, and green—are called the **additive primary colors.**

Where any two of the additive primary colors overlap, the subtractive primary colors are formed. Magenta is actually a combination of red and blue, cyan is produced from blue and green, and yellow is made up of red and green. In order to simplify terminology, some ink manufacturers and printers refer to magenta as "process red," cyan as "process blue," and yellow as "process yellow."

The idea of the visible spectrum as a part of the electromagnetic spectrum is discussed in detail in appendix B. The blue end (400 millimicrons) of the visible spectrum is made up of wavelengths shorter than those at the red end (700 millimicrons). Newton's experiment with the prism was a success because of this wavelength difference. Because each color is a different wavelength, the rainbow was easily produced as the white light was refracted through the prism.

Subtractive colors pass or reflect their own wavelengths and absorb or subtract their complement (opposite colors in figure 9.1 are complements). When cyan ink is printed on white paper, only blue and green light are allowed to reach the paper and are reflected back. Red, the complement of cyan, is absorbed and the combination of blue and green (cyan) reaches the eye (plate G). Where magenta ink is printed, only blue and red light reach the paper to be reflected back (plate H). Green, the complement of magenta, is absorbed, and the combination of blue and red (magenta) is seen by the eye. Yellow ink printed on white paper allows only green and red to be reflected (plate I). Blue, the complement of yellow, is absorbed. Green and red are perceived as the color yellow.

The importance of figure 9.1 cannot be overemphasized when learning these concepts. It is obvious that where additive colors overlap, subtractive colors are produced. As printers we work with subtractive colors on the printed page, and by controlling the amounts of cyan, magenta, and yellow (and black), we can form the illusion of any color of the visible spectrum.

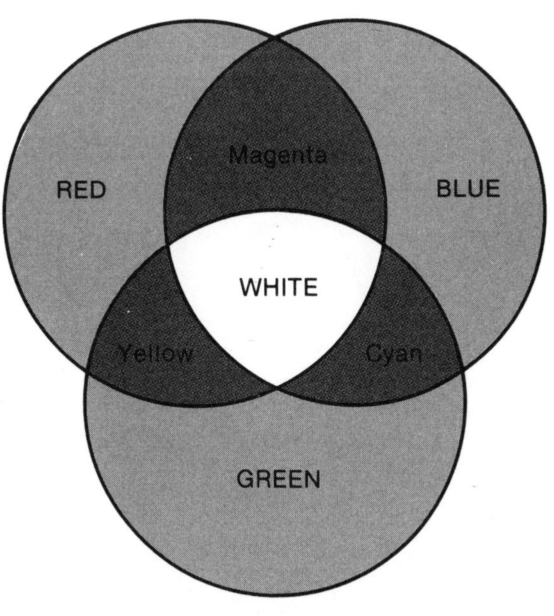

Figure 9.1. Process colors In process color photography, the primary additive colors are red, blue, and green. The primary subtractive colors are cyan, magenta, and yellow.

Color Separation

The task, then, of process color photography is to separate the hues of a continuous-tone color original into four negatives that represent the quantities of density that can be used to prepare cyan, magenta, yellow, and black printing plates. Figure 9.2 illustrates the basic concept of color separation.

When viewing this figure, it is important to keep two ideas firmly in mind:

1. A color filter transmits its own color and absorbs all other hues.
2. Light that reaches the film exposes the emulsion and becomes nonimage area; the actual reproducible image is that area of the film that has not been exposed to light.

In the color separation process, the primary additive colors, red, blue, and green, are used as filters to prepare cyan, magenta, and yellow separations. The separation process begins with a color original. The light from the original is directed through a red filter to produce the cyan separation negative (figure 9.2). Because a red filter (plate J) transmits its own color, the red patch is the only area of the original to form density on the film (figure 9.2). The unexposed areas then represent the combination of blue and green, which is cyan. The magenta printer is made by using a green filter (plate K). The wavelengths reflecting from the green patch of the original will be transmitted through the filter and will expose the film (figure 9.2). Red and blue light will be absorbed by the filter and will not expose the film. Red and blue combine to form magenta. The blue filter (plate L), transmitting

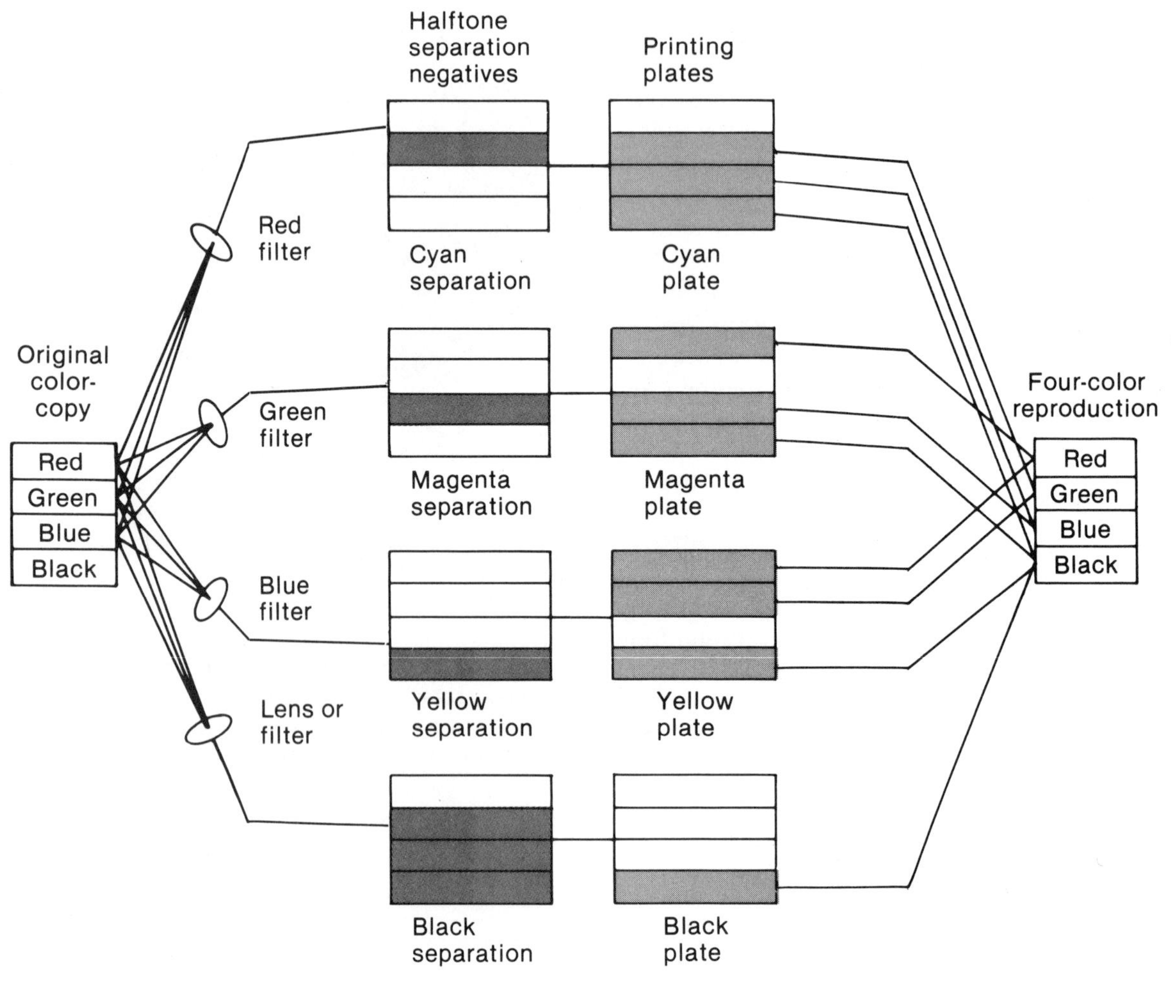

Figure 9.2. A basic diagram of color separation

only blue light, will produce the yellow printer by exposing the negative in all but the red-green areas (figure 9.2). The black printer is exposed in such a way that shadows or dark areas of the original are not recorded on the film, but the primary hues are recorded as density on the negative (figure 9.2).

After the negatives are exposed to printing plates, the clear areas on the film become areas of density on the plate. When the four plates are printed together in their proper combinations on a single sheet, the result should duplicate the range of hues of the original copy.

Halftone Dots and Color

Although figure 9.2 is a good conceptual view of the color separation process, it represents flat color and does not accurately show how the full range of hues is produced on the final printed sheet. Most color separation is done from continuous-tone color originals and must be screened during the reproduction process. Recall from chapter 7 that halftone photographs form the illusion of tones by the use of dots of varying sizes. For example, 15% dots surrounded by 85% white space will appear as light gray; 35% dots with 65% white space will appear to be a darker gray. That same dot structure will produce a range of values within a given subtractive color for process color reproduction. It is the overlapping of dots of varying size from the four different printers that produces the accurate representation of the color original. It is possible to illustrate this concept with a set of "progressive color proofs."

The yellow printer is actually a halftone represented in one hue (yellow), consisting of a limited range of values (plate M). The values of yellow are produced by many halftone dots of varying sizes. When the magenta printer is added to the yellow printer, additional hues and values become noticeable. By adding a cyan printer, the image looks complete. All the hues and values of hues seem to be visible. By adding a black printer, density will be increased in the shadow areas and the values of each hue will be strengthened.

Because the various values of each hue are produced by an overlapping dot structure, it is important that each halftone separation be prepared with dots at differing screen angles. If these angles are not properly controlled, an objectionable moiré pattern (see figure 8.3) could be formed. The cyan separation is typically made at a 45° angle, the magenta at 75°, the yellow at 90°, and the black at 105°. Angle control is discussed later in this chapter.

Masking

The purpose of **masking** is actually threefold:

- To compress the density range of the color original,
- To compensate for color deficiencies in process inks,
- To enhance the detail of the final reproduction.

A color mask is made by exposing the continuous-tone original to pan masking film (a continuous-tone film) through a special filter.

Color transparencies typically have a maximum density of around 2.60, and color reflection copy may reach 2.00. With four layers of ink on a single printed sheet, it is possible to match the 2.00 reflection density; but the 2.60 density of transparent images cannot be recorded during the separation process and cannot be reproduced on the press. With a mask the tonal range of the image can be compressed to a usable range without causing color imbalance.

An additional problem is inherent to printing inks. Although the concept is accurate, subtractive inks that are perfect absorbers cannot be produced. Plate B shows that cyan absorbs all red and reflects all blue and green. Unfortunately, cyan ink also absorbs some green and blue. Likewise, magenta absorbs some blue and red, and yellow absorbs some green. If cyan ink absorbs green and blue light, it is really acting like magenta ink. Therefore it becomes necessary to reduce the magenta separation negative in areas where

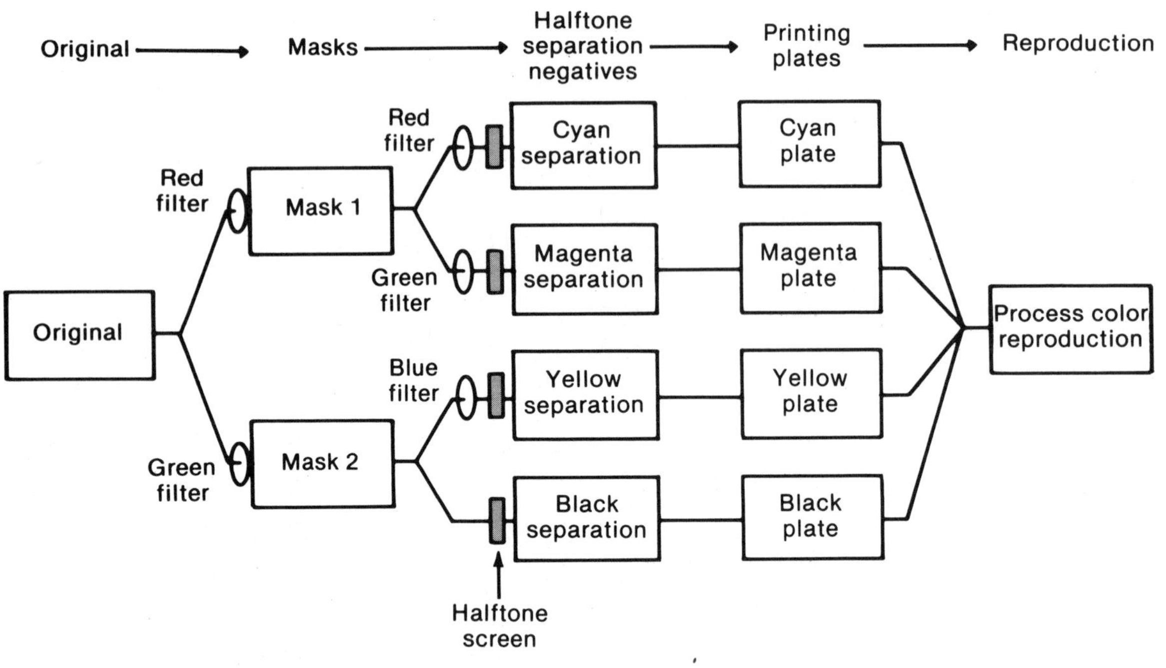

Figure 9.3. Diagram of direct screen color separation

cyan ink is also printed on the final reproduction. This interaction occurs between all colors. The process of masking reduces selected areas of the separation negatives in an attempt to overcome the deficiencies of process inks.

The third purpose of a color mask is to enhance the detail of the individual separation. An unsharp mask will produce a sharp separation. The mask is produced by placing a diffuser sheet (generally frosted acetate) between the original and the mask film during the mask exposure. The separation exposure is made with the mask in contact with the separation film. The diffused mask then slightly increases the contrast of the edges of the image, which in turn gives more detail to the reproduction.

A color mask, then, only compresses the density range, compensates for ink deficiencies, and enhances detail. A mask cannot overcome the limitations of a poor original nor can it hide the photographer's errors.

Methods of Producing Color Separations

There are basically only two methods of making color separations—the direct screen method and the indirect screen method.

LIGHT PRINTER

A
DUOTONE
(Dark plus
light printer)

DARK PRINTER

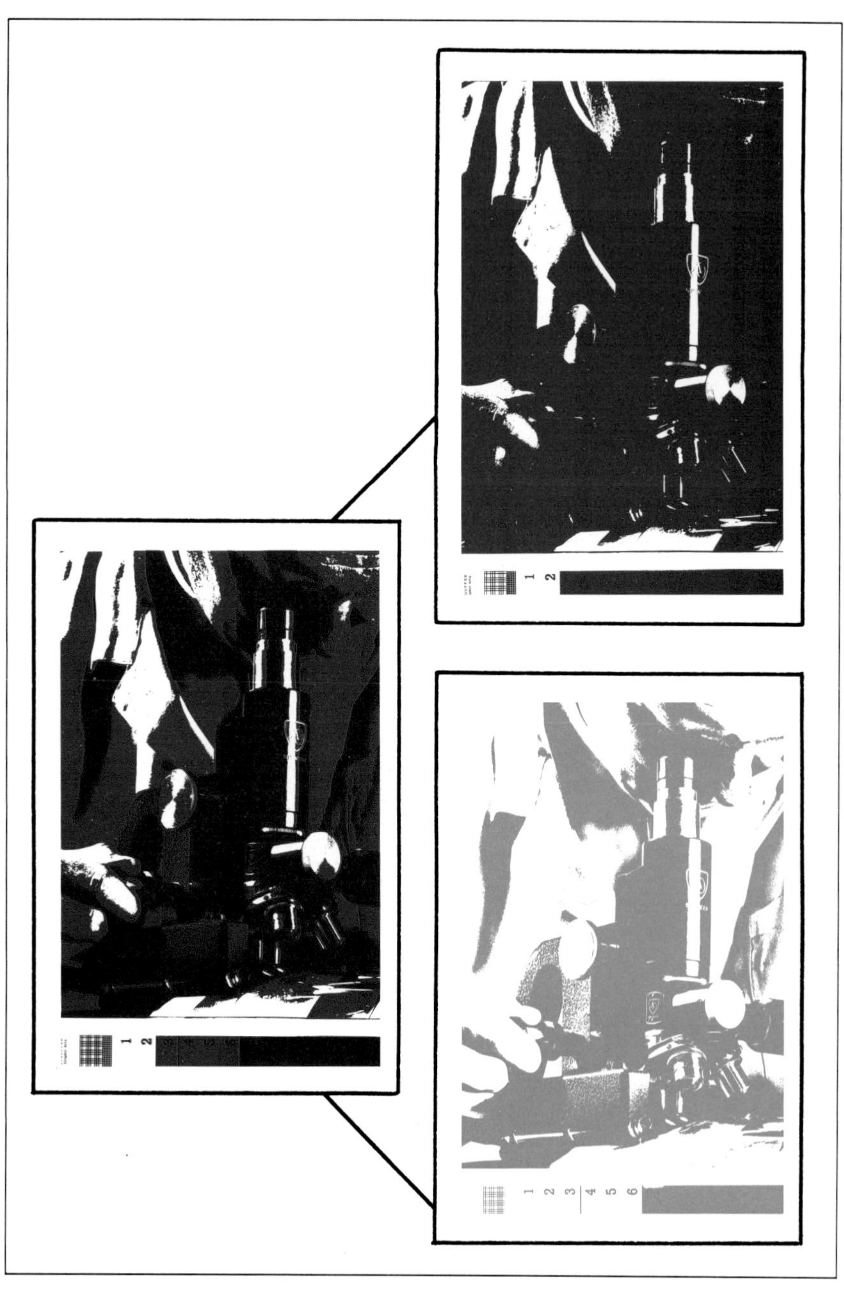

B
TWO-COLOR POSTERIZATION

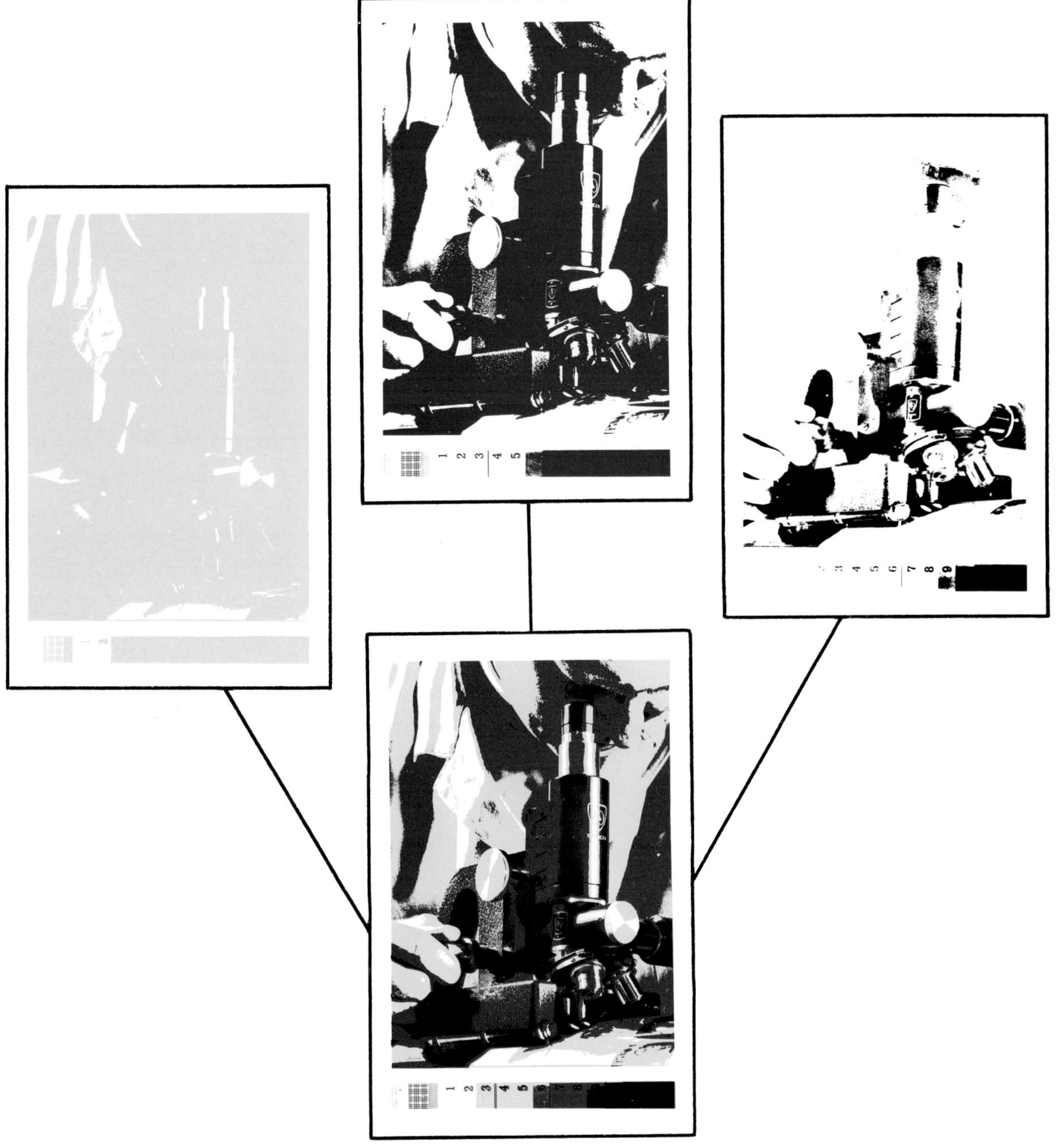

C
THREE-COLOR POSTERIZATION

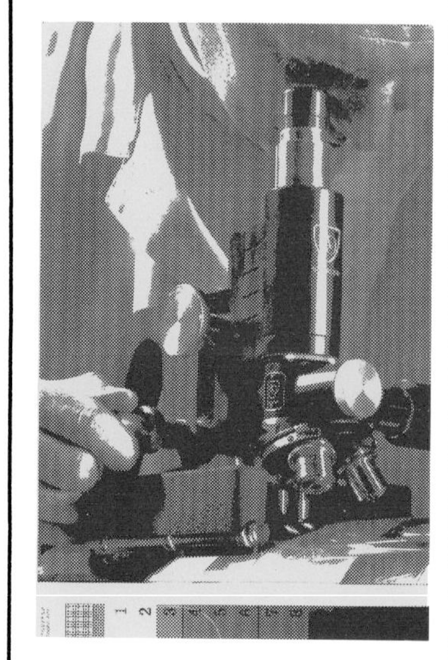

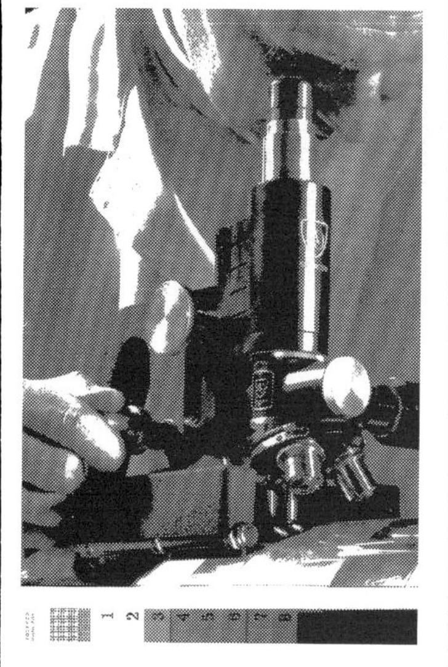

D

SINGLE-COLOR, THREE-TONE POSTERIZATION
(The yellow color represents a sheet of paper)

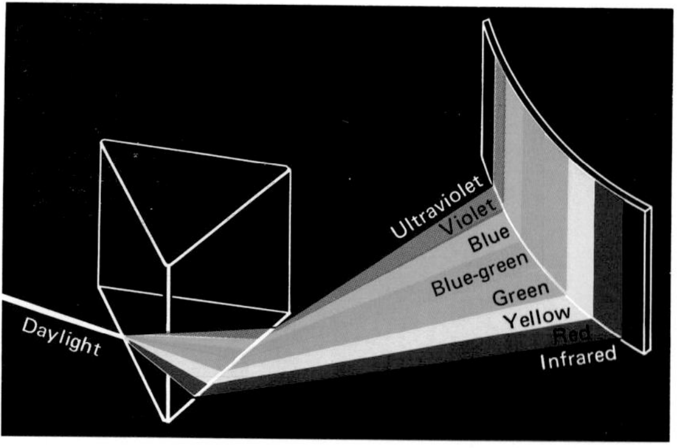

E
PRISM

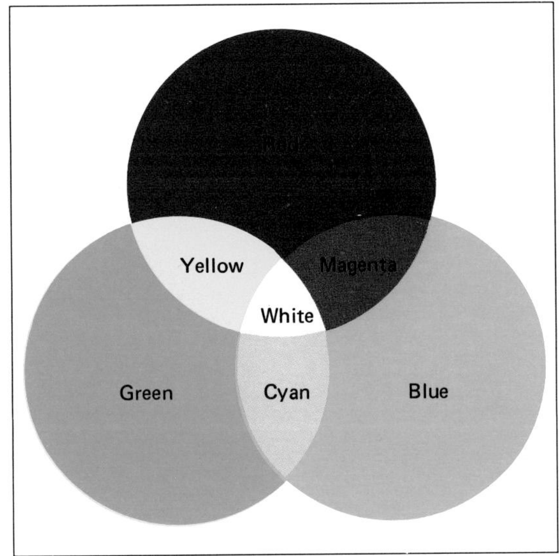
Yellow
Magenta
White
Green
Cyan
Blue

F

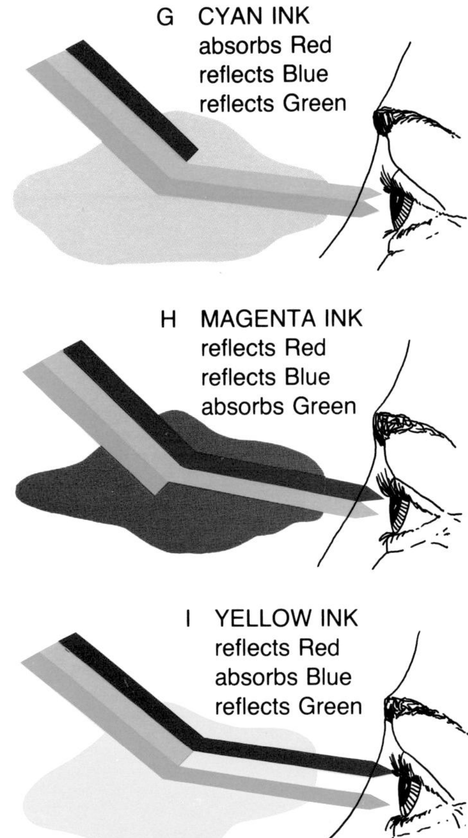
G CYAN INK
absorbs Red
reflects Blue
reflects Green
H MAGENTA INK
reflects Red
reflects Blue
absorbs Green
I YELLOW INK
reflects Red
absorbs Blue
reflects Green

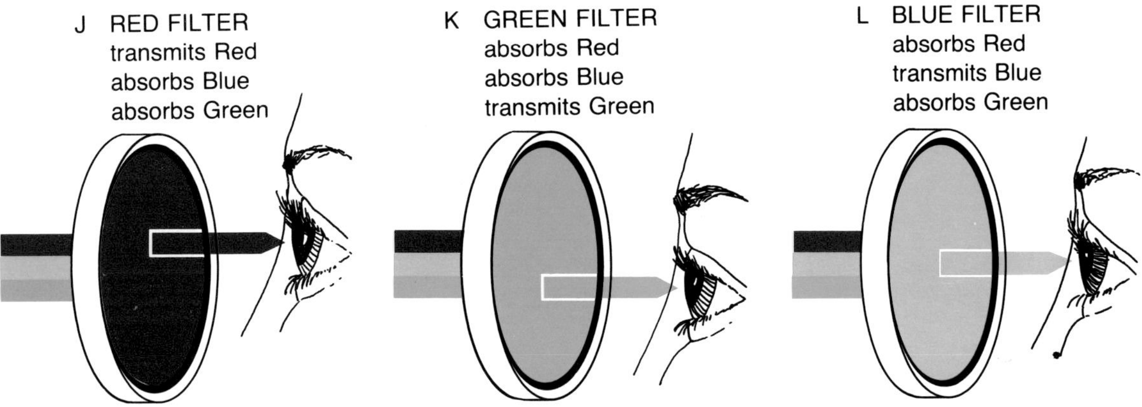
J RED FILTER
transmits Red
absorbs Blue
absorbs Green
K GREEN FILTER
absorbs Red
absorbs Blue
transmits Green
L BLUE FILTER
absorbs Red
transmits Blue
absorbs Green

Yellow proof

Magenta proof

Yellow plus Magenta

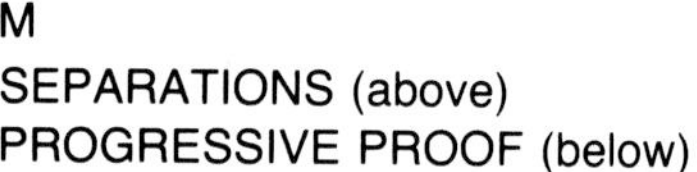

M
SEPARATIONS (above)
PROGRESSIVE PROOF (below)

From The Metropolitan Museum of Art, the Michael Friedsam Collection, 1931. (Detail)

Cyan proof

Black proof

Yellow, Magenta plus Cyan

Yellow, Magenta, Cyan plus Black

Ives early tricolor experiment. Original proof of tricolor halftone reproduction made by Frederic E. Ives about 1893. Perhaps the first three-color illustration ever produced with a crossline halftone screen. Courtesy of 3M Company, from the Joseph S. Mertle Collection.

Direct Screen Color Separation

The direct screen method produces color separation halftones in one step. In other words, the halftone and the color separations are made at the same time. This method has both cost and time advantages. Because the color separated halftone is produced in one step, fewer pieces of film are exposed, and operators spend less time producing a set of separations. Figure 9.3 (p. 196) illustrates the basic steps involved in the direct screen method. This method can be used with a contact system, an enlarger, or a camera.

The first step in any separation process is to produce the masks. Only two masks are made for direct screen separations. Figure 9.4 shows how each of the three systems—contact, enlarger, and camera—is set up to produce masks. These set-ups will be discussed in detail later in this chapter. The next step is to make the halftone and color separations using light that comes from the original and passes through the color separation filter, mask, halftone screen, and onto the film (figure 9.5, p. 206). The order of the items, through which light passes, will depend upon what type of equipment is used. Finally, the plates are made from the stripped negatives and run on the press.

Indirect Screen Color Separation

The indirect screen method first produces a continuous-tone separation negative (figure 9.6). Next, the continuous tone negative is screened to produce a halftone positive. The screened positive is then contact printed to make the final separation negative.

Each mask for this method is made exactly like direct screen separation masks are made (figure 9.4). The difference in making masks with the indirect screen method is that usually four masks, one for each separation negative, are made. After the masks are made, the indirect method completely differs from the direct method. A continuous-tone separation negative is now made from the original by using the appropriate mask and separation filter (figure 9.7, p. 208). The continuous-tone separation negative is contacted or projection printed to produce a halftone positive. The halftone positive can be made in a contact system or with a process camera (figure 9.8, p. 209). An enlarger is usually not used to produce the halftone positives because the continuous-tone negative is too large to fit in the negative carrier. Advantages of the indirect method are that the negatives can be retouched or enlarged. The opportunity to enlarge, for the second time, during the separation process allows the printer to produce large posters and display work.

Direct and indirect color separation can be done with a variety of equipment (such as a process camera, an enlarger, a contact printing system, or even an electronic scanner. A process camera can be used to separate either reflection copy, such as a color print, or transparencies (with a back-lighted copyboard). An enlarger or a contact printing system can only be used to separate transparent copy. A scanner can be used to separate either transparent or reflection copy.

Several variables need to be considered when selecting the method and equipment to use for color separation. Typical considerations include available money, type of copy to be separated, the enlargement-reduction factor required, and ultimate use for the separations. Fewer steps are involved with the direct method, so it is obviously faster than the indirect process. The additional steps can, however, be used to advantage for color correction and proofing. The fact that indirect separations are finally contacted to give the halftone negatives also produces a better dot structure.

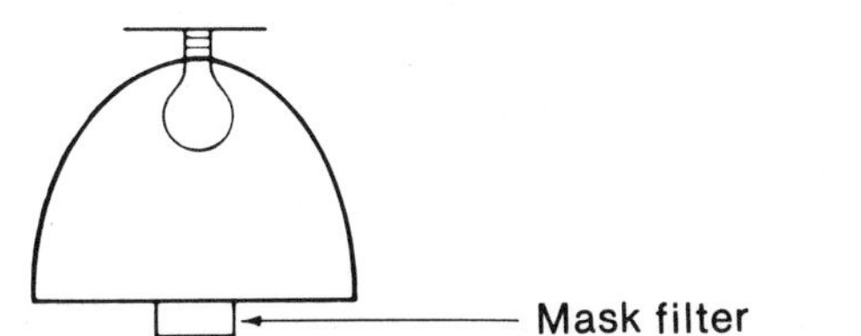

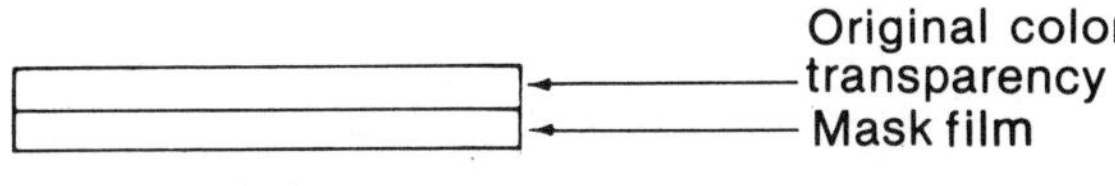

By contact printing and enlarger

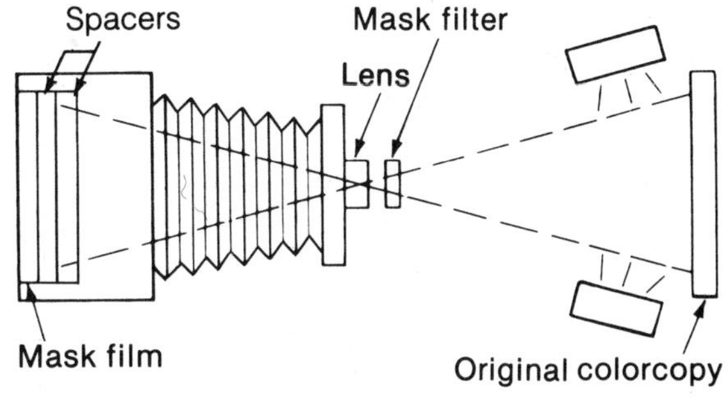

By camera

Figure 9.4. Making the color separation mask

Direct Screen Method—Transparent Copy

Using the direct screen method to make separations from transparencies is a very popular technique. The separations can be made using one of four ways: a contact system, an enlarger, a camera, or a scanner. The contact proc-

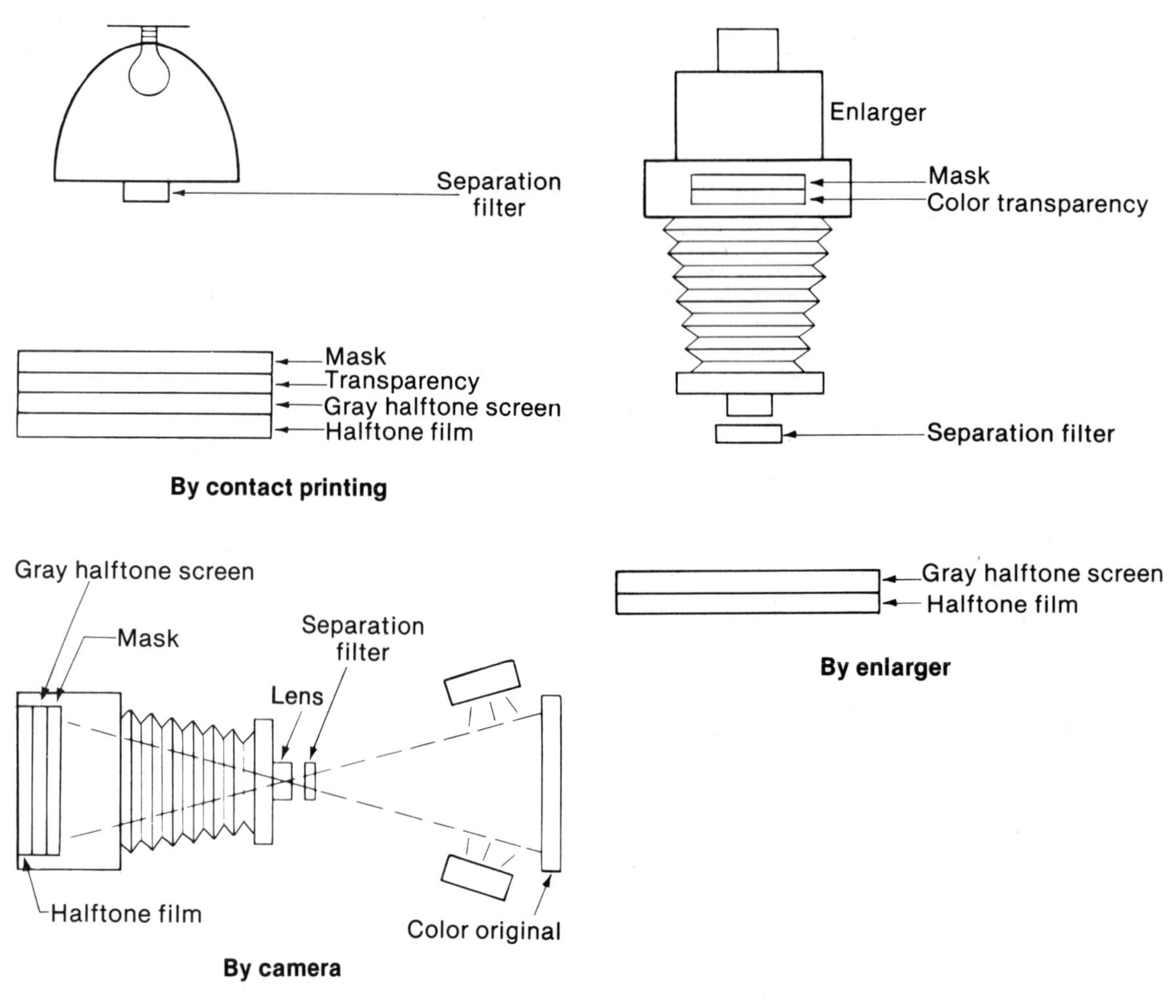

Figure 9.5. Making the color separation halftone negative

ess requires only a point light source with filter capability, filters, gray contact screens, and a vacuum frame or easel with a simple register system. The process is popular because the equipment is inexpensive to set up and frees the process camera for other production work.

With both the contact and the projection techniques, it is first necessary to produce a two-color correcting mask by contact printing from the transparency (figure 9.9a, p. 210). The final halftone separation negatives are made on high-contrast panchromatic film by using a sandwich of the transparency, mask,

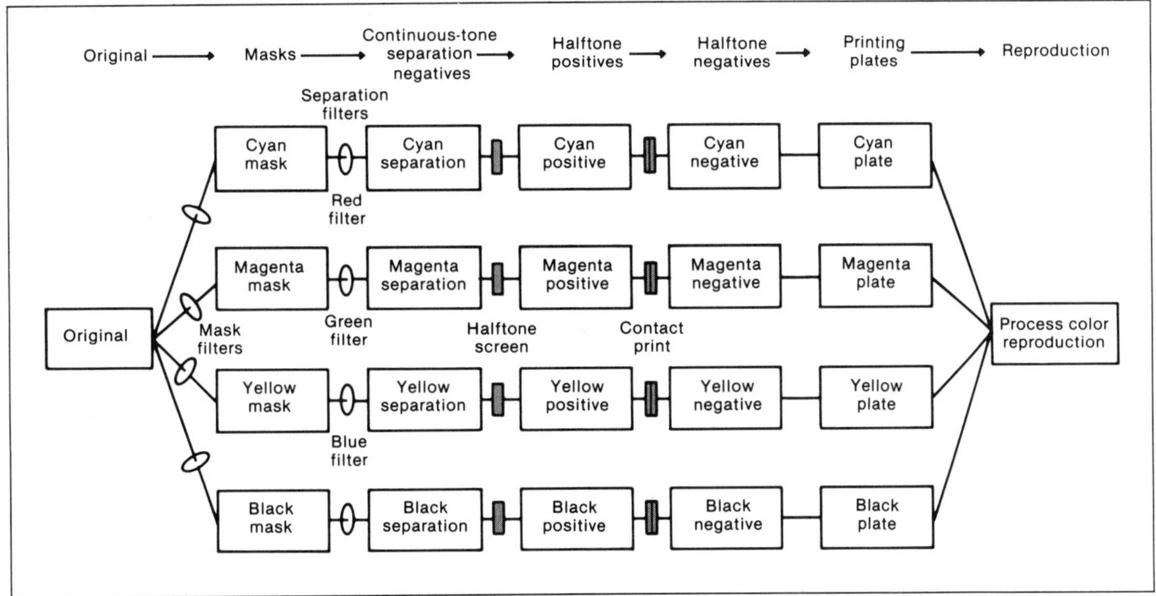

Figure 9.6. Diagram of indirect screen color separation

and gray screen with appropriate filtration (figure 9.9b). This process is described in detail in the last half of this chapter.

The projection direct screen method is generally used when a change from the original size is desired (figure 9.9c). The procedure is very similar to the contact method except that an enlarger projects the masked transparent image to the proper size through the halftone screen onto the film. An industrial enlarger is shown in figure 9.10, (p. 211).

If a change in size is necessary and no projection system is available, a duplicate transparency can be made to the proper size from the original and then separated by the contact technique. Several transparencies can be ganged together and separated at one time with the contact system, whereas only one image can be handled at a time with the enlarger.

Direct Screen Method —Reflection Copy

A process camera (or a scanner, but the scanner concept will be discussed separately) must be used to prepare color separations of reflection copy. Direct screen with a camera is not a popular method. With this process, the copy is placed in the camera copyboard and masks are produced to the desired size (figure 9.11a). Each halftone negative is made in a single step by exposing a sandwich consisting of the mask, halftone screen, and film through the appropriate filter (figure 9.11b). The main disadvantage is that the camera cannot be used for any other purpose until the entire set of separations is produced and approved. If the camera were moved, it would be impossible to reset it to the exact enlargement or reduction ratio.

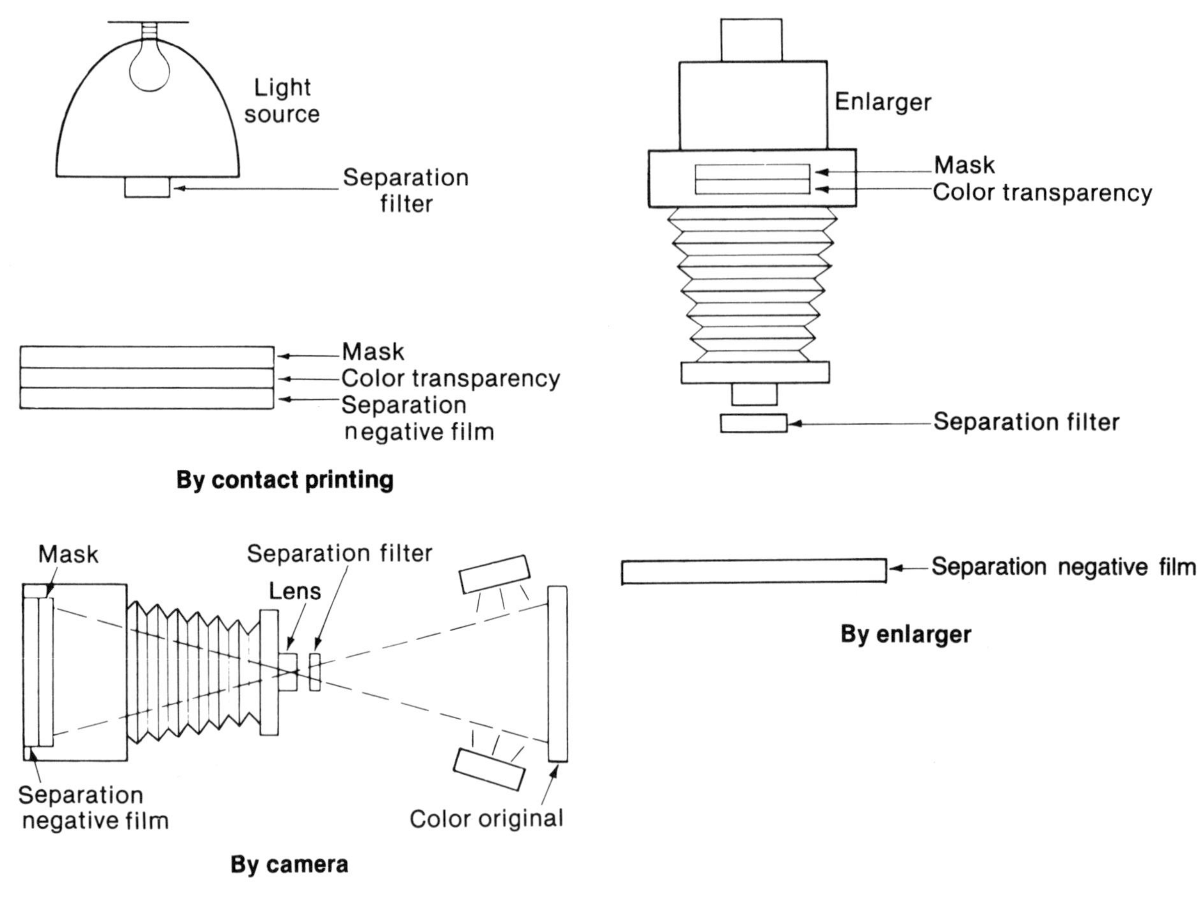

Figure 9.7. Making a continuous-tone separation negative

Indirect Screen Method—Transparent Copy

One of the oldest techniques of making color separations is with transparencies on a back-lighted process camera copyboard. Size changes can be made with an enlarger or can be allowed for on the camera. Masks are made with the proper filter by transmitting light through the transparency and the mask filter and onto the masking film (figure 9.12a, p. 213). Spacer film is used between the mask film and camera back. Spacer film moves the mask material away from the camera vacuum board a distance equal to the thickness of separation film. When the actual separations are made, the spacer film will be replaced by film material. In this way, there will be no size or focus distortion in the final product. Next, separation negatives are made by exposing

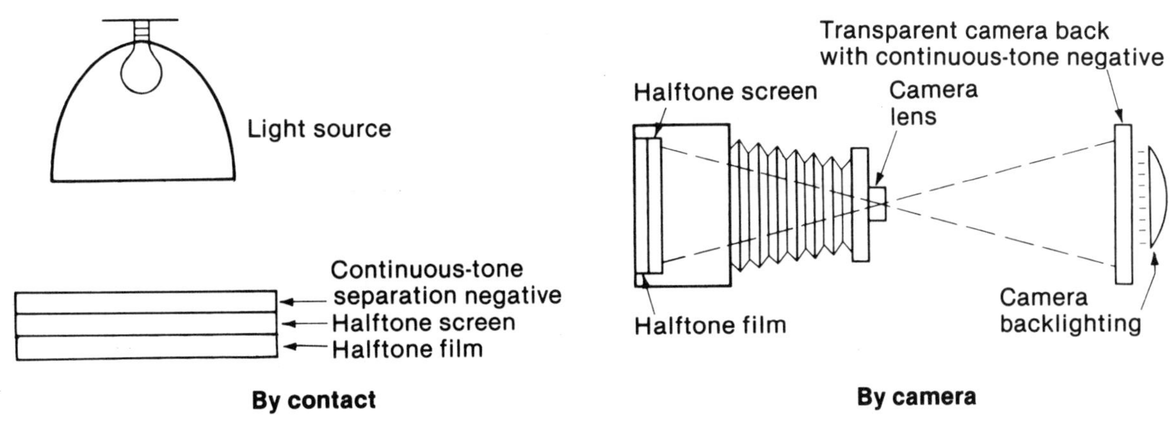

Figure 9.8. Making a color separation halftone positive

continuous-tone film through the proper filter and mask (figure 9.12b). The separation negative is then placed on the copyboard and exposed to ortho film through a halftone screen (figure 9.12c). The separation positive is then contacted to produce a halftone negative. Again, this technique requires that the camera be immobile during the entire process.

Indirect Screen Method —Reflection Copy

This technique is very similar to the indirect method for transparent copy. Masks are exposed by light reflecting from the copy (figure 9.13a, p. 214). A spacer film is placed behind the masking film so that the mask will be in focus when it is placed in front of the separation film in the following step. Next, continuous-tone separation negatives are made by photographing the original through the appropriate filter and mask (figure 9.13b). Positives can be made by contact printing or by placing the positives in the back-lighted copyboard (figure 9.13c). The final halftone negative separations are made by contact printing (figure 9.13d).

Color Separation by Electronic Scanning

The original concept of an electronic color scanner dates to around 1940, but it wasn't until 1949 that the first successful scanner was actually put into commercial operation. Until recently, industrial acceptance of scanners has been slow. It was the general feeling of the industry that contemporary photographic methods and color scanners were about the same in terms of final quality and cost. It was also obvious that scanners required a substantial initial investment. American printers did not accept the concept as readily as did the rest of the world. However, it is rapidly becoming a popular system for producing screened separation negatives directly from original color copy.

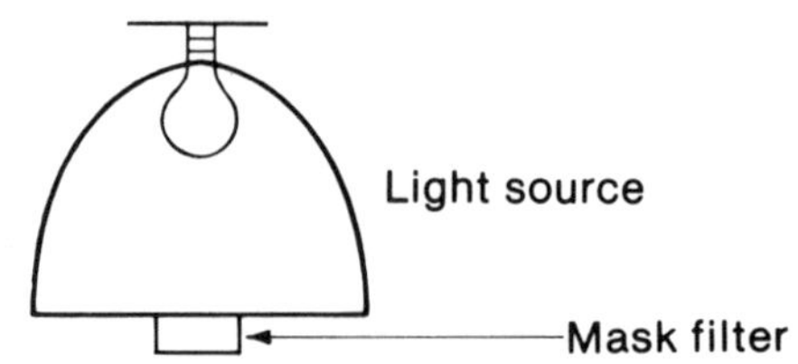

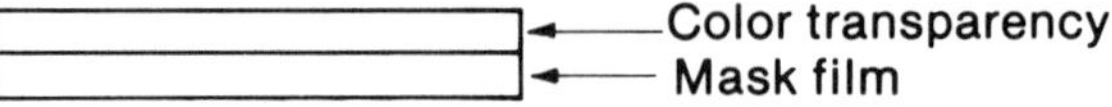

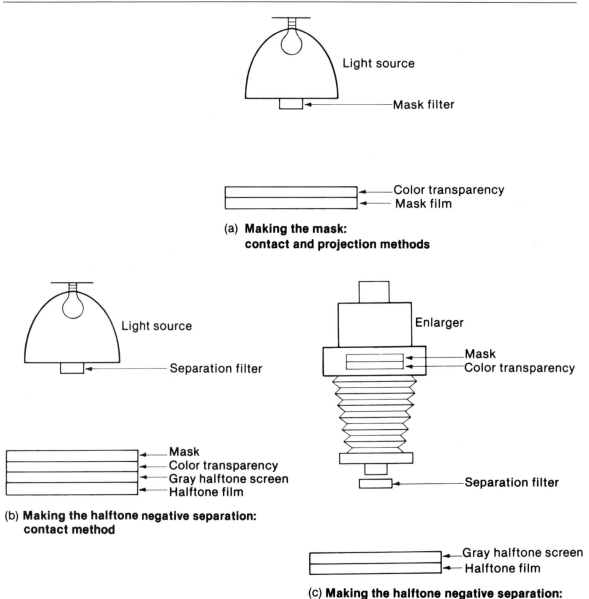

(a) **Making the mask: contact and projection methods**

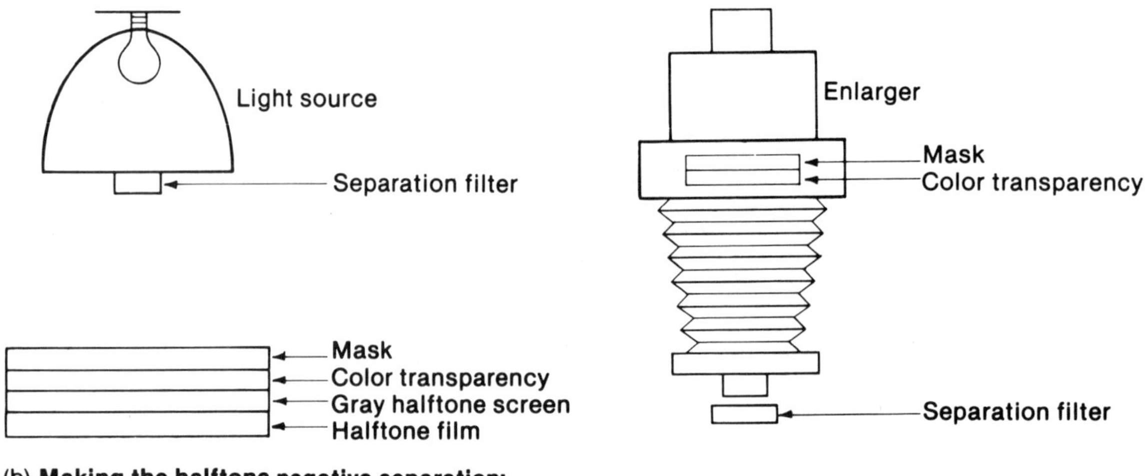

(b) **Making the halftone negative separation: contact method**

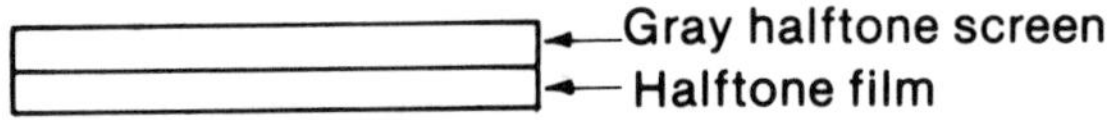

(c) **Making the halftone negative separation: projection method**

Figure 9.9. Contact and projection methods of direct screen color separation When the original copy is a transparency and the size of the reproduction is the same as that of the original, the contact method of separation is used. When the original is a transparency, but the size is changed in the reproduction, the projection method of separation is used.

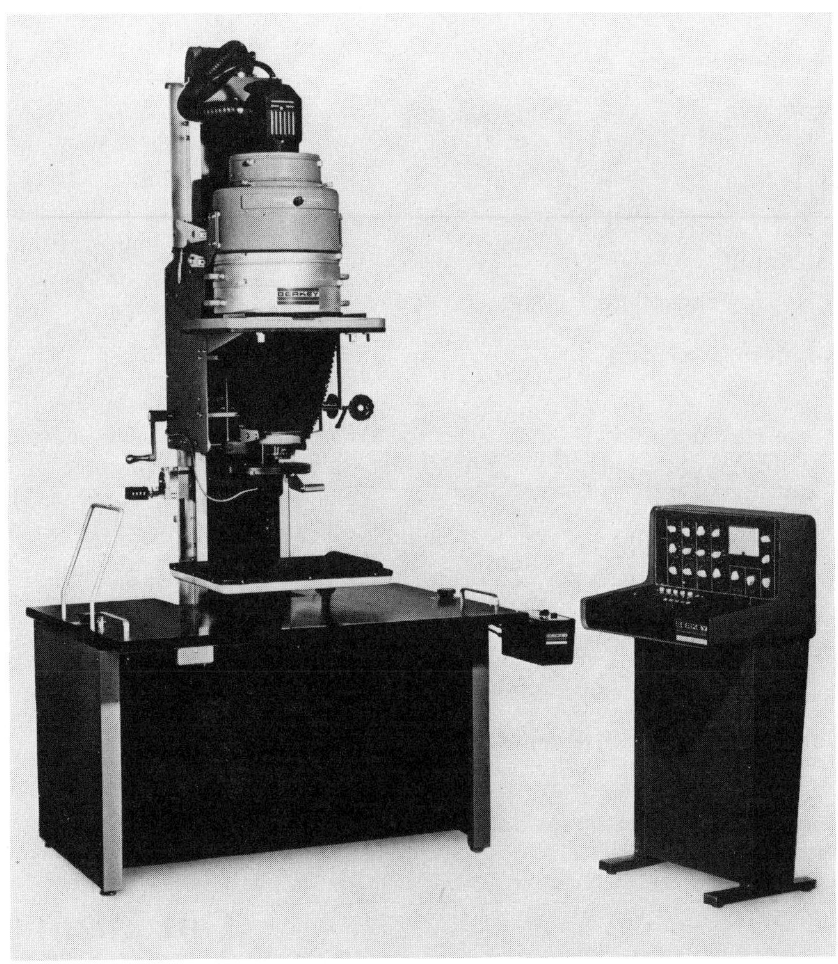

Figure 9.10. An industrial projection enlarger and color separator
Courtesy of Berkey Technical.

There are many reasons for the growing popularity of scanners. Electronics replaces several photographic steps. Separations can be output as continuous-tone or as screened halftones. Enlargements or reductions and negatives or positives can readily be programmed. Separations can easily be made from 35 mm transparencies and enlarged without grain exaggeration. Unlike the graininess produced when black-and-white negatives are greatly enlarged, electronic separations do not produce large-grain images. In addition, a scanner has the advantage of being able to compensate for deficiencies of the original copy, such as correcting poor color or tonal balance. The electronic color scanner (figure 9.14, p. 215) can accomplish the same operations done photographically

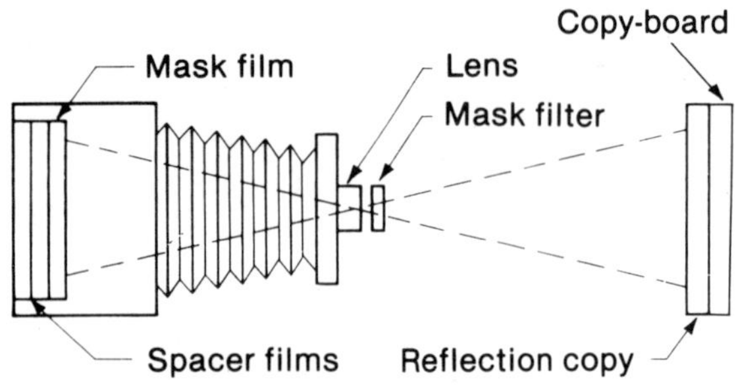

(a) **Making the mask**

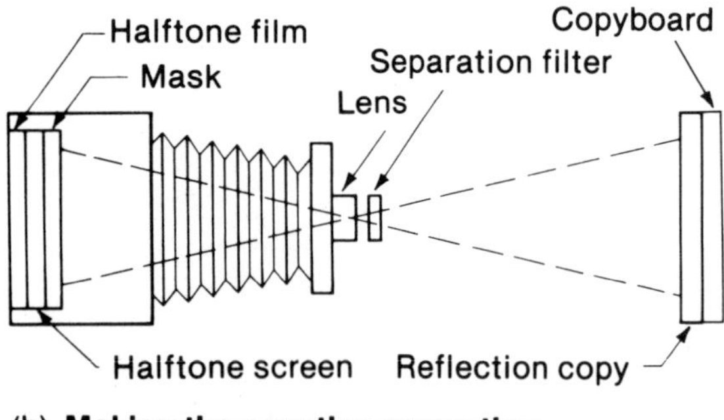

(b) **Making the negative separation**

Figure 9.11. Direct screen color separation from reflection copy

by the direct or indirect color separation methods. It separates the color original, whether transparent or reflection copy, into high-quality printers for the three subtractive colors and black.

Figure 9.15 illustrates the general principle of scanner operation. The scanner light source projects a narrow beam of light through transparent (or from reflection) copy through an aperture. Transmitted (or reflected) light is then gathered by three photocells covered with red, green, and blue separation filters. The cells generate signals that become the input for a computer. The computer then determines the amount of each printing ink needed to reproduce the scanned spot. At this point the program can control color correction or other modifications. The computer output then controls a lamp focused on photographic film. The lamp's exposure produces film density in proportion to the signal from the computer.

Figure 9.16 (p. 216) is a simplified schematic of the computer section. Incoming signals from the photocells are altered in the three sections of the computer. The first section converts the signals to amplified alternating current. The copy tonal range is then compressed to a usable range. Color correction and black printer calculations are performed in the second section. The signals entering this stage represent the amounts of additive colors (red, blue, and green) of the original. The signals leaving this stage represent the amounts of yellow, magenta, cyan, and black needed to reproduce the original.

Dot Etching

It is frequently necessary to alter individual separations to emphasize or deemphasize individual sections of color. The need for changes does not necessarily imply frequent errors or inexact processing controls, but rather is often done to specifications defined by the customer after seeing color proofs. **Dot etching** is a process that changes dot sizes on color separations with a liquid etch (a combination of potassium ferricyanide and sodium thiosulphate) that reduces the developed silver of the film emulsion.

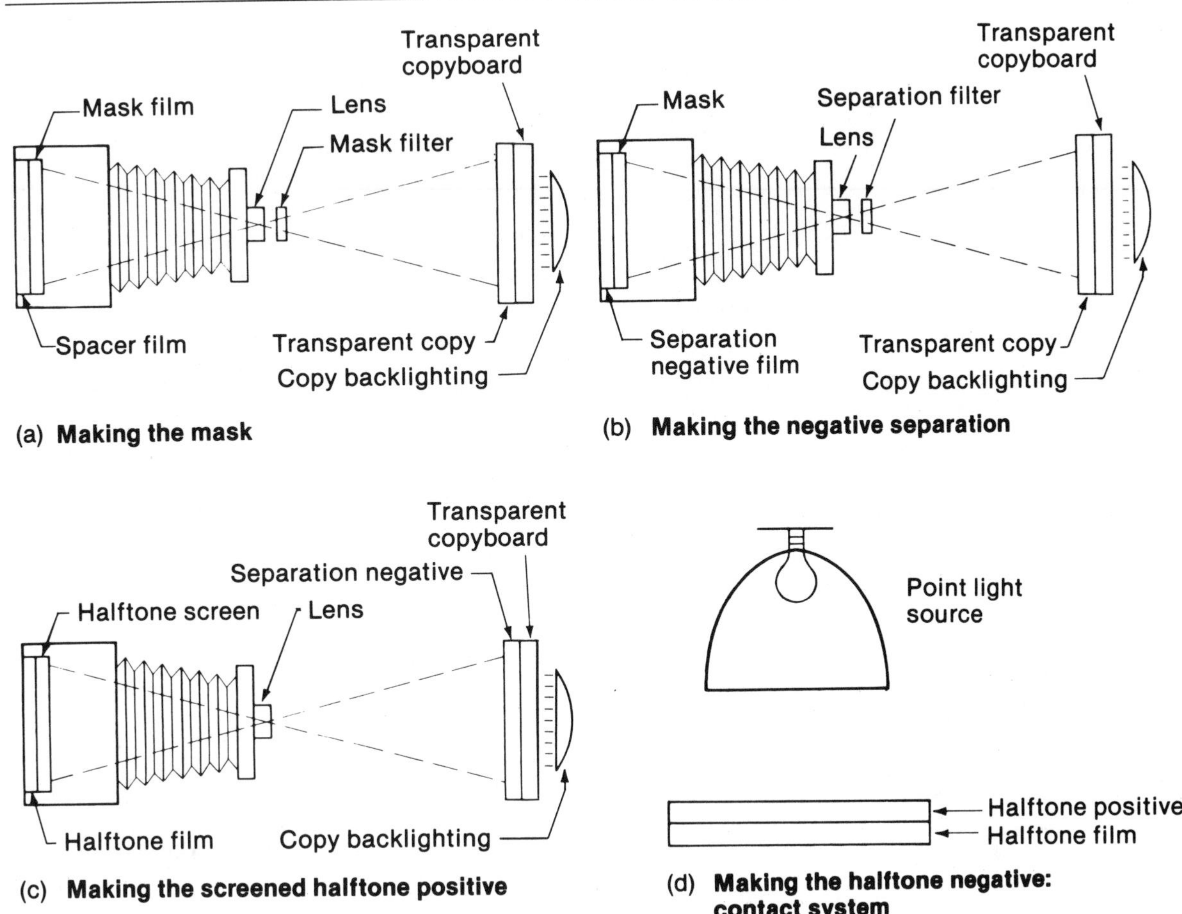

Figure 9.12. Indirect screen color separation from transparent copy

Both halftone and continuous-tone separations can be etched. Due to the shape of the halftone dot, the etch first affects the outer edges of the dot. Etching continuous-tone separations changes tonal values on the separation in order to obtain the desired dot size on its halftone reproduction. A diluted etch must be used because continuous-tone emulsions reduce rapidly.

Stain, a thin black liquid, is often used for adding highlight and shadow detail in small areas on continuous-tone images. Stain can also be used to reduce color on negatives or to add color on separation positives. **Re-**

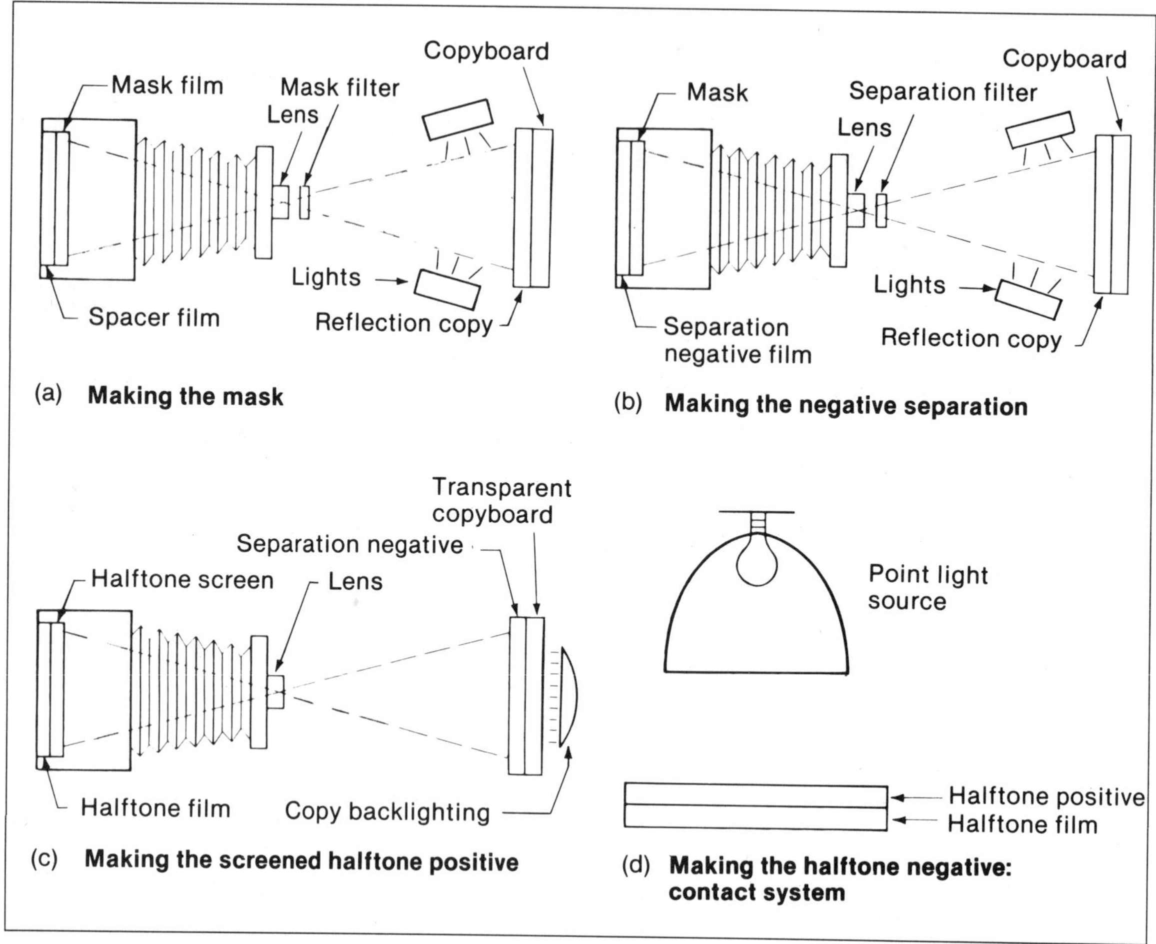

Figure 9.13. Indirect screen color separation from reflection copy

touching pencils are used to add fine line detail or to repair damaged film.

Once halftone positives are made, a set of proofs will indicate any necessary corrections. The areas needing correction are then marked. If the color needs to be increased in an area, a **staging solution** (an etch resist) is applied with a brush to all other parts of the film. To reduce the unstaged area, the film is immersed in a tray of etch solution (start with one-quarter potassium ferricyanide, one-quarter hypo, and one-half water).

Occasionally an area becomes over-etched. It is possible to bring up or restore an etched dot by an intensification process. The process requires two solutions: a bleach and a developer. The bleach is first applied to the

Figure 9.14. An industrial color scanner
Courtesy of HCM, Hell-Color Metal Corporation.

dot area needing intensification. The developer is then applied to the bleached area, and the original dot structure is made visible.

Making Color Separations By The Contact Direct Screen Method

Recall that the direct screen method can be used to produce screened separation negatives in one step, with the use of a camera, an enlarger, a scanner, or a contact printing system. The contact technique for direct screen color separation was chosen for closer examination for a number of reasons. The equipment requires the least amount of capital investment, uses fewer materials, and is

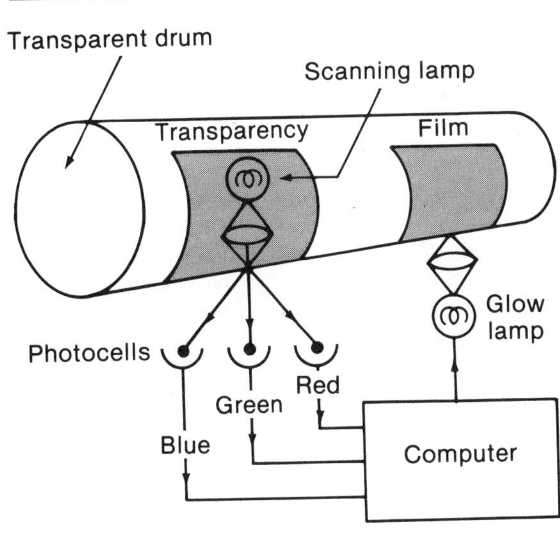

Figure 9.15. A schematic of scanner operation
Courtesy of Eastman Kodak.

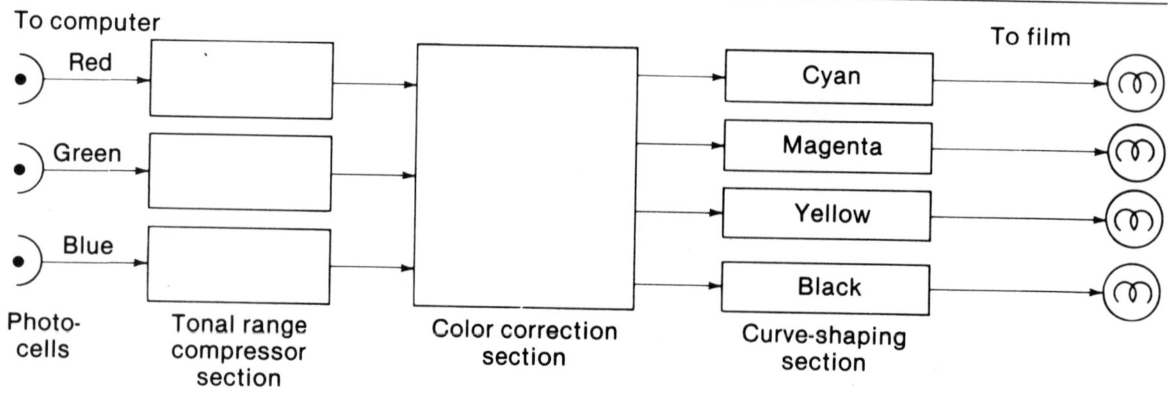

Figure 9.16. A simplified schematic of the computer section of a color scanner
Courtesy of Eastman Kodak.

faster than any other method. The process does not tie up a camera. Someone with little color experience can produce high-quality, final size screened negatives that are ready to be stripped and plated. The process requires the use of transparencies, which are enjoying increased popularity among commercial photographers.

Equipment

The primary concern is to set up a system that can produce repeatable and predictable results. Initial efforts will be spent in determining exposures or "calibrating" for various mask and separation exposures. If the voltage fluctuates and timers are inaccurate, the exposure will not be repeatable. A point light source (figure 9.17) with variable voltage controls (tap settings), an accurate timer (figure 9.18), and a line voltage stabilizer are recommended. Intimate contact between masks and screened separations is necessary, so a vacuum frame or easel is also recommended.

A halftone screen should be prepared so that it can be angled when producing the four separation negatives. This is done by cutting and punching the screen to obtain the proper screen angles. One combination of angles is cyan, 45°; magenta, 75°; yellow, 90°; and black, 105°. A template is available from the Eastman Kodak Company to help cut a contact screen. The authors use a set of preangled screens that can be purchased through a local graphic arts supplier.

Regardless of the screen type (preangled or cut), it is necessary to punch the material to fit a set of register pins in the vacuum frame. This requires the purchase of some type of **register punch** (figure 9.19). When punching preangled screens, place the reference edge indicated by the manufacturer against the head stops of the register punch.

It will be necessary to purchase a variety of filters to be used in the point light source. The authors use 3-inch Kodak gelatin filters mounted in filter frames. These filter packs can easily be pregrouped and placed in the

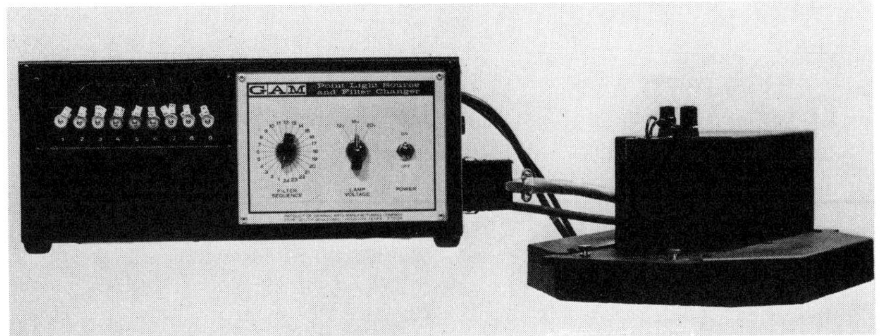

Figure 9.17. A point light source with variable voltage control and filter changer
Courtesy of Graphic Arts Manufacturing Co.

filter frame holder under the point light source as needed. If your contact system includes an automatic filter wheel, filter packs can be selected by the flip of a switch. The following filter packs are necessary when using Kodalith Pan Masking film 4570 to produce the required masks and Kodalith Pan film 2568 (Estar Base) for making the negative separations;

- Pack #1 (33) for making the cyan and magenta mask*
- Pack #2 (58) for making the yellow and black mask
- Pack #3 (23A + 1.60 ND filter) for making the cyan separation negative bump exposure
- Pack #4 (23A + .60 ND filter) for making the cyan separation negative main exposure
- Pack #5 (58 filter only) for making the magenta separation main exposure
- Pack #6 (47B filter only) for making the yellow separation main exposure
- Pack #7 (85B filter only) for making the black separation exposure
- Pack #8 (a total of 3.5 ND) for making flash exposures

*The numbers indicated refer to Kodak filter numbers. The letters ND stand for "neutral density."

Preparing the Transparencies for Color Separation

The transparencies must be of exact size to be separated by the contact direct screen method. If they are not of proper reproduction size and are positive transparencies, they can be commercially duplicated to the exact size. If the originals are reflection copy or negatives, they should also be photographically converted to reproduction size as positive transparencies.

The first step is to strip the exact-size transparencies along with some quality control devices into a **stable-base jig** (figure 9.20). The jig the authors use is a piece of ortho film exposed to a negative consisting of register marks and then developed. The jig was exposed to obtain a density of between 0.7 and 1.0 (the average density of a normal transparency). The chemical used for processing was HC–110 (dilution D). The jig was devel-

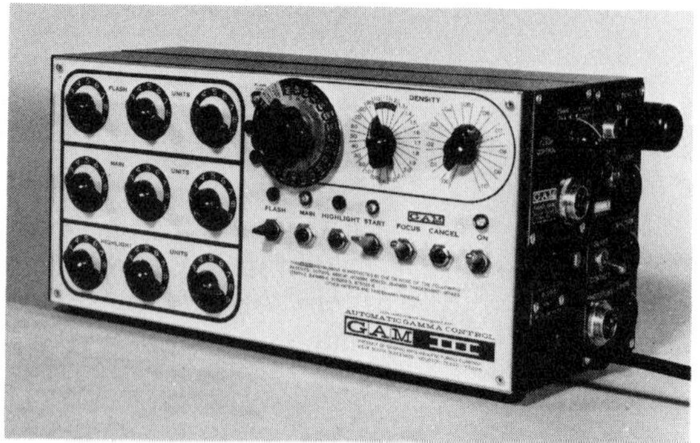

Figure 9.18. A sophisticated light control system
Courtesy of Graphic Arts Manufacturing Co.

Figure 9.19. A register punch
Courtesy of Berkey Technical.

oped for the recommended time of 3 minutes. The exposure was 15 seconds through a 1.0 ND filter at a 20V tap setting with a 3½-foot light-to-film distance.

The purpose of this average density jig is to prevent density distortion of the A, M, and B patches on the three-point transparency guide, which will be one of the control devices in the jig (figure 9.20). Possible distortion of these densities could occur from what is termed the **developer adjacency effect.** Whenever small patches are surrounded by large black areas, the patches receive less development because the large areas cause local exhaustion of the developer. It is not necessary to use such a jig, but it is important to surround any control device with at least 1 inch of average density. Use of the jig will eliminate any possibility of density distortion.

Figure 9.20 shows a jig containing two transparencies to be separated, a Kodak Three-Point Transparency Guide, and a transparent gray scale. Strip all items in the jig so they are in the right-reading position. Punch the jig for registration purposes. It would also be good practice to scribe additional register marks in the emulsion side of the transparencies' borders.

If there is an obvious density difference between the transparencies to be separated, visually balance them with neutral density sheeting. Place the jig on a light table and place the sheeting over the lighter one to obtain a rough visual match. Save these sheets for use when making the separation negatives. Neutral density sheeting can be made by exposing orthochromatic film at various times with the point light source and processing it in a continuous-tone developer such as HC–110 (dilution D).

Exposing, Processing, and Evaluating Masks

While the white lights are on, prepare the contact area to make the mask exposures. Carefully clean the table surface, vacuum frame glass, filters, and jig contents. Unacceptable separations will be produced if the entire system isn't spotlessly clean. Place filter pack #1 in the filter frame holder of the point light source and place pack #2 where it can easily be reached. A trial exposure time can be determined from the film manufacturer's recommendations. The authors use 50 seconds at a 15-volt setting to expose the #1 mask. Next, place the film (Kodak Pan Masking film 4570) and register punch in an area where working in total darkness will be easy. Then fasten register pins (usually two) to the base of the vacuum frame or easel. To obtain proper alignment, punch a used piece of film and use it as a guide to tape down the register pins. It is a good idea to check the pin position with the size of the halftone screen before finally securing them to the surface.

Turn off all the lights and punch a piece of pan masking film. Place the film, emulsion side toward the exposing source, on the register pins. Then position the jig, emulsion-side down, over the masking film, also on the register pins. With the jig and film in intimate contact by use of the vacuum frame, make the exposure. Place the exposed mask #1 in a box and remove filter pack #1. Insert pack #2 (58 + diffusion filter) and repeat the same steps as for mask #1. Cut off one corner of mask #1 and two corners of mask #2 so you can later identify the separate masks.

Develop the masks for 3¼ minutes in Kodak HC–110 (dilution D) developer at 68°F (20°C) with continuous agitation. After the film is dry, measure the A, M, and B patches of the three-point guide with a transmission densitometer and record the densities. It is important to keep accurate information on exposure times for all steps. A data sheet (figure 9.21) should be made in order to keep accurate records. The photographer is primarily concerned with two figures: the A–B

Figure 9.20. Example of a stable-base jig
Shown is a stable-base jig containing transparencies, a transparency guide, and a gray scale.
Courtesy of Kenneth E. Fay.

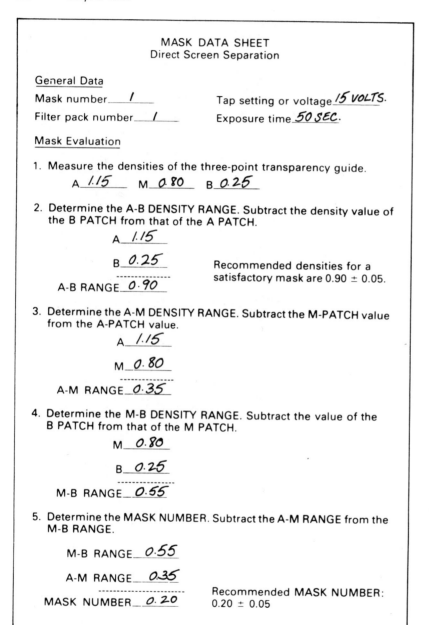

MASK DATA SHEET
Direct Screen Separation

General Data

Mask number 1 Tap setting or voltage 15 VOLTS.

Filter pack number 1 Exposure time 50 SEC.

Mask Evaluation

1. Measure the densities of the three-point transparency guide.
   A 1.15 M 0.80 B 0.25

2. Determine the A-B DENSITY RANGE. Subtract the density value of the B PATCH from that of the A PATCH.

   A 1.15

   B 0.25

   A-B RANGE 0.90

   Recommended densities for a satisfactory mask are 0.90 ± 0.05.

3. Determine the A-M DENSITY RANGE. Subtract the M-PATCH value from the A-PATCH value.

   A 1.15

   M 0.80

   A-M RANGE 0.35

4. Determine the M-B DENSITY RANGE. Subtract the value of the B PATCH from that of the M PATCH.

   M 0.80

   B 0.25

   M-B RANGE 0.55

5. Determine the MASK NUMBER. Subtract the A-M RANGE from the M-B RANGE.

   M-B RANGE 0.55

   A-M RANGE 0.35

   MASK NUMBER 0.20

   Recommended MASK NUMBER: 0.20 ± 0.05

Figure 9.21. Example of a mask data sheet

range and the mask number. The recommended densities for a satisfactory mask are an A–B range of 0.90 ± 0.05 and a mask number of 0.20 ± 0.05.

To determine the A–B density range, subtract the value of the B patch from the value of the A patch. The A–M density range is found by subtracting the M patch value from the A patch value. The M–B density range is obtained by subtracting the value of the B patch from that of the M patch. The mask number is calculated by subtracting the A–M range from the M–B range. If the mask number or A–B range is not within the allowable tolerances, the mask must be remade. The A–B range can be adjusted by increasing or decreasing development time. The mask number is adjusted by increasing or decreasing exposure time. By doubling or halving the exposure, a density change of 0.20 should occur. When properly exposed, mask B density should be between 0.10 and 0.30.

Problems will most likely be encountered when first determining proper exposures for the mask. Kodak's publication, Q–7A, *Silver Masking of Transparencies with Three-Aim-Point Control,* suggests detailed steps for mask corrections:

If The Mask Number is Low *and the A–B Range is Low:* Increase development time to increase the A–B range. If the mask number is only slightly low, no exposure change is needed. The increased development will raise the mask number slightly. If the mask number is very low, increase exposure time slightly.

and the A–B Range is Correct: Increase exposure time to raise the mask number. If you use a very large exposure increase, decrease development time slightly to hold the A–B range constant.

and the A–B Range is High: Increase exposure time to raise the mask number. Decrease development time to decrease the A–B range.

If The Mask Number Is Correct *and the A–B Range is Low:* Increase development time to increase the A–B range. This development increase will also tend to raise the mask number. Decrease exposure time slightly to hold the mask number constant.

and the A–B Range is Correct: No change necessary.

and the A–B Range is High: Decrease development time to decrease the A–B range. Since decreased development will tend to lower the mask number, you may need to increase exposure time slightly to hold the mask number constant.

If The Mask Number Is High *and the A–B Range is Low:* Decrease exposure time to lower the mask number. Increase development time to increase the A–B range.

and the A–B Range is Correct: Decrease the exposure time to lower the mask number. If you use a very large exposure decrease, you may need to increase development time slightly to hold the A–B range constant.

and the A–B Range is High: Decrease development time to decrease the A–B range. If the mask number is only slightly high, this development decrease will also tend to correct the mask number. If the mask number is very high, decrease exposure time slightly.

Kodak also suggests the following rough guides to adjustments:

> A change of 5% in exposure time will change the mask number by approximately 0.01.
>
> A change of 3% in development time will change the A–B range by approximately 0.02.

The basic problem with any system is first to determine the exposure and development times that produce consistent and predictable quality results. Once the first successful set of masks has been made, it is important to continue to use the same procedures. The only variation would come for transparencies with radically different densities and tonal ranges.

Exposing, Processing, and Evaluating Screened Negative Separations

With the normal room lights on, set up the contact system to expose the cyan separation negative. Insert filter pack #3 (23A + 1.60 ND filter) for the bump exposure. The pack contains an added 1.0 neutral density to produce a 10% bump effect. Pack #4 (23A + .60 ND filter) is without the added density and is intended for the second or main cyan exposure. Set the timer for a trial bump of 15 seconds and place the tap setting to 20 volts. Place the cyan mask (mask #1), film, screen (45° angle), #4 filter pack, and #8 filter pack near the vacuum frame so that everything can easily be found in the dark. Be certain that everything is dust free.

Turn off all the room lights and punch a sheet of film (the authors use Kodalith Pan film 2568). Place a sheet of punched pan film emulsion-side up on the register pins. Do not use diffusion sheeting when making the separation negatives. The transparency jig goes next, with the right-reading side against the emulsion side of the film. It will help you identify the correct side in the dark if the jig is notched like pan film. Place the cyan mask in register with the transparency (see figure 9.5b). Turn on the vacuum frame and make the bump (no-screen) exposure. While still under totally dark conditions, replace the #3 pack with the #8 (3.5 ND filter) set. Remove the mask and transparency and place the 45° angled halftone screen on the register pins (emulsion-side down) over the film. Set the timer for a 20-second flash exposure. Activate the vacuum frame and make the flash exposure. Next add the transparency jig and mask and insert filter pack #4 (23A + .60 ND filter). Again turn on the vacuum frame and make an exposure identical to the first bump time. Remove the film, cut off one corner for identification, and store the sheet in a spare box.

With the white lights on again, ready the system to produce the magenta separation. Insert filter pack #8 (3.5 ND filter) and set the timer for a trial flash exposure of 20 seconds. Place the 75° angled screen, the magenta mask, and the #5 filter pack where they can easily be found in the dark.

Turn off all the lights and put a sheet of punched pan film on the register pins. Place the halftone screen (75° angle) emulsion-side down over the film. Turn on the vacuum pump and make the flash exposure. Then place the transparency and the #1 mask over the film. Insert filter pack #5 (58 filter) in the filter frame holder, set the timer for 25 seconds, activate the vacuum pump, and make the main exposure. Notch two corners of the magenta negative separation and place it in the spare box with the cyan sheet.

Again turn on the room lights and set up the system to expose the yellow negative by using the procedures established for the cyan and magenta printers. Try a 20-second flash and an 80-second main exposure. Use pack #8 (3.5 ND) for the flash exposure and pack #6 (47B filter) for the main exposure. Place the screen at 90° and use mask #2 over the transparency when making the main exposure. Cut three corners off the yellow separation and place it in the box.

The black separation will require only a main exposure using filter pack #7 (85B filter) with mask #2 at approximately 20 seconds. Be sure that the screen angle is 105°.

Develop the separation negatives in Kodalith Super RT Developer for 2¾ minutes at 68°F (20°C). Use continuous agitation processing and follow the procedures recommended in the film instruction sheet.

The cyan separation is the key printer. First examine the highlight dot. The desired highlight dot size will depend on the printing process to be used and the quality of the system. When making separations for offset lithography, the cyan printer should carry a highlight dot of between 90 and 95%.

If the cyan highlight is not of the proper size, you must make an exposure adjustment. Remember that halftone highlights are controlled by the main exposure. The A patch will represent the highlight areas. You can determine a new main exposure time by using the Kodak Direct-Screen Color-Separation Dial. Use the "exposure adjustment dial" by setting the exposure of the first attempt opposite the dot area value of patch A that resulted from that time. As an example, assume that an exposure of 15 seconds produced a dot area value of 75%. Place the 15-second line opposite the 75% point. Without moving the dial, read the recommended exposure opposite a 90% dot. The second attempt should use a 22-second main exposure.

After obtaining the proper highlight dot for the cyan separation, read the A, M, and B patches on a transmission densitometer or dot area meter. Using the reverse side of the Kodak Direct-Screen Color-Separation Dial, set the percent dot value of the A patch at the black line in the A window of the cyan scale on the dial. The M and B windows will then give the recommended values for the M and B patches of the cyan printer. Check these recommended values against the actual M and B readings. If they do not agree with the aim points, the flash exposure must be adjusted. The exposure adjustment dial can also be used to determine new flash exposures.

Once the cyan printer has been correctly produced, the values for the magenta and yellow separations can be obtained by using the initial cyan settings. The separation dial will show at the cyan settings the recommended A, M, and B values for magenta and yellow and will also recommend the dot area value for the black printer in the B patch.

After a set of separations has been successfully produced within the tolerances of the aim points, they must be proofed. The following chapter deals with the problems and procedures of negative stripping and proofing.

The purpose of this chapter has not been to provide extremely detailed procedures for all aspects of process color photography. The basic concepts of light and color were reviewed, a conceptual overview of industrial techniques was presented, and one method of color separation was examined in detail. The information provided, however, is more than sufficient for individuals to set up a color system to prepare acceptable subtractive color separations. For those desiring more detailed or additional information, several resources are listed in the bibliography.

Key Terms

process color photography
subtractive primary colors
additive primary colors
masking
direct screen color separation
indirect screen color separation
dot etching
stain
retouching pencil
staging solution
stable-base jig
developer adjacency effect

Questions for Review

1. What are the subtractive primary colors?
2. What are the additive primary colors?
3. When using subtractive primary inks, what color would result from a combination of yellow and magenta?
4. What is the purpose of adding a black printer if a combination of three subtractive inks will approximate all colors?
5. What are the three purposes of masking in color separation?
6. What are the two general methods of making color separations?
7. What is the advantage of the direct screen contact technique of color separation?
8. What are several advantages of color separation by electronic scanning over other techniques?
9. What is the purpose of dot etching color separations?

Chapter Ten

Stripping and Proofing

Anecdote to Chapter Ten

Stripping refers to the process of preparing and positioning a piece of film for exposure to a printing plate. The term originally described a process, commonly used as recently as the 1950s, in which a wet emulsion was removed from a special "stripping film." Stripping film was cumbersome to work with when compared to today's flexible, stable-base photographic materials, but at the time it was considered an efficient, simple process.

The stripper could use a variety of techniques. One of the most common was to manufacture the film from existing materials in the darkroom. The process started with the careful cleaning of a sheet of glass. The glass was then polished with a soft rag and a powder called "French chalk." Next, substratum of rubber solution or egg albumen solution was poured on the glass, followed by a layer of rubber and naphtha. The final layer was a light-sensitive stripping emulsion.

While the emulsion was still wet, the plate was rushed to the camera and an exposure was made of the image to be reproduced. The

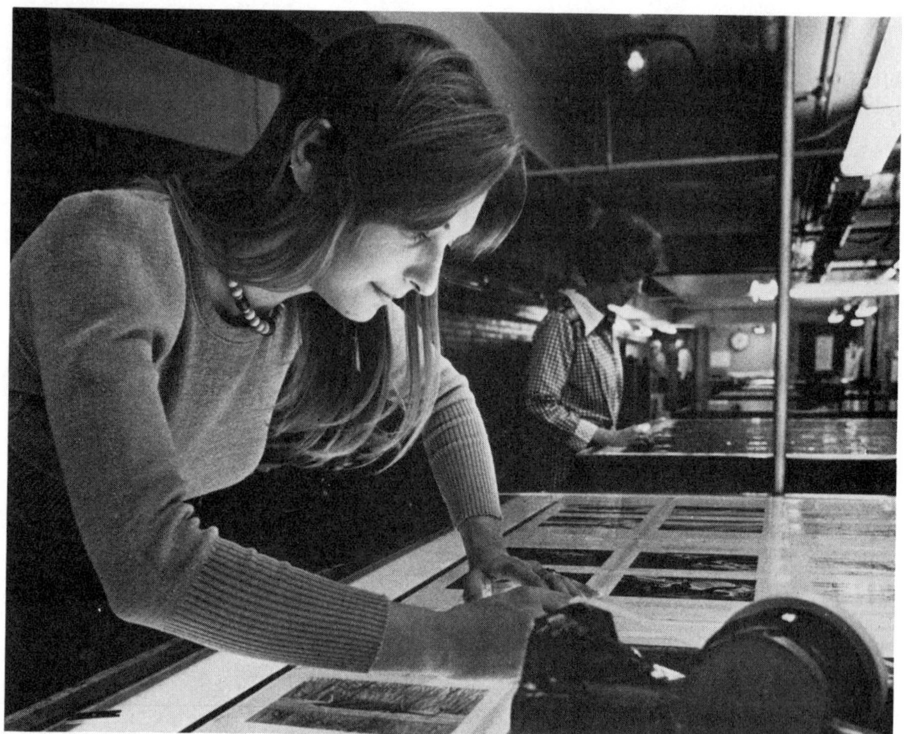

Stripping film on a light table
Courtesy of Kingsport Press, an Arcata National Company.

plate was then taken to the developing area and the image processed to the required depth. The wet plate then went back to the stripper, who immersed it in an acetic acid-water bath.

When the emulsion began to lift, the stripper started at one corner and actually stripped the membrane from the plate. While this was going on, another worker prepared a new glass plate by covering it with a small pool of gum solution. The wet emulsion was positioned on the second plate and finally squeegeed into place. Depending on the printing process used, the emulsion could be placed on the plate either right or wrong reading. If a halftone or new piece of line work needed to be added, the stripper used a sharp knife to cut away the unwanted area and put a new wet piece in its place.

Even though wet strippers would probably not recognize the materials used today, it would take little retraining for them to function at a modern light table. The task of positioning film images remains the same, and they would probably feel accepted because they would still be called "strippers."

Objectives for Chapter Ten

After completing this chapter you will be able to:

- Understand the purpose of stripping and proofing in the printing processes.
- Recognize the equipment and supplies used in stripping and proofing.
- Recall and explain the basic stripping steps.
- Describe several methods of multiflat registration that include common edge, snap fitter and dowel, and punch and register pin.
- Recall and explain the basic methods of preparing single-color proofs.
- Describe the techniques of preparing both opaque and transparent color proofs.

Introduction

This chapter is divided into two main sections. The first section describes the sequences of steps used to work with film, prior to making a printing plate. This operation is called stripping. The second section deals with methods of checking the quality and the accuracy of the position of the stripped film images. This process is called proofing.

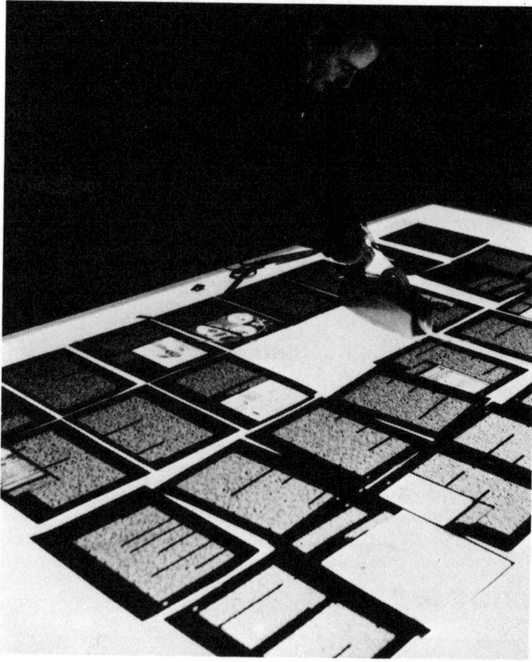

Figure 10.1. A glass-topped light table On this light table, negatives for a 32-page signature are being assembled and stripped.
Courtesy of Pre-Press Co., Inc.

Stripping is the process of assembling all pieces of film containing images that will be carried on the same printing plate and securing them on a masking sheet that will hold them in their appropriate printing positions during the plate-making process. The assembled masking sheet with attached pieces of film is called a **flat.** After the flat is stripped, it is generally tested on some inexpensive photosensitive material to check the image position and to ensure that no undesired light reaches the plate. This process is called **proofing.** If the proof is approved, the flat can be placed in contact with a printing plate, light passed through the film, and the plate exposed.

Most printers view the stripping process as the most important step in the printing cycle. The stripper can often correct or alter defects in the film image by etching away undesired detail. The stripper also directly controls the position and squareness of the image on the final page. If the film is not stripped square in the masking sheet, the image will appear crooked on the printed page. However, the stripping process cannot correct poor work that started on the mechanical or in the darkroom, no matter how skillful the stripper.

Stripping Transparent Materials

The Purpose of Stripping

After the final layout has been completed and converted to transparent film, the film image must be photographically transferred to the printing plate. Although the type of plate used will differ according to the method or process of reproduction (relief, lithography, screen, or intaglio), the stripping and proofing steps from the darkroom to the plateroom are basically the same.

Equipment and Supplies

The stripper uses a variety of tools that center around the use of a quality T-square and triangle. Tools made of plastic or other easily nicked materials are not used because the tools must serve as cutting edges for razor blades or Exacto knives when trimming pieces of film or masking sheets. Most printers use one quality steel T-square and one steel 30°–60°–90° triangle. Measurements can be made with an architect's scale and an engineer's scale. Stainless steel straightedges with frational gradations to one-hundredth of an inch are also commonly used. For greater accuracy, an ordinary needle or a special purpose etching needle is used to mark the masking sheet when laying out a flat. The etching needle can also be used to remove unwanted emulsion from a film negative or positive. Detail is added to a piece of film with a brush. Most strippers have an assortment of red sable watercolor brushes on hand. Start your collection of brushes with # 0, 2, 4, and 6 brushes. In addition, the stripping area should have such things as a scissors, a supply of single-edged razor blades, a low-power magnifying glass (10X), pencils (# 2H and 4H), erasers, and several felt-tip marking pens for labeling flats.

Almost all stripping is done on a glass-topped light table (figure 10.1). One side of the glass is frosted, and a light source (generally fluorescent) is located under the glass so that the surface is evenly illuminated. When a film negative or positive is placed on the lighted glass, it is easy to view the image and to detect any film defects. A variety of light tables are available. Most are equipped with accurately ground straight edges on each side to that if a T-square is placed on any side, lines will always be at right angles to each other. More sophisticated models, called mechanical **line-up tables** (figure 10.2), come equipped with rolling carriages, micrometer adjustments, and attachments for ruling or scribing parallel or perpendicular lines.

Several types of supplies are needed for the stripping operation. For negative stripping, **masking sheets** that do not pass light to the printing plate must be used. The most common material is "goldenrod paper," which blocks **actinic light** (any light that exposes light-sensitive emulsions) because of its color. For jobs that require greater dimensional stability, yellow-colored vinyl masking sheets are typically used. When you are stripping positives, the masking sheet and film must pass light in all but the image areas. Most positive stripping is done on clear acetate support sheets, although some special function shops use glass plates. In most positive stripping, tracing paper is used for the initial image layout. Transparent tape is used to secure the film to the flat. Special "red" translucent tape can be used to secure film negatives during stripping. This tape blocks actinic light. Opaque is a liquid material used to cover pinholes and other unwanted detail on film negatives. Red opaque is easier to apply, but black colloidal-graphic opaque is thinner and thus more efficient for extremely small areas, as when retouching halftones. Both water- and alcohol-based opaques are available.

All tools and supplies should be centrally located near the light table so the stripper can reach any item easily. If each item is located in a particular spot and is always returned there after use, much time can be saved. Disorder causes wasted motion and, over a period of time, increases the cost of each job.

Elementary Stripping Techniques

It is important to keep in mind that there is no single "correct" way to strip a flat. It sometimes seems, in fact, that there are as many different stripping methods as there are strippers. The techniques presented in this section are intended to introduce some basic stripping procedures, but it should be understood that they represent only one approach.

Several things must be considered before the actual stripping operation begins.

Figure 10.2. A mechanical line-up table
Courtesy of nuArc Company, Inc.

Most jobs arrive at the stripper's in a work envelope with a work order attached. The work order has been completed from information contained on the rough layout and from the printing customer when the contract was awarded. The rough should provide detailed specifications for all phases of production, but the stripper is concerned only with such things as the process of reproduction, plate size, paper size, final trim size, image position specifications, and detailed list of all pieces of film to be stripped. The stripper should check the contents of the packet against the list and examine each piece of film for quality. It is an expensive delay if the stripper has nearly completed a flat and then discovers that a piece of film is missing or is of inferior quality.

Masking Sheets

In order to place pieces of film in the correct printing positions on the final flat, you must identify the following four areas on the masking sheet:

- The cylinder line,
- The gripper margin,
- The plate center line,
- The point where the image begins on the printed piece (figure 10.3a).

The **cylinder line** identifies the area of the masking sheet that covers the part of the lithographic plate clamped onto the press to hold the plate on the plate cylinder. Most offset lithographic plates are flexible and wrap around a press cylinder called the "plate cylinder." The top and bottom portions of the plate are covered by the clamps that hold the plate in place, so no image can be printed from these areas (figure 10.3b). Recall from chapter 3 that the **gripper margin** is the area of the paper held by the mechanical fingers that pull the sheet through the printing unit (figure 10.3b). Since these fingers cover part of the paper, it is not possible to print an image in the gripper margin area.

The top of the uppermost image on the printed piece dictates how far down from the bottom of the gripper edge the film image is stripped onto the masking sheet. Information on this dimension should be included on the rough. The center line of the masking sheet is used to line up the center of the film image area so that it is exposed squarely in the center of the lithographic plate and consequently prints in the center of the press sheet. (There are instances when an image is to be printed off center on the final press sheet; but for these images, too, the center line of the masking sheet must be identified in order to correctly position the film.) Once these four areas are marked on the masking sheet, film can be stripped onto the sheet with confidence that the images will appear in the correct location on the printing plate and the final press sheet.

Masking sheets can be purchased with or without preprinted guidelines. Preprinted masking sheets are typically made in specific sizes for specific presses. For example, preprinted masking sheets can be purchased for an 11-by-17-inch offset duplicator. These numbers indicate that the press can print a page up to 11 inches wide and 17 inches long. The plate for such a press would be about 11 inches wide and slightly more than 17 inches long. The plate is longer than 17 inches to allow for space to clamp it to the plate cylinder.

The stripper's job is to create a flat by positioning the film on the masking sheet so the plate will transfer images in the required locations on the final press sheet. Press adjustments to change image location are possible, but they are time consuming and costly. Press adjustments for image location are also limited. For example, it is difficult, if not impossible, for a press operator to salvage a plate that has an image above the cylinder line. Often an incorrectly stripped flat must be completely restripped, and a new plate made. This wastes both time and money. The problem becomes even more critical when several flats are used to expose images on the same plate (see "Multiflat Registration").

Preprinted masking sheets of the type mentioned above are generally made only for small duplicator presses (images up to 11 by 17 inches in size). Stripping for larger presses requires the use of unlined masking sheets. Whether or not the masking sheets have preprinted guidelines, the stripper's tasks remain the same: the cylinder line, center line, gripper margin, and top image must be identified, and the images must be stripped into

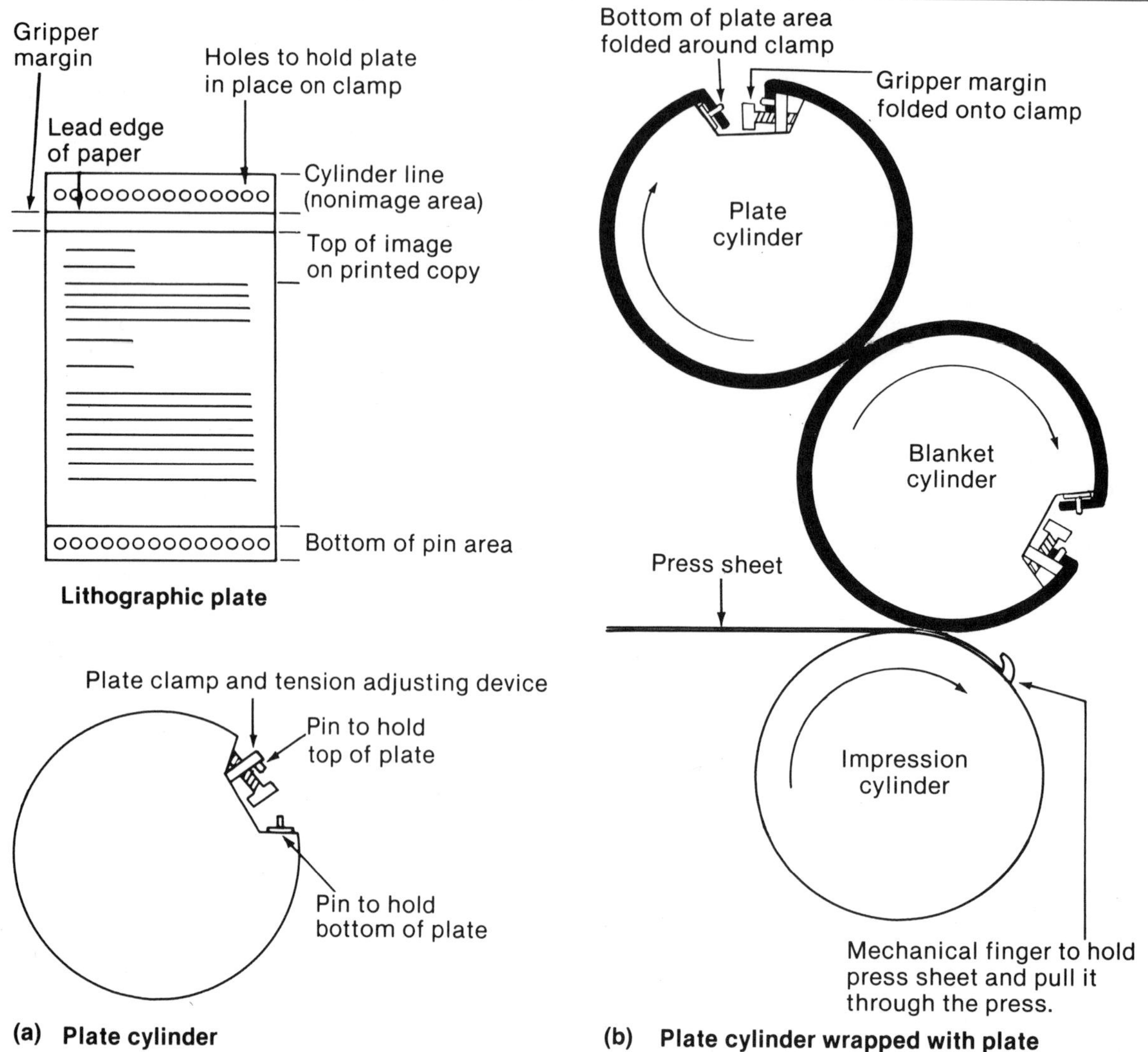

Figure 10.3. Diagram of printing plate and plate cylinder The plate is wrapped around the plate cylinder and held in place on the top and bottom with clamps.

their correct printing position (figure 10.4). Stripping for both lined and unlined masking sheets will be discussed. We will cover stripping procedures for lined masking sheets first.

Laying Out a Preprinted Masking Sheet

To begin our discussion, let's pick a simple one-color, single-flat stripping problem: a single image to be printed on 8½-by-11-inch paper on an 11-by-17-inch duplicator. For this example, we will be stripping a negative film image.

The stripper's first job is to select the correct masking sheet. If there is only one size of press in the shop, this presents no problem. However, if the shop has several different-sized presses, careful masking sheet selection becomes necessary. Our job requires a preprinted masking sheet for an 11-by-17-inch duplicator. Often the masking sheet will carry the name of the press manufacturer and a symbol code or size marking to identify which press the masking sheet is designed for. If your shop does not have masking sheets with this information, a simple measurement will help you locate the correct sheet; or you can compare the sheet to a plate from the press on which the job is to be run. The masking sheet should be the same size as or slightly larger than the plate that will be used with it.

Place the masking sheet on a light table and line up one edge of the sheet with a T-square. Tape the sheet securely in two places on the edge opposite the T-square (figure 10.5). Masking tape can be used for this purpose.

Our masking sheet is prelined in a ¼-inch grid. This grid can be used as a rough

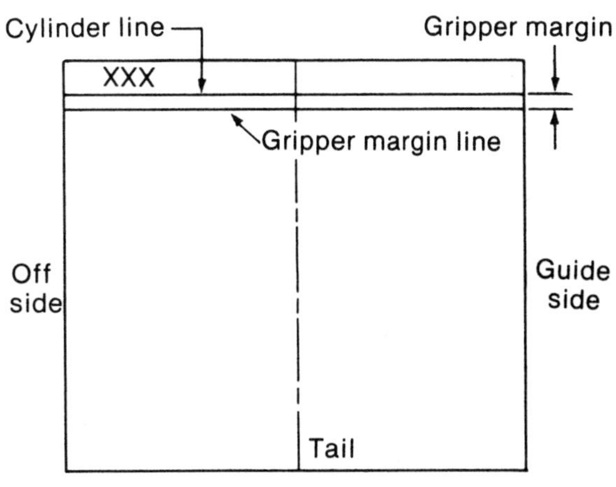

Figure 10.4. Marking blank masking sheets Many strippers layout blank masking sheets using the specifications for a particular press. The cylinder line, gripper margin and center line are carefully located. All layout is made from these three lines. Pre-printed masking sheets are also used with these guidelines provided.

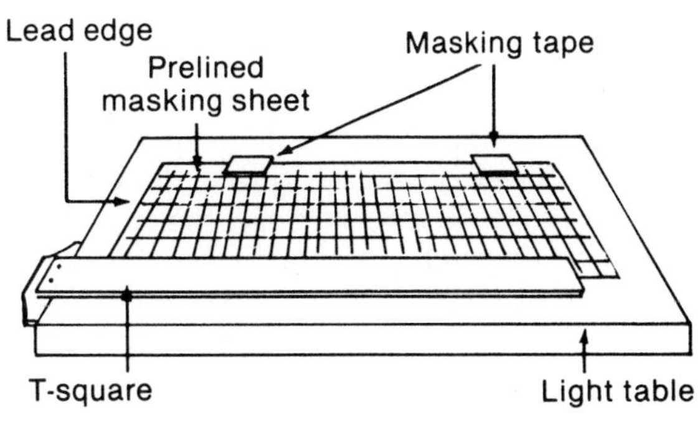

Figure 10.5. Placing the masking sheet on the light table Line the masking sheet up against the edge of a T-square and tape it on one side.

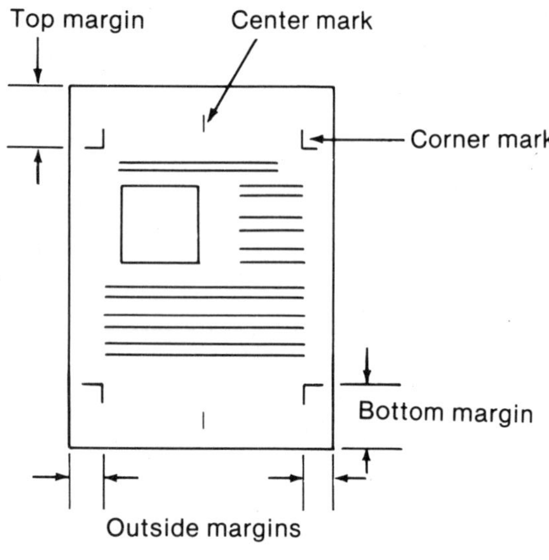

Figure 10.6. Rough layout with margins identified

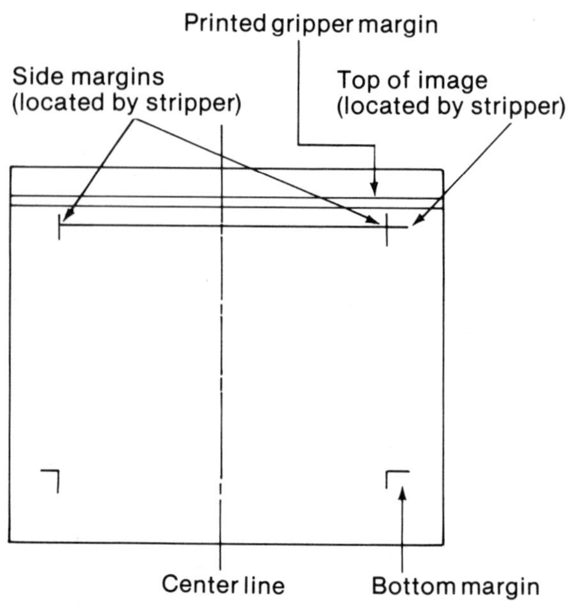

Figure 10.7. Diagram of a masking sheet Lines representing the top, sides and bottom margins are first drawn on the masking sheet. The top image margin should always be below the gripper margin.

indicator of measurements on the sheet, but exacting measurements should always be carefully made with a ruler. Not only is the ¼-inch grid not perfectly accurate, but we taped the masking sheet in place based on the location of the edge of the sheet against our T-square, not the printed grid. There is no reason to assume that the grid printed on the masking sheet is parallel to the edge of the masking sheet. It may be close, but probably not perfectly parallel. Using the T-square and ruler for all image location ensures that the images will end up correctly positioned and straight on the sheet.

After the masking sheet is taped in place, look it over carefully. As shown in figure 10.4, the cylinder lines, gripper margin, and center line should be clearly identified. It is often a good idea to draw a line over the bottom of the gripper margin line and down the center line on the masking sheet. This will help you refer back to these locations as you lay out the sheet.

Now check the rough layout to determine top margin: the distance from the top of the paper to the top of the image on the printed piece (figure 10.6). A line representing the top of the image should be drawn across the masking sheet, below the bottom of the gripper margin; lines representing side and bottom margins should also be drawn (figure 10.7).

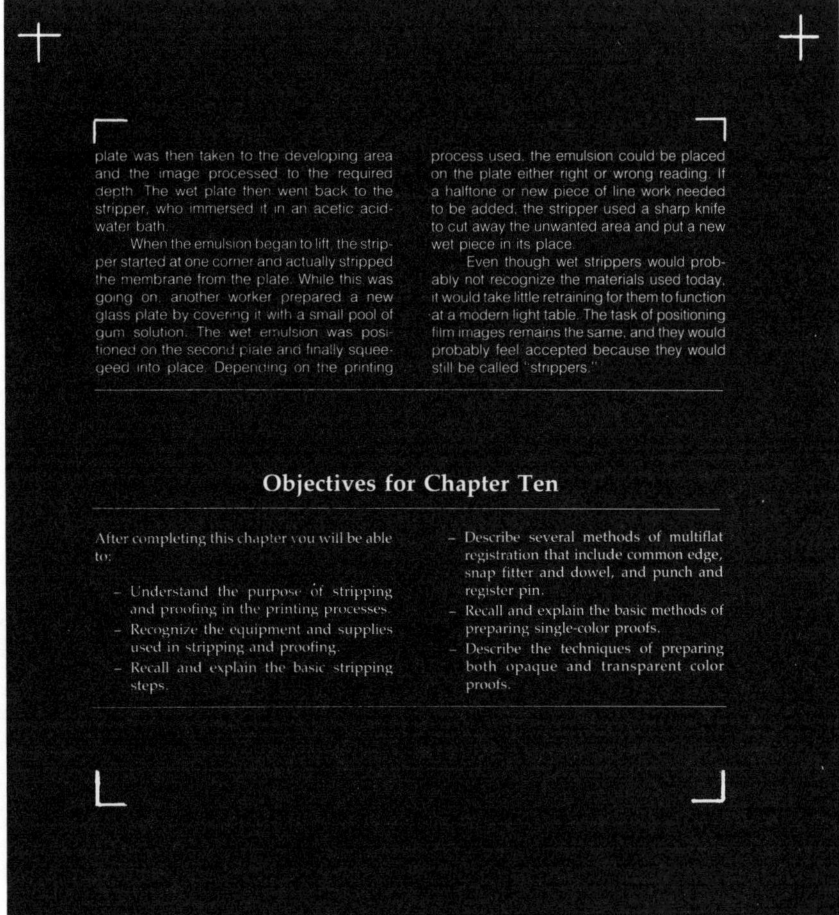

plate was then taken to the developing area and the image processed to the required depth. The wet plate then went back to the stripper, who immersed it in an acetic acid-water bath.

When the emulsion began to lift, the stripper started at one corner and actually stripped the membrane from the plate. While this was going on, another worker prepared a new glass plate by covering it with a small pool of gum solution. The wet emulsion was positioned on the second plate and finally squeegeed into place. Depending on the printing process used, the emulsion could be placed on the plate either right or wrong reading. If a halftone or new piece of line work needed to be added, the stripper used a sharp knife to cut away the unwanted area and put a new wet piece in its place.

Even though wet strippers would probably not recognize the materials used today, it would take little retraining for them to function at a modern light table. The task of positioning film images remains the same, and they would probably feel accepted because they would still be called "strippers."

Objectives for Chapter Ten

After completing this chapter you will be able to:

- Understand the purpose of stripping and proofing in the printing processes.
- Recognize the equipment and supplies used in stripping and proofing.
- Recall and explain the basic stripping steps.
- Describe several methods of multiflat registration that include common edge, snap fitter and dowel, and punch and register pin.
- Recall and explain the basic methods of preparing single-color proofs.
- Describe the techniques of preparing both opaque and transparent color proofs.

Figure 10.8. Example of a negative with corner marks If corner marks are placed on the paste-up board, they will appear as images on the film negative. These negative corner marks can then be lined up with the top, sides and bottom margins on the masking sheet.

For this example, there will be only one film negative. Lay it emulsion-side down near the masking sheet on the light table. Examine the negative carefully. Corner marks that indicate image extremes or center lines (or both) should be recorded on the negative (figure 10.8). These marks will help you position the film negative in the proper location under the masking sheet.

Attaching Film Negatives

With rare exception, all printing plates are exposed with the emulsion side of the plate against the emulsion side of the film. Recall from chapter 6 that negatives are right reading through the base. In other words, if the piece of film is placed on the light table so that the image can be read from left to right,

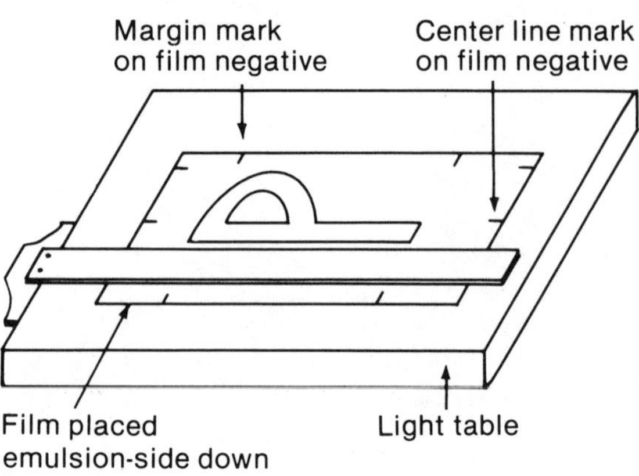

Figure 10.9. Positioning the negative on the light table

the base side is up and the emulsion side is against the glass. If there is any question about which is the emulsion side of a film negative, the emulsion side can be identified in one of two ways: by comparing the finish or by scratching the film edge. If the film is folded over on itself, the emulsion side will be the duller of the two sides (see figure 6.16). Also, the emulsion side of the film can be scratched. In fact, scribing the emulsion is a common method for adding image areas to a film negative. A small pin scratch on the edge of the film outside the image area will quickly determine which is the emulsion side of the film.

Begin by placing all negatives emulsion-side down on the masking sheet in their appropriate positions, with the images roughly falling in place with the image margins. Never allow pieces of film to overlap on the flat. If the overlap is near an image area, there may be some distortion as the plate exposure is made. With all negatives in place, mark where any pieces overlap. If possible, cut any overlapping sheets to within ½ inch of any film image. If, because of imposition (image location on the final press sheet), the cut must be less than ½ inch from an image area, delay trimming the film until both pieces have been attached. That procedure will be discussed shortly. After trimming, the negatives should be removed and set aside until they are needed again.

Because the masking sheet is translucent, it is possible to see through the material to the glass surface below. With right-reading stripping, untape the masking sheet and set it aside. Place the negative, emulsion-side down, on the light table. Accurately align the image margins or tick marks with a T-square and triangle and tape the film in place (figure 10.9). Next, move the masking sheet over the film until the image lines are positioned with the image margins on the negative. It should be easy to see both marks line up as you look down through the flat. Use a T-square to ensure that the margins and type lines run parallel to the edge of the masking sheet. After the negatives are in place, smooth the masking sheet down and cut two small triangular openings over the negative in the nonimage areas (figure 10.10). It is important that you cut only through the masking sheet and not into the film. Practice several times on a scrap sheet. Still holding the film in position under the masking sheet, place a small piece of red tape over each triangular opening and apply pressure. This will temporarily attach the negative to the flat (see figure 10.11). Continue the same procedure for all other negatives.

Before untaping the flat from the light table, again check all film images for position and squareness. Improper image placement at this stage will be reflected throughout the rest of the job.

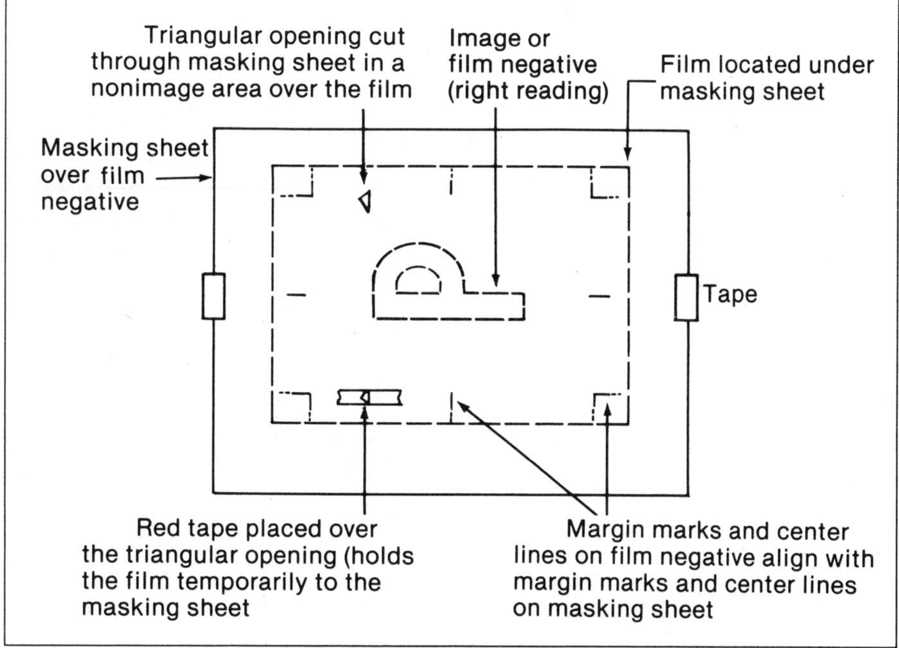

Figure 10.10. Cutting triangular openings Looking down through the masking sheet to the film negative below, cut two small triangular openings in the masking sheet covering a nonimage area in the film. Tape across these openings with red tape to temporarily hold the film to the masking sheet.

After all negatives have been temporarily attached and checked for accuracy, release the flat from the light table and carefully turn it over. Each negative should now be secured to the masking sheet at each corner with a small piece of cellophane tape (figure 10.11). Be sure to smooth each negative as the tape is applied to ensure that there are no buckles in the film. Once the film is securely taped in place, turn the masking sheet over again (lined side up) and recheck the image placement.

If two pieces of film overlap, it is necessary to cut the negatives so they will butt against each other. To do this without cutting into the masking sheet, insert a piece of scrap film or acetate beneath the overlapping portions and with a steel straightedge and a single-edged razor blade or frisket knife cut through both pieces of film (figure 10.12). Do not remove the straightedge until you are certain that you have cut completely through both sheets of film. Remove the loose pieces and the scrap of film and tape the negatives to the masking sheet. Tape the negatives on the nonimage edges only. Do not put tape over the image areas on a negative.

After all the negatives have been located and taped in place, turn the flat over again so that the film emulsion is against the light

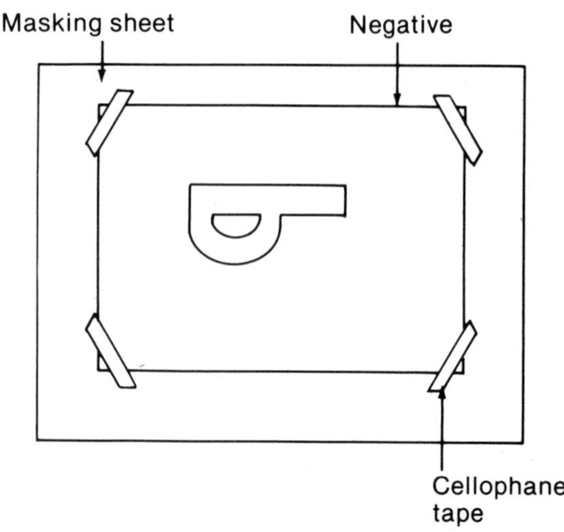

Figure 10.11. Taping the negative to the masking sheet Turn the masking sheet over and tape each corner of the film negative with cellophane tape.

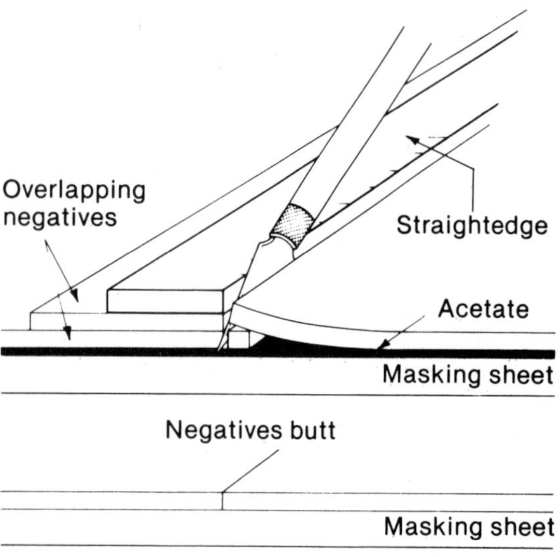

Figure 10.12. Cutting overlapping negatives

table and cut away the masking sheet in the image areas. Some strippers slide a piece of scrap plastic between the masking sheet and the film during this operation to ensure that only the masking sheet is cut. With practice and a sharp cutting tool (a single-edged razor blade or frisket knife), however, lack of a plastic insert should cause no problems. The masking material should be removed to within 3/8 of an inch of the image areas. The less open nonprinting area exposed, the better (figure 10.13).

Opaquing and Etching the Flat

Although theoretically the flat is now ready to be sent to the plating room, in actual practice there are usually small defects that must be corrected. The most common defect is **pinholes.** These are small openings in the emulsion that pass light. They may be caused by dust on the copyboard when the camera exposure was made or by dirty original copy. Whatever the reason, any openings in the film will pass light to the printing plate and will ultimately appear as ink on the final press sheet. Pinholes are undesired images and therefore must be blocked out with **opaque.**

Most opaques are water based. Alcohol-, turpentine-, or petroleum-based materials are also available. These opaquing materials dry more rapidly than water-based opaques. The opaque should be applied in as thin a coat as possible yet still block light through the negative. If properly mixed, water-based materials should dry on the film in 15 to 30 seconds. Although some printers opaque on the emulsion side of the film, the authors recommend opaquing only on the base side. The emulsion of any film is frail and cannot stand a great deal of manipulation. If opaque is mistakenly placed over a desired image on the base side of the film, the opaque can be washed off or scratched away with a razor blade without damaging the film emulsion. Such scratching on the emulsion side of the film would destroy the emulsion. Also, opaque on the emulsion side of the film will come into contact with the plate emulsion, thereby producing thick areas that could hold the film emulsion away from the plate emulsion during plate making and introduce image distortion (figure 10.14).

Novice strippers often have trouble deciding whether or not to opaque an area. As a rule of thumb, when someone standing over a light table looking straight down at an eye-to-flat distance of about 2 feet can see light through a pinhole, then the pinhole will probably pass enough light to expose the plate.

The fact that a film's emulsion is fragile can be used to advantage. There are frequent situations when detail needs to be added to a negative. Images can be created in the film emulsion by scraping away the emulsion with an etching tool. An overdeveloped area on a character can be opened with the tool and new letters or symbols can even be added, although they must be etched in reverse. Lines can be added by etching against a straightedge.

The final step, after all opaquing and etching are complete and checked, is to label the flat. The platemaker typically handles many flats in a single day, so each must be identified. Place all information in the trailing edge of the masking sheet, out of the paper limits. The notations made depend on the individual shop, but such things as the name of the account, job title or production number, sequence of the flat, ink color, or any special instructions such as the inclusion of a screen tint are all commonly included (figure 10.15).

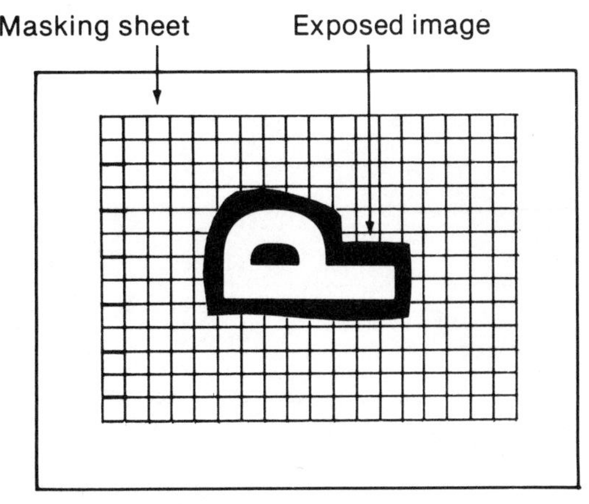

Figure 10.13. Exposing the image area The masking sheet is cut away to expose the image area of the film negative.

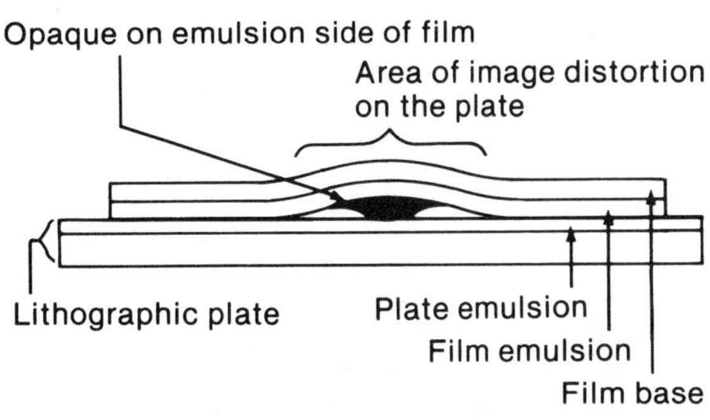

Figure 10.14. Opaque-caused image distortion Opaque used on the emulsion side of the film can hold the film away from the plate emulsion during exposure and thereby distort the image.

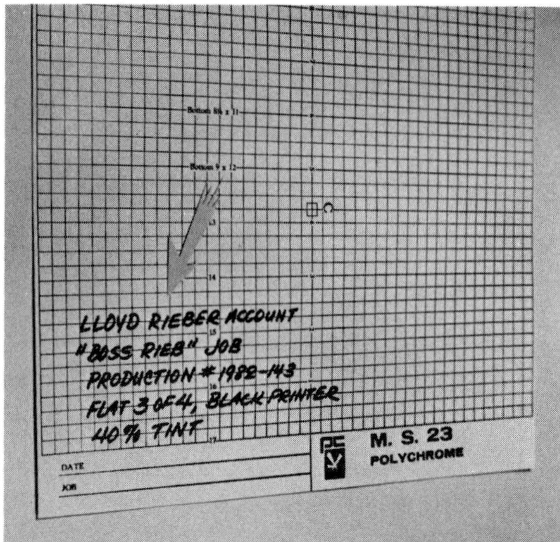

Figure 10.15. Identifying the film flat

Attaching Film Positives

There are several advantages to stripping film positives instead of negatives. Because a positive has the image as a black emulsion on a clear film base, it is easier to position the film on the support sheet and to register additional pieces of the film to the first piece for multicolor work. It is also possible to work with many small pieces of film, which would be difficult with negatives and goldenrod masking sheets. Finally, a positive halftone produces a higher-quality printing plate and is easier to strip than a negative halftone. This is because a negative halftone, made with a vignetted contact screen, produces a ghost image around each dot. When a negative is contacted to a new piece of film to make a film positive, a well-defined hard dot is produced because all ghosting is dropped from the first halftone.

The initial layout of all guidelines is made on a piece of tracing paper instead of a goldenrod or yellow vinyl masking sheet. When complete, the tracing sheet is turned over and mounted on the light table with the T-square. A clear sheet of transparent base material is then taped in place over the reversed layout. For low-quality jobs, a second sheet of tracing paper can be used. But a clear, stable plastic, such as vinyl, acetate, or a polyester-based material, is typically used. Notches are cut to indicate the plate limits to aid in placing the flat on the plate in the plate-making department.

All positives must be adhered emulsion-side up and in reverse on the support sheet so that all images will be exposed emulsion to emulsion in the platemaker. The emulsion of a positive is right reading when produced by contact printing from a film negative. For that reason, it is necessary to laterally reverse the image so that the final stripped flat will be emulsion to emulsion with the plate during plate making. "Duplicating Film Materials" in chapter 6 outlines the process in detail.

Trim each positive to within ¼ inch of the image, position it on the support sheet in line with the margin marks, and tape it in place with clear cellophane or polyester tape. The tape should not extend over any image area. When the film is too small or is too close to another piece of film to allow for taping, rubber cement can be used to secure the positive to the support material. To do this, position the positive and then lift one corner. Place a small quantity of thin rubber cement on the base side of the film and press the corner back into position. Repeat the operation with each corner of the positive. Be sure to use the cement sparingly and avoid any contact with the film emulsion.

As with negative stripping, individual pieces of film should not be overlapped.

Opaque can be used to add images or positives, and gentle etching can remove the emulsion. Pressure-sensitive materials as used in the preparation of mechanicals can also be used to add lines or borders to a positive image (see "Pressure-Sensitive Materials," chapter 4).

Stripping Halftones

Several techniques for adding halftone images to printed materials were discussed in chapter 4. One method suggested the inclusion of a red or black pressure-sensitive material on the paste-up that would reproduce on the film negative as a clear, open window. A halftone negative could then be added to the window at a later phase in production. It is the stripper's responsibility to combine the halftone negative with the negative holding the window on the flat. This must be done in such a way that the halftone will appear in the proper position on the final printed sheet and the added piece of film that carries the halftone image will not interfer with the existing images on the negative that has the window.

To add a halftone negative to a window in a main negative, first prepare the masking sheet, add the main negative(s), and complete all cutting, opaquing, and etching. Then turn the flat over on the light table so that the film is emulsion-side up. Trim the halftone that is to be stripped into the window so that it is larger than the window opening and yet does not overlap any image detail near the window. Position the trimmed negative over the window emulsion-side up, in line with the rest of the image detail on the flat, and tape it in place with clear cellophane tape. The halftone must be mounted in this position because the emulsions of both the main negative and the halftone negative must be in contact with the printing plate when the plate exposure is made (figure 10.16).

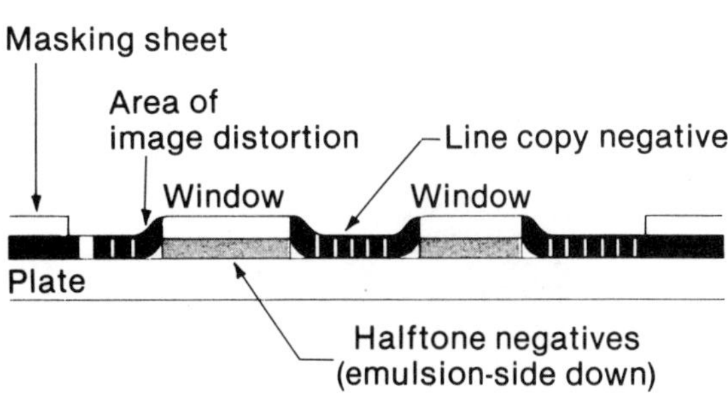

Figure 10.16. Positioning the negatives The emulsions of both the line copy and the halftone negatives must contact the emulsion of the printing plate.

Check to be sure that the halftone image completely fills the window. Any open area around the edges of the window will print as a solid line on the final reproduction.

When you are stripping positive flats, treat a halftone exactly as you would all other pieces of film. Cut it to size and secure it in place with clear tape or a thin layer of rubber cement.

It is often not possible to add a halftone negative to an existing flat without overlapping image detail and creating an area of image distortion. This happens when two halftones are to be butted together on the final printed sheet or the halftone window is positioned too close to other image detail. In such cases, the stripper cannot work with the halftone on a single flat. The solution is to use two **complementary flats.** One flat carries the main printing detail; the second holds the halftone image (figure 10.17). If properly stripped, each flat can be exposed in succes-

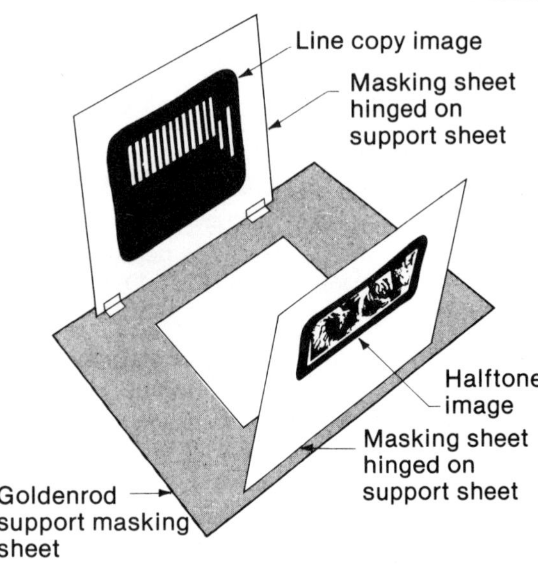

Figure 10.17. Complementary flats In this example of complementary flats, the two masking sheets are hinged on a larger support sheet.

sion in the platemaker in order to combine the two images in their proper positions on a single printing plate (figure 10.18). The section titled "Multiflat Registration" in this chapter is concerned with this problem of controlling the positions of film images that are mounted on more than one flat.

Laying Out Masking Sheets for Larger Presses

Masking sheets for offset presses larger than 11 by 17 inches are generally unlined. However, the stripper is still concerned with the four major areas on the sheet: the cylinder line, the gripper margin, the top of the image area, and the center line of the masking sheet. All images are positioned from these four dimensions.

The initial layout lines are located from specifications provided by the printing press manufacturer. Table 10.1 (p. 244) shows the specifications for the Harris LXG offset lithographic press. The following example will assume use of the Harris press, although the process is applicable to any printing process or press.

Begin by cutting the masking sheet equal to or slightly larger than the plate size. If you are doing positive stripping, cut a piece of tracing paper instead of goldenrod masking sheet. Tape the paper securely in place in the center of the light table; use a T-square to line up the top edge of the sheet accurately. Be sure that there are no buckles or loose portions that will cause inaccurate line rulings.

Mark the top edge with three Xs to identify the lead or gripper edge of the plate. Label the off (left), tail (back), and guide (right) sides (figure 10.19). From the press specifications, measure down from the top of the sheet the position of the cylinder line and prick the goldenrod with a needle or etching tool. Then draw a line through the point with a pencil (figure 10.20). From the same specification list determine the amount of gripper margin (or bite); mark the distance from the cylinder line to the bottom of the gripper margin and draw a second line parallel to the first (figure 10.21). The area between the cylinder and gripper line represents the gripper margin. The area varies in size from press to press, but the width is generally from 3⁄16 to 3⁄8 of an inch. It is important to remember that the gripper margin represents nonprinting area and can carry no printing image. The last initial layout line is a vertical line drawn in the center of the masking sheet (figure 10.22,

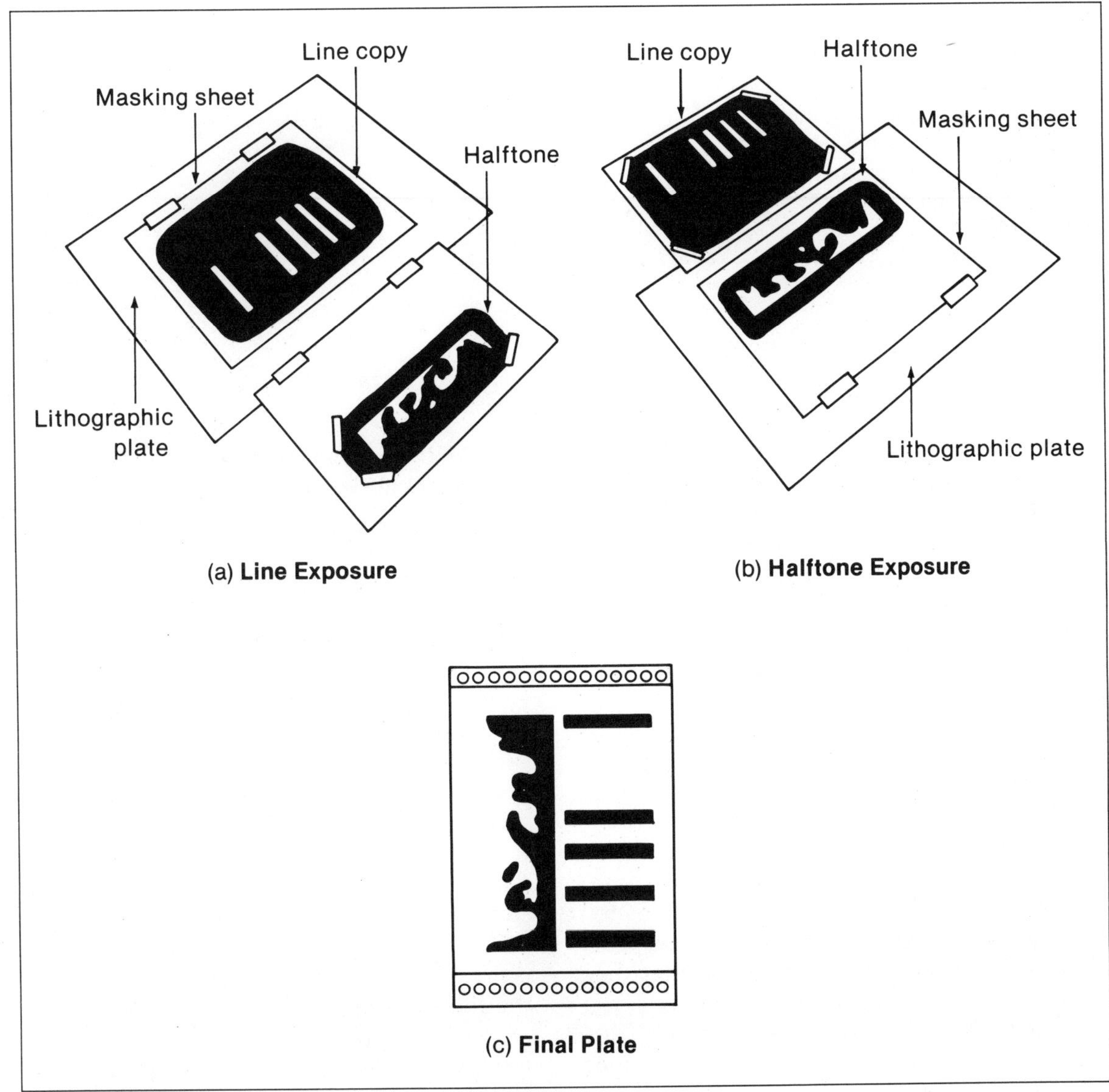

Figure 10.18. Using complementary flats for double exposures The complementary flat uses one exposure to record the line copy (a) and one exposure to record the halftone (b). The final plate carries both images (c).

Table 10.1. Harris LXG Press Specifications

Maximum Printing Area	22⅝ × 30
Maximum Sheet Size	23 × 30
Minimum Sheet Size	9 × 12
Plate Size	27 × 30
Distance from Lead Edge of Plate to Cylinder Line	1 13/16
Gripper Margin	5/16

p. 245). All vertical measurements will be made from this center line, and all horizontal measurements will begin from the cylinder line. With this technique there is little chance of error in image placement.

From the center line measure half the length of the plate in either direction, then cut notches as illustrated in figure 10.23. The top of the masking sheet and these two notches will serve as guides when the flat is placed on the printing plate during the plate exposure.

The next concern is to define the press sheet area. The work order should identify the paper size and the way in which the sheet is to be fed through the press. If a sheet is to be trimmed after printing and a choice is possible, lay out the masking sheet so that the lead or gripper edge of the paper will be trimmed. Position any register marks (for multicolor registration) or test scales in the trim area. Assume for this example that a 20½-by-24¾-inch sheet is to be fed through the Harris LXG. Measure 20½ inches down from the cylinder line and 12⅜ inches on each side of the vertical center line and draw the paper lines (figure 10.23). You must position all film images within this area, but do not extend them into the gripper margin.

With large sheet presses but small final printed sheet size, most companies gang several jobs on the same flat, with the intention of cutting the paper pile after printing. In large companies the ganging positions are decided by the planning section; in most small organizations the stripper makes all these decisions. Figure 10.24 illustrates the ganging several sheets on a larger press sheet. Notice that identical jobs are identified by similar numbers and that image margins are defined by the use of corner ticks. Again, measuring from the cylinder and vertical center line, the stripper places all final paper lines within the large press sheet paper lines and steps off the margin marks for each sheet (figure 10.25). After one check of all dimensions is made, the masking sheet is ready to receive the film negatives.

Most industrial stripping is done with the film negative emulsion-side up, facing the stripper. Begin by turning the masking sheet over on the light table. Accurately position the cylinder line with a T-square and tape the sheet in place. Check to be sure you can see the layout lines through the masking sheet (figure 10.26).

Position the first negative in the correct area, emulsion-side up, after checking the

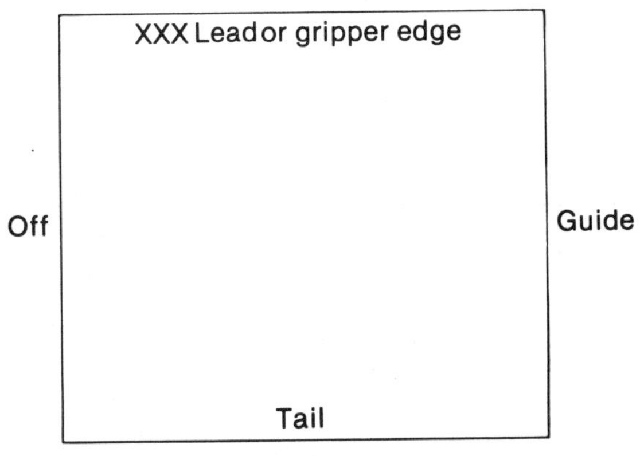

Figure 10.19. Goldenrod sheet with labeled edges

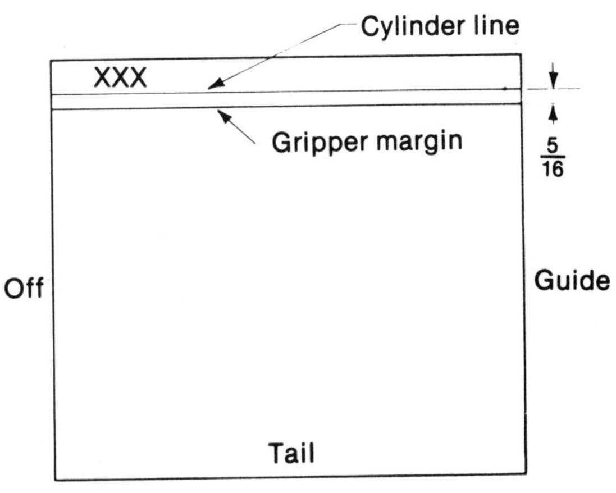

Figure 10.21. Goldenrod sheet with labeled gripper margin

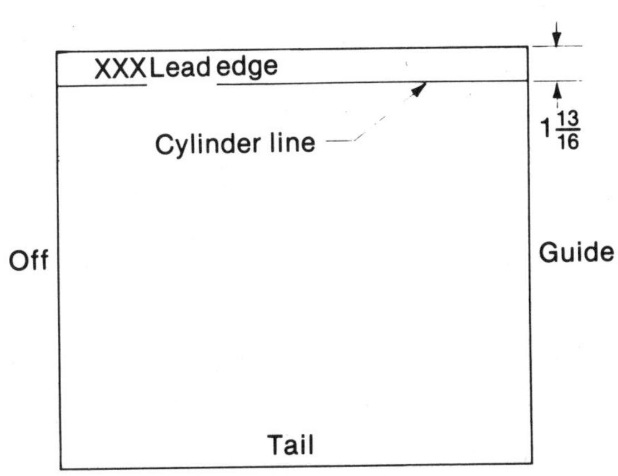

Figure 10.20. Goldenrod sheet with labeled cylinder line

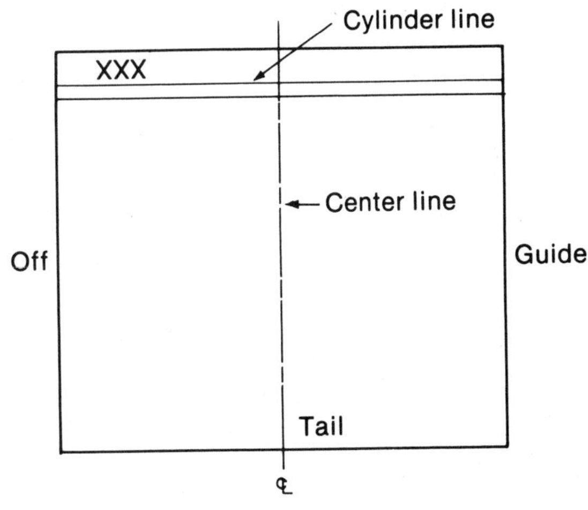

Figure 10.22. Goldenrod sheet with labeled vertical center line

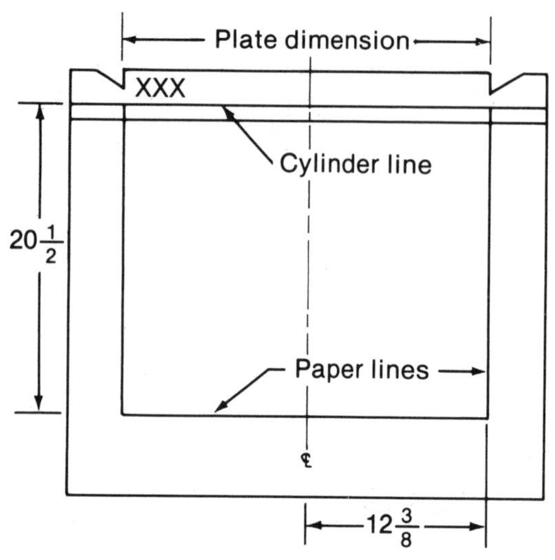

Figure 10.23. Goldenrod sheet with paper dimension added

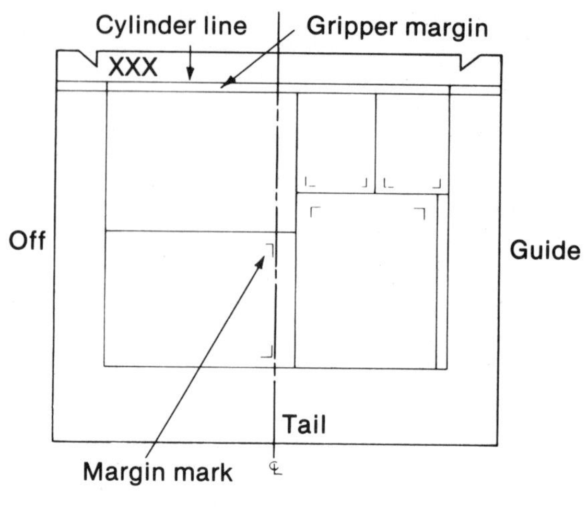

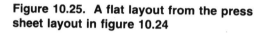

Figure 10.25. A flat layout from the press sheet layout in figure 10.24

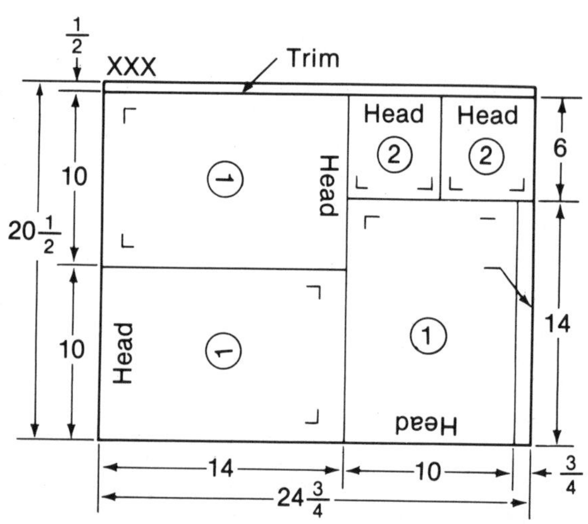

Figure 10.24. A press sheet layout

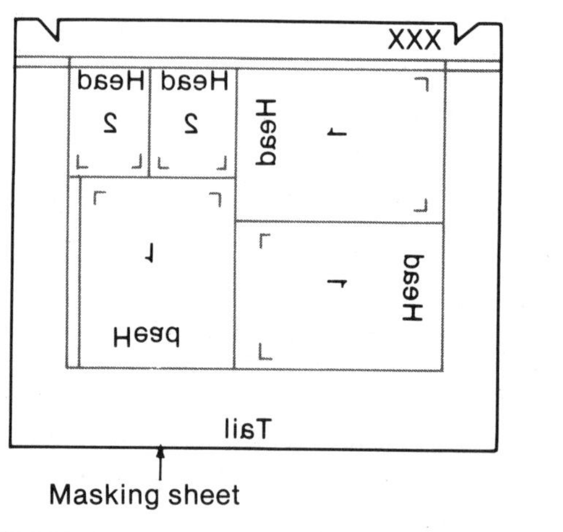

Figure 10.26. Layout lines as seen through the base of the masking sheet

rough layout. Place the side margins and top image in line with the head and side guidelines on the flat. Check with the T-square to ensure that the image is parallel to the cylinder line and then tape each corner of the negative with cellophane tape. Repeat the same procedure for the remaining negatives (figure 10.27).

When all negatives have been attached and checked for accurate position, turn the flat over and cut windows through the masking sheet to expose the film image openings. Opaque and etch as necessary.

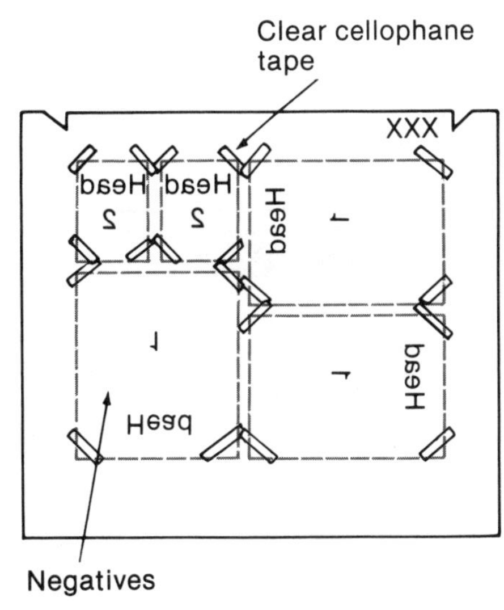

Figure 10.27. Positioning negatives on the masking sheet Position negatives emulsion-side up in line with head and side guidelines. Secure the negatives with cellophane tape.

Multiflat Registration

The Purpose of Registration Systems

It is important to realize that almost all printing plates can typically be exposed from five or six different flats before the sum effect of light passing through the goldenrod or yellow vinyl masking sheets begins to expose the plate emulsion in nonimage areas.

The problem of multiflat exposures is that of registration. The stripper must place the separate film images on each flat and then control the placement of the images from each flat on a single plate. When the plate is processed, all images must appear in their proper printing positions in relation to each other and to the limits of the printing press. Some form of mechanical punch or guide is generally used to aid in the multiflat registration process. These techniques will be discussed shortly.

Many situations besides complementary halftone flats require the stripper to deal with the multiple flat process. Commonly the stripper must print two separate screen tint values in the same color with the use of the same plate. It is possible to place both images on a single negative and to use folding masks to make the plate exposure (figure 10.28). Two separate exposures would be made with a screen tint between the flat and the plate during each exposure. Only the desired areas would be opened for each exposure, and the proper screen would be placed between the flat and the plate each time the plate was exposed. If the images are extremely close together, however, or if many different areas are spread over the entire flat, this technique is not usable. It is then necessary to place all images of common screen tint values or sizes on separate flats. With proper multiflat reg-

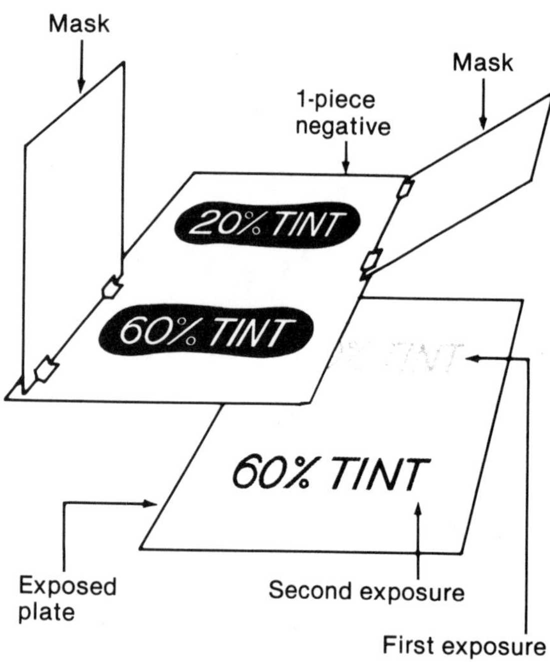

Figure 10.28. Using folding masks to control multiple plate exposures

istration techniques, these images can be assembled on a single plate in the proper tint values, screen angle, and position (figure 10.29).

Surprints and reverses were introduced in chapter 3 as a part of the design phase, but they are actually assembled by the stripper. Figure 10.30 (p. 250) illustrates the use of two flats with two separate exposures to produce a surprint over an image on a single plate. Figure 10.31 shows the registration of a positive image to create a reverse in an area during a single plate exposure. Multiple flats are often used to provide a mask or frame for a larger image (figure 10.32).

Certainly the largest application of multiflat registration techniques is in the area of process color reproduction. The four primary flats, representing cyan, magenta, yellow, and black detail, must be stripped so that the plates, when placed on the printing press, can be adjusted to "fit" the four colors together on the printed sheet, duplicating the original as closely as possible.

Basic Registration Methods

Several methods are used for multiflat registration. The ones discussed here include:

- The common edge method,
- The snap fitter and dowel method,
- The prepunched tab strip method,
- The punch and register pin method.

Common Edge Method. The simplest system is the **common edge** method. With this method the flat containing the greatest amount of detail is first stripped by using ordinary layout and assembly procedures. This first flat is called the main or **master flat.** All remaining flats are aligned with it. The second negative (or set of negatives) is then placed in position over the completed master flat and attached to a second masking sheet. It is important that both flats have at least two edges (generally the top and right or gripper and guide sides) that line up perfectly. Any number of flats can be registered with this method as long as each image on each flat is registered to the master flat and the masking sheets have a minimum of two common edges. When the plates are exposed, the top and right edges of each flat are placed in line with the top and right edges of the plate.

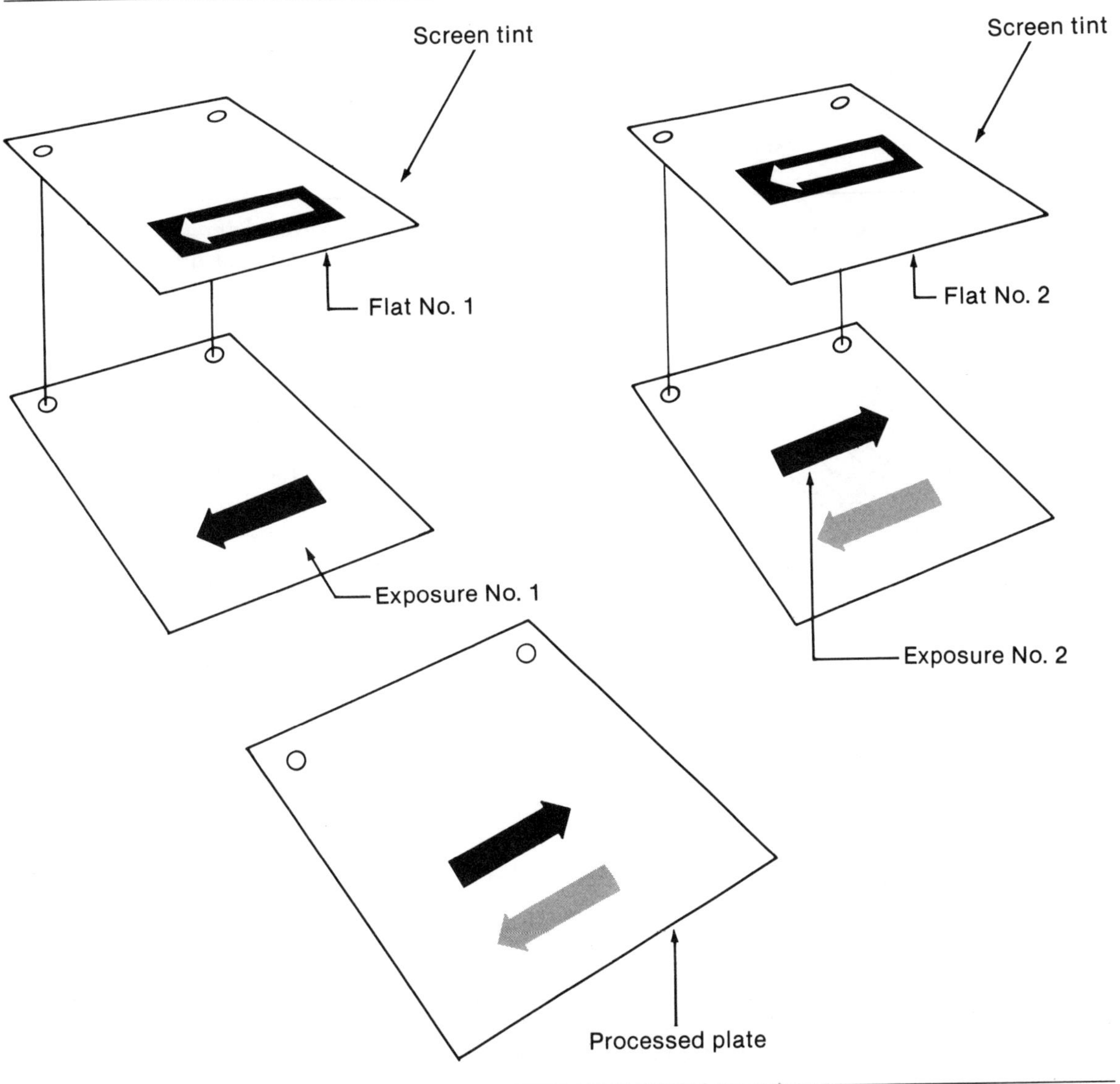

Figure 10.29. Using multiflat registration techniques to assemble different screen tints on the same plate

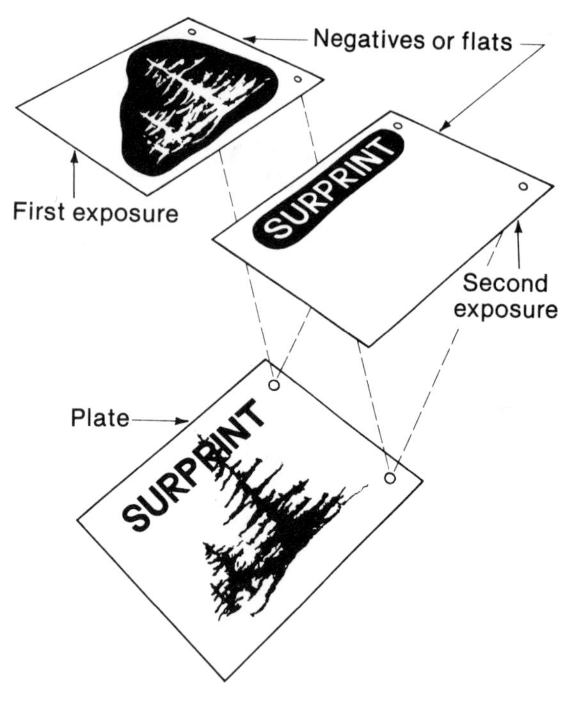

Figure 10.30. Using multiflat registration to place a surprint over another image

Snap Fitter and Dowel Method. A second technique is the use of **snap fitters and dowels.** With this system the main or master flat is stripped as usual. At the tail edge of the masking sheet, well away from any image or paper limits, two openings are cut and plastic snap fitters are taped in place (figure 10.33). The flat is then positioned on the light table with a T-square, and soft adhesive-backed pins (dowels) are pressed through the fitter openings onto the glass table surface (figure 10.34). The flat can then be removed, but the dowels will remain in place on the light table. When the snap fitters are inserted over the pins a second time, the flat has been returned to exactly the same position. To register additional flats, new snap fitters are cut into separate masking sheets and are stripped so that image detail registers to the first master flat (figure 10.35).

Prepunched Tab Strip Method. A less expensive method for control of multiflat registration is the use of **prepunched tab strips.** Most companies that employ this technique save their scrap or discarded sheets of film material and cut them into tabs approximately 3 inches wide and as long as their masking sheets. Three holes are then punched into each tab with a special mechanical punching device (figure 10.36, p. 254). Special register pins (generally metal) are then taped to the light table so that the punched tabs fall perfectly in line with the pins (figure 10.37). After the master flat has been stripped, a punched tab is taped to the tail edge. All subsequent flats are stripped in register to the main flat while it is secured to the register pins. Tabs are added to the tail of each additional flat to hold it in register with the master.

Punch and Register Pin Method. The most efficient approach for controlling registration is to apply the **punch and register pin** method from the camera to the press. With this method the camera operator uses a mechanical punch on each piece of film as well as register pins to hold it in position on the camera back. This is especially effective for process color separation work where the copy is not moved between exposures. Once the film is processed, the stripper works with opaquing and etching and mounts the film on a punched masking sheet if necessary. When used as a total systems approach, the printing plate is also punched to line up with the film or masking sheet holes before plate exposure, and register pins are placed on the printing press to receive a punched plate. If used throughout the process, the technique results in printed images that line up perfectly with few press adjustments. This significantly reduces costs in all areas.

Multiflat Stripping for Process Color Work

This section is primarily concerned with the specific techniques involved in stripping for four-color process printing. The general procedures are applicable to all other multiflat stripping, whether it is flat color, more than four colors (such as topographic mapping where five are used), or single color with the use of several flats to generate one plate.

It is generally accepted that registration for process color work is too critical to employ the common edge registration method. Some form of pin or dowel register system must be used. The most accurate method of positioning multiple flats is to use some type of master image stripped into a master flat as a guide for all subsequent images and flats. There are two basic approaches: blueline flats and single master flat.

Blueline Flat Method. With the **blueline flat** system a special flat is prepared. This flat holds any detail needed to position all film images for the job and includes all necessary registration marks. Negatives are generally used to assemble the blueline flat. The blueline master flat is then exposed to a special light-sensitive solution that has been coated on a piece of clear plate glass or plastic. The processed emulsion produces a blue image that will not expose a printing plate if the clear base is used for positive stripping. If you are

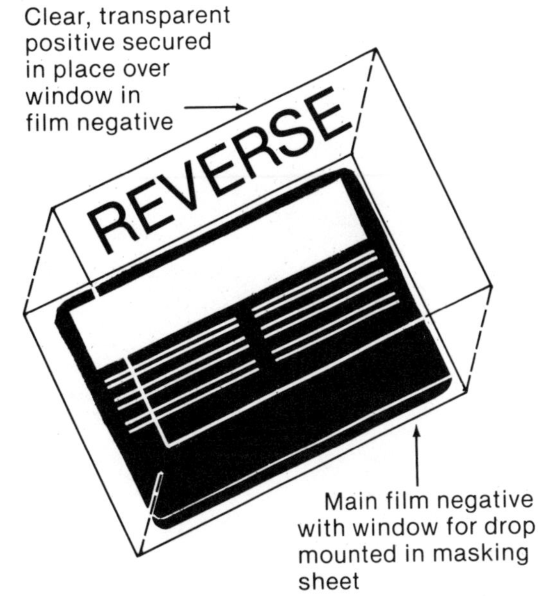

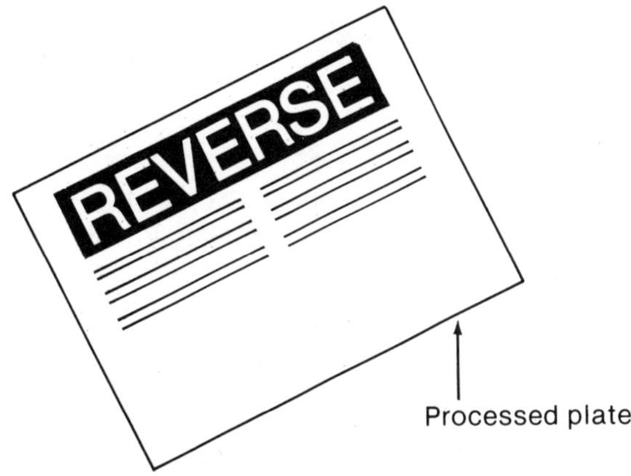

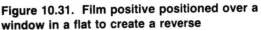

Figure 10.31. Film positive positioned over a window in a flat to create a reverse

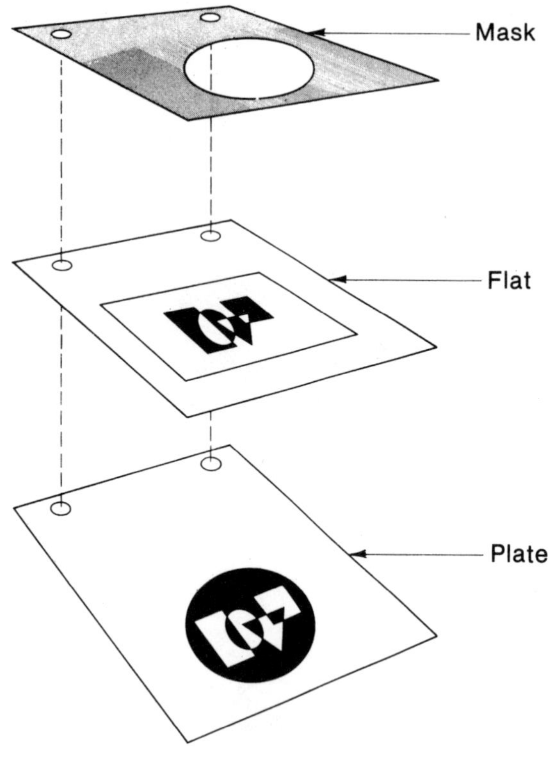

Figure 10.32. Using multiple flat registration to create a mask or frame for a larger image
The mask is registered in place over the film positive. Only one exposure is made.

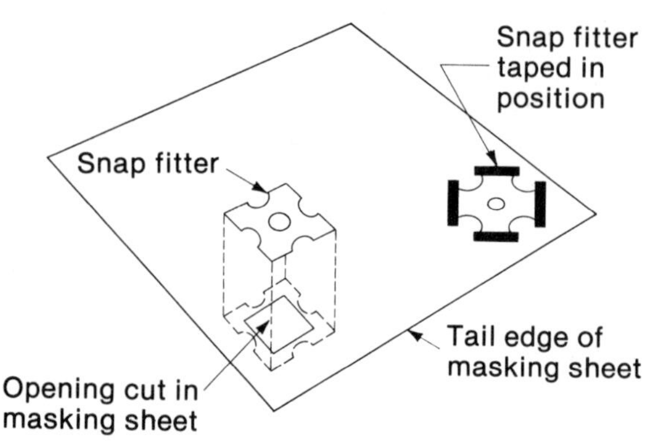

Figure 10.33. Using snap fitters on a masking sheet

stripping negatives, you can use the blueline image as a guide to register all flats. For positives, prepare a laterally reversed blueline for each flat. Then take the master flat apart and strip all pieces of film with their appropriate color.

Single Master Flat Method. The most common registration technique for color negative stripping is the use of a single master flat as a guide for all other flats in the job. For flat color, the master flat is generally the one that carries the greatest amount of detail. For four-color process work, the black printer is used. Four-color stripping with a master flat will be covered here.

Prepare the master flat with the black printer by using common stripping techniques. After opaquing and etching, apply some type of pin register device and turn the flat over on the light table with the emulsion side of the film facing you. Apply the pin system to a second masking sheet and position it over the first flat. Then place the second set of negatives, emulsion-side up, in register with the first image.

Recall from chapter 9 that register marks were placed with the original during the color separation process. Each piece of film carries duplicate halftone and register mark images for each of the four-color printers. The register marks become your first guides. As you superimpose the second negative over the first, the register marks on each negative are

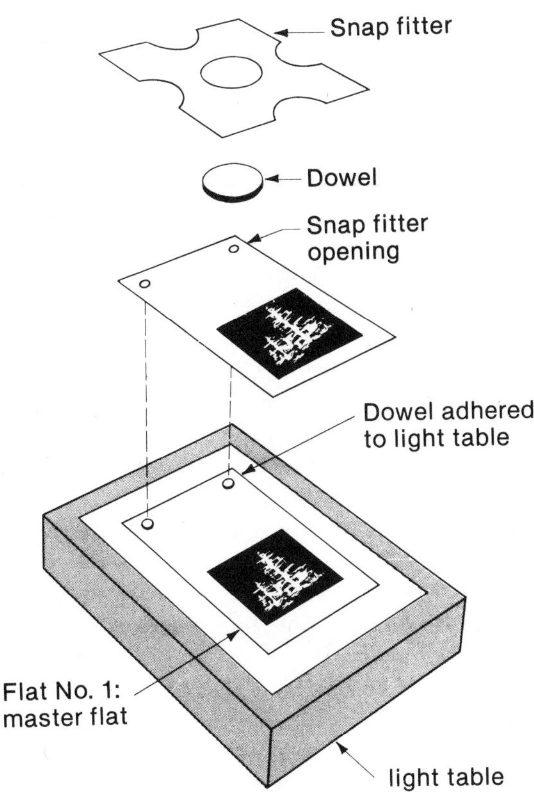

Figure 10.34. Positioning flat using snap fitters and dowels The snap fitter slides over the dowel and controls flat position.

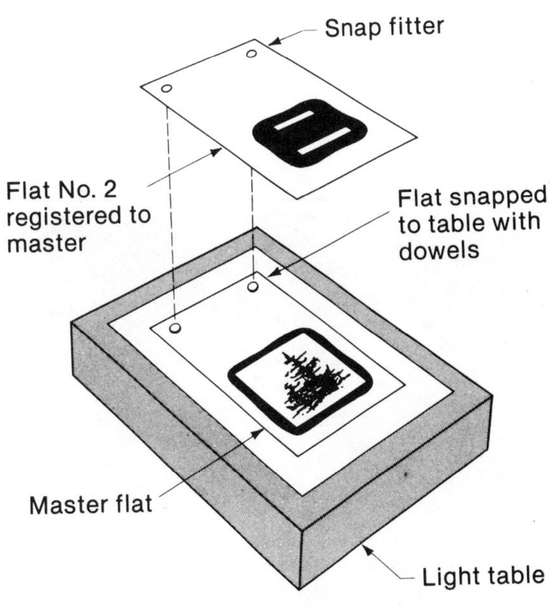

Figure 10.35. Registering additional flats

lined up. With four-color reproductions made up of halftone images, the alignment tolerance is extremely critical. If you view register marks at any but a 90° angle, the thickness of the film might cause a distortion that will put the two images out of register. To eliminate the possibility of this type of error, some strippers use a sighting tube to view the register marks (figure 10.38).

After all register marks are in line, hold the negative in place with some weighted material (often a leather bag filled with lead pellets is used) and examine the detail registration in the halftones themselves. The register marks should always be ignored in preference to accurate image alignment on the different negatives.

If the job is made up of only four flats to print as four different colors, all flats are individually registered to the master flat that carries the black printer. If there are more than four flats to be reproduced with only four colors (such as when using two different screen tint percentages in the same color, or when line copy falls too close to a halftone image to include it on one flat), the sequence of flat registration is important. Examine each color grouping. For each color, the flat that contains the greatest amount of image detail

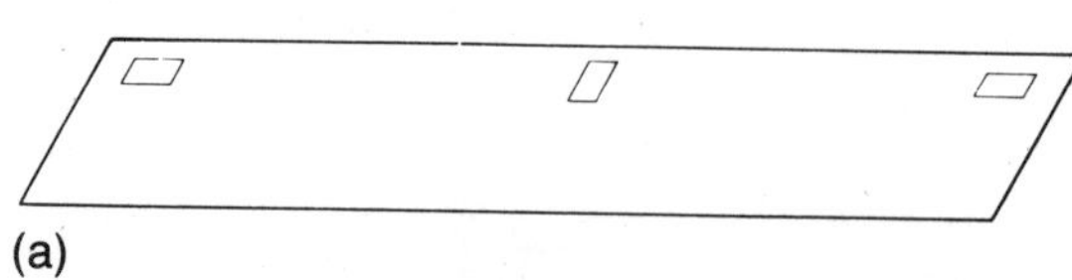

(a)

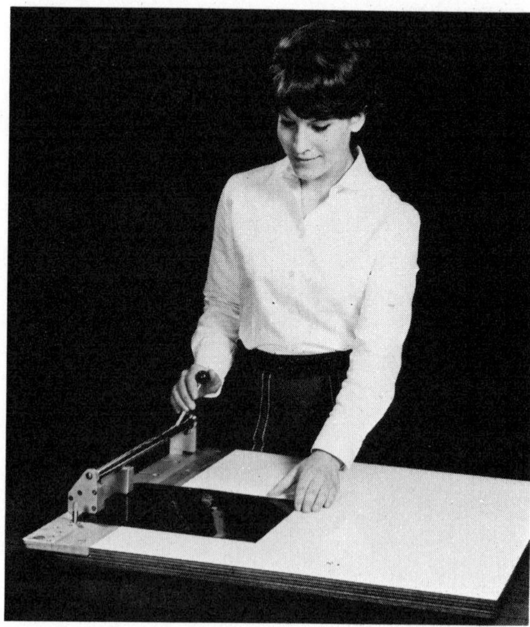

(b)

Figure 10.36. Example of a punched tab (a) and a mechanical punch (b)
Courtesy of Dainippon Screen Mfg. Co., Ltd., distributed by DS America, Inc.

becomes the key flat for that color. Register each key color flat to the master black flat and register all other flats in the color group to the key (figure 10.39). If there is more than one black flat, they are all registered to the master black flat.

Proofing Transparent Materials

The Purpose of Proofing

After the job has been stripped and checked, it is ready to be converted to some form of plate or image carrier. Generally, however, another step, proofing each flat, occurs before plate making. It is difficult to interpret the image on the flat. Both printers and printing customers are distracted by such things as the masking sheet, tape, opaque, notations, or instruction marks. Moreover, the image on the flat is often a negative. It is also not possible to fold a flat to check for accuracy of image position for a work-and-turn or a signature job. The function of proofing is to check for image location and quality and to obtain the customer's final approval to run the job. There are basically two ways to proof transparent materials: by using ink proofs and by using photomechanical proofs.

Ink proofs are associated with limited press runs using the same types of ink and paper that are to be used on the final job. Press proofing has the disadvantage of high cost. The costs of press time (set-up, make-ready, actual running time, and clean-up) and materials involved in press proofing must be borne by the customer. Therefore, press proofing is reserved for extremely high-quality, long-run jobs. However, with press proofing the customer can see how the final job will actually look (including the final colors).

Photomechanical proofs, on the other hand, require no large investment in special proofing equipment and generally use existing plate-making equipment. Most photomechanical proofing systems use a light-sensitive emulsion coated on some inexpen-

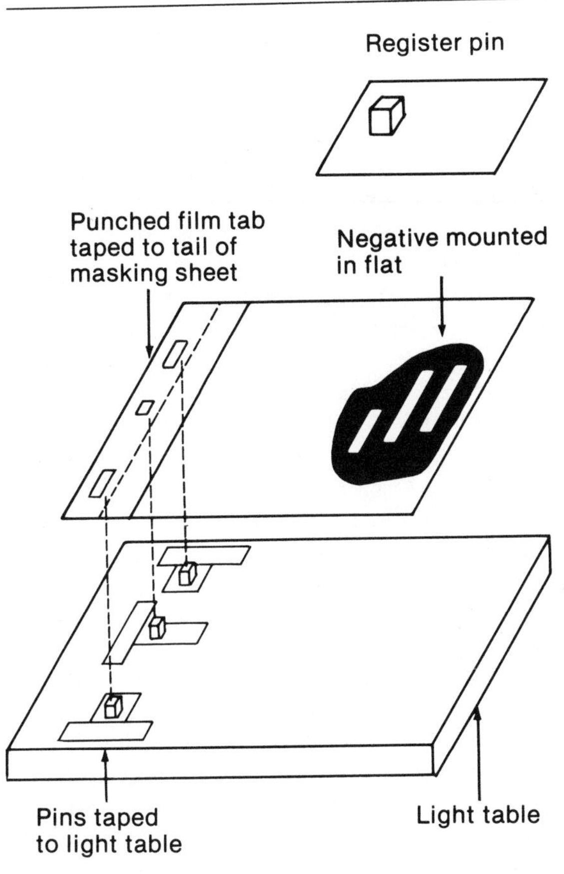

Figure 10.37. Using register pins to secure a flat to a light table Register pins are taped in place on the light table in line with the holes in the punched film.

sive carrier, such as paper or plastic, which is then exposed through the flat in the same way the plates will be exposed. The emulsion is then chemically processed to produce an image that represents the final press sheet. Contrary to what many proofing manufacturers claim, no photomechanical proof will match the quality and color of a press proof.

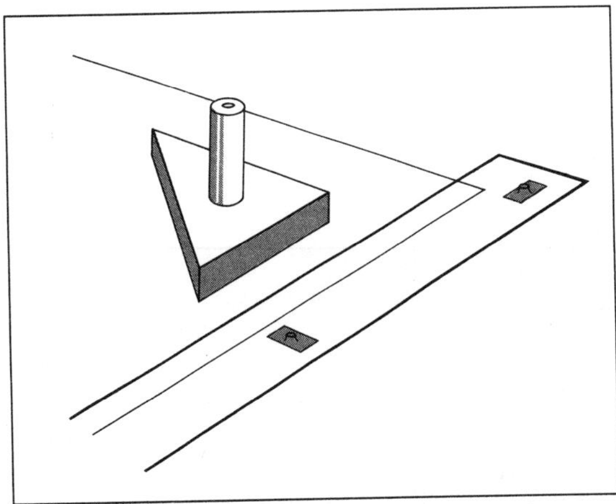

Figure 10.38. Example of a sighting tube

However, the low cost of photomechanical proofs vastly outweighs this disadvantage. Photomechanical proofs are generally classified as either single color or multiple color.

Single-Color Photomechanical Proofing

Single-color photomechanical proofing is the least expensive of all proofing systems. Most methods use a vacuum frame to hold the flat in contact with a light-sensitive coating on a sheet of paper and a light source to expose the emulsion. This equipment is discussed in detail in the following section. Single-color proofs do not show the actual ink color of the final press run. They are used only to check on such things as imposition, masking and opaquing, and image position. Four common types of materials used for single-color proofs are blueprint paper, brownlines, diazo, and instant image proof papers.

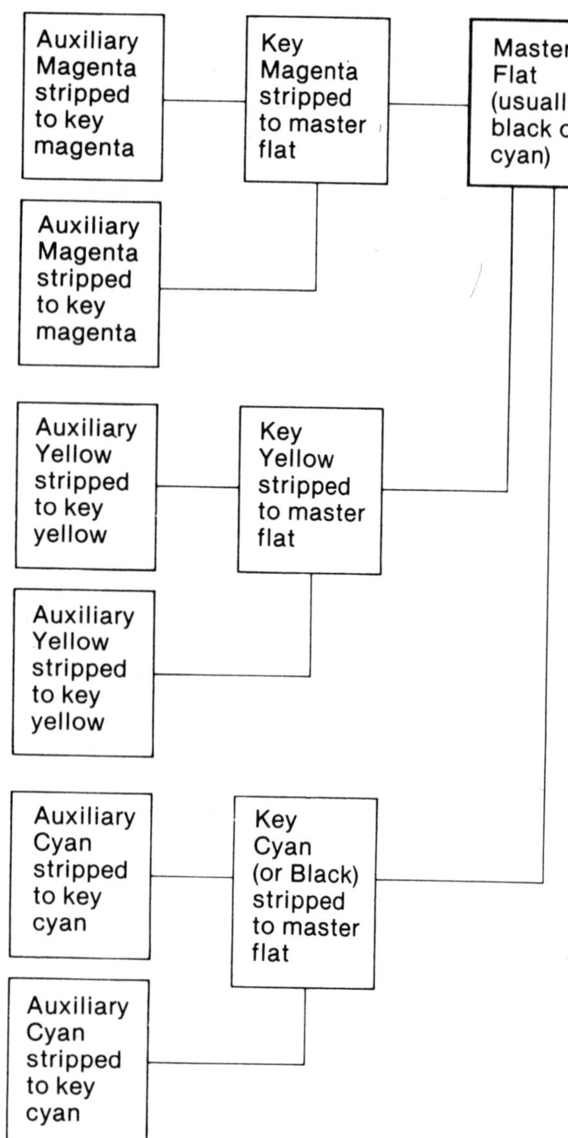

Figure 10.39. Example of a sequence of color flat registration for more than four flats A four-color reproduction may require more than four flats if two different screen tint percentages in the same color are specified or if line copy falls too close to a halftone image to include in one flat.

Blueprint paper is a low-cost material that produces positive images from transparent film negatives. The paper is coated with an organic iron compound (potassium ferricyanide) that changes structure when light strikes it. The proof is developed in water and dried by hanging it in the air. Unfortunately, blueprint paper is not dimensionally stable (which means that it can easily change size) and the image recorded on the blueprint tends to lighten with age.

Brownlines are formed on papers coated with a silver salt compound similar in structure to that used on photographic films. Brownlines form an image that becomes more intense the longer the exposure to the development chemicals. The proof is developed in water, fixed in hypo, washed in water to remove the fixer, and air dried. Although the image formed on a brownline is permanent, the paper is not dimensionally stable.

Diazo papers produce a positive image when exposed to transparent film positives. The exposed emulsion is developed when placed in contact with a special liquid or gas (generally ammonia fumes). The material has the advantage of relative dimensional stability because the paper is not moistened with water during development.

Instant image proof papers produce dry image proofs without the aid of processing equipment and chemicals. One example is DuPont's Dylux materials, which are exposed with ultraviolet light and produce a visible image without chemical processing. The proof can be fixed, or deactivated, after exposure by placing the proof under a bright white light. Dylux papers are available coated on one or two sides, with either a blue or near-black image. The material can be handled under normal room light for several minutes. Typical exposure light sources are Sylvania BLB lamps, pulsed xenon with an ultra violet filter, mercury vapor with a UV filter, or carbon arc with a UV filter. Different colors can be proofed for fit by using different screen tint values to represent each color.

Blueprints, brownlines, diazos, and instant image proofs can all be used to check imposition for jobs that involve image alignment on both sides of a press sheet. Most papers can be purchased from the manufacturer with both sides sensitized. The first flat to be proofed is positioned on the paper, small notches that line up with the center lines of the flat are cut, and an exposure is made. The proofing paper is turned over, the center lines of the second flat are placed in line with the small notches, and the second exposure is made. When processed, the proof can be folded or cut to approximate the final job. If paper that is sensitized on both sides is not available, two separate sheets can be blued together for the same effect.

Multiple-Color Photomechanical Proofing

It is possible to proof multicolor jobs in one color on a single-color proofing paper. Brownlines are often used for this purpose by varying the exposure time for each color. Because the intensity of the image recorded on a brownline varies with exposure time, each color is recognizable as a different shade on the paper, and is easy to check registration. The typical use for multicolor proofing, however, is to show the job in full color to predict how the final press sheet will look. Color proofing materials can be grouped as either transparent or opaque based.

Transparent color proofs. These proofs are generally formed from separate sheets of clear-based plastic (each carrying one color image) that are positioned over each other so that the total effect approximates the printed job. Many companies produce these materials. A commonly used product is Color-Key, manufactured by the 3M Company. Color-Key sheets are available as negative or positive acting. They produce transparent colors on a clear polyester backing. The sheets are exposed to a high-intensity light source with the emulsion of the negative or positive being proofed against the base side of the proofing sheet. The image is processed with a special 3M Color-Key developer, rinsed in water, and allowed to air dry (figure 10.40). When used for proofing four-color process negatives, the exposed and developed sheets are sandwiched yellow first, then magenta, cyan, and black last. Each sheet is placed in register with the previous sheet and is fastened on one side to hold all the sheets in register. One advantage of transparent proofs is that the potential press sheet can be placed under the transparent sandwich of colors to obtain an approximation of the appearance of the final job.

Opaque color proofs. This type of proof is prepared by adhering, exposing, and developing each successive color emulsion on a special solid-based sheet. A typical product is Cromalin by the DuPont Corporation. The Cromalin system uses a patented laminator to apply a special photopolymer to the proof stock. The laminated sheet is then exposed through a film positive by using a conventional plate-making system. After exposure, the top mylar protective layer is removed and the entire sheet is dusted with a color toner, which only the exposed areas accept. The dry toners are available in a wide variety of colors and usually can be mixed to match any press ink color. After all surplus toner powder has been removed, the proof sheet can be relaminated and exposed to additional flats to pro-

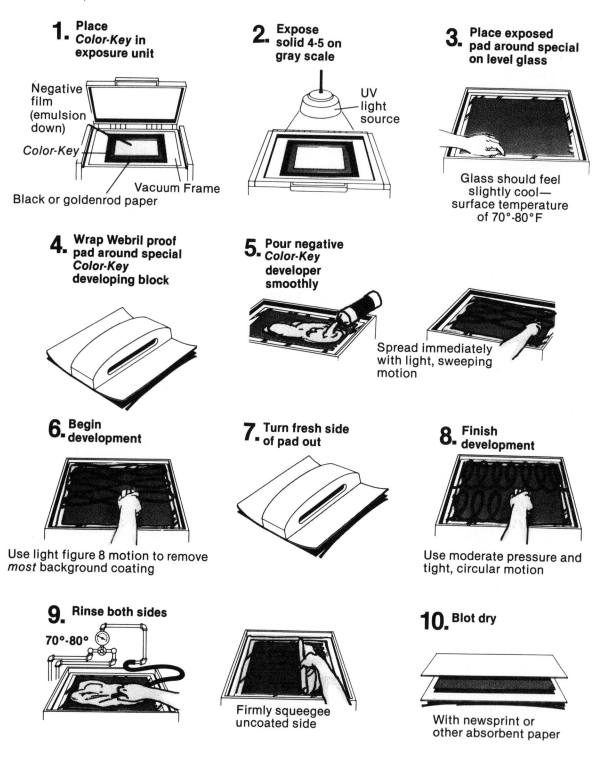

1. Place *Color-Key* in exposure unit

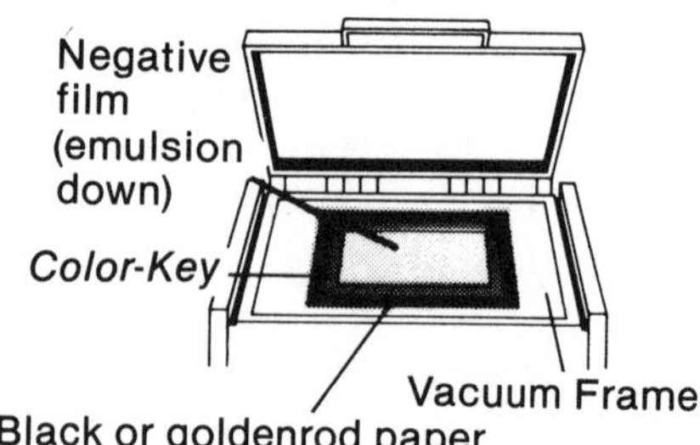

2. Expose solid 4-5 on gray scale

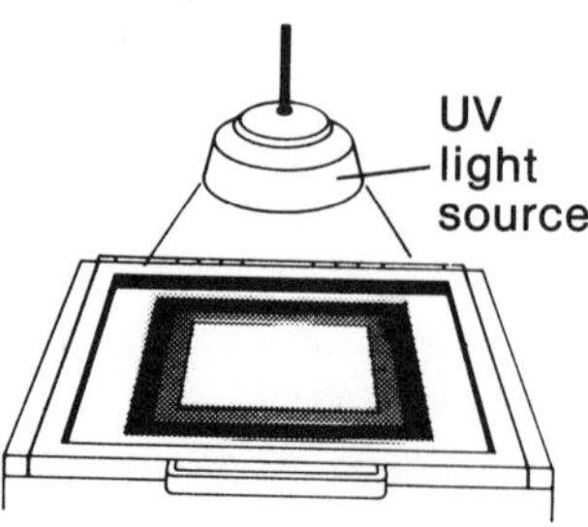

3. Place exposed pad around special on level glass

Glass should feel slightly cool—surface temperature of 70°-80°F

4. Wrap Webril proof pad around special *Color-Key* developing block

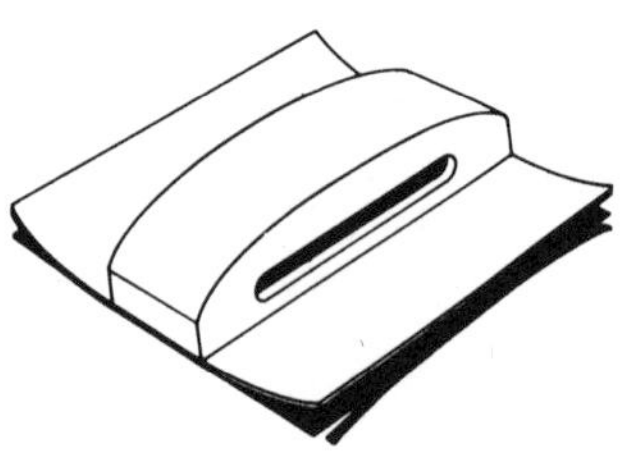

5. Pour negative *Color-Key* developer smoothly

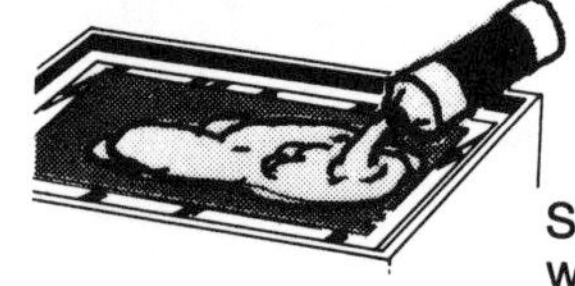

Spread immediately with light, sweeping motion

6. Begin development

Use light figure 8 motion to remove *most* background coating

7. Turn fresh side of pad out

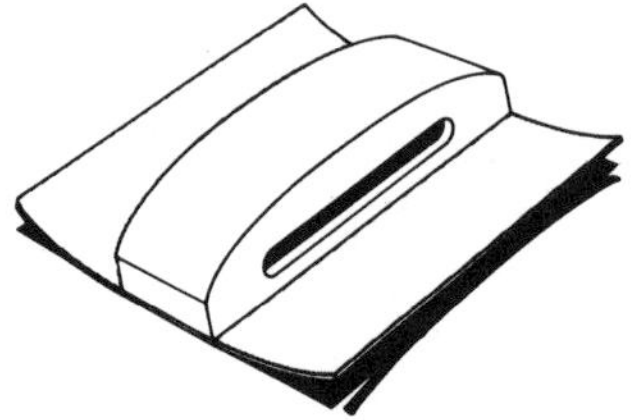

8. Finish development

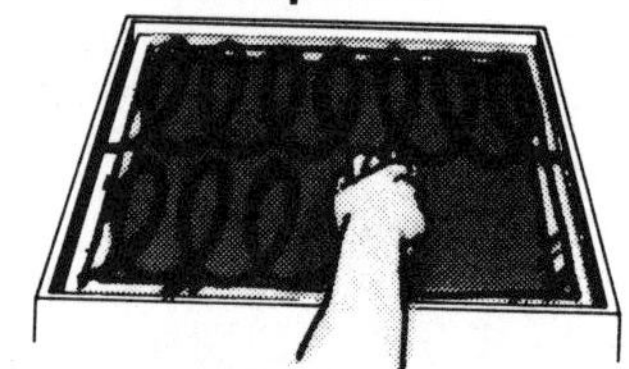

Use moderate pressure and tight, circular motion

9. Rinse both sides

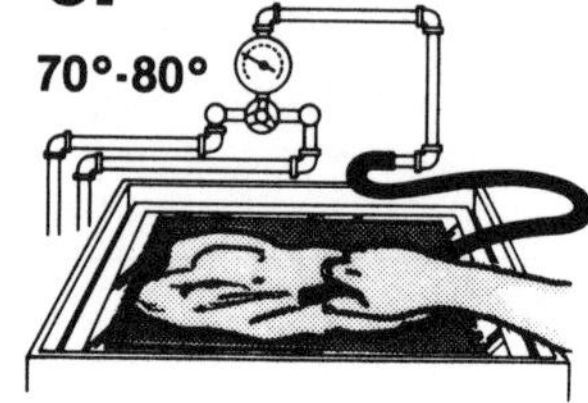

Firmly squeegee uncoated side

10. Blot dry

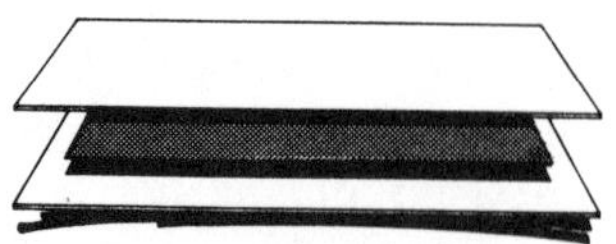

With newsprint or other absorbent paper

duce other color images on the same sheet.

It is important that all color proofs be viewed under a common light source. Any variation in color temperature, light intensity, amount of reflected room light, evenness of illumination, or surrounding color environment will change human judgment concerning color values. Many problems result when the printer and the customer use two different light sources or viewing situations to view color proofs. The industry has generally accepted 5,000°K color temperature emitted from an artificial source as the standard for color viewing. Several companies have developed viewing systems that meet the industry's specifications (figure 10.41).

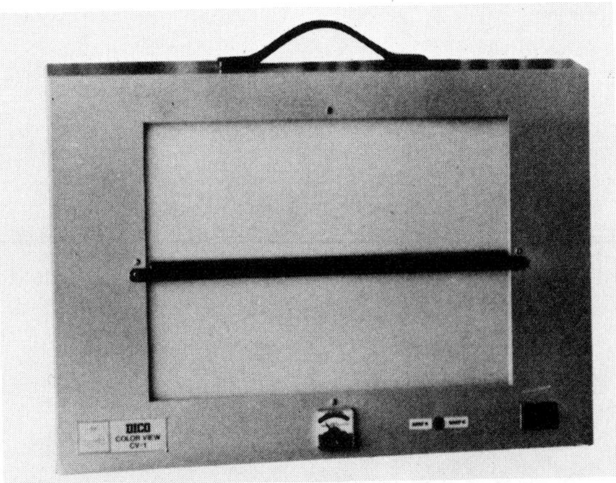

Figure 10.41. Example of a color viewer
Courtesy of Direct Image Corporation.

Equipment for Proofing and Plating

Exposure Systems

Most equipment for proofing and plating can be used interchangeably. In most industrial situations, one system meets both production needs. The simplest sort of exposure system is made up of a vacuum frame and some high-intensity light source. The vacuum frame holds the film or flat in contact with the proofing material or plate. The light source produces the actinic light that exposes the emulsion. Whether used for plating or proofing, most systems are referred to as **platemakers.** Some platemakers have the vacuum frame and light source set within a cabinet (figure 10.42). Other systems have the frame and lights on rolling stands that can be moved closer or farther apart.

Most proofing and plate photoemulsions have peak sensitivity in the blue and ultraviolet end of the visible spectrum (see "Light Sources," appendix B). The two most commonly used light sources for plate making are carbon arc and pulsed xenon. The main disadvantage of carbon arc lamps is the emission of fumes and dirt, which must be removed from the plateroom with a ventilation system. The carbon arc system is gradually being replaced with cleaner and more effective light sources, such as pulsed xenon and metal halide. Photoflood lamps, fluorescent tubes, and quartz iodine lights have also been applied to the platemaker's needs, but they are not often used.

The equipment for processing printing plates varies. The simplest type is merely a smooth, slanted hard surface set in a sink

◀ **Figure 10.40. Processing steps 3M Color-Key negative material**
Courtesy of Printing Products Division, 3M Company.

Figure 10.42. A fliptop platemaker
Courtesy of nuArc Company, Inc.

with a water source (figure 10.43). This type, called a **plate-making sink,** is generally used for hand processing lithographic plates, but it can also be used for developing several types of photomechanical proofs. Also available are several types of automatic processing units that produce plates ready for press without any hand finishing. A variety of special purpose platemakers and processing units are designed to be used with a specific process (such as an electrostatic platemaker for the electrostatic plate-making process).

Light Source Calibration

The control of exposure is the most important variable in the plating and proofing processes. The simplest form of platemaker control has a toggle switch that can be plugged into an automatic timer or manually controlled by an operator with a watch. The problem (as with line photography) is that accurate exposure is not necessarily related to time. Such variables as line voltage variation, the position of the light source, and the age of the lamp can all influence exposure. The most accurate technique for exposure control is a light integrator (figure 10.44). With a phototube sensing unit mounted on the platemaker vacuum frame, the integrator automatically controls the units of light reaching the plate or proof and alters exposure time with any line or light source variation. Such a system ensures that there will be no more than a 0.5% difference in the amount of light that strikes the plate from any two exposures made at the same time setting.

Whether you are using a simple toggle switch or an integrated system, the initial problem is to determine the quantity of exposure needed to produce a quality plate or proof image. Most plate or proofing material manufacturers will provide recommended exposures for general lighting situations. However, the actual exposure will differ for each working situation. To calibrate or to determine this actual exposure, you must use a transparent **sensitivity guide.**

The sensitivity guide is a continuous-tone density scale (in effect, a transparent gray scale). The density of each step increases from step 1 (around 0.0 density) to the last step (generally around 3.0 density). The scale passes progressively less light to the plate or proof as the step number becomes larger.

Figure 10.43. A plate-making sink
Courtesy of nuArc Company, Inc.

In addition to a suggested exposure, plate or proofing material manufacturers will also indicate a specific step reading that the exposure should record on the sensitivity guide. For example, for negative acting Color-Key, 3M recommends that the exposure be sufficient to pass enough light through a ten-step transparent sensitivity guide so that a solid step 4 or 5 will be recorded on the proof after development.

To determine the actual exposure for a specific working situation, place a test sheet of the plate or proofing material in the plate-

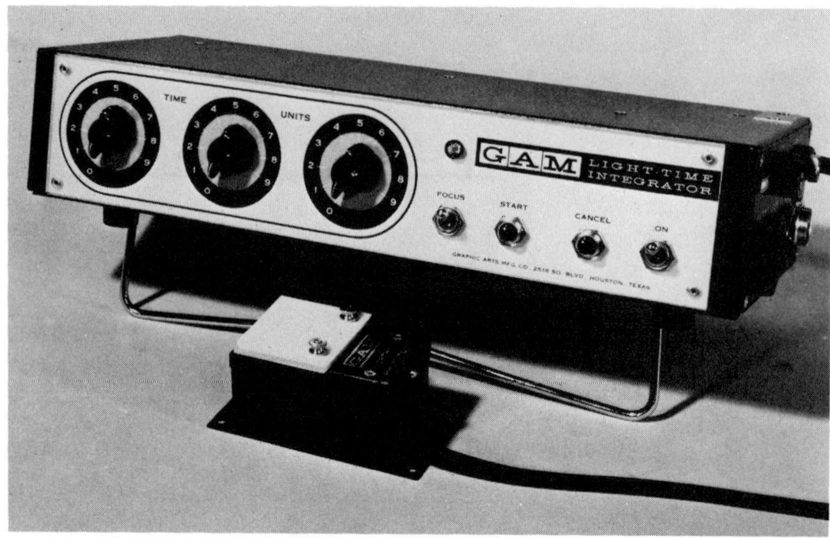

Figure 10.44. A light-time integrator
Courtesy of Graphic Arts Manufacturing Co.

maker, emulsion positioned as specified by the manufacturer. Place a transparent gray scale over the sheet with the right-reading side of the gray scale facing the exposure lamp. Mask all other areas of the emulsion with a masking sheet. Make an initial exposure by using the manufacturer's recommendations. Then process the material with appropriate procedures and controls. If the resulting image shows a step reading less than required, increase the exposure. If a higher step is recorded, decrease the exposure and run another test. Continue this trial-and-error technique until the desired step is reached. The exposure that produces the desired step density becomes the actual exposure for that specific material.

For greatest consistency of results, a sensitivity guide should be stripped into the flat margin for every plate. If variation occurs, each processing step should be reexamined for any variation, or the entire system should be recalibrated.

It is a general rule that the light source should be positioned from the plate a distance equal to the diagonal measure of the plate. Units that have the lamp a fixed distance from the vacuum frame are set for the maximum plate size that will fit the vacuum frame. There is no difficulty adjusting the distance when both the frame and light source are movable, but the exposure will vary. To recalibrate the exposure for each distance change is costly and time consuming. There is, however, a relationship that will show the new exposure, given a previous correct exposure time and distance. This relationship is expressed as follows:

$$\text{New Exposure} = (\text{Previous Exposure in seconds}) \times \left(\frac{\text{New Distance in inches}}{\text{Old Distance in inches}}\right)^2$$

$$\text{or NE} = \text{PE} \times \left(\frac{\text{ND}}{\text{OD}}\right)^2$$

where: NE = New exposure time in seconds
PE = Previous exposure time in seconds
ND = New distance in inches
OD = Old distance in inches

For example, if the original exposure was 40 seconds when the light source was at a distance of 50 inches, the exposure would be 160 seconds if the lights were moved to a new distance of 100 inches.

$$\begin{aligned} \text{New Exposure} &= 40 \times \left(\frac{100 \times 100}{50 \times 50}\right) \\ &= 40 \times \frac{10{,}000}{2{,}500} \\ &= 40 \times 4 \\ \text{New Exposure} &= 160 \text{ seconds} \end{aligned}$$

Step-and-Repeat Plate Making

Often a number of identical images must be placed on a single printing plate. One solution is to prepare a separate mechanical layout for each image and gang them all up on one illustration board. A second method is to prepare only one original image but produce a film conversion for each desired plate image. All pieces of film can then be stripped onto one flat. Unfortunately, both of these methods would take far too much time. To meet the need of identical multiple plate images, the industry has developed the **step-and-repeat platemaker** (figure 10.45).

With this approach, one paste-up and film conversion is prepared. The single negative (or positive) is then masked and fitted into a special frame or chase. When the chase is inserted in the step-and-repeat platemaker, the device can be manually or automatically moved to each required position on the plate and an exposure made. During each exposure, all areas of the plate except the portion under the chase are covered and receive no light.

Plate-Making Systems

Although not necessarily associated with a particular type of plate, several exposure systems that significantly increase productivity in the plate-making department have emerged in recent years. One interesting adaptation is the Paginator by the Royal Zenith Corporation (figure 10.46).

The Paginator is a total system that begins with a daylight-loaded camera console. The original copy is aligned with register guides and is recorded onto 35 mm high-contrast film. Image reductions and enlargements can be adjusted proportionally on the film. The exposed roll is then processed in an auxiliary unit and is inserted into the transport head of the platemaker. Control information, such as plate size, number of pages, image margins, and head positions for each page, is punched onto a paper tape. The plate is positioned on a vacuum platen, the punched tape is inserted into the tape reader, and the machine is turned on. The transport head automatically advances the film to the first frame, moves to the correct position over the plate, and projects the page image onto the plate emulsion. After each exposure, the next film frame is advanced, the head moves to the correct page position, and another image is exposed. After all pages have been projected onto the plate, the plate is removed and processed.

Figure 10.45. A step-and-repeat platemaker
Courtesy of Royal Zenith Corporation

Figure 10.46. The Paginator by the Royal Zenith Corporation
Courtesy of Ruth-Graphics Division, Sun Chemical Corporation.

Key Terms

stripping
flat
proofing
cylinder line
pinholes
complementary flats
master flat
snap fitters and dowels
photomechanical proofs
blueline flat
brownline
diazo
transparent color proof
opaque color proofs
platemaker
sensitivity guide
step-and-repeat platemaker

Questions for Review

1. What is the task of the industrial stripper?
2. What is the purpose of the masking sheet when preparing a negative flat?
3. What does the cylinder line represent on a flat?
4. Why can no printing image be placed in the gripper margin?
5. What is the purpose of opaquing a film negative?
6. What is the purpose of etching a film negative?
7. What are some advantages to stripping film positives rather than film negatives?
8. Why must a halftone negative be mounted in a window on the flat so that the halftone emulsion is facing in the same direction as the emulsion on the negative that carries the window?
9. What are complementary flats?
10. Briefly describe the approach of using the punch and register pin technique from the camera to the press in order to control registration.
11. What are the two basic approaches of multiflat stripping for process color work?
12. Describe the difference between a key flat and a master flat for multiflat stripping for process color work.
13. What is the purpose of proofing?
14. What are the three common types of single-color, photomechanical proofing?
15. What are the two basic groups of multicolor proofs?
16. What is the most important variable in the plating and proofing process?

Chapter Eleven

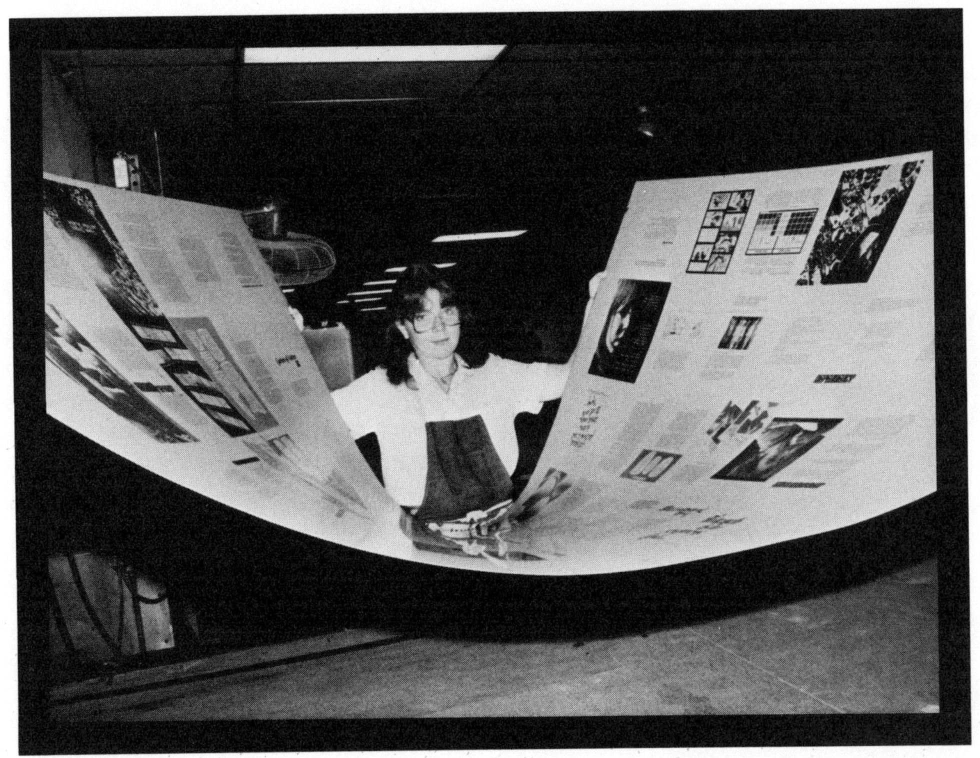

Offset Plate Making

Anecdote to Chapter Eleven

In 1789 a law student at the University of Ingolstadt in Bavaria, Germany, wrote a play entitled *Die Maedchenkenner* and had it published. After all printing costs were subtracted, he made a sizable profit and was convinced

Alois Senefelder
Smithsonian Institution, Photo No. 10577A.

his fortune was to be made on the stage. Alois Senefelder is little known to us today as a playwright, but he is recognized as the inventor of lithography.

After *Die Maedchenkenner,* Senefelder's plays were not well received, and he lost money on them. He was convinced, though, that it was not the quality of his writing but rather the high cost of the printing that caused his financial strain. After viewing printers at work one day, he decided printing was a simple task and resolved to learn the craft so he might write, print, and publish his own works. The common printing process where he lived was copperplate engraving. The images to be printed were carved in reverse into soft copper plates with a flexible steel tool.

Senefelder purchased the necessary tools and materials and began to learn the printers' craft. He soon learned that it was not as simple as he had assumed. He made many errors on the copper and finally had to invent a correction fluid (made from three parts wax and one part soap, mixed with a small quantity of lampblack, all dissolved in rain water) to use to correct his mistakes.

Unfortunately, even with the correction fluid, Alois's skills and finances were so small that he could not afford to continue practicing on actual copper plates. He tried tin as a substitute, but his resources dwindled with even that inexpensive material.

By chance he learned of a material called Kellhein stone—a limestone quarried at a local site. The stone had the unique quality that slabs of nearly any thickness could be easily cut. Kellhein stone, in comparison to copper, could be polished to a perfect surface with little effort. He resolved to practice writing in reverse on the stone to develop the skill necessary to be able to return to copper. With the stage set for a discovery, Senefelder relates in his book:

> *I had just succeeded in my little laboratory in polishing a stone plate, which I intended to cover with etching ground, in order to continue my exercises in writing backwards, when my mother entered the room, and desired me to write her a bill for the washerwoman, who was waiting for the linen; I happened not to have even the smallest slip of paper at hand, as my little stock of paper had been entirely exhausted by taking proof impressions from the stones; nor was there even a drop of ink in the inkstand. As the matter would not admit of delay, and we had nobody in the house to send for a supply of the deficient materials, I resolved to write the list with my ink prepared with wax, soap and lampblack, on the stone which I had just polished, and from which I could copy it at leisure.**

The result of that experience was an idea. Making a border of wax around the stone, Alois allowed an acid solution to stand on the entire stone surface for a short period of time and thereby etch away the limestone in any areas on which he had not drawn an image. The wax writing solution resisted the acid. After he removed the acid, he found that the coated, or image, areas were raised about 1⁄10 inch above the rest of the stone. By carefully rolling ink over the surface, he could ink only the image and easily transfer this ink to a sheet of paper with a little pressure.

Senefelder had invented an adaptation of the relief process—printing from a raised surface. Because of the low cost of stone, the ease of creating an image, and the simplicity of transferring the image to paper, he felt he could easily compete with local printers for jobs. He contracted with several people, notably music sellers, to produce musical scores and continued to experiment with his invention.

Senefelder called his invention "lithography," based on the Greek words *lithos,* meaning stone, and *graphein,* meaning to write. Although his discovery was a significant advance beyond copperplate engraving or even hand-set relief type, his greatest contribution was the refinement of what he called "chemical lithography."

After several years of experimentation, he observed that a solution of gum (gum arabic) and water, when coated over the stone, would clog the pores in the stone and would repel ink. As long as the gum-water mixture remained moist, an ink brayer rolled over the entire stone surface would deposit pigment only in the image area on the stone. By alternately moistening and inking the stone, he could build up a layer of pigment sufficient to transfer a perfect image to a sheet of paper.

It is this concept of moisture and ink repelling each other that is the basis for all contemporary lithographic printing.

*Alois Senefelder, *A Complete Course of Lithography,* reprint of 1819 edition (New York: DaCapo Press, 1968), p. 9.

Objectives for Chapter Eleven

After completing chapter 11 the student will be able to:

- Describe the characteristics of an offset printing plate.
- Define the term grain.
- Explain how offset plates are grained.
- Explain the basic components of light sensitive coating for offset plates.
- List and describe three major classifications of lithographic plates.
- Explain the difference between negative acting and positive acting plates.
- List various methods of imaging a direct image, nonphotographic plate.
- Discuss the characteristics of and identify the market for direct image photographic plates.
- Explain the process of preparing a wipe-on lithographic plate.
- List and describe two types of presensitized surface plates.
- List the steps involved in processing an additive lithographic plate.
- List the steps involved in processing a subtractive lithographic plate.
- Describe the construction of a deep-etch plate.
- Explain how a deep-etch plate is processed.
- List and describe four types of bimetal plates.
- Explain how a bimetal plate is prepared and processed.
- Explain how a transfer lithographic plate is exposed and processed.
- Discuss the basic procedure involved in making an electrostatic lithographic plate.

Introduction

The preparation and printing of most modern metal plates used in lithographic printing is based on the original concepts of stone printing developed by Alois Senefelder nearly two hundred years ago. Senefelder's invention was intended and used as an industrial process. Printers used this technique to reproduce images such as advertisements, business forms, maps, and many other printed products.

Lithography developed a reputation as a fine arts process in America through the products of the Currier and Ives Company that operated from 1835 to 1895. Today stone lithography remains an art process; historically it has formed the foundation for a major portion of the commercial printing industry. A brief review of the steps taken by a stone lithographer will help you understand all industrial approaches.

A slab of lithographic stone (generally limestone) is first cleaned and ground to a perfectly flat surface with a smaller stone and water mixed with carborundum. This process is called "graining." Once the stone is grained and dry, the artist-printer begins to draw on the surface with a lithographic grease crayon (a refinement of Senefelder's original correction fluid). This forms the printing image. The grease is absorbed into the pores of the stone. A gum arabic solution (generally mixed with a small quantity of nitric acid), called an etch, is then worked into the entire stone surface. The gum is absorbed into the nonimage areas and solidifies the grease, or image, areas. Etching seals the open parts of the stone against grease but keeps them receptive to water. After the residue crayon is removed with turpentine, the stone is ready to print.

A roller of ink is prepared and a layer of water is wiped on the stone with a damp cloth. The water is repelled by the grease crayon image, but it remains in the nonimage areas. As the ink roller moves over the stone, the film of water acts as a buffer that repels ink. Wherever there is no water (as on the crayon image), the ink remains.

If a prepared piece of paper is carefully positioned over the stone and pressure is applied, the image will be transferred to the sheet. A skillful stone lithographer can prepare a stone and pull one print every ten minutes.

Lithographic Printing Plates

The basis of all industrial lithography today is a combination of photography and Senefelder's original observation that oil and water do not mix. The degree of image control and the speed of preparation, however, have significantly increased.

Base Plate Materials

Almost all modern lithographic presses employ the offset principle and use as an image carrier a thin metal sheet, called a **plate,** that can be wrapped around a press cylinder. Plate thicknesses range from 0.005 inches to around 0.030 inches, depending on the size of the plate and the type of press. The entire plate must be of uniform thickness. It is generally held to a gauge tolerance of ± 0.0005 inches. Most metals for plates are cold rolled to the final plate gauge or thickness to produce a hard printing surface.

Zinc was the standard plate material of the industry for years, but it has been almost totally replaced by aluminum for all but special purpose plates. Some types of plates are made from such materials as steel, stainless steel, chromium, copper, and even paper, but aluminum enjoys the most widespread use.

Just as Senefelder had to prepare, or **grain,** the stone surface before an image could be added to it, modern lithographic plates must also be grained. On metal surface-printing plates, this is a roughening process that must be performed so that a uniform layer of photoemulsion will adhere to the plate. All graining processes can be classified as either mechanical or chemical.

Mechanical Graining. The simplest form of mechanical graining is accomplished by placing the plate in a rotating tub filled with steel ball bearings, water, and some form of abrasive material. Assembly line techniques have been applied to the process so that a continuous row of plates passes under a series of nylon brushes with a spray of water and pumice. Sandblasting has also been used, but this procedure presents some problems because small pieces of abrasive become embedded in the metal plate surface.

Chemical Graining. Chemical graining of lithographic plates is similar in operation to Senefelder's first trial acid etch of a piece of stone. The plate is submerged in an acid bath that causes surface roughness. One technique uses an electrolytic reaction in a solution of hydrofluoric acid. Almost all presensitized surface plates (see following sections) are formed from anodized aluminum. The surface is chemically treated and then sealed. The anodized surface is unaffected by almost all acids but remains water receptive.

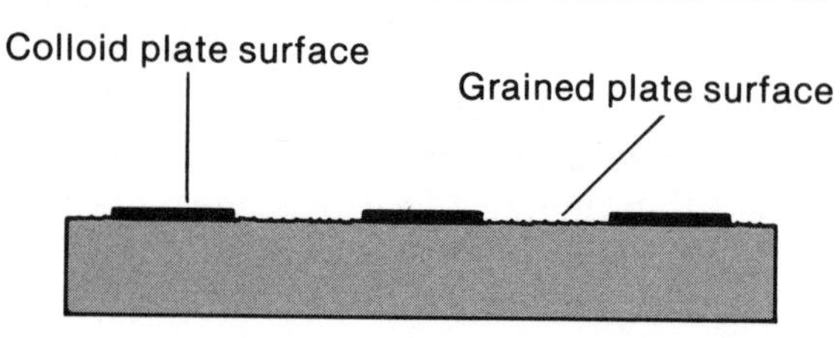

Figure 11.1. Cross section of a lithographic surface plate

Coating Materials

All modern lithographic metal plates have some form of light-sensitive material combined with a collodion coated on a grained metal surface. A **collodion** is an organic compound that forms a strong, continuous layer. When mixed with the light-sensitive solution and then exposed to light, the colloid becomes insoluble and forms a strong, continuous coating on the printing plate.

Ammonium bichromate combined with egg albumin was previously used as the photoemulsion in the photolithography process. Albumin has gradually been replaced by other solutions, until it is now very nearly obsolete. Popular industrial coatings are polyvinyl alcohol (PVA), diazo, and photopolymers.

Gum arabic is a collodion commonly used with deep-etch and some forms of bimetal plates (see following sections). It is also used for a variety of other purposes in the lithographic process. The material is harvested twice a year from the acacia tree that grows almost exclusively in the Sudan area of northern Africa. During the dry season, when a liquid gum forms under the bark of the tree, workers cut long gashes in the bark. The gum flows out and dries in the wound. The dried gum is then removed and shipped all over the world in either flake or powder form.

As taken from the tree, gum arabic is edible and is used as a main ingredient for some types of candy. Early lithographers would taste their gum solutions to check for freshness. If they smelled and tasted sweet, they were fresh. If they had a sour flavor, they were discarded.

Gum solutions are generally prepared by mixing the gum flakes or powder with water. The thickness of the mix is classified by a density scale called **baumé** (pronounced *bow-may*). Baumé can be measured with a special hydrometer designed to gauge liquids that are heavier (or denser) than water. (Specific gravity is a similar measure used to classify liquids that are lighter than water.) Pure water has a 0° Bé. Adding gum arabic increases the Baumé.

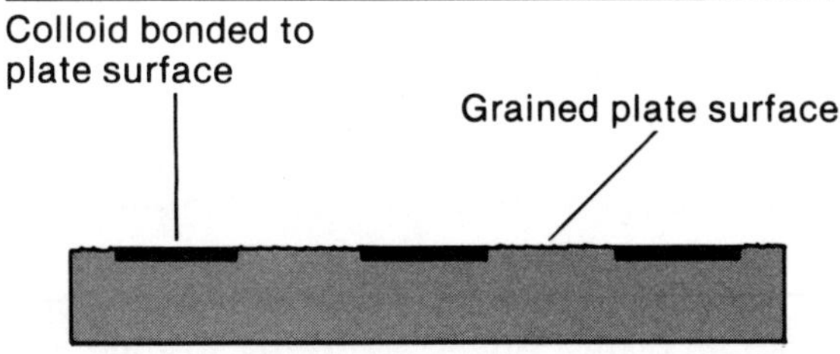

Figure 11.2. Cross section of a lithographic deep-etch plate

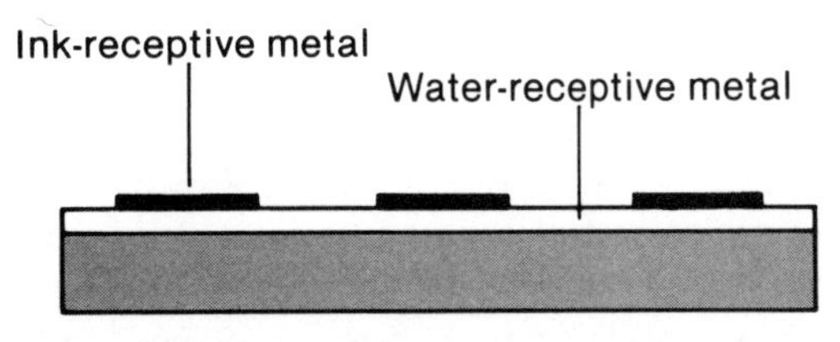

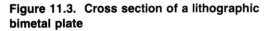

Figure 11.3. Cross section of a lithographic bimetal plate

Classifying Lithographic Plates

Lithographic plates can be classified in several ways. The most common method is to apply labels according to structure and action.

Lithographic plate structure can be described as surface, deep-etch, or bimetal. **Surface plates** can be visualized as being formed from a colloid sitting on the surface of the metal (figure 11.1). **Deep-etch plates** are formed by the actual bonding of the colloid material into the plate surface (figure 11.2). **Bimetal plates** are a recent development. They function through the adhesion of two dissimilar metals—one ink receptive and the other water receptive (figure 11.3). There are, of course, special purpose plates that defy classification with any one of these three. Surface, deep-etch, bimetal, and special purpose plates are discussed in detail in the following sections.

A second way to classify plates is by action. All industrial lithography uses the photographic process to produce the image area on the plate. Plate emulsions can be formulated for use with either negatives or positives. When the plate image is formed by passing light through the clear areas of a negative, the plate is called **negative acting.** When a positive is used to expose the plate, the plate is called **positive acting.** Plate action is not necessarily associated with plate structure. Surface plates can be designed for use with either negatives or positives, but only positives can be used with deep-etch plates.

Surface Plates

Direct Image Nonphotographic Surface Plates

The **direct image nonphotographic surface plate** is the closest remaining industrial link to the original Senefelder craft. Most current direct image base materials are either paper, acetate, plastic-impregnated paper, or thin aluminum foil adhered to a paper base. Whatever the base, however, almost all such plates have surfaces that are chemically treated to be especially grease receptive. For that reason, dirty or moist fingers touching the plate will reproduce as finger prints or smudges on the printed sheet.

Any oil-based substance can be adhered to the surface of a direct image plate. Images may be hand drawn with a lithographic crayon, a pencil, a pen and brush, or even a ballpoint pen. Probably the most common process is to type directly on the plate while using a carbon ribbon in an electric typewriter.

A special application of direct image plates is with short-run materials with standardized formats containing information that changes frequently. The format and constant information can be preprinted directly on the plate by using standing relief forms and a proof press or by actually printing master plates from a master plate on a lithographic press. These preprinted plates can then be stored. When there is a need for small changes, the new information can be typed directly onto the preprinted plate and the entire form printed. This approach is enjoying widespread use in bank check production. The basic check is mass produced on direct image plates. An individual's name and MICR (magnetic ink character recognition) number is added to one of the preprinted plates, and the completed checks are printed in a matter of minutes.

Initial layout lines or even rough image sketches can be placed on the plate surface with a special nonreproducing pencil or a water-based ink. During the printing operation only the oil-based materials will be reproduced. If an error is made, small images can be removed from the plate by erasing the area with a clean soft rubber eraser. There is danger of actually rubbing through the prepared surface, so only gentle pressure should be used. Large image areas can be removed with a special fluid available from the plate manufacturer.

In the actual running of a direct image plate, the plate is placed on the press and a special liquid etch is rubbed into the surface. The etch serves to make the image areas somewhat permanent and the nonimage areas water receptive.

The quality of direct image nonphotographic plates ranges according to their potential length of run. The most inexpensive are projected to yield a maximum of 50 press sheets before the plate image begins to break down. The highest-quality plates boast of up to 5,000 quality copies.

Direct Image Photographic Surface Plates

One of the most rapidly growing areas within the entire printing industry is "quick printing." Quick printing offers inexpensive short-run, low- to medium-quality prints from the customer's original copy. The growth in quick printing has been due largely to the refinement of **direct image photographic surface plates.**

The base material used for most direct image photographic plates is either paper or plastic. Plastic is typically used for plates requiring higher resolution capabilities than paper can give, such as reproducing prescreened halftones. Almost all direct image emulsions are of the silver halide type, which provides a very fast image response (light easily causes a chemical change in the emulsion) compared to diazo or bichromate solutions.

Most direct image photographic plates are exposed and processed in a special camera unit. The opaque original image is carefully positioned on the camera copyboard, and light is reflected from the image back through a lens system onto the plate surface. Most systems store the plate material in roll form and automatically advance and cut the required length prior to exposure.

A typical plate is structured with four separate layers: the base material, a developer emulsion layer, a sensitized emulsion layer, and a top fogged emulsion layer. The reflected light passes to the second layer and exposes the sensitized emulsion. Where light is not reflected from the copy (the image areas), the emulsion remains unexposed. The plate is then passed through a bath that activates the bottom chemical layer and causes the developer to begin to travel toward the top layer. The exposed portions of the second layer exhaust the developer, and the process is halted in the nonimage areas. Where the sensitized emulsion in the second layer was not exposed, the developer is allowed to pass to the top fogged area and changes the fogged layer to black metallic silver. Finally, the plate is delivered through a stop-bath, which halts the entire developing process.

The top surface of the plate, then, is made up of a hardened image area that is ink receptive and an undeveloped nonimage area that is water receptive. Most direct image photographic plate systems are totally automatic, self-contained units that deliver finished plates within seconds after the exposure has been made.

The advantages of this technique are speed and low cost. The entire film-stripping operation is eliminated because no film is made. The position of the original on the exposure unit determines the position of the image on the plate. The process, however, is intended for systems work where short-run, low- to medium-quality copies are to be run on presses set up for a standard paper size. Additions to and deletions of plate images are not typically attempted. Problem plates are usually remade.

Wipe-On Surface Plates

A refinement of the early attempts to sensitize a lithographic stone with a photographic emulsion is the **wipe-on metal surface plate.** With this process, an emulsion is hand or machine coated onto a pregrained plate immediately prior to plate exposure.

The base material is either aluminum or zinc. Aluminum has gained the widest acceptance. All plates are supplied to the printer with a fine-grain surface and are treated with a protective coating that acts as a link between the future emulsion coating and the base metal. The emulsion is generally mixed in small quantities shortly before it is to be applied. All current solutions are formed by mixing a dry diazo powder and a liquid base.

There are two techniques for coating the light-sensitive emulsion onto the plate: by hand and with a mechanical roller. With the hand process, the liquid is applied with a damp sponge (or cheesecloth) from which as much water as possible has been squeezed. A pool of the solution is poured into the center of the plate and is distributed in light strokes parallel to the long edge of the plate. Some manufacturers suggest a second series of strokes at right angles to the first, followed by air drying. Others direct that their materials be buffed dry, and still others recommend forced cold-air drying. Whatever the directions, the goal is to place a fairly uniform layer of emulsion over every portion of the plate surface.

The mechanical roller approach for wipe-on plates employs a dual roller device (figure 11.4). As the plate is passed between the two rollers, a perfectly uniform layer of emulsion is distributed over one side. The gap between

Figure 11.4. Coating a wipe-on surface plate
Courtesy of Western Litho Plate and Supply Company.

the rollers can be adjusted to put the desired thickness of emulsion on the plates, and there is no problem with consistency of coating or streaking, major difficulties with the hand process.

Work has been done in the past several years to develop a positive-acting wipe-on plate, but almost all systems now in use for actual production are negative acting (some positive-acting plates are currently used as image carriers for press proofing). Most wipe-on plates are exposed through a film negative, with the use of a vacuum frame and a high-intensity light source, as discussed in chapter 10. Specific times vary according to the individual plate and emulsion and the working situation. Manufacturers' specifications should always be followed.

Wipe-on plates are processed by one of two methods. The first technique is a two-step process. A pool of desensitizer gum is first poured onto the plate and rubbed into the entire surface with a damp sponge. The gum solution serves the dual function of removing any unexposed emulsion and making the nonprinting area water receptive. The excess desensitizer is removed. A second solution, made up primarily of lacquer, is then rubbed over the entire plate. Then the plate is washed with water.

The image area, which was hardened during exposure, would theoretically accept ink and could be used on the printing press. But adhering a layer of lacquer to the exposed areas greatly increases the number of copies that can be made from the plate. With the two-step process, a final layer of desensitizer gum is generally buffed into the entire surface until dry. This last step serves to protect the plate until the job is run on the press and also ensures that all unexposed emulsion has been removed.

The alternative wipe-on processing technique is a one-step process using a lacquer developer that removes the unexposed emulsion at the same time that lacquer adheres to the image areas. After being washed with water, the plate is buffed with a coating of gum arabic until the entire surface is dry.

Small images can be added to wipe-on plates by burnishing or scratching into the metal surface with a sharp instrument and then rubbing lightly with a commercial liquid

tusche (a lithographic drawing or painting material of the same nature as lithographic ink) or with the printing ink in the new area. Deletions can be made by gently rubbing away the emulsion with a **slipsnake** (an artificial stone available through lithographic suppliers) or a hard rubber eraser, and then rubbing the area with desensitizer or with a commercial scratch remover.

Presensitized Surface Plates

The first presensitized metal plate was introduced by the 3M Company in 1950. Since that time a score or more of manufacturers have developed similar plates. The advantages of presensitized plates are many. With their introduction, the lithographer no longer had to invest in or maintain emulsion-coating equipment (see "whirlers" in the following section), bother with mixing chemicals, or be concerned with freshness and quality. Presensitized plates are used by the platemaker directly from the manufacturer's wrapper with no surface preparation. In addition, the plates are processed with ease, have a reasonable long shelf life (generally up to six months) and can be produced for high-quality, long-run press situations.

The base material for presensitized plates can be paper, aluminum foil laminated to paper, or a sheet of aluminum. Paper and foil plates are generally used only for short-run situations. As discussed previously, the metal plates are typically grained by an anodizing process. The term *graining* is actually misleading because relatively little roughness is imparted to the surface. Aluminum plates can be sensitized on one or both sides.

Almost all emulsion-coating materials used today are of diazo formulation. The specific makeup of the solution varies from manufacturer to manufacturer, but the primary ingredient of all types is nitrogen. When the plate emulsion is exposed to a sufficient quantity of light (UV sensitive), the nitrogen is released and the material becomes insensitive to additional light. The insensitive emulsion then can readily accept dyes that become the printing, ink-receptive surface.

Presensitized plates are available in a wide range of capabilities, from short runs of less than 1,000 copies to emulsions that can easily produce as many as 300,000 impressions. With the anodized metal surface, the diazo emulsion, and mass production techniques, presensitized plates easily compete in quality and cost with other types of surface plate.

In addition to being either negative or positive acting, presensitized plates can also be classified as additive or subtractive. Recall that for wipe-on plates a lacquer was adhered to the image areas in order to increase potential plate life. The lacquer, then, is the surface that actually accepts the ink. The same concept is used with preparing the image areas for presensitized plates. When the printer applies a lacquer-like material to the image areas during plate processing, the plate is **additive.** When the printing surface is built into the emulsion by the manufacturer and the printer merely desensitizes the unexposed areas, the plate is **subtractive.**

Processing Additive Plates. Additive materials can be processed with a one- or two-step technique. With the two-step process the plate, after exposure, is first desensitized with a gum-acid solution. The chemical is distributed over the carrier with a moist sponge in order to remove the emulsion and/or make the unexposed emulsion area water receptive. The entire plate is then rubbed with a gum-water-lacquer mixture (plate developer) to

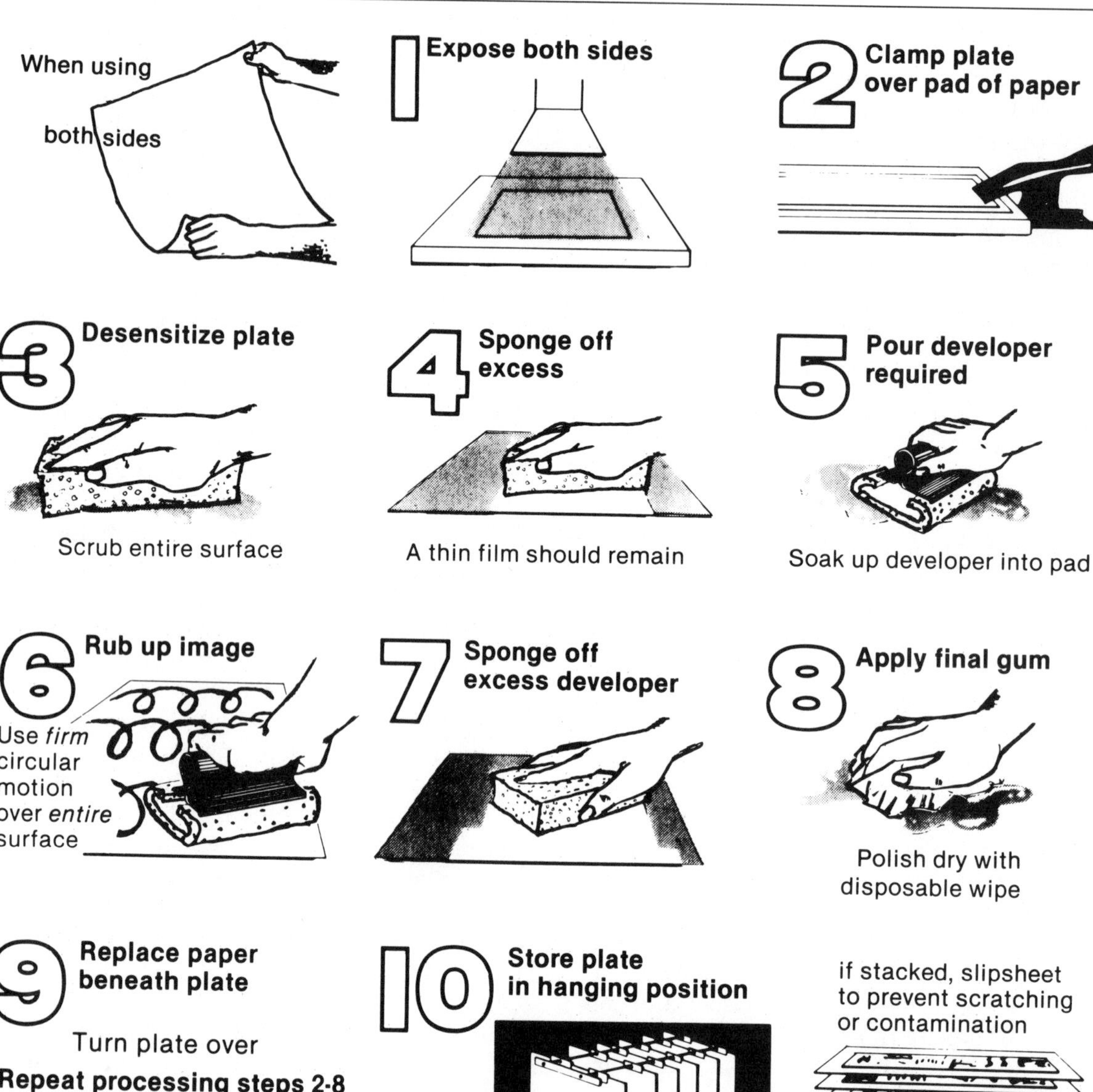

Figure 11.5. Processing additive lithographic surface plates
Courtesy of Printing Products Division, 3M Company.

build up the image areas. Finally, the plate is washed, squeegeed, and coated with a light layer of gum arabic (figure 11.5). With the one-step technique, the desensitizer and lacquer-developer functions are combined. The plate is developed with the single solution, washed, squeegeed, and gummed.

Negative-acting presensitized emulsions are exposed by light passing through the open or image areas of a film negative.

Processing Subtractive Plates. With negative-acting subtractive plates, only one developing step is used. After exposure, a special developer, supplied by the plate manufacturer, is used to remove the unexposed lacquer emulsion that was added during the presensitizing process. Again, the plate is washed and squeegeed, but a special subtractive gum must be used to coat the plate for storage (figure 11.6).

Positive-acting presensitized plates are exposed by light passing through the open or nonimage areas of a film positive. Positive-acting presensitized plates can also be classified as either additive or subtractive. In general, after exposure, the exposed emulsion of an additive plate is removed by wiping it with a special developer supplied by the manufacturer. The unexposed or image area remains in place. The developing action is then halted by a fixing agent. As with negative-acting additive plates, lacquer is rubbed into the plate. The lacquer adheres to the image areas and increases the potential length of the press run. After the plate is washed and squeegeed, it is coated with gum arabic and buffed dry. Subtractive positive-acting plates are processed in a similar manner, but without the lacquer step.

Several plate manufacturers have developed automatic processing units for presensitized plates (figure 11.7). Although the specific configuration varies from unit to unit, all systems provide for the exposed plate to be inserted at one end, use automatic drive rollers for uniform feeding, and deliver a finished, gummed, and dried plate at the other end. Automated processing has virtually eliminated the possibility of an uneven printing emulsion. This can be a problem with hand-lacquered additive plates.

Deep-Etch Plates

Defining Deep-Etch Plates

There is basically only one category of deep-etch plates. All are defined by the fact that the emulsion areas are bonded or etched into the base metal, unlike surface plates where the emulsion is merely adhered to the surface. This single characteristic permits a deep-etch plate to hold more ink than any other type of lithographic plate, which results in a greater ink density on the printed sheet. Halftones appear more brilliant with a superb tonal range representation.

The base material for deep-etch plates can be aluminum, zinc, or even stainless steel. The plate is fine grained, by a mechanical or chemical process. Some manufacturers have refined techniques that can use an anodized aluminum plate surface. Some types of plates can be regrained after one use and used a second time with no decrease in image quality.

The basic concept of the deep-etch plate is that of a stencil formed on the plate that covers the nonimage areas with a resist but leaves image areas as open base metal that can be etched with a special solution. Two types of coating materials are commonly used

1 Place exposed plate on smooth firm surface

Use yellow lighting in work area

2 Pour developer smoothly

Apply liberally to Pad and Plate

3 Spread developer with pad

Pause briefly to allow chemicals to work

4 Develop

Use firm pressure and tight circular motion

5 Clean pad

Remove loose coating particles

6 Squeegee plate and sink area

Remove *all* visible developer from *plate surface*

7 Rinse image side thoroughly

Use *disposable* paper wipe to mop surface while rinsing

8 Rinse under plate

To wash away developer and sensitizers

9 Squeegee plate

Face

Backside

10 Gum plate

- Place plate on dry surface
- Dry plate if still wet
- Pour on liberal amount of Gum
- Spread with disposable wipe
- Buff dry with fresh disposable wipe
- Turn plate over on clean dry surface
- Dry backside with wipe

Storage—Slipsheet processed plates to prevent scratching or contamination.

Figure 11.6. Processing subtractive lithographic surface plates
Courtesy of Printing Products Division, 3M Company.

to form the stencil: a bichromate gum solution and a bichromate polyvinyl alcohol (PVA) formulation. The gum compound provides greater exposure latitude, but the PVA is easier to process.

After the base plate is coated with the light-sensitive emulsion, a right-reading film positive is registered with the carrier in a vacuum frame and a high-intensity light source is projected through the clear, or nonimage, areas on the positive. The actinic light hardens the emulsion in the nonimage areas, but in the image areas no light reaches the plate and the coating remains soft.

Deep-etch plates are unrivaled for high-quality, extremely long-run press jobs. Runs of 500,000 impressions are common, and longer editions have been printed on quality machines run by experienced craftspeople.

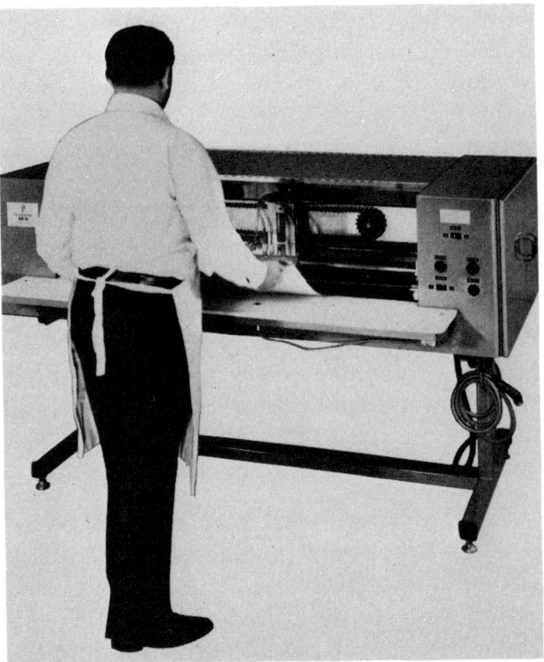

Figure 11.7. An automatic plate-processing unit
Courtesy of Western Litho Plate and Supply Company.

Preparing and Processing Deep-Etch Plates

Coating manufacturers all have specific directions for their material. The following is a description of the typical processing steps for a bichromated gum deep-etch plate.

1. The grained surface of all deep-etch plates must be cleaned before a light-sensitive emulsion can be adhered. First wash the plate with a stream of running water to remove any dust particles that might have become attached to the surface during storage. Allow a thin layer of an acid solution to stand on the entire plate surface for several minutes and then flush the mixture away with running water. A phosphoric acid and water mixture is generally used as this cleaning pre-etch. The diluted acid does not damage the plate grain.

2. The coating of most deep-etch plates is accomplished in a mechanical device called a **whirler,** a flat surface that turns (like a record player) and is contained within a box to prevent chemicals from being sprayed into the work room. Most whirlers also have a heating element to hasten drying. Some presensitized deep-etch plates have been developed in recent years, but they have not found widespread acceptance. The whirler remains the most common method of deep-etch plate coating.

The coating technique is simple, and the machine does most of the work. After cleaning, clamp the plate into the center of the whirler board. Then ready the coating material. Commercially prepared solutions are available or you can mix your own from an in-house formula. Turn on the machine to a speed of between 30 and 50 rpm. Strain the light-sensitive liquid through cheesecloth to remove any foreign particles and to break any air bubbles and pour it onto the center of the rotating plate. Centrifugal force pulls the solution to the edges of the plate surface and causes a uniform layer of emulsion to be formed. Some deep-etch chemical manufacturers recommend high rotation speeds and a small amount of heat during the last few seconds of spinning.

3. All deep-etch plates are exposed through film positives. Standard high-intensity light sources, such as carbon arc or pulsed xenon, are typically used (figure 11.8). Always strip a transparent gray scale into the flat so the image can be used to gauge development.

4. After exposure, cover any unwanted detail with a stop-out solution. Most solutions are lacquer- or shellac-based and are applied by hand with a soft bristle or camel's hair brush. Cover any unexposed areas, such as borders, dust spots, and shadows caused by the edge of the pieces of plastic film or pieces of tape.

5. The action of the developing solution removes the unhardened bichromate emulsion that was covered by the image areas of the film positive. Process deep-etch plates in a high-sided sink with a level, hard surface, such as a piece of glass built up from the bottom with wood or metal supports. The sink should also have a convenient water supply and a drain.

All emulsion manufacturers market a commercial developer that is compatible with their coatings. Pour enough liquid onto the plate to cover the entire surface. Rub the developer into the emulsion by hand with a clean, dry developing pad. Work over all areas of the plate, not merely the image areas. Several minutes of moderate rubbing should dissolve the unexposed areas. Then squeegee the plate clean and repeat the development with a second developer bath. The coating manufacturer will specify a solid sensitivity guide step number for its material. Continue development until the sensitivity guide reveals that step. It is important to closely follow the manufacturer's recommendation because additional development will reduce the thickness of the exposed image areas. After the second development, squeegee the plate again. It is now ready for the deep-etch step.

6. The function of the deep-etch step is to etch the areas of exposed metal (the image areas) into the actual plate surface and to provide a chemical bonding base for the lacquer coating. Lithographic suppliers usually can provide both the deep-etch coating and the etching solutions.

With the plate still in the developing sink, spread the liquid etch over the surface with a special etching pad. The etch is generally allowed to sit on the plate for several minutes and is then squeegeed off. Some manufacturers recommend that etching be followed by an application of the developer in order to neutralize the etching solution remaining on the surface and to remove any blind spots (iron deposits) caused by the etch in the nonimage areas.

7. It is next necessary to dissolve any remaining etching solution and to prepare the image areas to receive the lacquer coating. Rub anhydrous (water-free) alcohol into the plate with clean, dry paper wipes; be espe-

cially careful to cover the image areas. The alcohol will dissolve both the etch and the stop-out. Blot the plate dry with the paper wipes. Repeat the alcohol bath several times. A squeegee would allow alcohol to remain in the small recesses of the etched areas, but blotting with paper removes nearly all traces of the solution. Dry the entire surface with forced air.

8. Two steps are necessary to prepare the actual printing areas. First pour a quantity of deep-etch lacquer on the plate and buff it in with a dry lint-free paper or cloth wipe. Leave as much lacquer as possible, but don't allow any to remain on the hardened nonimage emulsion.

Place a layer of developing ink over the lacquer with a clean, lintless cloth rag. Developing ink is similar in formulation to actual press ink, but it is designed to adhere readily to the deep-etch lacquer. Developing ink is also significantly runnier than press ink. This final layer, then, forms the actual printing surface.

9. Remove the stencil, or hardened bichromated emulsion, by gently scrubbing the surface with warm water (around 90°F) and a soft bristle brush. After the nonimage areas have been cleared, direct a stream of cold water on the plate and rub the surface again with a clean paper wipe. The final buffing sharpens the image by removing any raggedness from the edges of the developing ink.

10. The last processing step is to move the plate to the gumming area and to make the nonimage areas water receptive. A phosphoric and gum arabic solution is generally rubbed over the entire plate surface. Be sure the plate is completely dry before applying the gum solution. Water will dilute the solution.

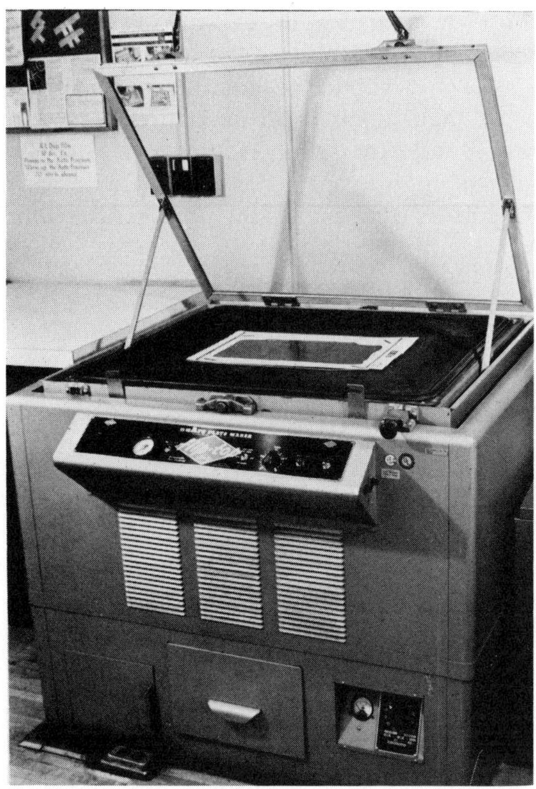

Figure 11.8. A carbon arc plate exposing unit.

The plate may be immediately placed on the printing press. If it is to be stored, coat the surface with a protective covering. Most printers use a gum-asphaltum mixture.

Small image areas can be removed with a slipsnake, but large areas become a problem. The processing steps must be reversed. The deep-etch is chemically removed, and the plate area is made water receptive. Additions can be made by several techniques, such as directly with plate tusche; by adhering plate lacquer; or by clearing an area, recoating with the bichromated gum, exposing it a second time, and then repeating the processing steps.

The deep-etch technique involves more steps than required for surface plate preparation and processing. However, the advantage of high quality, linked with extremely long press runs, makes the process appealing to large printing concerns.

Bimetal Plates

Defining Bimetal Plates

Bimetal plates function through the adhesion of two dissimilar metals—one ink receptive and the other water receptive. Bimetal plates appear similar to deep-etch plates in that there is an apparent difference of levels between the printing and the nonprinting areas. A common image metal is copper. Chromium is often used as the nonimage surface.

The Graphic Arts Technical Foundation classifies four types of bimetal plates by the methods used to produce and process them:

> *Type I.* An image metal is electroplated on a plate of a nonimage metal; an acid-resistant positive image is formed on the layer of image metal; the image metal is etched away from all areas except the image areas; the acid resist is removed from the image areas.
>
> *Type II.* A nonimage metal is electroplated on a plate of an image metal or on a plate which carries a surface layer of an image metal. A stencil or negative image is formed by means of acid-resistant coating on the layer of nonimage metal. The nonimage metal is etched away to lay bare the image metal in the positive image area. Then the protective stencil is removed from the nonimage areas.
>
> *Type III.* An acid-resistant positive image is formed on a plate of an image metal; a nonimage metal is electroplated on the remaining areas; and finally the acid resist is removed from the image areas.
>
> *Type IV.* A stencil or negative image is formed by means of an acid-resistant coating on a plate of a nonimage metal; an image metal is electroplated on the bare image areas; and finally the protective stencil is removed.
>
> While all four types have been tried, only Type I and Type II have been generally successful. Type III and Type IV gave trouble because of difficulties in finding photo-resists that could withstand the electroplating operation, and because of the inability to obtain uniform electro-deposits of metal.*

In all instances the operation of multimetal plates is due to the chemical properties of only two metals. However, there are plates that have been formed from three or more different metals. Zinc and aluminum are often used as a base to hold the image and nonimage metals. The basic advantage is a decrease in weight and cost over the copper-chromium combination.

Bimetal plates are more expensive to prepare and process than nearly any other

*Charles Shapiro, ed., *The Lithographer's Manual*, 5th ed. (Pittsburgh: The Graphic Arts Technical Foundation, Inc., 1974), P. 10:29.

form of lithographic plate. Their main attractions are the potential length of run and high image quality. More than a million impressions are commonly made from a single bimetal plate and up to 3 million impressions are not rare.

Preparing and Processing a Typical Bimetal Plate

There are four types of bimetal lithographic plates. The following is a brief summary of the preparation and processing of only one type. Detailed directions for any specific plate should be obtained from the manufacturer.

Recall that the common type of bimetal plate has copper (or other ink-receptive) metal electroplated on top of a water-receptive base, such as chromium. This type of plate is available with a presensitized emulsion or with only the two metals and a thin layer of gum to protect the top surface.

If the printer adds the light-sensitive coating, the chemicals and procedures are somewhat similar to deep-etch plate preparation. The gum is first washed away with warm water, and a pre-etch solution is allowed to stand on the copper to prepare it to receive the emulsion. Although the image layer has little grain, coating still takes place in a whirler, with standard whirling procedures. The light-sensitive emulsion is then hardened in the image areas by exposure through a film negative in a vacuum frame, with the use of a high-intensity light source.

The unexposed nonimage areas are removed with a deep-etch developer to expose the electroplated copper. The entire plate is then immersed in a copper etching bath until the base or water-receptive metal is revealed. The etch removes only the copper that is not covered with the hardened emulsion.

After it is washed, the image area coating is dissolved with an acid counteretch. The solution also sensitizes the copper so that it is more ink receptive. Finally, a developer ink is rubbed over the image area and the plate is gummed.

Presensitized bimetal plates are processed in similar manner, but without the coating steps.

Special Lithographic Plates and Systems

There are a variety of individual plates that, because of processing or structural characteristics, defy clear-cut categorization as surface, deep-etch, or bimetal. In the following sections transfer and electrostatic lithographic plates are discussed, but it should not be assumed that they are the only possible special lithographic image carriers or systems.

Transfer Plates

Transfer lithographic plates are formed from a light-sensitive coating on an intermediate carrier that is exposed and then transferred to the actual printing plate. The advantage of the technique is that the usual film and stripping steps are bypassed because the intermediate sheet can be exposed in a process camera or contact print frame or even on a special purpose electronic scanner. Several types of transfer systems are commercially available. The PMT (photomechanical transfer) Metal Litho Plate by the Eastman Kodak Company is one example.

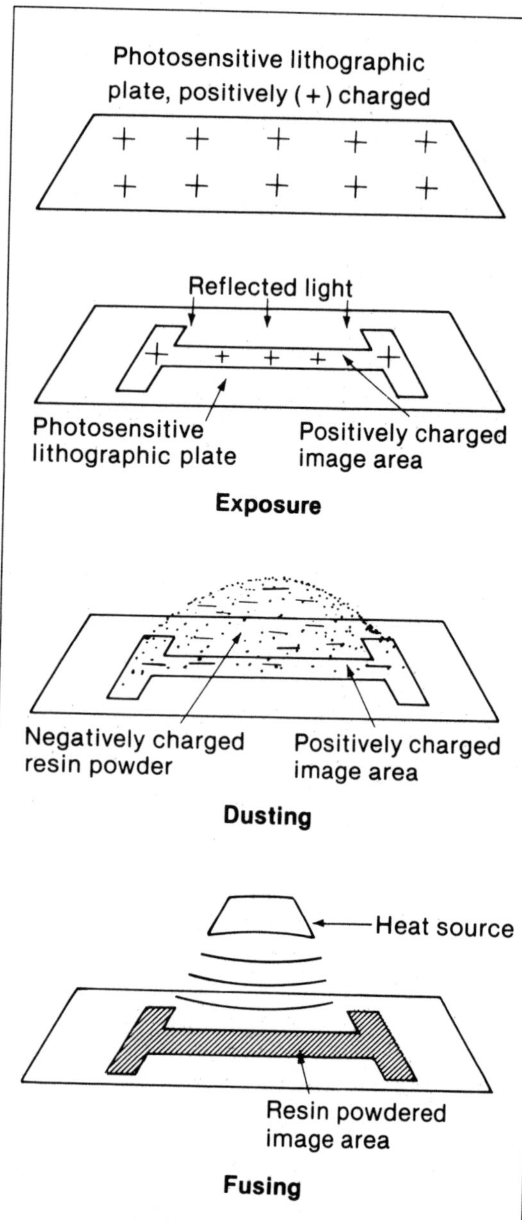

Figure 11.9. Electrostatic printing process Electrostatic printing uses a positively charged image to attract negatively charged resin powder. The resin powder is then fused in place with heat.

Recall from chapter 6 that the diffusion transfer process is a method used to produce quality opaque positives (either enlarged, reduced, or same size) from positive opaque originals on a process camera. The copy is positioned on the copyboard and the reproduction size and camera exposure are adjusted. A sheet of Kodak's PMT negative material is placed on the filmboard and an exposure is made. A sheet of PMT receiver paper is then positioned emulsion to emulsion with the negative and both are passed through an activator bath. After a short period of time the sheets are separated. A positive image is formed on the opaque receiver sheet and it is ready for paste-up.

In the plate-making process, an aluminum plate is substituted for the paper receiver sheet. The fine-grained plate need only be fixed and gummed before it is placed on the press. The PMT plate can produce up to 25,000 press copies with a quality that rivals a medium-run presensitized metal plate.

Electrostatic Plates

The process of making **electrostatic transfer plates** is based on the concept of xerographic image reproduction. The idea is commonplace in the office copier now marketed by the Xerox Corporation and others. The basic procedure involves the formation of an image by light striking a photoresponsive surface that has been charged with static electricity (hence the name "electrostatic").

In actual practice, some type of material is coated (selenium and zinc oxide compounds are two patented coverings) on the plate and then positively charged. When light (generally reflected light through a process type of camera) strikes the plate, the positive charge is lost in the nonimage areas, which leaves only the positively charged image area. The remaining charged area is then dusted with negatively charged resin powder. The powder, which clings only to the image area, is then fused to the plate to be run on lithographic presses (figure 11.9).

One interesting feature of the electrostatic system is that corrections can be made directly on the plate. The negative pole of a magnet is used to remove the resin powder from unwanted areas before the powder is fused to the plate. Resin powder can also be added in areas where it was not deposited during the initial process.

In recent years, several manufacturers have developed plate materials that can directly carry the photoresponsive surface. One such manufacturer, the Addressograph-Multigraph Corporation, has linked an electrostatic platemaker to an offset lithographic press. The original copy is inserted into the copier, and the plate is automatically prepared and delivered to the plate cylinder by a belt delivery system that attaches it to the press. The press automatically runs the required number of sheets, removes the plate, cleans the blanket cylinder, and turns the whole system off (figure 11.10).

Figure 11.10. A lithographic printing system with an electrostatic platemaker
Courtesy of Multigraphics Division, Addressograph-Multigraph Corporation.

The electrostatic process is receiving widespread acceptance for systems work in the printing industry. Although intended for low- to medium-quality short runs (up to 5,000 copies), the low cost makes it a viable plate-making system for many printers.

Key Terms

plate
grain
collodian
colloid
baume
surface plate
deep-etch plate
bimetal plate
negative-acting plate
direct image nonphotographic plate
direct image photographic plate
wipe-on metal plate
tusche
slipsnake
additive plate
subtractive plate
whirler
transfer lithographic plate
electrostatic transfer plate

Questions for Review

1. What is the basis of all industrial lithography?
2. What is the purpose of lithographic plate graining?
3. What are the three most basic types of lithographic plates?
4. What is the difference between a negative-acting and a positive-acting lithographic plate?
5. Briefly, what are several techniques that can be used to prepare direct image nonphotographic surface plates?
6. What are the advantages of the direct image photographic surface plate?
7. What is the difference between an additive and a subtractive plate?
8. What is the basic concept of the deep-etch plate?
9. What is the basic concept of the bimetal plate?
10. How are transfer lithographic plates made?
11. What is the advantage of electrostatic lithographic plates?

Chapter Twelve

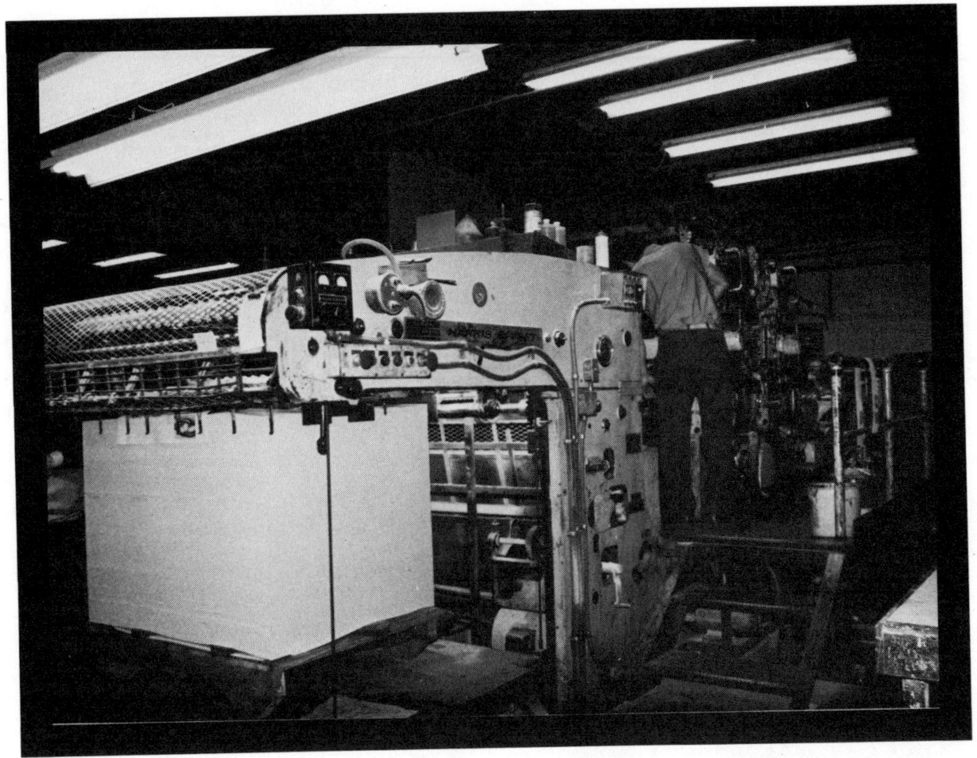

Printing Presses: An Overview

Anecdote to Chapter Twelve

A replica of Benjamin Franklin's press
Smithsonian Institution, Photo No. 17539–B.

The first high-speed printing press was designed around 1450 by Johann Gutenberg in Germany. Gutenberg tried several different designs, but he settled on the basic form of a wine press. He changed the bed around so that it could be rolled out from under the plate, activated the screw by a lever, and added a frame, or tympan, to hold the paper. With this device he printed his famous forty-two-line Bible (called the Gutenberg Bible). It took him just over three years to print two hundred copies.

The press worked so well that three hundred years later Benjamin Franklin used a similar device (see illustration). In practice, two men operated the press. The type was locked in place on the bed, the raised portions were inked, and the paper was positioned on the tympan frame and swung into place over the type. The bed was then rolled under the platen and the lever activated to press the sheet against the type. The press was then opened, the printed sheet was hung on a line to dry, and the entire process was repeated. Using this method, the press operators could make about three hundred impressions in a single twelve-hour workday. The basic steps of feeding the paper, registering the paper to the form, printing, and finally delivering the sheet remain to this day. Modern processes, however, are more accurate and more rapid than the wine press.

Objectives for Chapter Twelve

After completing this chapter, you will be able to:

- Recall the four units that make up any printing press.
- Identify typical controls on any automatic feeder unit.
- Recall the difference between fit and registration and identify common registration unit controls.
- Recall and recognize the common printing unit designs, including platen press, flat bed cylinder, rotary, offset, and perfecting.
- Identify common delivery unit designs.

Introduction

A printing press is a machine that transfers an image from some sort of plate or image carrier to an image receiver, such as paper. It is certainly possible to transfer images from a plate surface without the use of a machine—consider a rubber stamp or a stencil—but it is the printing press that made printing the most powerful influence on the social, scientific, and political history of humanity.

Gutenberg's refinement of a wine press could be operated at the then fantastic rate of one copy every three minutes. In combination with his casting device, the simple wine press operation magnified beyond human comprehension the quality and quantity of the printer's craft. Contemporary automatic presses operate at a medium speed of around 125 copies each minute (6,000 to 8,000 copies per hour). When the paper is fed from a continuous roll (called "web feeding"), the paper can pass under a printing plate as rapidly as 1,500 feet per minute.

The design of the wine press has been refined a bit, but press operators and presses still perform the same basic operations of feeding, registration, printing, and delivery that Gutenberg's workers followed more than five centuries ago. It is important to understand that every printing press is built from these four basic units (figure 12.1). Relief, gravure, screen, and lithographic presses all have a feeding system, registration system, printing unit, and delivery system. A firm understanding of press systems and component parts will simplify the task of running any type of printing press.

The **feeding** system can be as simple as a human hand picking up a sheet of paper or as complex as an air-vacuum device that automatically fans the top sheets of a paper pile and lifts a sheet with mechanical fingers. Whatever the method, the concern is to feed a single sheet of stock into the press rapidly and uniformly.

The **registration** system is designed to ensure that the sheet is held in the same position each time an impression is made. It is important that the printed image appear in

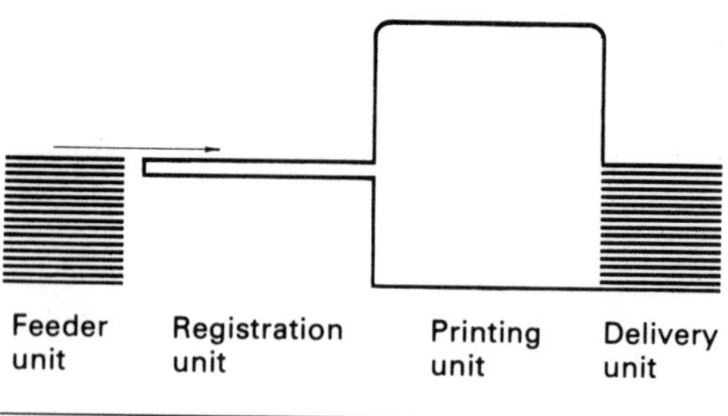

Figure 12.1. The four units common to all presses

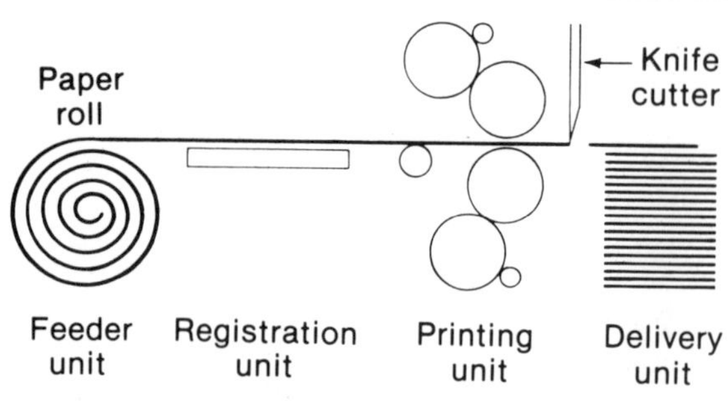

Figure 12.2. Diagram of a web-fed press

the same spot on every sheet. It would be a foolish method that randomly placed each sheet under a printing plate and then custom cut the sheets so that the pages would line up when bound together in a book. Registration is especially important for two-color designs that are to be formed by two different passes through a printing press. The different colored images would not line up if the position of the paper were not controlled during printing.

If the sheet is held firmly in the proper position, the image can be transferred from the plate to the paper in the printing unit. The placement of the plate or image carrier might vary with the type of printing (relief, screen, intaglio, or lithography), but there are general similarities with all presses.

After printing, the completed sheet must be removed from the press—a process called **delivery**. Gutenberg picked up each printed copy and hung it on a wire line to dry. Modern presses generally deliver a uniform stack of sheets that can be easily folded, collated, packaged, or cut.

Every printing press is made up of these four systems. The only differences are combinations, variations, or refinements of control within each system.

The Feeder Unit

One method of classifying presses is by the form of the material sent through the feeder system. When a roll of paper is placed in the feeder unit, the press is classified as **web fed** or simply web (figure 12.2). When the feeder unit picks up individual pieces from a pile, the press is classified as **sheet fed**. The primary concern of this chapter is sheet-fed presses.

Loading Systems

The simplest and most common sheet-feeding system is **pilefeeding** (figure 12.3). With this technique a pile of paper is placed on a feeder table while the press is turned off. The table is then raised to a predetermined feeder height and the press run begun. As each sheet is removed from the pile, the press moves the table up so that the top of the pile remains at a constant height.

Pilefeeding presents no difficulties when all the sheets for a single job can be placed in one pile. However, when the press must be stopped and started several times during an extremely long run to add more paper, problems are often encountered. When a job is first set up on a press, a certain amount of paper spoilage occurs during **make-ready** (or preparation work) to obtain a quality printed image. During a steady press run, it is relatively easy to maintain consistent quality. Whenever the press is stopped, however, not only is production time lost, but more spoilage could occur before the quality impression is again obtained (especially with lithography).

Continuous feeding provides a means of adding sheets to a feeder system without stopping the press in the middle of a run. There are two common continuous-loading designs. The oldest generally has a feed table located over the registration unit (figure 12.4). The printer fans the paper, and the pile is spread on the infeed table. A continuous belt then moves the pile around and under the feeder table to the registration unit. Additional paper is fanned and added to the moving pile as it is needed.

A second system provides continuous feeding by loading new paper under an existing pile while the press is running (figure 12.5). Before the pile has run out, temporary rods are inserted, and the fresh pile is elevated into position. The rods are removed, and a single stack of paper is again in the feeder unit.

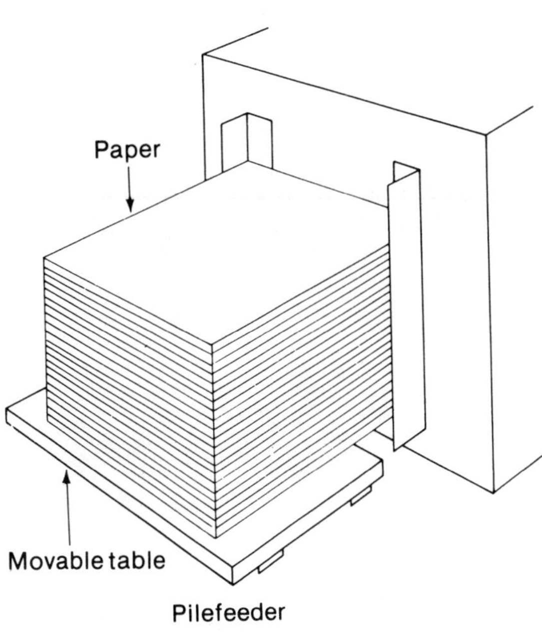

Figure 12.3. Diagram of a sheet-fed press

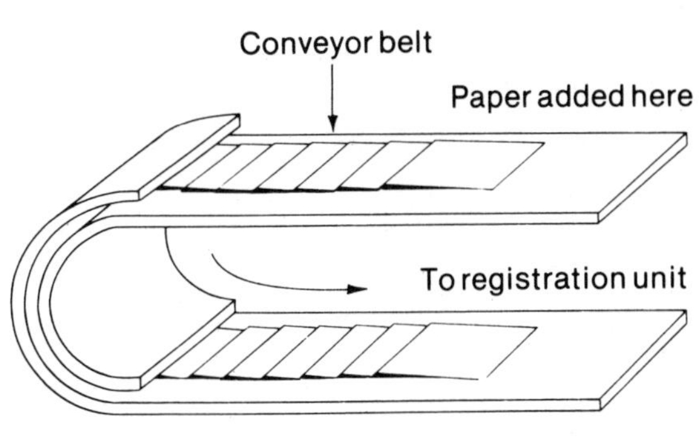

Figure 12.4. Diagram of a continuous-feeding system

Types of Feeders

The most common type of mechanical feeder is the **successive-sheet-feeding** system (figure 12.6). Mechanical fingers pick up one sheet from the top of the paper pile and direct it into the registration unit. The paper feed

Figure 12.5. Example of a continuous-feeding system that uses dual tables
Courtesy of Miller Printing Machinery Co.

Figure 12.6. Diagram of a successive-sheet-feeding system

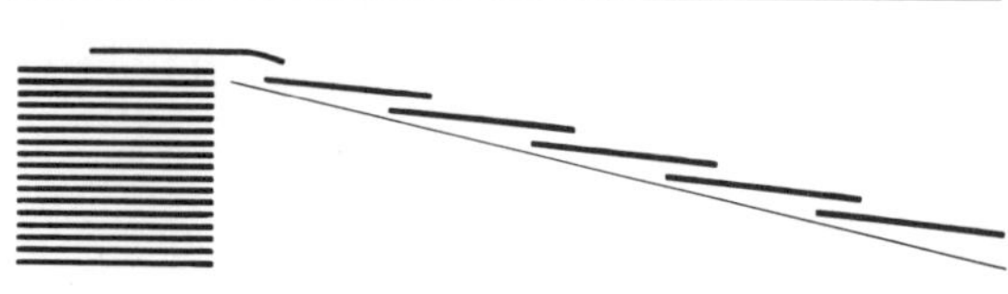

Figure 12.7. Diagram of a stream-feeding system

must be synchronized with the printing unit—each time an impression is made, the feeder must be ready to insert a fresh sheet. For high-speed presses with a successive-sheet-feeding system, the paper is literally flying through the registration unit in order to keep up with the printing unit. It is not easy to hold accurate registration when high-speed printing very lightweight papers. There is a possibility of the paper bouncing back as it enters the printing unit at a high rate of speed.

A **stream feeder**, on the other hand, overlaps sheets on the registration table, and the rate of sheet movement is significantly slower (figure 12.7). With a stream feed, sheets move through the registration unit at a fraction of the speed of the printing unit, and the resulting greater control makes accurate registration of any paper weight possible.

Automatic Feeder Controls

Whatever the method of paper loading or feed, there are common feeder system controls on all sheet-fed presses. When the paper pile is loaded into the feeder system, it is centered on a press. A scale is usually provided somewhere on the feeder to ensure accurate paper position. Once the pile has been centered, movable side and back guides are put into position just touching the paper so that the pile will not shift position during the run (figure 12.8).

The height of the pile can usually be adjusted and automatically maintained by the press. Usually some type of sensing bar touches the top of the pile immediately after a sheet has been fed and directs a gear-and-chain height control. The actual pile height is a variable that depends on such factors as the weight of paper, environmental conditions, and method of feed. The top of the pile must be as nearly level as possible for consistent feeding. This is usually a problem only with large press sheets. Wedges or blocks are often placed under the pile to keep it level.

To ensure that only one sheet is fed into the registration unit at a time, the top sheet must be separated from the rest of the pile. Various mechanisms are used on different machines, but they are all labeled **sheet separators**. The most common is a blast of directed air. Blower tubes, which can be directed at the front, side, or rear of a pile, place a blanket of air under the first few sheets (figure 12.9). Another common approach is to combine a blast of air with a mechanical **combing wheel**, which curls one edge of the paper above the rest of the stack (figure 12.10). With either technique, a mechanical device called a **sucker foot** telescopes to the top sheet and forwards it into the registration unit. Most sheet separators have at least two sucker feet. Both the volume of air to separate the top sheet and the amount of vacuum pull in the sucker feet can be adjusted for different paper characteristics.

The final consideration is to ensure that only one sheet is fed into the press from the feeder at a time. Multiple sheets can jam the press, give poor image impression, fail to be held in register, and even do damage to the printing unit. Most presses have a **double-sheet detector** (figure 12.11) to check for multiple sheets and either eject the paper from the registration system or stop the press. Usually the mechanism merely gauges the thickness of the material passing under a sensing switch. The gap under the switch can be set to any thickness. When the allowable gap is exceeded, the switch is tripped and the operator is signaled. If all adjustments have been properly made, the feeder should rarely misfeed multiple sheets.

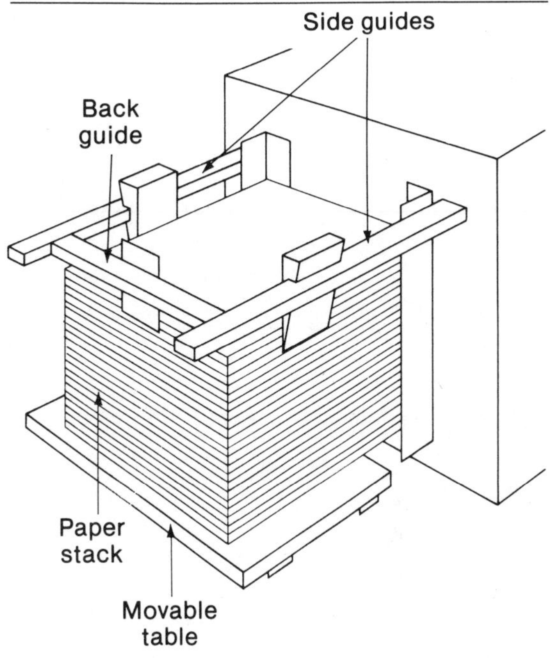

Figure 12.8. Diagram showing movable guides
The movable side and back guides hold the pile in position.

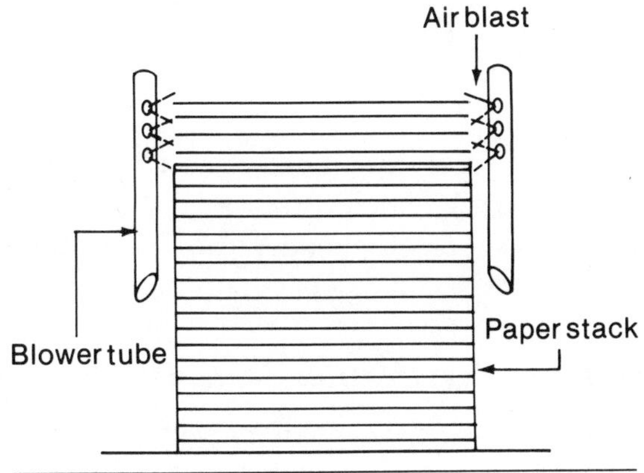

Figure 12.9. Diagram showing blower tubes
Blower tubes force a blanket of air under the first few sheets of paper and float them above the rest of the pile.

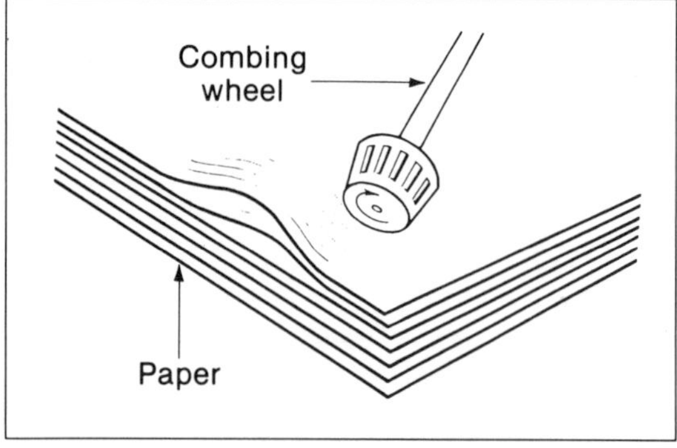

Figure 12.10. A mechanical combing wheel

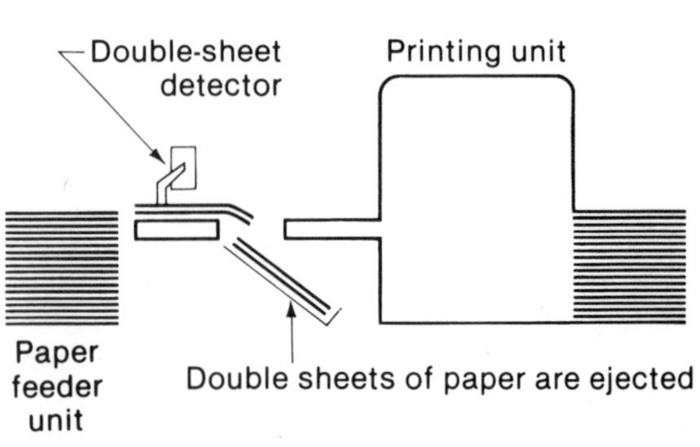

Figure 12.11. Diagram showing a double-sheet detector

The Registration Unit

Importance of Registration

Registration is the process of controlling and directing the sheet as it enters the printing unit. The goal of registration is to ensure absolute consistency of image position on every sheet in the delivery pile. When one color is to be printed over another on a single sheet, the image will not fit unless registration of all sheets is held throughout the press run. The ideas of registration and fit are often confused. **Fit** refers to the image position on the press sheet. Registration refers to the position of the sheet. Fit can be controlled by a variety of devices, some dependent on registration and others totally independent.

Typical Registration Systems

The press sheet usually is moved along the registration table by continuously moving belts. The actual operation of registering the sheet is performed just before it enters the printing unit. There are basically only two types of sheet-fed automatic registration systems: "three-point guides" and "rotary" or "roller guides."

In a three-point guide system the sheet is advanced along the registration board and is halted against movable front guides, called "**headstops**" (figure 12.12). Side guides then push the sheet into the proper position, the front guides move out of the way, and the sheet is moved into the printing unit. There is sometimes a tendency for heavy stock to bounce back as it comes into contact with the headstops and misregister. Extremely lightweight materials easily buckle with the push system.

The two-point pull rotary system reduces the possibility of the sheet misregistering (figure 12.13). The headstops still swing into position at the head of the registration table, but a single side guide is locked into position and does not move. As the sheet meets the headstops and comes to rest, a finger or roller is lowered against the stock and it is pulled by a rolling, or rotary, motion against the stationary side guide. Once in register, the sheet is moved into the printing unit.

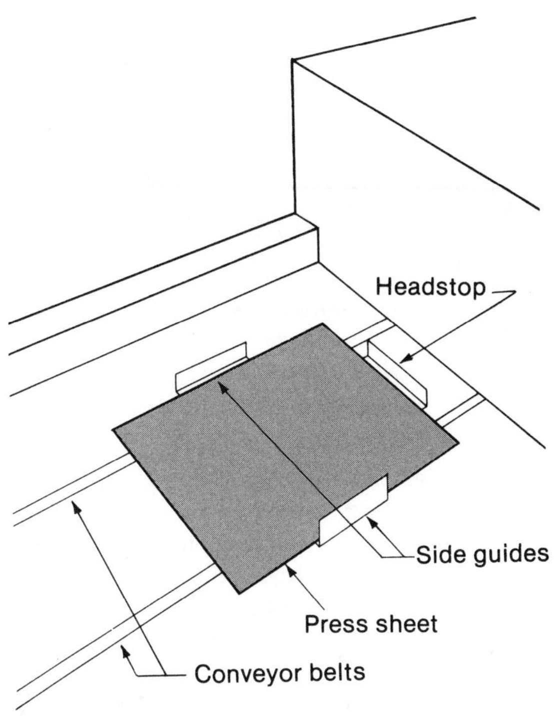

Figure 12.12. Diagram of a three-point guide system

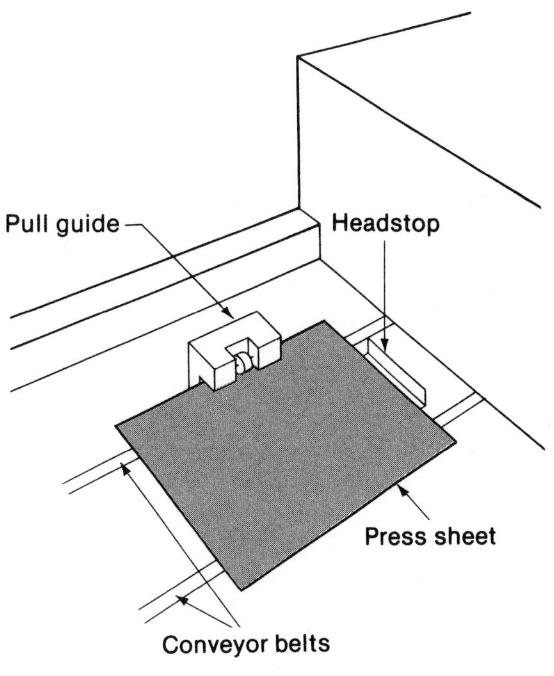

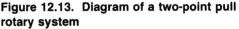

Figure 12.13. Diagram of a two-point pull rotary system

The Printing Unit

Several different mechanisms can be used to move the sheet into and through the printing unit.

Platen Press

If it were in operation today, Gutenberg's converted wine press would be labeled a **platen press**. On this type of press, the paper is placed between the typeform and a flat surface, called a "platen" (figure 12.14a). The typeform and the platen are then brought together, and an image is transferred to the sheet (figure 12.14b). Although the feeder, registration, and delivery units have been automated, the basic problems inherent in the platen design remain. The paper must be inserted, held in place, and printed, and it must remain in place until the platen opens sufficiently for the sheet to be removed. The process is slow.

Flat Bed Cylinder Press

The **flat bed cylinder press** is constructed so that the sheet rolls into contact with the typeform as a cylinder moves across the press (figure 12.15). Mechanical fingers, or "grip-

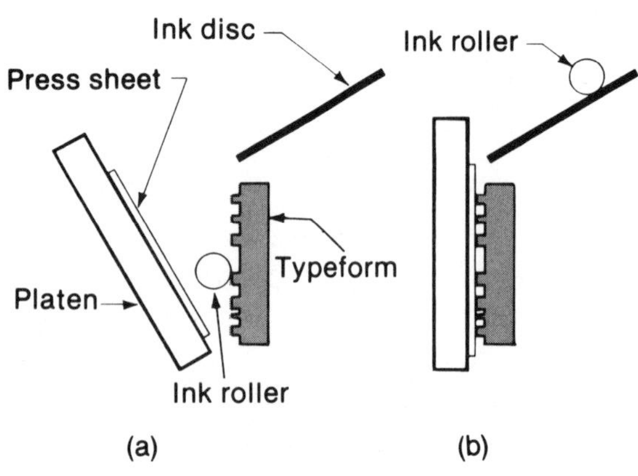

Figure 12.14. Diagram of a platen press A press sheet is positioned on a platen when the device is open (a), and the image is transferred when the press is closed (b).

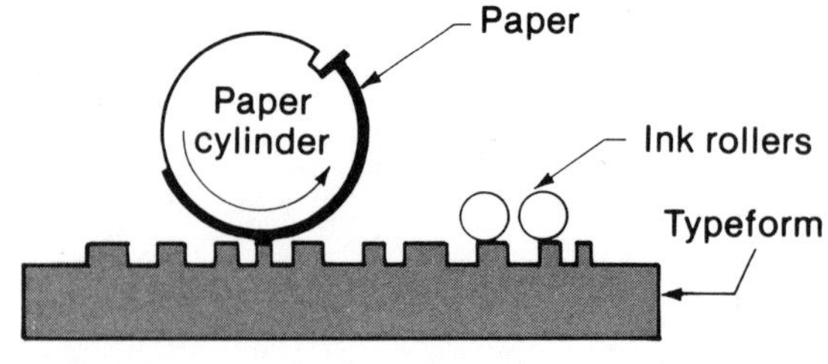

Figure 12.15. Diagram of a flat bed press A flat bed cylinder press rolls the paper sheet over the plate carrying the image.

pers," hold the paper in place during the trip and automatically open at the end of one rotation. Ink rollers are usually attached to the cylinder assembly so that as an image is being printed, the form is also being re-inked. At the end of one pass, the cylinder is automatically raised and rolled back to the starting point to receive another sheet. On some models the cylinder is stationary and the form moves.

One advantage of the flat bed cylinder design is that because only a very narrow portion of the sheet is being printed at any given instant, much less pressure is required to transfer the image than for the platen design. A slight modification is to place the form in a vertical position so that both the bed and the cylinder rotate in opposite directions. This cuts the printing time in half because the cylinder makes only a 180° turn for each impression. However, there is still wasted motion when the cylinder and/or the form return to their original position and no image is being transferred.

Rotary Press

The **rotary press** is formed from two cylinders. One holds the typeform while the other acts as an **impression cylinder** to push the stock against the form (figure 12.16). As the cylinders rotate, a sheet is inserted between them so that an image will be placed in the same position on every piece. Ink rollers continually replace ink that has been transferred to the press sheet. The impression cylinder can usually be moved up or down to adjust the gap to the weight or thickness of the material being printed.

The rotary press is an efficient design. Because one impression is made with each cylinder rotation, there is no wasted motion. It is the only press design that can transfer an image onto a continuous roll of paper (called "web printing"). The rotary configuration can

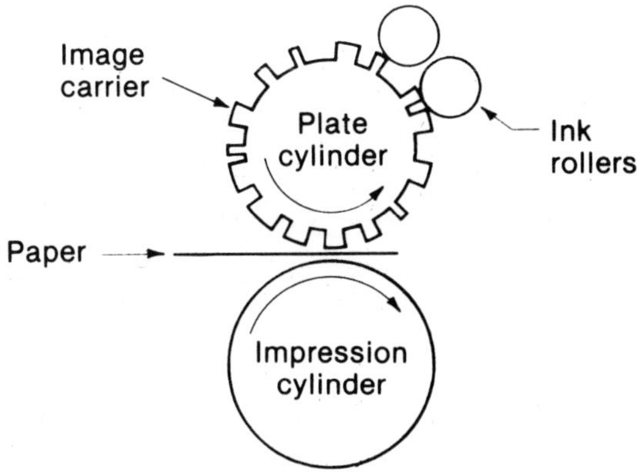

Figure 12.16. Diagram of a rotary press A rotary press moves the paper sheet between two cylinders—the plate cylinder, which holds the image carrier, and the impression cylinder, which pushes the piece against the plate.

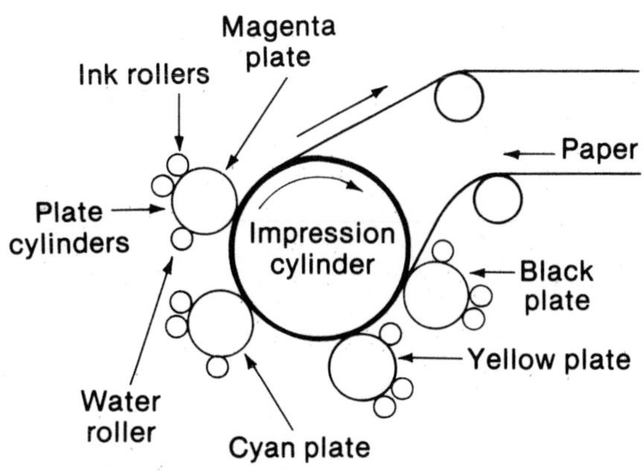

Figure 12.17. Diagram of a multicylinder rotary press A rotary web-fed press can be adapted to place several plate cylinders around a single impression cylinder.

easily be adapted to multicolor presswork. One common design is to place several **plate cylinders** around a single impression cylinder (figure 12.17).

Offset Principle

Offset is a common term used in the printing industry. It is generally associated with the lithographic process, but this is really not accurate because an offset image has little or nothing to do with the lithographic principle. An offset image is produced by transferring the image from an inked form onto a rubber blanket and then transferring the blanket image to some receiver sheet (such as paper). The offset principle can be applied to any press structure, but it is most commonly used as a third cylinder on a rotary lithographic press (figure 12.18).

This intermediate transfer cylinder—usually called a **blanket cylinder**—has several advantages. Paper has an abrasive effect on plates. Having the sheet contact only a replaceable rubber blanket lengthens the potential life of the plate. Whenever an image is transferred from one carrier to another, the symbols are reversed (recall that foundry type is cast in reverse). When a blanket cylinder is used on a press, the characters on the printing plate must be right reading. The characters will be printed in reverse on the blanket cylinder, then reversed again (back to right reading) on the press sheet. Right-reading characters are more convenient for people to work with and assemble during the compo-

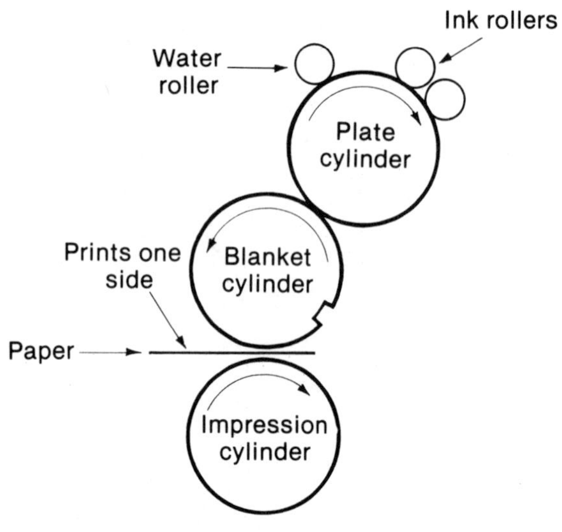

Figure 12.18. Diagram of an offset rotary press With the offset principle, the image is transferred (or offset) from the plate to the blanket cylinder, which reverses the image. The image is then passed to the press sheet as it moves between the blanket and impression cylinders.

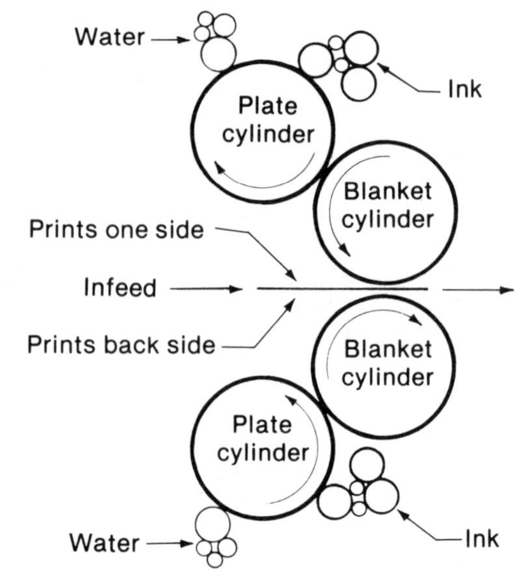

Figure 12.19. Diagram of a blanket-to-blanket configuration for a perfecting press

sition and stripping processes. A rubber blanket also tends to diminish unwanted background detail or "scum" that might accumulate on the printing plate.

Although the term *offset* is often used interchangeably with the word *lithography,* it is important to keep in mind that it describes only a particular press cylinder design.

Perfecting Principle

A **perfecting press** can print simultaneously on both sides of the paper as it passes through the printing unit (figure 12.19). The most common perfecting presses use the rotary configuration and can be adapted for either sheet-fed or web-fed reproduction. Multicolor web-fed systems are extremely versatile. Most can adapt the paper feed to print four colors on each side, seven on one and a single color on the other, or a variety of combinations between the two sides.

The Delivery Unit

Types of Delivery Systems

There are two common designs for press delivery units: gravity delivery and chain gripper delivery. **Gravity delivery** is the simpler and less dependable of the two. As the sheet

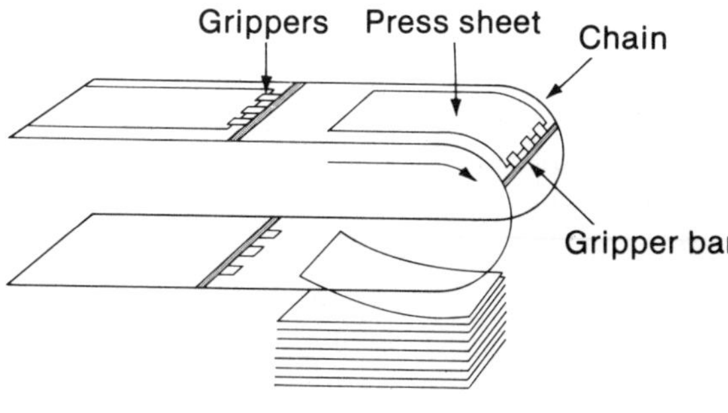

Figure 12.20. Diagram of a chain gripper delivery system

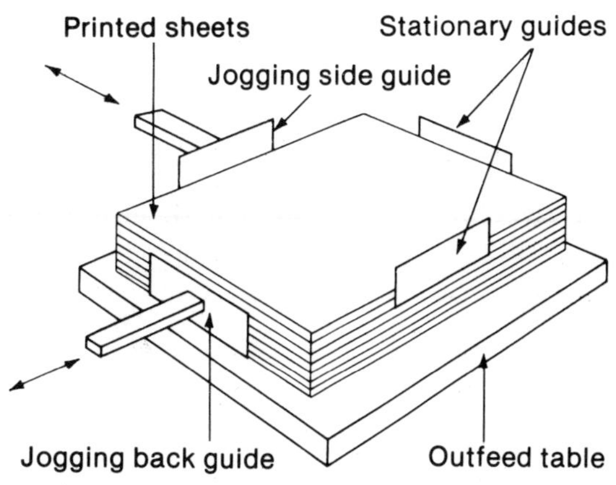

Figure 12.21. Diagram showing jogging side and back guides

leaves the printing unit, it is dropped into a tray or box. The basic limitation is that paper cannot be delivered faster than gravity can pull it into place. With lightweight papers, air resistance reduces the possible press speed even more. Gravity delivery is usually found on only the smallest, least expensive duplicators.

The most popular design for delivery units is the **chain gripper system** (figure 12.20). As the sheet leaves the printing unit, a set of mechanical fingers (grippers) grabs the leading edge of the sheet and pulls it out of the printing system. The gripper bar is attached to a continuous chain that moves the printed sheet to a paper pile, releases it, and moves the grippers back to receive another sheet. The chain moves at the same rate and in synchronization with the feeder, registration, and printing units. As one sheet is delivered, another sheet is being placed onto the registration board. Presses with chain gripper delivery systems can be adjusted to nearly any speed because the gripper chain moves the sheet and does not depend on gravity to remove it from the printing unit.

Delivery Pile Controls

Ideally, the delivery system will form a perfectly neat stack of paper on the outfeed table. If a perfect pile is formed, the printer can easily move it back to the feeder system to print another color, can stack it in a paper cutter to trim it to a finished size, can collate it with other sheets, or can punch, drill, fold, or package it.

Jogging side and back guides are usually used to control the outfeed pile (figure 12.21). As a sheet is dropped onto the stack, the guides are open. As the piece drops into position, the guides begin to close until they gently push the stock in place. Most systems are designed so that two stationary guides can be adjusted to the paper extremes. The jogging guides are adjusted to touch the remaining two paper sides on their innermost stroke. As the press operates, the delivery pile is continually touched by all four guides. This keeps the stack straight. The entire outfeed table is typically lowered automatically as the height of the delivery pile increases.

A static electric charge is frequently built up on a sheet as it passes through the printing unit. Charged sheets are difficult to control and often do not stack properly in the delivery system. The most common **static eliminator** is a piece of Christmas tree tinsel (a special copper tinsel attached to a thin copper wire is commercially available). A length of tinsel is stretched across the delivery unit so that each sheet must brush against it as the stock passes to the outfeed pile. The wire is grounded through the press and removes the troublesome charge.

Key Terms

feeding
registration
delivery
web-fed press
sheet-fed press
pilefeeding
make-ready
sheet separators
sucker foot
double-sheet detector
fit
headstops
platen press
flat bed cylinder press
rotary press
offset
blanket cylinder
plate cylinder
impression cylinder
perfecting press

Questions for Review

1. What are the four basic units of any printing press?
2. What is a web-fed press?
3. What is the purpose of a double-sheet detector?
4. What is the difference between a "successive-sheet" feeder and a "stream feeder"?
5. What is the difference between registration and fit?
6. What is an advantage of a flat bed cylinder press design?
7. How does a rotary press transfer an image?
8. How is an offset image produced?
9. What is a perfecting press?
10. What are the two common delivery unit designs?

Chapter Thirteen

Offset Press Operation

Anecdote to Chapter Thirteen

Alois Senefelder, the inventor of lithography, designed the first lithographic press sometime between 1798 and 1800. He borrowed the basic idea of a press that was used to reproduce copperplate engravings—a relief process. Senefelder took what was basically a flat bed cylinder design and added a tympan frame and frisket to hold the paper, a flexible blade instead of a roller to apply the pressure, and a lever-counterweight system to control the blade tension.

In actual production, two workers operated the device. They drew a design by hand on a slab of limestone with a grease crayon-like material and placed the "plate" on the movable bed of the press. They then covered the stone with a water and gum arabic solution. The liquid flowed off of the greasy image but covered the nongreasy stone surface. Then they vigorously rolled an ink-covered leather roller back and forth over the stone. The ink was repelled by the water film but attached to

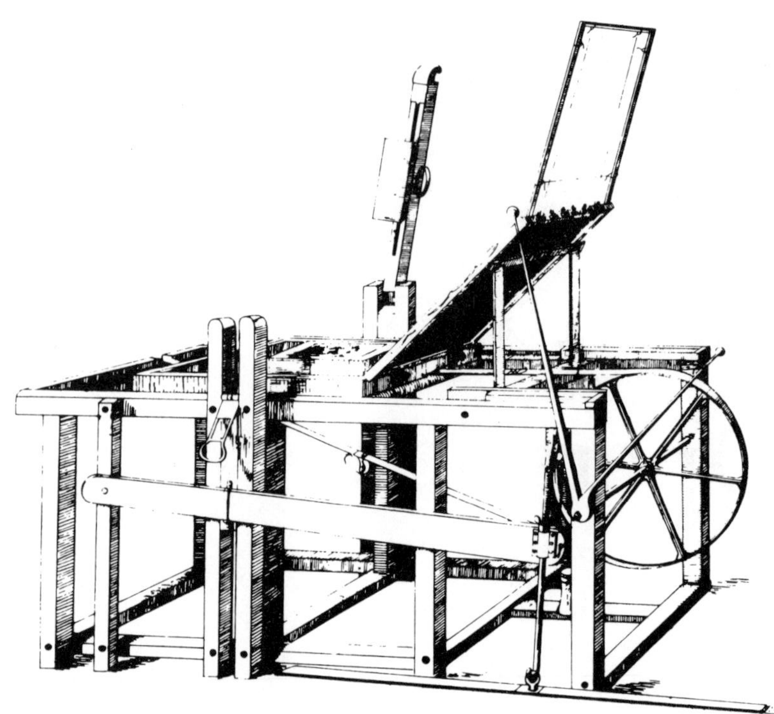

Original drawing of Senefelder's lithographic press design

the grease image. The stone was ready to print after the workers carefully wiped it with a clean cloth to remove any excess moisture.

They mounted a sheet of previously dampened paper on the tympan, closed the frisket to hold it in place, and lowered the frame into contact with the stone. Then they lowered the blade against the back of the tympan. One worker stood on the pressure lever while the other slowly turned a wheel to slide the bed under the blade. It was this scraping pressure that actually caused the ink to be transferred from the stone to the paper. There was always danger that too much pressure would be applied by the blade and the stone would be broken or that the sheet would slip under the scraping action. After one pass, they released the blade, hinged the tympan frame out of the way, and hung the sheet on a line to dry. Then they repeated the whole process.

Senefelder's press was considered a marvel of its time. In an average twelve-hour day, two craftsmen could produce perhaps fifty acceptable copies. His later designs included an automatic dampening and inking system and a lever scraper blade that moved across the stone instead of the stone moving under the blade.

Although steam power was applied to a litho press around 1866, Senefelder's basic design was not changed until the offset press was introduced in 1907.

Objectives for Chapter Thirteen

After completing this chapter, you will be able to:

- Classify offset presses and identify the four press units.
- Recall the different printing unit cylinder configurations.
- Recall the most common inking unit configuration and describe set-up operations.
- Recall the most common dampening unit configuration and describe set-up operations.
- Describe the basic steps in setting up and operating an offset lithographic press.
- Recall press concerns when printing process color on sheet-fed offset lithographic presses.
- Recall common roller and blanket problems and solutions and describe mechanical adjustments that are possible on most presses.
- Recall common press concerns.
- Recognize a troubleshooting checklist and be able to use it to suggest solutions to press problems.
- List common press maintenance steps.

Introduction

This chapter is divided into two sections. The first section covers the information necessary to run an offset press. The second section gives important information on press-trouble-shooting concerns.

SECTION 1

There are so many different offset presses on the market today with so many minute operational differences that it is easy for the reader to become bogged down trying to learn press operation by the "which-switch-does-what" method. The problem with this approach is that the operator is lost if moved to another type of machine.

An operation manual prepared by the press manufacturer is unexcelled for teaching "switches." Such a manual can provide more detailed on-the-job information for a production situation than any textbook could ever hope to provide. The purpose of this chapter is not to provide a "general operation manual," but to deal with fundamental understandings that will enable the reader to run any offset duplicator or sheet-fed press after a review of the manufacturer's operation manual.

Classifying Offset Presses

There are many manufacturers who produce offset lithographic presses. As described in chapter 12, all printing presses can be classified by feeding method, registration method, whether the device is a perfector (prints on both sides of the sheet), number of color heads, speed, and delivery method, among other characteristics. Although lithographic presses can be classified in the same manner, two additional distinctions are made: the machine is labeled as either a duplicator or a press.

Offset Duplicators

Duplicators are any offset lithographic transfer devices that can feed a maximum sheet size of 11 by 17 inches. A duplicator is assumed not to have the degree of control found on a press, although the feeder, registration, printing, and delivery units will always be present.

Table-top duplicators are designed for short-run forms work and can be operated by office personnel. Most such models have friction paper feed, control registration by the position of the paper pile, and use a simple gravity delivery system. Figure 13.1 shows a common pedestal type of duplicator. Pedestal duplicators are usually more rugged than table model duplicators and have a few more sophisticated controls than the table-top design. Such duplicators commonly have vacuum feeder systems, jogging registration, and chain delivery. Both types, however, seldom have more than two ink form rollers and a single dampening form roller. **Form rollers** are the rollers that transfer the ink and water to the plate. Because duplicators generally have only two ink form rollers, they are definitely limited in their ability to deliver a consistent layer of ink across a large image area.

An offset duplicator can do any job a press can handle, but there are differences in sheet sizes that can be handled and in image quality (image quality depends on the specific type of job being printed). Modern duplicators are available that can print on a variety of stock thicknesses at speeds of 10,000 to 12,000 impressions per hour. They are also available with a web-fed design and multicolor printing units.

Duplicators are versatile machines that meet the short-run demands of the industry. They have the same basic controls as offset presses yet are significantly less expensive. Duplicators are commonly used for introductory press training because of their similarity to presses.

Figure 13.1. A common pedestal type of duplicator

Courtesy of Multigraphics Division, Addressograph-Multigraph Corporation.

Offset Presses

Offset **presses** are any machines that can feed a sheet size greater than 11 by 17 inches. Presses are generally identified by the maximum sheet size that the device can handle. Sheet-fed presses are available in sizes from 12⅝ by 18 inches to 54 by 77 inches.

Figure 13.2 shows a common offset press. Such presses may include pull side guides for registration, a photoelectric sense switch that trips the printing unit onto impression as a sheet passes, an electronic double-sheet detector, adjustable front guides on the registration board, a pin register system that allows a plate to be automatically snapped into register on the printing unit, and many other features.

Most presses have between fourteen and sixteen rollers in the inking system, of which three or four usually function as ink form rollers. The dampening system will typically carry six rollers, with two form rollers. Combined with controls that perform minute adjustments, the printing unit can reproduce a quality ink layer for an image area of almost any size.

Figure 13.2. A common lithographic offset press

Courtesy of Miller Printing Machinery Co.

Perfecting offset presses are often equipped with two or more color units for both sides. Four-color sheet- and web-fed systems are common (see chapter 12).

Although "presses" and "duplicators" are technically different (the difference is based on the maximum sheet size printable with each), the word *duplicator* is rarely used to describe an offset lithographic printing device. Rather, all such devices are commonly referred to as "presses." This practice will be followed throughout this chapter.

Understanding Offset Press Operation

As mentioned in chapter 12, all presses are composed of four basic units: feeder, registration, printing, and delivery. It is crucial that you understand the process a sheet of paper goes through in its trip from the infeed pile through the registration system to the printing unit and finally to the delivery table, as well as the adjustments necessary for the correct operation of each system.

Feeder Unit

The feeder unit for offset sheet-fed presses must separate the top sheet of paper from the infeed pile, pick it up, and deliver it to the registration unit. This process must be done consistently for each sheet in the pile. Only one sheet can be fed at a time, and each must reach the registration unit at a precise moment to be registered and sent to the printing unit.

Usually, an **air blast** is used to separate the top sheet from the rest of the pile. This blast can be adjusted for papers of different weight and for different atmospheric conditions. On dry days, when the sheets tend to cling together because of static electricity, the air blast can be increased. Heavy papers require a stronger air blast than is needed for light papers. Coated papers, too, generally require a stronger air blast than is needed for uncoated papers. The air blast must be strong enough to "float" one piece of paper above the pile at a specified height below the sucker feet.

The sucker feet are small vacuum tubes that grab the floating top sheet and send it down the registration board, where the registration unit takes over. The amount of vacuum in the sucker feet can be adjusted for the weight of paper being printed. Heavy papers generally require more vacuum than is needed for light papers. The object is to adjust the vacuum so that only a single piece of paper is picked up by the sucker feet and delivered to the registration unit.

In actual operation, the sucker feet grab the top sheet from the pile and move it forward a short distance where it is picked up by pull-in wheels (or some other device) that put it squarely on a conveyer belt system on the registration board. The press automatically controls the precise moment when the sucker feet grab the top sheet, their movement toward the registration board, and the precise moment when the vacuum is cut off and the sheet enters the registration unit.

As the press removes paper from the infeed table, the height of the paper pile decreases. Yet the paper pile must be maintained at a constant distance from the sucker feet. This requirement is accomplished automatically by the press. As the press removes paper from the infeed pile, the infeed table is automatically moved up, which moves the infeed pile closer to the sucker feet.

The feeder system must be adjusted for air blast, vacuum, paper pile height, and upward movement of infeed table as the paper is used.

Registration Unit

The registration board consists of a conveyer belt system and some type of registration system. Both systems were discussed in chapter 12. The conveyer belts carry the paper to the registration unit, where it is momentarily stopped and squared to the plate cylinder along the top edge by a headstop. At the same time, it is either jogged or pulled slightly sideways and placed in the proper printing position. It is important to understand that before each sheet is printed, the registration system places it in exactly the same position as the preceding sheet. This position determines where the image will fall on the paper in the printing unit. The registration unit must be adjusted for paper width and image location.

Printing Unit

The printing unit places a water solution and ink on the plate, transfers the image to the paper, and delivers the paper to the delivery unit. The printing unit must be adjusted so that the proper amount of ink and water solution is deposited on the printing plate and that the image is transferred accurately, evenly, and consistently to the printing paper.

Delivery Unit

The delivery unit takes the paper from the printing unit and places it on an outfeed table. This step can be done by gravity feed or chain delivery. If chain delivery is used, the paper can be either pulled through the printing and delivery unit by the same chain system or transferred from the paper grippers on the impression cylinder in the printing unit to a different set of grippers on the delivery chain. Once the paper is on the outfeed table, it is jogged on one end and one side so that a perfectly even pile is formed. The delivery unit must be adjusted to form this even pile on the outfeed table.

Feeder, registration, and delivery units are common for most offset presses. The main difference in offset presses lies in the printing unit. Printing units vary in the type of cylinder systems they have and the type of ink and water systems they use.

The Cylinder Unit

Every offset printing unit is made up of the following three parts:

- The cylinder system,
- The dampening system,
- The inking system.

Each serves an important function in the total image transfer process and thus will be examined in detail.

Cylinder System Configurations

The cylinder system for any offset press has three functional groups: a plate cylinder, a blanket cylinder, and an impression cylinder. The function of the plate cylinder is to hold the plate and revolve it into contact with the blanket cylinder during the printing process. It generally has some form of clamping system that holds the plate squarely and firmly

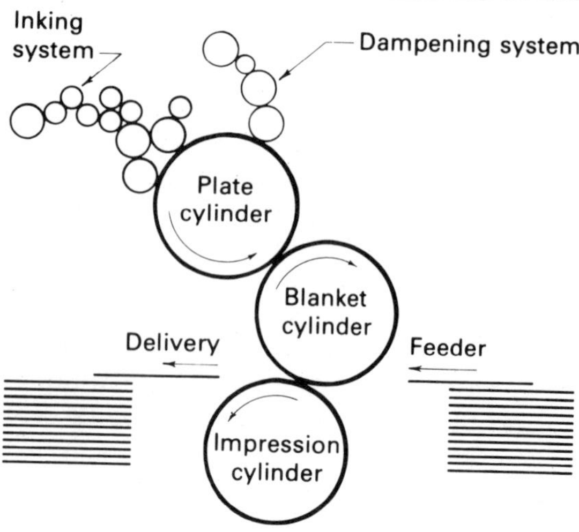

Figure 13.3. Example of a three-cylinder configuration

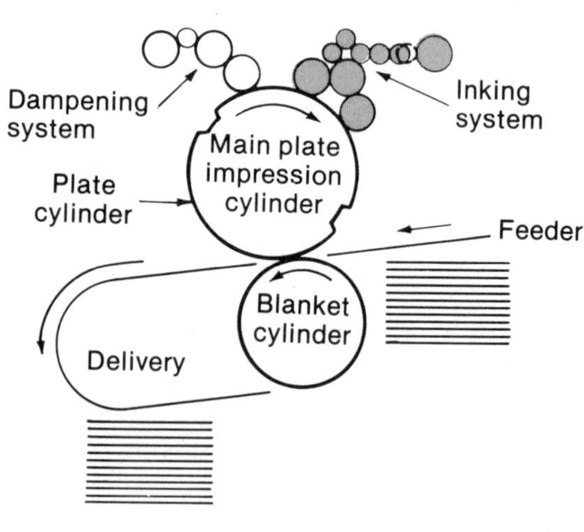

Figure 13.4. Example of a two-cylinder configuration

in place. Ink and water form rollers contact the plate while it is attached to the plate cylinder, thereby causing the image areas to be inked. The plate image is transferred on "offset" to the blanket cylinder, and the image is reversed. The press sheet or web paper is then passed between the blanket and impression cylinder, where the image is offset back to right reading. The impression cylinder applies the necessary pressure against the blanket and paper to transfer the image from the blanket to the paper.

Figure 13.3 shows one common configuration of plate, blanket, and impression cylinders, called the **three-cylinder principle**. Notice that because the blanket is above the impression cylinder, the paper travels in a straight line from feeder to delivery. Note also the direction of rotation of each cylinder and the logical placement of water and inking systems (remember that the plate must be moistened before it is inked).

Figure 13.4 illustrates an alternative cylinder configuration called the **two-cylinder principle**. With this design the plate and impression functions are combined to form a main cylinder with twice the circumference of the separate blanket cylinder. During the first half of the main plate/impression cylinder rotation, the image is offset from the plate section of the main cylinder to the blanket. During the next half-revolution, the press sheet is passed between the impression section of the main cylinder and the blanket cylinder. Because the blanket is beneath the impression device, the paper must be flopped by the delivery system in order to have the printed image face up on the outfeed table. This means that the sheets to be fed into the press must be placed on the infeed table upside down.

The three-cylinder configuration is commonly found on both duplicators and presses.

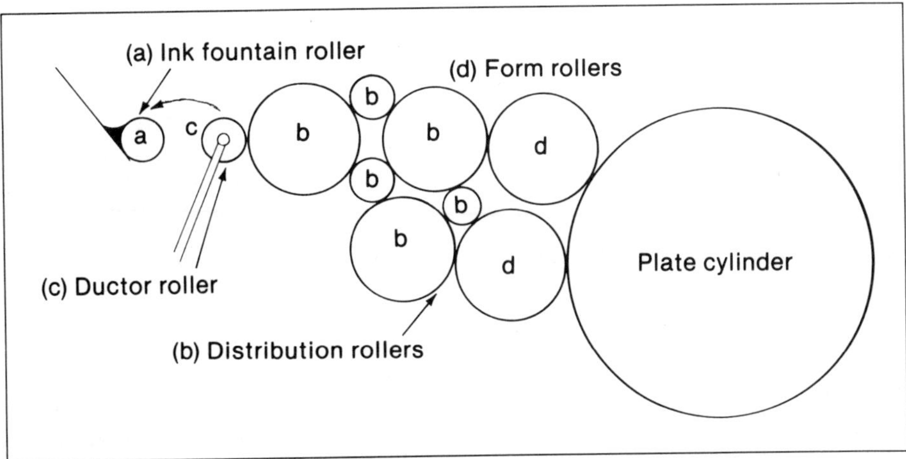

Figure 13.5. Example of a typical inking system The ink fountain (a), the distribution rollers (b), the ductor rollers (c), and the form rollers (d).

The two-cylinder design is rarely used on offset presses.

Impression Cylinder Adjustments

The gap between the blanket cylinder and the impression cylinder controls the final image quality. The pressure must be sufficient to transfer a dense ink image but not great enough to smash either the blanket or the press sheet. Controlling the amount of gap is referred to as adjusting **impression**. Each time the thickness of the paper being printed changes, the impression must be readjusted. Heavier papers need a wider opening than required for lighter papers.

On most duplicators, the impression cylinder can be raised or lowered by a simple set screw arrangement. On presses, impression is controlled by adding or subtracting packing from behind the blanket cylinder or by a cam adjustment attached to the impression cylinder.

The Inking Unit

The goal of any inking system is to place a uniform layer of ink across every dimension of the printing plate. The lithographic process is unique in that it requires the ink form rollers to pass in contact with the nonimage areas of the plate without transferring ink to them.

Inking Unit Configurations

All lithographic inking systems are made up of three main sections:

- Ink fountain and fountain rollers,
- Ink distribution rollers,
- Ink form rollers (figure 13.5).

The ink fountain stores a quantity of ink in a reservoir and feeds small quantities of ink to the rest of the inking system from the fountain roller. The ink distribution rollers receive ink and work it into a semiliquid state that is uniformly delivered to the ink form rollers. A thin layer of ink is then transferred to the image portions of the lithographic plate by the ink form rollers.

Inking Unit Operation

The ink **fountain** (figure 13.5a) holds a pool of ink and controls the amount of ink that enters the inking system. The most common type of fountain consists of a metal blade that is held in place near the fountain roller. The gap between the blade and the fountain roller can be controlled by adjusting screws to vary the amount of ink on the fountain roller. The printer adjusts the screws in or out as the fountain roller turns to obtain the desired quantity of ink. If the image to be printed covers only half the plate, half the fountain screws will be closed. If the plate image is even across the whole plate, all screws will be moved to place a uniform layer of ink on the ink fountain roller. Care must be taken not to form kinks in the doctor blade by turning one screw farther than the rest.

The ink distribution rollers spread the ink out to a uniform layer before it is placed on the plate (figure 13.5b). There are generally two types of distribution rollers: rotating distribution rollers and oscillating distribution rollers. **Rotating distribution rollers** rotate in one direction. **Oscillating distribution rollers** rotate and also move from side to side.

The ink is transferred to the ink distribution rollers by a **ductor roller** (figure 13.5c). The ductor is a movable roller that flops back and forth between the ink fountain roller and an ink distribution roller. As the ductor contacts the fountain roller, both turn and the ductor is inked. The ductor then swings forward to contact a distribution roller and transfers ink to it. The rate of rotation of the ink fountain roller and the gap between the ink plate and fountain roller control the amount of ink added to the distribution system. The rollers that actually ink the plate are called form rollers (figure 13.5d).

A simple indication of the quality of a printing press is the number of distribution and form rollers it has. The greater the number of distribution rollers, the more accurate the control of ink uniformity. It is difficult to ink large solid areas on a plate with only one form roller. With three (generally the maximum) it is relatively easy to maintain consistent ink coverage of almost any image area on the plate.

The Dampening Unit

Recall that most lithographic plates function on the principle of water-attractive and ink-attractive areas. In order for ink to adhere only to the image areas on the plate, a layer of moisture must be placed over the nonimage areas before the plate is inked. The dampening system accomplishes this by moistening the plate consistently throughout the press run.

Dampening Unit Configurations

There are no radical differences among the basic designs of most dampening systems (figure 13.6). Like inking systems, they all contain some form of fountain, a fountain roller, a ductor roller, distribution rollers, and one or more form rollers.

The functions of the dampening system and the inking system are distinctly different.

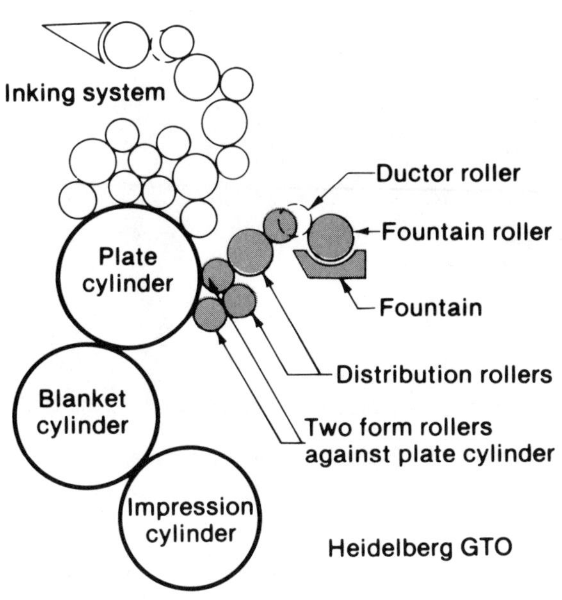

Figure 13.6. Diagram of a typical direct dampening system

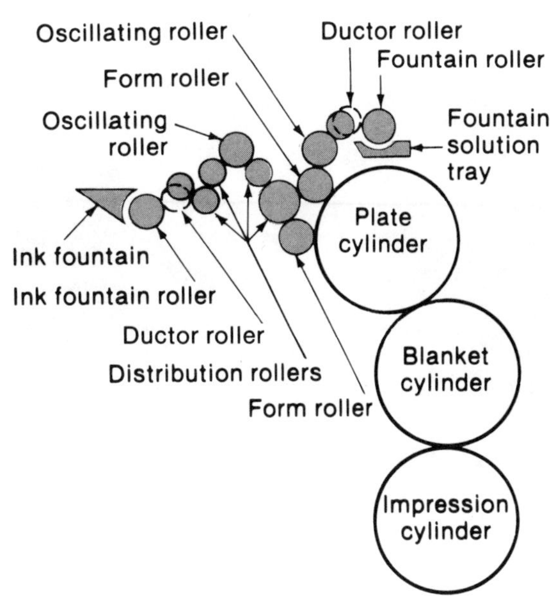

Figure 13.7. Diagram of an indirect dampening system

However, not all manufacturers use direct dampening systems where the ink and water rollers are separate. An indirect dampening system, such as the "aquamatic system" found on A. B. Dick duplicators, combines the ink and dampening rollers and carries the water solution to the plate on the ink-covered form rollers (figure 13.7).

Dampening Unit Operation

In a direct dampening system, the dampening fountain roller sits in a pool of fountain solution stored in the dampening fountain. As the press runs, the dampening fountain roller turns, picking up fountain solution from the fountain and holding it on its surface. A ductor roller jogs back and forth touching the fountain roller, where it picks up fountain solution, then touching a dampening distribution roller. The distribution roller(s) takes the fountain solution from the ductor roller to the dampening form roller(s), where it is transferred to the plate.

As mentioned above, in an indirect dampening system, the dampening distribution and form rollers are also the inking distribution and form rollers. In this system all the rollers in the **ink and water train** are inked; then fountain solution is added to the fountain. Because the dampener fountain roller and every other roller in the roller train in inked, the fountain solution literally rides on the surface of the inked rollers and is carried to the plate.

Figure 13.8. Fanning the press sheets The press sheets are fanned to remove any static electricity.

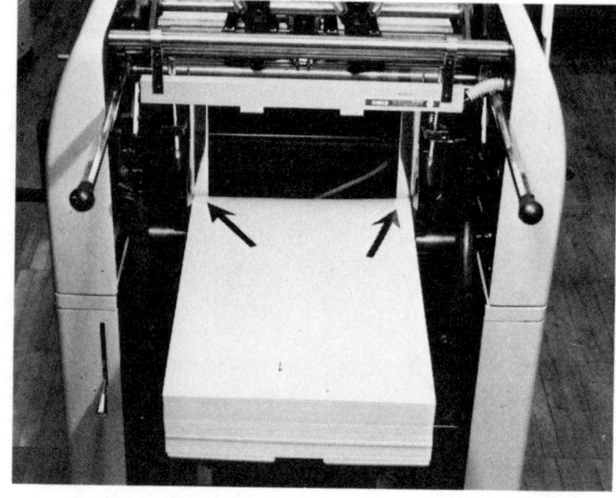

Figure 13.9. Adding paper to the feeder section Seat the pile of paper squarely against the front plate of the feeder.

On both systems, the rate at which the dampener fountain roller rotates in the fountain can be varied. The faster the fountain roller turns, the more fountain solution it delivers to the dampening system. In this way, the quantity of moisture reaching the plate can be adjusted.

Offset Press Operation

The purpose of this section is to examine the general operation of any sheet-fed offset press or duplicator. Refer to an operation manual for the details of operation for a specific machine.

Experienced printers typically set up the ink and water sections of the printing unit before adjusting the paper feed. In an industrial situation each machine is usually assigned one operator (or group of operators). Whoever is assigned to a press knows its characteristics and typically runs only a few standard sheet sizes. Novice printers, however, do not have the same advantages. In a learning situation the student is not familiar with the machine, is not aware of the sheet size previously run, and is generally hesitant when confronted with a machine as complicated as an offset press. For these reasons, the authors recommend that when learning press operation, students adjust the paper feed before adding ink or fountain solution to the printing unit. When the sheets are consistently passing through the press without jam-ups or misfeeding, students can direct their attention to obtaining proper ink-water balance.

Feeding the Paper

It is important that the pile of press sheets be accurately cut to the same size, be of the same thickness (paper weight), and not be wrinkled

Figure 13.10. Using wedges to level the paper Push wedges under the pile of paper to level the top surface of curled stock.
Courtesy of SUCO Learning Resources and R. Kampas.

Figure 13.11. Adjusting the pile height

or stuck together. Begin by fanning the pile to remove any static electricity that might be holding individual sheets together (figure 13.8). Place the pile in the feeder section of the press, slightly off center. When the sheet passes through the registration unit, it is generally jogged or pulled from ⅛ to $3/16$ inch and is then centered on the registration board.

Push the pile forward so that it is squarely seated against the front plate of the feeder when held by the side and back guides (figure 13.9). The top of the paper pile must be perfectly level and parallel to the registration board. If the stock sags, place a heavy board (such as a binder board cut slightly smaller than the paper size) under the pile. If the stock is curled, insert wedges at several points into the pile to make the top surface level (figure 13.10).

Next adjust the pile height below the feeding mechanism (generally sucker feet) (figure 13.11). Heavy paper must be closer to the sucker feet than is necessary for lighter material. To set the paper height, turn the machine on and allow the automatic pile height control to raise the stock to the previously set position. Turn the machine off and check the distance between the pile and the sucker feet when they are in the lowest position. If the distance is not between ⅛ and ¼ inch, lower the pile manually, readjust the pile height control, and allow the press to run and lift the paper pile to the new setting. Feeding problems will result if the pile height is not properly set. If the paper pile is too high, the sucker feet will pick up double sheets or jam-ups will result because the air and vacuum system is not allowed to do its job. If the pile is too low, the sheets will not be picked up or misfeeds will occur.

The purpose of the air blast is to float the top few sheets above the rest of the pile on a blanket of air. The amount of air blast needed will vary depending on the weight and size of the stock being printed. In general, the air blast should be adjusted to the point

Figure 13.12. Adjusting the air blast

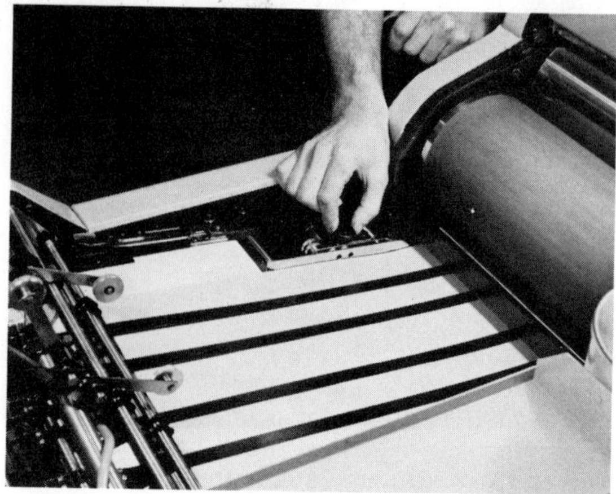

Figure 13.13. Adjusting the registration system Adjust the registration system by allowing a sheet of paper to move into contact with the headstop and position the sheet jogger or pull guide.

that the sheets do not vibrate and the topmost sheet nearly contacts the sucker feet (figure 13.12). Vacuum should be sufficient to draw the top sheet the short distance into contact with the sucker feet but not great enough to pick up more than one sheet.

Before allowing the feeder mechanism to send a sheet to the registration unit, the pull-in wheels (not on all machines) and the double-sheet detector must be set. Adjust the pull-in wheels to a uniform pressure so that each sheet is pulled squarely from the feeder onto the registration board. Double-sheet detectors either open a trap door and eject multiple sheets to a tray below the registration board or they mechanically (or electronically) cause the press to stop when a double sheet is detected. Set the device to pass the thickness of one sheet but to trip the press if more than one sheet is fed.

Next allow the press to feed a sheet into the registration unit and to stop it in contact with the headstop (figure 13.13). Line up the conveyor tapes, straps, or skid rollers to the sheet size. Then adjust the sheet jogger or pull guide to center the sheet on the press. The sheet should lie flat without binding or curling. Inch the sheet into the grippers that pull it between the impression cylinder and the blanket cylinder and allow it to be transferred to the delivery system.

Move the sheet to the delivery unit, but adjust the delivery table side guides before the sheet is released from the chain grippers (figure 13.14). Allow the sheet to drop onto the delivery table and position the table end jogger.

In order to check the entire system, start the machine and allow paper to pass from feeder to delivery. The sheets should be smoothly and consistently fed to the registration board. Each sheet should be uniformly registered and transferred to the printing

Figure 13.14. Adjusting the delivery side guides

Figure 13.15. Using make-ready sheets Notice that a marker is placed between the make-ready or scrap sheets and the clean press sheets.
Courtesy of SUCO Learning Resources and R. Kampas.

unit. The delivery system should remove each sheet and stack a perfect pile on the outfeed table. Final adjustments for image registration will be made after the printing unit has been inked and the first few proof sheets have been checked.

It is wise to place a quantity of make-ready sheets on top of the press sheet pile. Be certain that the make-ready sheets are of the same weight and surface finish as the final sheets (figure 13.15). These make-ready sheets can be used for initial press proofing.

Preparing the Printing Unit

Recall that basically two different systems are used to put water solution and ink on the printing plate: the direct system and the indirect system. In the direct system, moisture is transferred to the plate directly from a dampener form roller. In the indirect system, the water is transferred to the plate from the ink form rollers. The major difference in printing unit preparation for these two presses is that with the indirect system, the fountain solution cannot be added to the water fountain until after the press is completely inked. In the direct system, the ink and fountain solution can be put into the ink and water fountain during the same step. It is important to keep in mind which system you are working on as you read the following.

Adjusting the Ink Feed. Ink is transferred from the ink fountain reservoir by a ductor roller than contacts the fountain roller. The consistency of the ink layer over the fountain roller directly influences the amount of ink fed to the distribution section.

All ink fountains are set up with a thumbscrew system that allows the press operator to adjust the ink feed to allow for variation in ink coverage needed on the plate (figure 13.16). If large solids or halftones cover one section of the plate, it will be necessary

Figure 13.16. The ink fountain The fountain holds a pool of ink that is passed to the inking system by a controlled thumbscrew system.

to feed an additional quantity of ink to that area of the plate (figure 13.17).

When you are setting up an ink fountain, assume that the ink feed needs adjustment. Begin by loosening all the fountain keys, which will bring the ink fountain doctor blade out of contact with the fountain roller (figure 13.18). Reverse the process by gently tightening each key until you feel blade pressure against the roller. Then move the thumbscrews out slightly, allowing a small gap between the blade and fountain roller.

When the doctor blade is straight and parallel to the fountain roller, you can add ink to the ink fountain. To check for uniform ink distribution, manually rotate the ink ductor roller until it touches the fountain. Then turn the ink fountain roller and observe the appearance of the ink coverage on the ductor roller. If the surface is evenly covered, the keys are properly set. If heavy or light areas are noticeable across the system, make setscrew adjustments until the ink layer is consistent. If some areas of the plate require more ink than others, open the fountain keys in line with those sections to allow more ink to pass to the plate.

Once the first rough ink adjustments have been made, without bringing the water or ink form rollers into contact with the plate cylinder, turn the machine on and allow the systems to ink up. As the distribution rollers work the ink to a fine layer, make small adjustments to ensure ink train uniformity.

Adjusting the Water Feed. Fountain solution is added to most presses and duplicators from a storage bottle that keeps the water fountain full by gravity feed. This bottle should be located and tipped into place at this time. Remember, if you are operating an indirect dampening system, the fountain solution should not be added until the whole roller train is inked. In contrast, the fountain solution can be added to a direct dampening system before, after, or during ink adjustments.

Indirect systems have no covers on any of the ink and dampener rollers. Direct systems generally have cloth or fiber covers on the dampener ductor and form rollers. If these dampening covers are bone dry (as may occur after a long period of press shutdown), turn on the press, bring the dampener ductor roller into contact with the fountain roller, and turn the fountain roller by hand to add extra fountain solution to the water ductor. This action will speed up the dampening process. Be careful not to soak the ductor roller, however, as this will overdampen the press.

Another way to speed up the dampening process is to soak a cotton wipe in the fountain tray and squeegee the dampening solution onto the ductor roller. The form roller cover should be damp to the touch but

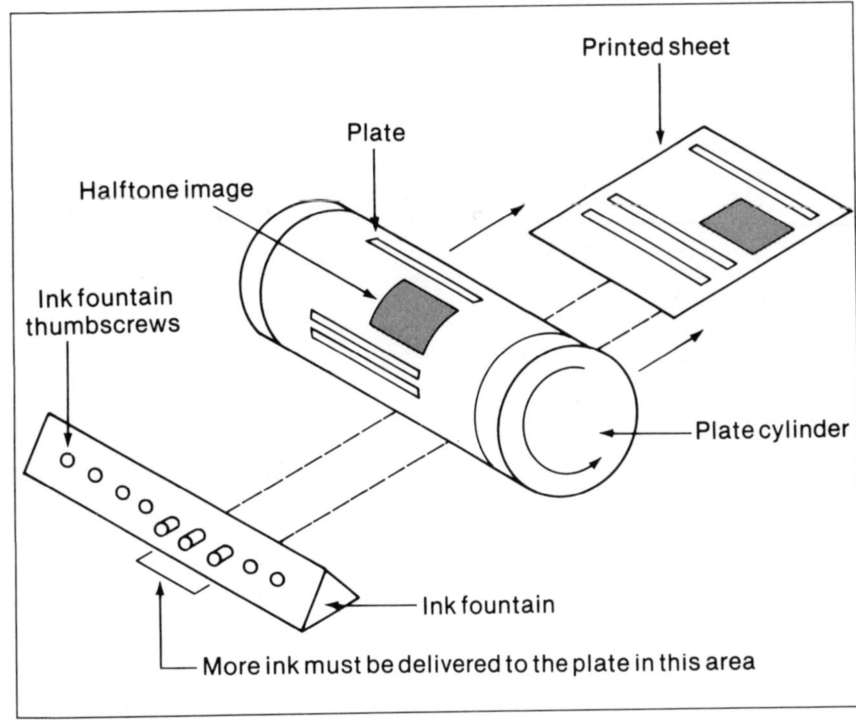

Figure 13.17. Adjusting the ink fountain In areas where large halftones or other kinds of dense copy are to be printed from the plate, the ink fountain thumbscrews must be adjusted to deliver more ink.

not dripping wet. Once the unit is adequately inked and moistened, stop the press and insert the plate.

Attaching the Plate. Mount the plate on the press by inserting the front edge of the carrier into the lead clamp of the plate cylinder and tightening it into position (figure 13.19). If packing is required, select and cut the appropriate material. Position the packing sheets between the plate and cylinder (if necessary) and rotate the cylinder forward so that the plate is curved into contact with the metal drum. When the rear plate clamps are exposed, insert the tail edge of the plate and tighten the clamp. The plate should be tight around the cylinder but should not be distorted or stretched.

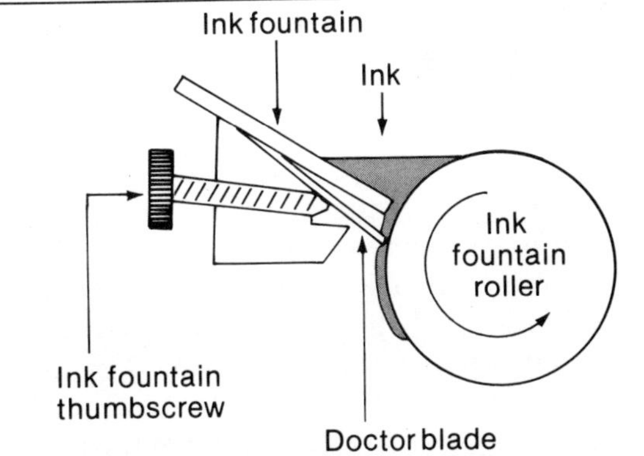

Figure 13.18. Diagram of an ink fountain thumbscrew As the ink fountain thumbscrew is adjusted, it moves the doctor blade either toward or away from the ink fountain roller and thereby decreases or increases the amount of ink that is deposited on the roller.

Figure 13.19. Mounting the plate on the press

Starting Up and Proofing

Most lithographic plates have had some form of gum preservative coating to protect the surface for the time between development and placement on the press. Moisten a sponge with plain water and wipe the entire plate to dissolve the coating. If a direct image plate is used, it is at this point that a special etch or starter solution must be used.

Inking the Plate. If you are operating an *indirect* system, start the press and allow it to operate for a moment; then move the form rollers into contact with the plate. The plate should pick up ink in the image areas and no ink in the nonimage areas. If no ink is picked up anywhere on the plate after several press revolutions, check to make sure that the form rollers are in contact with the plate. If they are, you must either cut back on the moisture or add ink until the image appears on the plate. To determine which adjustment is necessary, stop the press and observe the plate. If the plate is moist with only a thin film of fountain solution (not dripping), more ink is probably called for. If the plate is overdampened, adjust the water fountain to deliver less moisture.

If you are operating a *direct* dampening system, start the press, let it operate for a moment, and lower the dampener form rollers into contact with the plate. Release the rollers, stop the press, and check the plate. The surface should be moist, but dampening solution should not drip from the plate. If the plate is not moist, adjust the fountain system to deliver more moisture and repeat the process of dampening and checking. When the dampening form rollers are delivering enough moisture to the plate surface, lower the ink form rollers into contact with the plate. Ink should be transferred to only the image areas. If ink is deposited in nonimage areas, the problem is probably lack of moisture. Squeegee additional fountain solution onto the dampener form roller in the scumming area.

Press Proofing. Once the plate is properly inked, place the press on "impression" (the plate cylinder lowered into contact with the blanket cylinder) and allow several make-ready sheets to pass through the printing unit.

The initial concern is only with image position, not with image quality. Examine the first few sheets for consistency of image placement and compare the image position with the proofs or layout specifications for the job. All offset machines allow the press image to be raised or lowered on the sheet by moving the position of the plate image on the blanket. On most presses you can skew the plate on the plate cylinder to change the angular position of the image on the press sheet. The side-to-side image position can be adjusted by moving the registration system.

After obtaining the desired image position, start the press, lower the dampening and ink form rollers into plate contact, and begin the run with the make-ready sheets. As the sheets pass through the press, examine the image quality and make appropriate adjustments to the ink or water system and the impression cylinder. As the final sheets begin to be fed, set the sheet counter to zero and begin the press run.

Achieving Proper Ink-Water Balance. The ink-water balance is crucial in offset print. If not enough moisture is on the plate, the image will scum on the press sheet. If too much moisture reaches the plate, the image will appear light and washed out (not dense enough) on the press sheet. Adding ink to an overdampened plate will not correct the problem. In fact, it will make matters worse because once the correct amount of moisture is delivered to the plate, the press will be overinked.

It is important to remember that small changes made at the fountain rollers take a while to work their way through the distribution and form rollers to the plate. Most fountain rollers are adjusted by a ratchet arrangement. A lever is moved forward or back so many "clicks" along the ratchet to make the fountain roller turn faster or slower. Often the lever has a scale printed next to it. This scale does not refer to any specific quantity of ink or moisture, but rather is relative to the rate of fountain roller rotation at any given time. Moving the lever up the scale makes the fountain roller rotate more rapidly. Moving it down the scale causes the roller to rotate slower.

The water fountain roller alone controls the amount of moisture placed on the plate. However, on the inking system both the opening of the ink fountain keys and the rotation rate of the ink fountain roller control the quantity of ink reaching the plate. In order to achieve proper ink-water balance, the ink fountain keys, ink fountain roller rotation rate, and water fountain roller rotation rate must all be properly adjusted. When they are adjusted properly and the press can be run through several thousand impressions without the press operator touching the ink or water adjustments, the ink and water systems are said to be "in balance."

Ink-water balance can be achieved only while the press is actually printing. An inexperienced press operator may have to print quite a few make-ready sheets to achieve this balance. Even experienced press operators allow up to 6% spoilage for a run of 1,000 sheets. In other words, an experienced operator expects to print up to 60 press sheets before getting the press to feed properly and reaching the correct ink-water balance. These sheets, called the "spoilage allowance," are added to the 1,000 sheets needed for the final run and are paid for by the customer as part of the job.

The ink and water settings necessary to achieve proper ink-water balance differ with each job printed. One job may have large, dense image areas and require more water and ink than needed for another job. When colors are printed, whether process or flat color, proper ink-water balance must be achieved for each separate color. Thus the spoilage allowance is increased for color work.

The mark of an experienced press operator is the ability to get the press feeding and to reach ink-water balance with the least amount of spoilage. This takes practice and familiarity with a particular press. Novice printers do not have these advantages. However, the following considerations may make achieving ink-water balance a bit easier for the novice:

1. Remember that the gauge of the printing job is the actual press sheet. Experienced press operators watch the *outfeed table,* pulling out every twenty-fifth, fiftieth, or one hundredth press sheet and comparing it to their initial acceptable press proof. A quick check of the press sheet should show consistent density across the image area, no scumming or ink in the nonimage areas, and no "set-off" (printed image on the back of the press sheet). Watching the ink rollers and registration board will not help you determine whether the printed image is acceptable.

2. On direct system presses, the ink and water form rollers can be lifted off the plate separately. It is always a good idea to raise the form rollers off the plate when the ink or water system is being adjusted. This will help keep the plate from becoming overdampened or overinked while the adjustment is being made.

3. Most ink and water fountain rollers can be stopped without stopping the ductor or distribution rollers. If the press appears underdampened, but the ink quantity seems right, stop the paper feed, lift the form rollers, and turn off the ink fountain roller before adjusting the water fountain roller. It may take 50 to 100 press revolutions for a small change in the ink fountain roller adjustment to work its way down to the plate. If the press is inking all this time and no paper is being printed, the ink will build up on the ink rollers. Once the water system is properly adjusted, the press will be overinked.

4. Feed jam-ups are a frequent problem for inexperienced press operators. Generally a jam-up can be corrected in a short time simply by shutting off the press and removing the jammed paper. Occasionally, however, jam-ups take longer to clear. If the press is shut down for much more than two minutes during a run, ink-water balance will have to be reachieved before final sheets are again printed. This will increase spoilage unless new make-ready sheets are placed on the infeed table after the jam-up is cleared.

Remember that all the time the press is shut down, the dampener rollers are drying out. If the shutdown is lengthy, it may take several press revolutions before the dampening system is back up to proper moisture level. After a long shut down, it is best to run the press for a few minutes with the ink system shut off, the form rollers lifted off of the plate, and the dampening system on. Once the dampening system is back up to proper moisture, the dampening form roller(s) can be engaged to moisten the plate, the press briefly stopped, and the plate examined for moisture content.

Cleanup Procedures

With the availability of new inks, many small job shops clean the ink and water systems only once a week. Some operators only cover the press with a cloth to keep out dust; others spray the ink fountain and rollers with a commercial antiscum material that coats the ink with a thin layer of lacquer and, in effect, forms a seal that prevents drying. The disadvantage of this approach is that the buildup of paper lint and other impurities in the ink and water systems will eventually reach a level that affects production quality. Therefore, the most common procedure is to give the entire printing unit a thorough cleaning at the end of each workday.

Before the inking system is cleaned, the water fountain is generally drained. A tube

Figure 13.20. A doctor blade

Figure 13.21. Applying wash-up solution

leading from the water fountain is used for this purpose.

The ink clean-up system on all but the smallest offset duplicators is almost totally automatic. One common design moves a squeegee or "doctor blade" against a form roller or a separate transfer roller (figure 13.20). If the wash-up solution is applied to the press while it is running, the ink is dissolved and passes across the squeegee into a sludge tray.

There are specific procedures to follow when cleaning the inking system. First, remove as much ink as possible from the ink fountain with an ink knife. Next, remove the ink fountain and clean it by hand with ink solvent. On most presses, the rest of the system is cleaned automatically. While the press is turned off, attach or engage the squeegee or transfer roller cleanup device. Then start up the press and apply wash-up solution to one side of the distribution rollers (figure 13.21). Most of the ink rollers are driven by friction against two or three geared rollers. If solvent were applied across the entire system, friction would be reduced and not all the rollers would turn. Apply wash-up solution until half the system becomes clean and dry. Then apply the solvent to the remaining inked portion. Continue the procedure of applying solvent to one side of the system at a time until the entire system is clean.

The cleanup attachment will function more efficiently if the leading edge of the squeegee blade is wiped clean after each use. If ink dries and hardens on the blade, it will not contact the roller properly. Some cleanup attachments ae completely removed from the press after cleanup. Others merely hinge out of contact with the press rollers.

An alternative to the mechanical cleanup system is a blotter pad. Blotter pads are absorbent paper sheets that are cut and punched to the exact plate size for the press being used. To clean up the inking system, mount a pad on the plate cylinder, turn on the machine, and lower the ink form rollers into contact

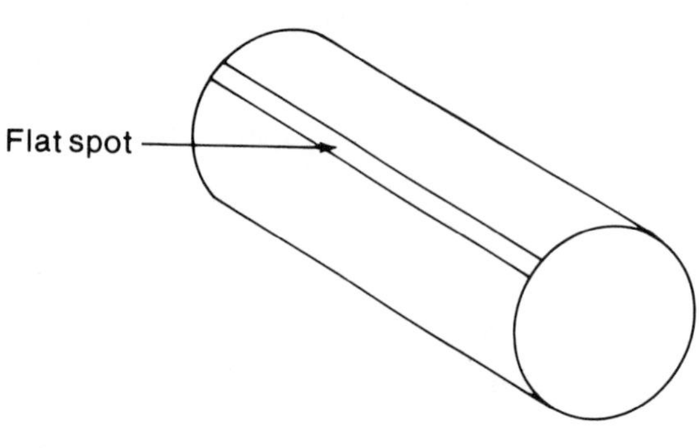

Figure 13.22. A roller with a flat spot

with the pad (take special care to raise the water form roller out of contact with the plate cylinder). Apply solvent much the same as you would when using a mechanical cleaning device, but with this approach the dissolved ink will be transferred to the blotter pad.

Many presses and duplicators have systems (often called "night latches") that separate the distribution rollers when the press is shut down. If the rollers are left in contact during lengthy shut-down periods, they will develop "flat spots" where they rest together (figure 13.22). Flat spots can cause uneven ink distribution throughout the roller train. Consult the operating manual for the press that you are running to determine whether there are night latches that should be set after the press is cleaned.

Printing Process Color on Sheet-Fed Offset Presses

Most offset lithographic presses can be used to reproduce quality process color work as long as good separations, plates, paper, ink, and, most important, a skilled operator are available.

Press Concerns

The concerns when working with four-color process printing are the same as for any quality single-color job: the sheets must be fed, registered, printed, and delivered. However, it becomes important that accurate and consistent registration be held throughout the entire run.

There is a simple method to check registration controls prior to printing a four-color job. Print a separate job that includes both line and halftone copy with the press set up for the most consistent feeding and registration. Without changing the press settings, remove the printed sheets from the delivery system and move them to the feeder system to be fed back through the press a second time. The goal is to print a second layer of ink—both halftone dots and line copy—over the first image with **dot-for-dot registration.** If, after two separate printings, only one sharp image is observed, quality registration is being held. If the image is blurred or if there is a double image, either the system is not properly adjusted or the press is incapable of quality color reproduction.

When a single press is used to reproduce four-color work, color contamination between runs is always possible. Even though an ink unit is thoroughly cleaned, residue ink may interfere with the purity of the next color. This is more of a problem when a dark color, such as black, is followed by a light color, such as yellow.

One solution is to ink the press first with a small quantity of the new ink and, after a uniform ink layer is obtained on all rollers, wash up the press. The press is then re-inked with the same color in proper quantities for the production run. With this procedure the press actually gets cleaned twice and there is little chance for color contamination. This technique is unnecessary when a light color is followed by black.

Sequence of Colors

Recall that process color involves the over-printing of four separate images whose combination can approximate the appearance of nearly any color in the visible spectrum. During printing, the sequence of colors can vary depending on the type of ink, paper, or press or the preference of the operator. There are, however, several common approaches.

The sequence of first cyan, then yellow, then magenta, and finally black is often used. Yellow, magenta, cyan, and black is another frequent order. The cyan printer generally resembles a normal halftone reproduction. In other words, if process blue (cyan) is the first color placed on the sheet, detail will usually be carried across the sheet wherever the final image will appear. Using progressive color proofs, it is possible to compare press sheets with each color to match density and detail positions, and it is relatively easy to fit all colors after cyan into their proper positions. One disadvantage with using cyan as the first color is with the quantity of ink laid down on the first pass through the press. With so much ink detail, all following colors tend to dry rather slowly because the paper has already absorbed ink over much of its area. With this technique there is also the possibility that as the paper becomes more ink saturated with each added color, adhesion can build up between the sheet and blanket.

Many printed jobs are made up of process color on the same page with other line copy, such as printed headlines or paragraph composition, which must appear in black. Often the color position on the page is defined by the location of this black detail. In this situation, it is necessary to print the black printer first and then fit all other colors in their correct position on the sheet. The typical sequence is black, yellow, magenta, and cyan. With this approach there is the added advantage that adhesion between the stock and blanket can be reduced because the colors typically carrying the least amount of ink detail are printed first. In instances where progressive proofs are not available, this sequence also enables the press operator to correct any color deviations on the first three colors by adjusting the cyan printer.

SECTION 2

This section covers some common press problems and concerns. Like all machines, presses need occasional adjustments in order to operate correctly. It is impossible to achieve proper ink-water balance or to print a quality image on a press that is not adjusted correctly.

Roller and Blanket Problems and Adjustments

Press operators often encounter several roller and blanket problems. Many of these problems can be corrected by relatively simple adjustments. Others require roller or blanket replacement. A press operator should be familiar with the adjustment procedures for most of the rollers in the roller train and be able to recognize solutions for many of the more common roller and blanket problems.

Blanket Considerations

Most offset blankets are formed from vulcanized rubber bonded to a fiber support base. Within the basic materials, however, a wide range of different blanket quality is available. There are special purpose formulations designed to be used with specific materials, such as ultraviolet drying inks or coated stock. Most printers do not change blankets every time a different ink or paper is fed through the press, but the importance of blanket compatibility with special materials must be stressed. Lithographic suppliers are prepared to identify the appropriate blanket for any press situation.

Blanket Problems

There are two common problems that occur with offset blankets that the press operator must be able to recognize and correct: glazing and smashes.

Glazing. Blankets become glazed as a result of long periods of improper cleaning or because of age. A very smooth, hard, glossy surface is created when the pores of the blanket fill with ink, ink solvent, or both. A glazed blanket will lose its ability to transfer enough ink to produce an acceptable ink density on the press sheet. Commercial deglazing compounds are available that will clear blanket pores, but the best measure is to prevent the problem by properly washing the blanket after each press run.

Smashes. Blankets become smashed when more material is passed between the impression and blanket cylinders than the gap will permit. Each time the press sheet is wrinkled or folded as it travels through the printing unit, the blanket becomes smashed or creased. If enough pressure is applied, the smashed areas will be pushed in too far to receive ink from the plate cylinder and unable to transfer an image to the press sheets. If the smash is small, a commercial "blanket fix" is available. When this is painted over the smashed area, it causes the surface to swell. If there are actual tears in the surface, the blanket should be replaced. If a large area has been smashed but there are no visible breaks, the blanket might be returned to a usable condition by removing it from the press and soaking it in a water bath for several days.

New blankets should not be stored near excessive heat. If a blanket is exposed to high temperatures, the rubber may lose its "give" or elasticity. Blankets should be stored in a flat position with a cover sheet to protect the surface from damage.

Plate-to-Blanket Packing and Adjustments

When the paper being printed passes between the impression and the blanket cylinders, the amount of pressure among the three must be uniform and sufficient to transfer ink. At the same time, it cannot be so great that the action becomes abrasive to the plate when the image is offset from the plate to the blanket.

The uniformity of the plate-to-blanket pressure can be easily checked by the operator. Turn off the dampening system and ink the entire surface of a used plate while it is mounted on the press. Stop the press and lower the plate cylinder into contact with the blanket cylinder (on "impression"). Separate the two cylinders and inspect the ink band that was transferred to the blanket. If the band is approximately 1/8 inch wide across the entire width of the blanket, the system is properly aligned. If the image is light, heavy, or irregular, consult the press manual for specific recommendations.

On most offset duplicators, plate and blanket cylinder pressure is either automatically controlled by spring pressure or can be changed by a manual screw adjustment.

On presses, plate-to-blanket pressure is usually adjusted by packing under the blanket and/or the plate. Improper packing of press cylinders could cause serious registration problems. Press manufacturers will specify appropriate packing for their equipment. Refer to the press manual for detailed procedure on plate-to-blanket packing.

Glazed Rollers

Even with the most efficient cleanup procedures, ink rollers can eventually become glazed with dried ink. **Glaze** is a buildup on the rubber rollers that prevents the proper adhesion and distribution of ink. Commercially prepared deglazing compounds are available that can be easily used to remove any dried ink from the rollers. One common technique is to apply a pumice compound to the rollers in the same manner as applying ink. Allow the pumice to work into the rollers by running the press for 5 to 10 minutes. Then wash the system with a liquid deglazing solution. Both the compound and the solution can then be removed by using wash-up solution and standard cleanup procedures. Many press operators deglaze their rollers on a regular basis as a part of a preventive maintenance system.

Dampening Rollers

Water does not readily adhere to smooth roller surfaces. Therefore, several dampening rollers are covered with some material that will easily carry usable quantities of the water fountain solution to the plate. The ductor and form rollers are typically covered. Two types of dampening covers are commonly used: molleton covers and fiber sleeves.

Molleton covers are thin cloth tubes that slip over the rollers and are tied or sewn at each end. It is important that the molleton uniformly cover the entire roller. If the ends are so tightly tied that a taper is formed in the roller, insufficient moisture will be delivered to the plate and the outside edges of the plate will scum with ink. A new molleton cover placed on a roller should be broken in. Soak the cover with water and squeeze out any excess water by rolling the covered roller over a sheet of uncoated paper. The breaking-in process removes any lint or loose threads.

Dampening sleeves are thin fiber tubes that, when dry, are slightly larger in diameter than the roller. To apply the sleeve, slide the dry sleeve over the clean roller and soak it with warm water. Within minutes the fibers shrink into position on the roller and the roller is ready to be installed on the press. Dampening sleeves are generally used only on form rollers. Because the tubes are exceptionally thin (when compared to molleton covers), the rollers must be oversize compared to those usually supplied with the press. Dampener sleeves are, however, easy to install, lintless, and easy to keep adjusted to the plate cylinder.

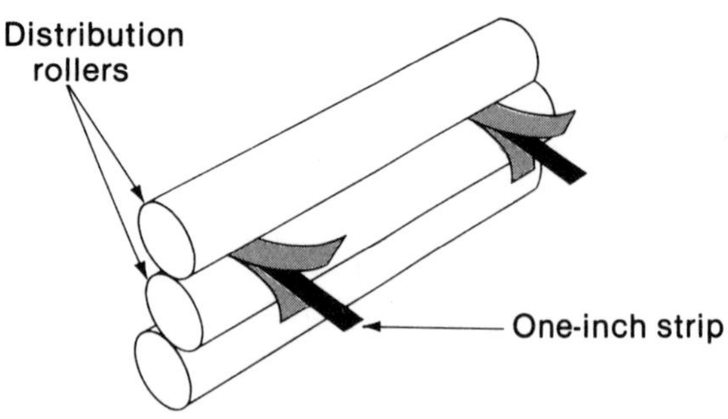

Figure 13.23. Adjusting the distributor rollers Distributor roller adjustment can be checked by placing a set of three pieces of paper under each end and then gently pulling out the middle strips. The strips should slide with some resistance.

Thin cloth sleeves that can be used to cover badly inked molletons are also available. Thin cloth and fiber sleeves react more readily to operator adjustments and make maintenance of consistent moisture control easier than with the traditional molleton cover.

At the end of each work day, remove the dampening solution from the water fountain tray. If the metal fountain roller becomes coated with ink, it can be cleaned with pumice powder and water. An occasional coating with any commercial desensitizing etch will ensure continued water transfer during the production day.

Cloth and fiber dampener covers can be cleaned with a commercial dampener roller cleaner. To clean the covers, first saturate the material with water so the cleaner will not soak into the fabric, then scrub the surface with a stiff brush and roller cleaner. Rinse the roller cover with water and allow the material to dry.

It is best to have two sets of dampener rollers for each press so a clean, dry roller will always be available. If the press has only one set and it is needed immediately after cleaning, roll the roller against blotter paper or cleaner sheets until no more water can be removed. Covers need not be cleaned on a daily basis, but only as necessary. They should be changed when the material in the cover will no longer accept water.

Distributor Roller Adjustment

All distribution rollers in the ink and water systems must be in uniform contact with each other to get proper ink and water distribution. Most rollers are adjustable in at least one direction and are relatively simple to move.

A common method for setting distribution rollers involves the use of strips of 20-pound paper. Cut six pieces, 8 or 9 inches long, four approximately 2 inches wide and two 1 inch wide. To check for uniform pressure between the two rollers, roll a set of three strips between a set of rollers at each end and then gently pull the middle pieces out (figure 13.23). The strips should slide with some slight resistance, but should not tear.

Form Roller Adjustment

The ink and water form rollers must all be adjusted so that they touch the plate with the correct amount of pressure, and so that the pressure is uniform across the width of the plate. Form rollers all have some type of easy adjustment for skew and pressure.

Dampening Form Roller Adjustment. If the dampener roller is not parallel to the plate cylinder, moisture will not be distributed evenly across the plate. If all portions of the

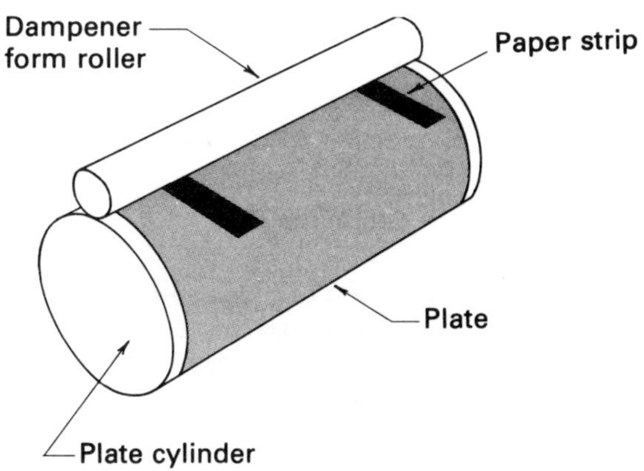

Figure 13.24. Checking the dampening form roller adjustment Dampening form roller adjustment can be checked by placing two strips of paper under each side and comparing resistance.

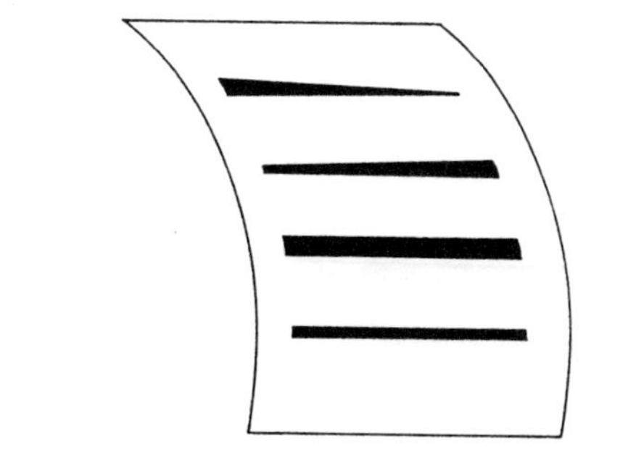

Figure 13.25. Examples of test strip checks for ink form roller-to-plate pressure The top two strips show rollers that are contacting the plate with uneven pressure. The third strip indicates too much pressure. The last strip is uniform and not too wide, indicating correct pressure.

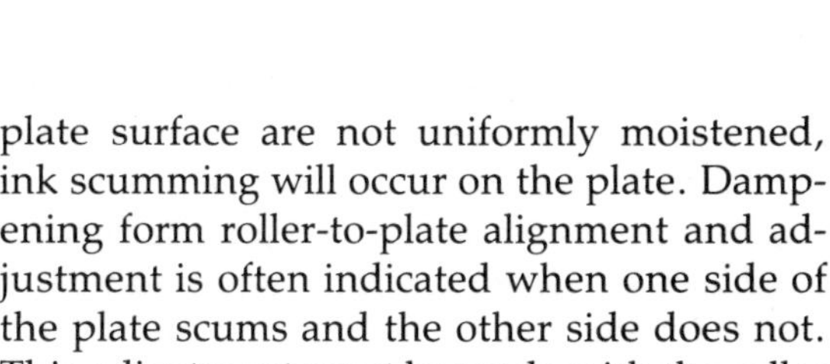

plate surface are not uniformly moistened, ink scumming will occur on the plate. Dampening form roller-to-plate alignment and adjustment is often indicated when one side of the plate scums and the other side does not. This adjustment must be made with the roller in place on the press.

Cut two 1-inch-wide strips of 20-pound bond paper and place one under each end of the dampening form roller (figure 13.24). Lower the dampening form roller into position against a plate. Slowly pull each paper strip while checking for uniformity of resistance. If unequal pull is observed, the roller is not parallel to the plate cylinder and must be reset. Both duplicators and presses have adjustments to control form roller-to-plate alignment.

Ink Form Roller Adjustment. Ink form roller-to-plate pressure is critical. Too much pressure will result in a blurred or enlarged image. Too little pressue will not transfer ink. Proper adjustment requires not only that you have the proper amount of pressure, but that the pressure be even across the width of the plate. Form roller pressure is checked by first inking the press and then turning the press off in such a way that the plate is located beneath the form rollers. With the plate in this position, bring the form rollers into contact with the plate by moving the press to the "print" mode. Immediately bring the press off ink and rotate the plate to a position where you can examine the ink tracks left on it by the form rollers (figure 13.25). As shown in figure 13.26, the first roller to contact the plate should have the heaviest ink line (1/8 to 3/16 inch) and the last should have the lightest (3/32 to 1/8 inch). All rollers should transfer a uniform width of ink across the plate. Figure 13.27a shows proper form roller positions

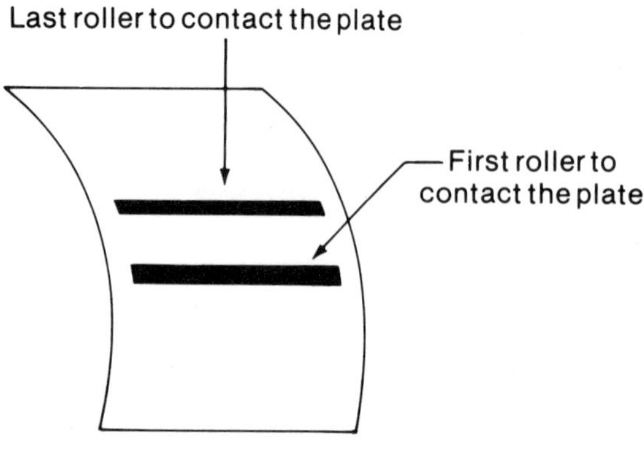

Figure 13.26. Examples of difference in tracks left by the first and last roller The ink track left on the plate by both rollers should be even across the width of the plate. The track of the first roller should be slightly wider than the track of the last roller.

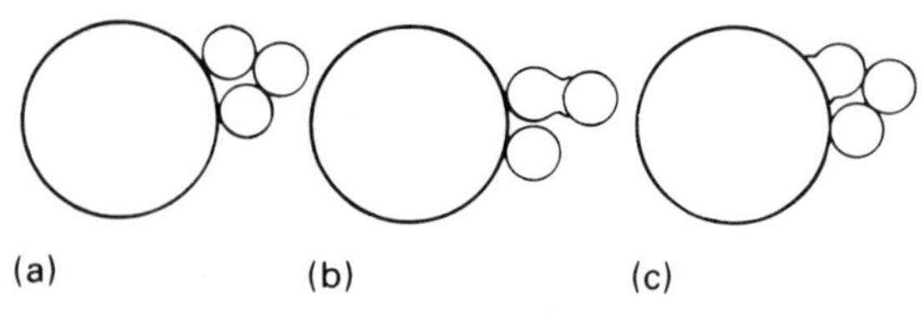

Figure 13.27. Diagram of ink form roller adjustment The proper adjustment of form rollers is shown in (a). Misalignment of form rollers is shown in (b) and (c).

against a distribution and plate cylinder. Figures 13.27b and 13.27c illustrate two possible adjustments that will diminish image quality on the final sheet.

Common Press Concerns

Many concerns are common to all press designs or models. This section does not contain an exhaustive list, but it should help you understand some basic press problems.

The Dampening Solution and pH

The moisture applied to the surface of a lithographic plate actually serves two functions. First, the presence of water in the nonimage areas repels ink. However, if only pure water were used as the dampening solution, the action of the ink would rapidly cause the nonimage areas to become ink receptive. The second purpose of the moisture, then, is to ensure that the nonimage areas of the plate remain water receptive. Alois Senefelder recognized the dual role of the moisture layer on the stone and used a solution made from a combination of water, acid, and gum arabic.

Dampening solutions are available ready-mixed from a commercial supplier or can be purchased as separate components and mixed by the printer. Most solutions are now made from an acid concentrate, gum arabic, and a gum preservative.

For lithographers, the most meaningful measure of dampening solution usability is the level of acidity of the liquid. The numeric scale that measures acidity in a range from 0 (very acid) to 14 (very alkaline, or a base) is called a **pH scale** (figure 13.28). The midpoint 7 is considered neutral. Plate manufacturers specify a recommended pH level to be used with their plates. A reading between 5.5 and 4.5 is acceptable for most plates.

The printer can measure pH in several ways. Litmus paper pH indicators are available from printing suppliers and give an acceptable level of acidity for most production

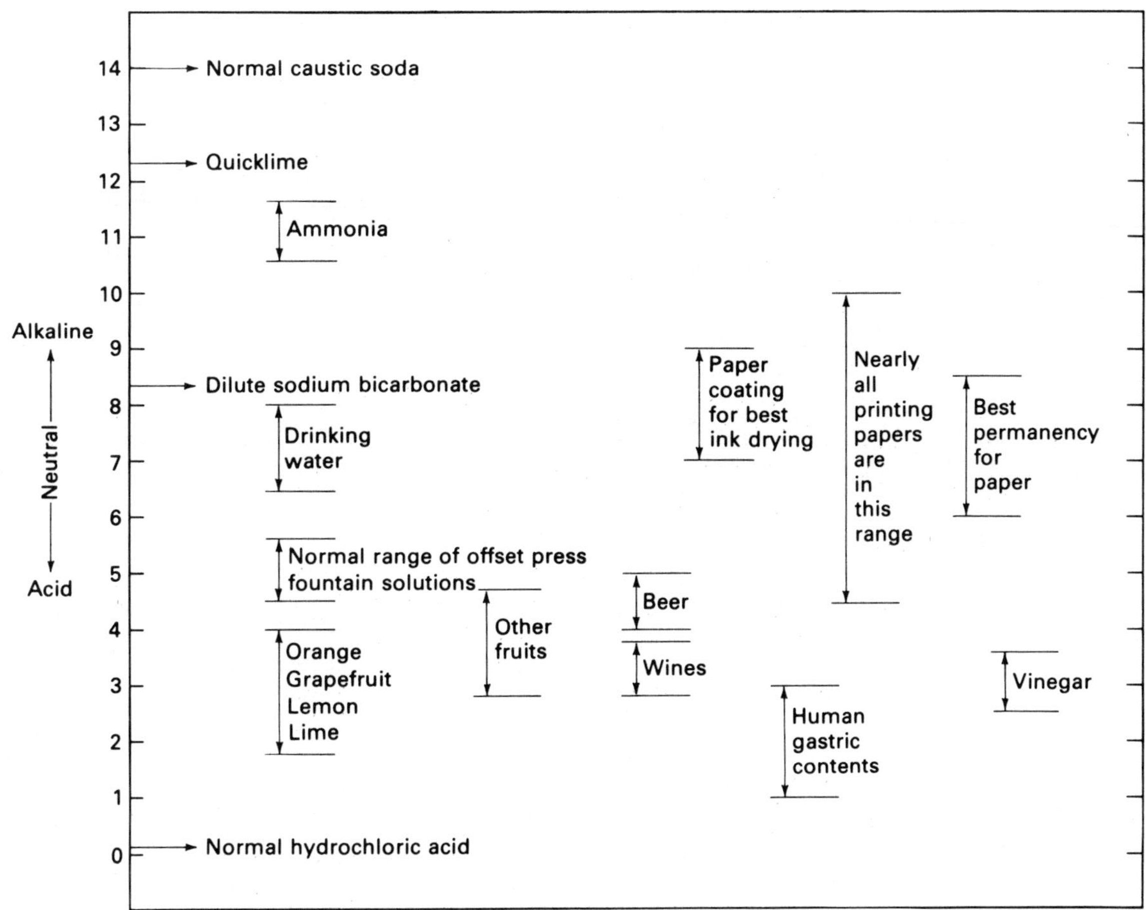

Figure 13.28. The pH values for various substances
Courtesy of Mead Paper.

situations (figure 13.29). To make a test, remove a small piece of litmus paper from the roll and dip it into the fountain solution. The wet paper will change color and can be matched to color patches supplied with the roll. A pH number will be identified next to each color patch. If the pH is not in the recommended range, remix the fountain solution.

Some presses have built-in sensors that continually monitor the pH level of the dampening solution. With such sensors, the required pH is dialed into the unit, and the device automatically compensates for any variation by adding water or acid concentrate.

A variety of problems can occur as a result of too acid a fountain solution (pH read-

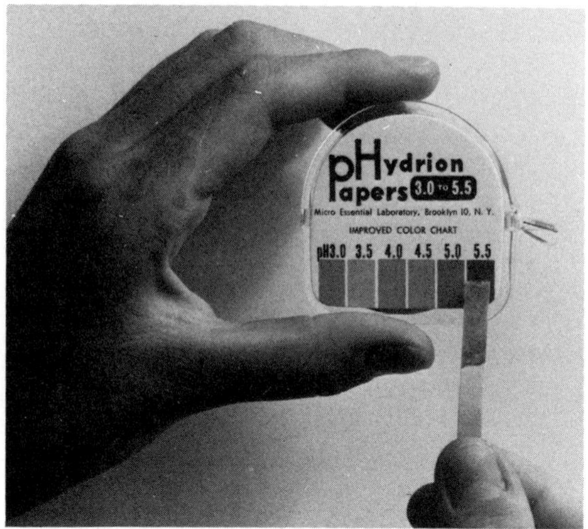

Figure 13.29. Example of a litmus paper pH indicator Litmus paper pH indicators are used to check the water fountain solution in most working situations.
Courtesy of Micro Essential Lab, Inc.

ings from 1 to 3). A strongly acidic solution can greatly shorten plate life. The acid tends to deteriorate the image area of all surface plates and can eventually make the image "walk off the plate." When the pressroom humidity is high, the action of acid with ink will cause drying problems on the press sheets (especially when running high-acid content papers). A high-acid bath will also break down the ink. The ink is attacked by the high acid content of the fountain solution, and the ink becomes paste-like, or **emulsified.** The rollers will appear glazed, and no quantity of ink that is added to the system will correct the problem. The rollers must be cleaned and the unit re-inked.

If the acid level if the dampening solution is too low (pH readings from 7 to 14), the action of the moisture layer on the nonimage areas will decrease water receptivity, and the plate will scum with ink.

Ink and Paper Considerations for Lithographic Printing

Ink and paper are probably the two most common ingredients for any printing job. The customer doesn't want to be bothered with the details of production problems, but the printer must live with ink and paper problems on a day-to-day basis. Some characteristics of these two important ingredients of offset litho press operation are worth examining.

Working with Lithographic Ink. Ink is affected by the paper it is put on. Many printers indiscriminately add materials, such as a drier or an extender, to their ink at the beginning of each workday, believing that they are improving the ink. There is a trend in ink manufacturing to supply inks that require no special mixing and that match each different type of press sheet and job characteristic. Under no circumstances should additives be mixed with any ink without consulting an ink supplier.

Troubleshooting Ink Difficulties. Beyond mechanical problems caused by inexact press adjustments, there are often difficulties resulting from ink characteristics that can be easily corrected by appropriate additives. Three common problems are tinting, picking, and slow drying.

Tinting is identified by a slight discoloration over the entire nonimage area—almost like a sprayed mist or the pattern created by a 5% or 10% screen tint. Generally, the situation is caused by a reaction between the ink and the water fountain solution. If the ink is too water soluble, it will bleed back into the water fountain through the dampening system. If tinting occurs, both the ink and the water systems should be cleaned and a different ink formulation used.

Picking is similar in appearance to small hickies over the entire image area of the press sheet (see figure 13.31). It can be caused by linty or poorly coated paper, but it is more commonly a result of ink that is too tacky. Small particles of paper are literally torn from the surface of each press sheet and fed back into the inking system. If picking is observed, the inking system should be cleaned and the ink mixed with a small quantity of reducer or nonpick compound.

Slow ink drying can be an elusive problem unless all possible causes are recognized. Simple drying problems can generally be eliminated with the addition of a drier compound to the ink, but too much drier can actually increase drying time. Overinking on a coated (nonabsorbent) stock can significantly increase drying time. On humid days, too high an acid content in the dampening solution (low pH) can cause difficulties. This combination of problems is almost impossible to solve without moving the sheets to a humidity-controlled environment. Delayed drying can be a special problem when the sheet must be flopped or turned to receive an image on the second side.

Paper Acid Content. In general, uncoated papers will not dry properly in a humid atmosphere if the pH is below 5 (see figure 13.28). Most coated papers have a pH of above 7.5. Coatings with a pH of between 6 and 7 would also cause ink-drying problems when linked with high humidity.

The pH testing of papers can be a cumbersome and time-consuming process. Acid content information for any paper lot is available from the manufacturer. If the room humidity is high and ink drying is a problem, consult the paper supplier for testing or information.

Paper Grain. Paper grain direction is an important characteristic that is most closely related to the ability of the individual sheets to be run through a sheet-fed lithographic press. Most paper is formed from the combination and interlocking of cellulose fibers. As paper is formed on the moving wire belt of the paper-making machine, a majority of the fibers are turned parallel to the direction of travel. Press sheets are defined as **grain long** when most of the paper fibers are parallel to the longest dimension of the sheet. **Grain short** means the paper fibers are at right angles to the longest dimension of the sheet.

A distinction should be made between feeding and printing as they relate to grain direction. Grain long feeding is with the grain direction parallel to the direction of travel through the press. Grain short feeding is with the grain direction at right angles to the direction of travel (figure 13.30). Grain long printing takes place when the grain of the paper is parallel to the axis of the plate cylinder. Grain short printing is when the paper grain is at right angles to the plate cylinder axis.

The Mead Paper Corporation suggests that cellulose fibers expand as they absorb moisture. The expansion can be up to five times as great across the width of a fiber as along its length. This fact should suggest to lithographers that the direction of grain feed could present significant registration problems when multicolor runs are printed on a single sheet-fed offset press. In other words, on a litho press, press sheets come into contact with moisture from the fountain solution. The individual fibers in the paper sheets can

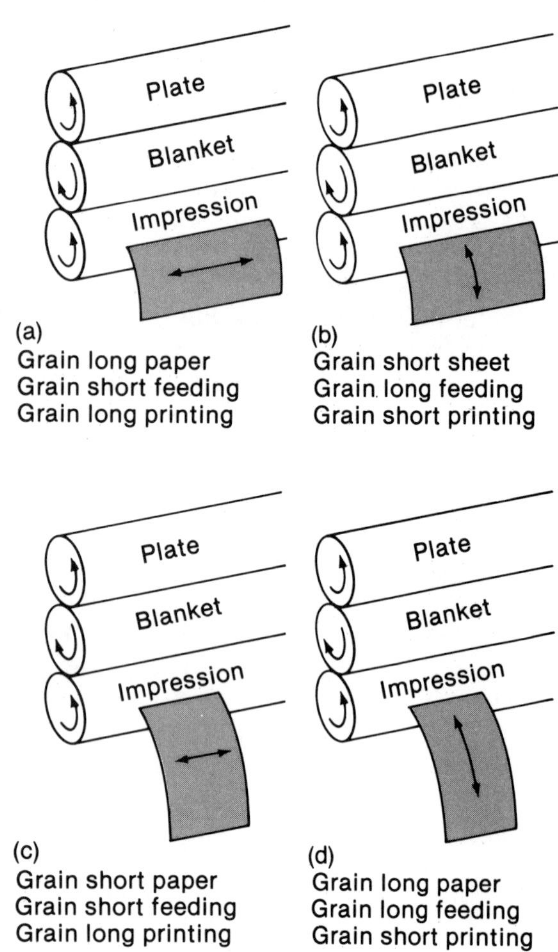

Figure 13.30. Grain direction in printing

then change size, with the greatest increase in the dimension across the grain. If the sheet has to be run through the press several times to receive different ink colors, each pass can add more moisture to the fibers and can cause different changes in sheet size. These changes can make it extremely difficult to fit one color image to another.

Almost all offset paper is supplied grain long. It is to the printer's advantage, when involved with multicolor runs, to print with the grain parallel to the axis of the plate cylinder. For most presses, the printing plate is longer across the cylinder dimension than it is around it. If the greatest paper expansion is going to take place across the grain, it is wise to feed the sheet so that the greatest change takes place across the smallest plate or image dimension. Also, on most presses, it is far simpler to make registration adjustments by rotating the printing cylinders than by moving the infeed pile.

It is important to understand that not all lithographic press work is done with grain long printing. Grain is of little importance for simple single-color runs or for multicolor images that do not have critical registration requirements. There are also instances when a multicolor job *must* be printed short grain. For example, when printed sheets are to be folded, grain direction is very important. Such jobs must generally be printed so that the fold is made parallel to the paper grain.

Surface Texture. A wide variety of textures can be formed on the surface of all papers. This texture is generally referred to as **finish.** Because lithography transfers an image from a flat printing plate, it is difficult to print a detailed design on a very rough paper surface. Ink would never reach the bottom valleys of rough textures. For this reason, almost all offset materials are relatively smooth. Lithographers are concerned with two main classifications of finish: coated and uncoated papers.

Almost all papers are formed by the interweaving of cellulose fibers. The surface of **uncoated paper** is made up of nothing more than the raw interlocking fibers. Although the fibers can be polished by **calendering** (pressing them between rollers or plates to smooth or glaze them), the ink image sits on and is often absorbed into the fibers. A **coated paper** surface has an added layer of pigment bonded to the original paper fibers to smooth out the rough texture of the natural material. Coated papers generally carry more printed detail and produce a better finished image, but they are more difficult to print than uncoated papers. Coated materials are available coated on one side (C1S) or coated on both sides (C2S). Both are made in at least two grades, and the surface appearance can vary from a dull to a high gloss.

There are several areas that lithographers have learned to watch when printing coated stocks. Most jam-ups occur because of static electricity between the coated sheets on the infeed table. The pile of paper should be carefully fanned and the feeding adjusted with start-up sheets before the actual run is begun. The blanket should be carefully checked for quality—specifically glaze buildup. Glaze has a tendency to pick and split or tear coated paper. Ink quantity is more critical with coated materials than with uncoated ones. Too much ink will cause **set-off** (the transfer of an image from the printed face of one sheet in the pile to the bottom face of the next sheet in the pile) of the image in the delivery pile. Overinking could also cause the paper to stick to the blanket cylinder and generally increases drying time. Roller and cylinder alignment is also more critical with coated stock and should be carefully checked.

A Troubleshooting Checklist

In theory, press set-up and operation are simple. Unfortunately, difficulties may develop in every situation and prevent a quality image from printing on the final press sheets. The true craft of the printer is to identify and correct the problems. This process is called "troubleshooting." The following sections identify common press and duplicator difficulties and outline probable causes and solutions.

Scumming

Too Much Ink. **Scumming** is a condition in which nonimage areas accept ink. If the press is overinked, the ink system rollers will appear highly textured and a hissing sound will often be heard from the rollers as the press is idling. To remove excess ink without a wash-up, turn the machine off and manually roll scrap sheets of paper between two of the upper ink distribution rollers. Repeat the procedure until the required amount of ink is removed.

Dampening System Difficulties. Scumming could also be caused by insufficient moisture, dirty dampener covers, dampener covers tied too tightly, light dampener form roller pressure to the plate, or low acid level of the fountain solution.

First carefully study the pattern of the scum and trace its position back to the dampener form roller. If the scumming covers the entire plate, it could be from overall lack of moisture (increase the fountain feed), poor form roller pressure (readjust), or a dirty dampening form roller cover (clean with a commercial dampener roller cleaner or replace). If the scumming pattern is on the outer edges of the plate, the form roller cover could be tied too tightly or the ductor roller cover may have slipped (retie or replace covers). If the plate is scumming in a band that extends around the circumference of the cylinder, that area of the dampener form roller might be inked and will not allow the moisture to pass to the plate (clean the form roller).

Blurred Copy (Double Image)

Loose Blanket. As blankets are broken in, and during a press run, they are pressed against the plate cylinder and tend to flatten or stretch out. If the blanket is new, immediately check for tightness.

Excessive Impression. Too much impression will tend to roll the blanket ahead of the impression cylinder and cause a set-off from the press sheet back to the blanket, resulting in a blurred image (back off impression).

Too Much Ink. Refer to the solution under "Scumming" above.

Gray, Washed-Out Reproduction

Too Much Moisture. If moisture is dripping off the plate or spraying onto the press sheets, water is flooding into the image areas and the plate cannot accept sufficient quantities of ink. Turn off the fountain ductor roller, lower the dampener form roller into contact with the plate, and allow the press to run. The process will allow the excess fountain solution to coat the plate and evaporate. If an extra set of dampener form rollers is available, it could replace the overmoistened ones. The rollers could also be removed from the press and rolled against clean, absorbent paper.

Not Enough Ink. If the inking system is carrying too little ink, a dense image cannot be transferred to the press sheet. Check the appearance of the ink coating and increase the ink feed if necessary.

Incorrect Plate-to-Blanket Pressure. If the blanket image is light but the plate is inking well, the plate-to-blanket pressure is insufficient and should be readjusted or the packing should be increased.

Incorrect Impression-to-Blanket Pressure. If the ink and water systems are set correctly and the blanket is receiving a good image, the impression cylinder position should be checked. Increase impression until a dense, sharp press sheet image is obtained.

Gray, Washed-Out Reproduction and Scumming

Glazed Ink Rollers. If the inking system rollers appear shiny and hard, glazed ink rollers are interacting with the moisture system and passing inconsistent or inadequate amounts of ink to the plate. Use a commercial deglazing compound to clean the ink system.

Glazed Blanket. If the blanket surface appears shiny and hard, clean it with deglazing compound.

Too Much Form Roller Pressure. If the ink and/or dampener form rollers are set too close to the plate cylinder, then sufficient ink or water solution transfer will not take place. Readjust the pressure.

No Reproduction on Press Sheet

Check for insufficient ink form roller pressure (readjust), not enough plate-to-blanket pressure (reset), not enough impression (increase impression), or too much moisture and glazed blanket and ink rollers (decrease moisture and deglaze blanket and rollers).

Figure 13.31. Example of a printer's hickey Hickies are defects in a printed image caused by small particles of ink or paper attached to the plate or blanket.

Printer's Hickey

Hickeys are caused by small particles of ink or paper attached to the plate or blanket (figure 13.31). The solution is to stop the press and clean the plate and blanket.

Press Maintenance

Maintenance is unfortunately often viewed as an activity that takes place after a problem occurs. Manufacturers always provide a recommended maintenance program for their specific machine. But several general areas of concern should be considered for every press.

The motor that provides motion for the press is often concealed in a position that would seem to challenge a professional contortionist's skills. The fact that it is out of sight does not diminish its importance. Check for lubrication points and examine the belt and pulley systems often.

Chains on infeed and outfeed tables need to be kept greased and free from paper pieces or dirt. Infeed rollers become smooth from use. A piece of fine-grit abrasive paper can be used to roughen and remove any dirt from the surface. Vacuum pumps usually have an oil reservoir that should be kept filled. The pump itself should be flushed out several times a year.

All roller and cylinder bearings must be lubricated, usually on a daily basis. Some presses have a single oil reservoir that continually delivers lubrication to bearing surfaces.

The importance of a consistent maintenance schedule cannot be overstated. It is far cheaper to spend time each day doing preventive maintenance than to wait until a major malfunction takes place and the press is "down" for several days waiting for new parts.

A printing press is a machine that is controlled by humans. Many printers claim that each press has a distinctive personality and accordingly assign human names and characteristics: "It's Monday and Harold is kind of sluggish" or "Mabel is mad at me today—she's throwing paper all over the place." However, a mechanism cannot perform "tricks" beyond what a human programs it to do. Every press problem has a cause and a solution. The printer works with a press, but it is the person, not the machine, who controls the situation.

Key Terms

duplicator
press
form rollers
three-cylinder principle
two-cylinder principle
impression
fountain
rotating distribution rollers
oscillating distribution rollers
ductor roller
glaze
molleton covers
dampening sleeves
pH scale
tinting
scumming
hickey

Questions for Review

1. What is the difference between an offset lithographic duplicator and an offset lithographic press?
2. What are the three main cylinders in any offset lithographic press?
3. What is the difference between the two-cylinder principle and the three-cylinder principle on a lithographic press?
4. What does the expression *adjusting impression* mean on an offset lithographic press?
5. What roller transfers ink from the ink fountain to the distribution rollers in a typical inking system?
6. What is the goal of any inking system?
7. What are the three main sections of all lithographic inking systems?
8. What is a solution to possible color contamination when running process colors in a lithographic press?
9. What causes a lithographic blanket to become glazed?
10. What is the purpose of dampening covers in the dampening system of a lithographic press?
11. Why is accurate alignment of form rollers against the image carrier (printing plate) so important?
12. How are printing inks formed?
13. What does the term *pH* mean?
14. What generally causes tinting on a lithographic press sheet?
15. What is the difference between grain short and grain long for press sheets?
16. What are two possible causes of scumming on a lithographic press?

Chapter Fourteen

Screen Printing Stencils

Anecdote to Chapter Fourteen

It is possible that observations of insects eating holes through leaves suggested stencil printing to primitive people. Examples of this idea can be seen in the early work of the natives of the Polynesian Islands. Designs were cut into green banana leaves, and dyes were forced through the openings onto bark cloth, or *tapa*.

Japanese stencil
Courtesy of the Art Institute of Chicago.

In Asia, the earliest existing stencils were produced during the Sung dynasty (AD 960–1280). Many examples of stencil printing that date from the same period are found in Japan. The Japanese have been extremely skillful in cutting detailed stencils from specially treated rice paper. It was easy to cut large open areas in the paper, but problems arose when the artist wanted to block out a portion of the open area. One solution was to glue center pieces or loose parts of the stencil together with strands of human hair. These strands were called "ties" because they tied the different parts of the stencil together. Fine pieces of silk fiber were later substituted for hair because of their greater strength.

In England during the late 1700s, stencils were used to decorate wallpaper, which had become popular in upper-class homes. European screen printers still used ties to hold the stencil pieces together, and it was difficult to create especially intricate designs.

During the early years of our own country's history, the stencil was a well-guarded secret. Traveling teachers often sold the idea to local printers and signmakers. The price depended on what the market would bear, but most printers were happy to pay almost any price for a process that was low cost and could be used to reproduce nearly any size image without being limited by the size of the available type or printing press.

In 1907, Samual Simon of Manchester, England, was granted a patent on his revolutionary new concept called a "tieless" stencil. His design used a piece of coarsely woven silk fabric to hold the stencil pieces in place. With the silk as a base, extremely intricate designs could be cut and then glued on the fabric. When ink was passed through the openings in the design, it would flow around the fabric threads and leave an image of the opening on the print.

It wasn't until the outbreak of the First World War that the method became a significant industrial process. It was ideal for rapid, high-quality, short-run signs and illustrations. With the development of photographic stencils, the process has been used for almost every conceivable application from printing tiny microcircuits in electronics to labeling cardboard cartons and even reproducing halftone photographs.

What began as a simple stencil probably more than thirteen centuries ago has moved into a position of significance in the printing industry. Many labels have been applied—stencil printing, silk screen serigraphy, and even mitography—but the term *screen printing* is now commonly accepted as the proper name for the process.

Objectives for Chapter Fourteen

After completing this chapter, you will be able to:

- Explain the basic concepts of screen printing.
- Classify types of screen stencils.
- Classify types of screen fabrics.
- Describe methods of stretching screens.
- List the steps in preparing and mounting hand-cut stencils.
- Describe the steps in preparing and mounting indirect photographic stencils.
- Describe the steps in preparing and mounting direct photographic stencils.
- Describe the different techniques of masking the stencil.
- Select the appropriate type of stencil, screen, and ink for different screen printing jobs.

Introduction

Of all the major printing processes, screen printing is undoubtably the oldest. The process was shrouded in mystery for centuries and remained a well-guarded secret until the first part of the twentieth century.

Screen printing is a generic term that

today includes a wide range of techniques and applications. Although such terms as "silk screen," "mitography," "serigraphy," and "selectine" might be classed within this framework, "screen printing" is the general label that the industry recognizes and uses.

Figure 14.1. Paper stencil cut with Ulano swivel knife
Courtesy of SUCO Learning Resources and R. Kampas.

Basic Concept and Classification of Stencils

The Stencil

The basic concept of screen printing is simple and is based on the idea of a stencil. By taking a piece of paper, drawing some outline or sketch of an object, and then cutting out the sketch, we can make a **stencil** (figure 14.1). By placing the stencil over another sheet, it is possible to paint, spray, or otherwise force ink through the opening (figure 14.2). When the stencil is removed, all that remains on the printed sheet is a reproduction of the opening on the stencil (figure 14.3). This process can be repeated as long as the original stencil holds its shape.

Today the advantages of screen printing are impressive. It is ideally suited for the low-cost production of high-quality short-run printed materials. Screen printing is extremely versatile. It is possible to print on nearly any surface, texture, or shape. The process is limited only by the size of the screen frame available. Fine line detail and even halftones may be reproduced by screen printing. Many types of ink are available, from acid etches to abrasive glues. Ink densities on the printed page are such that any color may be overprinted (printed over another color) without the first color showing through.

Types of Stencils

All stencil preparation can be classified into three groups:

- Hand-cut stencils,
- Tusche-and-glue stencils,
- Photographic stencils.

As the name implies, **hand-cut stencils** are prepared by manually removing the printing image areas from some form of base or support material. **Tusche-and-glue,** an art process, involves drawing directly on the screen fabric with lithographic tusche (an oil-based pigment) and then blocking out nonimage areas with a water-based glue material. **Photographic stencils** are generally produced by the use of a thick, light-sensitive, gelatin-based emulsion that is exposed and developed either on a supporting film or directly on the screen itself. Only hand-cut and photographic stencils are used in commercial printing.

Figure 14.2. Spraying ink through a paper stencil
Courtesy of SUCO Learning Resources and R. Kampas

Figure 14.3. A stenciled image
Courtesy of SUCO Learning and Resources and R. Kampas.

Screen printing preparation involves the selection and control of screen fabrics, screen frames, fabric stretch on the frame, fabric treatment to accept a stencil, stencil preparation, and stencil masking. As with all printing processes, it is most important to control every variable to produce a quality image on the final sheet.

Fabric and Frame Preparation

Screen Fabrics

There is no one fabric that can be used for all screen printing applications. The type of ink to be screened, the fineness of line detail, the quality of the material that is to receive the image, the number of impressions, and the type of stencil must all be considered when selecting the screen fabric.

Screen fabrics are made from either natural fibers, such as silk, or man-made fibers, such as polyester or nylon. They are all classified as either multifilament or monofilament materials. **Multifilament screens** are made up of strands of fibers twisted together into threads (figure 14.4). **Monofilament screens** are woven from single round strands (figure 14.5).

Silk was the first fabric used to carry screen printing stencils. Multifilament silk strands provide greater cross-sectional area than monofilament strands and allow for the strong adhesion of nearly any hand-cut or photographic stencil (figure 14.6). However, silk is not dimensionally stable, which makes it unsuitable for work requiring critical registration. Moreover, many special purpose inks, such as abrasives or chemical resists, can quickly destroy the silk fibers.

Although man-made multifilament fibers, such as multistrand polyester, do not have the natural coarseness of silk, they are stronger and can be woven more uniformly.

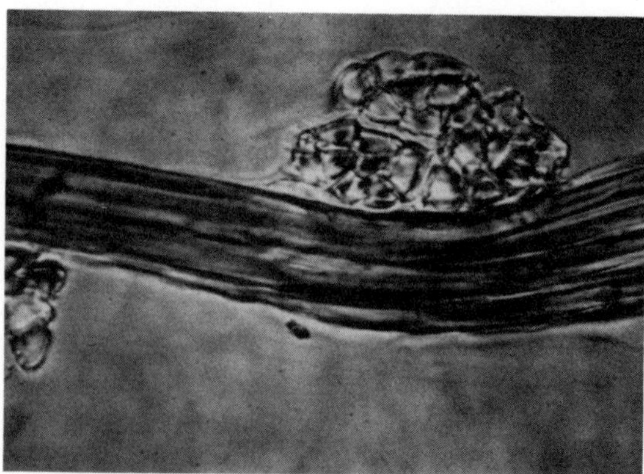

Figure 14.4. Magnified view of cross section of silk strand Notice that the strand is made up of individual fibers.
Courtesy of J. Ulano Company, Inc.

Figure 14.5. Magnified view of cross section of man-made monofilament strands
Courtesy of J. Ulano Company, Inc.

Polyester is useful for critical registration work because it can withstand many abrasive materials and pass a uniform layer of ink.

Monofilament fabrics, such as single-strand polyester, nylon, or wire cloth (copper or stainless steel), have a uniform weave and freely pass pigments through the mesh openings. Because of the smooth nature of the fibers, it is generally necessary to treat or roughen the filament surface to obtain good stencil adhesion (figure 14.7). Each fabric type has its own characteristics. Nylon tends to absorb moisture and will react to changes in room humidity. Metal screens absorb no moisture but react to temperature changes and will pass nearly any abrasive pigment with little difficulty. Monofilament polyesters have low moisture absorption rate, stability, and strength. They are also less expensive than most other screen materials, so they are rapidly becoming the main material for commercial work.

Screen fabric is purchased by the yard. Two systems of classification are used. Silk and multifilament polyesters are classified according to the ratio of open area to thread area per inch. Numbers ranging from 0000 to about 25 are assigned. The smaller the number, the larger the percentage of open or ink-passing area per inch. These materials are also assigned a strength indication. A 12XX fabric is stronger than a 12X. Most other fabrics, such as nylon and metal cloth, are classified according to the number of threads per inch. These materials are available in a range from about 60 threads per inch to a maximum of around 500 threads per inch. The two classification systems can be compared so that equivalent opening sizes can be identified (table 14.1, p. 346).

Specific recommendations cannot be made here about the type of fabric and mesh count to use in a given situation. Many variables can influence that decision. The first consideration is to identify the type of ink to be used and to consult the manufacturer's data for the screen material the manufacturer suggests be used with that ink. Manufactur-

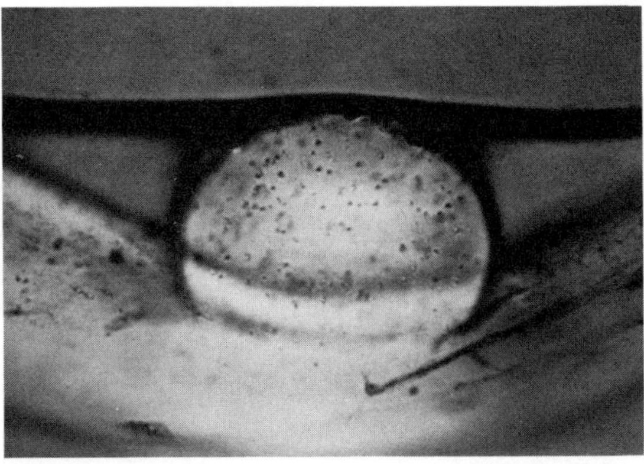

Figure 14.6. Magnified view of stencil applied to silk fibers
Courtesy of J. Ulano Company, Inc.

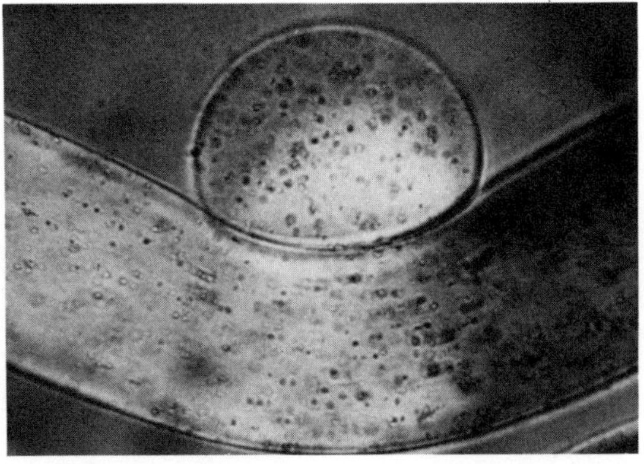

Figure 14.7. Magnified view of stencil applied to monofilament fibers
Courtesy of J. Ulano Company, Inc.

ers specify minimum screen mesh sizes based on the maximum pigment particle sizes in the ink (the particles naturally must be able to freely pass through the screen openings). Manufacturers also indicate whether the ink vehicle will interact with any commercial screen fabrics. The next step is to consider the fineness of the line detail of the image to be screen printed. A coarse screen mesh will pass a heavy layer of ink, but it will not hold a fine line stencil. In general, use a 12XX fabric for hand-cut and indirect photographic stencils with normal images and a 14XX and finer for photographic stencils containing images with fine line detail. Multifilament fibers are generally not suitable for halftone or extremely fine line reproduction.

Organdy is often used for short-run situations where bold line detail is wanted and reclaiming the fabric is not important. Organdy is an inexpensive, loosely woven cloth that can be purchased from any fabric shop. It has a strength of around 10X. Although its replacement cost is about one-tenth that of a commercial screen material, it does have certain drawbacks. The fabric is not as strong as silk or a monofilament fiber, so the squeegee action can rapidly wear away or fray the cloth. Also, because the weave is not perfectly uniform, some fine line detail might be lost.

Frames

There is no standard size or shape for a screen printing frame. The frame must hold the fabric without warping, be deep enough to hold the quantity of ink being printed, and be at least 4 inches wider and longer than the largest stencil to be reproduced.

Commercially constructed frames are available, but they are certainly not a requirement. Frames that are custom-made by the printer to meet individual needs are often better than their commercial counterparts. Most custom-made frames are made from wood because it is inexpensive, fairly stable, and easily cut to any dimensions. The high tension developed when modern synthetic

Table 14.1. A Comparison of Mesh Classification Systems

XX system used for silk and multi- or monofilament polyesters	Silk	Multifilament polyesters	Nylon	Monofilament polyesters	Stainless steel	Silk	Multifilament polyesters	Nylon	Monofilament polyesters	Stainless steel
6XX	74	74	70	74	70	47	43	45	34	55
8XX	86	86	90	92	88	45	32	42	42	48
10XX	109	109	108	110	105	40	20	43	39	47
12XX	125	125	120	125	120	32	28	45	30	47
14XX	139	139	138	139	135	30	26	47	35	47
16XX	157	157	157	157	145	31	25	41	24	46
18XX	166	170	166	175	165	31	31	38	34	47
20XX	173	178	185	—	180	28	29	43	—	47
25XX	200	198	196	200	200	23	26	44	32	46
			230	225	230			42	42	46
			240	245	250			39	38	36
			260	260	270			36	35	32
			283	280	—			37	34	—
			306	300	—			34	29	—
			330	330	325			30	27	30
			380	390	400			22	18	36

fabrics are stretched on a frame will warp wooden frames constructed with common butt joints, so the joint must be such that the frame cannot be sprung in any direction (figure 14.8). Wood frames are not recommended for close registration work because wood does have a tendency to swell and shift if it gets damp. When exact registration is required, as in printed circuits or color process reproductions, steel or aluminum is a preferable frame material.

Fabric-Stretching Techniques

Fabric manufacturers recommend the amount of tension that should be placed on their material. Generally, silk should be stretched 3% to 4% of its original dimensions in two directions, nylon from 4% to 7%, and polyesters from 1% to 4%. Most suppliers recommend the use of a mechanical stretching system. With this system it is easy to control the exact amount of tension for any frame.

The simplest method of attaching screen fabric is by tacking or stapling the material to the underside of the frame. Use number 4 carpet tacks or ¼-inch staples in a general purpose industrial staple gun. Space the fasteners approximately ½ inch (1.27 cm) apart in two rows. Start by placing the loose fabric over the frame so that the strands are parallel to the frame edges. The rough cut fabric should be at least 2 inches (5.08 cm) larger in each direction than the dimensions of the frame. Place three fasteners in the upper right-hand corner. Pull the fabric diagonally and fasten a second corner in place. Then stretch the upper left-hand corner and next the lower right. Now begin at the center of a long edge and space a row of fasteners completely around the frame. As you fasten, pull the material with fabric pliers so that all warps are removed from the screen surface. Go back and alternate a second row of fasteners just inside the first. (If staple tape is used, it will be easy to remove the staples when the fabric is replaced.) Finally, cut the surplus fabric from the frame with a sharp razor blade and mask over the staples with gummed tape (figure 14.9).

An alternative method for hand stretching fabric on a wooden frame is a starched cord and groove technique. Cut a single notch partially through each frame side with a saw (figure 14.10). The inside groove may have to be rounded to prevent cutting the fabric. An inexpensive piece of 3/16-inch woven clothesline will nearly perfectly fill the groove left by a standard table saw blade. By carefully working from one corner, you can stretch the fabric by forcing both the cord and the fabric into the groove (figure 14.11). Special tools have been developed to insert the cord (figure 14.12), but any device that will not tear the cloth is acceptable. Whatever method is used,

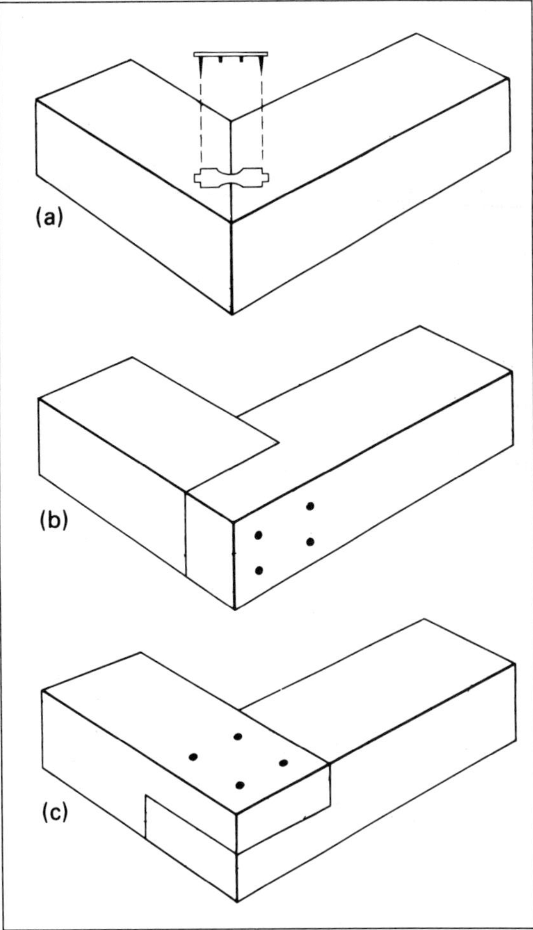

Figure 14.8. Common wooden frame joints Common joints used for custom-made wooden screen frames are a reinforced miter joint (a), a rabbet joint (b), and an end-lap joint (c).

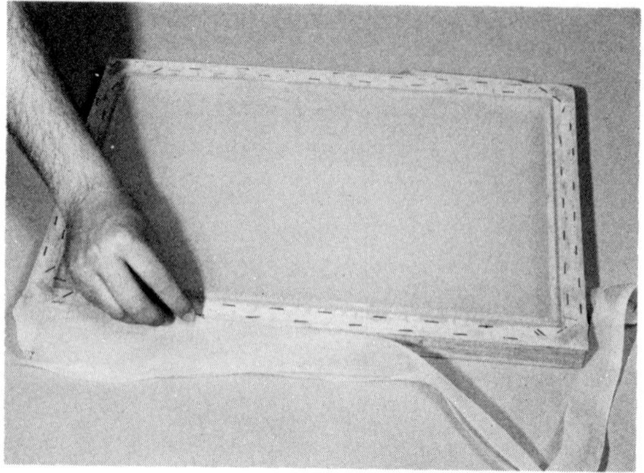

Figure 14.9. Cutting away surplus fabric
Courtesy of SUCO Learning Resources and R. Kampas.

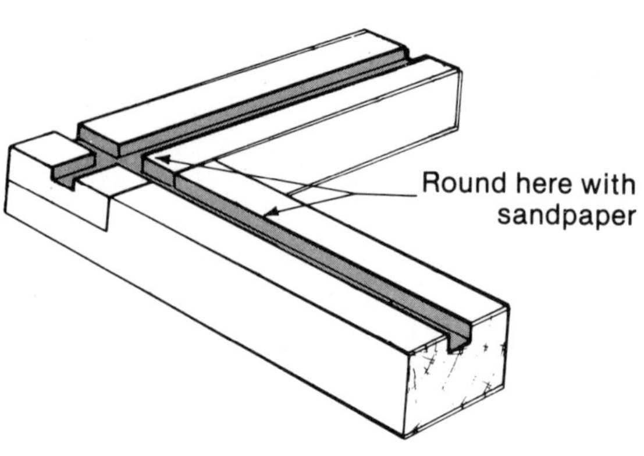

Figure 14.10. Wooden frame with sawed notch

the fabric should be "drumhead" tight, without warps or tears.

Fabric Treatment

Monofilament fabric, such as nylon or polyester, must be treated before a stencil can be adhered. A **tooth** must be produced on the smooth monofilament fibers so the stencil can be held in place.

To do this, slightly dampen the fabric with water and pour half a teaspoon of 500-grit silicon carbide for each 16-by-20 inch (40.64 × 50.8 cm) area on the back, or stencil side, of the screen. Carefully scour the fabric with a wet rag for 2 to 3 minutes. Scrub the entire screen surface. Then thoroughly rinse both sides of the screen with a strong water spray. The 500-grit silicon carbide will not clog even the smallest mesh screen opening. This operation must be repeated each time the screen is to be used.

Some printers use a very fine waterproof silicon carbide paper (sandpaper) to treat monofilament fabrics. Wet the screen and lightly rub the entire surface of the stencil side for 4 to 5 minutes. Then thoroughly rinse both sides of the screen with a strong water spray. This technique is recommended only if no alternative method is available.

All fabrics, whether new or used, must be cleaned and degreased to ensure proper film or emulsion adhesion. If it is an old screen, be sure that all ink has been removed and no foreign particles are clogging the mesh openings (figure 14.13). Ink manufacturers recommend the proper degreaser for their products. First, wet the screen with cold water and sprinkle both sides with powdered trisodium phosphate. Thoroughly scrub both sides with a soft bristle brush. Then rinse the screen with a powerful water spray. Allow the screen to drain and dry, but do not touch the fabric—skin oils on the fibers might prevent stencil adhesion. *Do not use* any commercial abrasive cleansers, such as "Ajax," because the cleanser particles can clog the screen on fine mesh fabrics and cannot be removed by the water spray. If trisodium phosphate is not available, use a commercial

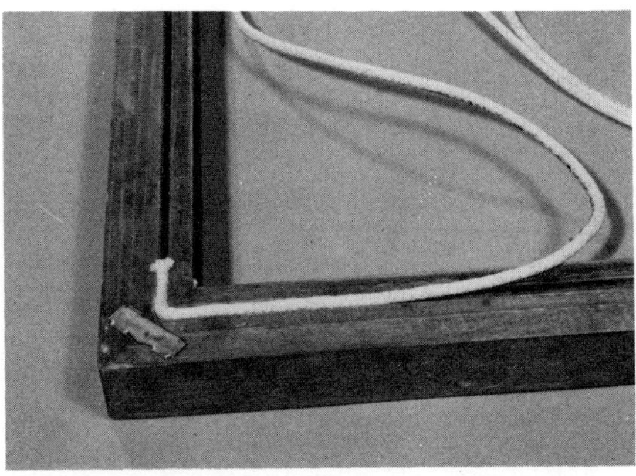

Figure 14.11. Cord forced into the notch to secure the screen
Courtesy of SUCO Learning Resources and R. Kampas.

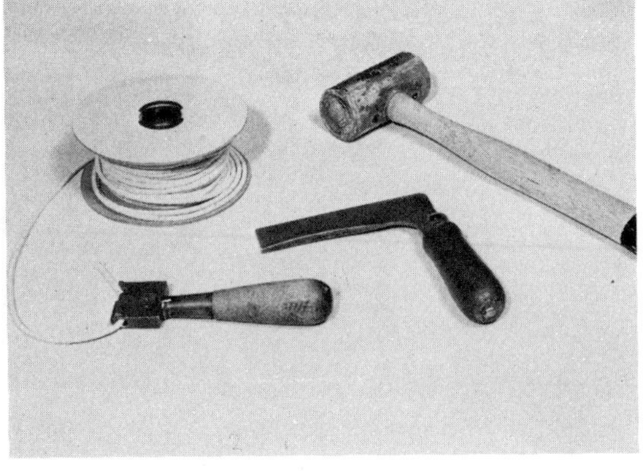

Figure 14.12. Tools used to insert cord into notch
Courtesy of SUCO Learning Resources and R. Kampas.

nonsudsing automatic dishwashing detergent.

After the fabric has been cleaned, it is ready to accept the stencil. It is important not to store the clean screen for a long period before attempting to adhere the stencil.

Hand-Cut Stencil Methods

The hand-cut process was the earliest method used to make screen stencils. Originally, pieces of thin paper were cut and glued to the underside of a screen. The process was tiring and time consuming, and it offered the printer only a limited number of impressions before the stencil simply wore out. Later, the paper was coated with shellac or lacquer to increase the stencil's durability, but the process was still slow.

In the early 1930s Joseph Ulano (founder of J. Ulano Company, Inc., now a leading screen printing supplier) made an interesting observation. He found that if a layer of lacquer was sprayed over a hard surface and allowed to dry, a thin sheet of lacquer could be pulled from the surface in one piece. This lacquer could be used as a stencil by coating it onto a support sheet and then cutting away the design, leaving a thin, clean stencil on the sheet. The lacquer could be applied to a screen and the support sheet pulled away. This method is the basis for nearly all hand-cut stencils in the industry today. It has the advantage of speed combined with sharp, crisp line detail.

The basic process of creating a hand-cut stencil is relatively simple. It involves only three steps:

- Cutting the stencil,
- Applying the stencil to the screen,
- Removing the support sheet.

Cut-film stencils are made up of two layers: a support sheet and a lacquer- or water-based emulsion. The problem is to cut away the emulsion without embossing or cutting the support sheet. As with all stencils, only

Figure 14.13. Magnified view of a clogged screen
Courtesy of J. Ulano Company, Inc.

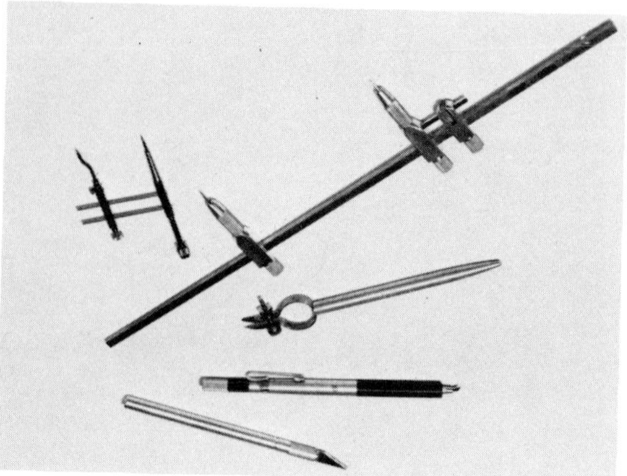

Figure 14.14. Common cutting tools From top counterclockwise: exacto knife or frisket knife, Ulano swivel knife, parallel bicutters, beam compass cutters.

the areas to be printed are removed from the base material.

Hand-Cutting Techniques

Place a line drawing of the desired stencil under a piece of cut-film material. Be sure that the emulsion side of the stencil material is up and that there are at least 2 inches of stencil film around all edges of the image. Tape the drawing and cut-film material securely in place.

A variety of tools are used in the industry to cut the film. A frisket knife is the cheapest and the most popular. Other useful tools are a swivel knife, bicutters (for cutting parallel lines), and a beam compass (figure 14.14). But none of these is absolutely necessary.

Several general techniques will ensure success with a hand-cut stencil. A razor-sharp blade is very important. The extra pressure needed with a dull blade rounds the film edge by forcing it down into the emulsion. A round edge will not properly adhere to the screen. Place the stencil material on a hard, flat surface. Apply light pressure while holding the blade at nearly a right angle to the film. The lower the angle of the cutting blade, the more danger of rounding the edges of the stencil material. Begin by practicing on a piece of scrap film. Cut only through the emulsion. A cut in the base will hold excess adhering solvent during the adhering step, which could dissolve part of the stencil material. Cut every line in a single stroke. It is extremely difficult to recut over a line. Where lines meet, always overlap the cuts (figure 14.15). This measure will produce sharp corners on the final print. The overcuts will always fuse together when the stencil is applied to the screen. As each image area is cut, remove the emulsion. Don't wait until all lines have been cut. The easiest method to remove a layer of cut emulsion is to stab it with the point of the knife and lift (figure 14.16). Remember to re-

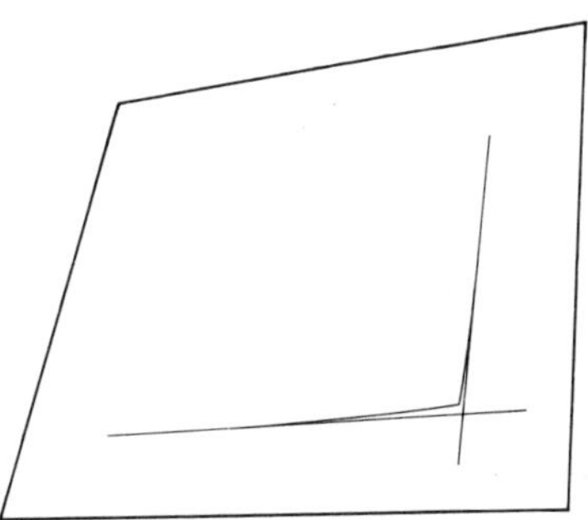

Figure 14.15. Overlapping cuts

Figure 14.16. Removing cut emulsion Stab a layer of cut emulsion with the point of a knife and lift it off the support base.

move the emulsion only in the areas where ink is to appear on the final print.

Adhering Water-Soluble Hand-Cut Stencils

There are two methods of adhering water-soluble hand-cut stencils. The first (figure 14.17a) uses a buildup board that is smaller than the inside dimensions of the frame. Place the hand-cut stencil emulsion-side up on the center of the board. Position the screen over the stencil and buildup board so that the screen fabric is against the emulsion of the stencil material. Saturate a sponge or cloth with water and slowly wipe the stencil in overlapping strokes until the entire surface is wet. Do not rub the stencil with the sponge. Allow only enough contact to moisten the stencil emulsion. With the frame still flat, dry the emulsion with a cold-air fan. To reduce drying time, excess moisture can be blotted out of the stencil with newsprint. The base material may be peeled off when the emulsion is dry. (See "Masking the Stencil" in this chapter.)

The second method (figure 14.17b) is to thoroughly wet both sides of the fabric with a clean sponge dampened with water. Roll the emulsion side of the stencil against the bottom of the wet screen. Using light pressure, move the wet sponge over the entire surface of the base material to adhere the stencil to the fabric. With the frame flat, dry the emulsion with a cold-air fan. To reduce drying time, blot up excess moisture with newsprint. The base material can be peeled off when the emulsion is dry. (See "Masking the Stencil" in this chapter.)

Adhering Lacquer-Solvent Hand-Cut Stencils

Lacquer-based hand-cut stencils use a commercial adhering fluid to soften the lacquer emulsion long enough to allow the stencil to adhere to the screen. The specific fluid used should match the specifications provided by

Traditional Adhering Technique

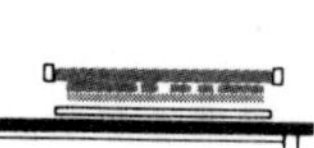

1. **Preparation.** Place cut stencil, film up, on your build up board, which is smaller than inside measurement of frame. Position the prepared screen, squeegee side up, over film.

2. **Adhering.** Saturate a sponge with water. Move the sponge slowly in one stroke over the fabric from the squeegee side. Slightly overlap the strokes until the entire surface is adhered. DO NOT RUB WITH THE SPONGE.

3. **Drying.** With the frame flat, dry the film from the squeegee side with a cold air fan. To reduce drying time, excess moisture may be removed by blotting with newsprint before drying with the fan. Peel off the backing sheet when film is dry. The adhesive will remain on the backing sheet.

(a)

New Simplified Adhering Technique

1. **Preparation.** This technique requires a clean, well stretched screen. Using a clean sponge, thoroughly wet both sides of the fabric with water.

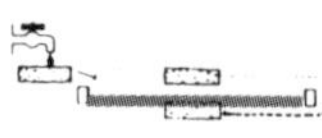

2. **Adhering.** Place the film side of cut stencil against bottom of the wet screen. Using light pressure, move the wet sponge over the entire surface of the plastic backing to adhere the film to the fabric.

3. **Drying.** With the frame flat, dry the film with a cold air fan from the squeegee side. To reduce drying time, blot excess moisture with newsprint before drying with the fan. Peel off the backing sheet when the film is dry. The adhesive will remain on the backing sheet.

(b)

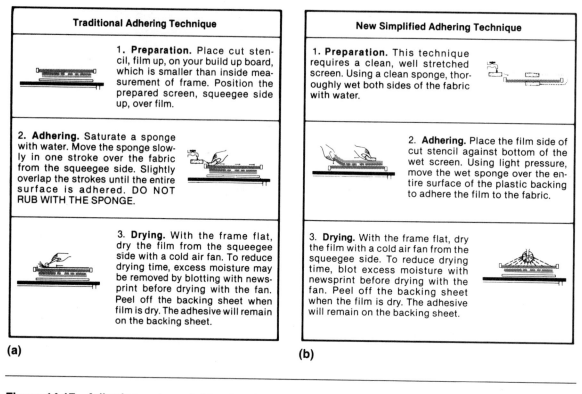

Figure 14.17. Adhering water-soluble stencils
Courtesy of J. Ulano Company, Inc.

the stencil manufacturer. To attach a lacquer stencil to the screen, place the stencil emulsion-side up on a buildup board. Position the screen over the stencil and board so that the screen fabric is against the emulsion of the stencil material. Place several weights on the frame to keep the stencil from shifting or, if possible, actually clamp the frame in place.

Take two clean, soft cloths and roll one into a tight ball. Moisten the cloth ball with a small quantity of adhering fluid. The cloth should not be so wet that the liquid drips from the ball. Begin in one corner of the stencil and moisten about a 4-inch square with the wet cloth. Use a blotting motion to saturate the area and then immediately wipe it dry with the second cloth. The moistened area should become darker in color than the rest of the stencil. That area is now adhered to the screen. Continue blotting and drying 4-inch squares over the rest of the stencil. Be extremely careful not to dissolve the lacquer with too much solvent, but use enough so that the entire stencil is a single uniform color. Lacquer-based materials dry rapidly. When the stencil is completely dry, the backing sheet may be peeled away. (See "Masking the Stencil" in this chapter.)

Photographic Stencil Methods

The primary reason for the growth of the screen printing industry has been the development of the photographic stencil. The idea is not new. The basic process was developed in Great Britain in 1850 by William Henry Fox Talbot. He found that certain materials, such as gelatin, egg albumin, and glue, mixed or coated with a potassium bichromate solution hardened when exposed to light. The areas not exposed remained soft and could readily be washed away. Talbot actually was concerned with a continuous-tone negative/positive process. It wasn't until 1914 that someone applied his work to the screen printing industry.

Today photographic emulsions far more sophisticated than egg albumin are available through commercial suppliers. However, whatever type of emulsion is used, the method is the same. Printers expose the light-sensitive material through a positive transparent image, and unhardened areas on the stencil are washed away. The stencil is fixed or made permanent, masked, and then printed.

The primary advantage of photographic stencils is the possibility for intricate and high-quality line detail. Step-and-repeat images, halftones, exact facsimile reproductions, and high-quality process color stencil prints are all possible and commonplace. The introduction of photographic screen printing allowed the screen printer to enter the field of packaged product illustration. A color image can be screen printed with any ink on any surface shape (flat, cylindrical, or irregular).

All photographic stencil processes are divided into three types:

- *Indirect* or transfer image method,
- *Direct* image method,
- Film emulsion or *direct/indirect* image method.

The **indirect process** uses a dry emulsion on a plastic support sheet. The stencil emulsion is sensitized by the manufacturer and is purchased in rolls or sheets. The stencil film is exposed through a transparent right-reading positive and is then treated with a developer solution. The areas that light reaches (the nonimage areas) are hardened during exposure. The remaining areas are washed away with a warm-water spray to form the image or printing areas. The stencil is adhered to a clean screen while it is wet, and the support sheet is removed after the stencil dries (figure 14.18).

The **direct process** uses a wet emulsion that is coated directly on a clean screen. The emulsion is exposed through a transparent positive to harden the nonimage areas. The image areas are washed away with a warm-water spray. When the emulsion is dry, the stencil is ready to print (figure 14.19). Direct emulsions have a limited shelf life when compared to indirect material.

The **direct/indirect process** combines the techniques of both the indirect and the direct photographic processes. An unsensitized film material is placed under the stencil side of the screen on a flat table. The stencil emulsion is stored in two parts, a liquid

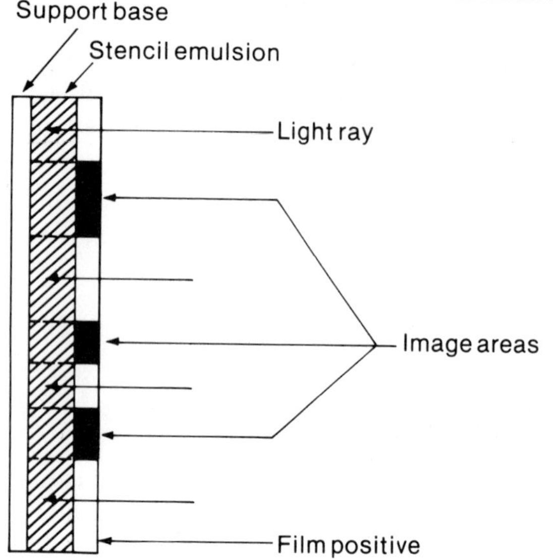

1. Exposure
No light strikes the photographic screen emulsion under the image areas on the transparent positive.

2. Development
Areas exposed to light during exposure are hardened during development.

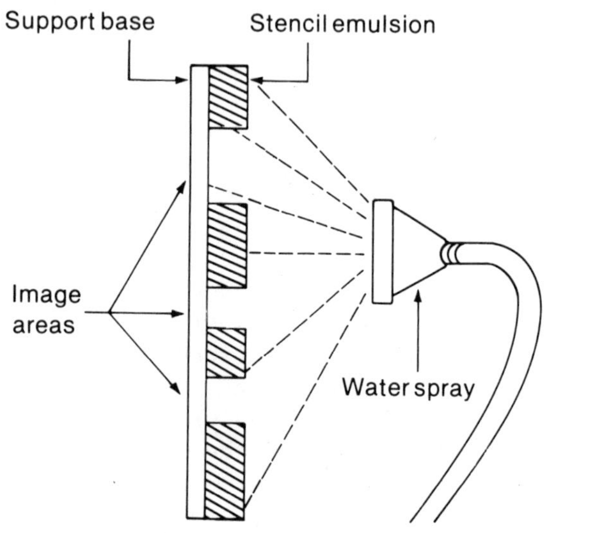

3. Wash
Unhardened areas (image areas) are washed away leaving open areas in the stencil.

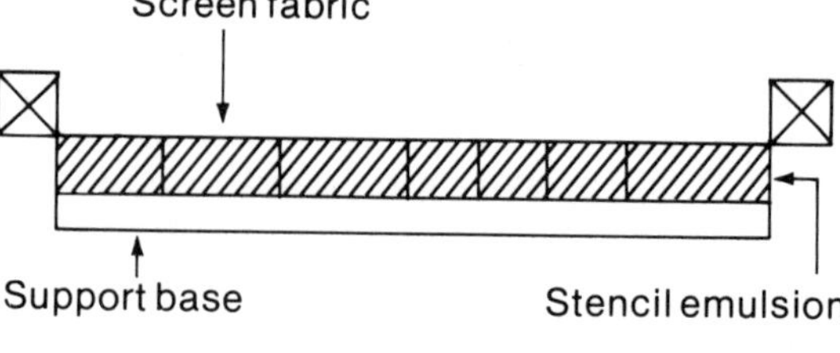

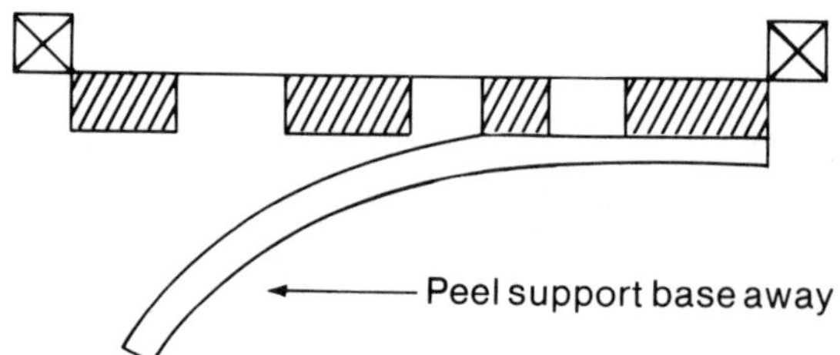

4. Adhesion
Adhere stencil emulsion to screen fabric, let dry, and peel support base away.

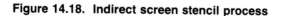

Figure 14.18. Indirect screen stencil process

emulsion and a sensitizer. When the two are mixed together, they become light sensitive and are coated through the screen to the film support. When the emulsion is dry, the backing sheet is removed and normal direct exposure techniques are carried out (figure 14.20). The main advantage of the process is the uniformity of the emulsion thickness. Because the direct/indirect process uses the procedures of both the direct and the indirect stencil methods, it will not be discussed in detail in this chapter.

Determining Photographic Stencil Exposures

Most photographic stencil emulsions have a spectral sensitivity that peaks in the ultraviolet-to-blue region of the visible spectrum (see "Light Sources" in appendix B). Because the stencil emulsion must be exposed through a transparent positive, good contact is important to ensure accurate line detail. Vacuum frames are generally used to hold the stencil and film in place during exposure.

Proper exposure is important for photographic screen stencils. An underexposed stencil will produce an emulsion that is too thin. A thin emulsion will have difficulty adhering to the screen material, with the possibility of passing ink in a nonimage area. An overexposed stencil will result in an emulsion that is too thick. A thick emulsion will close in the fine line detail and, if on an indirect stencil, might not adhere properly to the fabric.

A commercial **step wedge** manufactured by the J. Ulano Company, Inc. (figure 14.21, p. 358) can be used to calibrate correct stencil exposure. An alternative calibration device is a transparent positive made up of normal and hard-to-reproduce copy. The step wedge is preferable because it contains identified line weights.

In practice, a series of exposures is made through the step wedge to the photographic stencil. Most stencil manufacturers make time recommendations, but it is best to calibrate the exposure for a specific working condition. Begin with the manufacturer's recommended exposure time for the specific light source and distance. If no recommended time is identified, start with 60 seconds. From the recommended time, determine exposures that are 50%, 75%, 100%, 125%, and 150%. For example, if 60 seconds is the recommended time, then five separate exposures would be made through the step wedge: 30 seconds, 45 seconds, 60 seconds, 75 seconds, and 90 seconds.

If an indirect stencil is used, the emulsion must be exposed through the base material (figure 14.22). If a direct stencil is used, the transparent positive is exposed through the bottom side of the screen (figure 14.23).

A test exposure is easy to make if these time percentages are used. Place the transparent positive in contact with the stencil. First expose through the positive for the shortest exposure (for this example, the exposure would be 30 seconds). Then mask off ⅕ of the step wedge with opaque paper or masking film and expose the remaining uncovered portion for 15 seconds. Move the masking sheet to cover ⅖ of the wedge and again expose the uncovered area for 15 seconds. Continue this procedure until the entire step wedge has been exposed. Develop and wash out the stencil. (See the following sections outlining the specific procedures for each type of stencil.)

Mount the stencil on the screen that will be used in the shop, allow it to dry, and make a print with the desired ink. Examine the image in detail. First identify the step that has

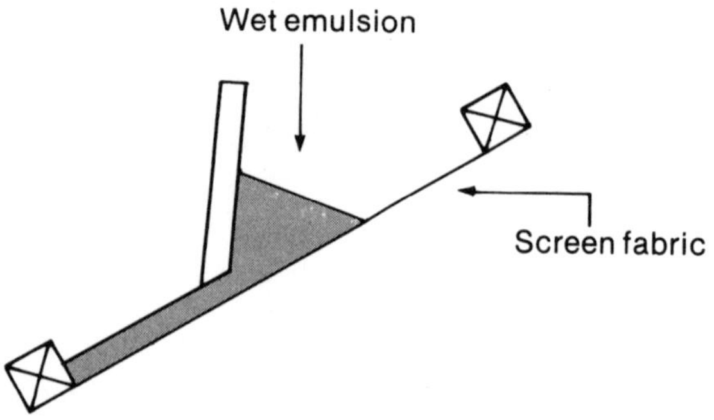

1. Coating
A wet emulsion is coated onto a clean screen.

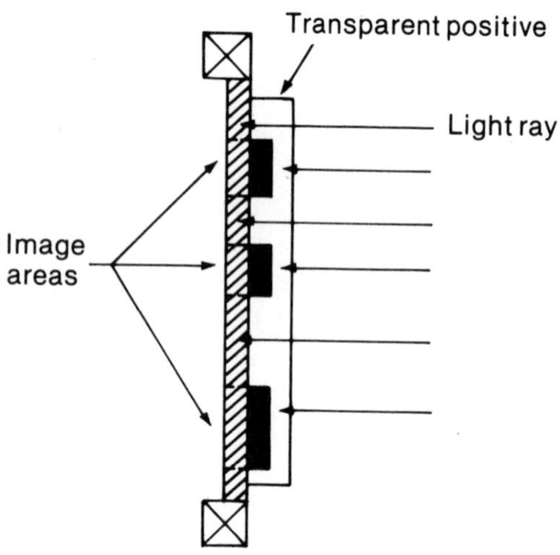

2. Exposure
Areas where light strikes the emulsion (nonimage areas) become hardened during exposure.

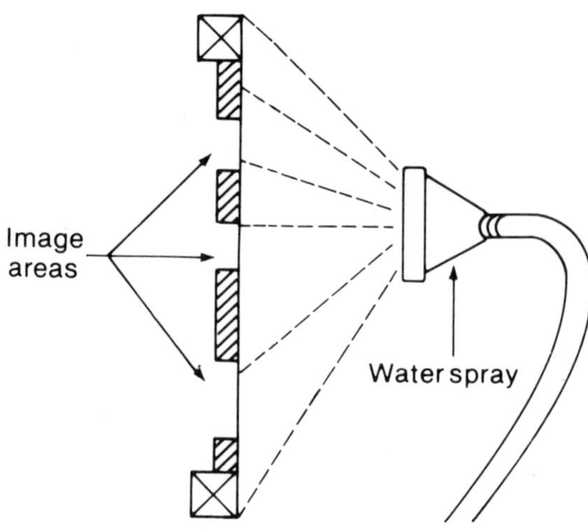

3. Wash
Unhardened areas (image areas) are washed away leaving open areas in the stencil.

Figure 14.19. Direct screen stencil process

most faithfully reproduced the original line detail. Consider the narrowest line that was reproduced, then select the exposure that has the thickest emulsion but has held that line dimension. If no step appears ideal, expose another stencil with a smaller percentage difference (such as 80%, 90%, 110%, and 120% of the recommended time).

Indirect Photographic Stencil Process

The indirect photographic stencil process is known by several terms in the industry: "transfer," "carbon tissue," and "pigment paper" are a few. The process is also identified by several trade names representing indirect stencil material that is supplied by individual dealers.

The indirect photographic stencil is exposed through a transparent film positive. Where light strikes the stencil, the emulsion is hardened. Where light does not strike the stencil, the emulsion remains soft and can be washed away. Logically, the better the positive, the better the reproduction. Chapter 6 provides detailed information on the production of positive film images.

An indirect stencil is the easiest of all the screen stencils to produce. It involves the following six steps:

1. Exposure,
2. Development,
3. Washing,
4. Application of the stencil to the screen,
5. Drying,
6. Removal of the base material.

Exposure. All indirect emulsions are coated onto a transparent support sheet by the stencil manufacturer. It is always necessary to expose the stencil through the support material. Some sort of contact frame is generally used to bring the positive into intimate contact with the presensitized sheet. It is important that the right-reading side of the positive be against the base side of the stencil. Place the positive on a table top so that the image reads exactly as it would on the final print. Place a sheet of stencil material over the positive so that the emulsion side is up. Be sure that the stencil extends at least 1 inch (2.54 cm) beyond all image extremes (figure 14.24, p. 360). Then pick up the sandwich of both pieces and turn them over. To expose the stencil, the light must pass through the clear areas of the positive. Place the two sheets in the contact frame and expose the stencil for the time that was determined from the test exposure.

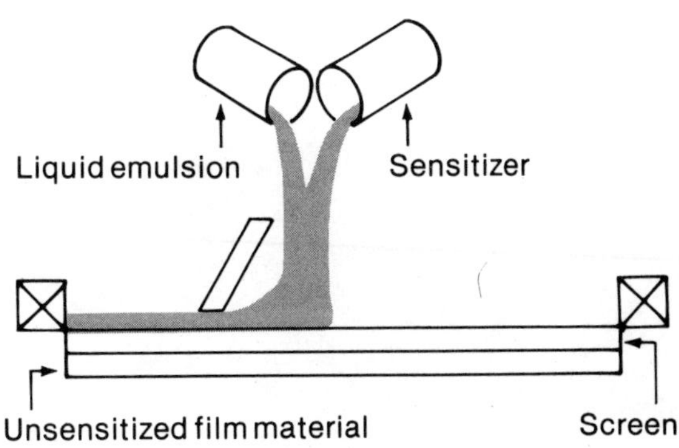

1. Coating
The two parts of the emulsion are mixed and coated on the screen material. Note the piece of unsensitized film material under the screen.

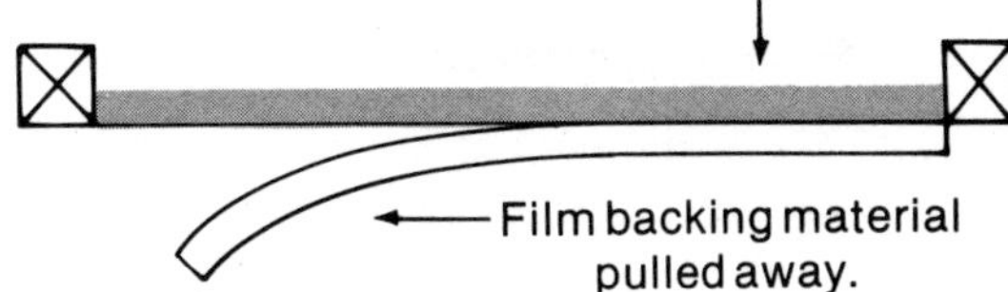

2. Removing the backing
The film backing is removed after the emulsion has dried.

Figure 14.20. Direct/indirect screen stencil process

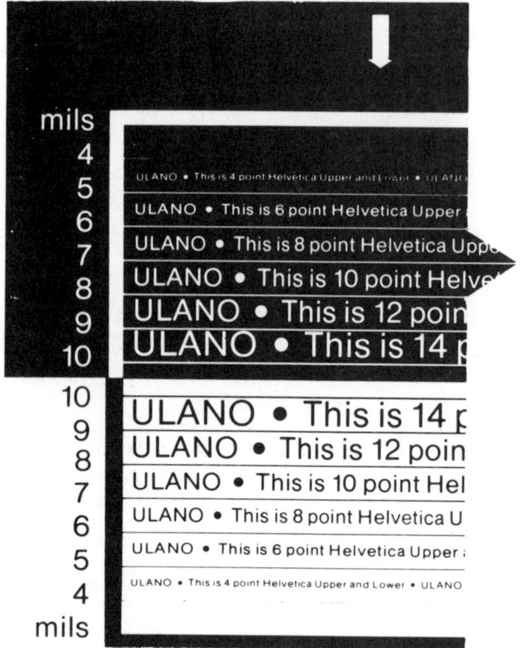

Figure 14.21. Ulano step wedge The Ulano step wedge is a precision tool that can be used to determine the correct exposure time for any type of photographic stencil. The illustration shown is only an approximation and in no way attempts to duplicate the quality of the original instrument.
Courtesy of J. Ulano Company, Inc.

Development and Washing. The process of developing removes all areas not hardened by exposure to light. Any area not covered by the positive image will be washed away. Depending on the type of emulsion, indirect stencils are developed by one of two techniques: a hydrogen peroxide bath or plain water.

Some emulsions require a hydrogen peroxide bath to harden the exposed areas. The stencil is placed in the solution emulsion-side up and is constantly agitated for 1 to 3 minutes, depending on the manufacturer's recommendations. The sheet is then removed and is sprayed with warm water (95°–105°F). The spray washes away the unhardened stencil areas, leaving a stencil outline of the image.

Other emulsions are developed in plain water immediately after being removed from the contact frame. A cool-water (70°F) spray is directed over the entire emulsion surface until the image areas are washed away.

With both methods the concern is with stopping all development as soon as the image areas are clear. Excess warm-water spray will remove the hardened emulsion and can

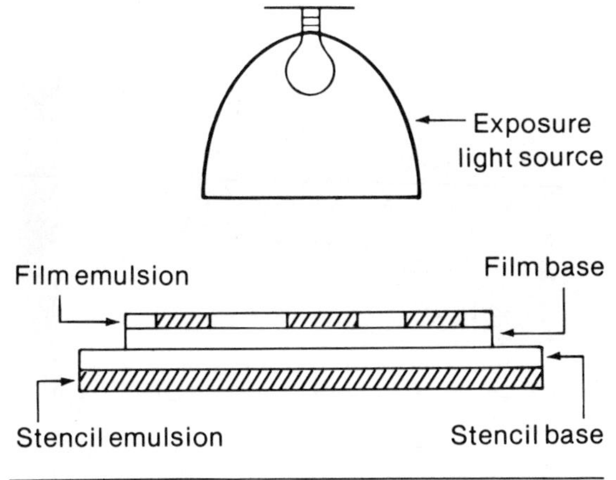

Figure 14.22. Exposing indirect stencils Indirect stencils must be exposed through the base side of the stencil material.

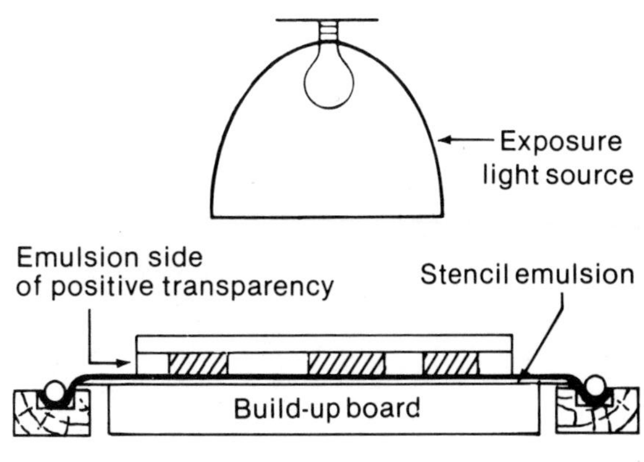

Figure 14.23. Exposing direct stencils A direct stencil is set up to be exposed through the bottom of the screen.

create a thin stencil. All indirect stencils are fixed by a stream of cold water (gradually decreasing the temperature).

Application. Indirect stencils adhere very easily to the screen fabric. Place the chilled stencil emulsion-side up on a hard, flat buildup board (figure 14.25). Position the clean screen over the stencil so that the clear printing area is in the center of the screen frame (figure 14.26). Do not move the screen once it has contacted the stencil and do not use excessive pressure—merely allow the weight of the frame to hold it in position. Excess moisture is removed from the stencil by blotting it with clean newsprint or inexpensive paper towels (figure 14.27). Gently wipe the newsprint with a soft, clean rag; *do not use pressure.* Keep changing the newsprint until it does not pick up moisture from the stencil. Excessive pressure during blotting will push the fabric threads into the emulsion, which could cause pinholes or a ragged sawtooth edge during printing. The function of blotting is to remove excess moisture and to "blot up" through the fibers the soft "top" of the emulsion.

Drying. Indirect stencils should not be forced dry with hot or warm air. Rapid drying could result in poor adhesion or could warp the stencil. To dry the emulsion properly, place the entire frame in a position so that air is allowed to flow over both sides—a gentle room air fan may be used. A spotty appearance of light and dark areas indicates that the stencil is drying. The emulsion is completely dry when the entire stencil area is uniform in hue.

Removal of the Base Material. When the emulsion is dry, the clear support base can be peeled off (figure 14.28). After printing, all indirect photographic stencils can generally be removed from the screen fabric with a

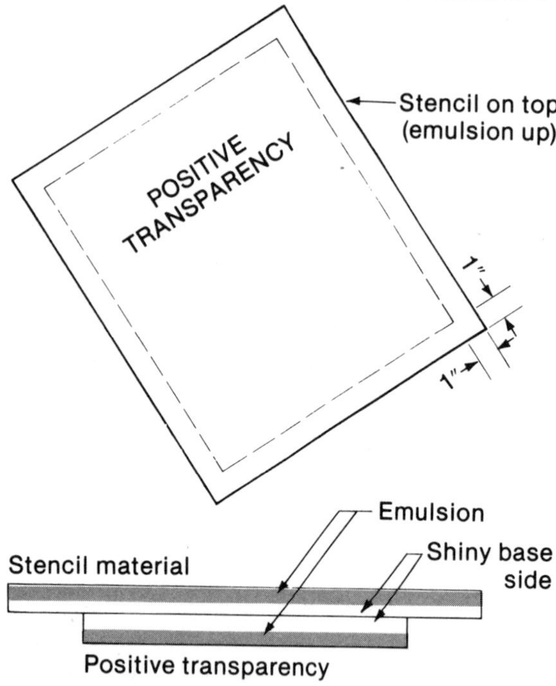

Figure 14.24. Positioning the positive transparency The right-reading side of the positive must be placed against the base side of the stencil.

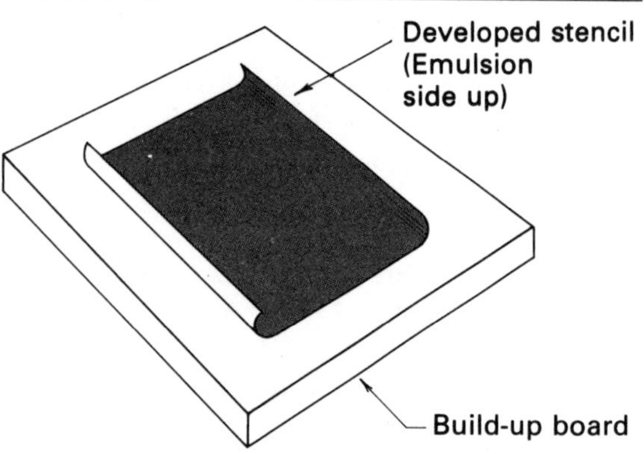

Figure 14.25. Placing the indirect stencil on a build-up board

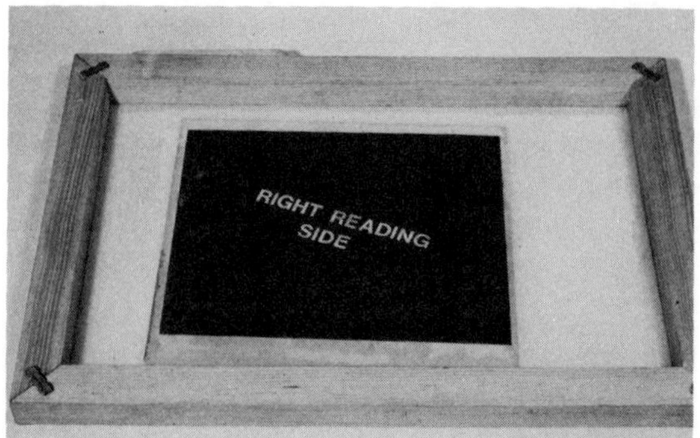

Figure 14.26. Positioning the screen over the stencil
Courtesy of SUCO Learning Resources and R. Kampas.

high-pressure hot-water spray. For difficult materials, enzymes are available that will help to dissolve the old material (on metal or synthetic screens, bleach is commonly used).

Direct Photographic Stencil Process

With the direct method of stencil preparation, a wet photographic emulsion is applied directly to the screen fabric by the printer. The entire screen is then exposed to a positive image, developed, and printed.

The main requirement of the direct process is some form of liquid light-sensitive emulsion. All currently used emulsions fall into the following types of chemical formulations:

- A synthetic-based material, such as polyvinyl alcohol;
- A gelatin-based chemical material;
- A combination of both synthetic and gelatin materials.

Figure 14.27. Removing excess moisture
Courtesy of SUCO Learning Resources and R. Kampas.

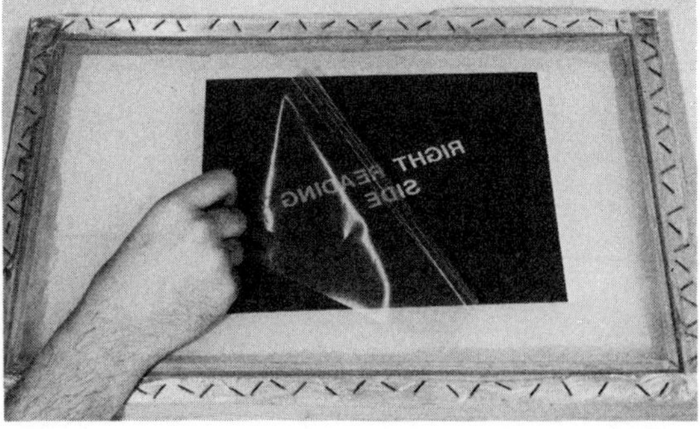

Figure 14.28. Peeling off the support material
Courtesy of SUCO Learning Resources and R. Kampas.

Most printers use commercially prepared emulsions rather than prepare their own. Commercial emulsions are more economical, higher in quality, and can be formulated by the supplier to meet any printing requirements. Commercial emulsions are available in two forms: presensitized and unsensitized liquids.

The steps in preparing a direct photographic stencil are relatively simple and involve five steps:

1. Preparation of the sensitized emulsion,
2. Application of the emulsion to the screen,
3. Drying the emulsion,
4. Exposure,
5. Development.

Preparation. Unsensitized, direct screen emulsions are provided by the manufacturer in two parts: a liquid unsensitized emulsion and a dry powder sensitizer. The dry sensitizer is first dissolved in warm water according to the manufacturer's recommendations. The liquid sensitizer is then added to the liquid emulsion to create an active solution. The mixture may be stored in a closed amber or light-tight bottle, but it usually must be applied to the screen as soon as possible.

Application. The screen should be coated with the liquid emulsion in a yellow or subdued light situation. One technique is to pour a quantity of the emulsion on one edge of the bottom side of the frame rather than on the screen itself, because then the liquid would rapidly seep through the screen mesh. With a round-edged scraper, squeegee the emulsion to the other end of the screen with smooth, continuous strokes (figure 14.29). Turn the frame over and immediately squeegee the inside of the screen until it is smooth. The quantity of liquid to apply for the first coat depends on the length of the screen, but it is better to apply too much and squeegee off the excess than to use too little and not totally cover the screen.

Figure 14.29. Using a squeegee on the emulsion
Courtesy of SUCO Learning Resources and R. Kampas.

Drying. Store the frame flat in a dark place. A circulating air fan can be used to hasten drying. When the first coat is dry, apply a second coat to the inside of the screen and allow it to dry. The thickness of the ink deposit can be somewhat controlled by the number of emulsion layers. If a thick ink deposit is desired, a third emulsion coating should be placed on the bottom side of the frame.

Exposure. Special contact frames must be used to hold the screen frame and film positive during exposure. Place the right-reading side of the transparent positive against the outside surface of the screen (see figure 14.23). The light must pass through the positive to expose the screen emulsion. Expose the screen stencil material through the positive for the time determined from the test exposures.

Development. The stencil image is developed by first wetting both sides of the screen in warm (95°–105°F) water, then gently spraying both sides with warm water until the image areas are completely clear (figure 14.30). Allow the frame to drain and blot the emulsion dry with newsprint.

Masking the Stencil

Preparing a Paper Mask

The idea of a stencil is that ink passes through any open areas on the screen. It is necessary to block out or mask those open areas of the screen not covered by the stencil material and not intended to print. There is generally a gap between the edge of the stencil and the screen frame that must be covered to prevent ink passage.

A paper mask works very well for short runs for blocking nonimage areas. Cut a piece of kraft paper slightly smaller than the inside dimensions of the frame. Lay the paper on the screen and with a pencil trace the rough outline of the image area. Remove the paper and cut out an area that is about 1 inch (2.54 cm) larger than the image extremes. Replace the masking sheet and apply gummed tape around the edges of the frame. Then tape the opening of the masking sheet to the stencil material. It is important that the tape be at

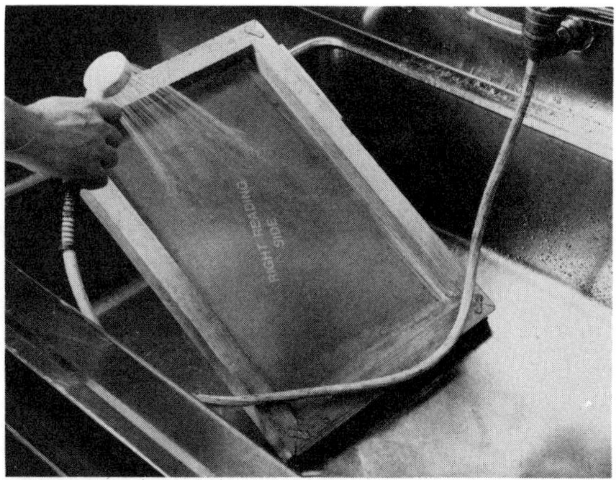

Figure 14.30. Developing the image Gently spray both sides of the screen with warm water.
Courtesy of SUCO Learning Resources and R. Kampas.

Figure 14.31. Using a liquid mask
Courtesy of SUCO Learning Resources and R. Kampas.

least ¾ inch (1.91 cm) from the nearest image and in perfect contact with the solid stencil.

Preparing a Liquid Block-Out Mask

A second method of masking employs a liquid block-out fluid (figure 14.31). These fluids are usually water based and are easy to use. Materials such as LePage's glue will work, but specially formulated commercial products are inexpensive and work much better. Brush or scrape one coat on the underside of the screen wherever the fabric is exposed but an image is not desired. Allow it to dry and apply a second coat on the inside area of the screen.

It is often necessary to touch up any imperfections, such as pinholes, that are in the stencil. The liquid block-out is ideal for small corrections and should be applied to the underside of the screen.

The processes of printing and cleaning the screen and stencil are discussed in detail in chapter 15.

Key Terms

screen printing
stencil
hand-cut stencils
tusche-and-glue
photographic stencils
multifilament screens
monofilament screens
tooth
indirect process
direct process
direct/indirect process
step wedge

Questions for Review

1. What is the basic concept of screen printing?
2. What are the three groups of stencil preparation methods?
3. How are screen fabrics classified?
4. Which mesh count will pass a coarser ink pigment, a 6XX or a 14XX fabric?
5. Why must a tooth be produced on a monofilament fabric and not on a multifilament one?
6. Why should commercial household abrasive cleansers *not* be used to clean or degrease a screen?
7. What are the three basic steps in creating a hand-cut stencil?
8. What is the primary advantage of photographic stencils?
9. What are the three types of photographic stencils?
10. Briefly outline the six steps necessary to prepare an indirect photographic stencil.
11. Briefly outline the five steps necessary to prepare a direct photographic stencil.
12. What is the purpose of masking?

Chapter Fifteen

Screen Printing

Anecdote to Chapter Fifteen

The illustration is a famous playing card called the "Knave of Bells" that dates from before the year 1500. There is some debate as to how the card was actually printed, but it was probably printed from a stencil. The "Knave" was a part of a set of forty-eight playing cards found in the inner lining of a book cover that was printed and bound sometime around the turn of the sixteenth century. Paper was such a precious commodity that discarded or inferior sheets were often used to stiffen book bindings. Many valuable early pieces of printing have been found in such hiding places.

As we understand the process today, the stenciled card was made by using a perforated metal plate. To create a stencil, many small holes were punched through the thin metal in the shape of the desired image. The "illuminator," as he was called, positioned the plate over the paper and applied the ink with a brush. The brush forced the ink through the small openings onto the page. Several different colors were often used, with a separate plate for each color.

The "Knave of Bells" A printed playing card from about 1500 A.D.

No one knows exactly when playing cards were invented, but the first documented evidence of their existence can be found in a 1392 account book kept by the treasurer of King Charles VI of France, in which a notation was made on the purchase of three packs of cards for the king. Several scholars, however, have found references to "games of hazard," as cards were called, in French poetry as early as 1328.

It is also difficult to trace the exact evolution of the printed card design. It is known that by 1550 printers had nearly universally adopted the four suits we know today as symbols of the four classes of society. Hearts symbolized the clergy. Spades were a refinement of the Italian *spada,* a sword, and were for the nobility. Clubs meant the peasantry. Diamonds symbolized the citizens or burghers.

There are some experts who suggest that playing cards were the first printed product ever produced in Europe. Some even believe that it was the widespread use of games of hazard that started an interest in learning for many of the uneducated peasants of the Continent. There is little doubt that a demand was created for a printed product.

Objectives for Chapter Fifteen

After completing this chapter, you will be able to:

- Identify important considerations when selecting a squeegee and ink.
- Explain basic screen printing techniques, including registration, on- and off-contact printing, printing, and clean-up.
- Recall multicolor printing techniques.
- List methods of ink drying.
- Recall methods of screen printing halftones.
- Classify high-speed production screen printing presses.
- Recognize special screen printing machine configurations.

Introduction

The basic process of screen printing has changed little in the last several hundred years. The standard printing device remains a stencil attached to a piece of fabric stretched over a wooden or metal frame. A flexible **squeegee** is used to force the ink through the stencil opening. Even though the basic printing device has changed little, the printer's understanding of the variables that affect image quality has substantially increased.

The term **printing press** might sound strange when associated with the most basic screen printing unit, but the screen printing frame is in every sense a press. The receiver must be fed and registered under the stencil. The ink must be transferred to the receiver. The printed product must be removed and stored for later distribution. Screen printing presses can range in complexity from an elementary homemade, hand-operated wooden frame (figure 15.1) to a sophisticated system that automatically inserts, registers, prints, and removes any material, including cylindrical surfaces.

Squeegee and Ink Considerations

Selecting Proper Squeegee

It is the squeegee (figure 15.2) that actually causes the image transfer to take place because it is the squeegee that forces the ink through the stencil and fabric openings onto the receiver. All squeegees have two parts: a handle and a blade. The handle can be of any design that is comfortable for the printer and meets his or her particular needs, but great

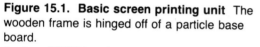

Figure 15.1. Basic screen printing unit The wooden frame is hinged off of a particle base board.
Courtesy of SUCO Learning Resources and R. Kampas.

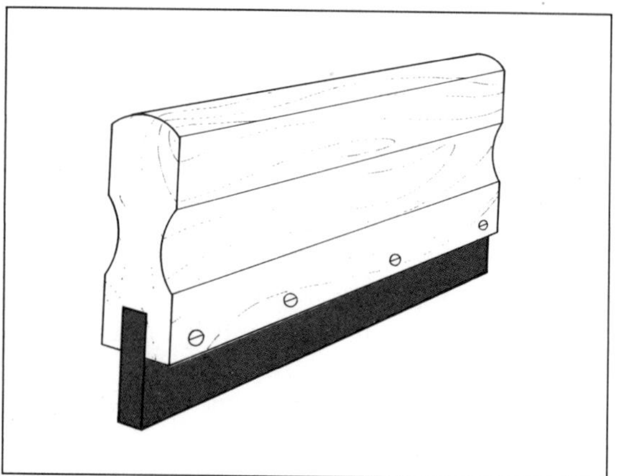

Figure 15.2. Printer's squeegee

care must be taken when selecting the squeegee blade. Three primary blade considerations must be examined prior to printing:

- Shape,
- Chemical makeup,
- Flexibility,
- Length.

Shape. The blade shape generally determines the sharpness and thickness of ink deposit. There are six basic blade shapes (figure 15.3). A *square* blade (figure 15.3a) is the most common and is a good general purpose design that can be used to print on flat surfaces with standard poster inks. A *double-bevel, flat-point* design (figure 15.3b) is good for working with ceramic materials such as glazes or slip. The *double-bevel* shaped form (figure 15.3c) is used for printing on uneven surfaces or for placing a fine layer of ink on a surface when stenciling extremely fine line detail. The *single-bevel* (figure 15.3d) is generally used when printing on glass. The *square-edge with rounded corners* (figure 15.3e) is generally used when screening light colors over dark backgrounds. The *round-edge* (figure 15.3f) works well with printing on fabrics. The round-edge design has the advantage of forcing an extra-heavy amount of ink through the screen. All but the special purpose printer will find the square form acceptable for almost every job.

Chemical Makeup. The chemical makeup of the squeegee blade is important. The base for some inks could actually dissolve the blade if the wrong type of blade were used. Most squeegee blades are cast from rubber or plastic. Blades that are designed for vinyl or acetate printing are water soluble and cannot be used with a water-based pigment. Synthetic blades, such as polyurethane, retain their edges longer and have more resistance to

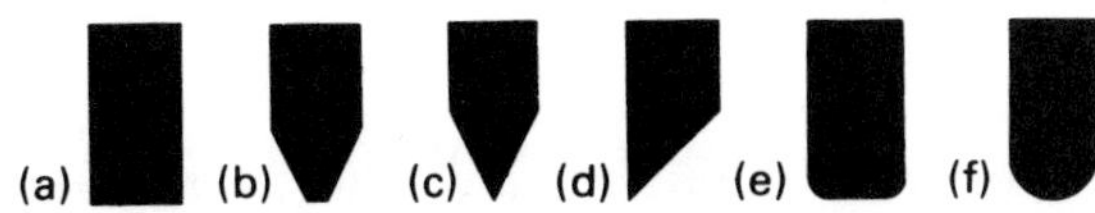

Figure 15.3. Basic shapes of squeegee blades The six basic shapes are square (a), double-bevel, flat point (b), double-bevel (c), single-bevel (d), square-edge with rounded corners (e), and round-edge (f).

abrasion than do blades of any other material, but they are significantly more expensive. A good general purpose blade is neoprene rubber. It can be used for vinyl, lacquer, oil, poster enamel, and ethocel inks. When selecting the specific chemical makeup of the blade, decide on the type of ink to be used, identify the ink base, and determine which blade formulation is acceptable.

Flexibility. The third consideration for squeegee blade selection is flexibility. Rubber hardness is measured in terms of **Shore Durometer** readings—an average blade for general use has a rating of 60 Shore A. Most squeegee manufacturers translate the value into the terms *hard, medium,* and *soft.* Soft blades (around 50 Shore A) will deposit a fairly thick layer of pigment. Hard blades (around 70 Shore A) will deposit a sharp, thin ink layer. A medium squeegee blade (60 Shore A) will meet most shop needs.

Length. The length of the squeegee is also an important consideration. As a rule of thumb, the blade should extend at least ½ inch beyond the limits of the stencil image, but it should be able to pass freely between the edges of the screen frame.

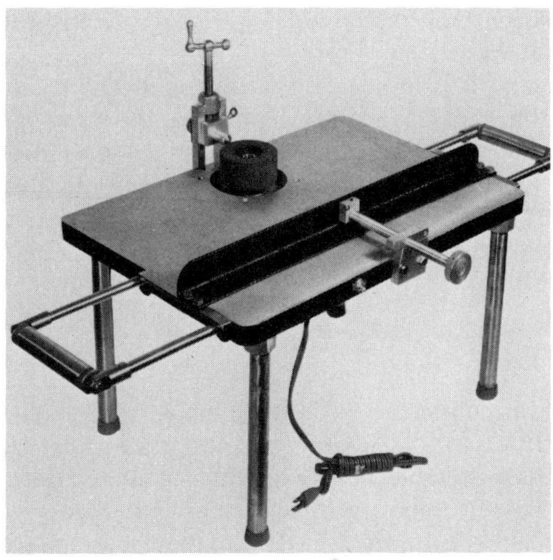

Figure 15.4. Commercial squeegee sharpener
Courtesy of Naz-Dar Company.

Squeegee Preparation

Whatever the shape, makeup, or hardness of the blade selected, the major factor controlling image quality is blade sharpness. Several types of commercial squeegee sharpeners are available that can be used to prepare any shape of edge (figure 15.4). Most machines operate with a moving abrasive belt or drum. The squeegee is mounted with a series of clamps, and the blade is passed against the cutting surface.

If a sharpening machine cannot be obtained, 6- and 8-inch widths of garnet cloth are suitable for sharpening square-edge blades. The cloth is mounted (generally with staples) on a hard, flat surface. The squeegee is held in a perfectly vertical position and is dragged back and forth over the abrasive cloth until a sharp edge is formed.

It is important that the squeegee be absolutely clean prior to printing. Any dry ink left on a blade from previous printing runs will contaminate the pigment used with other printing jobs. This is especially important when a dark color is to be followed by a light color.

Ink Selection

The pigment and vehicle must freely pass through screen fabric and still place an image of acceptable density on the receiving surface. Screen inks are thinner than letterpress or lithographic inks. Early screen inks were very similar to ordinary paint. The creation of new fabrics and stencil materials, the growth of printing on nontraditional materials (anything but paper), and the application of screen printing to specialized industrial needs (such as printed circuits) resulted in the development of a wide variety of screen inks.

There are so many different materials intended for so many different applications that both novice and experienced printers become easily confused. Choosing the appropriate ink becomes easier to understand if all elements of a particular job are examined in detail and several specific questions are answered.

Product Characteristics. The first area of concern should be the characteristics of the printed piece. What is the function of the final product? Will it be exposed to harsh weather conditions (as is a billboard)? Will it be in contact with harsh chemicals (as is printing on a detergent bottle or even a cola container)? Should the appearance of the image be a gloss or a flat finish? What will be the surface of the image receiver? Will the ink have to dry by absorption into the material? Will it need to be heat set? Will it have to air dry?

Production Limitations. After considering the characteristics of the printed piece, the printer must deal with the limitations of the production situation. Any material that can be ground into a fine powder can be mixed with a liquid vehicle and used as a screen ink. Ink manufacturers will recommend a minimum **screen mesh count** (or opening) that can be used with each of their materials. If the openings are smaller than the recommended minimum, no ink will pass through the screen. The solvents for the stencil and for the ink must not be the same. For example, if a water-based ink is used with a water-based stencil, the entire image carrier will rapidly become a puddle of ink and stencil on the screen.

By making a list of both product and production limitations, it is possible to eliminate all but a narrow category of possible ink choices.

Ink Preparation

Many manufacturers advertise that their inks are "ready to use directly from the can," but rarely does the printer not have to prepare the ink before printing. **Ink viscosity** (resistance to flow) is of major importance. The goal is to keep the ink as dense as possible to form an acceptable printed image. But at the same time, it must be thin enough to pass freely through the screen openings without clogging. The difficulty is that the required viscosity can be different for every job. The higher the mesh count, the thinner the ink must be. In very general terms, the ink should "flow like honey" off the ink knife. It should move slowly and smoothly and should not hesitate to flow when the knife is tipped.

Many different additives can be mixed with screen inks to yield certain ink characteristics. Viscosity can be decreased by adding a compatible thinner and/or reducer. The addition of a transparent base will make the ink somewhat translucent. An extender base will increase the quantity of usable ink without affecting density. The function of a drier is to hasten the drying of the ink on the receiver, but it can also increase the possibility of the ink drying in the screen fabric. A binder can be added to increase the adhesion of the ink to the stock. Individuals inexperienced with additives should always consult a screen ink supplier for information.

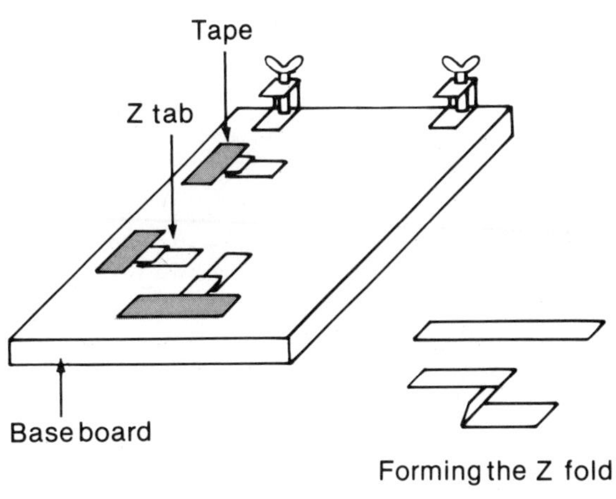

Figure 15.5. Making gauge pins Three Z tabs taped in place serve as gauge pins used to register the paper.

The Basic Printing Process

The basic techniques for screen printing will be discussed in terms of a hand-operated hinged-frame system. For this section it will be assumed that the printing frame is held with a pair of heavy-duty hinge clamps to a wooden or particle-board base. The hinges can be common butt hinges, or special hinges can be purchased from a screen printing supplier.

The sequence of steps, as with any press system, is to feed, register, print, and deliver the stock. Because the simple screen system is hand fed and delivered, this section will consider only registering the stock and printing the image. The processes of drying the image, cleaning the screen, and removing the stencil will also be discussed.

Basic Registration Techniques

As with all printing systems, registration is concerned with placing the image in the same position on every press sheet. Recall from chapter 12 ("Controlling Image Position on the Press Sheet") that three metal gauge pins were used on the tympan of a platen press to hold the sheet in place. It is possible to form "gauge pins" from a narrow strip of paper. These gauge pins will hold the sheet in register during printing. Cut three pieces of 20- to 40-pound paper ½ inch by 2 inches and make a simple Z fold. Tape the tabs to the base under the screen frame (figure 15.5).

Commercial printers use several methods to locate the image in the appropriate printing position. A simple method is to place the original drawing or film positive used to produce the screen stencil right reading on a piece of the printing stock. Tape it to the stock so that the image is in the desired printing position. Place the stock, with the taped image, on the base board and lower the screen frame into the printing position over the stock. Move the stock until the taped image

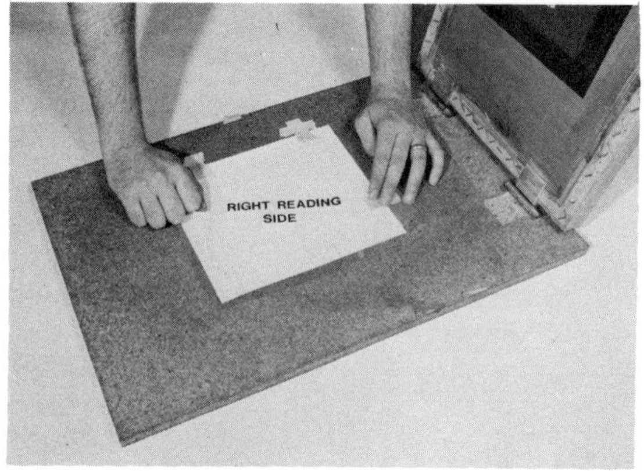

Figure 15.6. Setting the image position The Z tabs are placed against the positioned stock and carefully taped in place.
Courtesy of SUCO Learning Resources and R. Kampas.

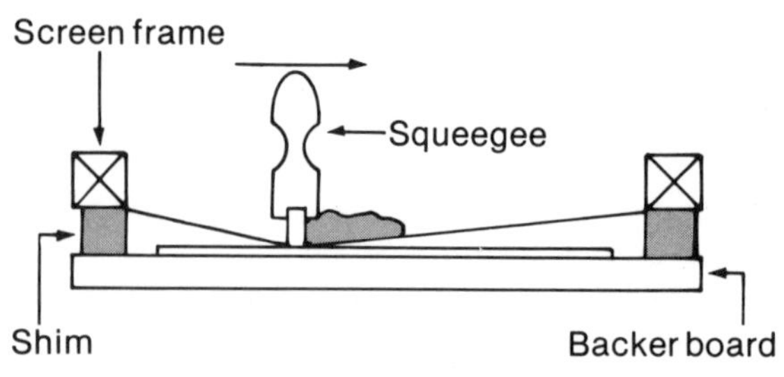

Figure 15.7. Diagram of off-contact printing In off-contact printing, the screen touches the paper only when the image is transferred by the squeegee.

aligns with the stencil opening, then carefully hinge the screen up out of the way. Without moving the stock, carefully insert the "gauge pins" and tape each one to the base (figure 15.6). The tabs should be positioned so that there are two pins on a long side of the paper and a single one on a short side. It is also important that the tabs be placed as far away from the image areas as possible. Remove the printing sheet and tape the inside portion of the Z-tabs to the base. If every piece of stock is seated against the inside of the three tabs, the image will be printed in the same position on each sheet.

On- and Off-Contact Printing

Two common printing methods are used for hinged-frame printing: on-contact and off-contact printing. With **on-contact printing,** the screen and stencil contact the printing material throughout the transfer process. With this method the press sheet sticks to the screen. After the image is transferred, the frame must be hinged up and the stock carefully peeled away. On-contact printing is the most common technique for small job shops or for short-run jobs that do not require an extremely sharp impression. However, off-contact printing should always be done if possible to avoid the problem of sticking. One method of preventing the stock from sticking to the screen with the on-contact approach is to place several pieces of thin double-backed adhesive in nonimage areas on the base board.

In **off-contact printing,** the screen and stencil are slightly (generally no more than ⅛ inch) raised away from the printing material by small shims, or spacing material, under the hinge and frame. With this technique the stencil touches the stock only while the squeegee passes over the screen. Once the image is transferred across the squeegee line, the screen snaps back away from the receiver (figure 15.7). Off-contact printing helps keep the press sheet from sticking to the screen and usually prevents image smearing. It is

Figure 15.8. Adding ink to the screen
Courtesy of SUCO Learning Resources and R. Kampas.

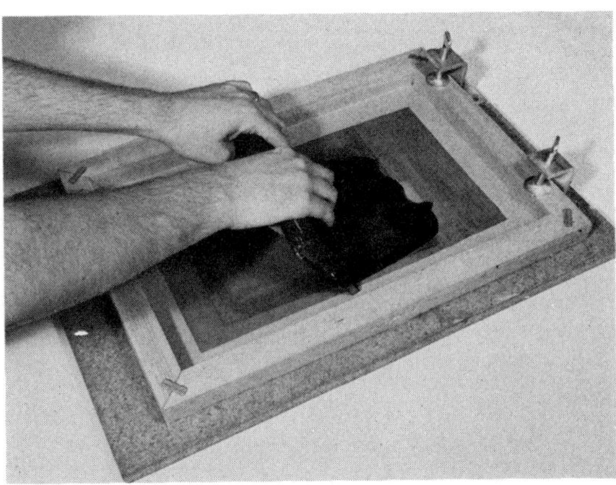

Figure 15.9. Distributing the ink
Courtesy of SUCO Learning Resources and R. Kampas.

often used as a technique to produce sharp impressions on smooth surfaces.

A vacuum frame base can be used with either on- or off-contact printing to help keep the stock from sticking to the screen. Vacuum bases are available as single units or tables and are found on most semiautomatic machines.

Printing the Stencil

Chapter 14 outlined several procedures for masking the nonimage portions of the screen. Before printing, two tasks remain. First check to ensure that there are no pinholes or other unwanted openings in the stencil. Block out any areas with the recommended block-out solution for the type of stencil being used. Second, seal off the inside edge, between the fabric and the frame. Sealing can be done with any wide commercial tape (a 2-inch width is recommended). If the run is exceptionally long or if special inks (such as water based) or abrasive materials (such as a ceramic glaze) are used, a plastic solvent-resistant, pressure-sensitive tape should be used. Otherwise, a water-moistened gummed tape will be sufficient.

Begin the printing operation by positioning a piece of stock in the registration system on the base and lowering the screen frame into position. Pour a puddle of prepared ink at one end of the screen, away from the image and in a line slightly longer than the width of the image (figure 15.8). Hold the squeegee at about a 60° angle to the screen surface and, pressing firmly, draw the puddle of ink across the stencil opening with one smooth motion (figure 15.9). It is important that the movement be uniform and that the motion not stop until the squeegee is out of the image area. Make only one pass. Remove the squeegee, raise the frame, prop the screen away from the image surface, and remove the stock sheet (figure 15.10).

Examine the printed image for correct position, ink uniformity, and clarity of detail. If necessary, readjust the registration tabs for

Figure 15.10. Removing the stock sheet
Courtesy of SUCO Learning Resources and R. Kampas.

proper registration. Ink clogging or drying in the fabric can cause the layers of ink on the image to be nonuniform or can actually cause loss of line detail. To correct this problem, remove as much ink from the screen as possible and add thinner to the ink. Clean the clogged portions of the screen by gently wiping the underside of the stencil with a rag moistened with thinner. Then re-ink and pull a second impression. Once an acceptable image is obtained, continue the process of inserting stock, passing the squeegee across the stencil, and removing the printed sheet until the job is completed.

Multicolor Printing

Multicolor screen printing presents no great difficulties. The primary concern is the method of registration. It is important that the first color be accurately placed. If the first image is printed with variation in page placement, it will be impossible to fit the second image to it.

A two-color job requires two separate stencils. Multicolor runs require careful planning of the sequence of printing and overlapping of the colors to eliminate gaps between them. When opaque colors are used, the images must overlap by at least 1⁄16 inch. It is not necessary to overlap transparent colors except where a third color is desired.

Several techniques can be used to control accurate color fit. Register the first color by using standard positioning methods, but mark the first sheet as a proof. While the proof sheet is still held by the Z-tabs, mark the position of the tabs with a pencil. Most press sheets are cut with some slight variation on the edges. If, for the second color, the tabs are placed in the same position as for the first color, the possibility of misregistration is lessened.

To position the second color over the first, mount a sheet of clear acetate over the base board and tape it from one edge so it can be hinged out of the way when necessary. With the acetate in place, swing the second stencil down into the printing position and pull an impression. When the frame is removed, the second image position will have been defined on the plastic. Slip the proof sheet from the first color under the acetate and line up both colors. Carefully hinge the plastic out of the way and mount the register tabs on the base board in line with the pencil marks. The two colors should now fit for the second printing. Any number of additional colors may be registered with this technique.

Problems with registration are not always the operator's fault. Fabrics that are loosely stretched on the frame tend to cause problems with multicolor registration. Frame hinges can become loose. If not taped securely, register tabs move out of position. Whatever the reason, when colors do not fit, all possible variables should be carefully examined.

Drying the Image

Most screen printing inks dry by absorption, aerial oxidation (air drying), a combination of both absorption and aerial oxidation, or by heat-setting action. Screen prints cannot be delivered from the press and stacked because all types of screen inks require some drying time. To save worker motion and conserve production space, a drying rack is often used to receive press sheets (figure 15.11). Racks are available in a wide variety of sizes, and commercial models come equipped with a spring system attached to floating bars that swing each shelf down into position as needed.

Inks that dry by absorption into the stock or by aerial oxidation can generally be stacked, dried, and shipped within 30 minutes. It is possible to hasten drying time by passing the sheet through a heat oven.

Heat-setting inks require an intense direct heat source. Some form of commercial curing or baking batch oven is generally used (figure 15.12). Most types are rated to about 320°F, have forced air circulation and a temperature control device, and are equipped with a variable-speed conveyor belt feeder system.

Figure 15.11. Floating bar print drying rack
Courtesy of Naz-Dar Company.

Cleaning the Screen

To clean the screen, first remove any large deposits of ink remaining on the screen and squeegee with an ink knife. It is generally wise to discard the ink from the screen surface and thereby avoid contaminating any fresh ink remaining in the can. Place ten to fifteen open sheets of newspaper on the base board and lower the screen into the printing position. Place a quantity of compatible solvent on the squeegee side of the screen. It is important to dissolve all the ink before any solvent is removed. If a rag were immediately

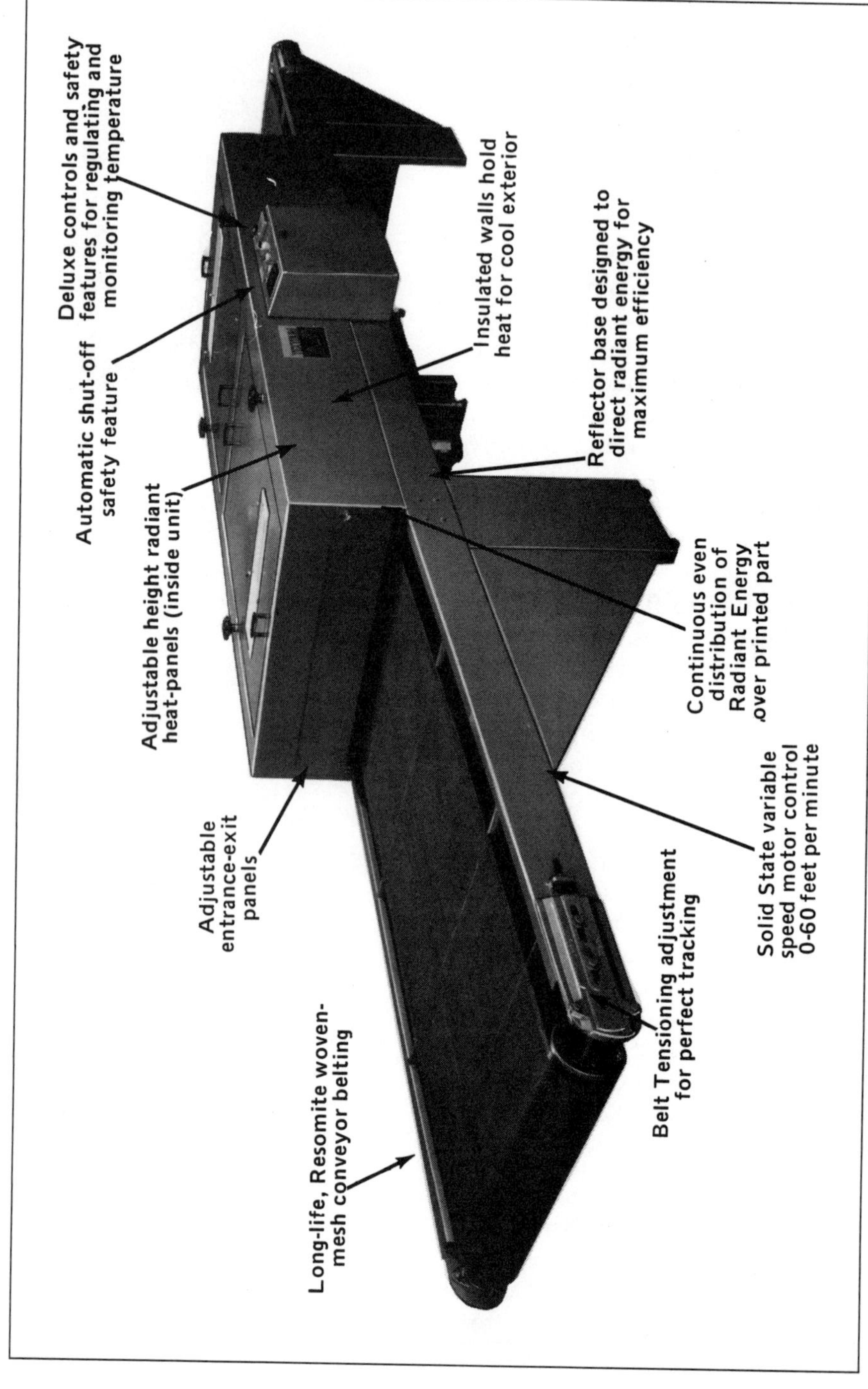

Figure 15.12. Commercial batch oven A commercial batch oven is used to dry heat-setting inks.
Courtesy of Advance Process Supply Company, Chicago.

applied to the screen, the solvent would be absorbed but no dissolving action would take place. Using your hand, rub the solvent into the entire surface of the screen. (Plastic gloves are practical during this process.) After all ink is dissolved, remove both the ink and the solvent with a dry cloth rag. Lift the screen and remove several layers of newspaper. Repeat the same operation until all ink has been removed. As a final step, moisten a clean rag with solvent and rub the underside of the screen to remove any remaining ink.

Commercial screen cleaning units (figure 15.13) are available that will dissolve all ink and leave the fabric perfectly clean. The frame is placed on a washing stand and a solvent spray is directed over it. The solvent drains back into a container where the ink and dirt settle or are filtered out, and the clear solvent is recirculated through the system.

There is a tendency for novice printers to mix dissimilar solvents during the cleanup operation. Stencil material and printing inks are chosen so that their bases will not dissolve one another. If the stencil is water based and the ink lacquer based and water is accidentally mixed with the ink, problems occur. The stencil may not wash away, but the ink will become emulsified and hopelessly clogged in the screen. It is important that the printer have a clear understanding of the printing materials and their solvents before starting any cleanup.

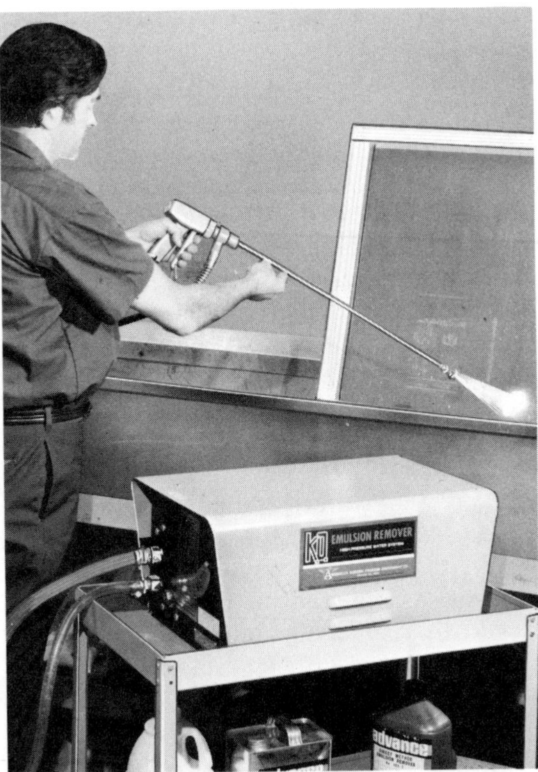

Figure 15.13. Commercial screen cleaning unit
Courtesy of Advance Process Supply Company, Chicago.

Removing the Stencil

After all ink has been cleaned from the screen and any remaining ink solvent has evaporated, the stencil can be removed. One of the great advances in recent years is the development of a quality water-based stencil material. Whether hand cut or photographic, most water-based stencils are designed to be removed with a hot-water spray. With some materials, a commercial enzyme is recommended.

Wet both sides of the stencil and sprinkle on the enzyme. After letting the material stand for 5 minutes (or whatever time is recommended by the manufacturer), spray the screen with hot water. It is necessary to neutralize the enzyme remaining on the wet screen by wiping the fabric with a 5% acetic acid or white vinegar solution. Thoroughly rinse the screen with cold water and allow it to air dry.

If nylon, polyester, or stainless steel fabrics are used with a water-based stencil, you can use a household clorine bleach presoak in place of the enzyme. One method is to wet both sides of the stencil with a sodium hypochlorite solution (bleach) and allow it to stand for 5 minutes. Carefully rinse off the bleach solution (avoid splashing or contact with the eyes) and spray with hot water. The technique should *not* be used if a natural fiber, such as silk, is used.

Lacquer stencils must be removed with lacquer thinner. Lay several layers of newsprint on a flat surface and pour lacquer thinner on both sides of the stencil. Allow the thinner to set for several minutes before rubbing with a cloth. Lacquer thinner has a tendency to dry very rapidly, so several applications of the solution might be necessary before the screen is clean.

Troubleshooting Clogged Screens

A clean screen is the first requirement when preparing to print. A clogged screen should not be used because a stencil will not adhere well; if adhered, the quality of the printed image will be very poor. In a learning situation, with many different individuals using the same equipment, it is not always possible to identify what material is clogging a screen. It could be stencil emulsion, block-out material, ink, or even some foreign substance.

There are several steps to follow to clean a clogged screen when you do not know what is causing the problem. First try the household clorine bleach mentioned in the preceding section (as long as the fabric is not silk) or a commercial enzyme (this should remove any water-based substance). Next try the solvent for the ink that was used for the last printing. If the screen is still clogged, try scrubbing the area with lacquer thinner, and finally try alcohol. It is important that the screen be thoroughly dried after each step. If, after all attempts, the fabric remains clogged, discard the material and restretch the frame.

Halftone Reproduction

Screen printing halftone images has several advantages over relief or lithographic processes. It is ideal for short-run posters or illustrations. It is less costly than any other method in terms of both time and materials. It can print extremely large image sizes. In addition, a wide range of inks can be used that have a brilliance, opacity, and texture unmatched by any other method.

There are, however, special considerations associated with screening halftones. Although 85- and 110-line halftones are commonly screened in the industry, a small job shop without critical controls with stencil preparation and printing should stay with rather coarse halftone screen rulings (85 lines per inch or coarser). Whatever ruling is used, however, the highlight and shadow dot structure must be carefully controlled and a film positive must be produced.

The reproducible halftone dot sizes of the final film positive should be 10% to 15% for highlights and 85% to 90% for shadows. Anything not within this limit will probably not reproduce on the final printed sheet.

Methods of Halftone Preparation for Screen Printing

The basic problem when preparing halftone images for screen printing is to work within the limit of production facilities. Although a

65-line contact screen is readily available from printing suppliers, it is not a common commodity in shops other than those preparing illustrations for newspaper production or screen companies that specialize in halftone printing.

Basically four methods can be used to prepare film halftone positives within a shop situation:

1. If a 65-line halftone screen is available, first make a film halftone negative to the reproduction size. Then make a contact film positive of the halftone negative.

2. Using an available halftone screen (such as 133-line screen), make a reduced halftone negative that can fit into a film enlarger (as used for making continuous-tone prints). Then project through the negative in the enlarger onto a fresh piece of high-contrast film to make a film positive at the reproduction size.

3. Using the available halftone screen, make a same-size film halftone negative from the original. Then place the negative on a back-lighted process camera copyboard and enlarge it to the required reproduction size on a fresh piece of high-contrast film.

4. Using an available diffusion transfer halftone screen (usually 100-line), make a diffusion transfer opaque halftone positive same-size from the original. Then enlarge the positive on a process camera to the required reproduction size by using either a second set of diffusion transfer materials with a transparent receiver sheet or high-contrast film to make a film negative. Then contact print a film positive.

If any but the first method is used, it is necessary to be able to calculate percentage changes in order to make halftones of the required screen ruling with available in-plant materials.

Assume, as an example, that a 5-by-7-inch continuous-tone photograph is required to be printed as a 9-by-12-inch halftone reproduction with a 50-line ruling. The available screen is a 133-line negative gray contact screen. It is decided to produce the final film positive by projection, with an enlarger (method 2).

First determine the necessary enlargement of a 133-line ruling to obtain 50 lines per inch by using the following equation:

$$\begin{aligned} \text{PE} &= \text{Percent Enlargement} \\ &= \frac{\text{Available screen ruling}}{\text{Desired screen ruling}} \times 100 \\ &= \frac{133}{50} \times 100 \\ &= 133 \times 2 \\ &= 266\% \end{aligned}$$

In other words, it is necessary to enlarge a halftone with a ruling of 133 lines per inch 266% in order to obtain a 50-line ruling.

An enlarger is to be used for this example, so it is necessary to determine the size of the first halftone negative. The easiest method is to refer to a proportion wheel. Set the wheel at 266% enlargement. Then read across from the required size (9″ × 12″) to obtain the size negative to be placed in the enlarger. For this example, the first halftone negative must be reduced to 3⅜″ × 4½″ from a 5″ × 7″ original. Calculations for all four methods can be made in similar manner.

Fabric Selection

When selecting the fabric for screening halftone images, the major concern is with the

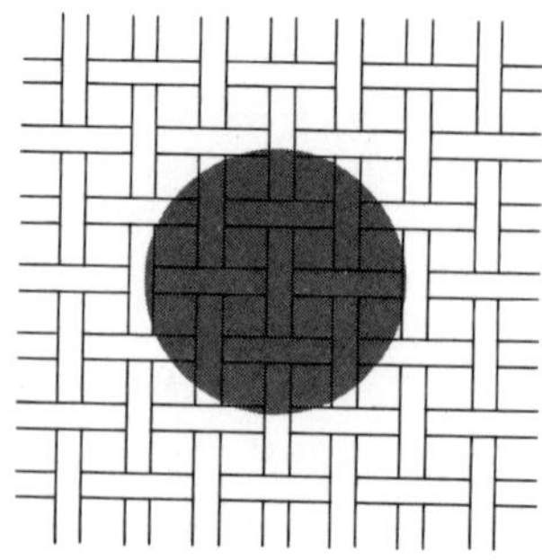

Figure 15.14. Halftone dot on screen printing fabric

cloth mesh count. In general, monofilament fabrics should be used with halftones. Choice of a specific mesh count depends on the halftone ruling of the film positive. The Ulano Company recommends that the halftone ruling be multiplied by 3.5 to 4.0 to obtain a usable fabric mesh range. For example, if the halftone ruling is 60 lines per inch, any mesh count between 210 and 240 can be used.

Whatever screen mesh is used, the smallest halftone dot must be attached to at least four fiber intersections (figure 15.14). For example, if a 133-line halftone stencil is attached to a number twelve fabric, which has approximately 125 threads to the inch, many individual dots would drop through the screen during the printing operation because there would be insufficient fabric support.

Moiré Patterns

A moiré pattern (an objectionable optical pattern discussed in Chapter 8) may be formed when two screen patterns are overlapped (such as a halftone image on the fabric screen pattern). This is a particular problem when the fabric mesh count is too coarse for the halftone screen ruling. A way to avoid the moiré pattern is to place the clean, stretched screen over the film halftone positive on a light table before making the stencil. Rotate the position under the screen until the moiré pattern disappears. Then mark the location or angle of the positive so that the stencil can be adhered in the same position.

Printing Considerations

Special inks designed for halftone reproduction are available from screen printing suppliers. Halftone ink is made from fine-ground pigment and can be purchased as either transparent or opaque ink. As with normal ink preparation, the material should be able to form a dense image on the receiving surface but should not be so thick that it clogs the screen. If the ink is too thin, the halftone dots may bleed together on the sheet, resulting in a loss of image detail in the shadow areas.

A double-bevel squeegee blade (see figure 15.3c) is recommended for halftone work. A sharp, square blade (see figure 15.3a) can be used, but the amount of pressure should be less than is typically applied for normal production runs.

When screening halftones, a vacuum base or off-contact printing will diminish the possibility of a blurred image as a result of the stock sticking to the bottom of the screen.

High-Speed Production Presses

The basic problem with any hand-operated, hinged-frame screen printing system is the small number of impressions that can be made per hour. Production is limited by how rapidly the printer can feed the stock, close the frame, position the squeegee, pull the impression, remove the squeegee, and deliver the stock. Even the most rapid operator is hard-pressed to screen print more than fifty impressions an hour with only a small stencil.

Low output was no problem with the early slow-drying inks. Most printers could not store an output of several thousand wet prints an hour that required overnight drying. With the introduction of fast-drying inks, however, greater production speeds became more important. High-speed screen printing presses can be classed as hand-operated, hand-fed, and hand-delivered; semiautomatic; or automatic units.

Lever-Action Hand-Operated Presses

Figure 15.15 illustrates one type of lever-action screen printing press. The advantage of the press is that a single operator can screen print images of nearly any size. The screen frame is counterbalanced over a vacuum frame that holds the paper. With light pressure the frame will swing down into position. The squeegee is attached to a lever that automatically springs up, out of contact with the screen. By grasping the lever handle, the operator lowers both the screen and the squeegee and, with a simple motion, drags the blade across the stencil.

Although the press is still hand operated, the action of lowering the screen, positioning the squeegee, and pulling the impression is significantly shortened. Large images are also easy to handle with the device because the lever action ensures uniform pressure across the stencil.

Figure 15.15. Lever action screen printing unit
Courtesy of Advance Process Supply Company, Chicago.

Semiautomatic Presses

Semiautomatic screen printing presses (figure 15.16) are generally hand fed and delivered by the operator, but the actual image transfer is automatic. The operator inserts and positions (registers) the stock. The machine then lowers the frame, draws the squeegee across the stencil, and raises the frame. Some devices have a 5- to 30-second built-in time delay for the stock to be fed. Others have a foot switch that is controlled by the printer to activate the squeegee. As with lever-action units, the speed of a semiautomatic machine is limited by the speed of the operator.

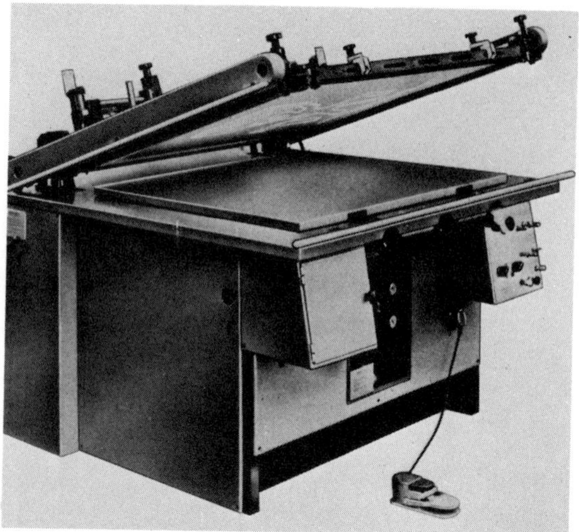

Figure 15.16. Semiautomatic screen printing press
Courtesy of Naz-Dar Company.

Automatic Presses

True high-speed screen printing is not achieved until the responsibility for feeding and removing each individual press sheet is taken from the operator and given to the machine. The techniques for the automatic screen printing press are the same as for any automatic press, except that the press uses no rollers or cylinders. The actual image transfer concerns are the same as for the hand-operated hinged system discussed earlier in this chapter.

One area of special importance, however, is the delivery system. Because wet sheets are being removed from the press at a high rate of speed, their handling becomes a problem. Devices are available that can be synchronized with any production press speed to deliver dry sheets that can be stacked or packaged.

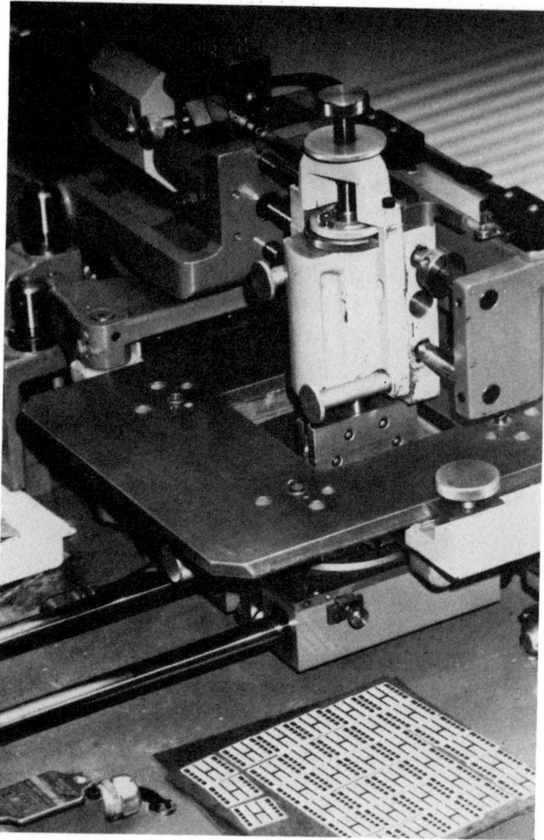

Figure 15.17. Automatic screen printing press This press is used to produce screen printed electronic circuits.
Courtesy of Electronic Products Division, E.I. Du Pont de Nemours and Company, Inc.

Special Machine Configurations

Screen printing has been applied to a wide variety of nontraditional materials and uses. One example is the production of printed circuits for the electronics industry (figure 15.17).

Major machine designs have been developed since World War II to meet the special demands of the screen industry and its customers.

Screening Cylindrical Surfaces

One major area of growth has been the printing of labels directly on cylindrical or conical containers such as bottles, cans, and drinking cups.

Whether automatic or hand operated (figure 15.18), all devices function according to the same basic principle. The familiar flat screen is always used as the stencil carrier.

Figure 15.18. Hand-operated cylindrical screen printing press
Courtesy of Naz-Dar Company.

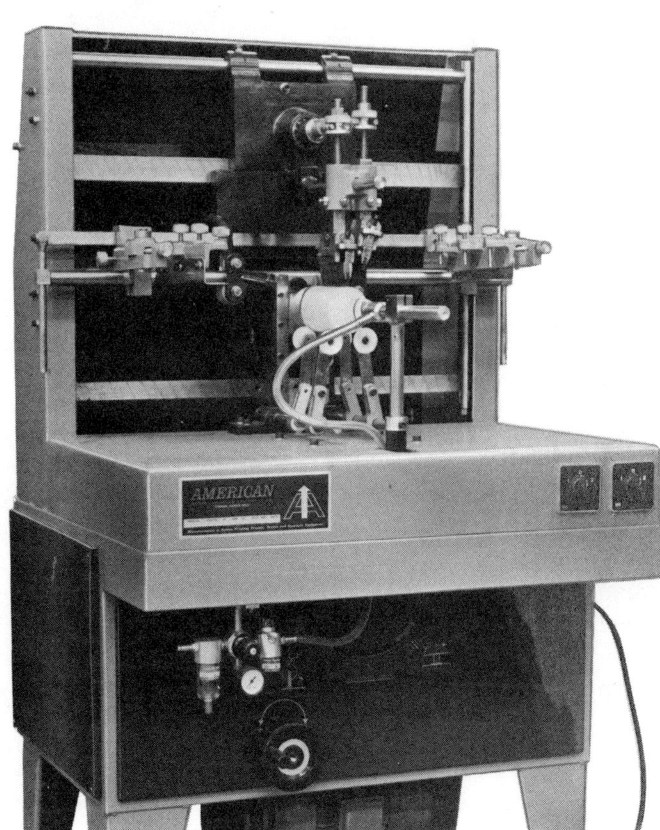

Figure 15.19. Automatic conical-shaped screen printing press
Courtesy of Advance Process Supply Company, Chicago.

Figure 15.20. Multicolor rotary screen printing press
Courtesy of Naz-Dar Company.

The cylindrical object is positioned beneath the screen and rests on ball bearings or some other system that allows the object to rotate. A squeegee is lowered into contact with the screen and the cylindrical object and is locked into position. To transfer the image, the screen frame is moved along a track. The pressure of the squeegee (which is not moving) pressing the screen against the cylindrical object also rotates the object.

Figure 15.19 shows a totally automatic screen printing press that can feed, print, and deliver 6,000 cone-shaped containers per hour. It operates with the same stationary squeegee and moving-screen idea.

Cylindrical Screens

There is a need for continuously repeating images on long rolls of such materials as wall-

Figure 15.21. Single-unit multicolor wet-on-wet screen printing press
Courtesy of Naz-Dar Company.

Figure 15.22. Automatic carousel printing system
Courtesy of Advance Process Supply Company, Chicago.

paper or bolt fabrics. A single flat screen stencil was traditionally used to meet this need. The stencil was carefully prepared so that the printer could step the image down the sheet. This method is still used with specially designed equipment, but it is a slow and costly process. Figure 15.20 shows a multicolor rotary screen printing press that is designed for continuous web printing. The stencil is carried by rigid screen mesh cylinders. Both the ink and squeegee ride inside the cylinders, which rotate as the line of material passes beneath them. With this approach a continuous multicolor image (up to sixteen colors with this model) can be placed on a roll of paper, plastic, or fabric at a rate of 240 feet a minute.

Carousel Units

A popular method of screening multicolor images, such as T-shirts, is **wet-on-wet printing** (figure 15.21). With this technique the individual pieces are mounted on **carousel carriers** that sequentially rotate under each different stencil color. The wet ink from the first color contacts the bottom of the second stencil, but because it touches in the same place each time, no blurring or loss of image detail occurs.

Registration is generally controlled with a pin system that accurately positions each screen stencil. Because the material is not moved until the entire printing cycle is complete, color fit should be perfect.

Some printers use automatic printing units with the carousel design (figure 15.22).

Key Terms

squeegee
on-contact printing
off-contact printing
carousel carriers
wet-on-wet printing
Shore Durometer
ink viscosity
screen mesh count

Questions for Review

1. Why is the chemical makeup of the squeegee blade important?
2. Why must the solvent for the ink be different from the solvent for the stencil base?
3. What is the difference between on-contact and off-contact screen printing?
4. Briefly describe the techniques that can be used to control accurate color fit when doing multicolor screening.
5. How do most screen printing inks dry?
6. What are the highlight and shadow reproducible dot sizes when screening halftone images?
7. How can a moiré pattern be prevented when mounting a stencil with a halftone image?
8. What is the advantage of a lever-action hand-operated screen press?
9. Briefly describe the operation of a semi-automatic screen press.
10. What is the advantage of a cylindrical screen?
11. What does the term *wet-on-wet printing* mean?

Chapter Sixteen

Hot Type Composition

Anecdote to Chapter Sixteen

The hot type composing room of a hundred years ago was a noisy, frantic place. The thundering rumble of the pressroom could be heard from the floor below as men and women ran from case to galley and back trying to meet production deadlines. The workday was long and tiring. The average workday was twelve hours, but during the industrial revolution few jobs were as desirable and more sought-after than that of printer. In the early etching of a typical work scene shown here, many different things are taking place.

The type cases are placed under the windows, where the light is best. The compositors are working quickly at their benches. Some are composing new forms. Others are distributing the type from jobs that have already been completed. When distribution is complete, another job will be set with the same type.

The center of the room is reserved for the stone tables. As compositors fill the composing stick, they move the contents to a metal galley (or tray) on the table and quickly return to the cases. When the entire job has been placed in the galley, it is locked in place so the individual pieces of type will not fall out and become printer's "pi."

The person with the large roller, to the right of the stone tables, is preparing to ink a completed form. Before the job is sent to the pressroom, a proof must be taken. The worker rolls a layer of ink onto the characters and then carefully places a thin sheet of paper over them. A variety of techniques could be used, but this fellow will probably rub the back of the paper with a *frotton* (a cloth bag stuffed with wool) and "pull a stone proof." The proof will be carefully checked by a skilled proofreader to ensure that the composition is perfect.

An early 1900s composition room

With all this running around, you would think that someone would have made the process simpler. After all, these people are using the same techniques that Gutenberg used, and that was three hundred years before this period. Many people did try to simplify the process. As early as 1682, Johann Joachim Becher patented a mechanism that duplicated hand composition by picking up cast characters and setting them in a stick. But the line still had to be justified by hand. In fact, the history of printing in the mid-1800s is a story of fantastic schemes and designs to automate the typesetting process. The author Samuel L. Clemens (Mark Twain) lost a fortune in developing and promoting a device called the Paige Compositor that unfortunately never paid off.

The first automatic typesetting equipment was still forty years away when this engraving was carved. New high-speed presses, however, were being developed and delivered. There was a tremendous need for vast quantities of type to keep the presses busy. All of it had to be set by hand.

Objectives for Chapter Fifteen

After completing this topic you will be able to:

- Identify foundry type and storage systems.
- Identify word-spacing and line-spacing material used in hot type composition.
- Explain the procedure for setting a line of foundry type.
- Explain the technique for centering a line of foundry type and for setting straight composition.
- Recall and recognize the two main types of hot type composition machines, including line-casting and character-casting.
- Describe the three main techniques of proofing hot type composition, including stone, galley, and reproduction proofs.

Introduction

Relief printing (printing from a raised surface) has long been one of the most important reproduction processes. Until recently, it accounted for almost all of the industrial printing done in the world. With the introduction of offset lithography, screen printing, and rotogravure, relief's share of the printing market declined, until today it accounts for only a small share of our industry. It is important, however, to understand the relief process. All of the terminology used by printers comes from the tradition of the relief press. There are also applications of relief printing in use today that cannot be accomplished by any other method.

Hot type composition is the preparation of any printing form used to transfer multiple images from a raised surface. **Cold type composition** is the preparation of any printing form that is intended to be reproduced photographically. The study of hot type composition is the basis for understanding all of relief printing.

Classifying Hot Type Composition

All hot type composition techniques can be classified into three broad groups:

- Hand-cut or block print composition,
- Hand-set foundry type composition,
- Machine type composition.

Contemporary block printing is basically an art process identical in technique to the methods used in China as early as AD 953. The traditional slab of fine-grained hardwood is often replaced with a piece of linoleum glued to a block of softwood. A design is drawn in reverse on the block surface, and special tools are used to cut away the nonimage areas. The remaining raised surface will readily accept a layer of ink, but the cutaway or sunken areas will remain clean. The process has little industrial application and will not be discussed further in this book.

Foundry type methods have changed little since the days of Johann Gutenberg. Individual characters are cast on separate bodies by type founders. The printer composes words and sentences by placing the appropriate symbols and spaces next to each other in a composing stick. Hot type foundry composition is discussed in detail in the following section.

Machine type composition is a refinement of the hand-set foundry type concept. Instead of individual pieces of raised type, matrices or dies are placed together to generate the words and sentences. Molten type metal is then forced into the matrices to form the raised printing surface. When the metal is solid, each matrix is returned to a storage system to be used again. Most machines use a keyboard (like a typewriter) to control the position of each matrix. After the type has been used, it may be melted and returned to the machine to be reused. Machine type composition is discussed in detail in the last half of this chapter.

Foundry Type

Identifying Foundry Type

To work with foundry type, it is necessary to be able to identify the significant parts of each cast character (figure 16.1). The actual printing surface is called the "face." The sides of the character are cast at an angle (called the "beard") for greater strength. The beard slopes down to the nonprinting shoulder and counter. The "feet" are planed perfectly parallel to the printing surface. The distance from the face to the feet is the "height to paper" or **type-high.** For most English-speaking countries, it is 0.918 inches. In Germany, France, and Spain, it is 0.928 inches. In Holland, it is 0.975 inches; and in Italy, 0.977. The variation is based on different definitions of the size of a point and makes international

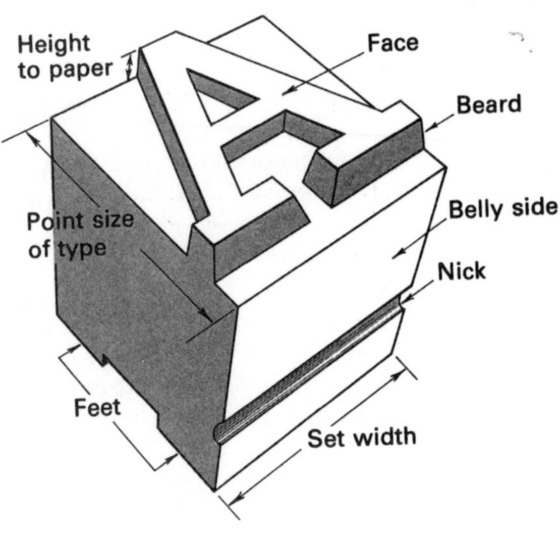

Figure 16.1. Example of a foundry type character Foundry type characters are cast on individual bodies.

Figure 16.2. Examples of dipthongs Dipthongs are a combination of two symbols into one graphic element, as are ligatures. Dipthongs differ from ligatures, however, in that they occur only in certain words, usually of Greek origin.

ﬂ ﬁ ﬀ

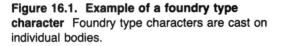

Figure 16.3. Examples of ligatures

exchange of foundry typefaces nearly impossible.

All characters in a single font (collection of type of the same style and size) have a nick cut in the same position on the type body. When setting a line of foundry type, it is easy to glance at the row of nicks. If one nick does not line up with all the rest, the printer knows it is probably a "wrong font" character. The nick side is often called the "belly side." The distance from the belly to the back side is the point size of the piece of type. Type size is defined by the point size of the body, not by the size of the character.

The distance across the nick or belly side of the type is an important measure called the **set width.** The letter *m*, for example, is a wider character than the letter *i*. Therefore, the set width of *m* is wider than that of *i*, or stated in another way, it is proportional to the size of the letter it is carrying. Most typewriters form "nonproportional" letters. It is possible to type the letter *m*, backspace, and type the letter *i* in the same visual space.

Special Characters

By using variations of the twenty-six letters of our Latin alphabet, many possible characters can be cast as foundry type to meet a special purpose. Gutenberg cast nearly two hundred and fifty different symbols to be used in his Bible. Some, such as "dipthongs" are no longer used; but others are still commonly found in every type storage case (figure 16.2).

A **ligature** is two or more connected letters on the same type body (figure 16.3). Ligatures are formed because of a visual or structural problem with some characters. The

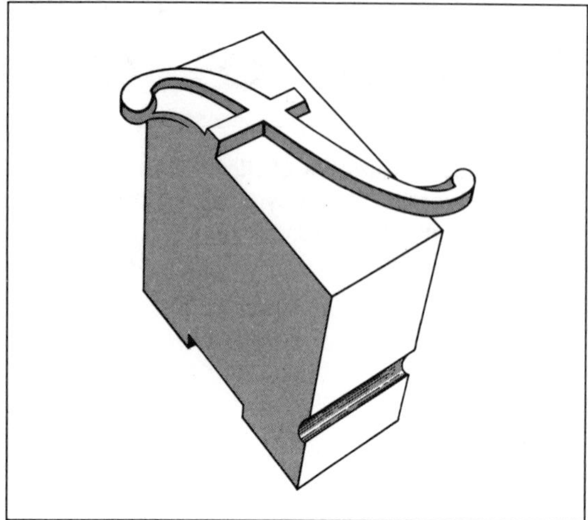

Figure 16.4. Example of a kerned letter

Figure 16.5. Example of a logotype

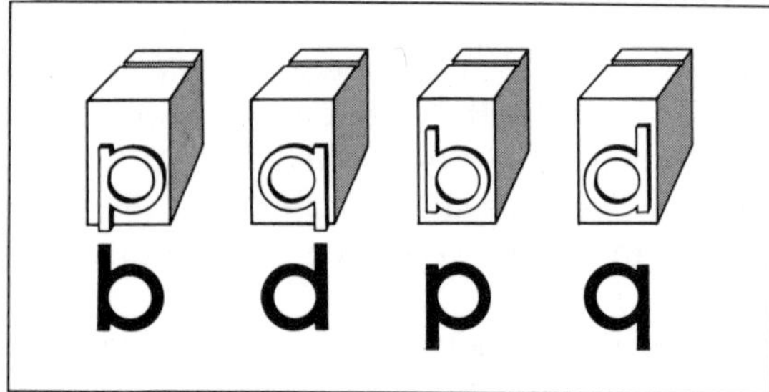

Figure 16.6. The demon letters

most common are *fi* and *fl* combinations. If these lowercase letters were set in a line as separate pieces of type, the visual space between the two would be too great because of their shape.

Whenever any portion of the printing face extends over the body of the type, the character is said to be **kerned** (figure 16.4). Kerns are very common in italic faces.

A **logotype** is two or more letters not connected but still cast on the same type body (figure 16.5). Logotypes are commonly found in situations where the same word or set of letters is to be frequently set in a job (such as a prefix, like "pre").

Novice printers often encounter problems with identifying a group of characters called **demon letters** (figure 16.6). Cast in reverse, the letters *p, d, q,* and *b* can be confusing because they are similar in structure. Foundry type is always set and read with the nick (belly side) up. With practice, visual accuracy can be gained if the pieces of type are always examined with the belly side up.

Type Storage Systems

The earliest relief printers stored identical characters in small compartments or bins. As the number of type styles grew, each font was stored in what was termed a "case."

A once-popular storage system was the **news case.** An entire font of letters was stored in two cases, capitals (or majuscules) in one and small letters (or minuscules) in another. The case with capitals was traditionally stored on a shelf directly over the case with small characters. When the master printer wanted a capital letter, he would call for a character from the "upper case." Our terms *upper-* and *lowercase* to indicate majuscule or minuscule date from the use of the news case.

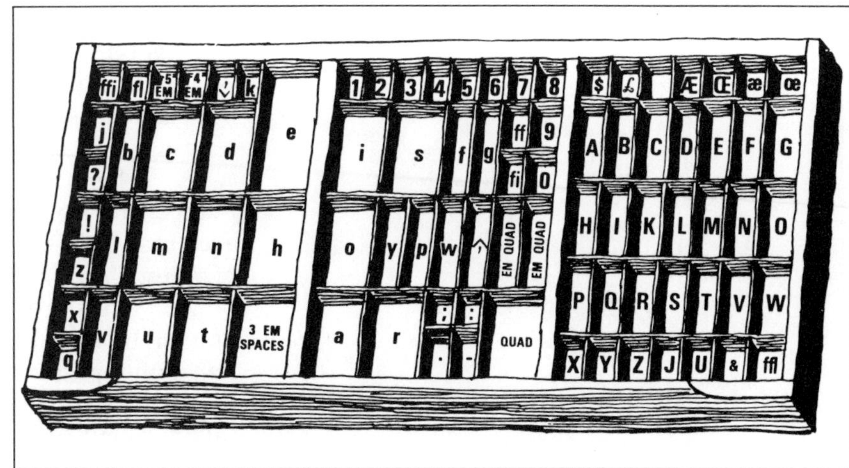

Figure 16.7. Example of a California job case
Courtesy of Mackenzie and Harris, Inc., San Francisco, Calif.

The most popular job case in use today is the **California job case** (figure 16.7). It is designed to hold one font of characters made up of upper- and lowercase letters, numerals, punctuation marks, ligatures, special symbols (such as $), and spacing material in a total of eighty-nine small boxes. The position of each symbol in the case is called the "lay" of the case. The capital letters are stored in the right-hand third of the case in alphabetical order, except for *U* and *J*, which were the most recent letters to enjoy wide use. Almost all other characters and spacing material are stored in the two left-hand sections. Lowercase letters are assigned positions and space in the case according to the frequency of their use.

Word-Spacing Material

The clear area of a printed page is often as important as the lines or symbols themselves. This is certainly the case with the use of spacing material between words. Without these open areas, the wordswouldblendtogether and our eyes would not receive visual cues that could be translated into meaning.

All hot type spacing material in a given font is of the same point size. Each space must match the point size of the type it is being used with and must be less than type-high (usually 0.800 inch or less) (figure 16.8).

Within any font size, then, is a collection of different pieces of spacing material. The basic unit of spacing material in each font is an **em quad,** sometimes called the "mutton quad." The size of the em quad depends on the point size of the font it is from. For example, an em quad from a 12-point font of type would be less than type-high and would measure 12 points by 12 points on the face; an 18-point font would contain em quads that are 18 points in each dimension on the face (figure 16.9).

All other spacing material in a font is based on the size of the em quad. Two **en quads,** or "nut quads," placed together equal the dimension of one em quad. For example, if the font size is 12 points, the en quad will measure 6 points by 12 points on the face. A

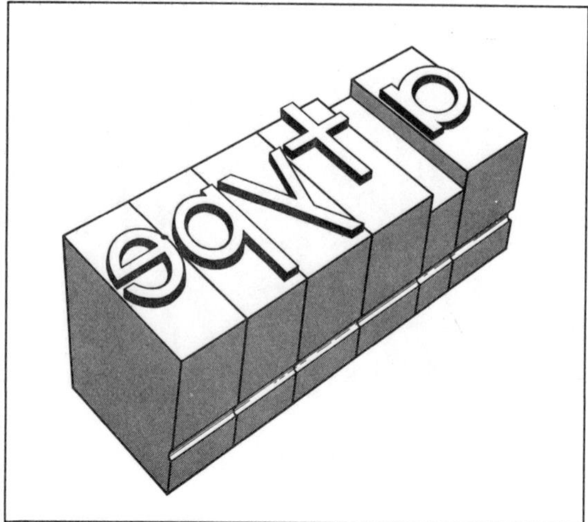

Figure 16.8. Example showing spacing material between words Spacing material used between words must match the point size of the type and be less than the height of the type.

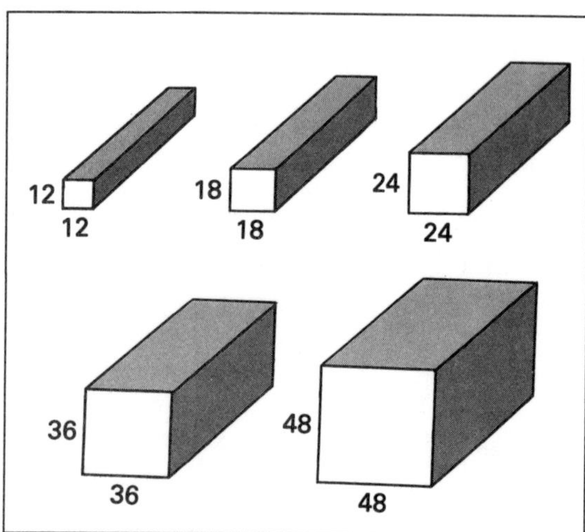

Figure 16.9. Examples of em quads The em, or mutton, quad is the basic word-spacing unit in each font.

3-em space (abbreviated from "three to the em") is one-third of an em. If the font is 18 points, the face of a 3-em space will measure 6 by 18 points. A 4-em space is one-fourth of an em. If the space is from a 24-point font of type, a 4-em space will measure 6 by 24 points. The smallest space typically found in a job case is the 5-em space, which is one-fifth of an em. If the font size is 30 points, the face of the 5-em space will measure 6 points by 30 points. In actual production, however, the size of the spacing material is usually rounded to the nearest half or quarter point (these are called "point-set" spaces). For example, a 3-em space from a 10-point font would in theory be 3⅓ (ten divided by 3) points wide, but it is cast to 3½ points.

Some spaces, such as the 2-em quad or the 3-em quad, are larger than the em quad. The 2-em and 3-em quads for a 24-point font of type would measure 24 by 48 points and 24 by 72 points, respectively.

For most composition, the em quad is used to indent the first line of a paragraph, the en quad is used between sentences, and the 3-em space is placed between words (some compositors use a 3-em space between sentences because of the extra visual space after the periods). Combinations of all spacing material are used to adjust equal line lengths of type composition.

There is one more class of spacing material called thin spaces. The most common thicknesses of thin spaces are ½ point, generally made of copper, and 1 point, usually made of brass. Two-point thin spaces are often cut from line-spacing material (see the following section). Thin spaces are generally only used in intricate hand-set work when spacing between letters (called "letter spacing") and when adjusting line lengths of large type sizes.

Line-Spacing Material

In addition to spacing between words, the visual space between lines must be controlled with line-spacing material. Line-spacing material is less than type-high and is generally cut from long strips to the length of line being set. All line-spacing material is classed according to thickness. **Leads** are generally 2 points in thickness, but anything from 1 to 4 points is termed a *lead*. **Slugs** are typically 6 points thick, but any piece up to 24 points (2 picas) is still labeled a *slug*. Both leads and slugs are made from type metal. Any line-spacing material that is 24 points in thickness or larger is called **furniture.** Furniture is made from type metal, wood (generally oak), or an aluminum alloy.

Composing a Line of Type

Foundry type characters are placed in a **composing stick** to form words and sentences. The most common composing sticks have slots that seat an adjustable knee to exact pica or half-pica positions. Type is always set with the right hand whereas the stick is held in the left (figure 16.10).

Begin by adjusting the knee to the desired line length and place a piece of line-spacing material in the stick. The first character of the first word is always seated against the knee of the composing stick, nick up. All other characters and spaces are set in order after this first character. The thumb of your left hand applies pressure against the last character set to keep the line from falling out of the stick.

When all characters have been set, it is necessary to fill out the remaining gap at the end of the line. The line must be held snugly in place within the preset line length. This is accomplished by filling the gap with spacing material. If the gap is large, begin with em quads or 2-ems until only a small space is left. Then select combinations of spacing to fill out the line perfectly. Ideally, the last space will slide in place with only slight resistance, and the entire composing stick can be turned upside down without the line falling out. This process of making the line tight in the stick is called **quading out.** To set another line of type, insert a piece of line-spacing material and repeat the techniques used for the first line.

Centering a Line of Type

The printer frequently wants to reproduce a series of centered lines, one over the other (figure 16.11). To do this, set the entire first line in the stick against the knee. Begin to quad the line out by placing equal amounts of spacing material on each side of the line. Adjust the spacing material so that the amount of spacing material on both sides of the line is the same. Insert a lead or slug and set the second line against the knee of the stick. Continue the process of balancing the spacing material on each side of the line.

Straight Composition

Straight composition or **justification** is the process of setting type so that both the left and the right margins form a straight line (figure 16.12). Almost all newspapers, magazines, and books are set by using straight composition. It is generally a more efficiently read design because it enables the eye to read predictable line lengths in short rapid glances. Hand setting justified copy is a slow process when compared with machine composition,

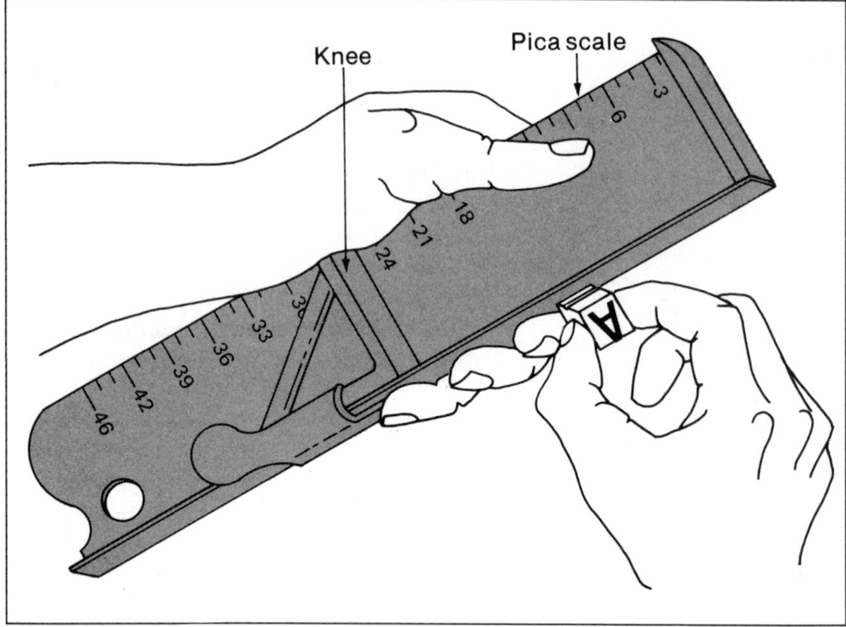

Figure 16.10. Example of a composing stick
When using a composing stick, hold the stick in your left hand and place the first character, nick up, against the knee. Always compose from left to right.

but both methods are based on nearly the same concepts. Hand-set straight composition involves setting each line of type against the knee of the composing stick, determining the amount of space left at the end of the line, and then dividing this space equally between the words in the line. Spacing material from the case is inserted between words in the line so that the words are separated from each other by a nearly equal amount and the line is tight in the composing stick.

The idea of totaling all spacing area and dividing it evenly between words is the concept underlying all mechanical or optical methods of straight composition.

Storing the Form

The process of composition creates what printers call a form. A **form** is the grouping of symbols and spaces that makes up a job or complete segment of a job (such as one page set to be printed in a book). There are three kinds of forms: live, dead, and standing.

A **live form** is any form that is waiting to be printed. All composition has been done, has been proofed and checked, and is ready to go to press.

A **dead form** has been printed and is waiting to be remelted or distributed (if hot type). It is generally held until the printed product has been shipped to the customer and approved or the bill has been paid.

A **standing form** is one that is never destroyed, melted, or distributed. Perhaps the printer has a standing order for the job or knows the job will be printed again at some time in the future. Instead of recomposing the form before each printing, the printer merely stores it until the next time.

Foundry typeforms are tied with string and stored in type trays called **galleys.** To tie

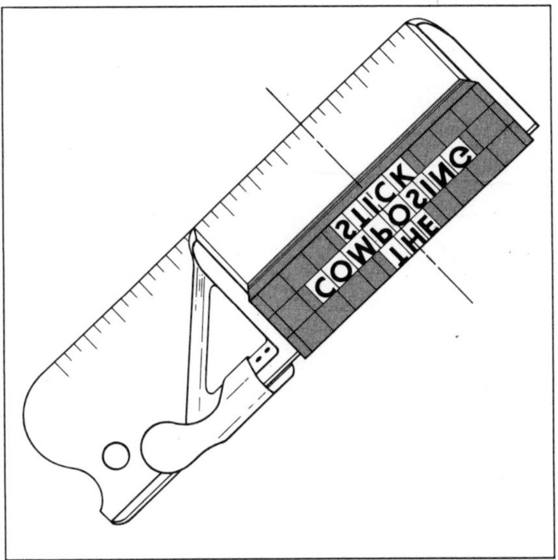

Figure 16.11. Example of type centered on a composing stick Centered lines are set in the composing stick by putting equal amounts of spacing material on each side of the type.

a form, cut a length of string long enough to go around the form several times. Begin along an edge with line-spacing material and wrap the string clockwise around the form. Pull firmly after the first several rotations. Never tie a knot. With a lead or the end of a rule, push a loose part of the string through the windings of the string against the form. To untie the form, merely pull the loose end of the string.

It is best never to lift a form of foundry type. Slide the form from the composing stick into the galley to be stored. Remove it from the galley in the same manner by sliding it into the stick or onto a table.

Many more topics could be discussed in the area of foundry type composition. The function of this section, however, has been to deal with only the most fundamental con-

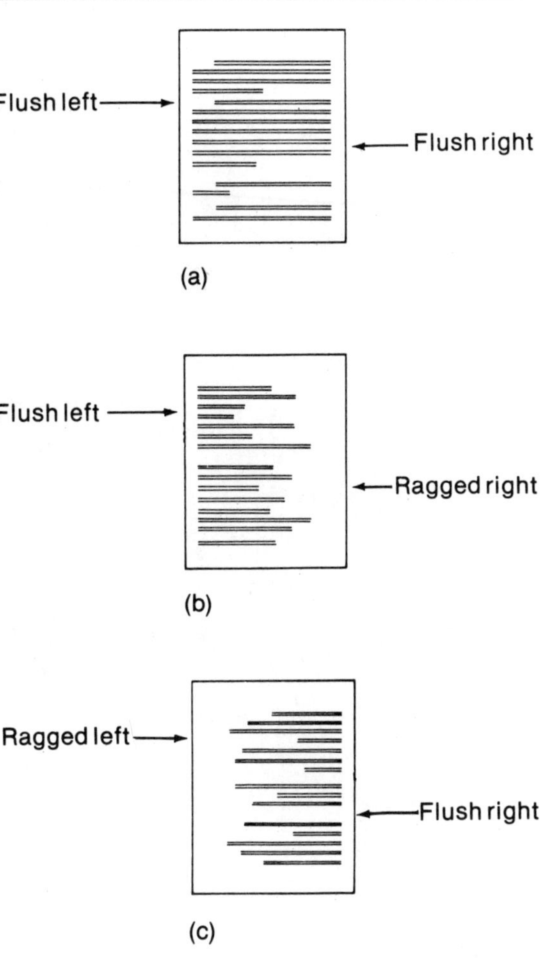

Figure 16.12. Examples of three styles of composition In straight composition the left and right margins are both justified; that is, set flush left and flush right (a). In (b) the left margin is justified, and the right margin is ragged. In (c) the left margin is ragged, and the right margin is justified.

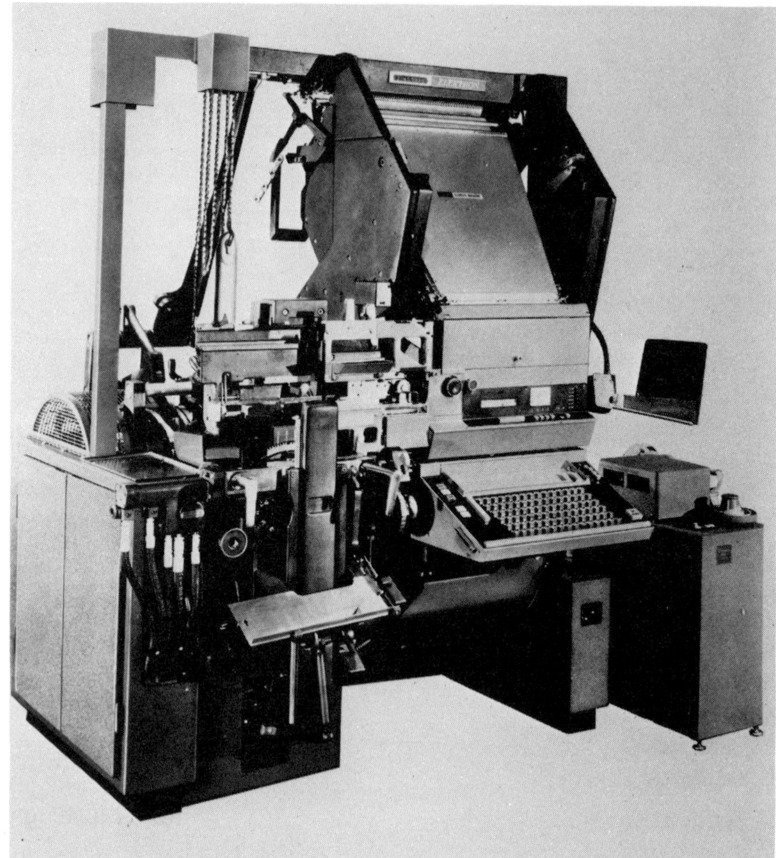

Figure 16.13. A modern Linotype machine
Courtesy of Mergenthaler Linotype Company.

cepts of hand-set procedures. Many people feel that no other process matches the image quality of foundry type. There is certainly a feeling of accomplishment as words grow heavy in the printer's hand—a feeling that can be found with no other process. However, the era of hand-set type as a standard of quality for the industry is past. It is easy to condemn change. Perhaps the block printers in 1450 saw movable type as a gimmick that sacrificed quality for the sake of speed. Printing technology has simply evolved new and faster methods.

Machine Composition

It probably wasn't long after the pages of Gutenberg's first Bible were dry that printers began thinking of ways to improve the speed of hand-set composition. Many ideas were tried even to the point of suspending a composing stick around the printer's neck so type could be set with both hands.

On July 3, 1886, the first truly automatic typesetting machine was demonstrated in the composing room of the *New York Tribune*. The device was designed by Ottmar Mergenthaler. His invention, the Linotype machine, has been called one of the ten greatest in the history of the human race (figure 16.13).

Line-Casting Machines

The success of the Linotype and later the Intertype is based on the concept of a recirculating matrix that is continually reused in the machine. The Linotype performs the following four basic operations with the matrices:

1. Matrices and spacebands are activated by keyboard control;
2. The line is justified;
3. The slug is cast;
4. Each matrix and spaceband is returned to its storage position.

The Linotype keyboard is made up of ninety keys, divided equally into three groups containing uppercase, lowercase, and special purpose characters. Each key controls one storage container for a particular matrix in the overhead magazine. When a key is depressed, a cam is activated that causes a matrix to be released and carried along a moving belt to be dropped into position on an assembler stick. A special wedge-shaped spaceband is dropped into position between all the words.

As the operator works at the keyboard, it is possible to view the physical length of each line being set as the matrices fill the assembler stick. Every matrix carries at least two faces. The operator can adjust the height of the matrix as it sits in the assembler stick and can therefore control which face is to be cast. When the physical limits of the preset line length are reached, the machine can be activated to removed the group of matrices and cast the slug body.

When the operator presses the proper lever, the group of matrices is automatically taken over by the machine. The line is first raised and passed along an intermediate channel to an elevator mechanism directly over the casting device where it is lowered into casting position. Vise jaws close to a preadjusted line length, and a justification block rises against the space bands, which expand to fill out the line.

The line of matrices is then positioned over the mold and is sealed into position. A plunger is activated, and the line is cast. The metal solidifies rapidly, and the matrices are almost instantly moved out of position. Special knives trim the slug to a preadjusted point size—line-spacing material is built onto the slug—and it is dropped into a receiving bin next to the operator.

An arm then swings into position to lift the line of matrices upward to the distributor box to be returned to the magazine. The spacebands are left behind and are automatically moved back into their storage position. The matrices are moved along a rail directly over the magazine. Each matrix has a different set of notches, called distributor teeth, that cause it to be dropped back into the keyed container that matches the notches.

As all this machine action is taking place, the operator can continue to activate matrices and spacebands, set additional lines, and repeat the entire operation. (See figure 16.14 for a diagram of the assembling mechanism of the Linotype machine.)

The Linotype can be, and probably has been, set up to do nearly every typesetting function in almost every language. It has a size limit of around 30-point characters, can hold as many as four different magazines, and is limited in speed only by the operator and the pull of gravity that returns each matrix to the proper magazine container.

A second contemporary line-casting machine (although not completely automatic) is the Ludlow, named after its inventor, Washington I. Ludlow (figure 16.15). The device was designed around 1888 and can cast type from 8- through 144-point characters from hand-set matrices. The line is set in a special stick from job cases similar in design to the California job case, although there are fewer matrices than there would be type. Spacing is adjusted by blanks. Centering is automatically adjusted by the stick. The assembled line is placed in the casting machine, and casting is automatic.

There are several advantages to the Ludlow system. It can cast an unlimited number of lines in sizes that would be too expensive in foundry type and impossible on the Linotype. The operator can cast varying sizes of display type on the same slug body, and duplicate lines can be cast from the same group of matrices. The process is faster than setting foundry type because of the matrix design, and italic characters can be formed without

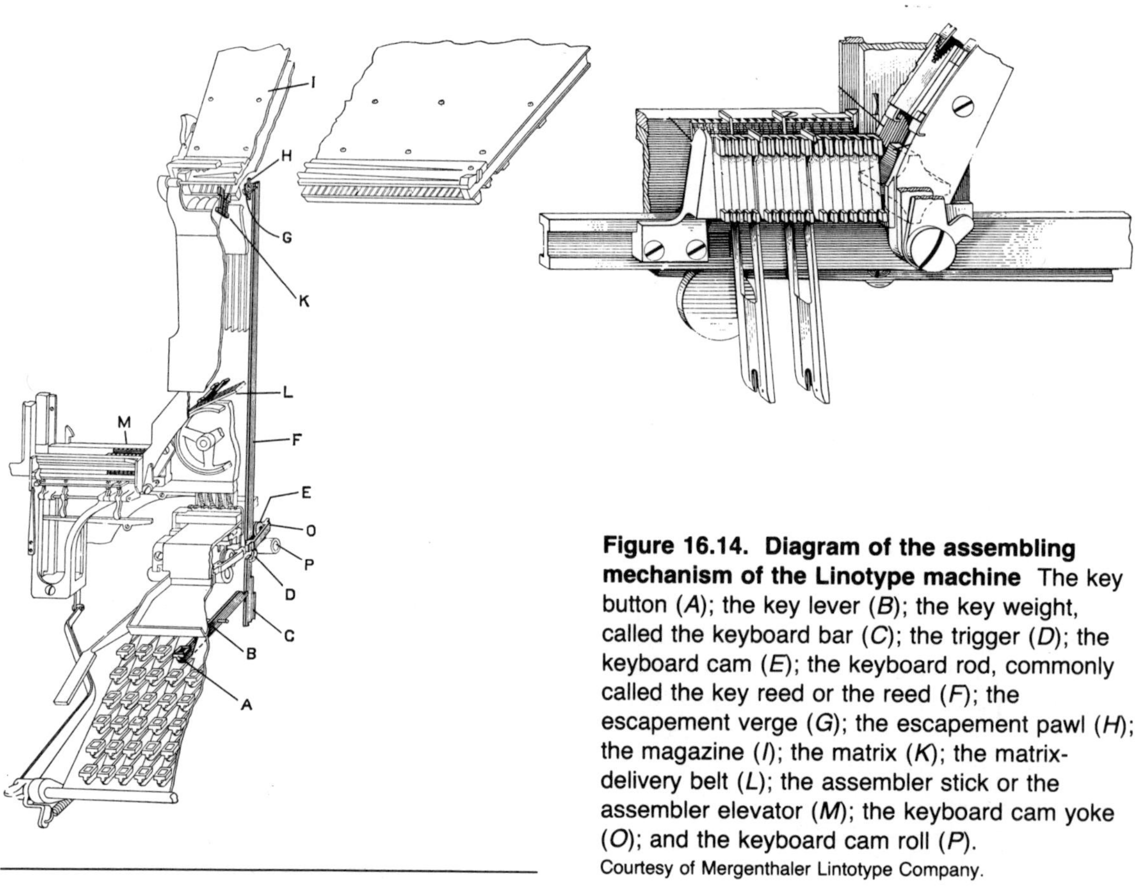

Figure 16.14. Diagram of the assembling mechanism of the Linotype machine The key button (*A*); the key lever (*B*); the key weight, called the keyboard bar (*C*); the trigger (*D*); the keyboard cam (*E*); the keyboard rod, commonly called the key reed or the reed (*F*); the escapement verge (*G*); the escapement pawl (*H*); the magazine (*I*); the matrix (*K*); the matrix-delivery belt (*L*); the assembler stick or the assembler elevator (*M*); the keyboard cam yoke (*O*); and the keyboard cam roll (*P*).
Courtesy of Mergenthaler Lintotype Company.

Figure 16.15. A Ludlow line-casting machine
Courtesy of Ludlow Typograph Co.

concern for the structure of fragile kerned letters.

Character-Casting Machines

The Monotype system was designed by Tolbert Lanston in 1889 to cast and assemble individual pieces of hot type in a line. The system is made up of two machines: a keyboard device that punches holes into a long paper tape and a casting mechanism that casts type automatically from the information on the tape (figure 16.16).

The arrangement of characters on the Monotype keyboard is similar to that of a standard typewriter. As the operator types, holes that are coded to each symbol are punched into a paper tape, and the width of each letter is recorded on a special justifying scale. The set width of letters is proportional to the size of the symbol. Specific dimensions are in units equal to one-eighteenth of an em quad. A bell rings when the end of the line has been reached, and the operator reads the total combined width of all letters. A scale then indicates the size of quading necessary to justify the line, and that information is added to the tape.

The perforated paper tape, or controlling ribbon, is then fed into the casting mechanism backward so the size of quading for each line is read into the machine first. The actual casting of each piece of type is done from a matrix held in a matrix case (figure 16.17). The holes in the controlling ribbon direct the proper character to come into line with the mold, and the symbol is cast. The metal is then cooled by water and is pushed into a galley until the entire line has been cast.

The matrix case holds 255 matrices and is usually set up to cast as many as three different faces. Character sizes up to 36 points and line lengths to 60 picas (90 picas with a special attachment) can be cast on the same machine. For small faces, up to 150 characters per minute can be formed. Because of the

Figure 16.16. A Monotype caster This machine reads the paper tape punched on the keyboard machine and casts individual characters.
Courtesy of The Monotype Corporation, Ltd.

machine's speed and versatility, several keyboards can be constantly functioning to feed a single caster.

The Monotype system is ideal for tabular work because corrections can be made by hand by changing a single character instead of recasting an entire line. The machine is also ideal for forming non-Latin symbols because the matrix case can hold more than twice as many matrices as the Linotype magazine can. The paper tape can be stored and reused at any time. Some Monotype models can be set up to do strip casting of lead and slug materials or even decorative borders. As in the Linotype, dead forms are returned to the melting pot.

The idea of a paper control tape led to the formation of the "Teletypesetter" (TTS). The TTS is a system in which an operator in a news center (such as New York City) encodes copy at a keyboard, and electrical impulses are sent across the country to be formed into paper tapes at receiving stations (such as small-town newspapers). The locally punched tape can then be placed on a caster and the day's production of hot type rapidly produced.

Figure 16.17. Example of a matrix case for the Monotype machine
Courtesy of the Monotype Corporation, Ltd.

Proofing Techniques

Once set, hot type composition is difficult to read because the characters are cast in reverse. Monstrous errors, both humorous and tragic, have been printed and distributed simply because the printer and the customer did not carefully check the form. For example, the following item appeared in a city newspaper:

> *OSWEGO—The City Republican Committee honored State Sen. H. Douglas Barclay yesterday with a plague citing his 10 years of service to his district and the state.*

The inclusion or exclusion of an unplanned character can radically change meaning: a "plaque" is an honor; a "plague" is not.

A sample print of type composition is called a **proof.** Printers check for typesetting errors by "proofing," which means comparing composed copy to the rough or manuscript copy provided by the customer. Most companies employ proofreaders to proof copy for errors. Over the past century a collection of special proofreader's marks or notes have been developed to communicate to the printer what corrections to make on the proof (figure 16.18). There are three kinds of proofs: stone, galley, and reproduction.

Stone Proofs

Stone proofs are images transferred from the form without the use of a machine. An ink brayer is rolled over the form, a sheet of paper is then positioned on the form, and a "planer block" (see "Typical Lock-up Procedures," chapter 17) is placed over the paper (figure 16.19). The block is then given a sharp rap, and ink is transferred to the paper sheet. A stone proof is a simple way to check page position (called imposition) when many forms are to be printed on a single sheet of paper and then folded as a signature in a book. However, the quality of stone proofs is generally poor.

Galley Proofs

A **galley proof** is "pulled" on a device called a galley proof press. The name comes from

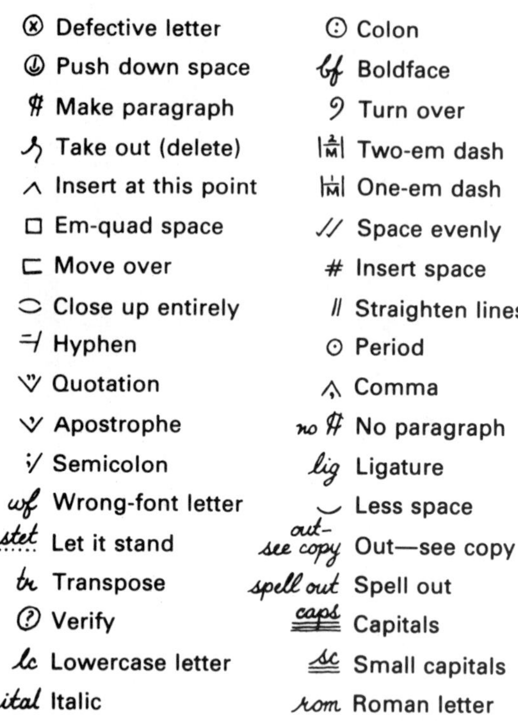

Figure 16.18. Examples of commonly used proofreader's marks Proofreader's marks are used to indicate on proof sheets corrections that must be made in type.

the fact that the distance from the bed of the press to the roller that passes over the form is type-high plus the thickness of the metal base of a printer's galley. The gauge of a composing stick base matches the thickness of a galley (0.050 inch).

The press is designed so that during composition the printer merely places the stick or a galley filled with forms on the bed, inks the type with a brayer, sets the paper on the form, and pulls the roller over the paper. Galley proofs are typically delivered to the

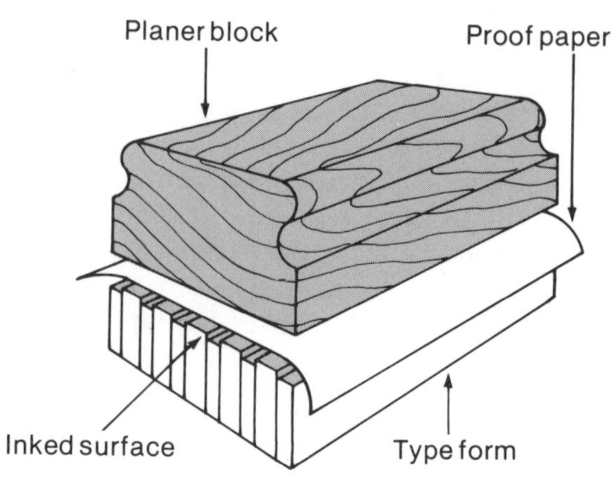

Figure 16.19. Diagram showing a stone proof set-up A planer block is used to tap paper against an inked typeform to produce a stone proof.

printing customer before the job goes to press. Many galley presses have a large piece of sheet metal that can be placed over the bed so that logotypes, or large pieces of display type, can be proofed without the use of a composing stick or galley.

Reproduction Proofs

Reproduction proofs are high-quality camera-ready proofs of hot type composition for cold type image assembly. They are made on a reproduction proof press (figure 16.20). There are primarily three considerations when pulling a reproduction proof: A precision press, quality type forms, and a good ink and paper combination.

In actual press operation, the type form is placed on the bed of the press (without a galley or composing stick) and is locked in

Figure 16.20. A reproduction proof press
Courtesy of Vandersons Corporation, Chicago.

place by a sliding hold bar. A moving cylinder can be rolled over the form, followed by a set of ink rollers. The cylinder is normally raised above the type form so that the power-driven ink rollers can place a uniform layer of ink over the type. When the form has been properly inked, the paper is attached to the printing cylinder. Most reproduction proof presses are equipped with cylinder grippers that hold the paper securely in place. A lever is tripped to lower the cylinder to type-high, and the paper is rolled over the form. At the end of the cycle, the paper is released and the cylinder is raised above the form and returned to the starting position.

As with all processes, the product will only be as good as the materials that form it. Because they are designed to be photographed, reproduction proofs must be pulled from perfect pieces of type. Many companies reserve special fonts of foundry type to be used exclusively for "repro" proofs. Others use only Linotype composition and return the forms to the melting pot immediately after a good proof has been pulled.

Reproduction proofs should be pulled on paper designed to receive this special image. It is best to use a coated, dull, or satin finish paper rather than a sheet with a high-gloss surface. An uncoated stock is not acceptable because the ink has a tendency to spread or "bleed" as it is absorbed by the paper fibers. It is desirable to use an ink that will dry rapidly on the sheet (in less than one minute). Most inks should not be allowed to remain on the press overnight because lint and dust will settle on the rollers and be transferred to the proof.

Some processes require reproduction proofs on clear, transparent acetate sheets. The concerns are the same as for normal reproduction proofs, except that a layer of lampblack is often dusted over the sheet immediately after it leaves the press. The loose powder adheres to the moist ink to form images of maximum density. Some presses are also designed with a system that will pull acetate proofs on both sides of the sheet—one side is printed directly from the type form, the other from an offset rubber blanket.

Key Terms

type-high
set width
ligature
logotype
demon letters
news case
California job case
em quad
en quad
lead
slug
furniture
composing stick
quading out
justification
form
galley
proof

Questions for Review

1. What are the three main hot type composition techniques?
2. What dimensions of a piece of foundry type define set width and point size?
3. What is a ligature?
4. Why is the lowercase *e* assigned the largest area in a California job case?
5. What are the dimensions (not height) of an en quad in a 12-point font of foundry type?
6. What are the two common line-spacing materials?
7. What is the difference between quading out and straight composition (or justification) when setting foundry type in a composing stick?
8. What is the difference between a line-casting and a character-casting hot type composition machine?
9. What is the difference between a stone proof, a galley proof, and a reproduction proof?

Chapter Seventeen

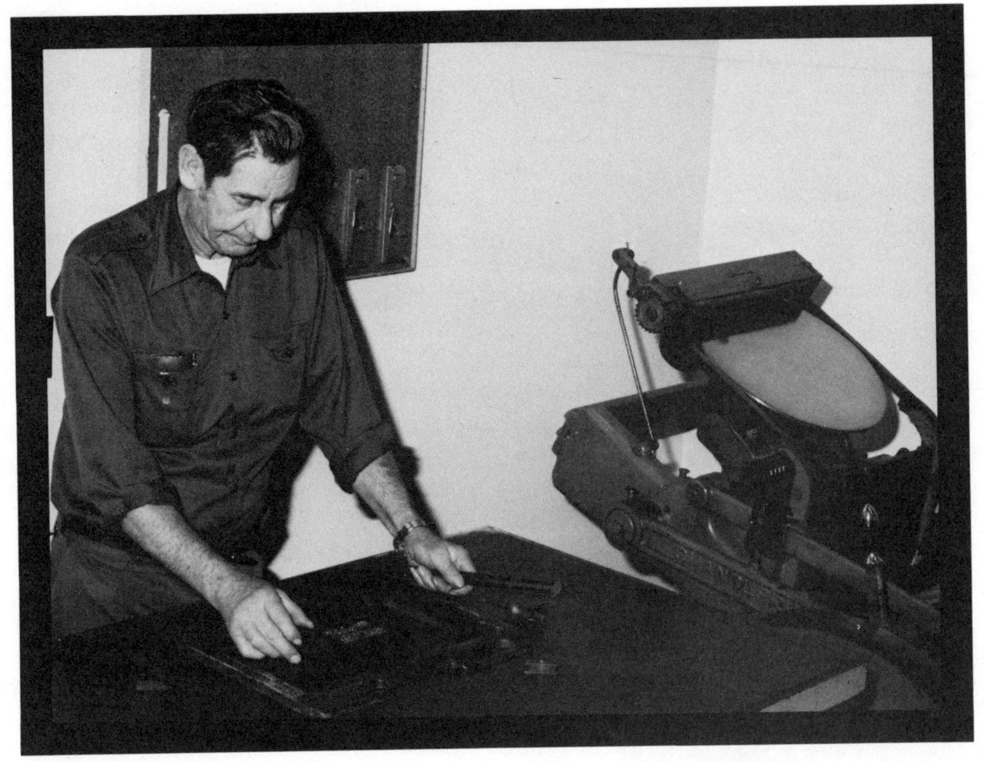

Relief Printing Plates

Anecdote to Chapter Seventeen

It is possible to trace the origins of relief composition to the use of seals to "sign" official documents as early as 255 BC, during the Han dynasty in China. A ceramic relief stamp was pressed into a sheet of moist clay. When dry, the imprint served as a means of certifying the authenticity of the document. When paper was invented, around AD 105, the transition to the use of the seal with ink was a natural one.

An early Chinese press The press was a low, flat table solid enough to hold the form in place.
The Bettman Archives

Early documents and manuscripts were copied and recopied by hand. Frequent copying mistakes were made from one edition to the next; copies often differ significantly from the author's original. Around AD 175, the Chinese began the practice of cutting the writings of important scholars into stone. The stones were placed in centers of learning, and students made "rubbings," or copies on paper from the carvings. The process was faster than hand copying, and all editions were identical to the first.

No one knows when the ideas of the seal and stone rubbings came together, but in China in AD 953, under the administration of Fêng Tao, a large-scale block-printing operation was begun to reproduce the Confucian classics. Block prints were generally slabs of a hard fine-grained wood that were carved to leave a well-defined raised image. The raised portions were inked, paper was laid over the block, and a pad was rubbed across the surface to transfer the ink to the paper.

During the Sung dynasty, around AD 1401, a common man named Pi Shêng invented movable type. Building on the ideas of block printing, he cut individual characters in small pieces of clay. The clay was fired to make it hard, and individual pieces were placed in an iron frame to create the printing form. Because the pieces did not fit together perfectly, they were embedded in a mixture of hot pine resin, wax, and paper ashes. When cold, all the pieces were held together perfectly tight, and the form was inked and printed. Reheating the resin mixture loosened the pieces of type so they could be reused.

Other materials, including wood, tin, copper, and bronze, were used for the same purpose. The idea of movable type traveled to neighboring countries. In Korea, in AD 1403, King T'aijong ordered that everything without exception within his reach should be printed in order to pass on the tradition of what the works contained. Three hundred thousand pieces of bronze type were cast, and printing began. It is interesting to speculate on the relationship between this event and a similar one that took place not more than fifty years later in northern Germany, which brought Gutenberg the title of "father of printing."

Objectives for Chapter Seventeen

After completing this chapter, you will be able to:

- Discuss the purposes of a primary relief plate.
- List and describe three types of primary relief plates.
- Explain the difference between a duplicate and a primary relief plate.
- List and describe three types of duplicate plates.
- Select and identify the necessary materials to lock up a relief form.
- Outline the procedure to lock up a simple relief form.

Introduction

The basic ideas of hot type composition were introduced in chapter 16. The tradition of hot type is the foundation for nearly all modern printing processes.

Chapter 4 introduced the ideas of cold type composition, which are based on the use of photography to manipulate and record images. It is important to realize that cold type composition methods can be used to prepare relief printing plates as well as hot type. This chapter is concerned with the process of taking the finished forms—whether in hot or cold type—and preparing relief printing plates from them.

There are only two main categories of relief plates: primary and duplicate (or secondary). **Duplicate plates** are made from master forms that are not intended to be used as a printing surface. Copies or duplicates of the master are made for the actual printing operation. This method has several advantages. In extremely long runs, when a single plate would wear out long before the job is finished, duplicate plates are ideal. When one plate begins to show signs of wear, a fresh duplicate is made to replace the old plate, and the run continues. There are instances, especially in newspaper production, where the master form is prepared in one location and duplicate plates are shipped to many plants across the country. The Sunday comics section is a prime example.

Primary plates, on the other hand, can serve two functions. They can be forms that are prepared to be placed directly on the printing press or they can be forms that are intended to be used only as master plates from which duplicates are made. The procedures of preparing the relief plate to print are basically the same for both primary and duplicate plates. They will be discussed in the last section of this chapter.

Primary Relief Plates

The original relief typeform, which will be used as a primary plate, can be generated by a variety of techniques. They can be classified into the following three main methods:

- Manually prepared plates,
- Photomechanical plates,
- Mechanically engraved plates.

Manually Prepared Relief Plates

Manually prepared relief forms should already be familiar to the reader because they were discussed in chapter 16. The three manual techniques are hand carving, foundry type, and machine composition.

Photomechanical Relief Plates

The steps in preparing any type of photomechanical relief plate are basically the same. A sheet of smooth plate material is coated with a light-sensitive emulsion. A film negative is placed in contact with the dry emulsion, and the plate is exposed by a powerful light source. When the plate is to contact the receiver directly (as opposed to an offset image), the image must be reversed and a laterally reversed negative must be used. The light passes through the open or image areas in the negative, hardening the emulsion, but it does not reach the covered or nonimage areas. This unexposed emulsion is easily washed away in a developing step, leaving only the image areas covered with a hard protective coating. The bare, nonimage areas are removed by chemical action until the required difference in levels between image and nonimage areas has been reached. The protective emulsion is then removed by a special solvent, and the relief plate is ready for the press or for further processing, depending on its intended use.

Any variation in the processing steps of commercial photomechanical plates is due to differences in the plate material or chemical formulation of the light-sensitive emulsion. Although many companies sell their own unique product, nearly all photomechanical relief carriers can be identified as either photoengravings or photopolymers.

Photoengravings. **Photoengraving** describes the traditional process of etching away with acid the nonimage portions of a metal plate. Zinc, copper, and magnesium have all been used as base materials; but presensitized magnesium alloys are now most widely used. As with all photomechanical relief plates, the emulsion of a photoengraving is exposed through a film negative in some form of contact frame. The light hardens the emulsion in the image areas but does not affect the nonimage portions. After development, the image emulsion acts as a resist that prevents the removal of metal by the acid.

Removing the nonimage metal from a photoengraving is called a **bite.** This step is performed in a special tank that sprays a liquid acid bath onto the plate's surface. The **depth of cut** (the difference between the levels of the image and nonimage portions of the plate) is typically between 0.020 and 0.040 inches, depending on the intended use of the plate. Nontraditional materials, such as plastic, bitumen, gelatin, casein, or even bimetal formulations, have all been substituted for the plate metal; but the process remains basically the same.

Photopolymers. A new idea, however, is the photopolymer relief plate. **Photopolymer plates** are formed from the simple bonding of a hard, light-reactive polymer (plastic) to a film or metal base. There are many different kinds of polymers. The one used in photopolymer relief plates reacts by hardening when exposed to an intense ultraviolet light. By placing a film negative in contact with such a material and directing an intense ultraviolet light source through the film openings, the image areas are polymerized, or hardened, but the unexposed or nonimage areas are not. When a warm alkaline spray is directed over the entire plate in a developing device, the unpolymerized areas are washed away (figure 17.1). The plate is then dried and can be additionally hardened by a second ultraviolet exposure or can be prepared directly for use on a press.

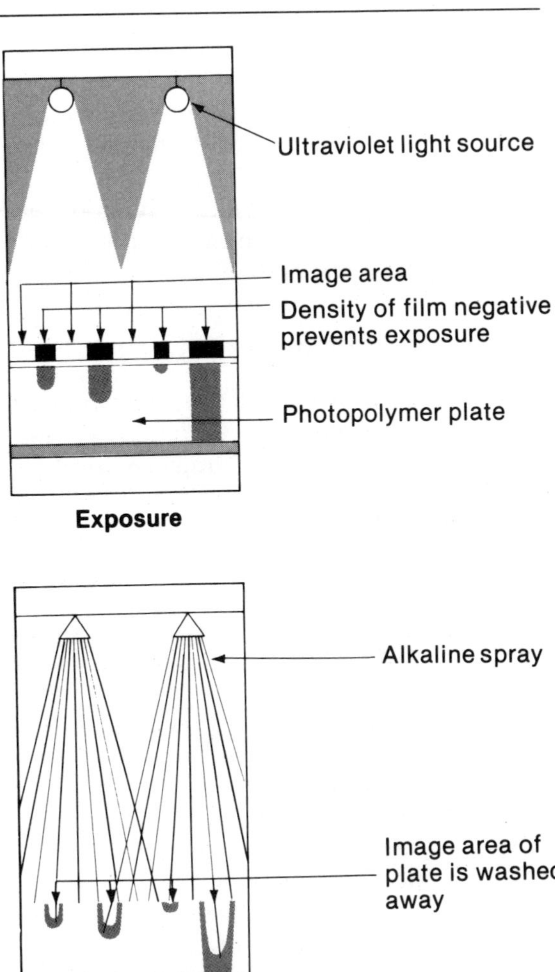

Figure 17.1. Diagram showing exposure and washout step for a photopolymer plate

Photoengravings and photopolymer relief plates can be mounted on blocks to raise them to "type-high"; they can be locked in a special "saddle" that clamps the plate in place on a press; or some materials (sometimes called "wrap-around plates") can be curved around a press cylinder (held in place by an adhesive or magnetism), thereby eliminating special preparation steps.

Mechanically Engraved Relief Plates

A third general method of preparing primary relief printing plates is by mechanical engraving (sometimes called **electromechanical engraving**). The process is relatively easy to understand, although the actual equipment is fairly sophisticated. Basically, the concept is similar to color separation by electronic scanning, discussed in chapter 9. A pulsating beam of light is directed at some cold type copy. Some devices have the copy mounted on a drum and rotate it past the light; others have a flat surface, and the light moves over the copy. A sensing unit receives the reflected light and converts it to electrical impulses. An amplifier intensifies those impulses, which results in mechanical motion by a special cutter head. The cutter action removes nonimage portions of a special form of plastic that is the plate material. Mechanical engraving represents an intermediate stage of relief plate development beyond foundry or machine composition.

Duplicate Relief Plates

Duplicate relief printing plates are made from master plates that are not necessarily intended to be used as an image carrier. Any primary plate (and some duplicate plates) can be used as a master, although some processes could damage plastic and photopolymer materials. It is possible to classify all duplicate plates into three types:

- Electrotypes,
- Stereotypes,
- Flexible molded plates.

Electrotypes

Electrotypes are considered the highest-quality duplicate relief plate, but they require a lengthy preparation process. There are many techniques, depending on the types of materials used. However, a general procedure can be examined.

The electrotyper begins with a master form that has been locked in position in a large metal frame (such as the lockup for a platen press shown in figure 17.19). The specific procedures for lockup are discussed later in this chapter. A mold is then made from the form by pouring or pressing a hot material against the form (figure 17.2). Wax and lead were once popular mold liquids, but both have been replaced by a special plastic material. When cool, the mold is carefully removed from the form. It is then a reversed, or intaglio, form (figure 17.3).

A thin layer of metallic silver is then sprayed over the mold surface. The silver is electrically conductive and makes the plastic ready for electroforming, the next step.

Electroforming is a process in which a thin layer of copper or nickel is deposited on the metallic silver by an electrochemical exchange. The copper or nickel and the mold are both lowered into a tank containing a plating bath called an "electrolyt" (figure 17.4). The mold is connected to the negative end of an electrical circuit (called the cathode), and

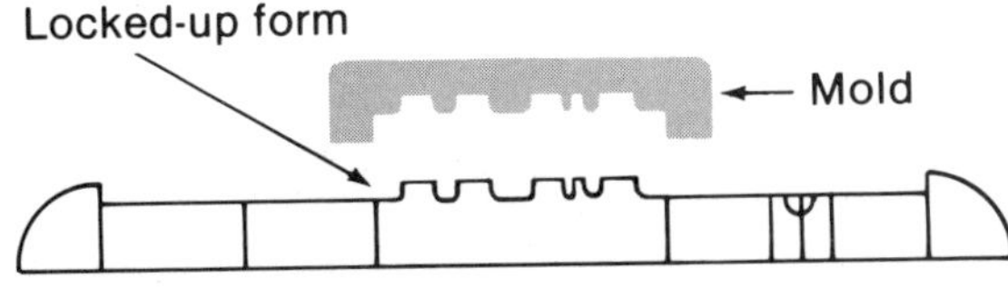

Figure 17.2. Making a mold from a locked-up form

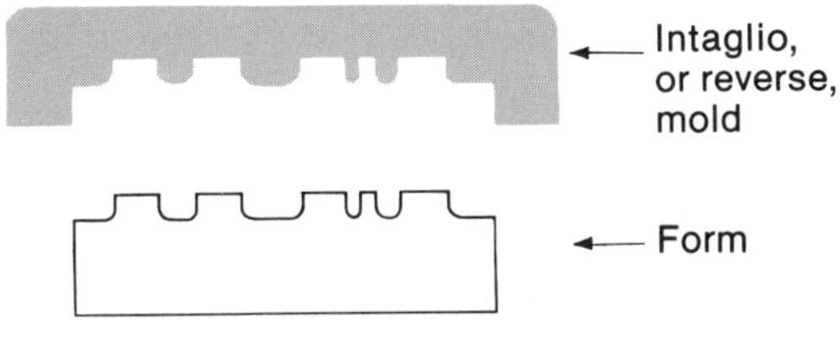

Figure 17.3. Diagram of a mold and a form
The mold made by pouring a hot plastic material onto the master form is the reverse shape of the original form.

the plating metal is attached to the positive end (called the anode). When an electrical current is passed through the circuit, the plate metal is electrodeposited on the metallic silver coating of the intaglio mold. In general, the longer the current is on, the thicker the deposit of plate material.

Several different metals are often deposited in one or more steps. For example, 0.0007 inch of nickel might be first transferred to the mold, followed by 0.010 inch of copper. A variety of metals and metal alloys can be used as the plating material to obtain different press characteristics. For example, chromium is a metal that gives extremely long press runs.

When the desired thickness of deposit has been reached, the mold is removed from the plating tank, dried, and separated from the plate metal, which is now an exact duplicate of the master plate. The electroformed duplicate shell, however, is fragile and could not be used on a printing press. To provide the necessary stability, the shell must be backed with some sort of support material. The most common procedure is to cast a layer of electrotype metal to the back of the duplicate (figure 17.5). The finishing process involves straightening, shaving away unwanted metal (with a "router"), or even building up weak areas after the piece is cold.

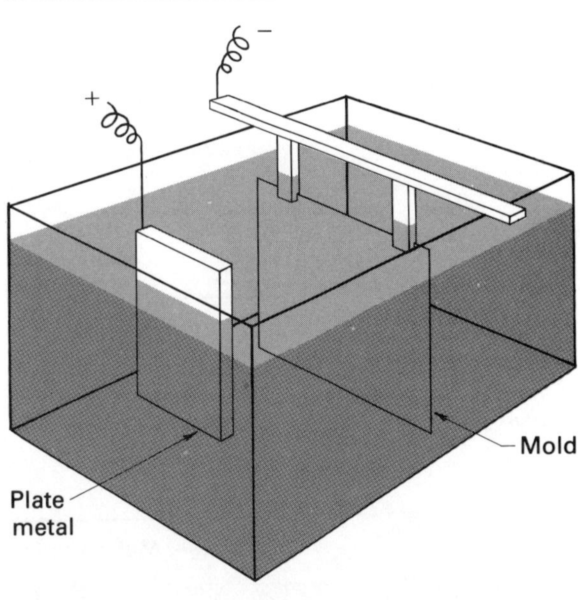

Figure 17.4. Diagram of an electroforming plating tank

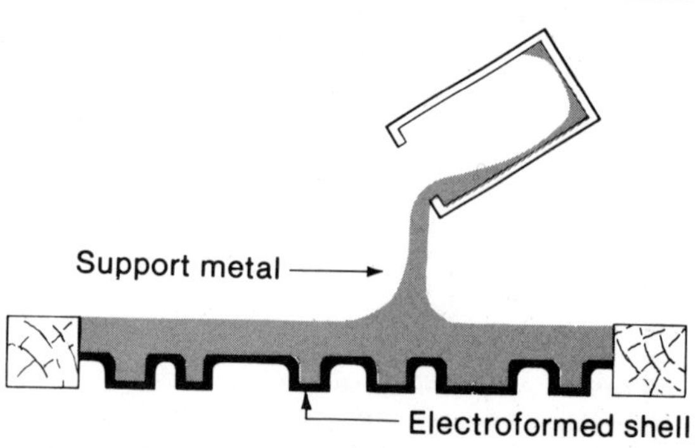

Figure 17.5. Diagram of an electroformed shell backed with support metal

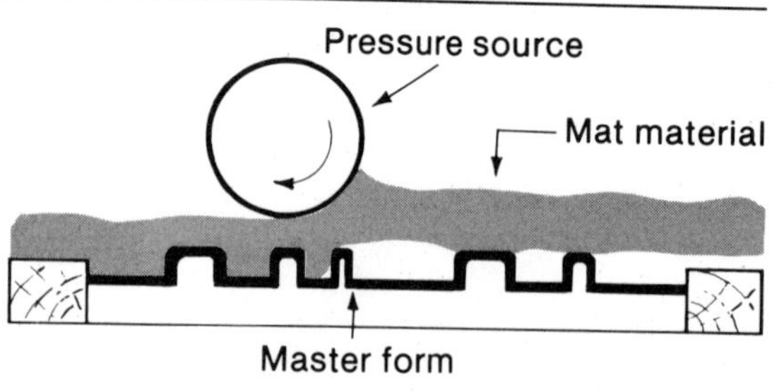

Figure 17.6. Making a stereotype mat Stereotype mat material is forced into the sunken areas of the master form. The resulting mat is a reverse copy of the original form.

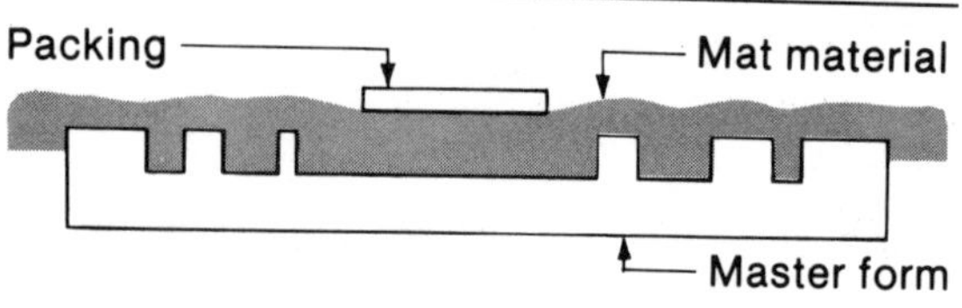

Figure 17.7. Reinforcing the mat Pieces of packing are glued to the back of the mat in the large open areas that could easily collapse during the casting step.

Electrotypes can be mounted on type-high material for use in a flat format, can be curved for use on rotary presses, or can be used as master plates from which other duplicates can be made.

Stereotypes

Stereotyping is a very old process used to produce duplicate, cast-formed, metal relief plates. Its widest use is in relief newspaper production, although it does find other applications in some commercial job shops.

As with electrotyping, the process begins with a master form that has been locked into position in a large metal frame. The first step is to prepare an intaglio, or reversed, copy of the master, called a **mat.** Mat material is specially prepared layers of extremely soft and flexible paper wood pulp. Several different techniques can be used, but it is basically a process of applying pressure to force the mat into the sunken areas of the form (figure 17.6). The mat can be removed from the master at this point or can remain in place until later in the process, depending on the materials and equipment being used.

There is some problem with large open areas, which could collapse during the casting operation. To reinforce these areas, pieces of packing are glued to the back of the mat (figure 17.7). New forms of mat material, called "packless," have been developed. But a certain amount of hand packing is almost always required.

After the mat has been packed, it is necessary to dry the sheet to remove excess moisture in the paper fiber. This step is called **scorching** and is extremely important because molten metal will be forced against the mat. Any drop of moisture could cause dramatic reactions—think what happens when a drop of water falls into a skillet of hot grease.

Scorching could present some problems because paper has a tendency to shrink as it dries. Some preshrunk materials are available that reduce the possibility of image distortion. Where such mats are not used, the amount of shrinkage is taken into consideration when preparing the form.

Stereotype mats can be cast either flat or curved, but the most popular format is for curved plates that can be used on rotary relief presses (see "Rotary Press," chapter 12). Some devices form a curved stereotype plate by means of vacuum pressure to draw the molten type metal against the mat image. Some casting mechanisms are designed to perform the scorching operation automatically as the mat is curved in preparation for casting.

Most curved stereotypes leave the caster ready for the press, although it is possible to perform some finishing operations (figure 17.8). The plate can be hand tooled to remove any unwanted image or can be nickel or chromium plated to improve the length of press run. Flat stereotypes can be cut into smaller components, can be hand tooled, can be plated, and can be mounted on blocks to raise them to type-high (0.918 inch).

Because of its several advantages over metal duplicate plates, the stereotype system has had continued popularity since as early as 1755. The paper mat is inexpensive and easy to use. The mat can generally be reused to form two or more duplicate plates from the same mold. Because of their light weight, the mats can be shipped economically to remote facilities. The design of stereotype equipment into a "system" approach also allows for nearly complete reuse of the plate metal. After a press run, it can be easily melted and returned to the casting machine. Stereotypes are generally used when less than the best quality image is necessary. Electrotypes are associated with extremely high-quality reproduction.

Figure 17.8. A cast stereotype plate

Flexible Molded Duplicate Relief Plates

Molded rubber or plastic relief plates are called "flexible plates" because they can be formed around almost any curved surface without distortion or damage. Flexible plates have been largely responsible for the growth of the process called **flexography,** which is used to print on nontraditional materials (such as thin sheet plastics) at high rates of speed. They are also used in indirect relief printing, and certain kinds can be used as plates for other duplicate plate-making processes.

The procedures for making a flexible molded plate can vary greatly, depending on

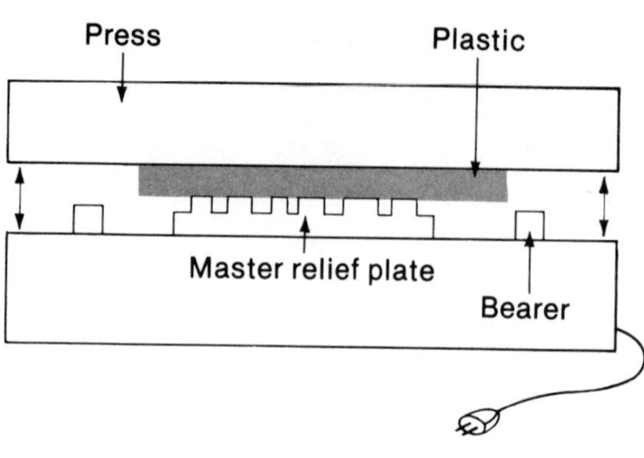

Figure 17.9. Preparation of a mold from a master plate The pressure of the press forces the heated plastic into the sunken areas of the mold until the type-high bearers have been reached.

the type of materials and the specific manufacturer's equipment and instructions. Here we will review the general techniques. All flexible duplicate relief plates are formed by the molding of a sheet of rubber or plastic, by both heat and pressure, into a mold that has been made from a master plate.

Most printers use a special hydraulic press to prepare the mold or intaglio matrix from the master plate. Efficient devices have been designed to control the temperature of the press surfaces that contact the mold and plate materials. A sheet of special plastic is placed over the face of a master relief plate in a press. Type-high bearers are then placed next to the plate to control the distance the press can be lowered and therefore gauge the proper thickness of the mold (figure 17.9). The press is then lowered into contact with the plastic, and heat is applied. As the temperature that causes the material to soften is reached, pressure is slowly increased until the bearers have been reached. The temperature is gradually raised, the matrix is allowed to harden, and it is finally taken from the press. When cool, the mold is carefully removed from the master plate and trimmed in preparation for the molding of the duplicate plate.

Both natural and synthetic rubber can be used to form flexible rubber plates. The choice is determined by the types of solvents used in the production situation. Rubber plates can be molded in the same press that was used to prepare the matrix. The intaglio mold is positioned on the bed of the press, the height stops are added, and a layer of uncured rubber is placed over the matrix. The press is lowered into contact with the rubber and is slowly heated. When the rubber is soft, the pressure is increased until the bearers have been reached. Continued application of pressure and heat will cause the rubber to conform to the outline of the matrix and also will cause the rubber to vulcanize, or harden (or "cure"). The mold is removed from the press, allowed to cool, and separated from the duplicate plate. Rubber is thermosetting material and cannot be reused. Plastic plates are formed in a like manner, with only a slightly more critical temperature range in the final stages.

The final step for any type of flexible molded plate is finishing. Any excess plate material (called flash) is trimmed away, and the thickness (or gauge) of the plate is checked. Plates that exceed the allowable thickness limits can be ground to meet the required tolerance. The plate must then be readied to be mounted on a press. Some manufacturers market a rubber plate that has been laminated to a magnetic layer that will easily attach to a steel press cylinder. Other methods are adhesion or special saddles that clamp the plate into place and fit into position on a cutout portion of the press cylinder.

The point of the detailed discussion on primary and duplicate relief plates was to classify the types of relief image carriers being used by today's printers. It is important to keep in mind that we can use either type as a vehicle for transferring an image. The only distinction is in the material and preparation steps.

Lockup for Relief Printing Plates

Lockup is the process of securely locking in place a relief plate in some type of clamping frame or holding system, commonly called a **chase.** Lockup can serve the following two functions:

- It can be used to hold a primary or master plate in position while a secondary or duplicate plate is prepared, as when making a stereotype matrix.
- It can be used to hold a primary or duplicate plate in the proper position on the press during the printing operation.

Chases are made in many forms, depending on their intended function. If the chase is to hold the plate in place on a press, it must be designed to fit into the bed of the press. If it is to be used to make an electrotype mold, the sides must be designed to contain the mold material.

The following sections examine one type of lockup, the traditional relief lockup procedures for use on a platen press. The procedures for any other, however, are similar.

The Materials of Lockup

Chases for presswork come in all sizes. The smallest is perhaps 6 by 9 inches, and some frames are as large as 6 feet square. Whatever the size, the requirements remain the same: the chase must be sturdy, must be designed to fit exactly the specific printing press to be used, and must lie perfectly flat on a smooth surface without wobbling.

The process of placing the relief form in the proper position within the chase so the images will be correctly placed on the final printed sheet is called "imposition." When more than several forms are to be printed on the same sheet (as in book production), the problem of page imposition can be very involved.

Lockup is done on a special table called an **imposing stone** or simply a stone table (figure 17.10). The name refers to early imposing tables that were made from polished granite. It is extremely important that the surface be perfectly flat. The granite was easily nicked, so it has been almost totally replaced by steel; but the original name remains.

Few relief plates are as large as the inside dimensions of the chase being used. Material called "furniture" (figure 17.11) is used to fill the unused portions. Furniture can be made from wood (generally oak), iron, magnesium, and even plastic. Some varieties are designed to be cut to fit the specific job situation, but the most common type is precut by the manufacturer and is intended to be reused. Most precut furniture is cut to 2-, 3-, 4-, 5-, 6-, 8-, and 10-pica widths, from 10 to 60 picas in length, in 5-pica increments. Wood is the least expensive, but it is also the least accurate furniture for very close imposition requirements because it expands and contracts with changes in room humidity.

Figure 17.10. An imposing stone or stone table
Courtesy of SUCO Learning Resources and R. Kampas.

Figure 17.12. Examples of quoins and quoin keys
Courtesy of SUCO Learning Resources and R. Kampas.

Figure 17.11. Examples of furniture
Courtesy of SUCO Learning Resources and R. Kampas.

The locks that hold the form in place in the lockup are called **quoins** (pronounced *coins*). Quoins are opened and closed by **quoin keys** (figure 17.12). Printers' quoins come in many forms, but they all operate in the same fashion. When a key is inserted and turned, the device expands or slides in two directions. When placed in a chase that has been filled out with a form and furniture, slight pressure from two quoins will hold everything in position until the printer chooses to remove them.

Reglets (figure 17.13) are thin pieces of wood that are always placed on either side of each quoin in a lockup. When wooden furniture is being used, the reglets serve as a means of protecting the large pieces of furniture from damage by the metal quoins. With metal furniture, reglets help prevent slippage of metal against metal. Reglets are intended to be reused after each job. They are

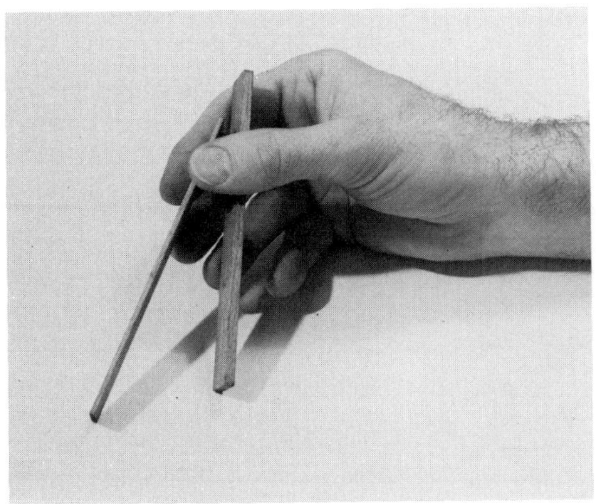

Figure 17.13. Examples of reglets
Courtesy of SUCO Learning Resources and R. Kampas.

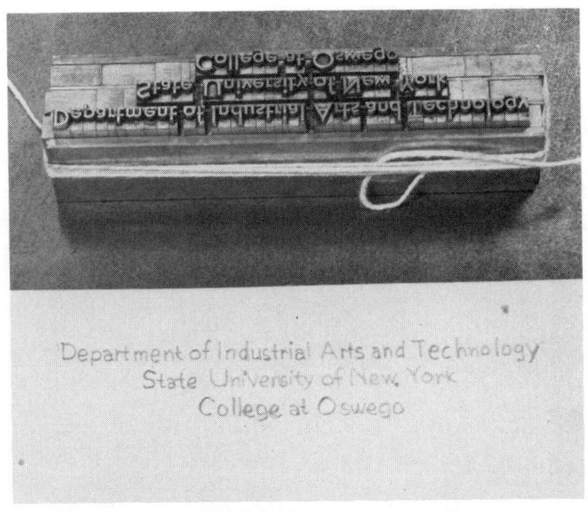

Figure 17.14. A rough layout and the corresponding typeform
Courtesy of SUCO Learning Resources and R. Kampas.

generally precut in pica increments and are 6 or 12 points in thickness.

Typical Lockup Procedures

Lockup is not a procedure that can be memorized and then performed with little thought. There are simply too many exceptions and problems with individual jobs for the process to conform to any set of laws. Fortunately, there is a general sequence of operations that is followed in every job. For this example we will assume that the foundry typeform shown in figure 17.14 is to be locked up in a chase to be printed. Notice, from the sketch lying next to the form, that the image is to appear at the top of a long and narrow sheet.

Recall that a printer never directly lifts a foundry typeform. You must slide it from place to place. To begin lockup, slide the form from the galley to the stone table surface; be sure there is no dust or lint under the form. Always place the chase over the typeform. Never place the chase down first and try to put the form inside it because the foundry type could be easily spilled. Every chase has a top and a bottom. Always place the top of the chase away from you as you stand at the stone table.

The typeform or plate also has a top (**head**) and a bottom (**tail**). The head of the form is identified by the first line that is to print at the top of the press sheet. Always place the head of the form at the bottom or to the left of the chase. This practice will make it easier to read the printed sheet as it comes off the press. The final direction of the head depends on the dimensions of the sheet to be run and on how it is to be fed through the press. On hand-fed platen presses, most printers run the sheet so that the longest dimension of the piece is parallel to the longest

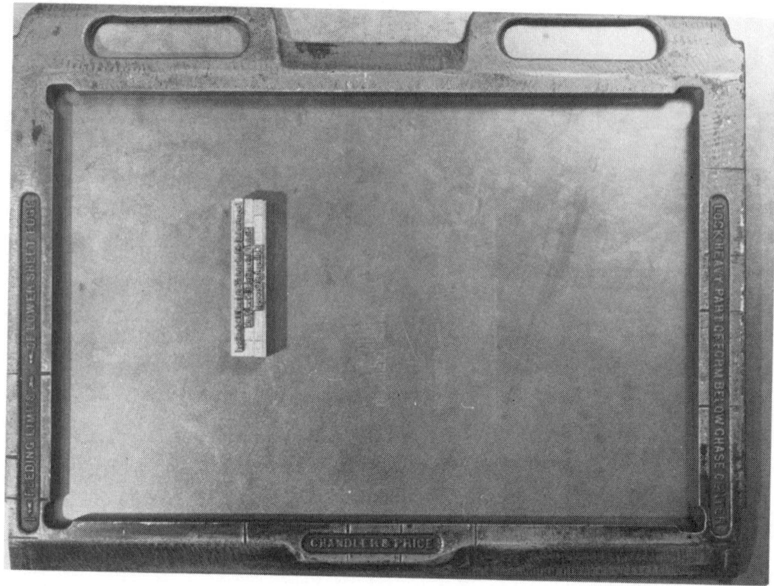

Figure 17.15. Placing the typeform in the chase
Courtesy of SUCO Learning Resources and R. Kampas.

dimension of the chase. From the rough layout shown in figure 17.14, the decision is to place the head of the form to the left of the chase (figure 17.15).

The specific location within the chase is determined by the size of the sheet. The form should be placed so that the image will be transferred to the page when it is held slightly above center on the platen of the press.

The next step is to block around the form with furniture. There are two common techniques, called the chaser, or overlapping, and the square, or furniture-within-furniture, methods (figure 17.16). With the square, or **furniture-within-furniture, technique,** the typeform must be in increments of picas that match the available furniture sizes. For example, if wooden furniture were being used, the width of the form would have to be built out with leading to a multiple of 5 picas. With the **chaser,** or **overlapping method,** each piece of furniture, in effect, chases the others around the form. The advantages of this layout are that it is simple and that it can be used with any typeform size.

After the form has been surrounded, build furniture out to the sides of the chase from the bottom and left sides (figure 17.17). Then place quoins to the top and right of the form (figure 17.18) and build more furniture out from the form to the top and right sides of the chase (figure 17.19). If there is string around the form, remove it at this point.

If the furniture has been properly placed, reglets should just slide into place on either side of each quoin. It might be necessary to vary combinations of furniture width in order to include the reglets, but they are a necessary addition.

The next step is very important. First insert a quoin key and tighten each quoin until slight pressure is placed on the form and

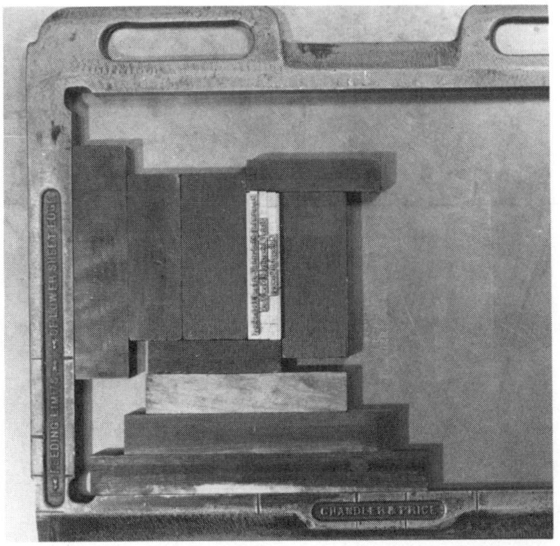

(a)

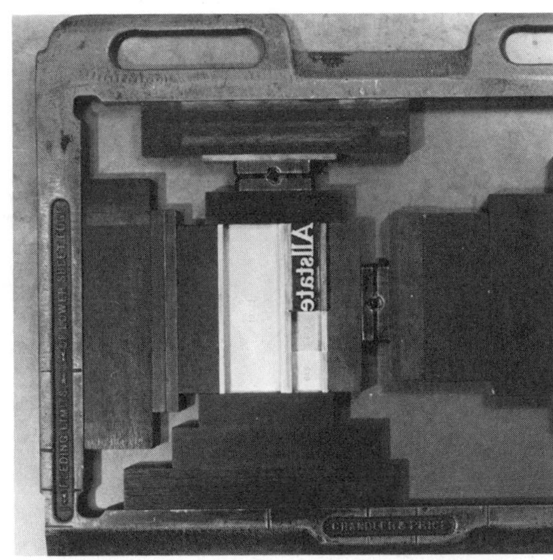

(b)

Figure 17.16. Examples of blocking with furniture The chaser placement can be used on any size of form (a). The square placement of furniture requires that the form be built out to an even 5-pica dimension (b).
Courtesy of SUCO Learning Resources and R. Kampas.

Figure 17.17. Building out the chase to bottom and left side From the blocked form, first build out with furniture to the bottom and the left side of the chase.
Courtesy of SUCO Learning Resources and R. Kampas.

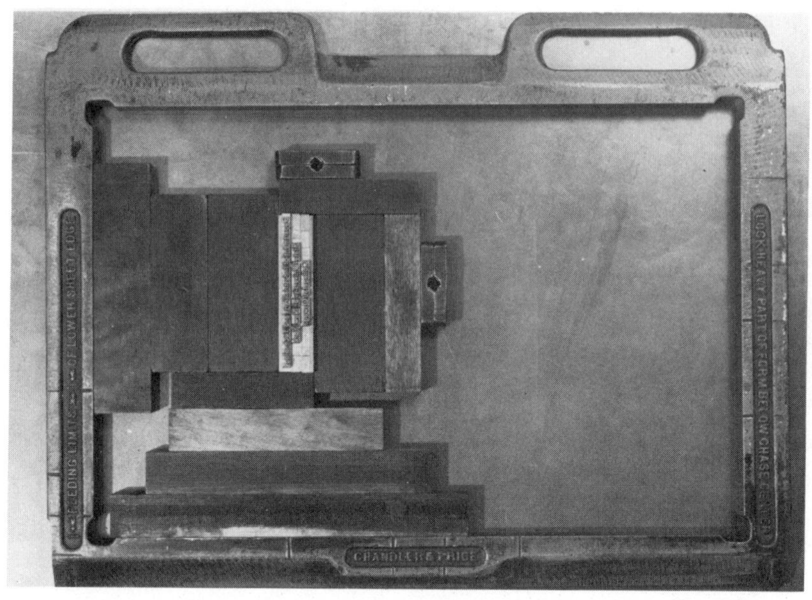

Figure 17.18. Using quoins in the chase Quoins are placed at the top and to the right of the form in the chase.
Courtesy of SUCO Learning Resources and R. Kampas.

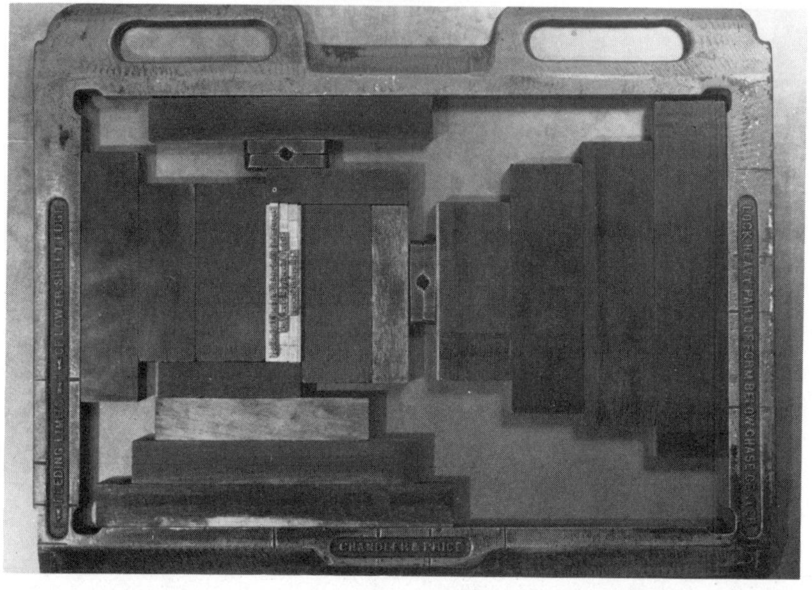

Figure 17.19. Building out the chase to top and right side With the quoins in place, build out the chase to the top and the right side.
Courtesy of SUCO Learning Resources and R. Kampas.

Figure 17.20. Securing the form and furniture Secure the form and furniture in place by carefully tightening the quoins.
Courtesy of SUCO Learning Resources and R. Kampas.

furniture (figure 17.20). A planer block is a piece of hardwood that can be used to seat each individual character and the entire form into position on the stone table (recall figure 16.23). If any part of the form is not properly seated against the stone, the printing faces will not be on the same plane, and image quality will be difficult to control on the press (figure 17.21).

If the planer block is gently placed on the face of the form and sharply tapped several times with a quoin key, each character will be jogged against the table (figure 17.22). Tighten the quoins a bit more, plane the form a second time, and turn the quoins to their outermost position with light resistance. Never force a quoin. It is possible to spring a chase out of flatness or even to damage it beyond

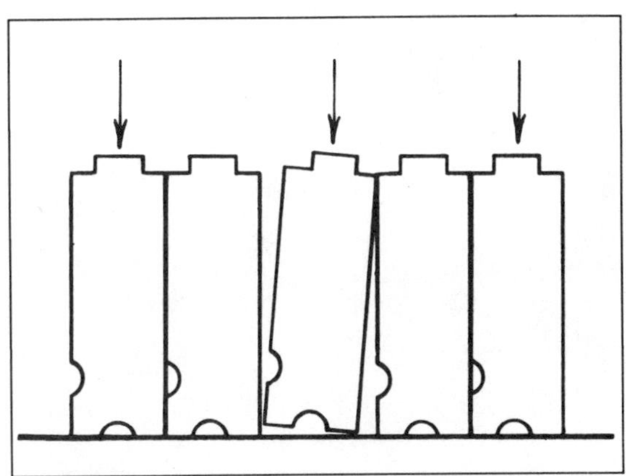

Figure 17.21. Diagram showing character before planing The purpose of planing is to knock each individual character squarely against the stone table.

Figure 17.22. Using a planer block Gently place the planer block on the face of the form and tap several times with a quoin key.
Courtesy of SUCO Learning Resources and R. Kampas.

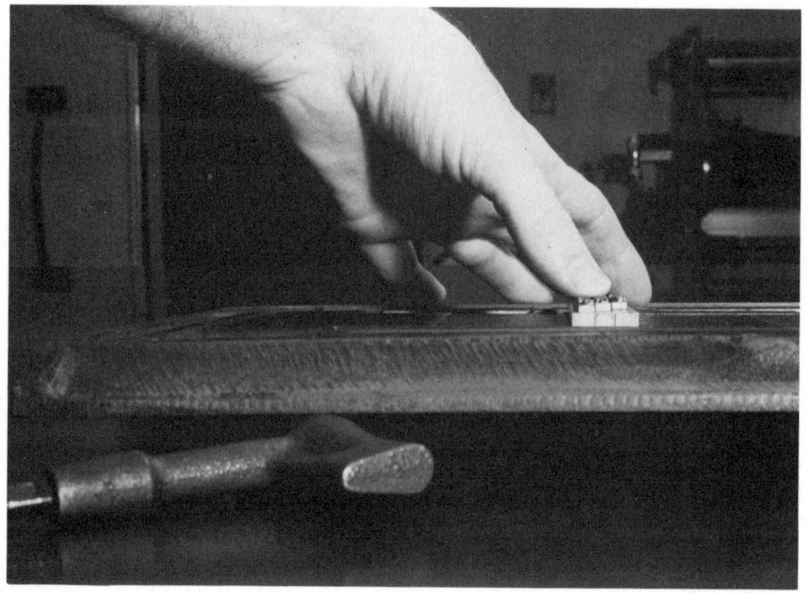

Figure 17.23. Checking for lift Check for lift by placing a quoin key under one edge of the chase and pressing with your thumb over the form.
Courtesy of SUCO Learning Resources and R. Kampas.

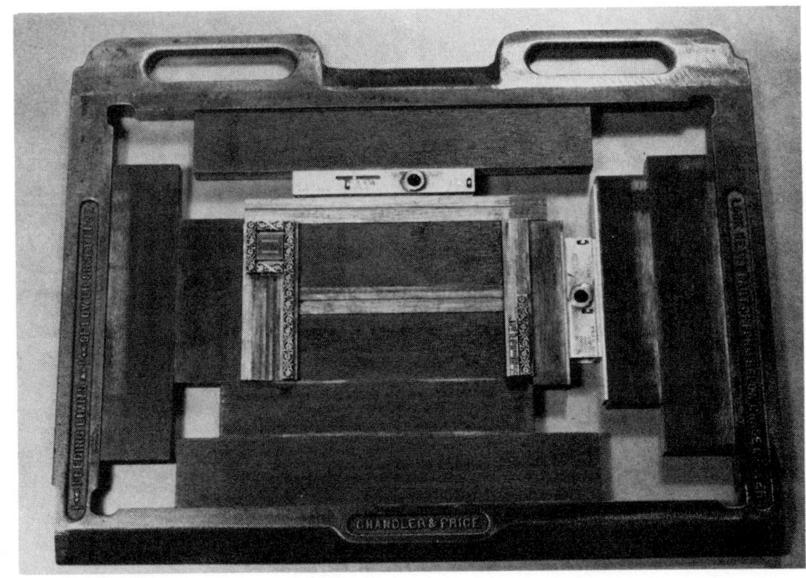

Figure 17.24. Example of a chase with more than one form More than one form can be locked into the same chase through the basic procedure discussed in this unit.
Courtesy of Robert Hollenbeck, SUCO Learning Resource, and R. Kampas.

repair by too much pressure. Be sure never to plane a form that has been completely tightened. Damaged type will be the only result.

The last step is to check that all parts of the form have been securely clamped in place. It is better to spend a few extra moments at this point than to have the form fly out of the chase in the middle of a press run. This process is called **checking for lift** (figure 17.23). Carefully lift one corner of the chase high enough to insert one part of a quoin key. With your thumb, gently press down toward the table over all parts of the form. If any portion moves, the lockup is not acceptable and must be corrected. The problem could be because of poor composition techniques when setting the original form, because of faulty positions of furniture around the form (particularly with a square lockup), or simply because the quoins are not tight enough. If the lockup passes the test for lift, the job is ready for the press.

After the press run, the form can be retied and the furniture, reglets, and quoins returned to storage until the next job. Most stone tables have areas to hold both furniture and spare chases. Chases with jobs locked up can also be stored, but it is wise always to return them to the stone table to repeat the final lockup steps before placing them on the press.

Although this example was a simple one with only a single form, the procedures for more complicated jobs are the same. Figure 17.24 shows a job with two unequal forms that have been locked in a chase through the same general sequence of steps. Chapter 18 deals with the procedures involved with actually running a relief job on a printing press.

Key Terms

bite
depth of cut
electroforming
mat
scorching
quoin keys
head
tail

Questions for Review

1. What are the two main categories of relief plates?
2. Under what category and methods of relief plates would foundry type be classified?
3. Briefly describe the steps in preparing any type of photomechanical relief plate.
4. What does the term *photoengraving* describe?
5. What is the difference between electrotype and stereotype duplicate relief plates?
6. Why are molded rubber or plastic relief plates called flexible plates?
7. What is the function of lockup?
8. What does the term *imposition* describe?
9. What is the difference between furniture and reglets?
10. What is the purpose of lockup quoins?
11. How is the head of the form identified?
12. What is the purpose of the planer block in foundry type lockup?
13. What is the difference between a chaser lockup and a square (or furniture-within-furniture) lockup?

Chapter Eighteen

Relief Printing

Anecdote to Chapter Eighteen

Although most small printers used equipment like the Franklin press through the beginning of this century, the fantastic growth of newspaper size and readership made demands for speed that could not be met by the hand-operated, adapted wine press. As early as 1790, an Englishman named William Nicholson took out a patent on a high-speed cylinder press. In his design, the relief type was attached to a revolving cylinder with a felt-covered impression cylinder to carry the paper. Unfortunately, Nicholson's press never moved beyond the drawing board because he could not perfect a means of holding the type in place and was unable to find a way to distribute the ink evenly (gelatin rollers were not yet invented).

The first practical power rotary cylinder press was patented in 1811 in Germany by Frederick König. It had a revolving cylinder that moved the sheet over a flat bed of type. It could print 1,100 sheets per hour. It was so much faster than other existing equipment that as soon as he learned of the invention, John Walter, publisher of the *London Times,* one of

An early cylinder press built by Robert Hoe

the largest newspapers of its time, secretly contracted with König to build one for his paper's use.

The press had to be constructed in secret because the pressroom workers had learned of the new invention and were bitterly opposed to anything that might change their job. On the morning of November 29, 1814, the printers arrived in the pressroom to begin work as usual and were told that they would have to wait because the foreign mail had not arrived on time and the composition was not yet ready. At 6 AM, when the presses usually started, Walter walked into the room carrying the first copy of the day's edition that had been printed on the new press. He told the workers what had taken place and warned them not to become violent because the new press was under police protection. He then paid them a full day's wage and assigned them all to new jobs in the plant. With the new machine the entire edition of the *Times* was printed in three hours rather than the ten it had taken with the old equipment.

In 1832, Col. Robert M. Hoe, a press manufacturer of New York, sent his engineer, Sereno Newton, to London to examine the König press and eventually began construction of cylinder presses. In 1847 Hoe built the first rotary press using stereotype plates. He called it the Patent Type-Revolving Printing Machine. By 1863 Hoe was building presses as big as the one shown here, with a single large plate cylinder as massive as 15 feet in diameter. This press had eight impression cylinders and required fifteen operators. Each impression cylinder had its own feeding and delivery system. An operator would pass a sheet into the machine and would then stack the sheets as they emerged. With eight impression cylinders, eight separate pages could be printed with each rotation. Then the piles had to be moved to another machine to be printed on the other side. With a steam-powered overhead belt to turn the big plate cylinder and fifteen fast-moving feeders and helpers, the press could turn out 16,000 impressions per hour.

Objectives for Chapter Eighteen

After completing this chapter, you will be able to:

- Identify and describe three types of relief printing machines.
- Outline traditional hand-fed platen press operation.
- Explain the procedure for adjusting the platen of a press to accept standard packing.
- Describe the procedure of adjusting platen press form rollers.
- List and define four special relief techniques.

(a)

(c)

Figure 18.1. Three basic designs of a platen press The hand-operated pilot press (a), the power-operated hand-fed press (b), and the power-operated automatically fed press (c).
Courtesy of SUCO Learning Resources and R. Kampas (a) and (b); Courtesy of Heidelberg Eastern (c).

(b)

Introduction

For nearly four hundred years Gutenberg's foundry type dominated all the printing trades in the Western world. It has only been in this century, and most notably in the last decade, that other processes, such as lithography, screen process, or intaglio, have moved to positions of importance in the industry. The decline of the relief process has been so rapid and pronounced that many printers consider relief either dead or almost so. Despite its decline, relief should not be viewed as an outdated process. A sizable portion of all printing in the United States is done by the relief method. Although declines might continue in some areas (such as relief newspaper production), it is unlikely that the process will disappear in the foreseeable future.

The relief printing process should be considered alive and well for several reasons. There are many areas in job printing where it can perform more efficiently and cheaply than any other process. The process is ideal for short-run, high-quality reproduction. Relief presses are easily adaptable to the problem areas of die cutting, creasing (or scoring), perforating, and foil stamping. There are also techniques (such as flexography and indirect relief) that, although not new, have emerged as viable industrial techniques.

As was discussed in chapter 4, the materials, presses, and language of all contemporary printing have closely followed the structure of the relief process. A thorough understanding of relief printing techniques is valuable knowledge for any printer.

Classifying Relief Presses

Chapter 12 introduced the most common printing press designs in a general manner, without reference to any particular process. It is important to recall that for every printing process, all presses perform the four basic operations of feeding, registering, printing, and delivering. The purpose of this chapter is to examine in detail some of the concerns involved with relief press work.

There are several ways to classify relief presses. One common way is to group them as either letterpress, newspaper relief, or special design relief.

Letterpress Machines

Letterpress is a common term that spans a wide range of devices and materials in the industry. In terms of machines, letterpress can be divided into three groups that were identified in chapter 12:

- Platen presses,
- Flat bed cylinder presses,
- Rotary presses.

At one time the hand-fed platen press was the backbone of every job shop in America. Some hand-fed devices still remain, but they have been largely replaced by automatic devices. The following three basic designs use the platen principle:

- Hand-operated pilot press,
- Power-operated hand-fed press,
- Power-operated automatically fed press (figure 18.1).

Figure 18.2 illustrates the basic components of a power-operated hand-fed platen press. The size on any platen press is determined by the inside dimensions of its chase. The most comon power presses are available in 10-by-15-inch and 12-by-18-inch sizes.

The flat bed cylinder press can print larger sheet sizes than the platen press can because of its method of impression. The image is transferred to only a small portion of the sheet at any given time by the force of the impression cylinder, so much less total pressure is needed and more printing area can be covered. There are two basic cylinder press designs. The vertical Miehle press is unique in that the bed holds the chase in a vertical position. The more traditional design has the bed and chase in a horizontal position (figure 18.3).

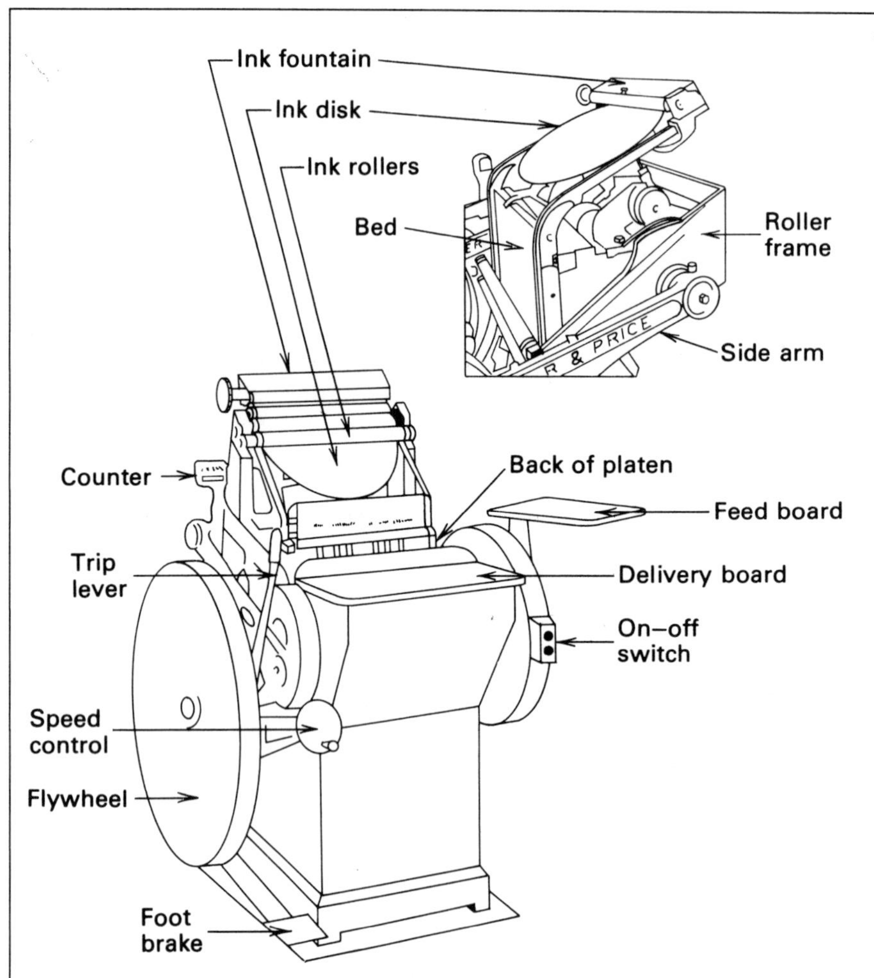

Figure 18.2. Diagram of the basic components of a hand-fed power platen press

Flat bed cylinder presses are described by the dimensions of the largest sheet the device is capable of printing. Almost all cylinder presses are automatically fed, registered, printed, and delivered.

Although both the platen and the flat bed cylinder presses can be adapted to web feeding, almost all devices are used as sheet-fed machines.

Recall from chapter 12 that image transfer takes place on a rotary press as the paper passes between an impression and a plate cylinder. Rotary presses have traditionally used cast duplicate plates (electrotypes and stereotypes) as the image carrier. With the decline in the use of hot metal composition to generate the printing plate, new forms of carriers have been developed. Chapter 17 discussed the range of possible relief plates, whether primary or duplicate, such as flexible photopolymer materials.

Flexible plates can be mounted on existing rotary relief presses in several ways. The basic problem is with "hold-down."

Figure 18.3. Example of a traditional flat bed cylinder press design
Courtesy of Heidelberg Platen Press.

There is a tendency for plates to fly off the rotating cylinder because of centrifugal force. One approach is to laminate the thin photorelief plate to an aluminum saddle that can be clamped in place as with hot metal cast plates. The thin plates can also be mounted on magnetic saddles and locked on the cylinder. Another alternative is to replace the conventional cylinder with a special magnetic cylinder or to mount the plate with magnetic tape or plate backings.

Newspaper Presses

All relief printing for newspaper production utilizes the rotary configuration with a web-feeding sytstem. The striking difference between the letterpress rotary design and the design for newspapers is size. A web newspaper press consists of many printing units. The number depends on the number of pages in the publication. All units perfect (print on both sides), and the entire system operates at a very high rate of speed. It is common for a single press to take up three stories of a building, with the paper rolls being mounted and fed from the first floor, image transfer occurring between the first and the second floors, and the trimming and folding done between the second and the third floors.

Newspaper relief presses are designed for a single function and are not readily adaptable to any other type of job. Rotary letterpress machines are characterized by ease of change-over to a wide variety of printing needs.

Special Design Relief Presses

There are several rotary relief presses that, because of the type of plate used or because of a slightly different configuration, are classed as special design machines. Two examples are indirect relief and flexography.

Flexography is a process that uses the traditional rotary press design but prints from a flexible rubber plate. Extremely fluid inks are used. The most common application is for printing nontraditional materials, such as nonporous plastic films. Flexo presses are rotary in design, with a high-speed web-feeding system.

A second special design relief process is termed **indirect relief.** All relief printing discussed to this point has been direct (the image is transferred to the paper by direct contact between the typeform and the paper). Recall that most lithographic presses print indirectly by the use of a rubber blanket. The technique is commonly referred to as "offset lithography." Indirect relief printing works from the same offset principle, without the problem of moistening the plate. For that reason, and to prevent confusion between relief and lithography, indirect relief printing is sometimes called **dry offset.**

The main advantage of indirect relief is that the plates can often be used on existing offset lithographic presses. There are, however, machines specifically available for dry offset plates. They are available as sheet-fed or web-fed devices.

A third form of special design relief press is called the **Cameron press** (figure 18.4). With this design, thin relief plates are glued to a flexible moving belt. The belt moves at high speed, passing the plates in direct contact with ink form rollers and then a web-fed paper roll. The image carriers are carefully positioned on the belt so that the paper can be cut, collated, and bound in a single operation. The advantage of starting with a roll of paper and ending with a finished book (with the whole process occurring at a high rate of speed) makes the Cameron design appealing to book printers.

It is sometimes difficult to understand the relationships of the three main categories of relief presses because of the complexity, and in some cases the similarity, of subcategories. Figure 18.5 shows one way to classify relief presses. It is important to understand the following main differences between groups:

- Letterpress is characterized by the wide diversity of potential jobs that can be run and by the rapid set-up and start-up time.
- Newspaper relief presses are limited to a single format and product.
- Special design presses, particularly indirect relief and flexography, are easily identified by materials or press designs different from the traditional forms of relief presses.

Traditional Hand-Fed Platen Press Operations

It is beyond the intent of this book to examine in detail the operation of all the different forms of relief equipment. The goal of this chapter is to provide enough information to allow the reader to transfer general understandings to specific operations with the assistance of a classroom instructor or a press operation manual.

The fundamental steps for hand-fed power platen press operation are similar to the procedures for any flat bed cylinder or sheet-fed rotary press. The following sections examine basic platen press techniques. The discussion is applicable to nearly any form of press. Readers interested in web operations should examine several of the sources cited in the bibliography.

Packing the Hand-Fed Platen Press

The platen press gets its name from the flat rectangular base that pushes the paper against the typeform during the printing operation. **Packing** is the material that is clamped on the platen by the bails (figure 18.6). It serves two functions. First, because the distance from the platen to the typeform is not easily altered (see "Press Maintenance" in this chapter), packing is the only means of controlling the overall impression (or amount of pressure) that the sheet receives. Second, the top sheet of the packing holds the mechanical fingers (called **gauge pins**) that receive the press sheet and hold it in place during the printing operation. (See "Controlling Image Position on the Press Sheet" in this chapter.)

If impression is too heavy, the type will emboss or punch through the paper. If impression is too light, a poor image will result. For impression to be perfect, the form

Figure 18.4. A Cameron press
Courtesy of Cameron Graphic Arts, Cameron-Waldron Division, Midland-Ross Corporation.

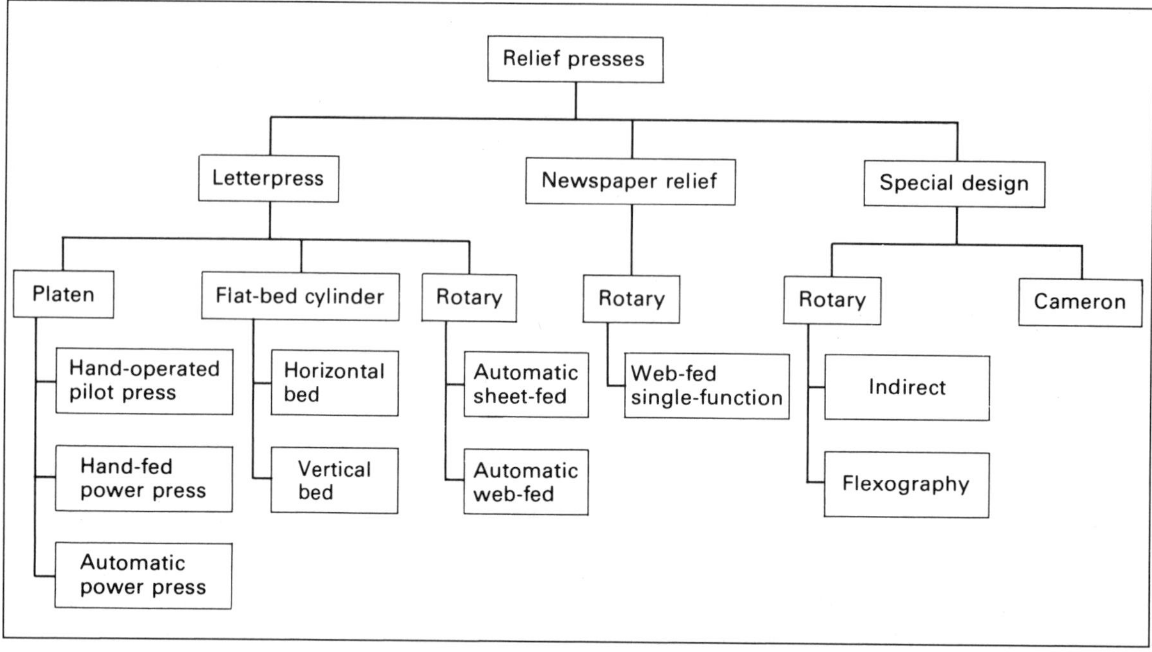

Figure 18.5. Classification diagram for relief presses

must press against the paper hard enough to reproduce its characters clearly and sharply but not so hard that the image can be felt on the back of the printed sheet. Control of proper impression can be difficult if the paper is thin, the equipment is not properly adjusted, or the form to be printed does not consist of pieces of type of uniform height.

All presses in a single shop are generally set for a standard packing, but the standard might vary from one shop to another. The standard packing is generally set up for the most common paper weight to be run. For example, in the authors' shops every press has been set for standard packing to print on a 60-pound paper. Each platen has been adjusted so that if one sheet of pressboard, three sheets of 60-pound book stock, and one drawsheet (tympan paper) are clamped in place, the impression on any 60-pound stock should be nearly perfect. Each operator knows to begin with the same standard packing. If the job calls for a lighter paper, such as 20-pound stock, packing must be added. For heavier sheets, packing must be removed.

The process of placing standard packing on the platen is called **dressing the press.** Using the authors' standard as an example, the first sheets to be positioned are the three sheets of 60-pound book paper, called **hanger sheets.** The hanger sheets are cut so that they will extend under the bottom bail but will not reach the top bail of the platen (figure 18.7a). Next the oil-treated manila **tympan sheet,** or **drawsheet,** is cut long enough to be held by both bails and is clamped with the three hanger sheets under the bottom bail (figure 18.7b). The last addition is the pressboard, which is

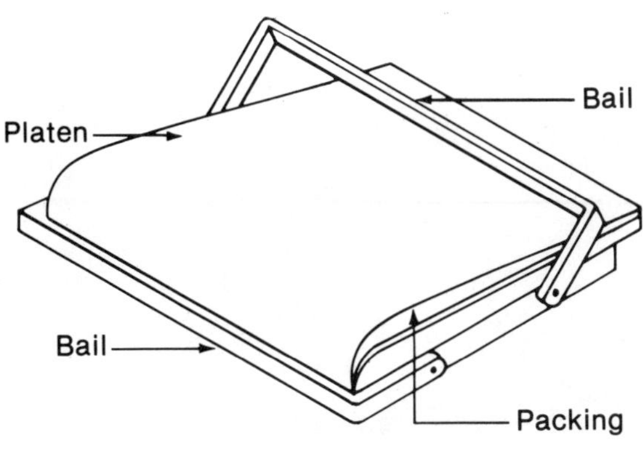

Figure 18.6. Diagram of press platen and bails

cut to the size of the chase and placed under the last hanger sheet but is not held by either bale (figure 18.7c). The **pressboard** is a heavy, hard paper sheet that gives a firm, flat, accurate base to the packing. With all materials in place, the tympan paper is drawn smoothly under the top bail and is clamped in place. If only the top bail is released during the make-ready operation (see following sections), the rest of the packing will be held accurately in place.

Inking the Press

Most power platen presses are equipped with an ink fountain that will automatically add ink to the ink disk during a long run. The procedures for setting up and adjusting any ink fountain were discussed in chapter 13. When the run is short and/or if several different colors are to be used on the same press during a single production day, it is foolish to go to the trouble of using the fountain system only to have to clean it up after a short time.

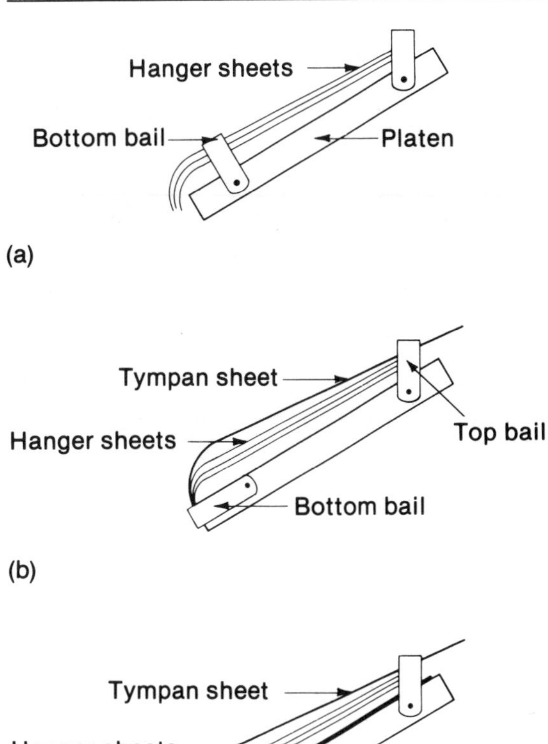

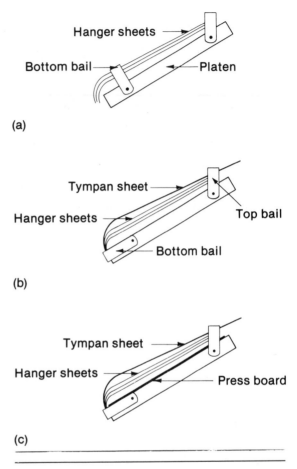

Figure 18.7. Diagram for dressing the press
Insert the hanger sheets under the bottom, but not the top, bail (a). Position the tympan paper over the hanger sheets and secure the bottom bail (b). Place a sheet of pressboard under the last hanger sheet (c).

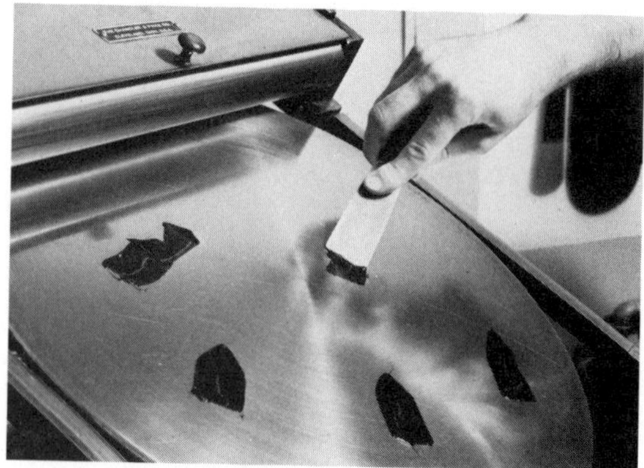

Figure 18.8. Hand inking the ink disk For short-run jobs, the ink disk can be inked by placing a small quantity of ink on the disk and allowing the press to idle.
Courtesy of SUCO Learning Resources and R. Kampas.

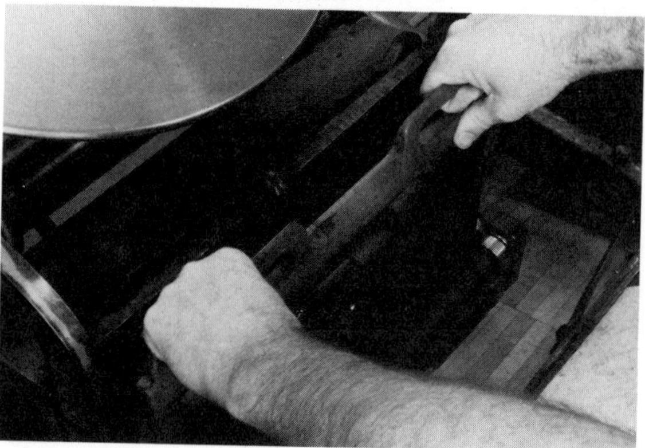

Figure 18.9. Inserting the chase Seat the chase in the bed of the press and lock it in place.
Courtesy of SUCO Learning Resources and R. Kampas.

When setting up the press for a short-run job, the ink disk can be easily inked by hand. The procedure is to distribute a small quantity of ink over several areas of the ink disk (figure 18.8). Then turn the motor on and allow the press to idle at a slow speed until the ink is evenly distributed over the entire disk.

Novice printers sometimes have difficulties judging the amount of ink to place on the disk. Too little ink will produce a gray, fuzzy image. Too much ink will result in a dense, blurred design. It is important to realize that the specific length of a run has little to do with the required ink quantity because there is a narrow range between too little and too much ink on the disk. Unfortunately, this judgment is one that comes with experience and varies with the quality and color of the ink being used. As a general suggestion, when inking by hand, place on the disk a bead of ink approximately the diameter of a pencil and about an inch long. If properly inked, the surface should look much like the texture of a ripe peach.

Inserting the Chase

After the press has been properly inked and dressed, it is ready to receive the chase. Turn the flywheel by hand until the platen is at its farthest point from the bed and the ink form rollers are in their lowest position. At the stone table, test the form for lift (see "Typical Lockup Procedures," chapter 17). Then move the chase to a vertical position and wipe the back of the form with a clean rag to remove any dust or lint that might prevent perfect contact against the bed of the press.

While the chase is still in the vertical position, carefully carry it to the press, place the frame against the bed, and lock it in position (figure 18.9). It is important that the chase be firmly held by the clamping device and perfectly seated against the bed's frame. Immediately check for any objects that might damage the form. In the case of a platen press, the primary concern is that the grippers do not line up with the form.

Controlling Image Position on the Press Sheet

Because the surface of the drawsheet on the platen is perfectly flat and smooth, some device is necessary to hold the sheet in the proper printing position during the printing operation. On automatic presses this is accomplished by grippers. On hand-fed platen presses gauge pins are used (figure 18.10). The basic problem is to attach the pins to the drawsheet so that each press sheet will be held in the same position and so that the printed image will appear in the correct position on every press sheet.

To determine the proper gauge pin positions, the form must first be printed on the clean drawsheet. This is called **pulling an impression.** The impression control for most hand-fed platen presses is the "throw-off lever" (figure 18.11). With the lever back (away from the operator), the platen will move against the form when the machine is running. With it forward, there will always be a slight gap. For the first few impressions the machine should be operated by hand. Throw the lever forward and turn the flywheel until the form prints on the tympan paper and the platen is returned to its farthest position. The image should be clear enough to determine the exact form position, but it need not be of reproduction quality.

Next it is necessary to identify the position of the lead edge of the stock by drawing on the drawsheet a line the proper distance from the printed form. This distance is determined from the rough or comprehensive.

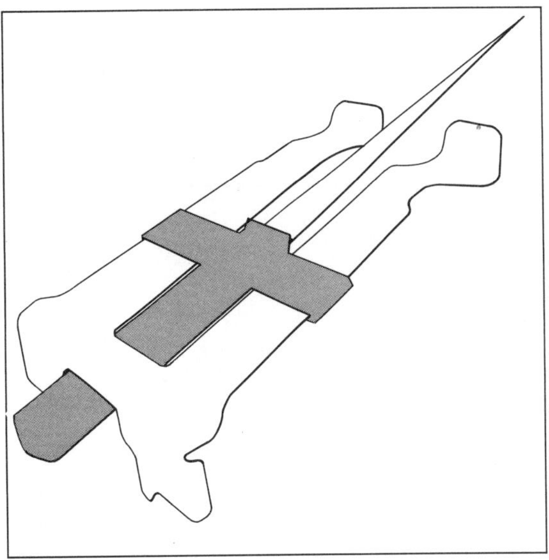

Figure 18.10. Diagram of a gauge pin

Figure 18.11. Throw-off lever The impression control for most hand-fed platen presses is a throw-off lever located at the side of the machine. Courtesy of SUCO Learning Resources and R. Kampas.

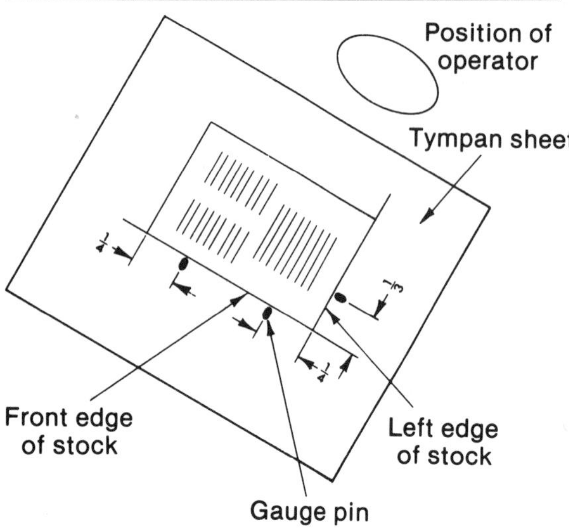

Figure 18.12. Determining the press sheet position Identify the position of the stock on the tympan by drawing paper lines to the front and left edges of the image. Place two gauge pins on the front edge of the stock at a distance of 1/4 the length of the sheet in from each edge. Place one on the left edge of the stock at a distance of 1/3 the width of the sheet in from the front edge.

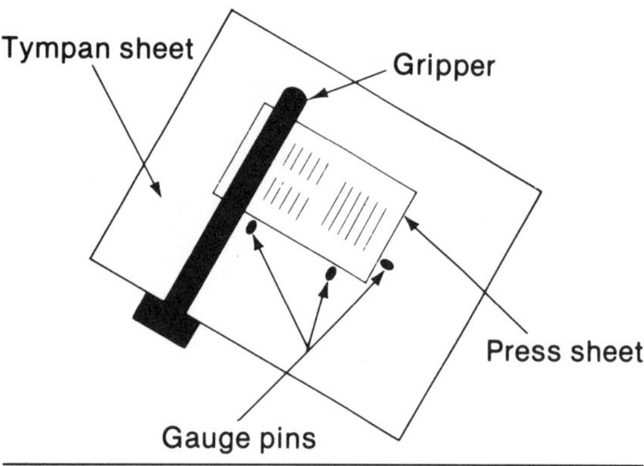

Figure 18.13. Using a gripper A gripper is placed in line with part of the sheet but not touching a gauge pin.

The line should be as nearly parallel to the lines of type as possible. The left edge (as the operator looks down on the platen) of the stock should then be drawn on the tympan at right angles to the first line. This distance can also be obtained from the rough or comprehensive. These two lines represent the position of the top and left edges of the press sheet during the printing operation (figure 18.12).

In order to hold the sheet on these lines, attach gauge pins to the drawsheet. Place two on the lead edge and one on the left-hand side (figure 18.12). To insert a pin, push the point through only the top tympan paper at a point about ⅛ inch below the paper line. Move the pin about ½ inch under the sheet and then push the point back through the tympan.

When all three gauge pins have been inserted in the tympan, check to ensure that the grippers do not line up with any pins. Then place at least one gripper in a position to catch part of the sheet (figure 18.13). The grippers prevent the sheet from moving during the printing operation and keep the sheet from sticking to the inked form as the platen moves back to deliver the finished product. There are many instances, such as with small press sheets, when it is not possible to place the grippers in contact with the paper. In such situations a sheet of paper (called a **frisket**) or a piece of string is often attached to the two grippers to hold the press sheet in place without touching an image area (figure 18.14).

The final gauge pin positions are located after a proof has been taken on an acutal press sheet. Small adjustments of one or more pins are always necessary so that the image appears parallel to one edge of the sheet and is in proper printing position. Once the exact locations are defined, push the nibs or feet of the gauge pins into the tympan paper so the gauge pins will not shift during production. This process, referred to as **setting the gauge pins,** is accomplished by lightly tapping the top of the pin with the back of an ink knife or some similar object.

Final Make-Ready

Up to this point in the discussion of hand-fed power platen presses, the concern has been only with the position of the image on the sheet. The final make-ready is the process of adjusting the impression to obtain the best possible image quality. After the gauge pins have been set, place a piece of job stock in the gauge pin fingers, pull the throw-off lever into the print position, and pull an impression by using the press motor. Examine the reproduction for image quality.

If many of the characters are not printing over the entire form, the press is probably underpacked. Add onionskin or another hanger sheet to the packing (between the last hanger sheet and the pressboard) by lifting only the top bail. Be careful not to overpack the press or the type will cut or emboss the tympan. If the drawsheet is impressed, it will be difficult to achieve a quality reproduction because there will no longer be a flat, firm base. If the drawsheet is embossed, it is best to change the packing and add a new drawsheet.

If the image shows an uneven impression across the sheet, a number of possibilities could be causing the problem. When the image is heavier at the lower portion of the form than at the top, the press may be overpacked. The bottom part is hitting the sheet harder than the top. When the impression is heavy at the top of the form, the platen is probably underpacked. Another possibility is that the chase could be warped. This situation commonly occurs when the form will not pass the

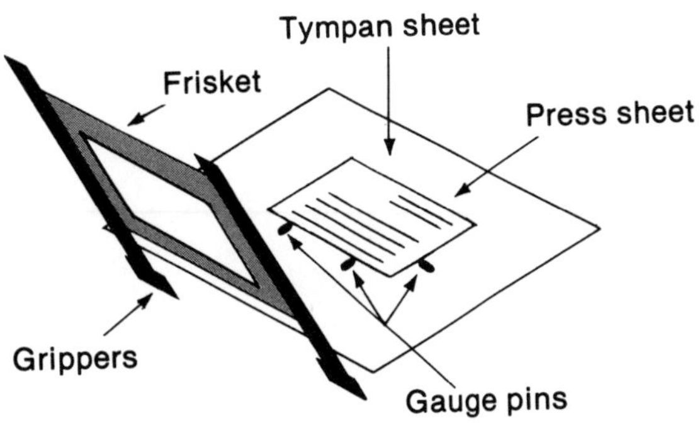

Figure 18.14. Using a frisket A frisket is taped between the grippers when the press sheet is too small to use grippers on it.

test for lift (see "Typical Lockup Procedures," chapter 17). Instead of correcting the problem, the inexperienced imposer will often try to overtighten the quoins. This only warps the chase.

In a shop that continually uses hand-set foundry type, some characters are used more often than others, with the result that in any given form there are characters with very slightly different heights. This problem does not occur when fresh hot type is used for every job, as with Linotype composition.

Regardless of the care taken during the prepress procedures, slight adjustments must nearly always be made to obtain quality reproduction. Two common techniques are "overlaying" and "underlaying."

An **overlay** is a sheet of packing that is added under the tympan sheet. This sheet is made up of built-up areas of tissue and book paper to increase impression or of cut-out portions to decrease impression in selected areas of the form. An overlay can be prepared by a variety of methods, including a mechan-

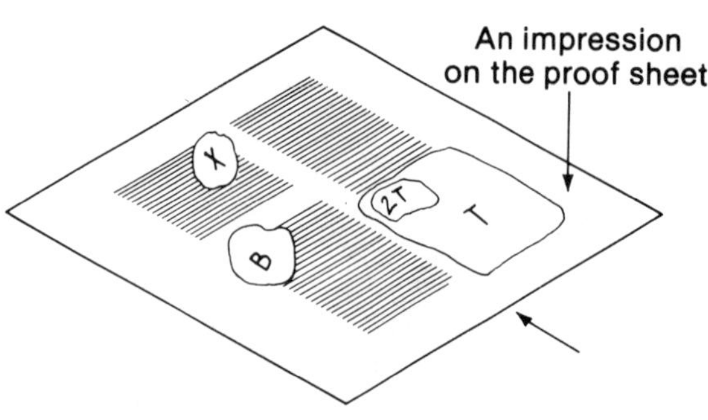

Figure 18.15. Marking a press proof for impression changes An overlay is marked where more or less impression is necessary. *X* means cut away, *T* means add one layer of tissue, *2T* means add two layers, and *B* means add a layer of book paper.

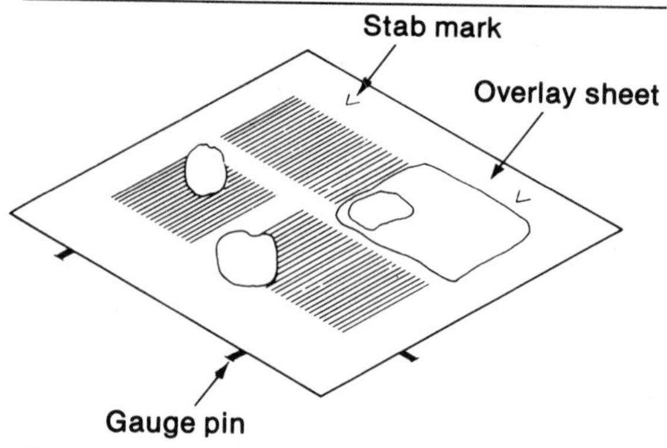

Figure 18.16. Hanging in the overlay Place the overlay in position on the gauge pins and cut out several *V* marks in the nonimage areas. The cuts will extend through the drawsheet and can be used to position the overlay under the tympan.

ical system. The most common procedure is to work from a press proof sheet.

The press operator first pulls an impression on a sheet of hanger paper that has been cut to the rough press sheet size. The proof is then examined, and the printer marks areas that need to be built up and areas that need to be diminished (figure 18.15). In this example, *X* indicates that the area is to be cut away. *T* means add one layer of tissue paper, *2T* means add two layers of tissue, and *B* means add a layer of book paper. The number of layers depends on the appearance of the image area. Judgment is largely a matter of experience. The actual process of pasting the tissue or book paper with make-ready paste is called **spotting up.**

After the overlay is prepared, the problem is to align the sheet perfectly under the drawsheet so that the proper amount of pressure will be added to or subtracted from the final press sheet image. This procedure is termed **hanging in the overlay.** First loosen the top bail and tear out one hanger sheet. Then clamp the bail back into position and place the overlay in the gauge pins as if it were a press sheet. With a make-ready knife or a sharp razor blade, cut two or three *V* marks in the nonimage areas through both the overlay and the drawsheet into the remaining hanger sheets in the packing (see figure 18.16). If the top bail is again released, the overlay can be pasted to the top hanger sheet so that the *V* cuts line up perfectly. After the drawsheet is clamped into place, the selected areas have been adjusted without affecting the properly impressed areas of the job.

An **underlay** is a piece of tissue or paper that is pasted under the form in areas that are light in impression. Underlaying is common in jobs that are made up of bold or solid areas mixed with fine lines or rule. An underlay is generally used rather than an isolated area spot-up to shim or level a typecut so that it is parallel to the paper.

Both overlaying and underlaying should continue until a quality printed image is obtained. Often a single job will need several overlays or underlays.

Feeding the Press

Several steps can be taken to feed the power platen press smoothly and without difficulty. First, fan the paper to remove any static electricity and then slant the pile to make it easier to lift only one sheet at a time. Place the stack on an easy-to-reach spot of the infeed table. Stand comfortably in front of the platen section within easy reach of both the paper and the platen areas. The actual feeding, printing, and delivering for a platen press is a two-hand operation, with the right hand feeding a sheet into the gauge pins while the left removes a printed sheet and stacks it on the delivery table.

With the press set at its slowest speed, lift a sheet from the infeed pile with the right hand and move it into contact with the two bottom gauge pins on the platen. Once the sheet hits, continue a leftward motion until the paper is stopped by the single pin. As the press begins to close to make an impression, the right hand immediately returns to the paper pile to pick up a fresh sheet. When the platen opens a second time, the left hand moves in to remove the printed sheet while the right positions another piece. Hand feeding is a continual process of inserting and removing press sheets. A skillful operator will glance at every tenth to fifteenth sheet to check for image position and quality without stopping the rhythm of feeding.

Inexperienced operators should practice feeding stock with the chase removed from the bed and with the press in an off-impression position. Skillful printers can feed some jobs at the rate of 5,000 cph (copies per hour), but the novice should concentrate on consistency, not on speed.

Cleaning the Press

Automatic-feeding platen presses generally have a built-in cleanup attachment that mechanically cleans ink from the ink form rollers, typeform, and ink distribution system. Hand-fed presses, however, must be manually cleaned because no cleanup attachments are generally available.

If the press was set up for a long run, first remove any ink remaining in the ink fountain with an ink knife and then clean the fountain system. Be sure to disengage the device so that the clean roller will not come into contact with the ink disk.

To clean the rest of the press, remove the chase and place it on the stone table to be knocked down or store it for further production. Then wash the ink disk with a rag saturated with wash-up solvent. For removing particularly heavy deposits of ink, use a soiled rag from the rag storage can. Then use a clean rag to remove the dissolved ink remaining on the surface. Next turn the flywheel by hand until the ink form rollers move to the top of the bed. With a saturated cloth, clean as much of the rollers as you can reach. Then begin to move the rollers across the ink disk. As the rollers turn, remove all remaining ink. With a clean rag, wipe both the ink disk and the rollers a final time and turn the flywheel until the rollers are positioned in the center of the bed. That midpoint position places the least amount of tension on the roller springs and will ensure that no flat spots are formed on the soft roller material.

Press Maintenance

Establishing Standard Packing by Platen Adjustment

Readjustment of the platen is not a frequent task, but there are times when it is necessary (for example, when establishing standard packing for a group of presses or when performing a semiannual maintenance check). The distance and angle of the platen from the bed of the press can be changed by means of four large bolts located under the platen (figure 18.17).

To establish standard packing, mount the tympan paper, the pressboard, and the desired number of hanger sheets (the authors recommend three) on the platen as described in the preceding section. At the same time, ink the press with a quality-job black ink. Next lock several large characters in each corner of a chase and mount it in the press. Insert gauge pins into the drawsheet in positions so that a single large sheet can be held in place.

Determine to what weight of paper the standard packing is to be established. The most commonly run weight in the shop is generally selected. If one press is set aside to handle only 110-pound stock for business cards, the gap should be set for the thickness of that material.

To check the existing settings, insert a sheet of the standard material and pull an impression. Examine the images for uniformity of appearance around the four corners. If one corner is lighter or heavier than the others, adjust the bolt under that corner. Most machines have a two-nut combination. One serves as a locking nut; the other actually controls the position of the platen. Make the necessary adjustment, lock the position, and pull another proof. Continue the same procedure until a uniform impression is obtained. The next concern is to adjust the gap for the packing and standard sheet. Examine the last proof sheet for quality of impression. As with any press job, the goal is to obtain the best image without indenting or scoring the sheet. If the proof sheet is not of acceptable quality, all four lock nuts should be loosened and the same adjustment must be made for each control nut. Then lock all four back in place and pull another proof. The process should be continued until the desired impression is obtained.

Care and Adjustment of Rollers

The ink form rollers on relief presses are generally made from a base material of either natural or synthetic rubber. The most frequent problem with form roller condition or adjustment is called **slur.** A slurred image is inconsistent in density and often gives a streaked appearance beyond the outline of the character design. The situation commonly occurs when the rollers have become glazed with dried, hardened ink because of inadequate cleanup procedures. A commercially prepared regeneration paste can be applied to the rollers and allowed to set overnight. The paste will dissolve the glaze without affecting roller shape, tackiness, or elasticity. The rollers should be thoroughly cleaned with wash-up solvent before the next day's production begins.

Image slur can also be caused by imperfectly round form rollers. When rollers become warped or out of shape from misuse or pressroom conditions such as high humidity, they should be replaced.

When the form rollers are hitting the typeform with too much pressure, slur will be a major problem. Excessive pressure causes a heavier ink deposit on one side of the form than on the other. To relieve excessive roller pressure, the form roller tracks must be adjusted. Most platen presses have adjusting devices under the tracks (figure 18.18). A special **type-high gauge** is available for making accurate form roller adjustments.

To adjust form roller impression, manually turn the flywheel until the rollers move to the bottom portion of the bed. Position the type-high gauge against the bed and move the roller into contact with the tool. In printer's language, the roller should touch the gauge with "kiss" pressure. This means that the roller should just brush the gauge without indenting the roller material. Adjust both tracks at the lower portion of the bed. Then move the form rollers to the upper portion of the bed and repeat the procedure.

A common error when performing a daily or weekly press maintenance is to allow oil to drip on the roller tracks and bed. As the rollers move up and down the track, the oil will be distributed along the path and will cause the rollers to slip. Oil on the press bed will raise the height of the typeform and could cause impression difficulties.

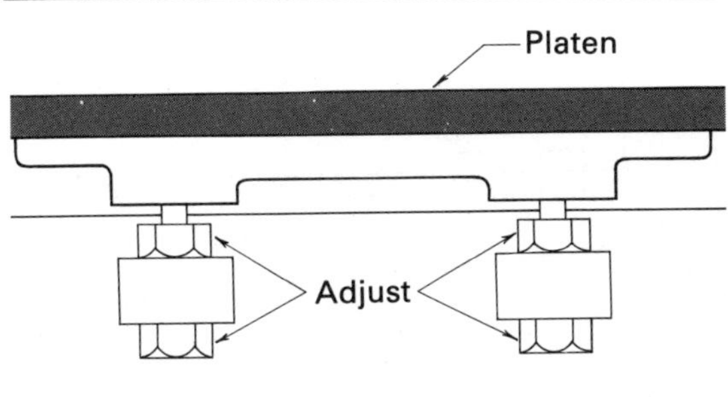

Figure 18.17. Platen adjustment bolts The four large bolts under the platen control its position.

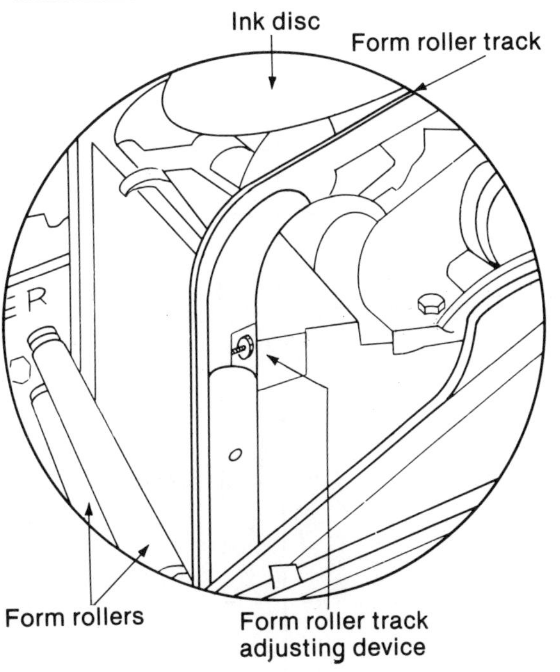

Figure 18.18. Adjusting the form roller tracks

Adaptation of Platen Presses for Special Techniques

Up to this point in the discussion of relief presses, we have discussed only the use of ink to form the image. Several other opera-

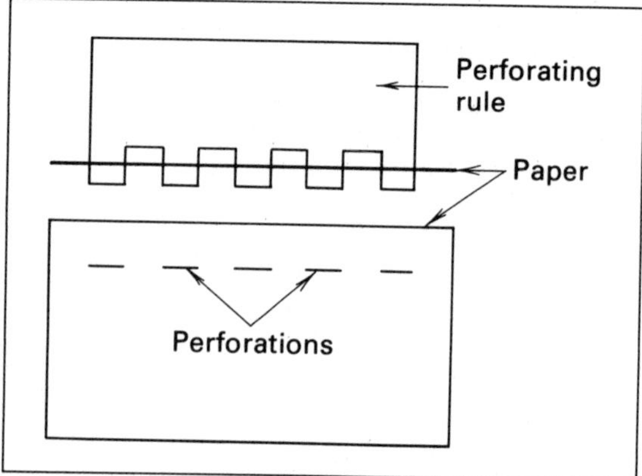

Figure 18.19. Diagram of a perforating rule

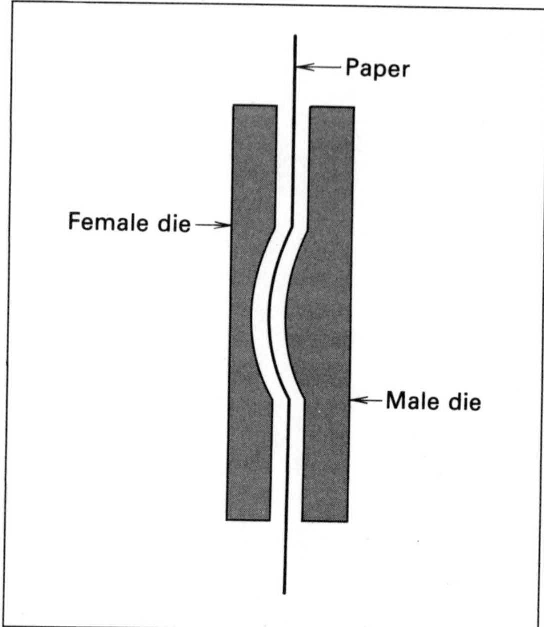

Figure 18.20. Diagram of embossing dies
Embossing creates a three-dimensional image between a male and a female set of dies.

tions can be performed with a relief press that use no ink but create an image or contribute to the final image design. Some of the possible techniques are creasing, perforating, embossing, and die cutting.

Perforating and Creasing

Perforating is a common requirement in jobs where portions of the piece are to be removed by the consumer (such as a ticket with a removable stub). In the perforating process, a series of very short slits are cut in the stock, leaving only a small bridge of paper in place. A perforating rule is a strip (generally about 2 points thick) of hardened steel that is made up of a series of equally spaced teeth that are driven through the stock by the motion of the press (figure 18.19).

Creasing is a process that uses a solid strip of hardened steel to crush the grain of the paper to create a straight line for folding. The process is also referred to as **scoring.** A ragged or cracked fold can occur when the printer tries to fold a heavy paper or when the job requires that the sheet be folded against the grain.

The make-ready procedures for creasing and perforating are similar. First remove the ink form rollers from the press. Because both perforating and creasing rules are slightly greater than type-high, the rule would cut into the roller and damage it. Dress the press with standard packing. Some presses have special metal plates that fit on the platen, under the drawsheet, when scoring is to be done.

Mount the rule in a chase by using standard lockup procedures and place the chase in the press. Pull an impression so that a slight indentation of the drawsheet can be

Figure 18.21. A female die
Courtesy of Heidelberg Eastern.

Figure 18.22. A male die
Courtesy of Heidelberg Eastern.

observed. Then position the three gauge pins as you would for any platen press job. After the pins have been set, adjust the impression with packing to obtain the desired result. The pressure of the perforating rule must be such that the teeth are pushed entirely through the sheet. The impression for the scoring rule must be set so that the blade only smashes the sheet, causing it to fold easily at the crease.

Embossing

Embossing is a process that creates a three-dimensional image by placing a sheet of paper or other material between a concave and convex (sometimes called female and male) set of dies (figure 18.20). The concave die (figure 18.21) is usually made of 3⁄16-inch or 1⁄4-inch brass and is mounted on a metal plate so that the topmost surface is type-high. The convex die (figure 18.22) is usually formed from the concave, which has been mounted in a chase and placed on the press.

Several methods are commonly used to form the convex die. Two are the manual technique and the pasting technique.

Manual Technique. For the manually formed male die, paste a piece of mat board (slightly larger than the final press sheet) to the platen. Then manually ink the nonimage areas of the female die with a brayer and pull an impression on the mat board. This image will be used as a guide on which a male die will be manually constructed. If a distinct impression is not made on the board, add packing behind the female die. Re-ink the die and pull another impression on a clean sheet of blotter paper (0.028 inch thick). Cut away the inked areas of the blotter sheet, pressing the outline of the uninked or image area. Paste this cutout portion to the image area on the mat board mounted on the platen. Pull another impression on blotter paper and again cut and paste

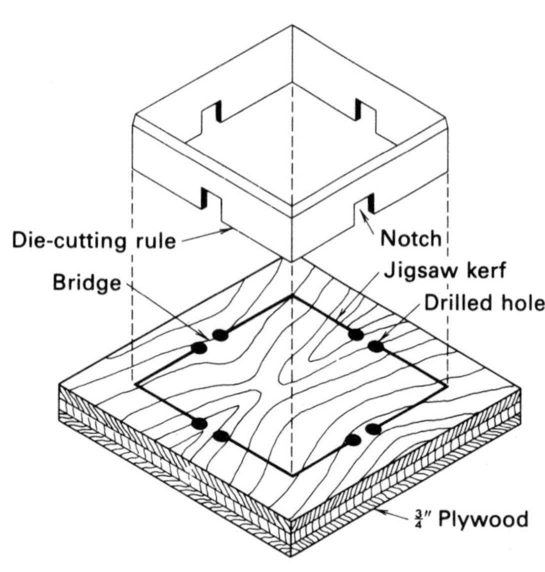

Figure 18.23. Making a simple die form

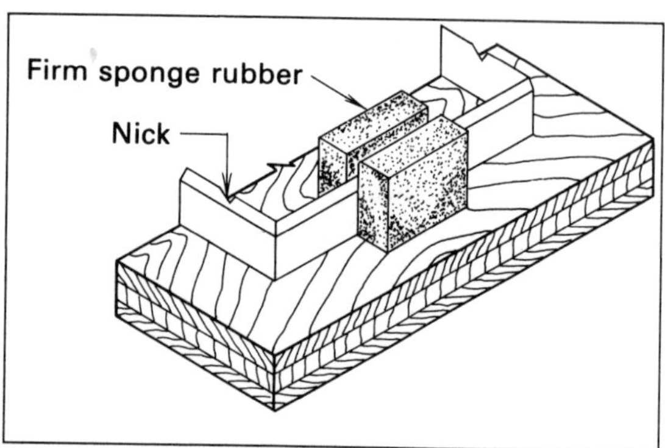

Figure 18.24. Ejecting the sheet after each cut Nicks are cut in the rule so the interior portions will remain with the main sheet, and sponge rubber is glued around parts of the rule to push the sheet back against the platen.

the image area. Repeat this procedure until the entire female die image is embossing the blotter sheet. Spot up weak areas on the male die by pasting small pieces of tissue paper directly over them on the blotter sheets. The manual forming technique is well suited to working with broad, open image areas.

Pasting Technique. When the female die contains fine or minute detail, a different technique should be used to produce the male die. One method is to use a mixture of plaster of paris, calcium carbonate, and gum arabic (2:3:2) to produce a doughy paste. Spread the paste on a sheet of mat board that has been glued to the platen of the press. Place a light coat of oil on the female die to prevent the paste from adhering to the metal surface. Pull the control lever of the press to the on-impression position and manually turn the flywheel until light contact has been made with the paste. Scrape off the excess compound squeezed out from the die. As the paste hardens, gradually increase impression by turning the flywheel until the platen is at the innermost position against the die. After the compound is completely dry, carefully open the press, dust the male die with talcum powder, and allow the material to harden overnight.

Die Cutting

Die cutting is a process that uses a razor-sharp steel rule to cut or punch various shapes (typically irregular) in the press sheets. It is possible for the local printer to produce basic die forms, but complicated designs should be prepared by commercial firms that are tooled-up to work the hard steel rule.

A simple die form can be made by bending the commercially available die-cutting rule to the desired shape, setting the formed rule in place on a piece of ¾-inch plywood, and tracing around both the inside and the outside of the metal with a pencil (figure 18.23). Cut between these lines with a band-saw to make an opening that will securely hold the rule. When making the cut, leave several bridges of wood in place so that the center portion will not drop out. Then mark the positions of these bridges on the rule and make notches so the metal will fit into place.

Because the die is actually cutting through the sheet, there is always a problem with the inside piece remaining attached to the form and not returning with the platen to the press operator. To eject the sheet after each cut, glue small pieces of firm sponge rubber to the plywood base in several spots around the steel rule (figure 18.24). The rubber is higher than the rule, so it compresses for each cut and then pushes the sheet back against the platen.

It would be a cumbersome working situation if the interior portion of each cut were allowed to fall free as the platen moved back out of the way of the die. After several thousand impressions, the pile of cut pieces would probably begin to interfere with the motion of the machine or could possible catch in the flywheel and send a cloud of confetti into the operator's face. The standard procedure is to cut small nicks in the cutting edge of the rule so the interior portion of the cutout will remain attached to the press sheet. After the job is completed, the scrap portions are removed in one operation.

The press make-ready procedures are the same as for creasing or perforating except that the rule must cut entirely through the sheet. Special die-cutting plates that fit over the platen are provided by most press manufacturers to protect the surface from the knife-like edges of the rule.

Key Terms

drawsheet
pulling an impression
setting the gauge pins
spotting up
hanging in the overlay
type-high gauge

Questions for Review

1. What are the three types of letterpress machines?
2. What is flexography?
3. What are the two functions of packing on a platen press?
4. What does the expression *dressing the press* mean?

5. Briefly describe the process of controlling the image position on a platen press.
6. What does the term *final make-ready* mean on a platen press?
7. What is the difference between an overlay and an underlay?
8. What does *spotting up* on a platen press mean?
9. What is the purpose of a type-high gauge for platen press roller adjustment?
10. What is the difference between creasing and perforating?
11. What does the term *embossing* mean?

Chapter Nineteen

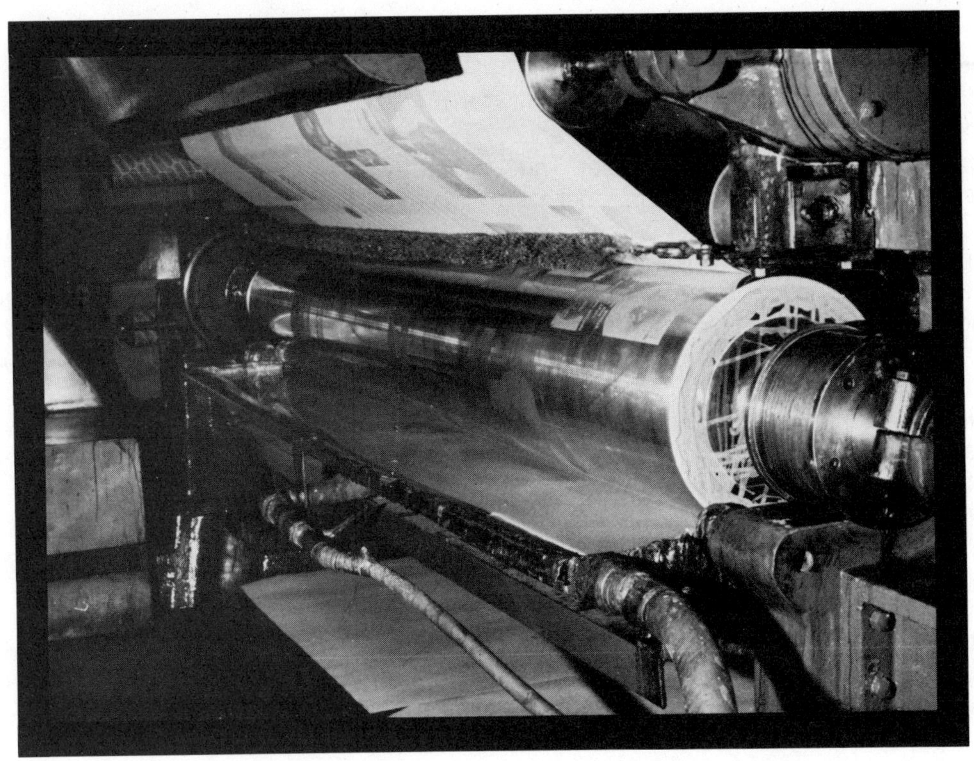

Gravure

Anecdote to Chapter Nineteen

The history of gravure printing begins with the work of creative artists during the Italian Renaissance, in the 1300s. Fine engravings and etchings were cut by hand in soft copper. The designs were cut away, leaving a channel, or sunken area, to hold the ink during printing. The term *intaglio,* which we use today to describe a class of printing, is an Italian word meaning to print with a sunken pattern or design.

The process quickly gained widespread recognition as a rapid, high-quality printing process that could be put to many different uses. The French artist Jacques Callot developed his reputation by sketching the fighting on battlefields and then rushing back to his studio to print etchings of the scenes. He would sell the etchings only a few days after the battle. Callot is sometimes called the first photojournalist because of the speed with which he distributed copies of his sketches.

The first photographic intaglio prints were made by Joseph Nicephore Niépce in about 1814. Niépce, who called his process heliography, printed the products on a copperplate press. Fox Talbot refined Niépce's work and, in addition to developing the first film negative, also worked on heliography.

The recognized inventor of modern gravure printing, however, is Karl Klič (born Klitsch). Klič began experimenting with photographic copper etching in 1875. By about 1879 he had refined the process and made a formal announcement of his "heliogravure" process to the Vienna Photographic Society. He produced very high quality reproduction for art collectors but gained little recognition outside his own country because he wanted to keep the techniques secret. He eventually sold his "secret," but continued to refine the process, even to his death in 1926. He made the revolutionary move from flat printing plates

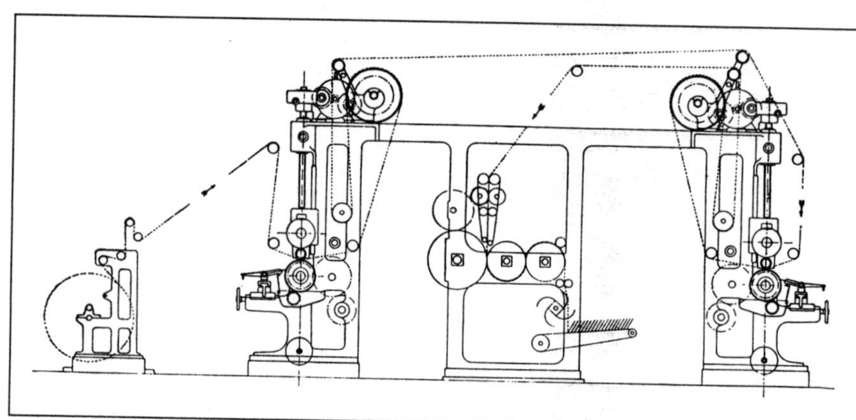

An early patent design for a French rotogravure press

to printing from a cylinder. He developed the first doctor blade and even designed a method of printing color on a web press. He is the one who originated the term *rotogravure* for printing from a cylinder.

After Klič shared his methods, other individuals became interested in rotogravure and began designing and building equipment for the process. By the beginning of this century, rotogravure had developed a relatively widespread reputation for fine reproductions. By 1920 huge presses were in use with four or five units for color gravure. Postcards, calendars, illustrations for books, and even magazines were being printed in full color.

One of the major uses of the process that began in the 1920s was the printing of the supplement section of the Sunday newspaper. The section carried human-interest stories, many advertisements, and lots of color photographs. The section was, and continues to be, a favorite item that readers look forward to each week. The supplement section and rotogravure printing gained such widespread public recognition that a Broadway play was even produced that used the two as a theme.

Irving Berlin was one of America's most famous songwriters. Few people, however, remember his 1934 Broadway play, *As Thousands Cheer*. However, almost everyone remembers the play's opening song, called "Easter Parade." The most famous lines mention both rotogravure printing and the Sunday supplement because the two terms had come to mean the same in the public's eye:

> *On the Avenue, Fifth Avenue, the photographers will snap us, and you'll find that you're in the rotogravure.*

Objectives for Chapter Nineteen

After completing this chapter, you will be able to:

- Understand the organization of the gravure industry and the importance of professional associations in its growth.
- Recall the major methods of cylinder preparation, including diffusion etch, direct transfer, electromechanical, and laser cutting.
- Recognize the variables in gravure printing, including well formation, film positive quality, etching and plating techniques, cylinder balance, cylinder and doctor blade considerations, and impression rollers.
- Recall the major steps in cylinder construction and preparation.
- Recall the major steps in placing an image on a cylinder by using the conventional gravure techniques.
- Recognize the parts of a gravure press and recall cylinder, doctor blade, and impression roller functions.

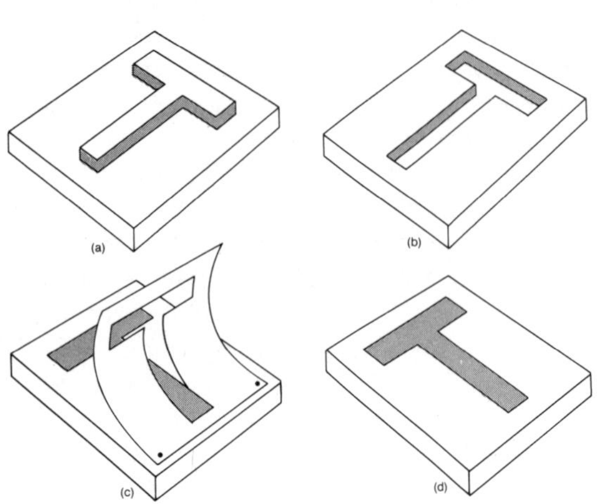

Figure 19.1. The four major printing processes Relief printing (a), intaglio printing (b), screen printing (c), and lithographic printing (d).

Introduction

Intaglio is a term that was introduced in chapter 1 in a simple comparison of the following four major printing processes (figure 19.1):

- *Relief,* which forms an image from a raised surface;
- *Screen,* which passes ink through openings in a stencil;
- *Lithography,* which prints photochemically from a flat surface;
- *Intaglio,* which transfers ink from a sunken surface.

Terms associated with intaglio include *etching, engraving, drypoint,* and *collagraphy.* Artists use these terms to describe images printed from lines cut into the surface of metal or plastic.

Industrial intaglio is called **gravure** printing, or **rotogravure.** *Roto* means "round." All industrial intaglio transfers an image from sunken areas cut into the surface of a cylinder (figure 19.2). Except for small proof presses, most industrial gravure presses are web-fed (figure 19.3). As the plate cylinder turns, a continuous roll of paper, foil, or plastic is passed through the press to receive the image. After printing, the paper is either rewound back onto a roll for shipment to the customer or cut into sheets at the end of the press by a device called a slitter.

The Gravure Industry

Gravure is a major printing process. Twenty percent of all printing in this country is done by gravure. The gravure industry has enjoyed a steady growth rate and, with recent technical advances, will continue to gain a larger share of the printing market. Several important characteristics make gravure an ideal process for jobs requiring high quality and extremely long press runs:

- Gravure is the simplest of all printing systems, with the fastest press start-up and the most direct press controls.
- Gravure's easy press control results in very little paper waste. Gravure has less than half the paper spoilage rate of lithography.
- Gravure press speeds are extremely fast. The largest gravure presses can operate as rapidly as 45,000 impressions an hour.
- Gravure cylinders are especially hardy. Several million impressions from the same cylinder are common. Some printers report press runs as long as 20 mil-

lion copies without the cylinder wearing out.

- Gravure gives the highest-quality image of the four major printing processes. It has the reputation of delivering excellent color and ink density even on low-quality printing papers.

The only significant disadvantage of gravure is the length of time required to prepare the printing cylinder. New equipment has been developed to automate much of the process, but most cylinders are still produced by the specialized craft of gravure engravers. Jobs with press runs of less than 60,000 to 70,000 impressions are generally not considered an effective use of the process. The cost of cylinder preparation is so much higher than other processes that some companies refuse jobs of less than a million copies.

Figure 19.2. A gravure press cylinder Rotogravure means printing from a cylinder.

Figure 19.3. A web-fed gravure press Almost all production gravure presses are web-fed. Courtesy of the Morrill Press.

Industry Organization

Gravure printing is divided into three broad product areas, each with its own special problems and solutions. The first group is **packaging printing.** This area includes folding cartons, bags, boxes, gift wrappers, labels, and flexible materials that will eventually be formed into containers.

The second area is **publication printing.** Publication printing includes newspaper supplements, magazines, catalogs, and mass mailing advertisements. Gravure is ideally suited for the long press runs required for the Sunday newspaper supplement sections that are distributed on a national basis.

The third area of gravure printing is **specialty printing.** In this area gravure is used to print such materials as wallpaper, vinyl, floor coverings, and even textiles for both decoration and clothing fabrication.

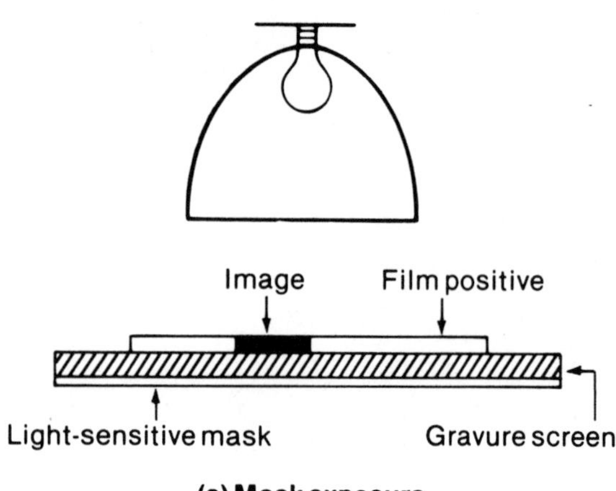

(a) Mask exposure

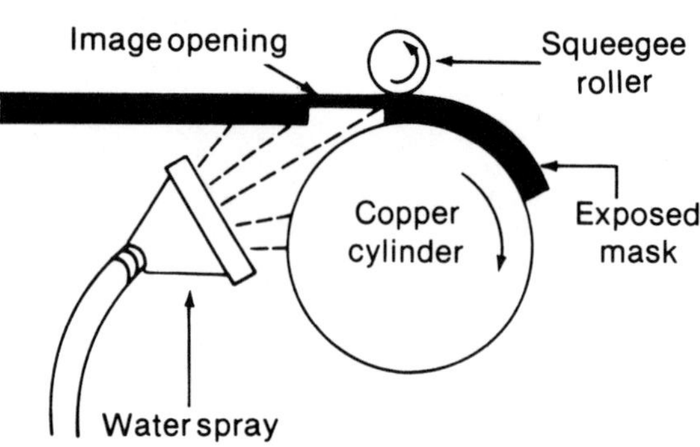

(b) Attaching the mask to the cylinder

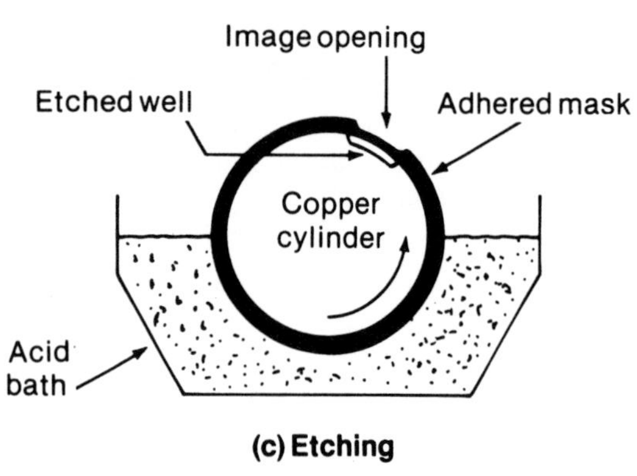

(c) Etching

Companies have found that they become more efficient and cost-effective by limiting the jobs they accept to a specific product area.

The Gravure Technical Association

One reason for the steady growth of gravure printing in the United States has been the cooperative efforts of gravure printers, suppliers, and manufacturers, focused through the **Gravure Technical Association** (GTA). GTA provides consultative assistance, publishes a wide range of technical materials related to all phases of gravure production, has worked to establish industry standards, supplies technical aids, and has a tradition of collegial efforts to educate printers and to disseminate information on gravure printing. Much of the information contained in this chapter was compiled through the courtesy and cooperation of the Gravure Technical Association. Individuals interested in using GTA's services or in becoming affiliated with the organization should write to the Gravure Technical Association, 60 East 42nd Street, Suite 2201, New York, N.Y. 10017.

Key Ideas

Gravure differs in several ways from other printing processes. Before the techniques of cylinder preparation are explained in detail, it is important to review several key ideas.

◀ **Figure 19.4. Cylinder preparation: diffusion etch** The three main steps in the conventional gravure process are mask exposure (a), attaching the mask to the cylinder (b), and etching (c).

Methods of Cylinder Preparation

There are basically four ways to prepare a gravure cylinder:

- By diffusion etch,
- By direct transfer,
- By the electromechanical process,
- By laser cutting.

Diffusion-Etch Process. In the **diffusion-etch process** (figure 19.4), a special mask is prepared by exposure first through a special gravure screen and then through a film positive of the printing image. Next the mask is applied to a copper gravure cylinder and is developed on the cylinder. After development, the mask is thick in the nonimage areas of the cylinder and is thin where an image is to carry ink. The cylinder is then placed in an acid bath. The acid penetrates through the thin areas of the mask and eats or etches away the copper. The last step is to apply a thin layer of chrome over the entire cylinder by an electroplating process. The purpose of the chrome is to extend the life of the surface areas.

Direct-Transfer Process. The second method of cylinder preparation is called **direct transfer.** The main difference between diffusion etch and direct transfer is the way in which the cylinder mask is exposed. In direct transfer, a light-sensitive mask is sprayed or applied over the cylinder surface. The mask is exposed by directing light through a halftone positive as it moves past the cylinder, which turns the same rate that the positive is moving (figure 19.5). The final steps of developing, etching, and chrome plating are the same as in the diffusion-etch technique.

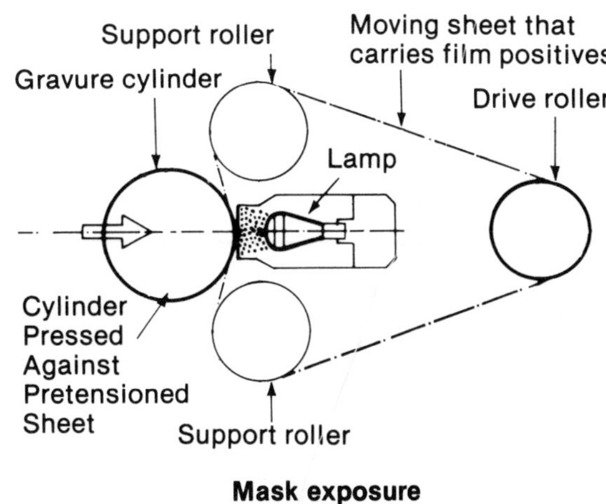

Figure 19.5. Cylinder preparation: direct transfer In the direct-transfer process, the light-sensitive mask is exposed by passing light through a halftone positive as it moves in contact with the rotating cylinder.
Courtesy of Southern Gravure Service.

Electromechanical Process. Another way of preparing a gravure cylinder is by the **electromechanical process.** In this process, a clean copper cylinder is mounted in a special engraving machine. Like a scanner used in color separation (see chapter 9), the original copy is ready by a beam of light. The information from the light is stored in a computer and is then translated into the motion of a cutter head (figure 19.6). A special diamond stylus actually cuts into the surface of the copper as the cylinder rotates. After cutting, the cylinder is chrome plated and is then ready for the press.

Laser-Cutting Process. The fourth technique of gravure cylinder preparation is called **laser cutting.** In this process, a series of small holes or wells is chemically etched over the entire surface of a clean copper cylinder. The wells are then filled with a plastic material

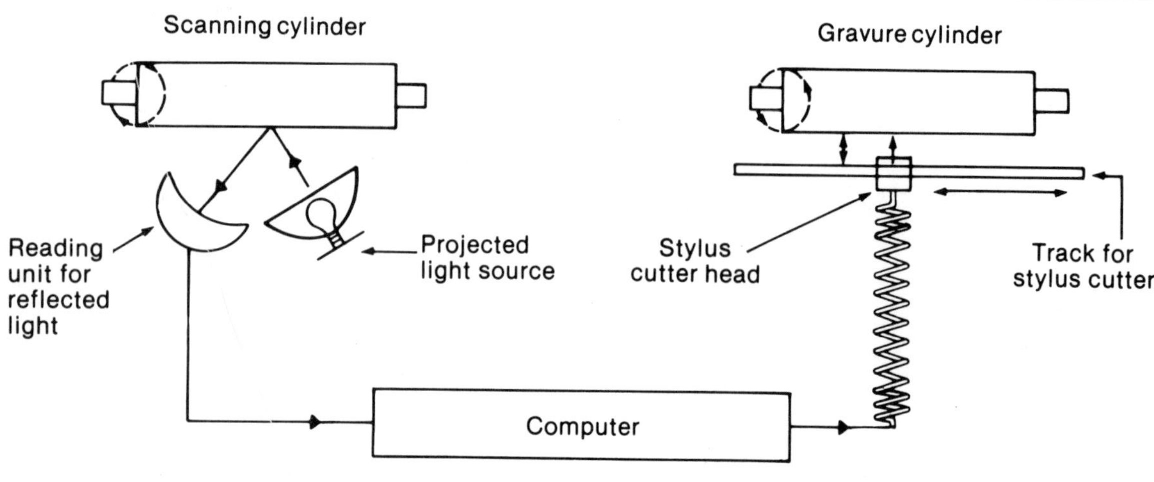

Figure 19.6. Diagram of the electromechanical process The cylinder is cut by using a diamond stylus in the electromechanical process.

until the cylinder again has a smooth, uniform surface. Like the electromechanical method, the original copy is scanned by a beam of light. This process, however, uses the narrow beam of a laser to remove parts of the plastic from individual wells rather than a diamond tool to cut away metal. The cylinder can be sprayed with a special electrolyte and plated with chrome.

Of the four cylinder preparation processes, diffusion etch is the oldest and is still the one most widely used by the industry. Recent advances with the laser process, and techniques still in the early research stages, point to changes in the near future that will revolutionize gravure cylinder preparation.

Well Formation

Gravure transfers ink from the small wells that are etched or cut into the surface of the cylinder (figure 19.7). On the press, the cylinder rotates through a fountain of ink. The ink is wiped from the surface of the cylinder by a doctor blade. The cup-like shape of each individual well holds ink in place as the cylinder turns past the doctor blade. The formation of perfect wells is the main concern of the gravure engraver. There are several important ideas to understand about gravure wells.

Every **gravure well** has four variables (figure 19.8):

- Depth,
- Bottom,
- Opening,
- Bridge.

The *depth* is measured from the *bottom* of the well to the top surface of the cylinder. The *opening* is the distance across the well. The

bridge is the surface of the cylinder between wells. The doctor blade rides against well bridges as it scrapes ink from the cylinder.

Within the diffusion-etch technique are two basic types of well design:

- Conventional gravure design,
- Lateral hard-dot process désign.

In the **conventional gravure** design, every well on a cylinder has exactly the same opening size (figure 19.9a). The amount of ink to be transferred to the paper is controlled only by the depth of the well. When reproducing photographic material, a continuous-tone film positive, rather than a high-contrast halftone, is used to expose the mask.

The second major type of well design with diffusion etch is called the **lateral hard-dot process** (sometimes called **halftone gravure**) design. Two separate film positives are used to expose the mask with the lateral hard-dot process. The first is a continuous-tone film positive, as with conventional gravure. A second exposure is then made with a halftone film positive that falls in the same position on the mask as that of the first exposure. The result is a well formation that varies in both opening size and depth (figure 19.9b).

The direct-transfer method of cylinder preparation produces yet another well design. A single halftone positive is used to expose the mask. The dot formation in the halftone defines the opening size of each well (figure 19.9c). The depth of each well is the same.

Electromechanical well formation is a bit different from diffusion etch or direct transfer. In the electromechanical process, each gravure well is created by the action of a diamond stylus as it pushes into the soft copper surface of the cylinder (figure 19.10). A direct relationship exists between the depth of cut

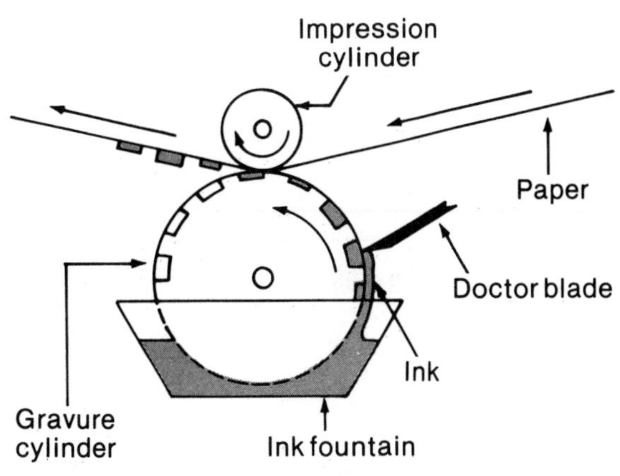

Figure 19.7. Diagram of the gravure printing process Etched wells in the printing cylinder pick up ink from the fountain. The excess ink is wiped from the surface of the cylinder by the doctor blade before the ink is applied to the press sheet.

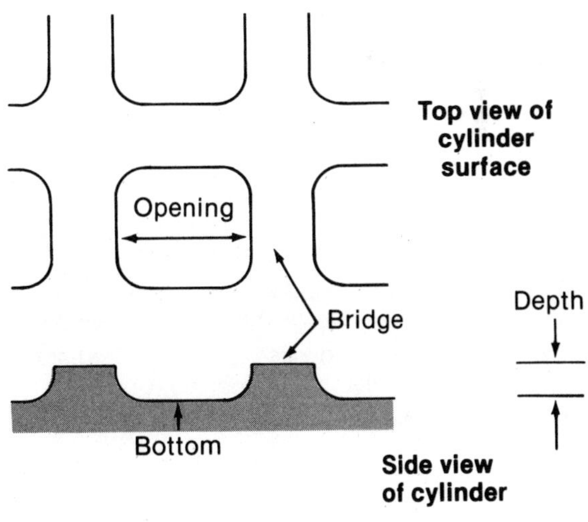

Figure 19.8. Diagram of gravure cylinder wells A gravure well has four variables—depth, bottom, bridge, and opening.

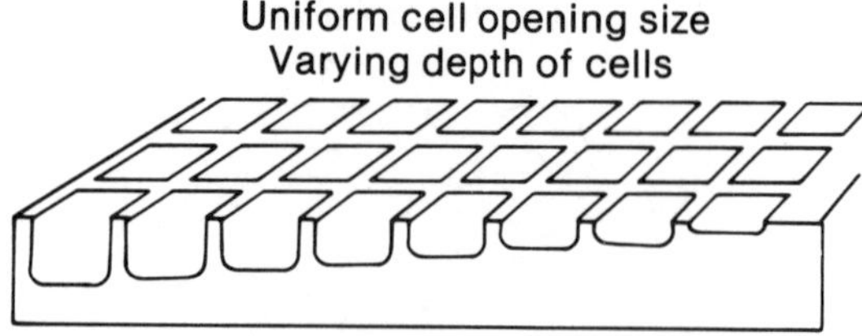

Uniform cell opening size
Varying depth of cells

(a) Conventional Gravure

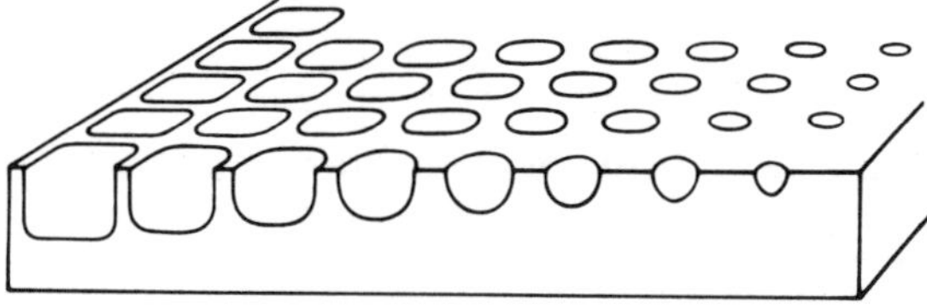

(b) Lateral Hard Dot

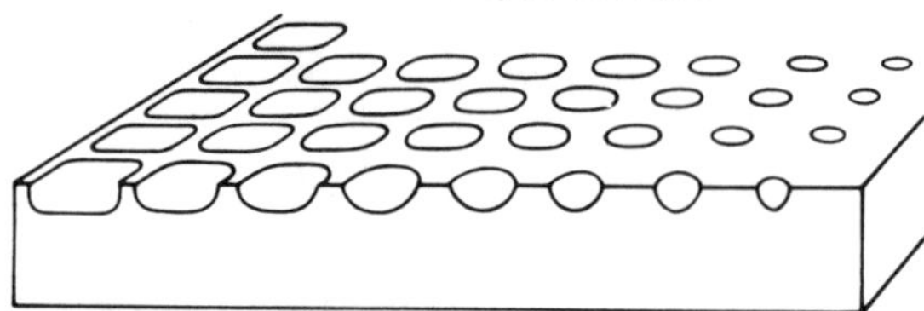

(c) Direct Transfer

Figure 19.9. Three examples of gravure wells Conventional gravure wells vary in depth, but all have the same opening size (a). Lateral hard-dot wells vary in both depth and opening (b). Direct-contact wells vary in opening size, but all have the same depth (c).
Courtesy of the Southern Gravure Service.

and the opening size. As the stylus pushes deeper, it also increases the opening. This action influences the volume of ink that the well can carry. In photographs, shadow area wells are much deeper than highlight wells.

Film Positives

Most artwork is delivered to the gravure engraver in the form of film positives. The characteristics of film images used by gravure are somewhat different from those used in other printing methods. The main difference is the image density range (see chapter 6 for a review of densitometry). Wells are etched or cut in proportion to the density of the corresponding area on the film positive.

There is a minimum depth that will hold ink during the printing process. If the well is too shallow, the action of the doctor blade and the rapidly spinning cylinder can actually pull ink from the well. Film positives must be prepared with a minimum density so that each well will be deep enough.

For continuous-tone images, the Gravure Technical Association recommends a density range of 0.30 to 1.65. This range means that the highlight areas of the positive will have a transmission density of 0.30 and a shadow reading of 1.65. The difference between the two measurements produces a basic density range of 1.35, which is acceptable to commercial photographers and still exceeds the range of most halftone negatives used in lithography.

Line images, such as type, ink, or line borders, are also supplied in positive form. Line image density should be near the same 1.65 shadow area density for continuous-tone images. Positives are often supplied to the engraver with both continuous-tone and line images on the same piece of film. The most common approach is first to prepare each type of image separately, in negative form, and then to make several contact exposures onto a new sheet of film to create a single film positive.

Cylinder Construction and Preparation

The quality of the final gravure image depends first on the construction of the cylinder. Almost all cylinder cores are made from steel tubing. Some packaging printers prefer extruded aluminum cores because they are much lighter, less expensive, and easier to ship than steel is. A few companies use solid copper shells, but steel remains the most popular core material.

A steel cylinder is used when printing with adhesives or other corrosive materials. In most gravure printing, however, a thin coating of copper is plated over the steel core to carry the image. Copper is easier to etch than steel and can easily be replaced when the job is finished.

Cylinder Design

There are five important parts to identify on a gravure cylinder (figure 19.11):

- Axis,
- Shaft,
- Diameter,
- Circumference,
- Face length.

The *axis* is the invisible line that passes through the center of the length of the cylinder. The **shaft** is the bearing surface as the cylinder rotates in the press. If you look at

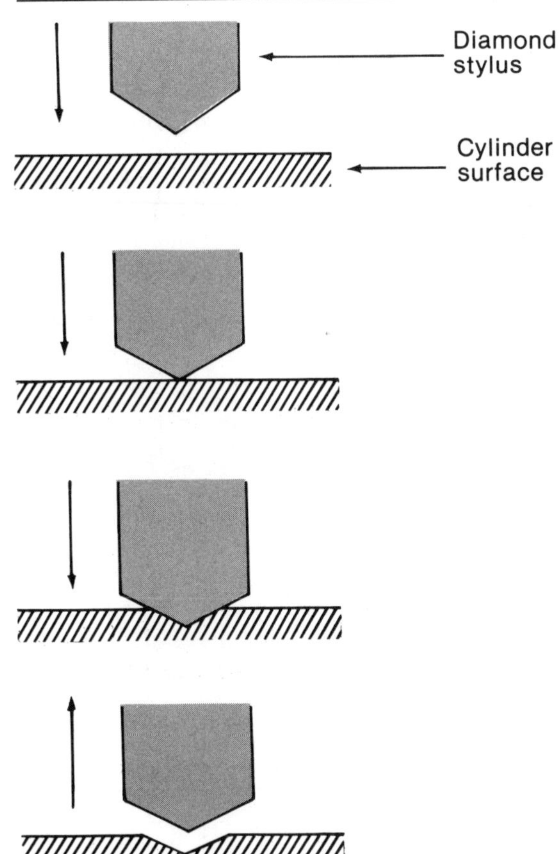

Figure 19.10. Cutting a cylinder surface In the electromechanical engraving process, wells are cut in the cylinder as a diamond stylus moves into the copper and then moves back.

the end view of a cylinder, it appears as a circle. The *diameter* is the distance across the circle, through the center of the shaft. The *circumference* is the distance around the edge of the end view. The *face length* is the distance from one end to the other, along the length of the cylinder.

The face length of the cylinder limits the width of paper to be printed. The circumfer-

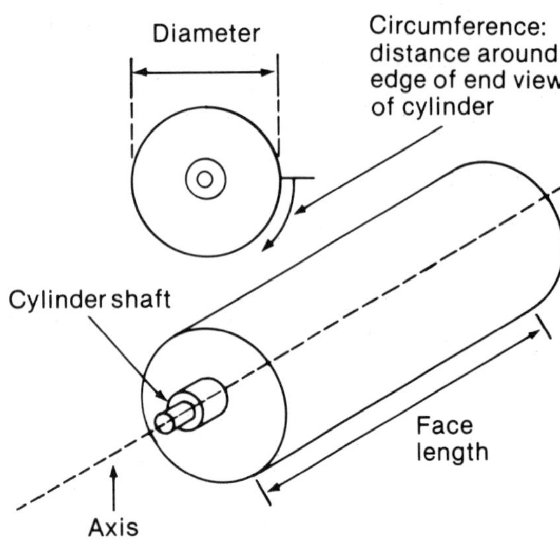

Figure 19.11. Parts of a gravure cylinder The most common identification parts of a gravure cylinder are diameter, circumference, shaft, axis, and face length.

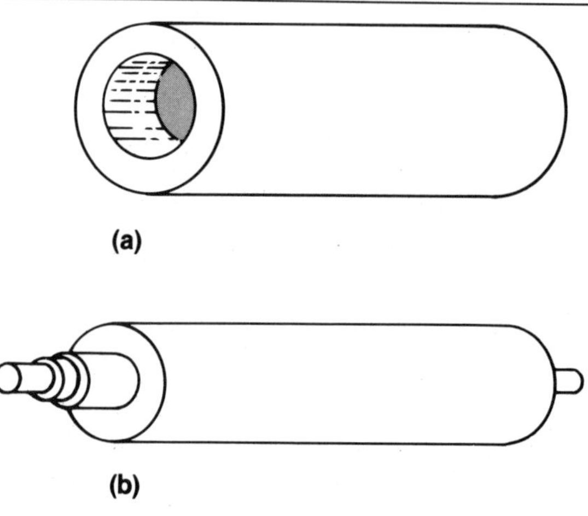

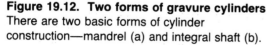

Figure 19.12. Two forms of gravure cylinders There are two basic forms of cylinder construction—mandrel (a) and integral shaft (b).

ence limits the size of the image. One rotation of the cylinder around its circumference is called one **impression.** Continuous images can be etched on a cylinder, without a seam, so the design is repeated without a break. Wallpaper designs are commonly printed by this technique.

There are two basic cylinder designs (figure 19.12):

- Integral shaft,
- Mandrel.

In the integral shaft design, the shaft is permanently mounted on the cylinder. The cylinder is first formed, and then the shaft is either pressed or shrunk in place. The shaft is permanently attached by welding and is not removed during the life of the cylinder.

A mandrel cylinder (sometimes called sleeve or cone cylinder) is designed to have a removable shaft. Most holes are tapered so that the shaft can be pressed in place and then easily removed.

Integral shaft cylinders are more expensive than mandrel cylinders but are generally considered to produce higher-quality images.

Balancing the Cylinder

A major concern during printing is vibration caused by an unbalanced cylinder (figure 19.13a). A great deal of vibration can bounce the cylinder against the doctor blade and result in a poor image. Vibration can also damage the press. GTA identifies two types of imbalance: static and dynamic.

Static imbalance occurs when the cylinder is not perfectly round or has different densities within a cross section (figure 19.13b). Static imbalance can be caused by such defects as air holes, impurities in the steel core, or improper copper plating and polishing.

Dynamic imbalance occurs when the cylinder differs in density or balance from one end to the other (figure 19.13c). Dynamic imbalance is the greatest cause of cylinder vibration at high press speeds. Both static and dynamic imbalance can be corrected by either cutting away from or adding weight to each end of the cylinder.

Copper Plating and Polishing

Electroplating is the process of transferring very small bits (called **ions**) of one type of metal to another type of metal. The process takes place in a special liquid **plating bath.** The ions are transferred as an electrical current is passed through the liquid. The longer the current flows, the more new metal will be plated onto the cylinder.

The first step in the gravure electroplating process is to thoroughly clean the surface of the cylinder. The cylinder is cleaned by brushing or rubbing it with special cleaning compounds and then rinsing with a powerful stream of hot water (figure 19.14). Some plants use special cleaning machines. The goal is to remove all spots of grease, rust, or dirt so that a perfect coating of copper can be applied over the entire surface. Areas not to be plated, such as the cylinder ends, can be coated with asphaltum or other staging materials.

To add a layer of copper, the cylinder is suspended in a curved tank and then rotated through the plating bath (figure 19.15). The electric current is allowed to flow from the copper anode (the plating metal) through the bath to the cylinder (base metal). Zinc sulfate, copper sulfate, or cyanide solutions are common plating-bath liquids. Six-thousandths inch (0.006″) to thirty-thousandths inch (0.030″) is the common thickness range for the copper layer on a gravure cylinder.

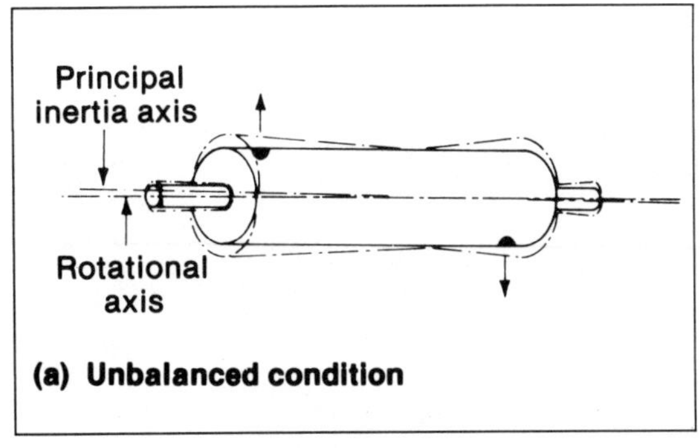

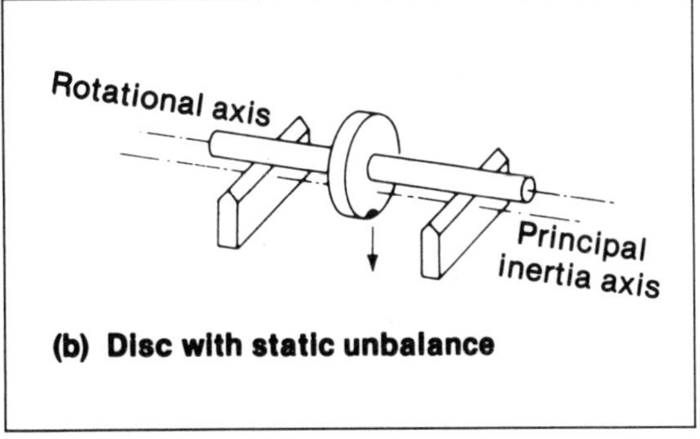

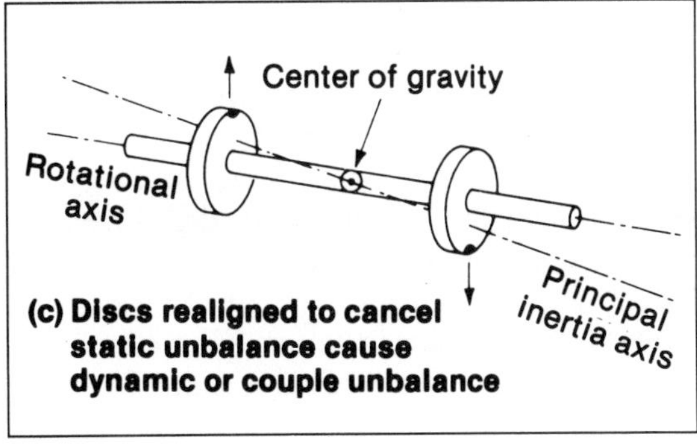

Figure 19.13. Examples of cylinder imbalance
Courtesy of Gravure Technical Association.

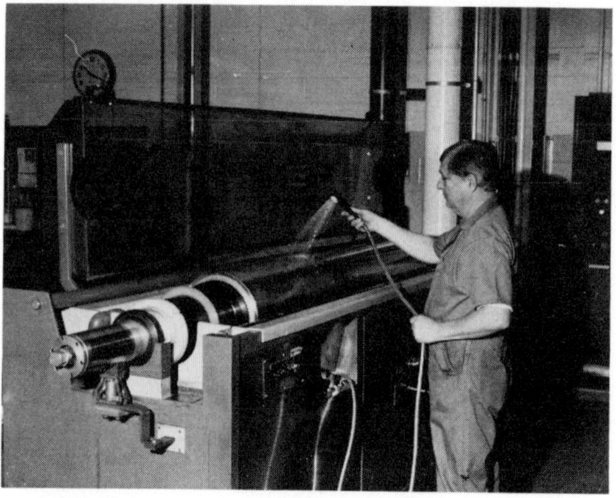

Figure 19.14. Cleaning the cylinder surface It is important to remove all spots of grease, rust, or dirt so that a perfect layer of copper can be applied to the cylinder surface.

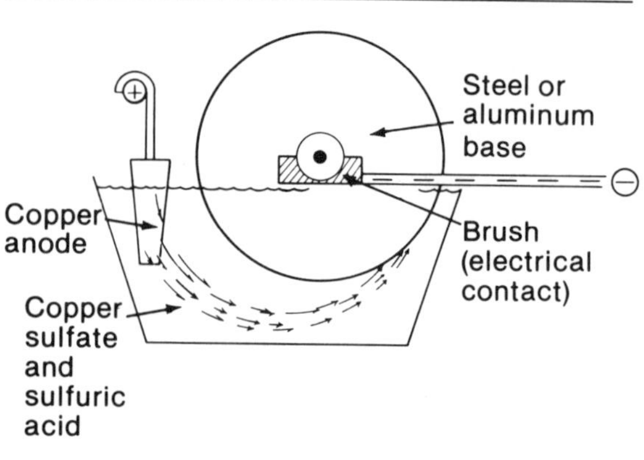

Figure 19.15. Diagram of the electroplating process An electric current passes from the copper anode through the plating solution to the steel or aluminum cylinder until the desired thickness of copper is plated on the cylinder. Courtesy of Southern Gravure Service.

A **newage gauge** is a device used to test the hardness of copper. Copper hardness is measured by pushing a diamond point into the copper surface. The diagonal length of the opening created by the diamond is measured and then compared with the amount of force required to push the diamond into the copper. The result is expressed in D.P.H. (diamond point hardness). Most printers look for a D.P.H. between 93 and 122.

The last step in the construction of a gravure cylinder is to bring the diameter (and circumference) to the desired size and at the same time to create a perfect printing surface. The cylinder must be not only perfectly round but also perfectly smooth and uniform across its length. If the cylinder is not uniform, the doctor blade will not be able to remove excess ink from the nonprinting surface (figure 19.16).

The newly plated cylinder is mounted in a lathe and prepared for final turning. Some plants use a diamond-cutting tool to bring the cylinder into round; then they use separate grinding stones to polish the surface (figure 19.17). Other plants use specially designed precision machines to both cut and polish at the same time. With this method, cylinders can be cut within one ten-thousandths inch (0.0001″) of the desired size and surface. After the final turning, the cylinder is ready for image etching.

Reuse of Cylinders

Gravure cylinders can be reused many times. One approach is to cut away the old image on a lathe. This involves removing only two- to three-thousandths inch. The cylinder is then replated with copper and again cut or ground to the original diameter.

Another technique is simply to dissolve the chrome coating (added as the final step

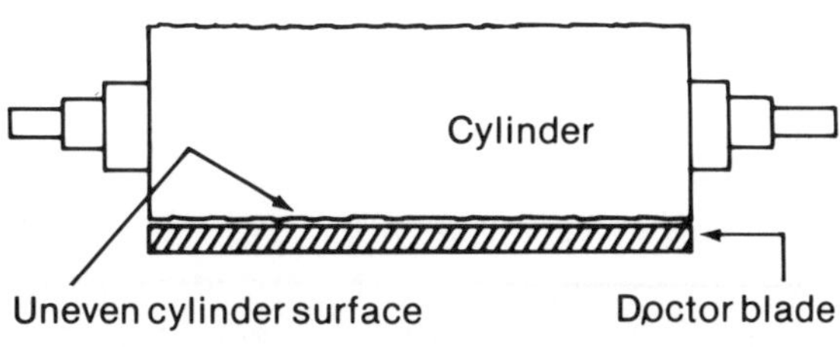

Figure 19.16. Diagram of a doctor blade against an uneven cylinder If the cylinder is not uniform, the doctor blade will not be able to remove excess ink from the nonprinting surface.

in cylinder preparation to protect the soft copper on the press) and then to plate over the old image with new copper. The replating process fills in the image areas above the level of the original surface. Excess copper is then cut or ground away, and the cylinder is returned to the desired diameter size.

Ballard Shell Cylinders

The **ballard shell process** is a special technique used by many publication printers that allows easy removal of a copper layer after the cylinder has been printed. The cylinder is prepared in the usual manner, including copper plating, except that it is cut twelve- to fifteen-thousandths-inch undersize in diameter. The undersized cylinder is coated with a special nickel separator solution and returned to the copper plating bath. A second layer of copper is plated onto the cylinder over the first layer. The cylinder is then cut or ground to the desired size, given an image etch, and printed.

The difference between most gravure cylinders and ballard shell cylinders is seen when the cylinder has been printed and is ready to receive another image. The second copper layer can be simply ripped off the ballard shell cylinder base. A knife is used to cut through the copper to the nickel separator layer, which allows the shell to be lifted away. The cylinder can then be cleaned, a new nickel separator solution applied, and another shell plated to receive the image.

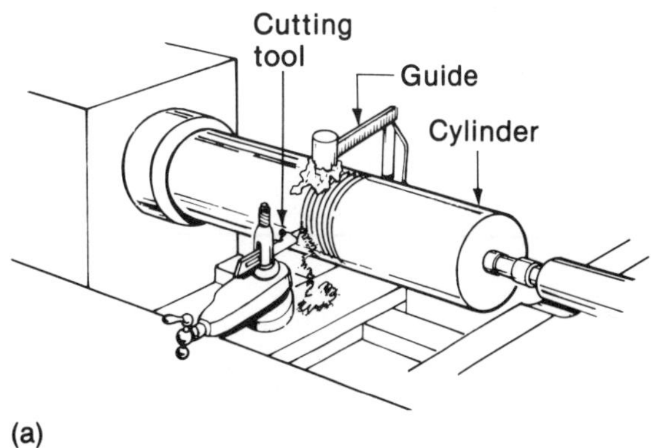

(a)

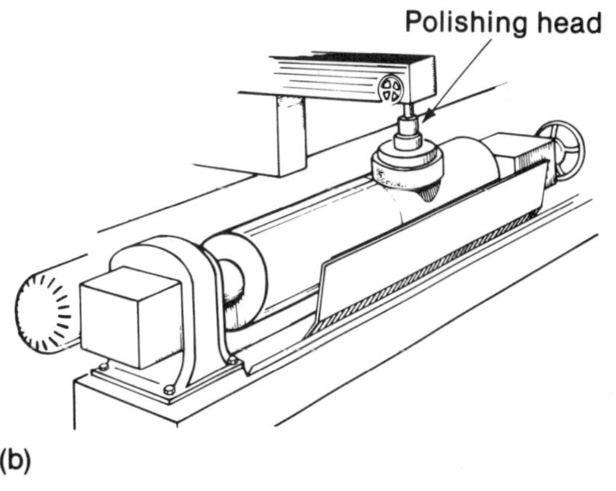

(b)

Figure 19.17. Final turning of a plated cylinder The cylinder is first cut to rough dimensions (a) and then it is ground or polished to the final size (b).
Courtesy of Southern Gravure Service.

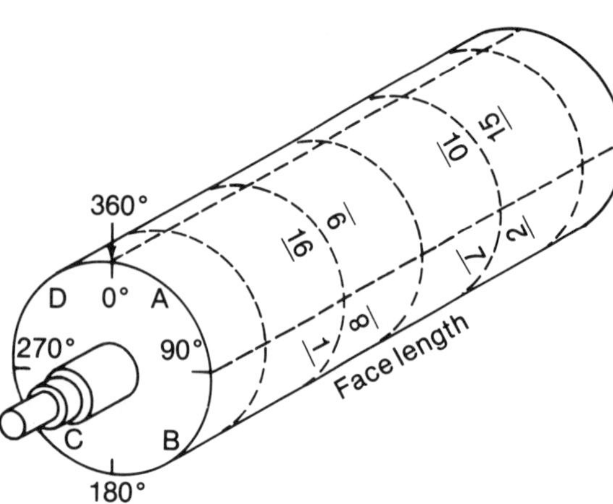

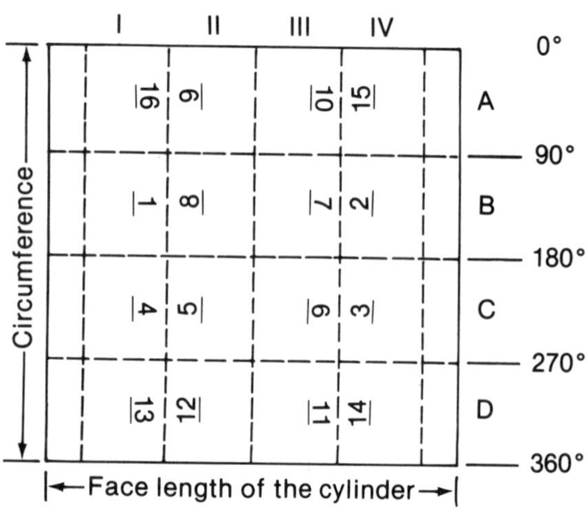

Figure 19.18. A 16-page cylinder layout

Conventional Gravure

There are several different ways to prepare a gravure cylinder. Four techniques were briefly described at the beginning of this chapter (diffusion etch, direct transfer, electromechanical, and laser cutting). A detailed explanation of the steps for each method is beyond the scope of this chapter. It is valuable, however, to examine one technique as an example of methods used in the gravure industry.

The diffusion-etch process is widely used in the industry. The steps involved in the process are somewhat similar to those used in direct transfer and lay a foundation for understanding the other methods of cylinder preparation. The following sections detail the procedure of etching a cylinder by diffusion etch, using conventional gravure with carbon tissue.

Cylinder Layout and Film Assembly

Most jobs arrive at the gravure printer in film format, with a dummy showing final page position. (See chapter 3 for a review of signature layout and use of a dummy.) The first step in gravure printing is to lay out the cylinder and identify page or image positions.

Figure 19.18 shows the layout for the first two cylinders that will be used to print a 16-page advertisement. The face length of the cylinder is one dimension of the layout, and the circumference is the other. The pages are identified by Roman numerals (along the face length) and by letters of the alphabet (around the circumference). For example, position III–C is page 6 of the job. Page positions are determined by how the job will be folded and are always provided with the job materials. Notice that for this job a second cylinder will be used to print the other side of the paper. The web will then be slit and folded to form two separate rolls. The layout will be used as a guide for assembling the different pieces of film.

If the job arrived as film negatives, then the printer must prepare contact positives. To make film positives that will fall into the cor-

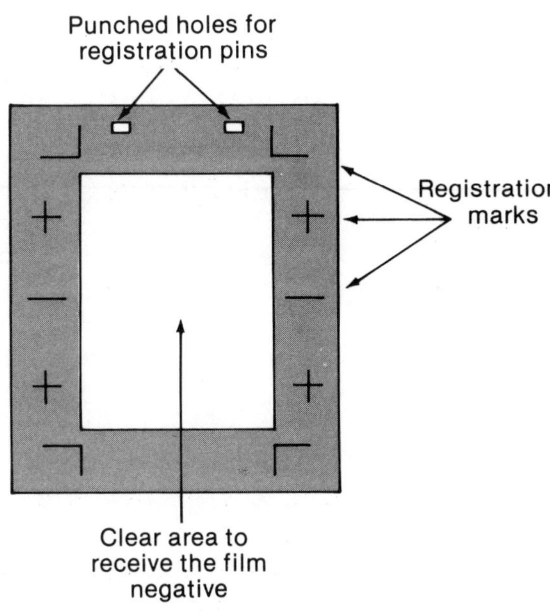

Figure 19.19. Diagram of a cab (cabriolet) A cab is used to register the film negative.

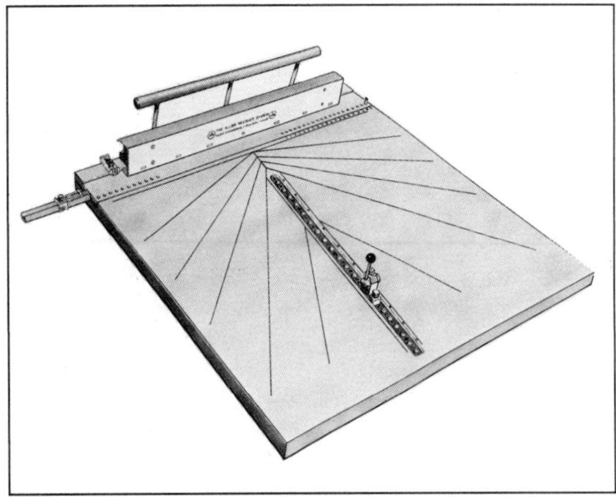

Figure 19.20. A Berkey stripper punch A two- or three-hole punch is used to punch both the cab and the unexposed film.

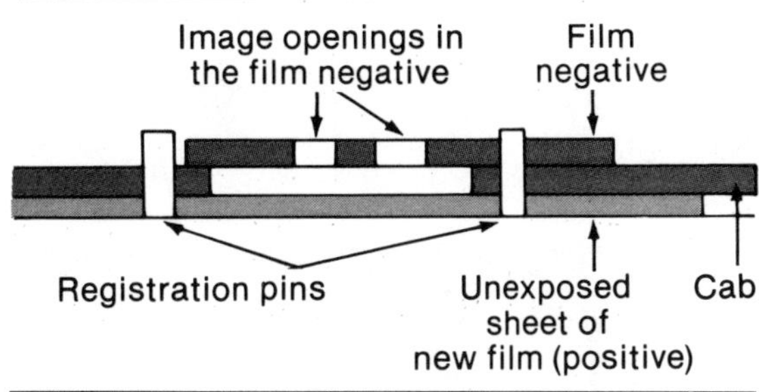

Figure 19.21. Using a cab to make a film positive The cab holds the film negative on registration pins when the negative is contact printed to a new sheet of unexposed film.

rect position on the cylinder, special carriers or cabs (cabriolets) are used. **Cabs** are special film masks that are punched and marked so they can be used as guides for the images (figure 19.19).

Each cab carries special registration marks and has a clear, open area to receive the negative image. The negatives are stripped to the cab's registration marks and then contact printed to a new sheet of film. The unexposed film is punched on the same device used to punch the cab (figure 19.20). When contacting is done, both the cab and the film are dropped onto registration pins (figure 19.21). The processed film positive will then fall into place on register pins mounted on a master plate.

The **master plate** is a frame with register pins that hold the film positives in correct printing position during exposure to the cylinder masking material. For color printing, each set of separations is exposed to the cylinder mask with the same master plate to ensure perfect color fit.

When the positives are completed and in position on the master plate, several additional positives are added before exposure

Figure 19.22. A cross-line gravure screen A cross-line gravure screen is used to create the well openings in conventional gravure.

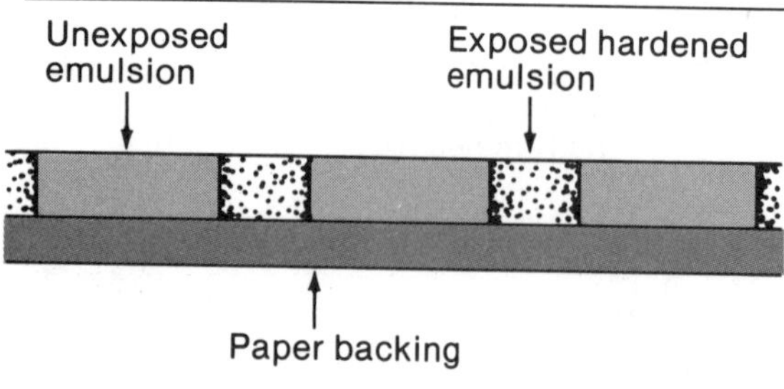

Figure 19.23. Side view of carbon tissue after exposure to a cross-line screen

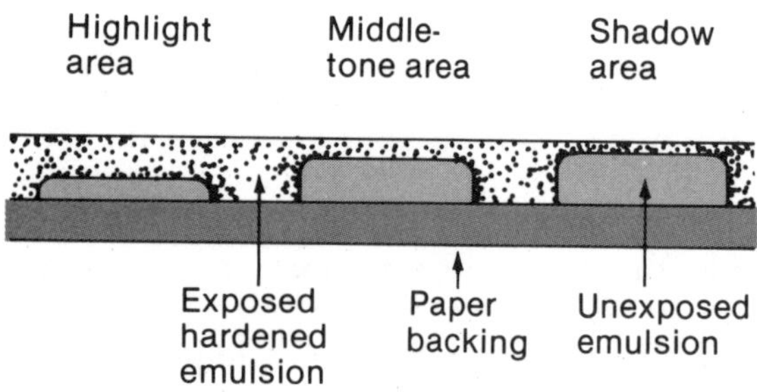

Figure 19.24. Side view of carbon tissue after exposure to a continuous-tone film positive

to the cylinder masking material. Registration on many gravure presses is monitored by special electronic eyes that sense misfit and automatically make press adjustments. **Electronic-eye mark** film positives are added to the master plate so that the marks will be etched into the cylinder, out of the image area on the paper web.

Some jobs require blank pages. Where no image is required, pieces of film, called burner film, are added to the master plate. **Burner film** is a piece of transparent film that allows full passage of light to the cylinder mask. This hardens the light-sensitive mask and does not allow acid to reach the copper cylinder. If acid does not reach the surface, the area is not etched and will not carry ink to the paper.

With all positives in position on the master plate, the job is ready for carbon printing.

Carbon Printing

The process of transferring the positive image to the cylinder mask is called **carbon printing.** The point of the process is to create a resist that can be adhered to the cylinder. A **resist** is material that will block or retard the action of the acid on the copper. There are two basic types of resist material for diffusion etch: carbon tissue and rotofilm.

Carbon tissue is a gelatin-based material coated on a paper backing. The emulsion can be sensitized so that it "hardens" in proportion to the amount of light that strikes it. Carbon tissue must be made light sensitive by the engraver. The second material is called rotofilm and is manufactured by the DuPont corporation. Rotofilm has the same characteristics as carbon tissue but comes to the engraver presensitized and ready for use.

Carbon tissue is sensitized by immersing the material in a 3% to 4% potassium bichromate solution. The sheet is placed in the solution, emulsion-side up, for 3½ to 4 minutes and then squeegeed onto a plexiglass sheet to dry. The squeegeed sheet is dried under circulating cool air for several hours and is then placed in storage for 8 to 10 hours to "cure."

The sensitized carbon tissue is placed emulsion-side up on a vacuum frame for exposure. In conventional gravure, the carbon tissue will receive two separate exposures. The first is a screen exposure, and the second is the image exposure.

Recall that with conventional gravure the well openings are all the same size and vary only in depth (see figure 19.9). A special gravure screen is used to create the outline of each well (figure 19.22). A sharp screen pattern is formed on the carbon tissue by allowing an intense light to harden the outline of the well bridges (figure 19.23).

For most work, printers use a 150-line screen (150 wells per inch). Gravure printers are also concerned with the ratio of opening to bridge dimensions. A ratio of 2½ or 3 to 1 (3:1) is common. This means that for each unit of well thickness there will be 2½ or 3 units of opening.

Carbon printing is done by exposing the master plate (with the film positives in place) to the carbon tissue. Registration to the cylinder is commonly controlled by a lug system. Both the carbon tissue and the master plate are dropped over special lugs or pins on the vacuum frame. The punched carbon tissue can then be mounted on the cylinder with a corresponding lug system.

The gelatin compound hardens in direct proportion to the amount of light that reaches the emulsion. The emulsion hardens first at the top of the gelatin layer. As light continues to reach the carbon tissue, the emulsion hardens down toward the paper base.

With line work, little light reaches the carbon tissue, so the emulsion is hardened only at the top layer. The varying densities of a continuous-tone photograph affect the emulsion differently. Highlight areas pass a great deal of light, so the hardened emulsion is very thick in those areas. Shadow areas pass little light, so the hardened emulsion is thin in those areas (figure 19.24). A highlight area on the positive, with a density of 0.35, passes 50 percent of the light that strikes the film; 50 percent is absorbed by the image density. In the middle tones, an area with a density of 1.0 will pass 10 percent of the light. At a density of 1.65 (a shadow area), only 2½ percent of the light reaches the carbon tissue.

Tissue Laydown and Development

The process of attaching the carbon tissue to the copper cylinder is called **tissue laydown.** The tissue can be laid down as a single piece of the same size as the cylinder. More commonly, however, tissue is applied to the cylinder in several separate pieces.

Before laydown the cylinder must be cleaned. Any traces of tarnish or grease will prevent tissue adhesion. Most companies use an electrolytic degreasing machine (see figure 19.15).

Most laydown is done on a special laydown machine. The clean cylinder is placed in the device and positioned by a special control gauge. A fixed metal lug bar holds the carbon tissue in register with the cylinder position (emulsion side of the carbon tissue against the cylinder) (figure 19.25a). A layer of distilled water is poured on the cylinder, and a rubber squeegee roller is brought into contact with the carbon tissue, against the cylinder (figure 19.25b). The carbon tissue is cut from the lug bar, and distilled water is poured between the tissue and cylinder as the rubber squeegee roller turns. After one rotation the carbon tissue is adhered to the cyl-

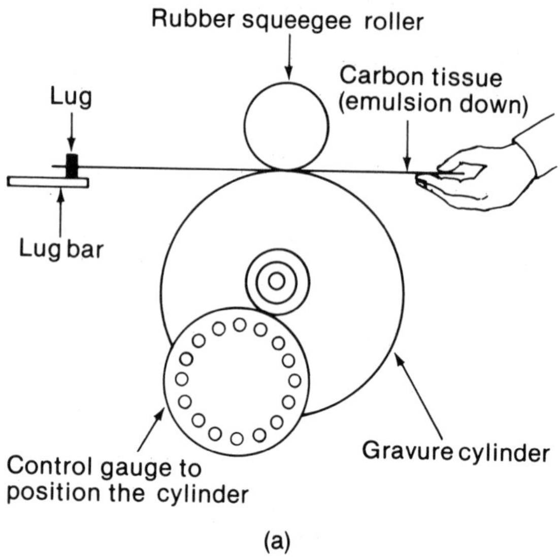

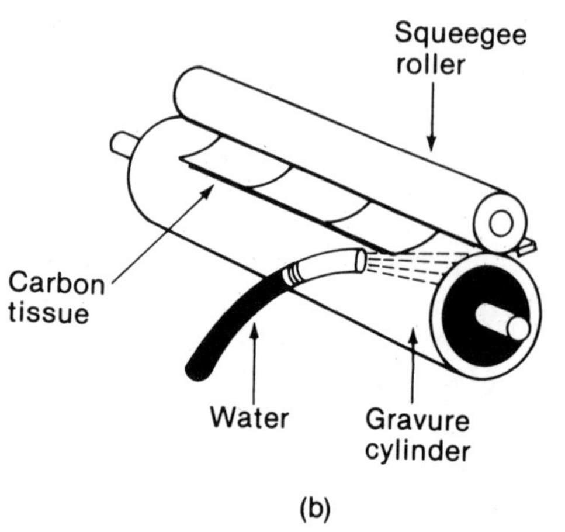

Figure 19.25. Mounting the carbon tissue on the gravure cylinder A special laydown machine is used to mount the carbon tissue on the gravure cylinder.

inder. If several pieces of tissue are to be applied to the cylinder, the operation is repeated for each section. After all pieces are mounted, the paper backing is soaked with cold water and then gently squeegeed by hand. The backing is then allowed to dry thoroughly (usually from 5 to 10 minutes with fan driers). This method is called **dry laydown.**

When the paper backing is completely dry, development can begin. The first step is to swab the paper with an alcohol solution. This solution rapidly soaks through the backing and begins to loosen it from the gelatin emulsion. The cylinder is then partially submerged in a water bath and slowly rotated so that all parts of the surface are kept uniformly wet. As the water temperature is gradually raised, the paper loosens from the cylinder and can be pulled away.

The goal in development is to remove all portions of the unhardened gelatin emulsion (figure 19.26). Some engravers gently spray the cylinder as it turns in the warm-water bath. Others use an automatic system that changes the water in the bath by a low-pressure water spray located in the bottom of the tray.

Development is completed when no more gelatin can be removed and the surface is hard to the touch. The emulsion is fixed by first cooling the cylinder below room temperature and then pouring an alcohol solution over the surface. A soft rubber squeegee is then used to remove all alcohol from the cylinder, and the emulsion is allowed to dry.

Staging and Etching

Some areas of the cylinder often are not covered after laydown and development. The edges and ends of the cylinder must be protected from the action of the acid. Other areas must be also protected. When two or more

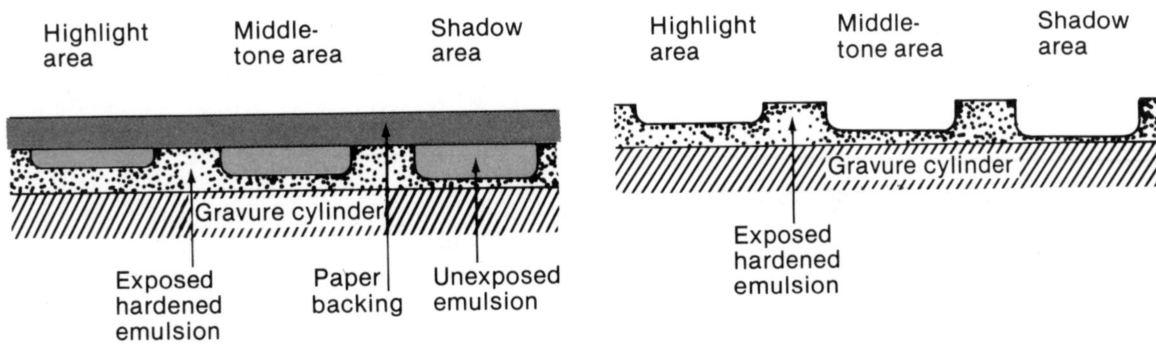

Figure 19.26. Side view of carbon tissue attached to a gravure cylinder showing unexposed emulsion to be removed

Figure 19.27. Side view of carbon tissue attached to a gravure cylinder showing emulsion that the acid bath must penetrate

pieces of tissue are applied to the cylinder, the area where they meet often shows bare metal. If acid reaches the metal at this union, a line will be etched and will appear as an image on the press.

The process of covering bare metal or thin areas on the tissue is called **staging.** The most common staging material is asphaltum. **Asphaltum** is a tar-like material that is acid resistant. The engraver paints the stage in unprotected areas by hand with a small brush or pen. After etching, the asphaltum can be dissolved with turpentine.

In etching, an acid bath penetrates through the resist to the copper (figure 19.27). When the acid reaches the surface, it dissolves a portion of the copper metal. The highlight areas of the resist are thick and therefore allow little acid to reach the cylinder. Highlight wells are shallow. The shadow areas of the resist are thin and allow a great deal of acid to penetrate to the copper. Shadow wells are deep.

Etching a cylinder is as much an art as a technical process. Conventional gravure typically involves five or six separate etching solutions, each of different acid strength. The acid used in the etching bath is perchloride of iron. The acid arrives at the engraver in large containers, usually at 48° Baumé (pronounced "48 degrees bomb-a"). Recall that Baumé is a system of measuring the density (or specific gravity) of a liquid. As the degrees Baumé fall, so too does the acid concentration, or strength. A 48° solution is much stronger than a 38° solution. For conventional gravure, separate etching solutions of 46°, 44°, 42°, 40°, 39°, and 37° Baumé are commonly used. The action of each bath penetrates the gelatin emulsion with different degrees of effectiveness. Figure 19.28 shows the action of the acid as it gradually penetrates through the carbon tissue to cut highlight, middle-tone, and shadow wells. Some efforts have been made to automate the process, but successful etching of a cylinder still requires the practiced eye of a skilled engraver.

The last step in the etching process is to remove the carbon tissue and staging material. The cylinder is rotated through a hot

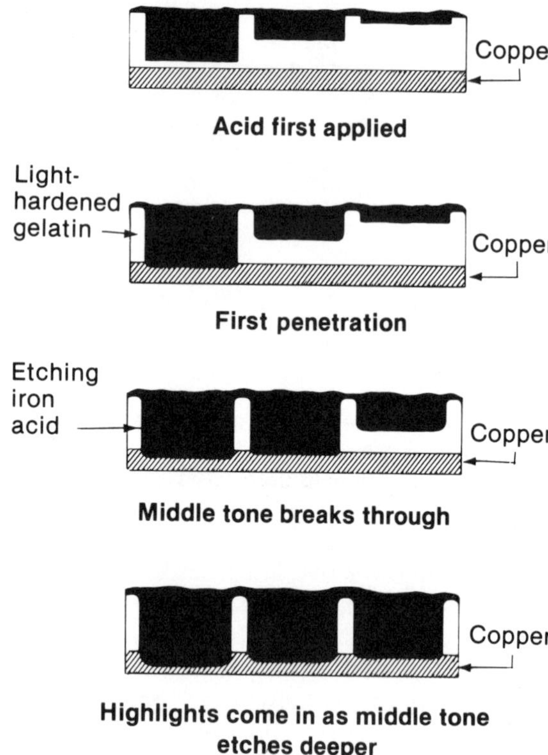

Figure 19.28. Stages of acid etch of a cylinder
The several different etching solutions gradually penetrate through the gelatin emulsion to form the wells
Courtesy of Southern Gravure Service.

acetic acid saltwater bath. The action of the hot bath dissolves all traces of the carbon tissue layer. The staging is dissolved with turpentine.

Cylinder Proofing, Correction, and Chrome Plating

The final steps in gravure cylinder preparation (with conventional gravure) involve proofing, correction, and chrome plating.

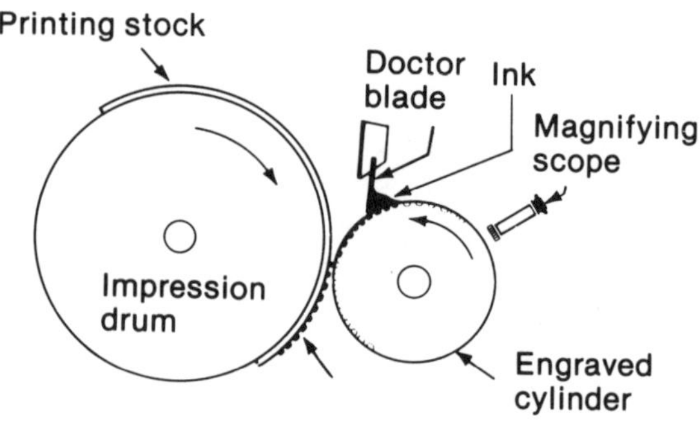

Figure 19.29. Diagram of a proof press
Special proof presses are used to duplicate the quality of the production press.
Courtesy of Southern Gravure Service.

Proofing. The cylinder is mounted in a special proof press that duplicates the quality of the production press (figure 19.29). Ink is applied, and several proofs are pulled from the cylinder. Color proofs are always judged under special viewing lights—usually 5,000° K (see chapter 6 for a discussion of color viewing).

Correction. Several methods are used to correct defects in the cylinder or to improve image quality to meet the customer's approval. It is possible to do hand tooling on a cylinder. A skilled engraver can reduce contrast by using an abrasive to rub away well walls. It is also possible to burnish or cut new wells into the cylinder with tools called a graver and a roulette wheel.

Sometimes it is necessary to fill in etched wells with new copper and then re-etch a new image. This is accomplished by spot plating. A **spot plater** is a machine that passes an electric current to the cylinder through a handheld electrode. The electrode is covered with cotton or gauze and then soaked in a plating solution. As the electrode is held against the

Figure 19.30. Rollup of a gravure cylinder

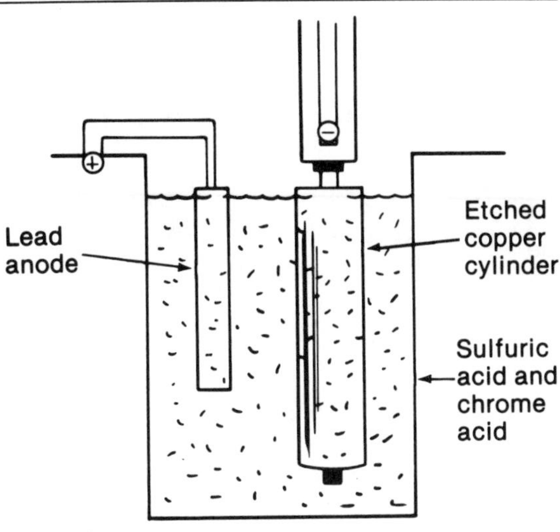

Figure 19.31. Plating the cylinder Electric current passes from the anode through the chrome plating solution to the cylinder.
Courtesy of Southern Gravure Service.

cylinder, a small area of copper is built up on the surface. Spot plating can be used only to correct small areas.

Sometimes the entire cylinder must be re-etched to increase overall well depth. A technique called **rollup** is used to cover the cylinder in the nonimage areas. A special brayer is carefully rolled over the surface to apply a layer of rollup ink (figure 19.30). After rollup, the cylinder can be returned to the etching room or the engraver can apply an etch to selected areas by using cotton soaked in acid.

Chrome Plating. After the press sheets have been approved by the customer, the cylinder is ready for chrome plating. Several different machines are used for chrome plating. All are designed to place a thin layer of chrome over the surface of the cylinder.

The cylinder is first cleaned to remove all traces of ink or grease from the proofing operation. The edges are staged or a special cover is applied to protect the cylinder shaft and face edge. The cylinder is then suspended in a solution of chrome and sulfuric acid (figure 19.31). Lead is commonly used as the anode. Electric current is passed from the anode through the plating bath to the cylinder. By controlling both time and amperage, a layer of chrome is deposited over the copper surface. Most chrome layers are between 0.0002″ and 0.0007″ thick. The desired thickness is detemined by the type of screen and the depth of well etch.

After all traces of the plating bath are washed away and the cylinder is dry, the cylinder is ready to be sent to the pressroom.

Gravure Presswork

Gravure presswork is similar to press operations for both relief and lithography. Almost all gravure printing is done on web-fed presses

Figure 19.32. A printing unit of a web-fed press
Courtesy of the Morrill Press.

Figure 19.33. Slitting the printed paper Some jobs require that the web be slit into smaller rolls at the delivery end of the press.
Courtesy of The Morrill Press.

(figure 19.3). Paper or some other material (called a substrate) is fed from large rolls to the printing unit through an intricate system of tension and registration controls (figure 19.32). The paper passes between the image cylinder and an impression cylinder. Some companies use offset gravure, but most transfer the image directly from the cylinder. After the paper leaves the printing area, it might pass through a set of driers to set the ink or it might follow an intricate set of rollers to dry by aerial oxidation and absorption. As the paper enters the delivery end of the press, it might be slit (figure 19.33), cut into sheets and folded (figure 19.34), or rewound back onto a roll for shipment to the customer (figure 19.35).

Many of the concerns in gravure web-press operation have already been discussed in previous chapters. Chapter 12 dealt with press design and operation, which are applicable to the basic procedures for any printing method, including gravure. Chapter 18 dealt with ink and paper and discussed the special characteristics of gravure ink. Some elements, however, are unique to gravure press operation. The two main areas of cylinder and doctor blade adjustment and impression rollers will be examined to complement the information presented in other chapters.

Cylinder and Doctor Blade Considerations

The function of the doctor blade is to wipe ink from the surface of the plate cylinder, leaving ink in only the recessed wells. A great deal of research has been done on materials, angles, and designs for doctor blades.

Several different materials are used for blades. The goal is to minimize blade wear and reduce heat generated by the rubbing of the blade against the turning cylinder. Plastic, stainless steel, bronze, and several other metals have been used with success. The most common blade material, however, is Swedish blue spring steel. Blades are usually between 0.006″ and 0.007″ thick. The blades must be relatively thin to reduce wear on the cylinder, but strong enough to wipe away ink.

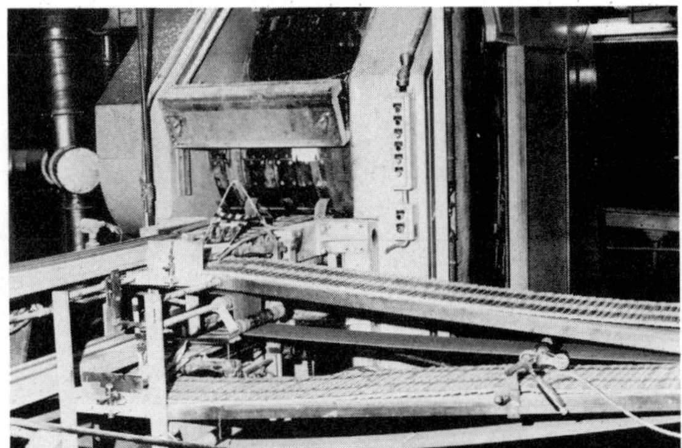

Figure 19.34. Folding unit of a web press Some jobs are cut into sheets and folded in line on the press.

Figure 19.35. Rewinding printed paper Some jobs are rewound back onto a roll after printing. Courtesy of The Morrill Press.

Blade angle is an important consideration. The angle between the blade and the cylinder is called the **counter** (figure 19.36). There is much discussion on the proper counter for the best image quality. The "best" counter depends on the method used to prepare the cylinder. For example, with electromechanically engraved cylinders, image quality decreases as the counter increases. Most angles are set between 18° and 20°. After the blade is placed against the cylinder and production begins, the counter generally increases to around 45°.

Another way to set the blade angle is by using the reverse doctor principle. With this approach the doctor blade is set at a large enough angle to push the ink from the surface (figure 19.37). The principle is not widely used, but it is gradually gaining acceptance in the industry.

Several different doctor blade designs are used by gravure printers (figure 19.38). The most popular are called conventional and MDC/Ringier. Care must be taken to keep the

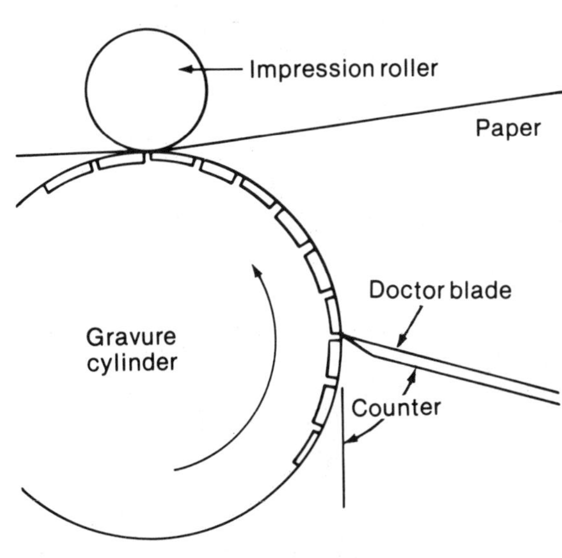

Figure 19.36. Diagram showing the counter The counter is the angle between the doctor blade and the cylinder surface.

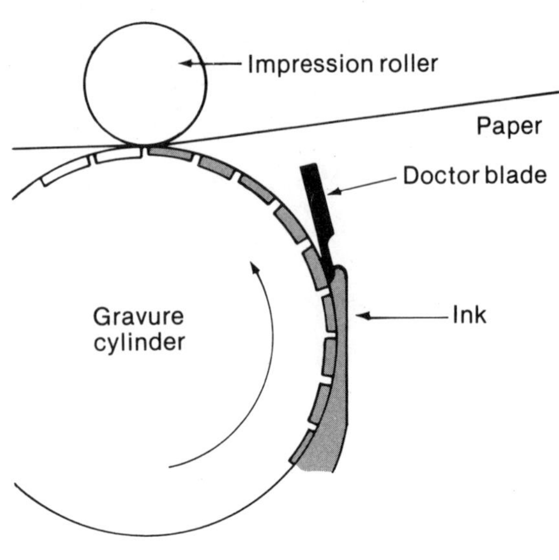

Figure 19.37. Diagram showing a reverse doctor blade A reverse doctor blade pushes ink from the cylinder surface.

conventional design sharp and uniform. Most printers hone the blade by hand with a special stone and then polish it with a rouge or emery paper to get a flawless edge.

The MDC/Ringier design has a longer working life than the conventional form has and requires much less press down-time for blade cleaning and repair.

The action of the doctor blade against the cylinder is of special concern. The blade rides against the cylinder with pressure. Pressure is necessary so that the ink does not creep under the blade as the cylinder turns. The most common method of holding the blade against the surface is by air pressure. The blade fits into a holder, which in turn is mounted in a special pneumatic mechanism. Most printers use a pressure of 1¼ pounds per inch across the cylinder length.

Most doctor blades are not stationary. As the cylinder rotates, the blade oscillates, or moves back and forth, parallel to the cylinder. The oscillating action works to remove pieces of lint or dirt that might otherwise be trapped between the cylinder and the blade. Dirt can nick the blade, which then allows a narrow bead of ink to pass to the cylinder surface. Blade nick is a major defect that can ruin the image or scratch the surface of the cylinder.

A **prewipe blade** is commonly used on high-speed presses to skim off excess ink from the cylinder (figure 19.39). This device prevents a large quantity of ink from reaching the doctor blade and ensures that the thin metal blade will wipe the surface perfectly clean.

Impression Rollers

Use of an impression roller is the second main difference between gravure presses and other web-fed machines. The purpose of the impression roller is to push the paper against the gravure cylinder to transfer ink from the image wells (see figure 19.18). The major considerations for impression rollers are pressure, coating and hardness, and electrostatic assist.

Most impression rollers are formed from a steel core coated with rubber or a synthetic material, such as DuPont's Neoprene. Rubber hardness is measured by a Shore Durometer (discussed in chapter 15). Values are given in "Shore A" readings. Hardness increases as Shore A numbers get larger. Different types of paper or substrates require different degrees of hardness for the impression roller. Material such as cellophane might require 60 Shore A, but Kraft paper or chipboard might need 90 Shore A.

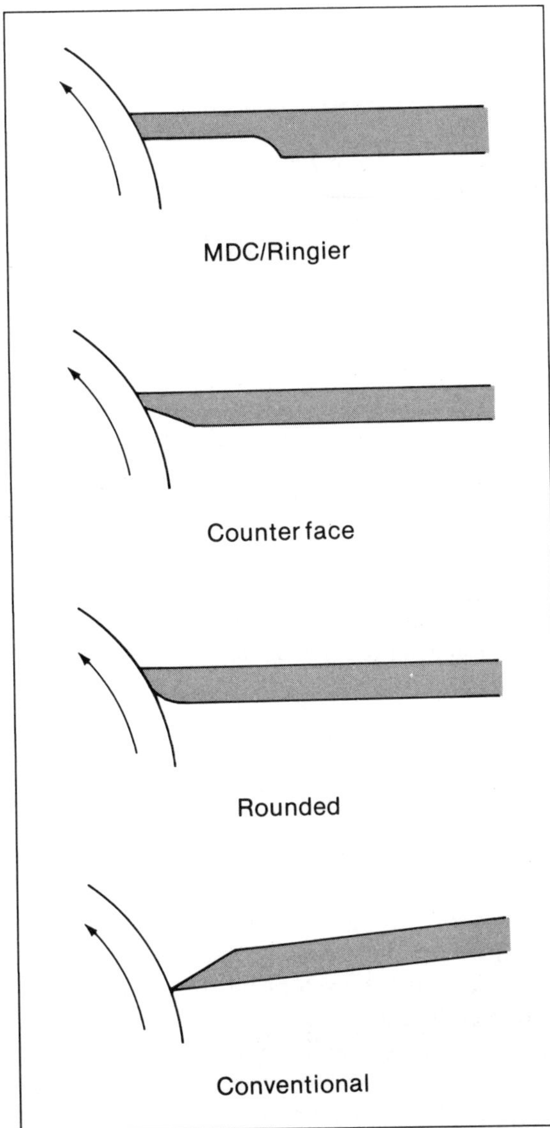

Figure 19.38. Examples of different doctor blade designs

Ink is transferred to the web by pressure of the impression roller. More pressure does not always give better image quality. Pressure might vary from 50 to 200 pounds per linear inch (p.l.i.). The amount of pressure the operator sets is determined by previous tests for the kind of paper being printed. Whatever setting is selected, it is critically important that uniform pressure be applied over the entire length of the cylinder.

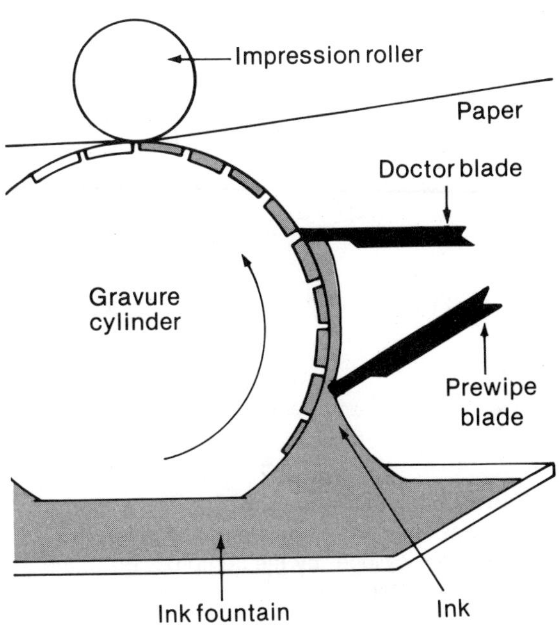

Figure 19.39. Diagram of a gravure cylinder showing prewipe and doctor blades Most presses use a prewipe blade to skim off most of the ink before the cylinder reaches the doctor blade.

The area of contact between the impression roller and the cylinder is called the **nib width,** or flat (figure 19.40). The amount of nib width is determined by the hardness of the impression roller and the amount of pressure. The nib width is important because it is the area of image transfer to the paper or

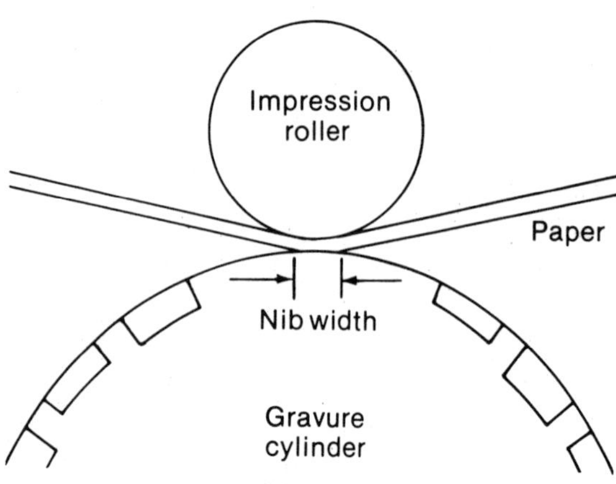

Figure 19.40. Diagram showing the nib width The nib width is the area where the paper contacts the cylinder by the compression of the impression roller.

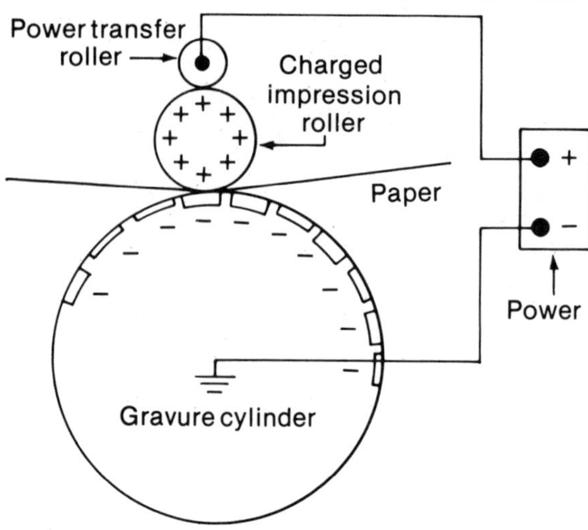

Figure 19.42. Diagram of electrostatic assist printing Electrostatic assist printing charges the impression roller and gravure cylinder so that the ink is electrostatically lifted from the cylinder to the paper.

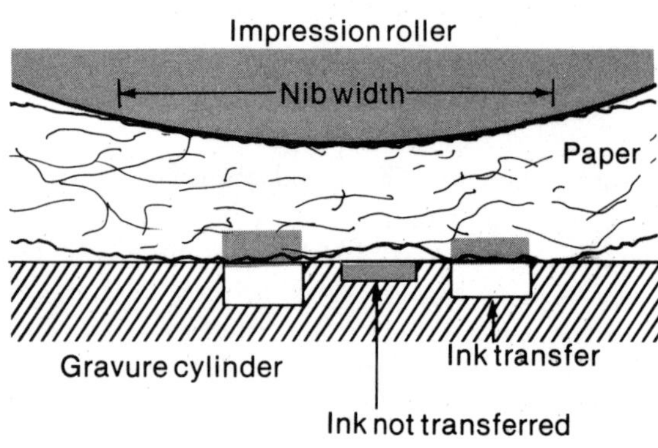

Figure 19.41. Diagram showing inking on defective paper If defects in the paper prevent contact with the gravure cylinder, ink will not be transferred.

plastic web. The nib width is adjusted to give the best-quality image on the web stock.

A great advantage of the gravure process is that it allows the printing of high-quality images on low-grade papers. Problems do occur when the paper surface is coarse and imperfect. Ink transfers by direct contact. If a defect in the paper prevents the contact, then no image will be transferred (figure 19.41). The Gravure Research Association designed and licensed a special device, called an **electrostatic assist**, to solve this problem and improve image transfer. With this technique, a power source is connected between the cylinder and the impression roller (figure 19.42). A conductive covering must be added to the impression roller, but no special problems are caused by this addition. An electric charge is created behind the web, which forms an electrostatic field at the nib. The charge pulls the ink around the edges of each well, which causes the ink to rise and transfer to the paper. Most presses are now equipped with electrostatic assist devices.

Gravure printing presses are sophisticated devices that have a wide range of controls to ensure high image quality. New presses are in use that reach speeds as high as 2,500 feet per minute. It is this high speed, linked with outstanding image quality, that makes gravure printing one of the major printing processes in this country.

Key Terms

gravure
rotogravure
packaging printing
publication printing
specialty printing
diffusion etch
direct transfer
electromechanical process
gravure well
bridge
lateral hard-dot process
electroplating
master plate
electronic-eye mark
conventional gravure
carbon printing
resist
carbon tissue
staging
counter
electrostatic assist

Questions for Review

1. What are the main characteristics of rotogravure printing?
2. List four characteristics of gravure that make it ideal for high-quality long-run jobs.
3. What is the Gravure Technical Association?
4. List the four basic methods of gravure cylinder preparation.
5. What are the most common identification parts of a gravure cylinder?
6. What is the difference between static and dynamic balance?
7. What are the two basic forms of cylinder construction?
8. What is electroplating?
9. What is a newage gauge?
10. What is the ballard shell process?
11. What is the purpose of a cab in cylinder layout?

12. What is a master plate?
13. What is carbon printing?
14. What is a resist?
15. What is "tissue laydown"?
16. What is the purpose of staging?
17. What is the purpose of chrome plating prior to printing a gravure cylinder?
18. What is the purpose of a doctor blade on a gravure press?
19. What is the difference between a conventional doctor blade design and a MDC/ Ringier?
20. What is the purpose of an impression roller in gravure presswork?
21. What does "electrostatic assist" refer to in gravure presswork?
22. What is the "nib width" on a gravure press?

Chapter Twenty

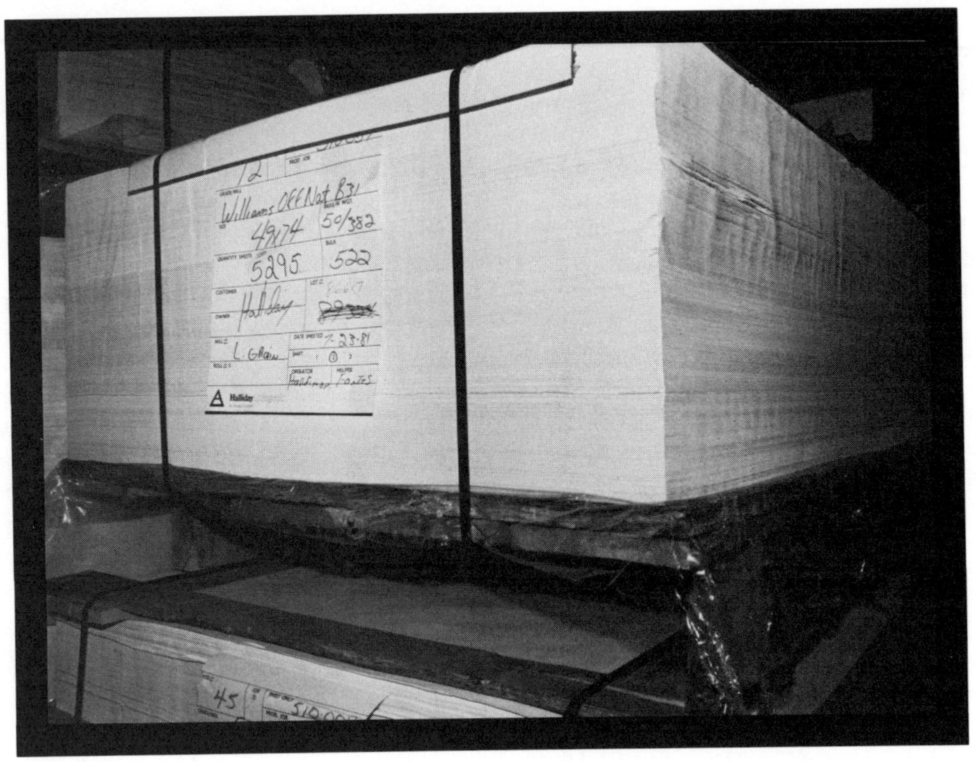

Ink and Paper

Anecdote to Chapter Twenty

Throughout the history of printing, demand for paper has constantly increased. The paper industry has evolved to meet this growing demand. It is the craft of early papermakers that allows us today to hold Gutenberg's first Bible, five hundred years after the sheets left his press.

The first paper-like material, called papyrus, was invented by the Egyptians about five thousand years ago. Their "paper" was made from the papyrus plant, which grew along the banks of the Nile River. The pith, or center of the plant, was cut into strips. These were then glued together in thin, crosswise layers to form sheets. After pressing and drying, the sheets were ready to use. They are still readable after more than five millennia.

The first truly modern paper was invented in China by a eunuch named Ts'si Lun in AD 105. He first shredded cloth fibers into a special hot-water solution. The fiber solution was then poured into a frame covered with a loosely woven cloth screen. The water drained through the cloth, leaving fine interwoven fibers on the screen. The frame was then placed in the sun to dry. The remaining water evaporated from the fibers, and the result was paper. Later, Ts'si created "laid" papers by immersing the screen in the fiber solution and gently raising the frame to the surface. The

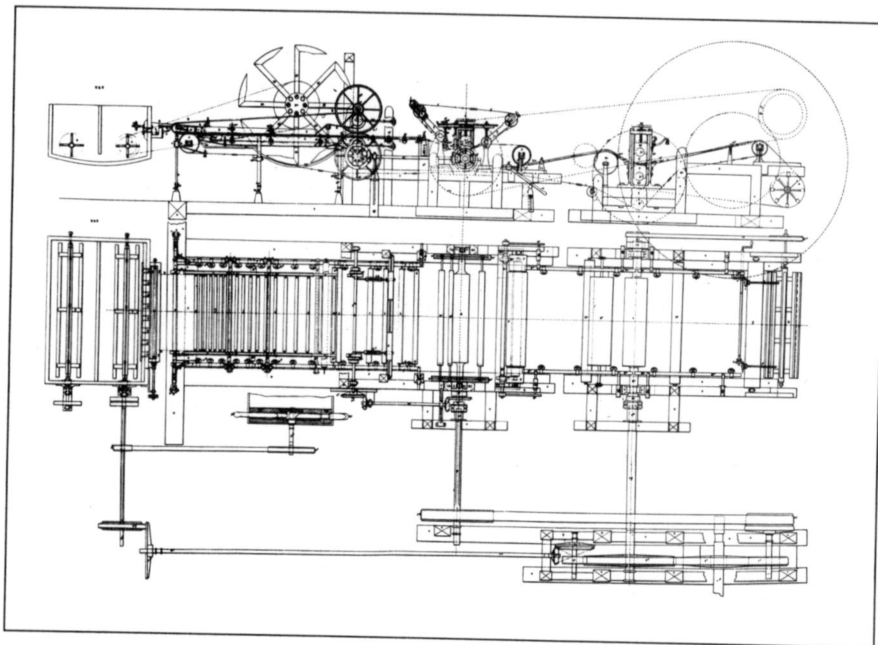

The patent drawing for the Fourdrinier papermaking machine.

laid technique produced a better quality of paper than the earlier method did. This basic hand process was used to produce all paper until around 1800.

The first automated process was developed in 1798 in the paper mill of M. Didot, a member of a famous printing-publishing family, in Essonnes, France. Nicolas Louis Robert, a superintendent in Didot's mill, developed the idea of making paper by pouring the fiber solution onto a continuously moving wire belt. After the water drained through the wire, the paper was passed between felt-covered rollers. The machine worked very well and, with time for improvements, would have been a commercial success. However, the French Revolution, and several lawsuits with his employer, prevented Robert from reaching his goal.

In 1801 an associate of the Didot family, John Gamble, joined the brothers Fourdrinier in a partnership to develop Robert's idea in England. By 1807 they had designed and constructed the first fully automated, continuous paper-making machine.

The fiber solution, called "stuff," was deposited from a special box onto a finely woven copper wire belt. The belt moved both forward and side to side. The belt's copper web was 54 inches wide and 31 feet long. The full length of the machine, including driers, was almost 100 feet. It took seven workers to operate and could produce a continuous roll of paper at the rate of more than 600 feet an hour.

The machine operated better than expected and created great excitement. At long last, here was a way to meet the ever-growing demand for printing papers. Like so many other creative people, the men who perfected one of the greatest contributions to modern printing died in poverty. The Fourdriniers lost a fortune in attempting to market their device. Although by 1860 thousands of tons of paper were being produced on automated machines all over the world, none of the paper-making machine pioneers ever benefited financially from the effort.

While many refinements and improvements have been made, the basic design of the 1807 machine is still used today to produce all paper. The machine is called a fourdrinier in honor of the brothers and the partnership that gave the world the supply of paper it needed.

Objectives for Chapter Twenty

After completing this chapter, you will be able to:

- Classify paper into four common groups and recognize the characteristics of each.
- Recognize and define common paper terms, such as ream, M, M weight, substance weight, and equivalent weight.
- Calculate press sheet cuts from standard paper sizes.
- Use a paper merchant's catalog to calculate the cost of paper for a job.
- List and define the properties of ink, including viscosity, tack, and drying time.
- List the common groups of ingredients

of printing ink, including pigment, vehicle, and additives.
- Describe the characteristics of lithography, screen printing, letterpress, flexographic, and gravure inks.
- Recognize the Pantone Matching System as a tool in selecting inks.

Introduction

Two of the most important ingredients for the printing processes are ink and paper. Traditionally printing consisted of images set in dense black ink on white paper. For many years, the problems of creating the ink and paper were so troublesome and time-consuming that no one bothered about using different colors.

Today, however, the printer and printing customer are faced with another problem. There are so many diferent kinds of paper—with different colors, textures, finishes, thicknesses, and weights—that it is hard to make a choice. So many different kinds of ink, each formulated for a specific process, problem, or paper, are available in any color of the spectrum that the printer is hard-pressed to understand even a fraction of the possible choices (table 20.1).

The purpose of this chapter is to organize the information on paper and ink into an understandable form. It is divided into two sections. The first deals with paper; the second, with ink. Each classifies materials and examines ideas that are important for a novice printer to understand.

SECTION 1: PAPER

Classifying Paper

There is no standard way to categorize the thousands of different papers available to the average printer through a supplier. One workable way is to classify all types under one of the following five headings: book, writing, cover, bristol, and an "other" category.

Table 20.1 Ink Mileage chart

Grade of Stock	Black	Purple	Haven Blue	Sky Blue	Kelly Green	Yellow Lake	Opaque Orange	Fire Red	Antique Red	Opaque Base	White
Enamel	360	320	330	330	200	275	250	300	250	310	250
Litho Coated	300	300	280	300	175	240	180	240	200	265	200
Label	240	250	250	220	155	190	160	190	165	195	165
Dull Coated	205	200	200	205	120	160	130	170	140	190	140
Newsprint	150	155	150	140	160	110	140	130	105	110	104
Antique Finish	135	120	130	120	140	95	115	110	90	95	90
Machine Finish	180	170	180	170	180	100	140	130	125	120	120

The numbers indicate the approximate number of thousand square inches of area that one pound of offset litho ink will cover on a standard sheet-fed press.

Table 20.2 lists these five categories with a further breakdown.

Book paper is the most common type of paper found in the industry. It is used as a general purpose material for such things as catalogs, brochures, direct mail, and books. **Writing paper** is generally a high-quality material that was originally associated with correspondence and record keeping. Today it includes a wide range of qualities and uses, such as stationery, inexpensive reproduction (such as for the ditto or mimeograph processes), and tracing or drawing. **Cover paper** is commonly used for the outside covers of brochures or pamphlets and is generally thicker than both book and writing paper. Common applications are booklets, manuals, directories, and announcements. **Bristol paper** comprises stiff, heavy materials that find wide usage for such things as business cards, programs, menus, file folders, and inexpensive booklet covers. The "other" category is a holding bin for anything that cannot be classified under the first four headings. Common examples are newsprint, lightweight materials such as onionskin, or items that meet a special purpose, such as NCR (no carbon required) paper.

All papers within each category are further classified (and sold) according to weight. The system is called basis weight. **Basis weight** is the weight in pounds of one **ream** (500 sheets) of the basic sheet size of a particular paper type. Unfortunately, all paper types do not use the same basic sheet size to determine weight. The **basic sheet sizes** of the four common paper classifications are:

- Book paper: 25 × 38,
- Writing paper: 17 × 22,
- Cover paper: 20 × 26,
- Bristol: 22½ × 28½.

Table 20.2 One Way to Classify Types of Paper

Book Papers
Offset
Opaque
Converting
Writing Papers
Bond
Duplicator
Mimeograph
Ledger
Tracing
Cover Papers
General Purpose Cover
Duplex
Bristol Papers
Tag
Index
Post Card
Other
Groundwood (newsprint)
Lightweights
Special Purpose

Most papers are available in a variety of basis weights. For example, the most common weights for uncoated book papers are basis 40, 45, 50, 70, and 80. One ream of basis 40 book paper measures 25 by 38 inches and weighs 40 pounds. A basis 80 book paper has the same dimensions, but one ream weighs 80 pounds. Within each category, then, the greater the basis weight, the heavier the sheet. It is not possible, however, to make the same generalization when dealing with different categories (such as book and cover) because the sizes of the sheets to be weighed are not the same.

Sometimes a basis weight is converted to **M weight,** which is the weight of 1,000 sheets (rather than 500) of the basic sheet size of a particular paper type. A paper's M weight

Table 20.3. Regular Sizes for Book Papers and the Corresponding Equivalent Weights

Basis	**40**	**45**	**50**	**60**	**70**	**80**	**90**	**100**	**120**
Sizes	**Equivalent M Weights**								
17 × 22	31	35	39	47	55	63	71	79	94
17½ × 22½	33	37	41	50	58	66	75	83	99
19 × 25	40	45	50	60	70	80	90	100	120
22½ × 29	55	62	69	82	96	110	124	137	165
22½ × 35	66	75	83	99	116	133	149	166	199
23 × 29	56	63	70	84	98	112	126	140	169
23 × 35	68	76	85	102	119	136	153	169	203
24 × 36	72	82	90	100	128	146	164	182	218
25 × 38	80	90	100	120	140	160	180	200	240
26 × 40	88	98	110	132	154	176	198	218	262
28 × 42	100	112	124	148	174	198	222	248	298
28 × 44	104	116	130	156	182	208	234	260	312
30½ × 41	106	118	132	158	184	210	236	264	316
32 × 44	118	134	148	178	208	238	266	296	356
33 × 44	122	138	152	184	214	244	276	306	366
35 × 45	132	150	166	198	232	266	298	332	398
35 × 46	136	152	170	204	238	272	306	338	406
36 × 48	146	164	182	218	254	292	328	364	436
38 × 50	160	180	200	240	280	320	360	400	480
38 × 52	166	188	208	250	292	332	374	416	500
41 × 54	186	210	234	280	326	372	420	466	560
41 × 61	210	236	264	316	368	422	474	526	632
42 × 58	206	230	256	308	358	410	462	512	616
44 × 64	238	266	296	356	414	474	534	592	712
44 × 66	244	276	306	366	428	490	550	612	734
46 × 69	268	300	334	400	468	534	602	668	802
52 × 76	332	374	416	500	582	666	748	832	998

is twice its basis weight. M weight is used merely as a convenience for paper calculation.

Although the basic size of book paper is 25 by 38 inches, other sizes are available to the printer. If the order is large enough, the printer can specify the required size to the manufacturer. In order to meet the needs of small jobs, local paper suppliers generally stock a variety of sizes within each paper type. These common sizes are called **regular sizes.** The left column in table 20.3 shows some regular sizes for book papers. Regular sizes are also stocked in each of the common basis weights.

Although a ream of basis 40 paper of the basic sheet size weighs 40 pounds, a ream of the same paper in any other sheet size (regular size) will not weigh the same. The weight of these regular size reams is defined in terms of **equivalent weight.** Equivalent M weight

Table 20.4. Regular Sizes for Writing Papers and the Corresponding Equivalent Weights

	Substance Weights								
	13	16	20	24	28	32	36	40	44
Sizes	**Equivalent M Weights**								
8½ × 11	6.50	8	10	12	Sizes and weights normally used for business papers—often called cut sizes				
8½ × 14	8.25	10.18	12.72	15.26					
11 × 17	13	16	20	24					
16 × 21	23	29	36	43	50	57	65	72	79
17 × 22	26	32	40	48	56	64	72	80	88
17		41	51	61	71	81	92	102	112
18 × 23	29	35	44	53	62	71	80	89	97
18 × 46	58	70	88	106	124	142	160	178	194
19 × 24	32	39	49	59	68	78	88	98	107
19 × 48	64	78	98	118	136	156	176	196	214
20 × 28	39	48	60	72	84	96	108	120	132
21 × 32	46	58	72	86	100	114	130	144	158
22 × 34	52	64	80	96	112	128	144	160	176
23 × 36	58	70	88	106	124	142	160	178	194
24 × 38	64	78	98	118	136	156	176	196	214
28 × 34	66	82	102	122	142	162	184	204	224
34 × 44	104	128	160	192	224	256	288	320	352

is twice the equivalent ream weight. Table 20.3 is a chart that printers and paper manufacturers use to determine equivalent M weights for regular sizes of book papers.

As an example, locate the basic sheet size for book paper (25″ × 38″) in table 20.3. Notice that the M weight for basis 40 is 80 pounds. One ream (500 sheets) weighs 40 pounds, and 1,000 sheets weigh 80 pounds. Now find the 38″ × 50″ regular sheet size (which is double the basic sheet size of 25″ × 38″) and find the equivalent weight of 160 pounds. One thousand sheets of 38 × 50 basis 40 book paper have an equivalent weight of 160 pounds.

There are two general exceptions to this vocabulary of papers when dealing with the four main types. Some bristol and cover papers are described not by weight but rather in terms of thousandths of an inch—called "points." An 11-point bristol is a sheet that is 0.011 inch thick. Common thicknesses are 8, 10, and 11 points. Most bristols and covers, however, are classified by the more common basis weight designation.

The second general exception deals with writing papers. Within this category, the term *substance weight* is used instead of *basis weight*, but the terms mean the same thing. **Substance weight** is the weight in pounds of one ream of the basic sheet size (17″ × 22″) of one particular type of writing paper. Table 20.4 shows some equivalent M weights of a list of regular sizes of writing papers.

When printers buy paper for a job, they order it from the supplier according to total pounds, type, and basis weight.

Determining Paper Needs

When printers deal with sheets on the press, they do not deal in pounds. Suppose we had a job that required 500 sheets of substance 40, 28- × -34-inch writing paper. How many pounds must be ordered from the supplier? By referring to table 20.4 we see that the equivalent M weight (remember, that means 1,000 sheets) is 204 pounds. Half of 1,000 is 500. Therefore, if we multiply 204 pounds by one-half, we get a paper weight of 102 pounds. If an identical job required 715 sheets, the paper would weigh 145.86 pounds (715 is 0.715 of 1,000, 204 × 0.715 = 145.86).

Not every job will use regular size press sheets that are easily obtained from the paper supplier. Most printers stock only a few sizes of each type and then cut them to meet the needs of individual jobs. Others purchase the most efficient regular sizes but often have to gang several jobs together on a single press sheet. In either case, the printer is faced with the task of calculating the most efficient method of cutting smaller pieces from available stock sizes.

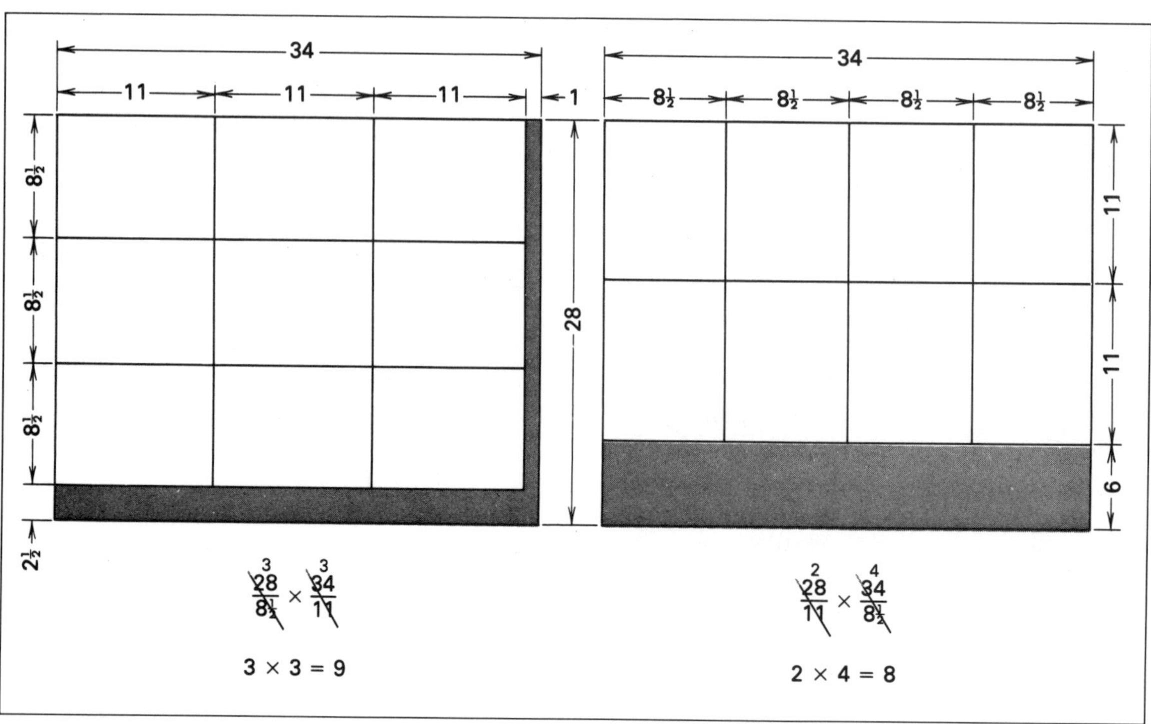

Figure 20.1. Example for calculating the number of sheets to be cut from a stock sheet by dividing or by drawing

To illustrate the process, consider an example. A printer is to cut a press sheet size of 8½ × 11 inches from a regular sheet that measures 28 × 34 inches. What is the maximum number that can be cut from the larger piece? Figure 20.1 shows the two common ways of figuring the problem. In the first case, the width and length of the stock sheet are divided by the corresponding width and length of the press sheet. The two answers are then multiplied to show that 9 sheets are possible. The same result can be obtained by simply drawing a picture of the large sheet and blocking out the maximum number of press sheets. In the second case, the width and length of the larger sheet are divided by the length and width of the smaller sheet. The result with this method is only 8 sheets. The printer would obviously cut the paper to obtain 9 press sheets to gain the maximum number of press sheets from the regular sheet.

Is it obvious, though, in the example above that the maximum number of sheets is 9? The procedure of dividing corresponding dimensions and then alternate dimensions of the stock and press sheets is rather straightforward, but paper calculation is not always that simple. Drawing a picture of the calculations can make the process easier and often can show where additional gains can be made.

Drawing and working with the placement of press sheets on the stock reveals that the example above (figure 20.1) can be cut to obtain 10 instead of 9 sheets (figure 20.2). It is necessary, though, to tell the paper cutter the sequence of cuts. This process of manipulating the positions and order of cuts to gain an additional sheet is called making a **nonstandard cut.** In an era when paper and other material can account for more than half the cost of a job, a nonstandard cut can often

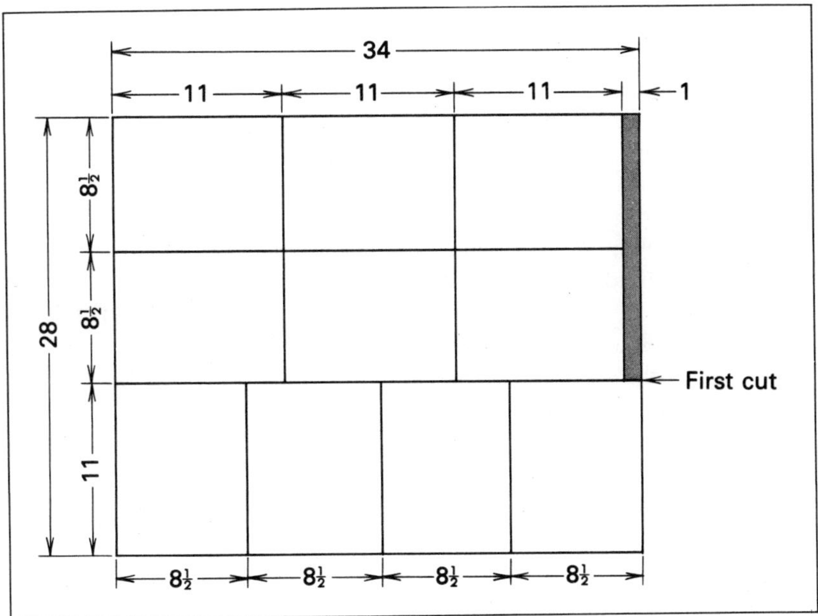

Figure 20.2. Example of a nonstandard cut It is necessary to specify the sequence of cuts to be made by the paper cutter when a nonstandard sequence is to be followed.

mean the difference between profit and loss.

A very important consideration when calculating the paper needs of a specific job is spoilage. All printing processes require some start-up to get the press feeding properly and the printed press sheets up to proper ink density. This is called make-ready. Beyond this, it is a rare job that does not have some waste because of something as frustrating as a machine jam-up or as foolish as spilled coffee on a finished pile. It is necessary, then, to give the press or bindery operators more sheets than the job actually requires to allow for start-up and printing problems. These extra sheets are called the **spoilage allowance.**

Table 20.5 shows a typical spoilage allowance chart that an estimator might use to calculate the average number of wasted sheets for different types of jobs.

For example, if 5,000 copies, two colors on one side, are to be run on a two-color lithographic press, the operator must begin the run with 5% more press sheets than the job requires (see table 20.5)—or $(5{,}000 \times 5\%) + 5{,}000 = 5{,}250$ press sheets.

Many printing presses are designed to print from rolls of paper that are cut into sheets after printing. This is called web printing. Even if their presses use sheets, many printers feel it is more economical to buy paper by the roll and have a machine (a slitter) that cuts individual sheets attached to their press.

The problem, again, is that rolls are sold by the pound, but the printer wants to count sheets. When estimating a job, the printer must determine the number of finished press sheets that can be obtained from a given roll.

Assume that a printer has an 800-pound roll of 25-inch-wide basis 50 book paper wound on a 3-inch wooden core. The printer wants to know how many 17- × -24-inch press sheets can be cut from the roll. To find the number of linear feet in the roll, use the following formula:*

$$\text{linear feet} = \frac{(\text{weight of roll}) \times (\text{basis size}) \times (500 \text{ sheets})}{(\text{width of roll}) \times (12 \text{ inches}) \times (\text{basis weight})}$$

or to find linear inches:

$$\text{linear inches} = \frac{(\text{weight of roll}) \times (\text{basis size}) \times (500 \text{ sheets})}{(\text{width of roll}) \times (\text{basis weight})}$$

The basis size of book paper is 25″ × 38″, so for this example:

$$\text{linear inches} = \frac{800 \times 25 \times 38 \times 500 = 304{,}000}{25 \times 50}$$

Because the press sheet size is 17″ × 24″, the printer can cut the 24-inch dimension out of the 25-inch roll width.** To determine the number of press sheets, divide the 17-inch sheet width into the total number of linear inches in the roll:

$$\frac{304{,}000}{17} = 17{,}882 \text{ press sheets}$$

A Sample Problem

In order to tie together the ideas presented so far, let's consider a sample problem of paper estimating.

*This formula applies only to rolls with a 3-inch core. Consult your paper salesperson for alternative formulas for other core diameters.

**The decision on which dimension to choose depends on grain direction (see "Paper Grain," chapter 13).

Table 20.5. Paper Spoilage Allowances
(Percentage Represents Press Size Sheets, Not Impressions)

Lithographic	**1,000**	**2,500**	**5,000**	**10,000**	**25,000 and over**
Single-Color Equipment					
One color, one side	8%	6%	5%	4%	3%
One color, work-and-turn or work-and-tumble	13%	10%	8%	6%	5%
Each additional color (per side)	5%	4%	3%	2%	2%
Two-Color Equipment					
Two colors, one side	—	—	5%	4%	3%
Two colors, two sides or work-and-turn	—	—	8%	6%	5%
Each additional two colors (per side)	—	—	3%	2%	2%
Four-Color Equipment					
Four colors, one side only	—	—	—	6%	5%
Four colors, two sides or work-and-turn	—	—	—	8%	7%
Bindery Spoilage					
Folding, stitching, trimming	4%	3%	3%	2%	2%
Cutting, punching, or drilling	2%	2%	2%	2%	2%
Varnishing and gumming	7%	5%	4%	3%	3%

The figures above do not include waste sheets used to run up color, as it is assumed that waste stock is used for this purpose.

Use the next higher percentage for the following papers:

1. Coated papers when plant does not usually run coateds.
2. Papers that caliper .0025 and less.
3. Difficult papers such as foil, cloth, plastic, etc.

Letterpress	**1,000**	**2,500**	**5,000**	**10,000**	**25,000 and over**
Single-Color Equipment					
One color, one side	7%	5%	4%	3%	3%
One color, two sides or work-and-turn	13%	9%	7%	5%	5%
Each additional color (per side)	6%	4%	3%	2%	2%
Two-Color Equipment					
Two colors, one side	—	—	4%	3%	2%
Two colors, two sides or work-and-turn	—	—	7%	5%	5%
Each additional two colors (per side)	—	—	3%	2%	2%
Four-Color Equipment					
Four colors, one side	—	—	—	6%	5%
Four colors, two sides or work-and-turn	—	—	—	8%	7%
Bindery Spoilage					
Folding, stitching, trimming	4%	3%	3%	2%	2%
Cutting, punching, or drilling	2%	2%	2%	2%	2%
Varnishing and gumming	7%	5%	4%	3%	3%

These paper spoilage allowance charts have been reproduced through the courtesy of the "Printing Industries of Metropolitan New York" and demonstrate how paper spoilage is calculated by printers belonging to this association.

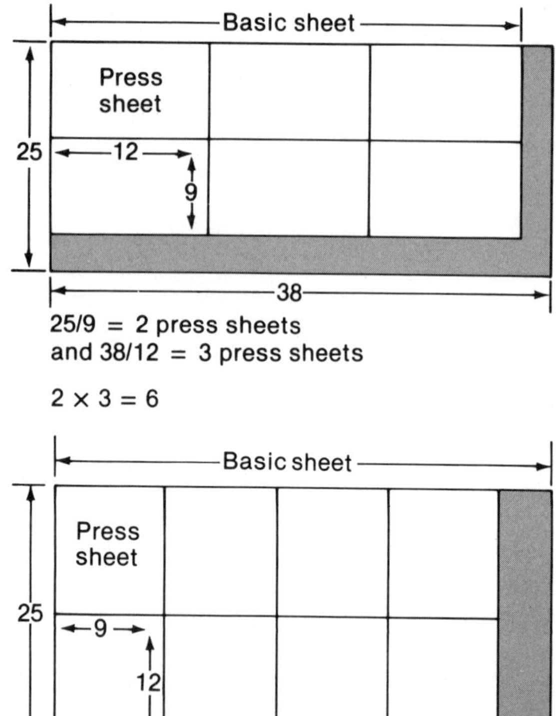

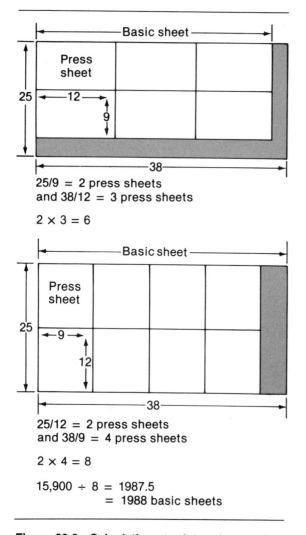

Figure 20.3. Calculations to determine number of basic sheets needed to cut 15,900 press sheets

A printer has been asked to bid on a job that requires 15,000 copies of a two-color poster to measure 9 by 12 inches. The printer has in stock a basis 60 book paper in a 25-by-38-inch regular sheet size left over from a previous job. The printer has only a single-color lithographic press and wants to run the job in the 9″ × 12″ size. How many pounds of paper must be purchased to bid on the job?

1. How many press sheets must be given to the press operator?

   The printer must deliver to the customer 15,000 sheets plus a 6% spoilage allowance (4% for the first pass through the press plus 2% for the second color) of 900 sheets.

$$15{,}000 \times .06 = 900$$

$$15{,}000 + 900 = 15{,}900$$

1. A total of 15,900 press sheets must be given to the press operator to ensure getting 15,000 good sheets for the customer.
2. How many basic sheets will be needed in order to cut 15,900 press sheets (figure 20.3)?

   If 8 press sheets can be cut from each stock sheet, then:

$$15{,}900 \div 8 = 1987.5$$

   But because partial sheets cannot be bought, we must always go to the next full sheet, or 1,988 regular sheets.

3. How many pounds does 1,988 sheets of basis 60, 25-by-38-inch book paper weigh?

   Referring to table 20.3, the equivalent weight is 120 pounds per 1,000.

   We need 1.988 M (thousand sheets).

$$120 \times 1.988 = 238.56$$

   To bid the job, the printer must determine the purchase cost of 238.56

Adams Brilliant Book

Shown in Sample Book number two.

Processes-- Offset and Letterpress
Color-- White
Finish-- Vellum and Coral
Packed-- Unsealed in Cartons
Basic Size-- 25 x 38

BA	Size, M Wt	G	Per Ctn	16 Ctns	4 Ctns	1 Ctn	Less Ctn
				Per 1,000 sheets			
Vellum Finish							
50	17.5x22.5- 41M	L	3600	14.04	15.09	17.26	25.89
50	23 x 35 - 85M	L	1800	29.11	31.28	35.79	53.68
50	38 x 50 - 200M	L	800	68.50	73.60	84.20	126.30
60	17.5x22.5- 40M	L	3200	17.13	18.40	21.05	31.58
60	19 x 25 - 60M	L	2400	20.55	22.08	25.26	37.89
60	23 x 29 - 84M	L	1800	28.77	30.91	35.36	53.05
60	23 x 35 - 102M	L	1500	34.94	37.54	42.94	64.41
→ 60	25 x 38 - 120M	L	1200	41.10	44.16	50.52	75.78 ←
70	17.5x22.5- 58M	L	2400	19.87	21.34	24.42	36.63
70	19 x 25 - 70M	L	2000	23.98	25.76	29.47	44.21
70	23 x 29 - 98M	L	1600	33.57	36.06	41.26	61.89
70	23 x 35 - 119M	L	1200	40.76	43.79	50.10	75.15
70	25 x 38 - 140M	L	1000	47.95	51.52	58.94	88.41
70	35 x 45 - 232M	L	600	79.46	85.38	97.67	146.51
80	23 x 35 - 136M	L	1100	46.58	50.05	57.26	85.88
80	25 x 38 - 160M	L	1000	54.80	58.88	67.36	101.04
80	35 x 45 - 266M	L	600	91.11	97.89	111.99	167.98
Coral Finish							
70	17.5x22.5- 58M	L	2400	21.66	23.26	26.59	39.90
70	19 x 25 - 70M	L	2000	26.15	28.07	32.10	48.16
70	23 x 35 - 119M	L	1200	50.80	54.54	62.36	93.57
70	25 x 38 - 140M	L	1000	52.29	56.14	65.19	97.64

Figure 20.4. A sample tear sheet from a price catalog for paper

pounds of book paper, basis 60, measuring 25 by 38 inches.

The task of calculating paper needs can become more complex than in this example, but the basic procedures are always the same:

1. Determine the spoilage allowance and find the total number of press sheets to run the job.
2. Calculate the most efficient method of cutting the stock sheets and figure the number of stock sheets required.
3. Find the total weight by referring to the paper's equivalent M weight.

Determining the Price of Paper

It is sometimes necessary to refer to a manufacturer's or distributor's price schedule to estimate the cost of the paper for the job without contacting a salesperson. Figure 20.4 shows a typical tearsheet from a price catalog.

(The prices here are samples only and do not represent current paper costs.) It is important that the estimator have an understanding of price differences according to the quantity of paper ordered. It is often economical to buy more paper than is needed for the specific job. Consider an example.

Assume that we need 1,100 sheets of 25″ × 38″ size for a job we are to print. The line from figure 20.4 that interests us most is:

	16 Ctns	4 Ctns	1 Ctn	less Ctn
25 × 38	41.10	44.16	50.52	75.78

Just as with most manufactured products, the more we buy, the less the unit cost. If the supplier has to split open a carton to meet our needs, we pay more because of handling and the storage of the unused portion.

This is basis 60 paper, so the weight is 120 M (120 pounds per 1,000 sheets). There are 1,200 sheets per carton. We require 1,100, so we will figure the split-carton price. If the price is $75.78 per M, the cost per pound is $0.6315 ($75.78 divided by 120 pounds per M). The 1,100 sheets we need weigh 132 pounds (120 pounds per M × 1.1M). The cost of 1,100 sheets when purchased from a broken carton is $83.36 (132 pounds × $0.6315 per pound).

A quick glance at the carton price, however, shows that the price of an unbroken carton is over $30 less and we would get 100 more sheets if we bought a full box. The estimator must be aware of such price differentials and must spend time to calculate potential differences.

SECTION 2: INK

It is ink that forms the images you see as words and pictures in this book. Whatever the printing process, ink is transferred to the paper in the shape of the lines on the image carrier.

Not all ink images, however, are transferred to paper. While paper is the most common printing material, many other surfaces are used, such as metal foils, sheet laminates, plastics, and even wood veneers. Since surfaces other than paper are also used to receive ink, a special term is employed. A **substrate** is any base material used in printing processes to receive an image transferred from a printing plate. The term *substrate* will be used throughout the rest of this chapter.

Properties of Ink

Three properties of ink that control the ease and quality of image transfer are viscosity, tack, and drying quality.

Viscosity

The term **viscosity** is used to accurately describe the "body" of ink. Some inks are heavy (offset and letterpress inks) and some are light (flexographic and gravure inks). Viscosity, or resistance to flow, can be measured and is a term universally accepted in the printing industry.

Tack

Tack, or stickiness, is a property of ink that must be controlled in order to transfer images and deliver the sheet through the press. Tack can cause paper (especially coated paper) to adhere or stick to the blanket of an offset press. Ink that is excessively tacky may also pick the surface of the paper and cause misfeeding. (Recall that to pick means to lift or tear small pieces of the paper's surface.) Tack increases as one color is printed over another. When printing multicolor and process color work, decrease the amount of tack on successive runs. The first run should have the most tack. Each successive run should be printed with ink of less tack.

Drying Quality

The final, and extremely important, property of ink is its drying quality. There are two stages in the drying process. First, ink should instantly **set** or stick to the paper. When ink on the press sheet is set, is can be handled without smearing. If ink does not set as it is stacked in the delivery side of a press, the image will transfer to the bottom of the next sheet. This transfer of wet ink from sheet to sheet is called **set-off.**

The second stage in the drying process is called **hardening.** When ink has hardened, the vehicle (or solvent) has completely solidified on the paper surface and will not transfer. The time it takes for liquid ink to harden to a solid state is called the **drying time.**

Most natural or synthetic inks that contain a drying oil set and harden by a chemical process called **oxidation.** To oxidize is to combine with oxygen. By combining with the ink's drying oil, the oxygen of the air changes the vehicle of the ink from a liquid to a solid.

When an ink is printed on an absorbant substrate, drying results from a physical process called penetration. When ink dries by **penetration,** most of the vehicle is absorbed into the substrate. The ink vehicle is not changed to a solid state in this drying process. Inks that rely heavily on drying by penetration are not popular because the ink never hardens. Handling work printed with penetrating-drying ink usually results in ink transfer to the hands.

Some inks dry by **evaporation.** Resinous and other film-forming solutions in the ink vehicle pass off as vapor during the drying process. Drying by evaporation is much like drying by penetration. The volatile solutions disappear (by evaporating instead of penetrating), leaving an ink film on the surface of the substrate.

Ingredients in Ink

All printing inks are made from three basic ingredients: pigment, vehicle, and special additives. The **pigment** is the dry particles that give color to ink. The **vehicle** is the fluid that carries the pigment and causes it to adhere to the substrate. **Additives** are compounds that control ink characteristics such as tack, workability, and drying quality.

Pigments

The same basic pigments are used to produce all inks for the various printing processes. To some degree the pigment type determines whether the ink will be transparent or opaque. It also determines image permanency when exposed to various solvents such as water, oil, alcohol, and acid. Pigments are divided into four basic groups: black, white, inorganic color, and organic color pigments.

Black Pigments. Black pigments are produced by burning natural gas and oil onto a collecting device. The by-products from the burning process are called *thermal* black and *furnace* black. Furnace black, the most popular pigment, is made from oil in a continuous furnace. Sometimes furnace black is combined with thermal black, which is made from natural gas. Each type of black pigment has unique properties. The pigments are used individually or mixed to produce the best pigment for the specified printing process.

White Pigments. White pigments are subdivided into two groups: opaque pigments and transparent pigments. White ink containing "opaque" pigments (through which light cannot pass) is used when transferring an image to cover a substrate or when overprinting another color. Opaque whites are also used for mixing with other inks to lighten the color or hue.

"Transparent" white pigments (through which light can pass) are used to allow the background material or ink to be seen. Transparent whites are used to reduce the color strength of another ink, to produce a tint of another color, and to extend or add to some of the more costly materials in the ink's formula. Transparent pigments are often referred to as "extenders" or "extender base."

Color pigments are produced from inorganic materials. Minerals such as lead, iron, cadmium, and mercury, modified with other compounds, are used to produce a wide range of colors for printing inks.

Vehicles

The printing process and drying system determine the vehicle used in the manufacturing process. The vehicle of an ink is the liquid portion that holds and carries the pigment. It also provides workability and drying properties and binds the pigment to the substrate after the ink has dried.

Each vehicle used in the manufacture of ink has a slightly different composition. Nondrying vehicles used in newspaper and comic book production are made from penetrating oils such as petroleum and rosin. Resins are added to the oil base to control tack and flow.

Most letterpress and offset inks dry by oxidation. Linseed oil and litho varnish are the most widely used drying vehicles for these inks. The way in which the oil and varnish are "cooked" or prepared determines the viscosity of the final ink.

Gravure inks for paper consist of hydrocarbon solvents mixed with gums and resins. This combination causes rapid evaporation with or without heat. Naturally, evaporation rate increases with the use of heat. Plastic, glassine, foil, and board inks are made with lacquer solvents and resins.

Alcohol and other fast-evaporating solvents combined with resins or gums are used to produce flexographic inks. Flexographic and gravure printing are capable of imaging many substrates. The substrate's surface characteristics will actually determine the final ingredients of the vehicle.

Screen printing inks dry by evaporation and oxidation. Therefore, a solvent-resin vehicle is used in their manufacture.

Offset and letterpress "heat-set" inks are made from rosin ester varnishes or soaps and hydorcarbon resins dissolved in petroleum solvents.

"Quick-setting" inks used for offset and letterpress consist of resin, oil, and solvent. During the drying process the solvent is absorbed by the substrate, leaving an ink film of resin and oil that dries by oxidation.

Additives

Some materials are added to ink during the manufacturing process, and some in the pressroom, to give the ink a special characteristic. Additives can reduce ink if it is too stiff. They can make ink less tacky or shorten its drying time. Additives should not be used carelessly. Many inks are "ready to use" and in normal situations will image best as they are. When you do use additives, be sure they are compatible with the ink's vehicle. The following list identifies major additives and describes their uses:

- *Reducers:* Varnishes, solvents, oils, or waxy or greasy compounds that reduce the tack or stickiness of ink. They also aid ink penetration and setting.
- *Driers:* Metallic salts added to inks to speed oxidation and drying of the oil vehicle. Cobalt, manganese, and lead are commonly used metallic salts. Cobalt is the most effective drier.
- *Binding varnish:* A viscous varnish used to toughen dried ink film. Can increase image sharpness, resist emulsification, eliminate chalking, and improve drying. Emulsification occurs in offset lithography when excessive fountain solution mixes with the ink. The result of emulsification is an ink that actually appears to break down and becomes greasy looking.
- *Waxes:* Usually cooked into the vehicle during the manufacturing process or can be added to the ink later. Paraffin wax, beeswax, carnauba wax, microcrystalline, ozokerite, and polyethylene are commonly used. Wax helps prevent set-off and sheet sticking. Wax also "shortens" the ink—that is, limits its ability to stretch or web.
- *Antiskinning agents:* Prevent ink on ink rollers from skinning and drying. If these agents are used excessively, the ink will not dry on the paper.
- *Cornstarch:* Can be used to add body to a thin ink. Also helps prevent set-off.

Lithographic Inks

There are many ink formulations to serve lithographic printers. Table 20.6 charts various ink formulations for different presses and substrates. Lithographic inks are used on sheet-fed and web-fed presses. A variety of vehicles are required because of the differences between sheet and web feeding and because of the many substrates on which the printer must transfer images.

The viscosity of lithographic ink varies according to the vehicle and pigment formulation. Viscosity means resistance to flow. Some inks appear fluid, while others are stiff and viscous. An ink that appears stiff does not necessarily require an additive such as a reducer. Some inks are "thixotropic": they become stiff and heavy when left standing in their containers. The ink is conditioned and milled by the ink train of the press before it reaches the printing unit. The ink that reaches the substrate is not as stiff and heavy as it was when it came from the can. The thixotropic phenomenon is typical in rubber-base ink formulations.

Rubber-Base Offset Ink

Rubber-base ink is a heavy formulation that gives quick setting and drying on both coated and uncoated paper. A good all-purpose off-

Table 20.6. Lithographic Inks and Substrates

Lithographic Inks	
Sheet-Fed Presses	**Web-Fed Presses**
Substrates	*Substrates*
Paper Foil Film Thin Metal	Mostly Paper
Ink Vehicle Class	*Ink Vehicle Class*
Oxidative—Natural or synthetic drying oils.	Oxidative—Drying oil varnish.
Penetrating—Soluble resins, hydrocarbon oils & solvents, drying and semidrying oils and varnishes.	Penetrating—Hydrocarbons, oils & solvents, soluble resins.
Quick Set—Hard soluble resin, hydrocarbon oils and solvents, minimal drying oils and plasticizers.	Heat Set—Hydrocarbon solvents, hard soluble resins, drying oil varnishes, and plasticizers.
UV Curing—Highly reactive, cross-linking proprietary systems that dry by UV radiation.	UV Curing—Highly reactive, cross-linking proprietary systems that dry by UV radiation.
Gloss—Drying oils, very hard resins, minimal hydrocarbon solvents.	Thermal Curing—Dry by application of heat and use of special cross-linking catalysts.

set and letterpress ink, it can remain on the press for long periods without skinning. It is also compatible with aquamatic or conventional dampening systems (see chapter 13).

Rubber-base ink can be left on the press and will stay open overnight. After standing overnight, the ink on the rollers might appear to be setting or stiffening. To overcome this problem, leave a heavy ink film on the rollers. This can be accomplished by simply placing extra ink on the large oscillating roller and running the press. When starting up again after the long shutdown, run the press at idle speed. If the press is an aquamatic type, remove the dampening solution. If the press is slightly overinked, **sheet off** the excess with scrap sheets of paper. Sheet off ink by manually feeding paper in and out of the ink train. The paper will collect the excess ink and bring the ink train to a normally inked condition.

Rubber-base ink works well with aquamatic dampening systems in which the ink and water travel on the same rollers. The high tack and viscosity of rubber-base ink are well suited to this system. When inking-up, use just enough ink to cover the ink rollers and run low on the dampening solution. Then increase both ink and water to acquire the desired density. Do not overink and/or overdampen. It is also important to keep the pH (acid content) of the fountain solution between 4.5 and 5.5. The pH factor keeps the nonimage area of the plate clean. The use of additives with rubber-base inks is not recommended under normal conditions.

Nonporous Ink

Ink such as Van Son's Tough Tex is an example of an ink with a nonporous formulated vehicle. This ink is suited for plastic-coated or metallic types of papers. It dries by oxidation rather than by absorption. It is important not to overdampen this ink. Since the substrate is nonporous, the fountain solution remains in the ink. Excessively dampened ink will not dry or set and will easily smear or set off to the adjacent sheet. An acid level of less than 4.5 will also retard drying. Ink additives are not recommended with this ink formulation. To prevent set-off, do not allow a large pile to accumulate in the stacker and use small amounts of spray powder.

Quick-Set Ink

Quick-setting, low-tack ink is formulated with the color and process printer in mind. Quick-set ink is usually available in a full range of process colors that will trap in any sequence. **Trapping** refers to the ability of one ink to cover another. Successful trapping depends on the relative tack and thickness of the ink films applied. Quick-set ink usually has very good drying qualities. It also produces an accurate color and is scuff and rub resistant.

Additives for Litho Ink

The five ink characteristics that can be controlled with ink additives include tack, flow or lay, drying quality, body, and scuff resistance. The following list identifies major litho ink additives and describes their effects and use:

- *Smooth lith:* A liquid that controls lay and set-off. Smooth lith also reduces tack, which prevents picking. Since it is a colorless solution, it will not change the hue of the ink. It will also aid in the drying process. Use approximately one capful per pound of ink. If you are using small amounts of ink, add smooth lith with an eyedropper.
- *Reducing compound:* Cuts the tack of ink without changing its body. This compound is used to alter the ink's viscosity. About ½ ounce of reducer to each pound of ink is a starting recommendation (a heaping tablespoon is approximately ½ ounce).
- *#00, #0 litho varnish:* A thin-bodied compound that rapidly reduces the ink's body. Use approximately ¼ ounce of varnish to each pound of ink (a teaspoon is about ¼ ounce).
- *#1 litho varnish:* Reduces tack and body. It is used as a lay compound and prevents picking.
- *#2, #3, #4, and #5 litho varnishes:* Increase ink flow without changing the ink's body. Use about ¼ ounce of varnish to each pound of ink.
- *Overprint varnish:* A gloss finish used to print over already printed ink. Also used as an additive to help prevent chalking on coated paper. When overprinting with varnish, use it directly from the can. When using overprint varnish as an additive to prevent chalking, add 1½ ounces to each pound of ink.
- *Cobalt drier, concentrated drier, and three-way drier:* Basic types of driers. Cobalt

and some concentrated driers are recommended for jobs that will be cut or folded soon after printing. These driers should not be used for process colors or inks that will be overprinted. Some concentrated driers are rub proof or binding. They are excellent for package printing where rough handling is anticipated. The ink's body can be built up with additives such as luster binding base, aqua varnish, and body gum.

- *Luster binding base:* Builds up viscosity, gives ink a luster finish, and makes ink more water repellent. Mix about 1½ ounces of binding base to each pound of ink.

- *Aqua varnish:* Builds up body and tack of ink. Works well for inks used in aquamatic types of press. Aids the ink in repelling water and helps prevent emulsification (ink breakdown). Use approximately ¼ ounce of aqua varnish to each pound of ink.

- *Body gum:* A heavy varnish that increases the ink's body, tack, and water repellency. Use ¼ ounce of body gum for each pound of ink.

- *Gloss varnish and wax compound:* Increase the ink's resistance to scratching and scuffing. Gloss varnish gives ink a bright finish and helps prevent chalking on coated papers. Use about ½ to 2 ounces of gloss varnish to each pound of ink, depending on the ink's color strength. In addition to improving scratch resistance, wax compound also reduces tack and picking. It should not be used when ink is to be overprinted. This additive is good for package or label printing. Use about ¼ to 1 ounce of wax compound to each pound of ink.

Troubleshooting Litho Ink Problems

Many problems that occur on press are ink related. Set-off, scumming, slow drying, chalking, hickies, and scuffing are just a few. There is seldom a single cause for each problem. Table 20.7 outlines common problems and their possible solutions.

Screen Printing Inks

Inks for screen printing are available in a rainbow of colors. Each type of screen printing ink has a binder suited to a specific class of substrate. Screen inks are formulated to be short and buttery for sharp squeegee transfer. Ink solvents should not evaporate rapidly. Rapid solvent evaporation would cause screen clogging during the printing process. Table 20.8 lists the many types of ink and substrates available to the screen printer.

Poster Ink

Inks whose end use is to produce "PoP" displays, posters, wallpaper, outdoor billboards, greeting cards, and packaging materials are classified as poster inks. The following list identifies major poster inks and describes their uses:

- *Flat poster ink:* Recommended for printing on paper and board stocks. Dries by solvent evaporation in about 20 minutes or can be force dried with special driers in seconds. Produces a flat finish and is used for displays, posters, and wallpaper.
- *Satin poster ink and halftone colors:* Recommended for printing on paper and cardboard displays. Dry by solvent evaporation in about 20 to 30 minutes or can be force dried in seconds. Are

Table 20.7. Troubleshooting Litho Ink Problems

Problem	Cause	Cure
Set-off in delivery pile	Acid fountain solution	Test pH; keep between 4.5 and 5.5
	Overinking	Adjust fountain roller speed or fountain keys
	Not enough drier	Add three-way or cobalt drier
	Ink not penetrating paper	Add smooth lith or #00 varnish
	Too much paper in delivery pile	Remove small piles from press
	Paper pile being squeezed before ink sets	Handle with care
	Using wrong ink	Consult literature, manufacturer or vendor
Scumming or Tinting	Bad plate	Make a new one
	Overinking/ underdampening	Adjust ink/water balance
	Incorrect pH	Keep between 4.5 and 5.5
	Too much drier	Change ink; use less drier
	Dirty molleton or dampening sleeve	Change cover or sleeve
	Soft ink	Add binding base, body gum, and aqua varnish
Slow ink drying	Incorrect pH—too acid	Test pH; keep between 4.5 and 5.5
	Bad ink/stock combination	Check with your paper or ink vendor
	Too little drier	Add drier
	Acid paper	Use different grade
Chalking	Too little drier	Add three-way or cobalt drier
	Wrong ink used	Overprint with varnish
	Ink vehicle penetrated too quickly	Add body gum or binding base
Hickies	Dust from cutting paper	Jog and wind paper before printing
	General dirt and dust	Clean, vacuum, and sweep press and press area
	Dried ink particles	Do not place drier or skinned ink into ink fountain
Scratching and scuffing	Overinked	Adjust ink fountain roller or keys
	Too little drier	Add drier concentrate or cobalt
	Wrong ink used	Overprint with varnish
	Ink not resistant enough	Add wax compound or scuff-proof drier

Table 20.8. Screen Printing Inks and Substrates

Ink Types	Substrates
Water soluble	Paper
Lacquer	Cardboard
Plastics	Textiles
Enamels	Wood
Metalic	Metal & foil
Ceramic	Glass
Electrical conducting	Lacquer-coated fabrics
Etching	Masonite
Luminescent	All Plastics
Fluorescent	

used to print "PoP" displays, posters, outdoor billboards, greeting cards, and packaging materials. Standard colors are opaque, and halftone colors are transparent.

- *Gloss poster inks:* Produce a hard gloss finish and are formulated for paper and board stocks. Are used to print "PoP" displays, posters, greeting cards, corrugated displays, and packaging materials. Dry by evaporation in about 15 to 20 minutes or can be force dried in seconds.
- *Economy poster inks:* Much like flat poster ink series but lack the outdoor durability of flat poster ink. Made for supermarket and chain store applications. Dry to a flat finish in about 20 to 30 minutes by evaporation or can be force dried in seconds.
- *24-sheet poster ink:* Formulated mainly for outdoor use. Are waterproof and flexible and can withstand finishing processes such as die cutting, creasing, and folding. Recommended for poster, outdoor displays, sign cloth, and bumper stickers. Dry by evaporation in about 20 to 30 minutes or can be force dried.

Enamel Ink

Enamels are inks that flow out to a smooth coat and usually dry slowly to a glossy appearance. Since they penetrate the substrate less than poster inks do and dry mainly by oxidation, drying times are much longer. Enamel inks include gloss enamel (normal and fast dry), synthetic gloss enamel, and halftone enamel.

Gloss Enamels. Gloss enamels are used to image substrates such as wood, metal, glass, paper, cardboard, and fiber drums and as an adhesive base for flocking or beads as a decoration on a variety of products. Normal gloss enamels dry by oxidation and should be allowed to stand overnight. Fast-dry gloss enamels are commonly used to image polyethylene bottles and lacquer-coated fabrics in addition to the substrates listed for gloss enamel. This formulation will air dry in approximately 60 minutes or can be cured (dry and usable) in about 5 minutes at 180°F (82°C).

Synthetic Gloss Enamels. Synthetic gloss enamels have high durability and are excellent outdoor inks. The synthetic vehicle adheres to a wide variety of surfaces. These enamels are great for imaging metal, wood, masonite, glass, anodized aluminum, some types of plastics, novelties, synthetic decals, and packaging containers. They dry by oxidation in 4 to 6 hours or can be cured at 180°F (82°C) in about 30 minutes.

Halftone Enamels. Halftone enamels are formulated to give the special hues required for halftone process work. They are made to be durable under outdoor conditions. Halftone enamels are used on the same substrates as synthetic gloss enamels. Halftone vehicles dry to a satin finish (instead of a gloss finish) in 4 to 6 hours or can be cured in 30 minutes at 180°F (82°C). All halftone enamels are transparent inks.

Lacquer Ink

There are basically two types of lacquer inks:

- A general industrial lacquer ink that can produce a gloss or flat, hard finish with excellent adhesion to a wide variety of finishes,
- A lacquer ink specifically formulated for making decals or printing on a specific substrate.

Industrial Lacquer Inks. Industrial lacquer inks have numerous applications where chemical and abrasion resistance is important. They are used to image enamel, baked-urea or melamine-coated metal parts, and many polyester finishes. Because of their high opacity, lacquer inks are also popular for printing on dark-colored book cover stock. In addition, they are used to image lacquer and pyroxylin surfaces, many plastics (cellulose acetate, cellulose acetate butyrate, acrylics, nitrocellulose, ethyl cellulose) and many polyesters. Wood, paper, and foils can also be imaged with lacquers. Lacquer ink dries by solvent evaporation in about 30 minutes or can be jet dried in seconds. It can be cured for 10 minutes at 250°F (93°C) for industrial applications.

Decal Lacquers. Decal lacquers are made for printing decalcomanias. **Decalcomania** is the process of transferring designs from a specially printed substrate to another surface. Decalcomanias can also be printed on any surface where a flexible lacquer ink is needed. Consult the manufacturer's literature on printing procedures. Decal lacquer dries by solvent evaporation in 1 to 2 hours.

Printing on Plastic

Because so many plastics are being manufactured, a complete line of special inks is needed by screen printers. Plastic materials are either thermoplastic or thermosetting. A **thermoplastic** material is one that can be reformed. A **thermosetting** plastic cannot be altered once it has been formed and cured. Table 20.9 lists several thermoplastic and thermosetting materials and some of their uses. Inks used to print on plastic include acrylic lacquer, vinyl, mylar, and epoxy resin inks.

Acrylic Lacquer Inks. Acrylic lacquer inks are general purpose formulations for imaging thermoplastic substrates such as acrylics, cellulose butyrate, styrene, vinyl, and ABS (acrylontile, butadiene, and styrene). They are used to image vacuum-formed products; in fact, adhesion and gloss are improved by vacuum forming. They dry by solvent evaporation in about 30 minutes or can be force dried.

Vinyl Inks. Vinyl inks are naturally formulated for both rigid and flexible vinyl substrates. These include novelties, inflatables, wall coverings, and book covers. They dry by evaporation in approximately 30 minutes or can be force dried. The vehicles can be formulated to produce a flat, a fluorescent, or a gloss finish. Gloss vinyl inks can be vacuum formed.

Mylar Inks. Mylar inks are formulated to image untreated mylar and other polyester films. They dry by solvent evaporation in about 30 minutes or can be force dried.

Table 20.9. Screen Printing Inks, Plastic Substrates, and Uses

Screen Printing Inks	
Print on Thermoplastic Substrates	**For End Use**
ABS (Acrylontile, Butadiene, & Styrene)	Safety helmets, automotive components, refrigerator parts, & radio cases
Acrylics	Outdoor signs
Cellulose Acetate	Packaging, toys, book cover laminations, lampshades, & toothbrush handles
Cellulose Acetate Butyrate	Outdoor signs & packaging materials
Polyethylene	Cosmetic packaging
Polypropylene	Housewares, medicine cups, luggage, & toothpaste and bottle caps
Polystyrene	Construction, insulation, packaging, signs, displays, & refrigerator liners
Vinyl	PVC bottles, book covers, decorative tiles, & building components
Thermosetting Substrates	
Melamine and Urea	Cosmetic packaging & electrical components
Phenolics	Electronics and appliance industry (excellent insulators)

Epoxy Resin Inks. Epoxy resin inks are formulated for difficult-to-print surfaces such as phenolics, polyesters, melamines, silicones, and nonferrous metals and glass. Epoxy inks dry by a chemical process called **polymerization** and require a catalyst prior to use. Once the catalyst is properly added, the ink must stand approximately 30 minutes. This period of time allows the catalyst to become part of the solution and to activate the polymerization process. The polymerization drying process takes approximately 2 to 3 hours and about 10 days for maximum adhesion and chemical resistance. The ink can be cured in 30 minutes at 180°F, 10 minutes at 250°F, or 4 minutes at 350°F. Epoxy inks that require no catalyst must be cured or baked and are not recommended for outdoor use. They are used on thermosetting plastic, glass, and ceramics. They dry to a flat finish and must be baked at 400°F for 3 minutes or 350°F for 7 minutes. This type of epoxy ink is very suitable for nomenclature printing on circuit boards that must be soldered.

Ink for Printed Circuits and Nameplates

Resist inks include alkali removable resist, solvent removable resist, vinyl plating resist, plating resist and solder resist inks.

Alkali Removable Resist Inks. Alkali removable resist inks are ideal for print-and-etch boards. They are less expensive than solvent removable resist ink and can reproduce fine lines. They cure at 250° to 265°F (120° to 130°C) in about 3 or 4 minutes. Air drying takes about 4 or 5 hours. Alkali removable ink can be removed from the board after etching with a 1% to 4% solution of sodium hydroxide.

Solvent Removable Resist Ink. Solvent removable resist ink, only black, is formulated for plating etch-resistant operations such as circuit boards or nameplates. It has excellent adhesion and printability and resists acids such as ferric chloride, ammonium persulphate, and other common etchants. Removable etch resist air dries in 30 minutes or can be dried in 5 minutes at 200°F (93°C).

Vinyl Plating Resist Inks. Vinyl plating resist inks are also formulated for plating or etch resist operations. They air dry in approximately 30 minutes or in 10 minutes at 200°F (93°C). They can be removed after etching with trichlorethylene or xylol.

Plating Resist Inks. Plating resist inks are formulated specifically for plating operations. The inks are recommended for long plating cycles. Curing takes about 30 minutes at 200°F (93°C). The resist can be removed from the substrate with trichlorethylene or xylol.

Solder Risist Inks. Solder resist inks are alkyd melamine formulations for printing on copper or copper-treated coatings. Solder resist inks cure in 20 minutes at 250°F (140°C), 10 minutes at 300°F (150°C), and 5 minutes at 350°F (160°C).

Textile Ink

The three basic inks available to the textile printer are standard textile, plastisol, and dye inks.

Standard Textile Inks. Standard textile inks are formulated for cotton and other nonsynthetic fabrics. Ease of application makes these the most widely used inks for natural fabrics. They dry to a flat finish in about 45 minutes or can be cured in 5 minutes at 275°F (135°C).

Plastisol Inks. Plastisol textile inks are formulated for woven or knitted cotton and some synthetic fabrics. These inks can be printed directly onto the fabric or onto a coated release paper. When printing directly onto the fabric, cure for 3 minutes at 300°F (150°C). When printing onto release paper, cure for 1½ to 2 minutes at 225° to 250°F (107° to 120°C). Images on release paper can be transferred to fabric with an iron or a heat transfer machine. Be sure to allow the release paper and fabric to cool before peeling away the paper backing.

Dye Inks. Dye textile inks are water-in-oil concentrated pigments that must be mixed with a clear extender. The proportions in the mixture determine the color strength. These inks are used to image cotton, rayon, linen, some nylon, and other synthetic blends. Dyes dry in 3 minutes at 300°F (150°C) and in 5 minutes at 250°F (120°C). Water-soluble stencil material cannot be used with dyes because of the water content of the dyes. For best results use knife-cut lacquer or a direct emulsion when preparing the stencil.

Letterpress Inks

Letterpress was once the major printing process. Much of what is known about ink today was discovered for the letterpress process. Although letterpress is gradually being replaced by other processes, it is still used to produce newspapers, magazines, packaging, and some commercial printing.

Some letterpress inks are much like offset inks. They are viscous, tacky compositions that dry mainly by oxidation. Letterpress inks include job, quickset, gloss, moisture-set, and rotary inks.

Job Ink

Job inks are standard items kept in most shops. They must be formulated to be compatible with a wide variety of presses and papers. By using additives, their characteristics can be altered to be short-bodied for platen press work, to flow well on faster automatic presses, or to set properly on different papers. In many shops a rubber-base offset ink is a common job ink for both general printing on platen letterpresses and small duplicator machines.

Quick-Set Ink

Quick-set inks are used when it is necessary to immediately print another run or color or to subject the substrate to finishing operations. They are used mostly on coated papers and boards. The ink's vehicle is a resin-oil combination. It dries by a combination of oxidation, absorption, and coagulation. When printed, the oil penetrates the stock and leaves the heavy material on the surface to dry by oxidation and coagulation (thickening).

Gloss Ink

Gloss inks are made of synthetic resins (modified phenolic and alkyd) and drying oils that do not penetrate the substrate as other inks do. This resistance to penetration is what produces the high gloss. A combination of gloss ink with a paper that resists penetration will produce the best ink finish. Since the ink does not penetrate the substrate rapidly, it must dry mainly by oxidation and coagulation.

Moisture-Set Ink

Moisture-set inks are used mainly in printing food packaging. Because they are free from odor, they are used to print wrappers, containers, cups, and packaging materials. The ink vehicle is actually a water-insoluble binder dissolved in a water-receptive solution. The ink sets as the water-insoluble binder adheres to the paper when the water-receptive solvent is exposed to humidity. Atmospheric humidity or the moisture in the stock might be sufficient to cause setting on some substrates.

Rotary Ink

Rotary inks are used mainly to print newspapers, magazines, and books. These publications require different substrates. Book papers range from soft to hard and are coated or uncoated. Rotary book-printing inks flow well and are quick setting to be compatible with these substrates. Magazines are usually printed on coated or calendered paper, which often requires a quick-drying heat-set ink. Heat-set inks are composed of synthetic resins dissolved in a hydrocarbon solvent. Presses using heat-set inks must be equipped with a heating unit, cooling rollers, and an exhaust system.

Flexographic Ink

Flexography is a relief process much like rotary letterpress. This economical process is now printing a variety of substrates with a fast-drying volatile ink. "Flexo" printing is commonly used to transfer an image to plastic films for laminating to packaging, glassine, tissue, kraft, and many other paper stocks. It is also a popular process for printing wrapping paper, box coverings, folding cartons, and containers.

Flexographic ink is formulated with alcohols and/or esters and a variety of other solvents. Plasticizers and waxes are used to make the ink flexible and rub resistant. These volatile ingredients cause the ink to dry extremely rapidly by evaporation.

Water-base inks are also used to print paper, board, kraft, and corrugated substrates. There are many different water-base vehicles, such as ammonia and casein. Water-base inks are limited, however, to absorbent stocks, rather than nonabsorbent materials such as foil or plastic, because of the ink's slow-drying and low-gloss characteristics. Water-base inks are popular because of ease of use and low cost.

Gravure Inks

Gravure printing uses two major kinds of ink: publications ink and packaging ink. Both are available in a full range of colors and properties. Publications ink basically consists of modified resins, pigments, and hydrocarbon solvents. Most packaging ink is formulated with nitrocellulose and various modifiers.

Because of the increased popularity of gravure printing on a variety of substrates, ink making and ink classification has become confusing. Many resins and solvents are used to make the ink, and most are not "compatible" or cannot be mixed together. In order to know which solvents are to be used with the inks purchased, a major ink suppplier initiated the classification of various types of inks by using letters. In this system, all inks of a single type are compatible. Types of inks are identified by letters as follows:

- A-type inks are low-cost aliphatic hydrocarbons,
- B-type inks use resins and aromatic hydrocarbons,
- C-type inks are made up of modified nitrocellulose and an ester class of solvent,
- D-type inks consist basically of a polyamide resin and alcohol,
- E-type inks are based on binders thinned with alcohols,
- T-type inks consist of modified chlorinated rubber reduced with aromatic hydrocarbons,
- W-type inks use water and sometimes alcohol as a reducing solvent.

This method of classification indicates which solvents should be used to obtain the proper viscosity. When you are mixing ink, carefully examine the technical data sheets, since ink suppliers frequently use trade names rather than "type" classifications.

The Pantone Matching System (PMS)

The **Pantone matching system (PMS)** is a method universally accepted for specifying and mixing colors. Using this technique, artists and customers can select any of the more than 500 hues from a "swatch book." The printer can then mix the desired color by using the swatch number and referring to a "formula guide." The guide gives the formula for making the color. It identifies the basic colors involved and indicates how much of each to mix together. The ten basic colors in the pantone matching system are rhodamine red, purple, reflex blue, yellow, warm red, rubine red, process blue, green, black, and transparent white.

Key Terms

basis weight
ream
M weight
equivalent weight
substance weight
nonstandard cut
spoilage allowance
substrate
viscosity
tack
set-off
oxidation
penetration
evaporation
pigment
vehicle
additives
trapping
thermoplastic
thermosetting
Pantone Matching System

Questions for Review

1. What are the three major expenses in the printing industry?
2. What are the five main paper types?
3. What is basis weight?
4. What is M weight?
5. Why is spoilage always considered when calculating paper needs?
6. Briefly outline the general procedures for calculating paper needs.
7. Define the word *substrate.*
8. List six factors that will slow down the ink-drying process.
9. Define the words *chalking* and *polymerization.*
10. Describe the difference between an inorganic and an organic ink pigment.
11. What is an ink vehicle? List an example for each of the following inks:
    a. Offset
    b. Screen
    c. Letterpress
    d. Flexographic
    e. Gravure
12. Define the words *emulsification* and *thixotropic.*

13. Match the cure to the following ink-related problems:

— Set-off	a. Jog paper and clean press area well.
— Scumming	b. Adjust ink/water balance.
— Chalking	c. Remove small piles from the press.
— Hickies	d. Add wax compound or scuff-proof drier.
— Scratching	e. Add body gum or binding base.

14. What screen printing ink or inks would be best for printing an outdoor sign on the following substrates?
    a. Paper
    b. Plastic
    c. Metal
    d. Wood

15. What plastic ink or inks would be used for printing the following substrates or products?
    a. Dark book cover
    b. Polyester film
    c. Drinking glasses
    d. Printed circuit
    e. Iron-on for a T-shirt made of woven cotton and polyester
    f. Directly onto a sweatshirt

16. Briefly describe the properties of the following inks:
    a. Letterpress
    b. Flexographic
    c. Gravure

Chapter Twenty-one

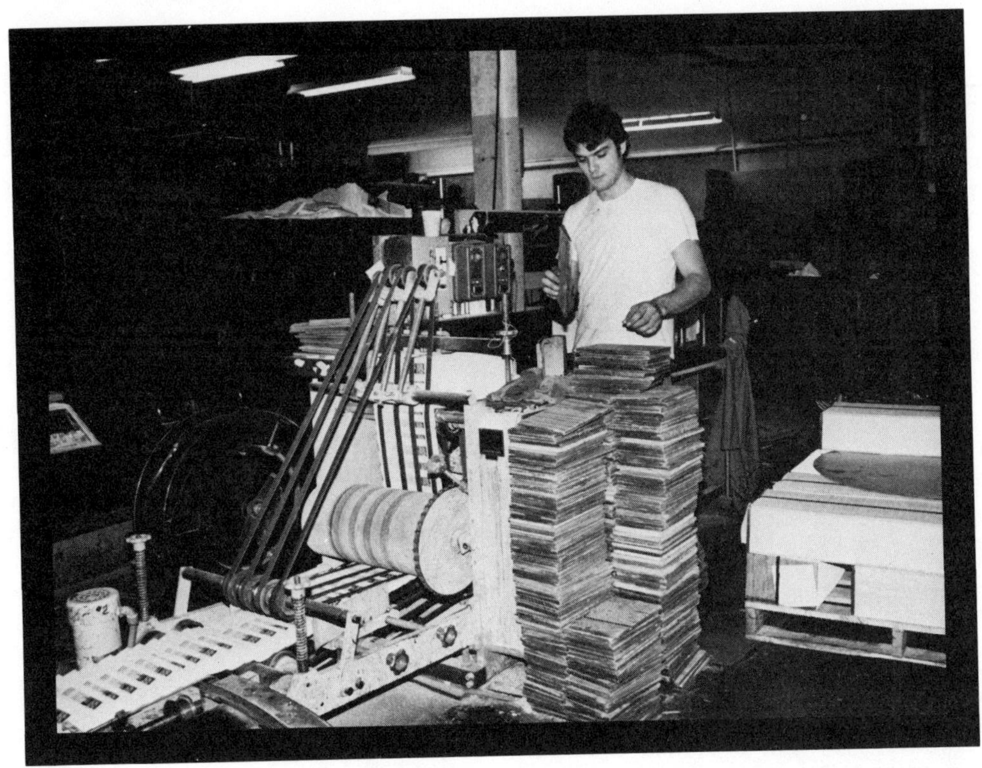

Finishing Operations

Anecdote to Chapter Twenty-one

Around AD 800, Charlemagne, the Frankish king who ruled from 742 to 814, ordered every abbot, bishop, and count to keep in permanent employment a copyist who would reproduce books by hand, writing in only roman letters. The bound books that the scribes lettered were to be stored in special rooms called "scriptoriums," which later evolved into what we know today as libraries.

Binding the finished pages together was a process nearly as important as copying. It was felt that just as each page of a manuscript needed to be decorated, so too did the case that held the pages together. The more valuable works were often encased in bindings of precious metal, such as gold and silver. They were sculptured works of art. These books were often so cumbersome that special lecterns were built just to hold them while they were being read. There is even a recorded instance when a reader accidently dropped a well-bound, sculptured book and was seriously injured. He almost had to have his leg amputated.

By the 1400s, bookbinding had grown into a profession with several special subdivisions. The person who sewed the pages and built the cover was called the "forwarder." The binding was passed to a "finisher," who ornamented the cover. When a book was des-

An industrial binding operation from around 1880

tined for a great deal of use, hog skin was frequently used as the binding. If it was to be a more expensive, carefully handled volume, calf or goat skin was often the choice. Large, inexpensive works were often bound in thin planks of wood.

The process of binding books remained a slow, specialized craft until the eighteenth century. The illustration shows one part of an industrial binding operation from around 1880. Several activities are taking place in this room. The women at the right are hand folding press sheets that will become signatures. Each is using an "ever-in-hand paper-folder," which today we would call a bone knife, to crease each edge as a fold is made. The two rows of tables hold the folded signatures, which are piled in the proper sequence as they will appear in the finished book. The women gather the book together as they walk down the rows, picking up one signature from each pile. After the signatures are gathered, three holes are punched through the edge of each one by the "stabbing-machine." The seated women in front of the large power wheel are all involved with hand sewing the signatures together by passing thread through the punched holes. On the floor below, the sewed books are trimmed, glue is applied to the backs, and covers are put in place.

The bindery of 1880 looks a bit crude to us today, but it was a big step beyond the tedious book work of five hundred years before. The work that took months to complete in 1400 took only days in 1880. The same job can be done today in only a few minutes.

Objectives for Chapter Twenty-one

After completing this chapter, you will be able to:

- List the steps in safely operating an industrial paper cutter, including identification of machine parts, safety steps, size adjustment, and actual cutting.
- Describe the basic folding devices, including the differences between knife and buckle folders.
- List and define the common assembling processes, including gathering, collating, and inserting.
- List and define the common binding processes, including adhesive binding, side binding, saddle binding, self-covers, soft covers, and casebound covers.

Introduction

Few printing jobs are delivered to the customer in the same form as the one in which they leave the printing press. Some work, such as simple business forms or posters, requires no additional handling other than boxing or wrapping. But the vast majority of printed products require some sort of additional processing in order to meet the job requirements. Those operations performed after the job has left the press are called **finishing.** Finishing might be performed by a separate company specializing in those operations; it might be handled by "in line" equipment that receives each piece as it leaves the press; or it might be handled in a special section of the shop.

The most common finishing operations are cutting, folding, assembling, and binding. Techniques such as embossing, perforating, scoring, and die cutting were discussed in chapter 18 ("Adaptation of Platen Presses for Special Techniques"), but they are often called finishing procedures. The tasks do not follow any certain order or sequence and are not necessarily all performed on the same job (although it is certainly possible). The following sections examine some basic techniques within each of the four common operations. Because paper is the most widely used printing receiver, the discussions will be restricted to devices and techniques used to finish paper materials.

Cutting

The Basic Device

The basic paper-cutting device used in the industry is called a **guillotine cutter,** or simply a "paper cutter" (figure 21.1). Guillotine cutters are manufactured in all sizes and degrees of sophistication. Size is defined by the widest cut that can be made. Sophistication is described by the speed with which the machine can be set up and a cut taken.

The bed of the cutter is the flat table that holds the paper pile. The back guide, or fence, is movable and is usually calibrated with some measurement system that tells the operator the distance of the guide from the knife (figure 21.2). The side guides are stationary and are always at perfect right angles to the edge of the bed. The clamp is a metal bar that can be lowered into contact with the paper pile before a cut is made. Its purpose is to compress the pile to remove air and to keep the paper from shifting during the cut. The cutter blade itself is usually mounted up away from the operator's view and hands. When activated, the blade moves down and across to cut the pile in one single motion.

The simplest sort of guillotine cutter is called a **lever cutter** and obtains its power from the strength of the operator. The worker moves a long lever that is directly linked to the cutter blade. The most common device is a power cutter, which automatically makes the cut at the operator's command. A frequent source of power is an electric motor, which operates a hydraulic pump.

The mere movement of paper onto and off the bed of the cutter is the most fatiguing part of the paper cutter's job. Consider that a single ream of paper might weigh 200 pounds and that several tons of paper are usually cut in a single day. Many devices are equipped with air film tables that work to reduce the fatigue factor. With this system, the paper is supported by a blanket of air that escapes from small openings in the table to allow for easy movement of any size of paper pile over an almost frictionless surface (figure 21.3).

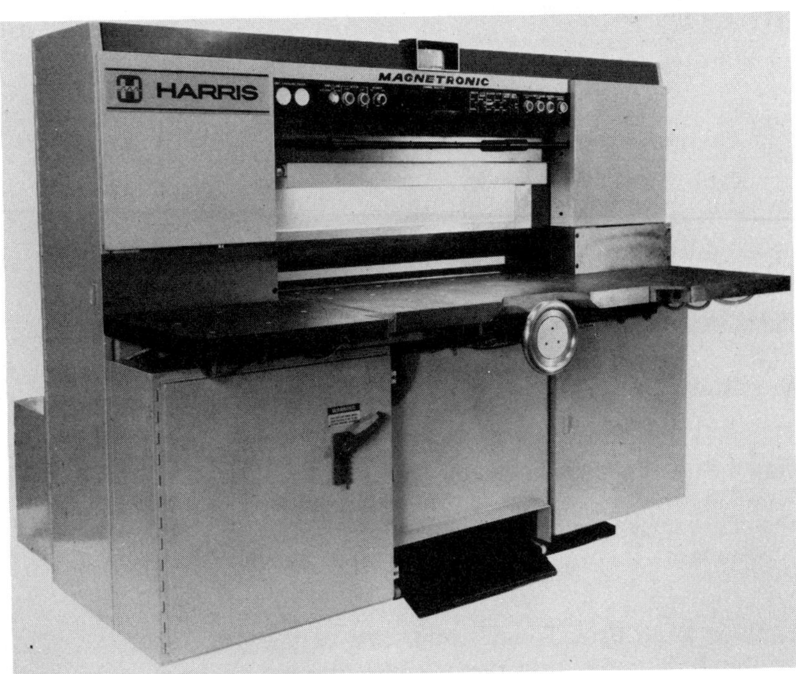

Figure 21.1. An industrial paper cutter
Courtesy of Harris Corporation.

One of the most time-consuming actions when making a series of different cuts is resetting the fence, which controls the size of cut to be made. Automatic spacing devices can be programmed to "remember" the order and setting for as many as twenty different cuts. As the operator removes a pile, the machine readjusts the back fence and is ready for the next cut by the time the new pile is in place. Some cutters can split the back fence into three sections and then independently control each position so that three different lengths can be cut with one motion of the cutter blade.

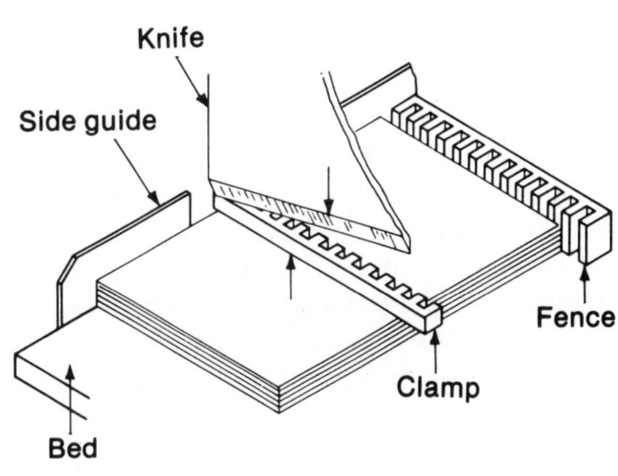

Figure 21.2. Diagram of a guillotine cutter
The blade of a guillotine cutter moves down and across to cut the paper pile.

Cutting Safety

The guillotine cutter is named after the infamous "guillotine" that so efficiently removed

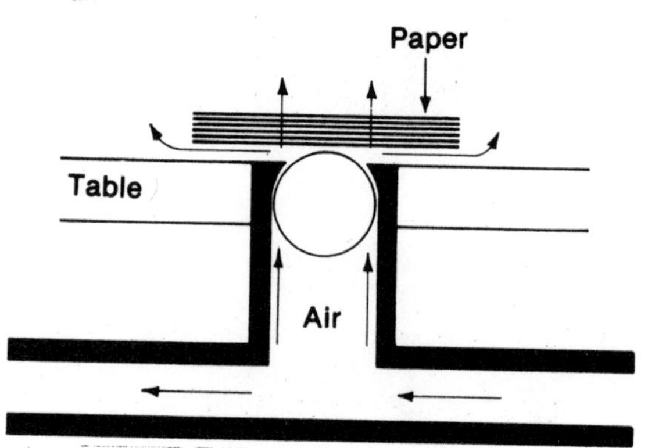

Figure 21.3. Side view of an air film table A sketch of the side view of an air film table shows one of the small openings that release air onto the table surface.

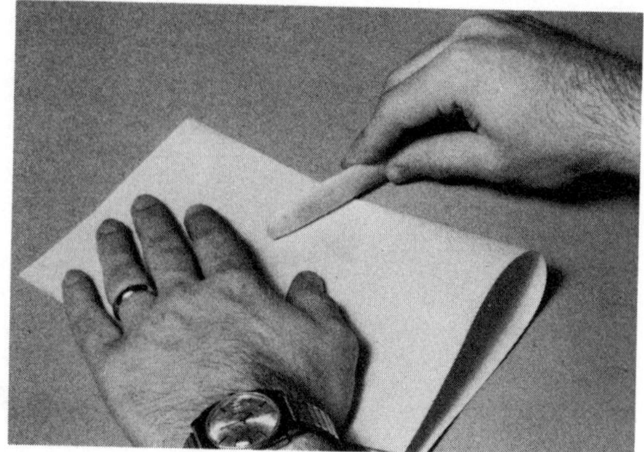

Figure 21.4. Example of a bone folder
Courtesy of SUCO Learning Resources and R. Kampas.

heads in times past. Today's guillotine cutter is intended to cut only paper. But, like its ancestor, it will easily cut almost anything placed in its path.

Today's paper cutters require an operator to use both hands to activate the cutter blade. Early machines had no such safety feature. As a result, many operators lost fingers or hands. No device is foolproof, so it should be a standard procedure to keep hands away from the blade and blade path at all times.

It is also a wise practice never to place anything but paper on the bed of a cutter. A steel rule or paper gauge can cause damage by chipping the blade's cutting edge. This will require resharpening the blade.

Operating a Paper Cutter

Paper cutting is a critical operation. The time and effort that go into every job can be made useless by a single sloppy cut. The fence and side guide of a paper cutter are similar in function to the side guide and headstop of a printing press (see "Typical Registration Systems," chapter 12). If the pile is in contact with both guides, the sheet will be cut square and to the proper length.

Every job delivered to the paper cutter should have a cutting layout attached to the pile. The **cutting layout** is generally one sheet of the job that has been ruled to show the location and order of the cuts. Sequence does not seem important at first thought, but if the cutting layout is not faithfully followed, some part of the main sheet will be damaged and a job will have to be done over.

Determine the length of the first cut from the cutting layout and adjust the back fence to that dimension. Place a pile on the cutter table and seat it carefully against both the fence and the side guide. Activate whatever control system the machine uses and make the cut. Remove the scrap (generally to be binned and sold back to the paper mill) and pull the cut pile free. If the job is large and the cutter is not equipped with automatic spacing, the same cut might be repeated for the entire pile. Then the fence would be adjusted for the next cut, and the entire pile would be cut again. If automatic spacing is used, the cutter goes to the next position at the operator's command.

Folding

The Basic Devices

The most basic type of folding device is called a **bone folder.** Printers have used it for hundreds of years to do hand folding. The process is simple. The printer registers one edge of the sheet with the other and then slides the bone folder across the seam to make a smooth crease (figure 21.4). Bone folders are used today only for very small, prestige jobs. Nearly all industrial folding is now done by high-speed machines. The two common folding devices are called knife and buckle folders.

Knife folders operate by means of a thin knife blade that forces a sheet of paper between two rotating rollers. The action takes place in two steps. First the sheet is carried into the machine and comes to rest at a fold gauge (figure 21.5a). Just as in a press, the sheet is positioned by means of a moving side guide. Next the knife blade is lowered between the two rotating rollers until the knurled (ridged) surfaces catch the sheet, crease it, and pass it out of the way so the next sheet can be moved into register (figure 21.5b). If sets of rollers and knives are stacked one over the other, many folds can be made on the same sheet as the piece travels from one level to the next.

Buckle folders (figure 21.6) operate on a similar notion of the sheet passing between two rotating rollers. The technique that directs the piece, however, is a bit different.

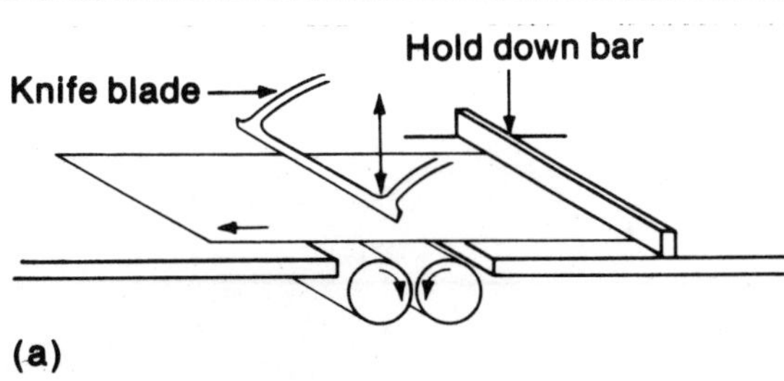

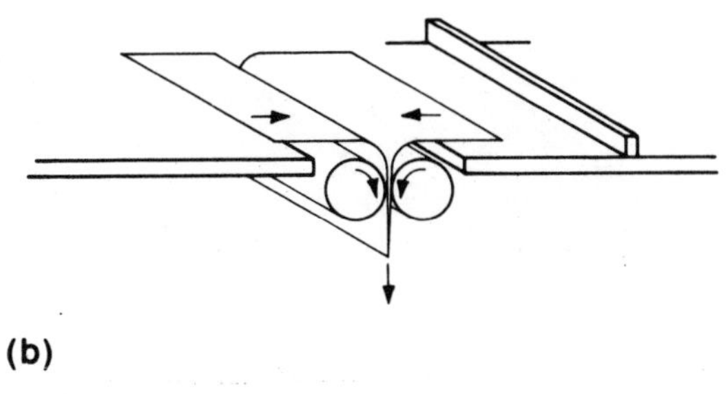

Figure 21.5. Diagram of a knife folder operation

Instead of a knife or some other object contacting the paper and causing the crease, the sheet is made to buckle or curve and passes by its own accord into the rollers. The sheet is passed between two folding plates by a drive roller until the sheet gauge is reached. The gap between the plates, however, is so slight that the paper can do nothing more than pass through the opening. As the piece hits the sheet gauge, the drive roller continues to move the sheet, which buckles directly over the folding rollers and passes through the two to be creased and carried on to the next level.

Sequence of Folds

Two important terms must be understood when discussing the sequence of folding. They are "right-angle" and "parallel" folds.

Figure 21.6. A buckle folder
Courtesy of Bell and Howell/Baumfolder Division/Philipsburg Division.

Figure 21.7a shows a traditional formal fold, called a **French fold,** that is frequently used in the production of greeting cards. To make a French fold, first crease a sheet across its length. Then make a second fold at a right angle to the first across the width. A French fold is a **right-angle fold** because it has at least one fold that is at a right angle to the others. Figure 21.7b illustrates an accordion fold that is commonly used in the preparation of road maps. An **accordion fold** can be made in a number of ways, but each crease is always parallel to every other crease and is therefore called a parallel fold.

Ideally, all parallel folds should be made with the crease running in the same direction as (parallel to) the grain of the paper. Great stresses are involved with folding, and grain direction should be considered whenever possible (figure 21.8).

The final folding product is a result of the use of either parallel or right-angle creases or a combination of the two. The sequence of folds is an important consideration that must be taken into account throughout the printing process.

In chapter 3 ("Imposition") the ideas of signature, work-and-turn, and work-and-tumble imposition were discussed. When laying out for imposition, the order of folds in the bindery room dictates the position of each paper or form on the press sheet. Figure 21.9

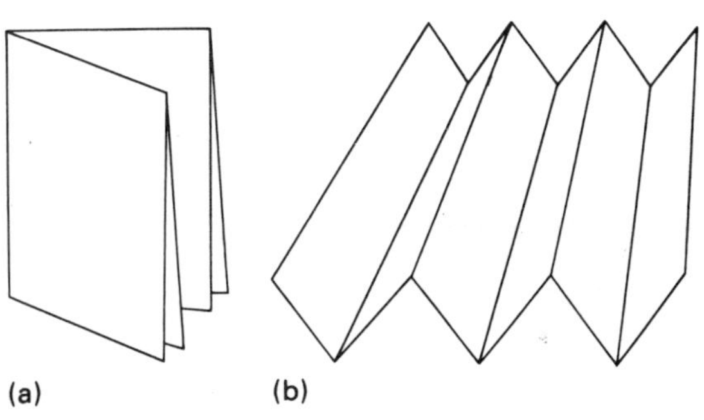

Figure 21.7. **Examples of French and accordian folds** A French fold (a) is often used for greeting cards. An accordion fold (b) is often used for road maps.

reviews four different ways that a single sheet can be folded to produce a sixteen-page signature. It also shows the page layouts for one side of the sheet. If the job is laid out for one sequence of folds but another sequence is actually used, the final result will be unusable. The wisest procedure is always to prepare the dummy by using a signature that has been folded on the piece of equipment and in the same sequence that will be used on the final press sheets.

Assembling

Understanding Terms

Assembling is a term that is generally used to describe several similar operations that have the same final goal. Before a printed product can be bound, the separate pieces must be brought together into a single unit. For a casebound book, the unit might be made up of ten signatures; for a pile of NCR forms, it might be only two sheets. Whatever the size

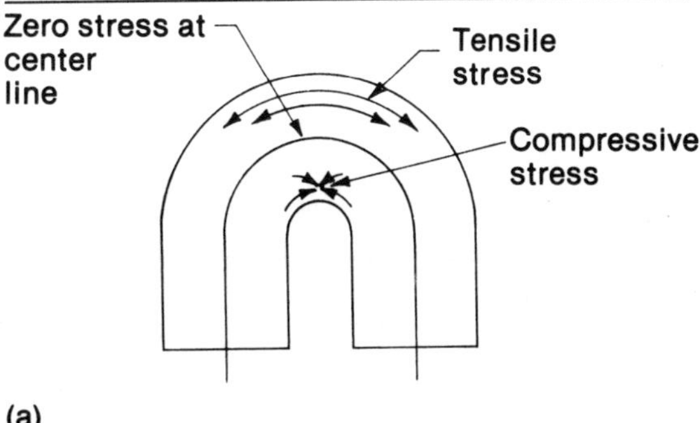

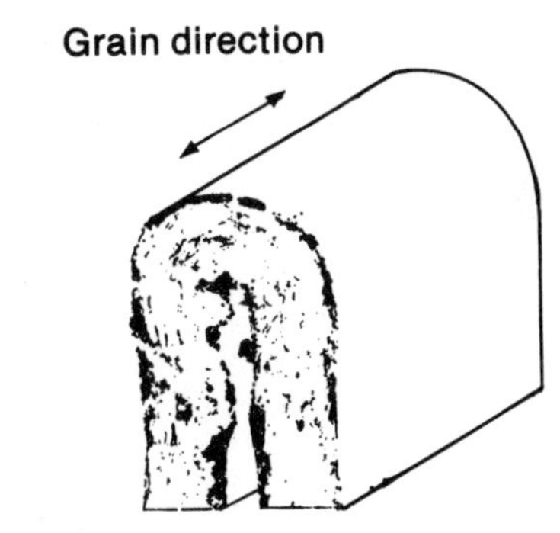

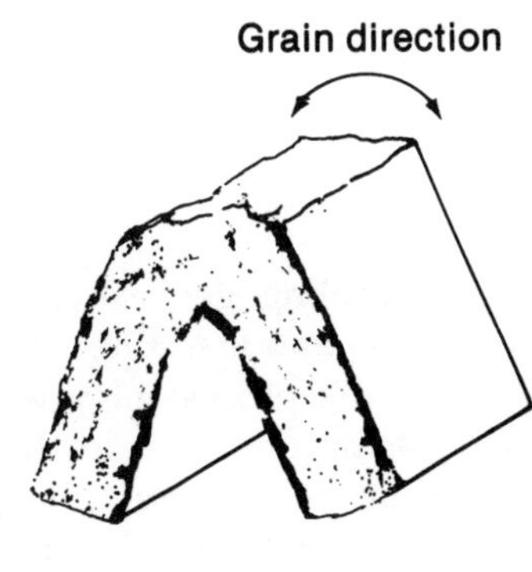

Figure 21.8. Diagram showing areas of stress in folding Fibers bend easily with the grain (b), but tend to bread break because of the stresses when folding against the grain (c).
Courtesy of Mead Paper.

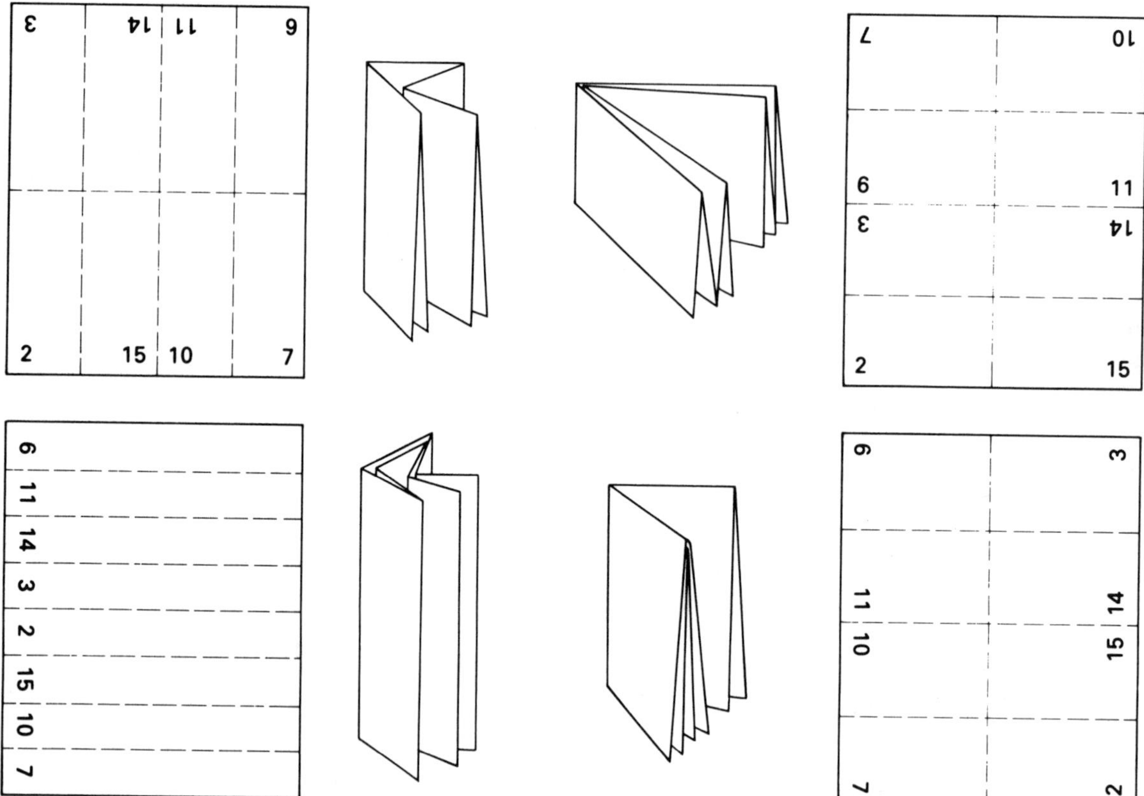

Figure 21.9. Four ways to fold a sixteen-page signature

of the unit, assembling generally includes gathering, collating, and inserting.

Gathering is the process of assembling signatures by placing one next to the other (figure 21.10a). Gathering is commonly used to prepare books whose page thickness will be greater than ⅜ inch (0.95 cm).

Collating once meant checking the sequence of pages before a book was bound, but now it means gathering individual sheets instead of signatures.

Inserting is combining signatures by placing one within another (figure 21.10b). Inserting can be done for pieces whose final page thickness will be less than ½ inch (1.27 cm).

Basic Assembling Techniques

Assembling procedures are either manual, semiautomatic, or totally automatic.

Manual Assembly. Manual assembly is exactly what the term implies. Piles of sheets or

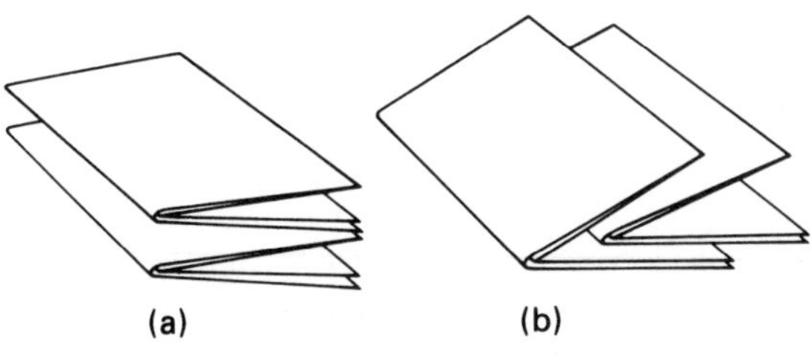

Figure 21.10. Two ways of assembling signatures Gathered signatures are placed next to each other (a). Inserted signatures are placed one within another (b).

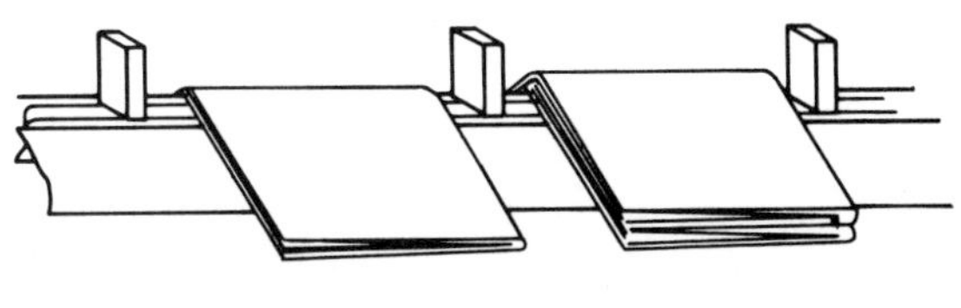

Figure 21.11. Diagram of open signatures placed at saddlebars on a conveyor

signatures are laid out on a table, and workers pick up one piece from each stack and gather, collate, or insert them to form bindery units. Equipment is available that improves the process a bit by having the worker stationary and moving the piles of a circular table. But the process is still slow and clumsy. Manual assembly is reserved for either extremely small jobs or for work so poorly planned that it cannot be assembled in any other way. Nearly all contemporary industrial assembly is done with semiautomatic or automatic equipment.

Semiautomatic Assembly. Semiautomatic assembly machines require no human interaction with the devices except to pile the sheets or signatures in the feeder units. In semiautomatic inserting, a moving chain passes in front of feeder stations. At each station an operator opens a signature and places it on the moving conveyor at "saddlebar" (figure 21.11). The number of stations at the machine will be the same as the number of signatures making up the unit or book. By the time each saddlebar has moved past every station, an entire unit has beern inserted or assembled and the saddle pin pushes the unit off the machine. The unit can then be moved in line with a bindery unit for fastening or can be stacked for storage and later binding. Little gathering or collating is done with semiautomatic equipment, but the same general principle is used as for inserting.

Automatic Assembly. Automatic assembling machines use a conveyor device moving past feeder stations. But a machine instead of a person delivers the sheet or signature. Almost all automatic systems are in line with bindery equipment so that assembly and fastening are accomplished at the same time.

Two designs of feeder mechanisms are used on automatic gathering devices (figure 21.12). Both allow for continuous loading of signatures because pieces are delivered from the bottom of the stack. With the swinging arm device, a vacuum sucker foot lowers one signature into position to be received by a gripper arm. The arm, with signature in hand, swings over the conveyor system and drops the piece in place on the belt. The rotary design uses the same suction system, but a rotating wheel with gripper fingers removes the signature and delivers it to the moving chain. With each rotation, the device can gather two signatures and is therefore considered a faster system than the swinging arm mechanism.

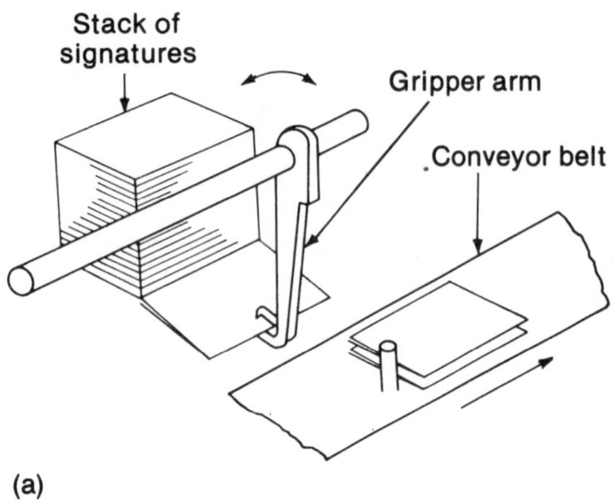

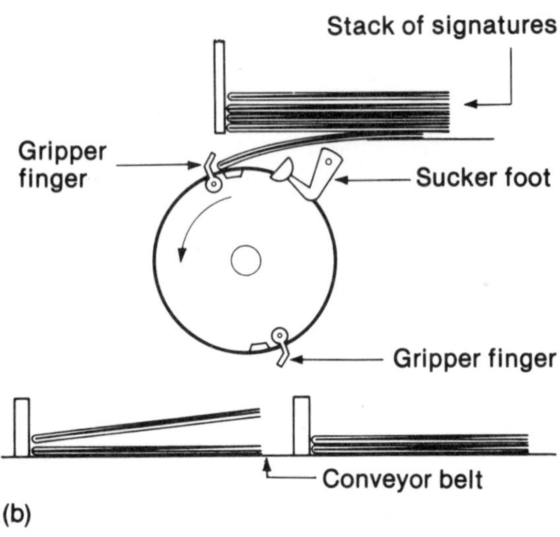

Figure 21.12. Two types of feeder mechanisms used on automatic gathering machines A swinging arm mechanism and suction action are used to move signatures onto a conveyor belt (a), or a rotating wheel with gripper fingers serves the same purpose (b).

Automatic collating equipment is similar in design to gathering machines, except that feeding is generally done from the top of the pile, as with most automatic printing presses (see "Loading Systems," chapter 12). Even though the machine must be stopped to load the feeder units, the device is nearly as efficient as continuous devices because a great many single sheets can be placed in the same area that only a few large signatures would take up.

Automatic inserting devices are almost always linked with a closed system of operations that extends from the composition room through plate preparation, press, on past assembly to fastening, trimming, labeling for mailing, and even bundling of piles by zip code order. Magazines such as *Time* and *Newsweek,* with editions of sometimes a million copies and little allowance for production time, require accurate planning, speed, accuracy, and a tightly controlled closed system of production. High-speed inserting is done by a combination of vacuum and grippers that removes the signature, opens it, and places it in the proper sequence with the other signatures in the job.

Binding

It is difficult to categorize neatly all the methods used by the printing industry to fasten together the assembled unit into its final form. The type of cover used on the printed piece is often confused with the actual method of attaching the pages. Sheets or signatures can be fastened together by using such techniques as adhesive, side, or saddle binding. The fastened pages can be covered with self-soft, or casebound covers.

Adhesive Binding

The simplest form of **adhesive binding,** called **padding,** is found on the edge of the common notepad. In the adhesive binding process, a pile of paper is clamped together in a press and a liquid glue is painted or brushed along one edge. The most common material is applied cold and is water soluble while in a liquid state, but becomes insoluble in water after it dries. Individual sheets can be easily removed by pulling one away from the padding compound.

The popular "paperback" or "pocket" book is an example of an adhesive binding technique called **perfect** or **patent binding.** The perfect fastening process is generally completely automatic (figure 21.13). If signatures rather than individual sheets are combined, the folded edge is trimmed and roughened to provide a greater gripping surface. The liquid adhesive (generally hot) is then applied, and a gauze-like material called **crash** is sometimes embedded in the pasty spine to provide additional strength.

Figure 21.13. An automatic perfect fastening machine
Courtesy of Gane Brothers and Lane, Inc.

Side Binding

A common office stapler is probably the most familiar method of **side binding.** With this technique, the fastening device is passed through the pile at a right angle to the page surface. In addition to the wire staple, side binding can be accomplished by mechanical binding, looseleaf, or side sewing.

Mechanical Binding. Mechanical binding is a process that is usually permanent and does not allow for adding sheets. One of the most common forms is a wire that resembles a spring coil. The wire runs through round holes that have been punched or drilled through the sheets and cover. The coil is generally inserted by hand into the first several holes of the book. Then the worker pushes the wire against a rotating rubber wheel that spins the device on the rest of the way.

Looseleaf Binding. Looseleaf binding devices are considered permanent, but they allow for the removal and addition of pages. The casebound three-ring binder is a popular item, but there are a great many other forms. Binder posts, spring back, and expansion posts are only three examples. An increasingly popular technique is a plastic comb binder (figure 21.14). With this system, a special device is used to punch the holes, and another device expands the plastic clips so the pages can be inserted on the prongs. The binder can be opened later to add sheets or it can be removed completely and used to fasten another unit.

Side-Sewn Binding. One pattern for the side sewing of a book is shown in figure 21.15. With hand sewing, the pile is drilled (always an odd number of holes) and then clamped in place so the individual pages will not shift. A needle and thread is passed in and out of

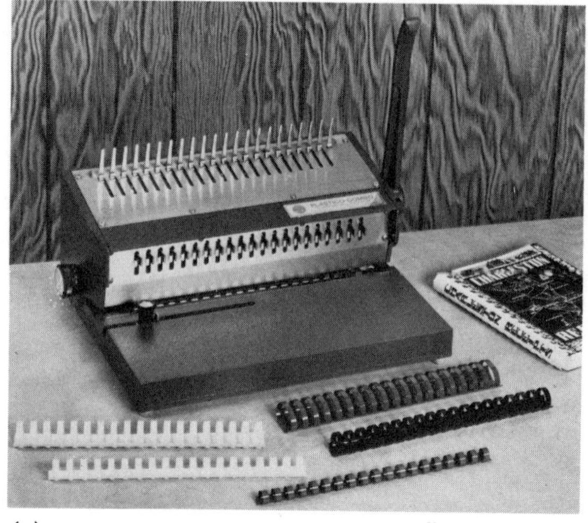

(a)

(b)

Figure 21.14. A hand-operated plastic punch and binder (a) and a power-operated punch (b)
Courtesy of Plastic Binding Corporation.

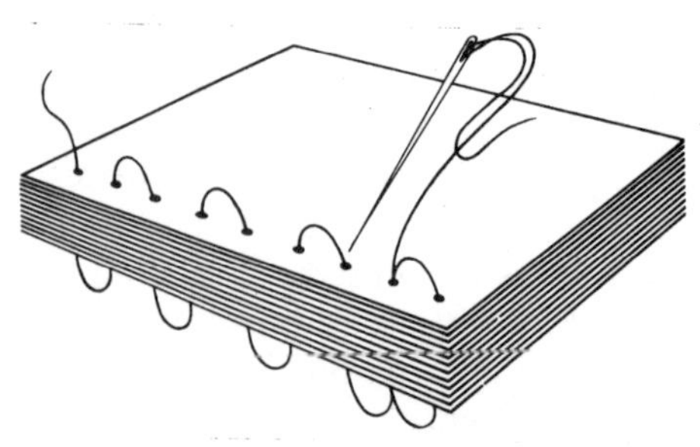

Figure 21.15. Diagram of hand side sewing of a book

each hole from one end of the book to the other and then back again to the last hole, where the cord is tied off. Automatic equipment has been designed that produces a side-sewn book rapidly and accurately, although with a different thread pattern than the hand technique (figure 21.16). The main drawback to side-sewn or wire-stapled side binding is that the book does not lie flat when open.

Saddle Binding

Saddle binding is the process of fastening one or more signatures along the folded or backbone edge of the unit. The term comes from the fact that a signature held open at the fold resembles—with some imagination—the shape of a horse's saddle.

Popular news magazines are fastened by saddle wire stitching. With large editions, the stitching is done automatically in line with the inserting of signatures. Saddle wire stitching can also be done by hand with large staple machines. It can be performed semiautomatically: the operator merely places the signature over a support, and the wire is driven through the edge, crimped, and then delivered (figure 21.17). This method of wire fas-

Figure 21.16. An automatic side-stitching device
Courtesy of Harris Corporation.

tening is generally restricted to thicknesses of less than ½ inch (1.27 cm).

Saddle sewing is commonly considered the highest-quality fastening technique in the world today. Sometimes called "center-fold" sewing, the process produces a book that will lie nearly flat when it is opened. Nearly all saddle-sewn books are produced on semiautomatic or completely automatic equipment. Semiautomatic devices require an operator to open each signature and place it on a conveyor belt that moves it to the sewing mechanism and combines it with the rest of the book. Automatic machines are usually in line with a gathering mechanism that delivers a single unit to the sewing device.

Self-Covers

Self-covers are produced from the same material as the body of the book and generally carry part of the message of the piece. Newspaper and some news magazines have self-covers. The method requires no special techniques to assemble or atttach the cover to the body of the work. The process is generally restricted to the less expensive binding techniques, such as wire side or saddle fastening.

Soft Covers

Soft covers are made from paper or paper fiber material with greater substance than that used for the body of the book. Soft covers rarely carry part of the message of the piece. They are intended to attract attention and to provide slight, temporary protection. Paperback books are one example of their use. Soft covers can be glued in place, as with perfect binding, or can be attached by stitching or sewing. The covers are generally cut flush with the pages of the book.

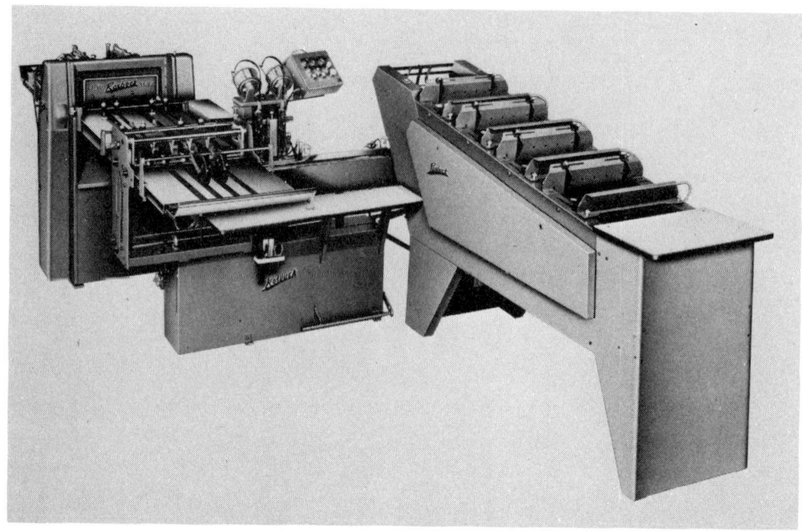

Figure 21.17. A semiautomatic saddle-stitching device
Courtesy of F.P. Rosback Company.

Casebound Covers

A **casebound cover** is a rigid cover that is generally associated with high-quality bookbinding. The covers are produced separately from the rest of the book and are formed from a thick fiber board glued to leather, cloth, or some form of moisture-resistant impregnated paper (figure 21.18). A casebound cover extends over the edge of the body of the book by perhaps ⅛ inch (0.32 cm). This "turn-in" provides additional protection for the closed pages.

In order to casebind a book, several operations, called forwarding, are necessary. First, the signatures are trimmed, generally by using a three-knife device that cuts the three open sides in a single motion (figure 21.19). The back or fastened edge of the book is then rounded. Rounding gives the book an attractive appearance and keeps the pages within the turn-in of the cover (figure 21.20). Backing is accomplished by clamping the rounded book in place and mushrooming-out the fastened edges of the signatures (figure 21.21). The purpose of backing is to make the rounding operation permanent and to provide a ridge for the casebound cover. Next the book goes through a "lining-up" process, which consists of gluing a layer of gauze (called "crash") and strips of paper (called "backing paper") to the backed edge. The crash and backing paper are later glued to the case and provide additional support for the book. A headband is a decorative tape that can be attached to the head and tail of the back of the book to give a pleasing appearance. This is not always done. All forwarding can be completed on automatic equipment.

The actual case is made from two pieces of thick binder's board glued to the covering cloth. The cloth can be printed before gluing to the board or after by such processes as relief hot stamping or screen printing. The binder's board is cut so that the piece will

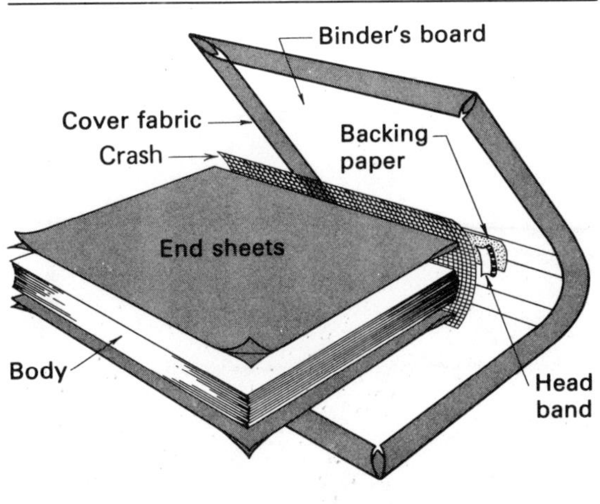

Figure 21.18. The anatomy of a casebound book

extend over the body of the book by at least ⅛ inch (0.32 cm) on each open edge and will miss the backed ridge by the same distance. The cloth is cut large enough so that it will completely cover one side of both boards and will extend around the edges by at least ½ inch (1.27 cm) (see figure 21.18). The positions of the two boards on the cloth are critical and must be carefully controlled. Automatic equipment exists that cuts both the board and the cloth and joins the two pieces in their proper positions.

The final process of joining the forwarded book with the case is called casing in. The two are attached by two sheets called **end sheets** (see figure 21.18). End sheets can be the outside leaves of the first and last signatures or can be special pieces that were joined to the pages during the assembling and fastening operations.

To case in a book, the end sheets are coated with glue, the case is positioned in

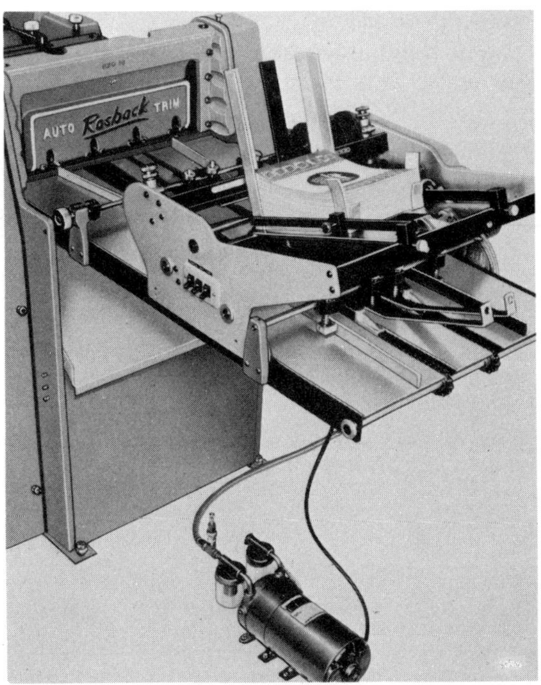

Figure 21.19. A three-knife trimming machine
Courtesy of F.P. Rosback Company.

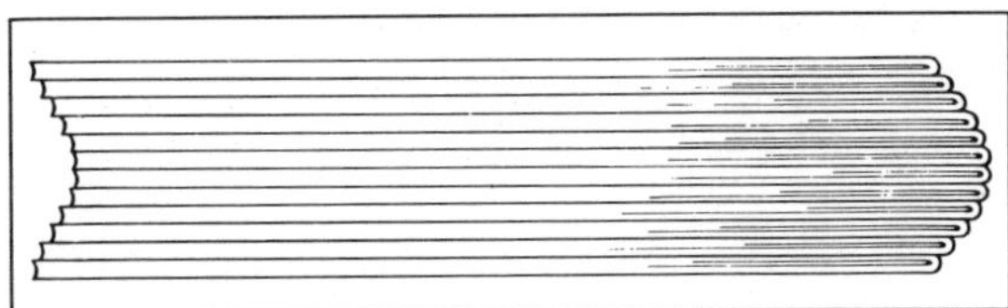

Figure 21.20. Rounded signatures of a book

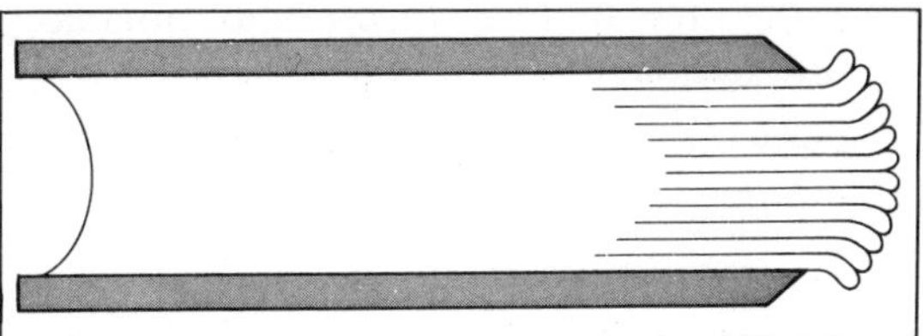

Figure 21.21. Backing the edges of the signatures

place, and pressure is applied. The pressure must be maintained until the adhesive is dry. This was traditionally accomplished by stacking the books between special "building-in" boards (figure 21.22). This technique has been gradually replaced by special heat-setting adhesives that dry in a matter of seconds as the end sheets contact the case.

When the book is complete, it can be jacketed (put in a protective paper cover) or boxed and delivered to the customer. Equipment exists that automatically case binds books from the forwarding operations to the final steps of sealing and labeling the cases used to ship the final product.

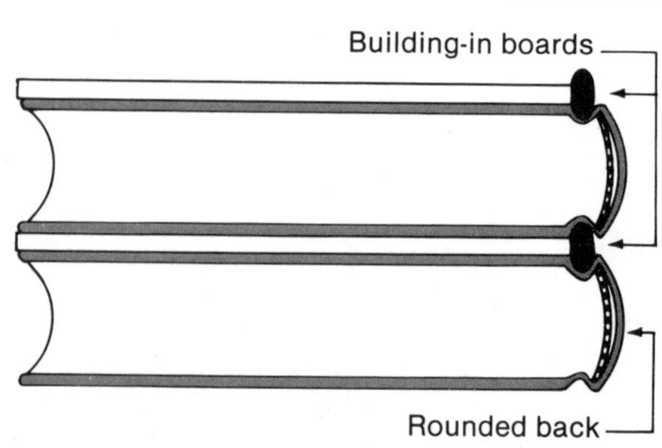

Figure 21.22. Diagram of the use of traditional building-in boards

Key Terms

finishing
guillotine cutter
knife folders
buckle folders
French fold
right-angle fold
accordion fold
parallel fold
assembling
gathering
collating
inserting
adhesive binding
perfect binding
patent binding
side binding
saddle binding
self-covers
casebound covers

Questions for Review

1. What are the most common finishing operations?
2. How is the size of a guillotine paper cutter defined?
3. Explain the difference between the operation of a knife folder and that of a buckle folder.
4. What do the terms *right-angle fold* and *parallel fold* mean?
5. What is the difference between gathering, collating, and inserting?
6. What does the term *perfect binding* mean?
7. Give three examples of side binding.
8. What is the process of saddle binding?
9. Explain the differences between self-covers, soft covers, and casebound covers.
10. What does the term *forwarding* describe?

Chapter Twenty-two

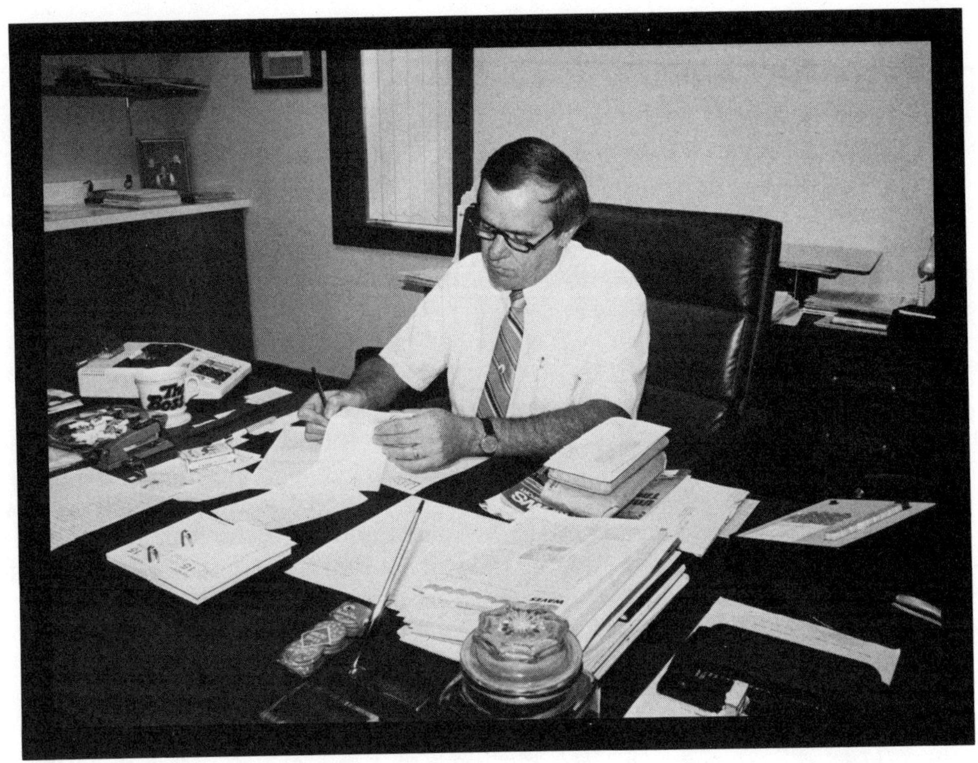

Estimating and Production Control

Anecdote to Chapter Twenty-two

Printing has made many contributions to our written and spoken language. Before printers came on the scene, there was no consistency of spelling or punctuation. When books were hand written by medieval scribes, words, sentences, and even paragarphs could be runtogetheronthe whim of the artist. They could become very difficult to read. Spaces between words, commas, periods, and other marks were invented by early printers to act as signals to the reader. There are also many examples of printers' language used in everyday conversation. One example is the use of the terms *uppercase* and *lowercase* to describe captial and small letters in our alphabet.

One of the early methods of storing pieces of foundry type was in a case of individual bins called a "news case" (see illustration). Two cases were necessary to store a complete alphabet. There was one case for the minuscule, or small letters, and another for the majuscule, or capitals. In actual practice, the printer placed one bin or case over the other. The case holding the capitals was placed above the case containing the small letters.

When the master printer wanted a certain letter, he would call out to his "devil" (a worker with less status than an apprentice) "get me a *C* from the upper case." When he was trying to save time he would shout, "Get me an upper case *C*."

The terms *uppercase* and *lowercase* have been accepted as the nicknames for the capital and small characters in our alphabet and are a direct result of the language of the early relief printers.

One of two news cases necessary to store a complete alphabet

Courtesy of Mackenzie and Harris, Inc.

Objectives for Chapter Twenty-two

After completing this topic you will be able to:

- Explain how estimates are determined for the length of time required to complete a task and how to use a unit/time standards form.
- Explain how fixed costs are identified and determined in production costs.
- Outline the basic job estimating process.
- Discuss the use of a job work order to direct a job through scheduling and production control.

Introduction

Both novice and experienced printers sometimes become so concerned with the craft that they lose sight of what is involved in operating any company beyond the manufacturing of the product. The purpose of this chapter is to examine the important problem of determining operating costs.

Determining the Cost of Labor

No industry can function by guesswork. At each level in a printing organization, it is important that the supervisor or manager know how long it takes to perform a specific task and how much it costs. Without information on time and cost standards, it is impossible to predict accurately the cost of a job. A bid would be either so low that the company loses money or so high that a competitor gets the job.

A variety of techniques are used by the printing industry to determine these important standards. The complexity or simplicity of the procedures depends on the size and diversity of the business. A small "quick print" company that uses only one sheet size sold in units of 100 will have a single standard—a set amount of dollars per hundred sheets. A large job shop, on the other hand, might need to set labor requirements and prices for as many as a thousand different operations. This section deals with the procedures that a medium-sized job shop might use to determine labor costs.

Figure 22.1 shows a typical form used in any section to determine unit/time standards. The section supervisor would maintain a form for each piece of equipment or operation. Every job or only a random sample of each week's work could be recorded on the

Standards Sheet

Description	Section	Equipment	Unit Quantity
Labor	Press	17x22 offset	1,000 sheets

No.	Date	Employee	Units	Total Hours	Average Hours per Unit
1	5/8	Faux	5	1.13	.23
2	5/11	Adams	7	1.44	.21
3	5/19	Roehrich	2	.38	.19
4	5/22	Gartner	4	.82	.21
5	5/23	Roehrich	10	2.10	.21
6	5/26	Faux	5	.98	.20
7	6/1	Gartner	2	.90	.18
8	6/2	Adams	6	.44	.22
9	6/3	Faux	5	1.20	.20

Total 1.85

Total(1.85)/No. of Entries(9) = .21

Standard = .21hrs/1,000 shts

Figure 22.1. A typical unit/time standards form

sheet. In each instance, the standard is nothing more than the average time to complete an operation.

The example in figure 22.1 is concerned with determining the average labor time to print 1,000 sheets of paper in the press section on a 17-by-22-inch offset press. On May 8, press operator Faux ran 5,000 sheets in 1.13 hours. That averages to 0.23 hours per 1,000 sheets. The press supervisor has taken a random sample of work on the 17-by-22-inch press for four different press operators. In each case the average time per 1,000 sheets was determined.

Industry has found that it is more convenient to record time in units of hundredths instead of hours, minutes, and seconds. It is far simpler to multiply $5.00 per hour times 1.13 rather than 1 hour, 7 minutes, and 48 seconds.

1 hour, 7 minutes, 48 seconds
48/60 = .8 minutes

1 hour, 7.8 minutes
7.8/60 = .13 hours

1.13 hours

When the labor standards sheet was full, the

"average hours per unit" column was totaled (1.85 in figure 22.1) and then divided by the number of entries (9) to give the standard time needed to print 1,000 17-by-22-inch sheets (0.21 hours per 1,000).

This procedure can be duplicated in each section, or cost center, of the company, and then a master list can be compiled for the estimator to use when preparing job bids (figure 22.2). Some companies continually keep track of production standards and update their master list on a weekly basis. Others merely spot-check their standards on a monthly or quarterly basis.

Determining Fixed Costs

It is relatively easy for a manager to determine the cost of the materials and labor that go into a given job, but in any business there are expenses that are hard to determine when making a job estimate. How many paper clips should be charged to that job? What was the cost of the electricity used to operate the camera lights for five negatives? How much water was used to wash the press operators' hands at the end of the day, and what job should be charged? All of these items are small alone. But when they are summed over the span of a year, they become significant. They are expenses and must be considered in the total cost of each job.

One approach is to add a certain percentage, called *overhead,* to each job. If the management had determined that 4% of their yearly costs were a result of these "unmeasurable" expenses and a job was calculated to cost $1,000, the 4% or $40 would be added to the bid.

An alternative procedure to the single overhead figure is to add a fixed amount to each productive hour spent on every job. The determination of that fixed amount is a bit involved, but it is a fairly accurate method of accounting for difficult-to-measure expenses of any business. It is necessary to use an example to illustrate the process.

Consider figure 22.3, a floor plan of Spartan Graphics, a typical—although imaginary—medium-sized printing company. From the accounting office, the president has determined that they have $8,000 fixed building costs each year. By measuring the plant, the president finds that there are 2,000 square feet in the building, which means that it costs the business $4 per square foot each year just to operate the building.

If the square foot area of each section is determined from the floor plan, it should be possible to assign a portion of the fixed building costs to each. The first three columns of table 22.1 have determined the "fixed building costs per square foot by department."

Another cost that is difficult to proportion out to each job is **depreciation.** Somehow the cost of the presses, platemakers, cameras, and all the other equipment must be paid for; but their cost is so great that no single job could cover it. Depreciation is arrived at by dividing the total cost for each piece of equipment by the number of years it should be productive. Table 22.2 shows the annual depreciation in the press section. The equipment manufacturers have determined that with proper maintenance and service the four presses that the business owns will last ten years. The total cost is then divided by ten to determine the annual charge that must be set so that at the end of the life of each press a new press can be purchased.

Column four in table 22.1 lists the equipment depreciation for each section. This is added to the fixed building cost in column five. That total represents the amount that

STANDARD LABOR PER UNIT		
SECTION	UNIT	STANDARD
Composing	Body composition, 35 square inches, 6–10 point	0.10 hour
	Headlines, 50 inches	0.15 hour
Camera	Negatives	
	up to 17 × 22	0.12 hour
	17 × 22 and up	0.18 hour
	Halftones	
	up to 4 × 5	0.23 hour
	4 × 5 to 8 × 10	0.32 hour
	Contacts	0.09 hour
Stripping	Flats, single color	
	12 × 19	0.25 hour
	19 × 24	0.48 hour
	For each added color	
	12 × 19	0.34 hour
	19 × 24	0.58 hour
Plate	Plates, surface	
	12 × 18½ (1 side)	0.20 hour
	19 × 24 (1 side)	0.22 hour
	For each added exposure	0.09 hour
Press	11 × 17 press, 1,000 sheets	0.18 hour
	17 × 22 press, 1,000 sheets	0.21 hour
	For each added color	
	11 × 17 press	0.22 hour
	17 × 22 press	0.27 hour
	Wash-up per color	0.35 hour
Bindery	One fold and staple, 1,000 sheets, saddle	0.15 hour
	Two folds and staple, 1,000 sheets, saddle	0.19 hour
	Trim, wrap and carton, 1,000 sheets	
	11 × 17	0.09 hour
	17 × 22	0.11 hour
	Trim and skid only, 1,000 sheets	
	11 × 17	0.05 hour
	17 × 22	0.06 hour

Figure 22.2. Example of a master list used by estimators to prepare job bids

Fixed building costs per year:	
Cost of building (lease)	$5,500
Building maintenance	1,200
Insurance (building and contents)	200
Taxes	150
Power (light, heat, etc.)	950
Total	$8,000

Fixed building costs per square foot:

$8,000 ÷ 2,000 square feet = $4 per square foot

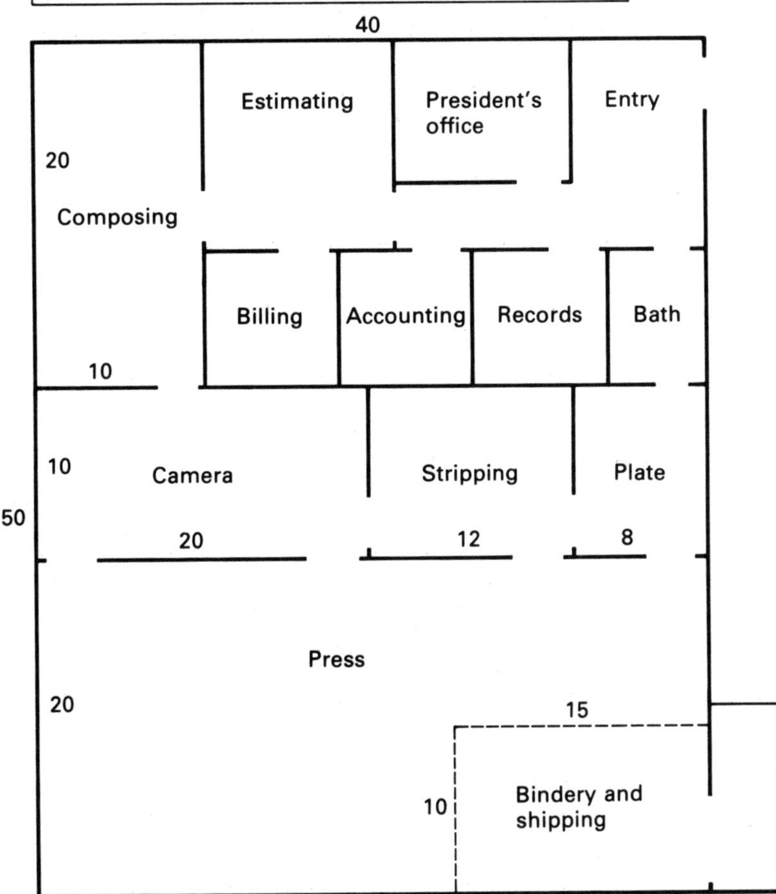

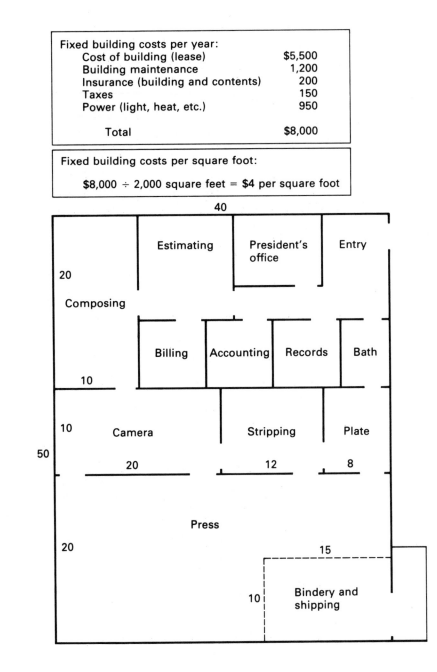

Figure 22.3. Floor plan of typical printing company

Table 22.1. Determining Fixed Costs

Department	Sq. Feet of Dept	×	Cost per Sq. Foot	=	Fixed Bldg. Cost per Sq. Foot by Dept	+	Equip. Deprec. by Dept	=	Total Fixed Costs per Dept per Yr	÷	Total Prod. Hrs per Yr	=	Fixed Hour Cost	+	Fixed Office Factor	=	Total Fixed Cost per Prod. Hour
Office	600	×	$4	=	$2,400	+	$1,400	=	$3,800	÷	9,150 hrs	=	$ .42				
Composing	200	×	4	=	800	+	1,200	=	2,000	÷	3,660	=	.55	+	$.07	=	$ .62
Camera	200	×	4	=	800	+	1,100	=	1,900	÷	1,830	=	1.03	+	.07	=	1.10
Stripping	120	×	4	=	480	+	500	=	980	÷	3,660	=	.27	+	.07	=	.34
Plate	80	×	4	=	320	+	1,000	=	1,320	÷	1,830	=	.72	+	.07	=	.79
Press	650	×	4	=	2,600	+	6,400	=	9,000	÷	10,980	=	.82	+	.07	=	.89
Bindery	150	×	4	=	600	+	2,600	=	3,200	÷	1,830	=	1.74	+	.07	=	1.81
Totals	2,000 sq ft				$8,000	+	$14,200	=	$22,200								

Table 22.2. Depreciation, Press Section

Equipment	Original Cost	Annual Depreciation
17 × 22 press (2)	$40,000	$4,000
11 × 17 press (2)	23,000	2,300
Miscellaneous Tools	1,000	100
		$6,400

Table 22.3. Productive Hours Per Year

(40 hours per week) × (52 weeks) =		2,080 hours
less:		
1) 2 weeks paid vacation	80 hrs	
2) 5 paid holidays	40 hrs	
3) 1 paid sick day (average)	8 hrs	
4) 30 minutes paid break per day (2½ hrs per week × 49 weeks minus 30 min for sick day)	122 hrs	
		−250 hours
Maximum productive hours		1,830 hours

must be distributed throughout the entire year for each productive hour worked in each section.

In table 22.3 the total number of available productive hours per worker per year has been calculated. (It is interesting that more productive hours are lost through coffee breaks than by two weeks of paid vacation.) In table 22.4 that number has been multiplied by the number of employees in each section to determine the total productive hours each year. Those figures have been transferred to column six in table 22.1. If the total fixed costs are divided by the total productive hours, the fixed hour cost has been determined (table 22.1, column seven).

A difficulty arises with the fixed hour cost for the office area. It is not possible to identify how much office time was devoted to each individual job. Also, time is spent estimating jobs that the company does not get, and that cost must be absorbed somewhere in the operation. Much office time is either nonproductive or not associated with particular jobs. To solve the problem, the fixed office cost is divided equally among all the other sections. In this case, $.42 was divided by 6 (six sections), and $.07 was added to the fixed hour cost for each section. When all these calculations have been completed, a total fixed cost per productive hour is determined that can be added to each estimate according

Table 22.4. Productive Hours per Year by Section

Section	Number of Employees	×	Productive Hours/Year	=	Total Productive Hours/Year
Office	5	×	1,830	=	9,150
Composing	2	×	1,830	=	3,330
Camera	1	×	1,830	=	1,830
Stripping	2	×	1,830	=	3,660
Plate	1	×	1,830	=	1,830
Press	6	×	1,830	=	10,980
Bindery	1	×	1,830	=	1,830

to the number of hours worked in each section.

Preparing the Job Estimate

Each company uses those estimating procedures that work best for its type of organization. There are published pricing guides, such as the *Franklin Printing Catalog*, that give "average" costs for nearly all operations or products of a typical printing company. Computerized programs are available that require sales personnel only to enter information on the job into a computer terminal. The estimated costs are displayed on a television-like screen above the keyboard. Some companies prepare price schedules for items that they frequently work with to avoid re-estimating every job. Whatever the method—computer, pencil and paper, or published guide—certain procedures are always followed to obtain a final price estimate. The following are the eight basic steps for making any estimate. Some authors might expand or reduce the number by combining or separating items, but the basic process will always remain the same.

1. Obtain accurate specifications.
2. Plan the job sequence.
3. Determine material needs and convert to standard units.
4. Determine time needed for each task.
5. Determine labor costs.
6. Determine fixed costs.
7. Sum costs and add profit.
8. Prepare formal bid contract.

The Basic Estimating Process

It is important, when predicting the cost of a job, to have all the information about what the customer wants. As emphasized in chapter 1, what one person has in mind might not always be what the other understands. It is the job of the sales personnel to obtain all job specifications and to ensure that the company meets the job requirements, all within the final formal price estimate.

It is impossible to estimate printing costs without knowing how the job is to be produced. It is necessary to outline the sequence of operations so time and material requirements can be easily determined. If an operation is forgotten or estimated incorrectly, the cost of that operation must come out of the profits. Customers will not pay more than the contracted bid price unless, of course, they contract for extras after accepting the bid.

Once the sequence of operations has been determined, it is a simple task to determine the quantities of materials needed for each task. These are then converted to unit amounts. From the standard units (see figure 22.2), the estimator can calculate the amount of time necessary to complete each operation. Labor costs, which are usually paid on a per hour basis, are then determined for each operation. Fixed costs, or overhead, are then added, usually based on the time needed for each task. All of these figures are then summed, and a fixed percentage of profit is added to the total. This final sum is the proposed cost of the job.

As a last step, the estimator usually prepares a formal bid that acts as a binding contract for the company, stating that the company will print a specific job for the stated amount. The customer commonly has a fixed number of days to accept the bid before the contract offer becomes void.

A Sample Job Estimate

For the sake of clarification, it is valuable to follow through the procedures of estimating a sample job. Assume that a salesperson for our hypothetical company—Spartan Graphics—has called on a customer who would like to have an information brochure printed to explain the details of their training program to employees. They would like to know how much the job will cost before Spartan Graphics gets the job. Our salesperson records all the important information about the job on a standard estimate request form (figure 22.4). Spartan has found that it is valuable to have the standard form so the sales personnel do not foget an important fact that might influence the job's final cost.

From figure 22.4, it can be seen that the brochure is to be an eight-page saddle-stitched booklet printed in one color on both sides of the page and trimmed to 8½ by 11 inches. The customer will supply only the manuscript and a rough layout of the job. Spartan Graphics will compose, print, fold, staple, and trim and will pack the paper-wrapped final product, 1,000 copies to the carton. Markert Enterprises, the customer, will pick up the boxes on or before November 4.

With all this information, the salesperson returns to the office to calculate the job's cost. Either alone or with the production manager, the salesperson plans out the sequence of steps. The list of steps is as follows:

1. Composing:
   - set body type
   - set headlines
   - paste up camera-ready copy
2. Camera: shoot negatives of paste-up copy
3. Stripping: strip flats
4. Plate making: burn plates
5. Press:
   - print job
   - wash-up press
6. Bindery:
   - fold and staple brochure
   - trim and box wrapped brochures

A decision must be made as to which press will be used because that will influence the sheet size and how the job is to be pasted up, folded, and stapled. In this case, the 17-by-22-inch lithographic press is to be used, with a sheet size of 17½ by 22½ inches. All of this information is then recorded in the first three columns of the Spartan Graphics standard estimate sheet (figure 22.5).

Spartan Graphics **Estimate Request**

Customer Market Enterprises Date 7/11/— Bid due 7/16/—
Address 147 Market Blvd. Market, NY 13126
Job Title Information Brochure Quantity 7,000

Description:

No. of pages eight Self Cover ☒ Plus Cover ☐

		1	2	3	4		
Cover Stock	colors	☐	☐	☐	☐	1/s ☐	2/s ☐
Text Pages Stock offset book - 60 #	colors	☒	☐	☐	☐	1/s ☐	2/s ☒
	colors	☐	☐	☐	☐	1/s ☐	2/s ☐
	colors	☐	☐	☐	☐	1/s ☐	2/s ☐

Art Work Supplied yes ☐ no ☒ Composition Supplied yes ☐ no ☒
Proofs Required yes ☐ no ☒ Type

Halftones: Square Finish Line Illustrations:
Silhouette
Screen Tints

Bindery: Fold to 8 3/4 x 11 1/4 Collate
Trim to 8 1/2 x 11 Punch
Stitching - saddle ☐ side ☐ other

SHIPPING:
To: Will Pick-Up Via:

Wrap in: Paper ☒ water-proof cover ☐
Pack in: cartons ☒ skids ☐ 1,000 sht each

SPECIAL INSTRUCTIONS: Text composition — 8-pt Century Schoolbook
Headlines — 14 pt Schoolbook Bold
Rough layout supplied

Previous Bid Number Previous Job Number
Reprint Likely yes Hold Plates or Ship Hold
Required Delivery Date 11/4/— Special Terms

Figure 22.4. Sample estimate request form

The next step is to determine the materials needed for each stage of production. Columns three through six on the estimate sheet identify the number of units of work and the total cost for each step. Refer to figure 22.2 and table 22.4 to recall where the units came from. The salesperson obtains the cost per unit from the suppliers' current price lists. The total material cost is determined by multiplying the number of units by the cost per unit. Figure 22.6 shows how the number of paper units is determined.

The labor necessary to complete each unit is obtained from figure 22.2. The total labor units are a product of the labor standard times the number of units. For the sake of simplicity, in this example we have assumed that all labor is paid at the rate of $5 per hour.

Spartan Graphics — **Estimate Sheet**

Sequence	Section	Description	No. of units	Cost/ unit	Material cost	Standard labor/unit	Total labor units	Labor cost/ hour	Total labor cost	Fixed cost/ hour	Total fixed cost	Total operation cost
1	Composing	Body Comp	8	$1.05	$8.40	.10 hrs	.80 hrs	$5.00	$4.00	$.62	$.50	
		Headlines	1	.25	.25	.15	.15	5.00	.75	.62	.09	
		Paste-up	2	1.40	2.80	.25	.50	5.00	2.50	.62	.31	
					$11.45				$7.25		$.90	$19.60
2	Camera	17x22 negs	2	$5.40	$10.80	.18 hrs	.36 hrs	$5.00	$1.80	$1.10	$.40	
					$10.80				$1.80		$.40	$13.00
3	Stripping	19 x 24 flats	2	$2.10	$4.20	.48 hrs	.96 hrs	$5.00	$4.80	$.34	$.33	
					$4.20				$4.80		$.33	$9.33
4	Plate	19x24 plates	2	$21.00	$42.00	.22 hrs	.44 hrs	$5.00	$2.20	$.79	$.35	
		(Single Exposure)			$42.00				$2.20		$.35	$44.65
5	Press	17½x22½ - offset book - 60#	7.77 M			.21 hrs	1.63 hrs	$5.00	$8.15	$.89	$1.45	
		388.5 lbs			$142.60							
		Ink			5.60							
		Wash-up	1	$2.10	2.10	.35	.35	$5.00	$1.75	$.89	$.31	
					150.30				$9.90		$1.76	$160.96
6	Bindery	Fold & Staple	7	$.60	$4.20	.19 hrs	1.33 hrs	$5.00	$6.65	$1.81	$2.41	
		Trim & Box	7	1.10	7.70	.11	.77	5.00	3.85	1.81	.20	
					$11.90				$10.50		$2.61	$25.01

sub-total ($272.45) x profit (.12) = $32.69

sub-total	$272.45
plus profit 12 %	32.69
total	$305.14

Estimate made by J. Michael [illegible] | Checker BK | Date 7/12/[illegible] | File No. 196-24

Figure 22.5. Sample estimate sheet

It should be understood that in the actual industry the rate of pay depends on the type of job and the level of individual skill (also assume that the office labor costs have been averaged into the $5 figure). The total labor cost for each production step can be found by multiplying the total number of labor units by the labor cost per hour.

Next the fixed operations cost must be determined. From table 22.2, the fixed cost per hour for each section is recorded on the estimate sheet (figure 22.5, column eleven). The total fixed cost is found by multiplying column eleven by column eight (total labor units).

For each step in the production sequence, the material, labor, and fixed costs are totaled and recorded in the last column of the estimate sheet. The total operation costs for each step are then summed and entered in the subtotal blank at the bottom of the page. Spartan Graphics has set 12% as their desired rate of profit. Therefore, multiply .12 times the subtotal to obtain the actual dollar amount. This quantity is then added to the subtotal to find the total estimated cost of the job.

The final step is to prepare a formal bid contract to be sent to the customer. In the contract letter used by Spartan Graphics, the details of the job are again specified so that both parties understand the conditions, and the total price is given (figure 22.7). The actual estimate sheet is generally not sent to the customer. It is retained by the printer to be used at a later date if the job contract is received.

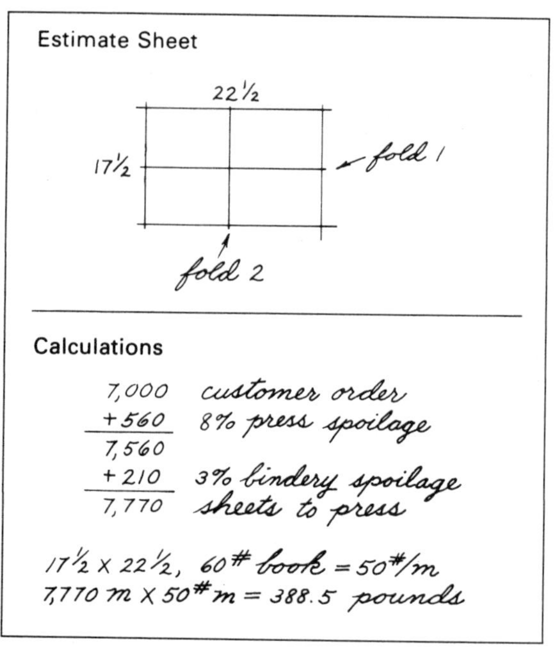

Figure 22.6. Sample estimate calculations

Implementing Printing Production

Before any job can go into actual production, it is necessary to carry a bit further the preliminary work done with the estimate. Work does not automatically flow through the shop. Every job requires continual planning, guidance, and follow-up. The following list outlines the typical steps involved in actually implementing printing production:

1. From estimate request sheet and estimate, prepare production work order.
2. Determine in-house availability of materials and order if necessary.
3. Prepare detailed job schedule.
4. Merge detailed schedule into production control schedule.
5. Coordinate materials with job's arrival in each section.
6. Put job into production.
7. Check quality control and production as necessary.
8. Reschedule as necessary.
9. Remove job from production control schedule and send all records to accounting.

To follow through with the logic of a typical printing job, let us assume that the brochure that was bid in the previous example was awarded to Spartan Graphics.

The Work Order

After the customer has accepted the bid and any legal contracts have been signed, the production manager takes control of the job. The first step is to transfer the information from the estimate request and estimate sheet to a production work order (figure 22.8). The work order will be the road map that will

Spartan Graphics

1359 West Third Street
Athens, New York 11476
July 14, 1982

Ms. L. Markert, President
Markert Enterprises
147 W. Markert Blvd
Markert, New York

Ms. Markert:

In reference to your request for an estimate, we are pleased to submit the following information:

Job Title:	Information Brochure
Quantity:	7,000
Format:	$8\frac{1}{2}$ x 11 inches, 8 pages, printed two sides, saddle stapled on 11 inch side.
Composition:	Manuscript to be supplied by Markert Enterprises; Spartan Graphics to set body in 8 point Century Schoolbook, headlines in 14 point Century Schoolbook Bold--according to layout specifications previously supplied by Markert Enterprises.
Packaging:	Brochures to be wrapped in paper and boxed, 1,000 copies per carton.
Shipping:	To be supplied by Markert Enterprises.
Terms:	Net thirty days.
Total Cost:	$305.14 plus applicable local tax.

We are looking forward to your acceptance of this bid. If additional information can be provided please do not hesitate to call on me personally.

Sincerely yours,

J. M. Adams

J.M. Adams
Sales Manager

Figure 22.7. Sample letter of bid

Spartan Graphics				Work Order
Customer Market Enterprises				# 196-24
Stock 17½ x 22½ offset Book - 60#	Ink Black	In Date 11/30/[illegible]	Fold Size 8¾ x 11¼	Quantity 7,000
		Out Date	Final Trim 8½ x 11	Start-up 7,770
		Due Date 11/4/[illegible]	Bind Saddle	Run sheet-wise

Sequence	Section	Operation	Standard Time	Time in	Time out	Actual Time	Remarks
1	Composing	Body	.80 hrs				
		Headlines	.15 hrs				
		Paste-up	.60 hrs				
2	Camera	17 x 22 negs - 2	.36 hrs				
3	Stripping	19 x 24 flats - 2	.96 hrs				
4	Plate	19 x 24 - Type M-2	.44 hrs				
5	Press	17½ x 22½	1.63 hrs				
		wash-up	.35 hrs				
6	Bindery	Fold & staple	1.33 hrs				
		Trim & Box	.77 hrs				

Figure 22.8. Sample production work order

chart the job through all the production steps. It will also be used by the production control section to check on the progress of the job. Each supervisor will log the time that the job arrives and the time it leaves the section. The form can also serve as a means of updating the labor standards (see figure 22.1) if the actual time varies significantly from the standard or estimated time.

At the same time that the work order is completed, the inventory control staff should check to determine that all the required materials are on hand and are not committed to another job. If they are in storage, they are reserved. If the supplies are not available in-house, they are ordered, and information about the expected delivery date is sent to those responsible for job scheduling.

Job Scheduling and Production Control

Job scheduling is a problem of coordinating the most efficient combination of materials, machines, and time. The skillful production manager will schedule jobs in a sequence that will require minimum machine changes. For example, if four jobs are to be run on a single press next Tuesday—two with black ink, one with yellow, and another with red—it would be wise to schedule the order to run the yellow first, then the red, and then the two black. The lightest colors should be run first (which makes for an easier roller cleanup), and the two black runs paired together. Likewise, it would be foolish not to schedule jobs with the same sheet sizes back to back.

The first step in the orderly scheduling of individual jobs is to prepare a detailed job schedule sheet (figure 22.9). Again the sequence of operations is listed, with the number of estimated hours in each section identified. A sort of diagram of times is then laid out so the planner can get a visual impression of the required times and sequence. If the job requires more than one day, additional sheets are used.

The individual job diagram is then

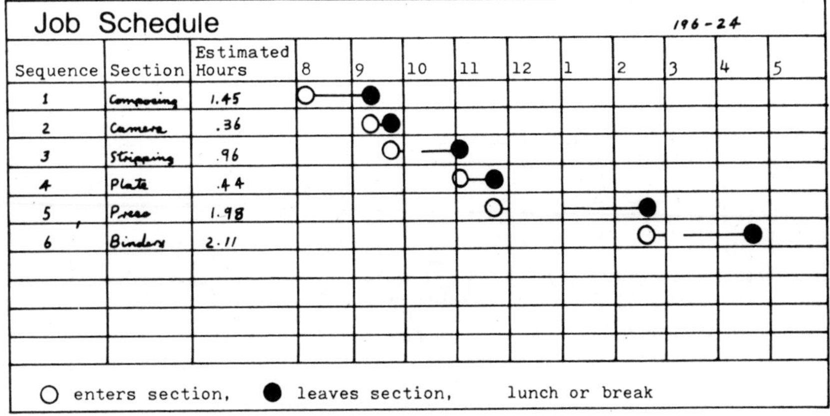

Job Schedule 196-24

Sequence	Section	Estimated Hours	8	9	10	11	12	1	2	3	4	5
1	Composing	1.45										
2	Camera	.36										
3	Stripping	.96										
4	Plate	.44										
5	Press	1.98										
6	Bindery	2.11										

○ enters section, ● leaves section, lunch or break

Figure 22.9. Sample job schedule

merged into the overall shop production control schedule (figure 22.10). The goal is to match time blocks efficiently with available personnel, materials, and common sizes, colors, or types of jobs. The production manager will prepare detailed production control schedules well in advance for each day's work. With a job scheduled as far as a week in advance, it is possible to coordinate the required materials with each section as the job flows through the shop.

The frustration of production control is that jobs do not always conform to the estimated time. Perhaps the camera burns out a bulb, which must be immediately replaced. Paper might jam in the press, and thirty minutes are wasted removing the scrap. Materials might not arrive in the section on schedule, and time is wasted checking on the problem. At any rate, a delay at one point in the schedule is felt throughout the shop. It is therefore necessary continually to alter and adjust the flow of jobs to make up for time gains or losses.

With the work order, manuscript copy, and rough layout, our sample job enters production on the appropriate day and should emerge as a completed brochure at day's end. If there are problems, the production manager must make adjustments. It is also the production manager's task to know the stage of each job at almost every moment in the day. When customers call and want to know how their material is progressing, it is important to be able to give an immediate and accurate answer.

When the job has reached the last production step and is waiting to be picked up or is on its way to the customer, all records are sent through the production control office to the accounting or billing office. The job is removed from the production control schedule, and any materials that are to be stored, such as the original paste-up copy, negatives, or printing plates, are filed and new jobs enter the system. A bill is sent to the customer, and payment is received.

Spartan Graphics										Production Control		
	Composing		Camera	Stripping	Plate	Press				Bindery		
Time	Comp	Paste-up				No. 1 17x22	No. 2 17x22	No. 3 11x17	No. 4 11x17	Collating	Bind Drill	Trimming Packaging
8:00												
8:15	196-24											
8:30	.956											
8:45												
9:00												
9:15			196-19									
9:30		196-24 .50hrs	[illegible] hrs									
9:45	196-19											
10:00	[illegible]		196-24 .96									
10:15												
10:30												
10:45		196-21		196-24								
11:00		[illegible] hrs		.96 hrs								
11:15												
11:30					196-24 .44 hrs							
11:45												
12:00												
12:15												
12:30												
12:45												
1:00												
1:15												
1:30												
1:45						196-24						
2:00						1.95 hrs						
2:15												
2:30												
2:45												
3:00												
3:15												
3:30												
3:45										196-24		
4:00										1.33 hrs.		
4:15												
4:30												
4:45												196-24 .77hrs
5:00												
over time												

Figure 22.10. Sample production control sheet The control sheet shows the example job sequenced across a single workday.

It is important to understand that the printing industry is more than just the production tasks of running a printing press or operating a process camera. Planning printing production requires a thorough understanding of production, but it also demands individuals with many skills beyond the manipulation of ink and images. This chapter gave you a brief overview of those skills.

Key Terms

overhead
depreciation
Franklin Printing Catalog
job estimate
work order
job scheduling and production control
job schedule

Questions for Review

1. What is the advantage of a uniform price schedule?
2. Why is a review of the sequence of operations an important part of the estimating process?
3. What is the purpose of a production work order?
4. What is job scheduling?
5. What is a production control schedule?

Appendixes

Calibrating and Using Graphic Arts Tools

Appendix A

Basic Exposure Calibration for Line Photography

Basic exposure is the camera aperture and shutter speed combination that produces a quality film image of normal line copy with standardized chemical processing. Once determined, basic exposure is used to predict or calculate new times for such things as enlargements and reductions or times for when the characteristics of the copy material vary from normal.

The following information complements the concepts introduced in chapter 6. Basic exposure must be calibrated for every camera in a facility and recalibrated every time any variable in the darkroom situation changes.

1. Select as a test image camera copy that exhibits characteristics of the material that will typically be reproduced in the darkroom situation. For line work, we recommend a sheet of photo composition. The lines should be about 12 to 18 points in size, should extend across the dimensions of the sheet, and should have sharp, distinct serifs. Center the sheet on the camera copyboard and clean and close the glass cover. This is the only camera exposure that will not require the use of a gray scale.

2. Set the camera for 100% reproduction by moving the percentage tapes or by adjusting the size control gauges. Open the camera lens two stops from the largest opening. The best camera resolution is typically obtained from that setting. For example, if the range of possible stops on the camera is f/64, f/32, f/22, f/16, f/11, and f/8, use f/16. Then adjust the camera lights for even copyboard illumination. A general recommendation is to set the lights at a 30° angle from the copyboard frame. Illumination can be checked by turning the camera on focus and examining or measuring the evenness of intensity across a ground glass screen at the back of the camera. Some types of reflection densitometers can be used to make this measurement.

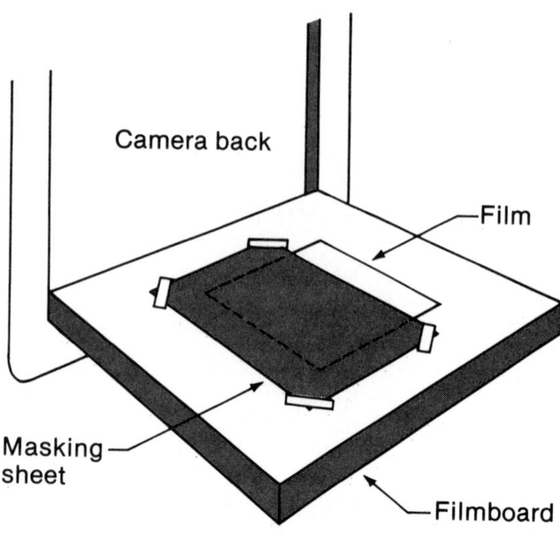

Figure A.1. Film set-up for calibrating basic exposure An opaque sheet is taped over the film. The sheet is moved to expose more of the film after each 5-second exposure.

Flare is an exposure problem caused by the uncontrolled reflection of stray light. If the camera is contained in the darkroom itself, the wall near the copyboard should be painted 18 percent gray so as not to reflect the camera lights. If the copyboard is in a normal room light situation, the room illumination should always remain the same for every camera exposure. Flare can also be caused by the base material of the camera copy, so paste-ups should always be done on mat-white illustration board. Some new continuous-tone print papers "fluoresce" (give off excessive ultraviolet radiation).

3. Set the camera timer for a 5-second exposure and place a sheet of film centered emulsion-side up on the film camera filmboard. Tape it in place or otherwise ensure that it cannot move. Tape a sheet of opaque material to the filmboard, covering all but a 1-inch (2.54 cm) strip of the film (figure A.1). Close the back and expose the film for 5 seconds. Then open the camera and move the opaque material another inch (2.54 cm) without shifting the film, so that a total of 2 inches (5.08 cm) of the film is uncovered. Close the back and expose for another 5 seconds. The first inch of film has now received a 10-second exposure and the second inch a 5-second exposure. Repeat this procedure of moving the film and exposing it for 5-second intervals until the whole sheet has been exposed. When completed, the film will have received a series of step exposures beginning with 5 seconds and extending in 5-second increments to 40 seconds.

4. Remove the film from the camera and process it with absolutely consistent techniques. Use the chemicals that will always be used in the darkroom situation, be within ±½° of the recommended temperature (68°F or 20°C), agitate with reproducible motion, remove the film from the developer exactly at the end of the recommended development time, and then stop, fix, and wash as usual. Examine the dry negative and select the strip that represents the best possible reproduction of the original copy (figure A.2). This can be done by a visual comparison or the film can be exposed to a printing plate and printed on the press that will always be used, and then the printed sheet compared to the camera copy.

5. After an ideal camera time has been determined, return to the camera and this time insert a gray scale in the center of the copy. Make a second camera exposure by using that ideal camera time and again processing with absolutely consistent time-temperature-agitation techniques. When the film

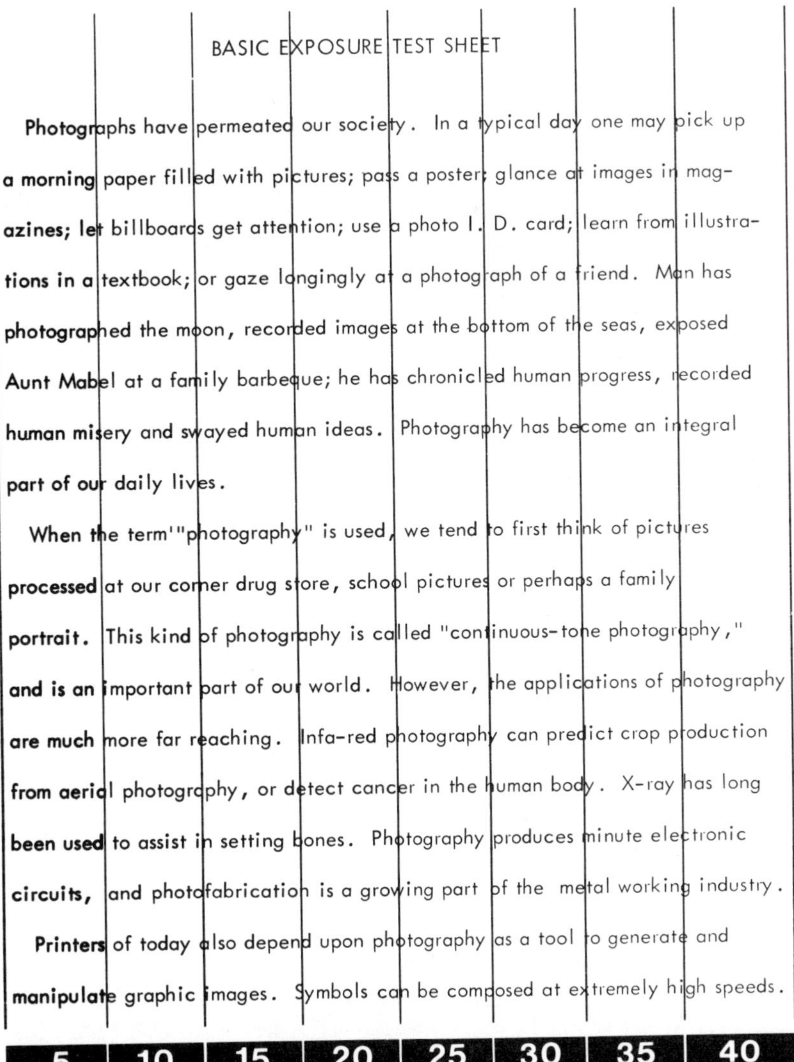

BASIC EXPOSURE TEST SHEET

Photographs have permeated our society. In a typical day one may pick up a morning paper filled with pictures; pass a poster; glance at images in magazines; let billboards get attention; use a photo I. D. card; learn from illustrations in a textbook; or gaze longingly at a photograph of a friend. Man has photographed the moon, recorded images at the bottom of the seas, exposed Aunt Mabel at a family barbeque; he has chronicled human progress, recorded human misery and swayed human ideas. Photography has become an integral part of our daily lives.

When the term '"photography" is used, we tend to first think of pictures processed at our corner drug store, school pictures or perhaps a family portrait. This kind of photography is called "continuous-tone photography," and is an important part of our world. However, the applications of photography are much more far reaching. Infa-red photography can predict crop production from aerial photography, or detect cancer in the human body. X-ray has long been used to assist in setting bones. Photography produces minute electronic circuits, and photofabrication is a growing part of the metal working industry. Printers of today also depend upon photography as a tool to generate and manipulate graphic images. Symbols can be composed at extremely high speeds.

5	10	15	20	25	30	35	40

Figure A.2. Example of a test sheet proof A proof of the test negative will reveal the best exposure. The exposure time for this test sheet was 5-second intervals from 5 to 40 seconds.

is in the stop-bath, examine the gray scale to determine the densest step, then fix, wash, and dry. This step—usually step 4 on a 12-step scale—becomes a visual cue that will indicate the stage of film development. Slight changes in processing time can be made to ensure that the proper level of density in the negative has been reached.

The basic exposure time becomes a constant for all normal copy. If the camera has a diaphragm control, only the aperture will be adjusted for percentage changes from

100%. If the camera has no diaphragm control, the basic exposure time is multiplied by an exposure factor—generally provided by the camera manufacturer—for enlargement or reduction.

Ideally, an f/stop and shutter speed combination will be selected that will give the best camera resolution but will not be too long. If the exposure is over 60 seconds in length, the f/stop should be adjusted to bring the time into a more realistic range that does not shorten the camera lights' life. However, the time should be long enough for the camera timer to accurately reproduce the period for every exposure. Because times less than 5 seconds are generally not reproducible (in process cameras), the aperture should be readjusted so the basic exposure is longer than 10 seconds.

Key Terms for Appendix A

basic exposure

flare

Appendix B

Light and Light-Sensitive Materials

The Nature of Light

Visible light is electromagnetic radiation. All radiation, whether cosmic rays, visible light, or heat, travels in waves and differs only by the length of the wave. Wavelength is measured by the distance from one wave crest to the next (figure B.1). X-ray radiation has a very small wavelength; radio waves have a very large wavelength. Figure B.2 illustrates the relationship of visible light to the spectrum of known electromagnetic radiation.

Because light waves are small, they are generally measured in millimicrons (mμ) (one millimicron = one-billionth of a meter, or twenty-five millionths of an inch) or in Angstrom units (Å or A.U.) (one millimicron = ten Angstrom units). Each color of the visible spectrum has a unique wavelength. White light is the balanced presence of all radiation from the visible spectrum.

It is this radiation that causes the chemical reaction on a sheet of film. As printers, we are concerned with the quantity and quality of light that creates that reaction. The sun is an ideal source of white light. For years it was the only source printers used to produce photographic images. In line photography, huge rooms were set aside with large overhead windows and mirrors that could direct sunlight onto the movable cameras below. Quality photographs were produced—unless it rained or was cloudy or was night or was the wrong time of year. It was difficult to control and predict the sun, so artificial light

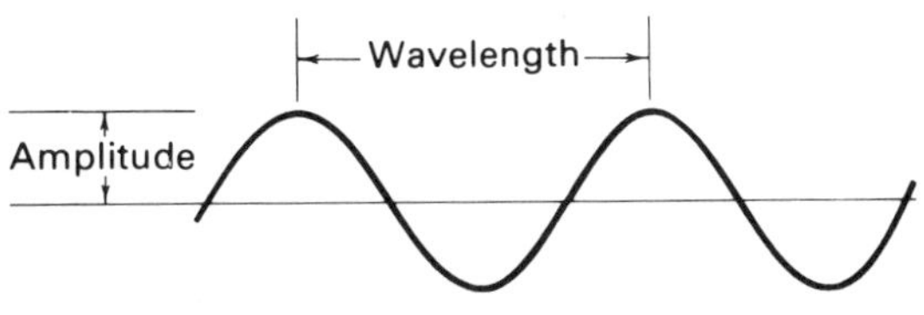

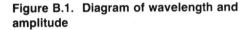

Figure B.1. Diagram of wavelength and amplitude

sources were developed. Although more controllable, these artificial devices were far from perfect. Improvements have been made, but the printer now is even more concerned about how to control the quality of light that reaches the film through the camera lens.

Light Sources

If we were to plot a graph of the relative intensity of natural white light across the visible spectrum, it would look something like figure B.3a. There would be nearly equal amounts of energy from all wavelengths of the spectrum. Contrast the natural white light curve with a similar distribution of energy emitted by a 40-watt white tungsten lightbulb (figure B.3b). The artificial source is not made up of equal amounts of energy from the visible spectrum. Tungsten light is composed of much more red light than blue. This imbalance of radiation can cause significant problems for the line photographer if the sensitivity of the film does not match the emission of the light source.

Carbon arcs have been used as a light source for nearly every photographic application in the graphic arts industry. Light is generated by passing an electric current between two carbon rods, much as in the arc-welding process. The electromagnetic emis-

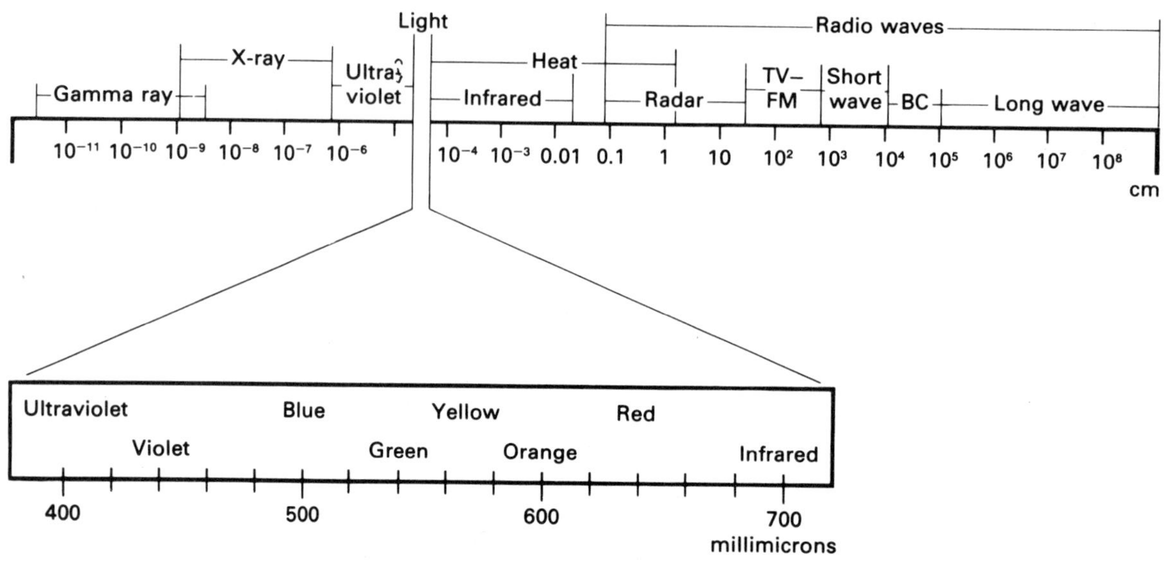

Figure B.2. Wavelengths of different colors of the visible light spectrum

sion of carbon arc light is continuous across the visible spectrum, but it is heavy in blue and violet light (figure B.3c). The quality of light is controlled by the inclusion of metallic salts in the core of each carbon rod. This peaking of energy in the blue end is actually an advantage because the sensitivity of most printing films and plates is greatest in that area (see "Classifying Light-Sensitive Materials" in this appendix). However, carbon arcs have several disadvantages. Voltage changes can cause unstable variation in color temperature and light output. Noxious fumes are released and must be ventilated. A great deal of dirt is generated in an area that must be kept as clean as possible. A brief warm-up period is required (60 seconds) before peak intensity is reached. There is always a potential fire hazard because of the open carbon flame.

Mercury vapor lamps operate by passing a current through a mercury gas in a quartz envelope. The vaporization and ionization of the gas generate light. The electromagnetic distribution is discontinuous across the visible spectrum (figure B.3d). There are massive peaks of emission in the blue-violet (b-v) and ultraviolet (u-v) regions, but radiation is practically nonexistent in all other areas. If images with colors other than b-v or u-v are being photographed, it is very difficult to record a film image. This characteristic makes it useless for color separation but causes no problems for monochromatic line photography, blue-sensitive emulsions, and plate making. The lamps require a 2-to-3-minute warm-up time and are generally operated on a dual exposure system—a standby voltage and a full-intensity voltage. Once the lamp is extinguished, it has to cool down before it can be started again. However, additives to the mercury vapor can improve its light quality and significantly extend the lamp life.

Pulsed xenon lamps were first introduced in 1958. They were developed as an application of photographic electronic flash techniques. The lamp is formed by filling quartz tubing with low-pressure xenon gas. The xenon is charged and discharged at the rate of the power line frequency—120 times each second. Even though the lamp is pulsed, the frequency is such that the light appears continuous across the visible spectrum, with no radical peaks of emission (figure B.3e). Although lower in blue-violet output, it has several overriding advantages for line photography. The lamp reaches peak intensity instantly, has constant color temperature, has a spectral output very close to sunlight, is economical to operate, and is very clean.

The **metal halide** is a recent development. It is basically a mercury lamp with metal halide additives. The electromagnetic emission peaks extremely high in the blue-violet area (figure B.3f). This output matches the maximum sensitivity of many printing materials. It has been successfully applied in plate making, proofing, photofabrication, screen emulsion exposures, and gravure work. It is not applicable for color separation, but within monochromatic line exposures it provides extremely short exposures and at least four times more **actinic output** (energy that activates or hardens light-sensitive coatings) than any other light source.

Color Temperature

Color temperature is a term bandied about by both printers and photographers, often without accurate understanding. Light sources are often classified according to color tempera-

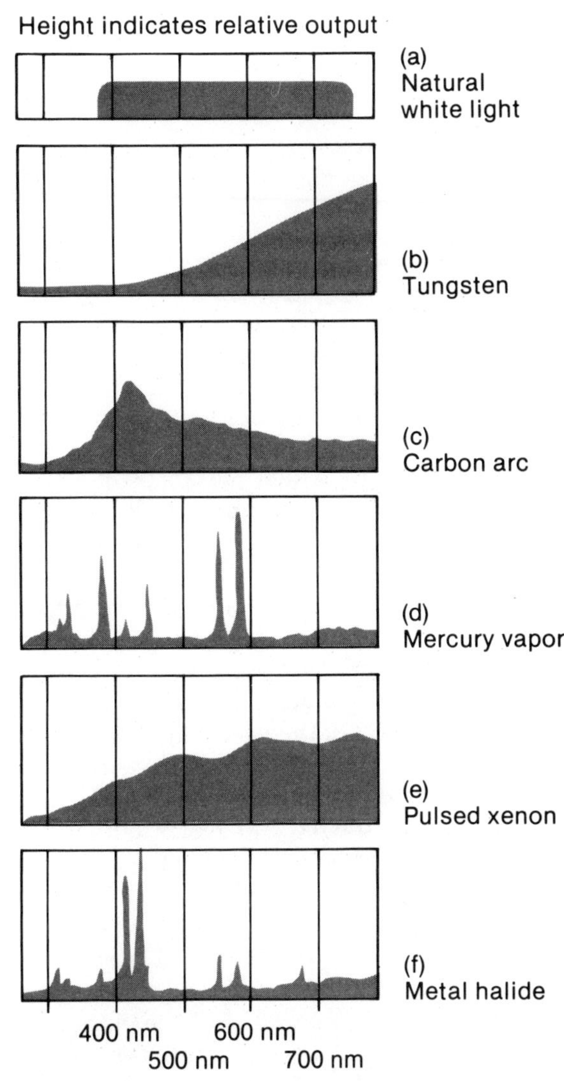

Figure B.3. Electromagnetic energy distribution of five artificial light sources and natural white light

Table B.1. Color Temperature of Various Light Sources

Light Source	Color Temperature
Clear blue sky	15,000°K to 30,000°K
Sun	5,100°K
Partly cloudy sky	8,000°K to 10,000°K
Fluorescent lights, daylight	6,500°K
Pulsed xenon	6,000°K
Quartz-iodine (high level)	3,400°K
Carbon arcs, white flame cored	5,000°K
Incandescent, 100-watt	3,000°K

Source: *Handbook of Tables for Applied Engineering Science*, CRC, 1970.

ture (table B.1), which makes people think that it is a primary concern for all photography—which it is not. Color temperature is not a concern in black-and-white process photography, but it is of paramount importance for color work, whether original photography or color separation.

Color temperature is a measure of the sum color effect of the visible light emitted by any source. The blue end of the visible spectrum is rated as having a higher color temperature than the red end. Color temperature is theoretically defined by heating a perfect radiator of energy or "black body." As the temperature increases, the color of the body changes. Each color of the visible spectrum is then assigned a temperature that corresponds to the temperature of the black body for that color. Color temperature is measured in degrees Kelvin (°K), which is derived by adding 273 to the temperature in degrees Centigrade (figure B.4). Color temperature is not such an unusual idea. Blacksmiths for centuries visually judged temperature by the color a piece of metal displayed as it was heated.

It is important to realize that color temperature describes only the visual appearance of a light source and does not necessarily describe its photographic effect. Both a tungsten and a fluorescent light source might be rated at the same color temperature. But because of difference in spectral emissions, they might produce totally different results on a piece of film.

Most color films are balanced for a particular color temperature. In other words, they are designed to record images accurately under certain color conditions. If a film is rated around 5000°K, it should faithfully record color balance as viewed under natural sunlight. If rated around 3000°K, it is designed to be used under artificial incandescent light, as found in the average home.

Graphic arts films are rarely identified as being balanced for a particular color temperature. However, when working with color originals, the graphic arts photographer has to be certain that the reflected light that reaches the film is faithfully describing the color balance of the copy being reproduced. For that reason the industry has even adopted a color temperature standard for viewing and judging color proofing and printing (5000°K) to ensure consistent human color perception. Figure B.4 is an example of a standard view-

Figure B.4. Color transparency viewers
Courtesy of Kollmorgen Corp., Macbeth Color and Photometry Division.

ing device. It ensures that each transparency viewed will be illuminated with a light source used throughout the industry.

Classifying Light-Sensitive Materials

All light-sensitive materials, whether films or plates, can be classified according to three main variables:

- Color sensitivity,
- Contrast,
- Film speed.

Color Sensitivity. **Color sensitivity** describes the area of the visible electromagnetic spectrum that will cause a chemical change in a particular silver halide emulsion. A **wedge spectrogram** is often used to show a film's reaction to light across the visible spectrum (figure B.5). A spectrogram corresponds in design to the diagrams used to describe a light source output. Figure B.5a uses a wedge spectrogram to describe the relative sensitivity of the human eye to the visible spectrum. The eye can perceive electromagnetic radiation from around 400 mμ to around 700 mμ but has a maximum sensitivity at the middle or green portion.

There are basically three types of light-sensitive emulsions: blue-sensitive, orthochromatic, and panchromatic materials. **Blue-sensitive** materials are often called "color blind" because they react to only the blue end of the spectrum (figure B.5b). On a negative they record high densities from blue materials, but they record very little from the green or red end. This characteristic is useful because the film can be used outside the darkroom and is ideal for copying black-and-white

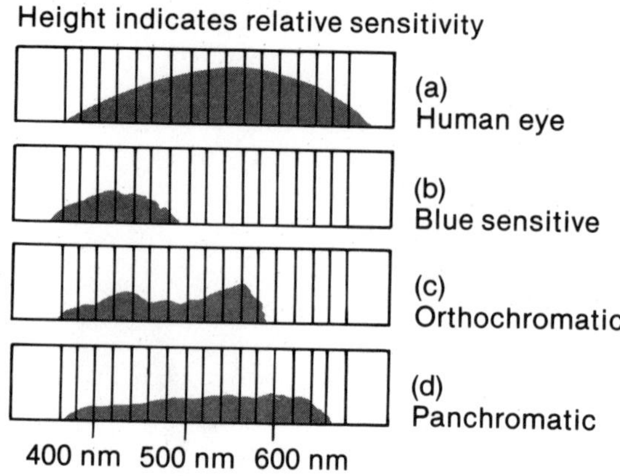

Figure B.5. Examples of wedge spectrograms
A wedge spectrogram shows a film's reaction to light across the visible spectrum.

photographs. Most photographic print paper is blue-sensitive.

Orthochromatic material is not red-sensitive, but it is sensitive to all other portions of the visible spectrum (figure B.5c). This characteristic increases the range of possible applications, including black-and-white originals, use of a magenta screen, and some filter manipulation. Orthochromatic material is significantly faster acting than blue-sensitive materials. "Ortho" films can be safely handled under a red darkroom safelight.

Panchromatic films approximate the sensitivity of the human eye (figure B.5d). They are sensitive to all visible colors and faithfully reproduce natural tonal variation. "Pan" film is ideal for reproducing color originals in monochromatic form. It fully responds to filter manipulation, but it must be processed in total darkness.

Most film manufacturers will provide a wedge spectograph for each of their films. Figure B.6 illustrates the sensitivity of Kodak's Kodalith Ortho Film, 2556, type 3 (ESTAR base). The most efficient and accurate photographs will always be obtained when the peak sensitivity of a film's spectograph corresponds to the peak output of a light source. For example, from figure B.3 it is obvious that tungsten light has its lowest output in the range where Ortho 3 has its peak sensitivity. Carbon arc or a metal halide light source would produce significantly better results.

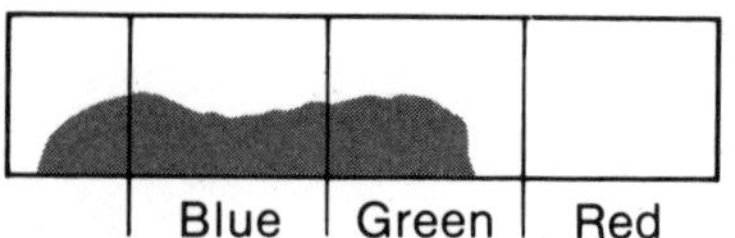

Figure B.6. Wedge spectrogram for Kodak Kodalith Ortho film 2556, type 3 (ESTAR base)
Courtesy of Eastman Kodak Company.

Contrast. **Contrast** is a term that describes the compression or expansion of the shades or tones of the original copy on the film or plate. Contrast is described by a film's **characteristic curve,** also called a "Log E curve," "H & D curve," "Density-Log E curve," "D-Log_{10} E curve," or "sensitometric curve" (figure B.7). Individuals interested in working in depth with Log E curves should have experience with common and natural logarithms, but it is *not* necessary to be on friendly terms with the manipulation of logarithms to be able to interpret the information the curve provides.

A simple characteristic curve can be drawn for any film by photographing a graphic arts gray scale, measuring the density of each step of the original and the density of each step of the film reproduction, and plotting the results on a graph. As photographers, we are

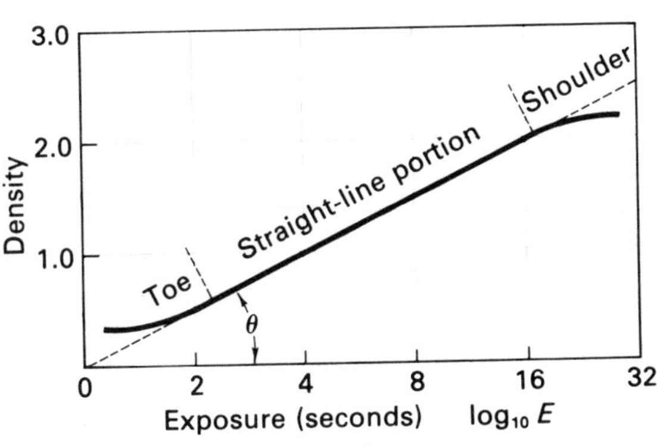

Figure B.7. Example of a film's characteristic curve The toe of the curve is a gradual incline because a light sensitive material does not produce a predictable density when exposed by a small amount of light. In other words a predictable amount of density is not developed until a specific exposure time is reached. The straight line portion represents an expected density development for each exposure. Eventually the curve will shoulder off even as exposure is increased—that is, the film will fail to produce an expected amount of density as the exposure increases. The film fails to reciprocate.

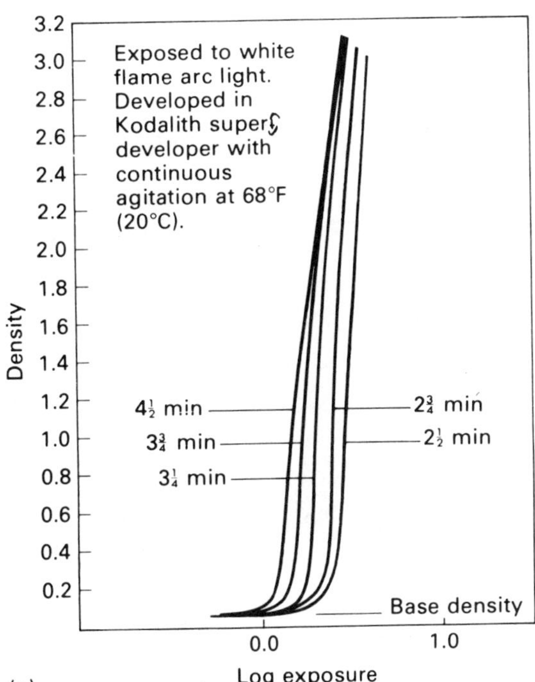

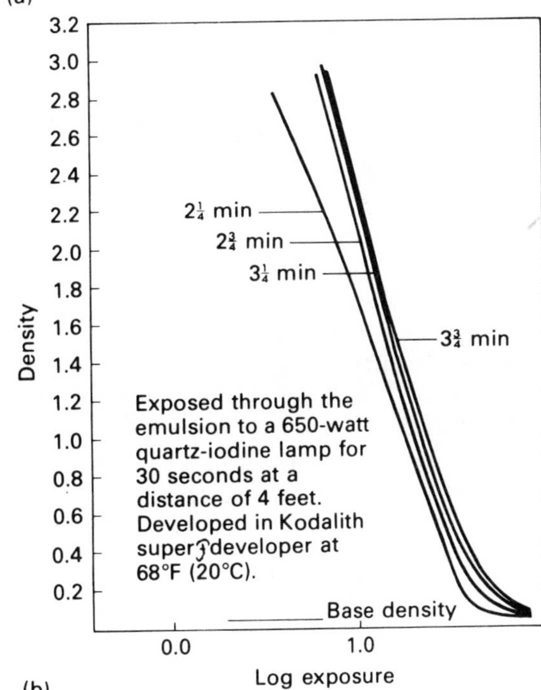

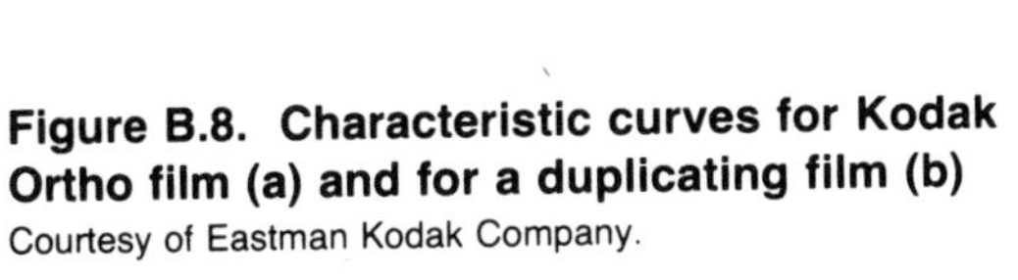

Figure B.8. Characteristic curves for Kodak Ortho film (a) and for a duplicating film (b)
Courtesy of Eastman Kodak Company.

Table B.2. Exposure Indexes for Meters Marked for "ASA" Speeds or Exposure Indexes.

White-Flame Arc	Tungsten or Quartz-Iodine	Pulsed-Xenon*
10	6	10

* This value indicates the relative speed of this material to pulsed-xenon illumination as measured by a conventional time-totalizing device.

Note: Example of Exposure—When making a same-size (1:1) line reproduction under average shop conditions, with two 35-ampere arc lamps about 48 inches from the copyboard, expose for about 10 seconds at *f*/32.

Source: Eastman Kodak Company.

primarily concerned with the angle of the straight-line portion of the curve. A mathematical interpretation of this angle (the trigonometric tangent of the angle) is often referred to as the film's "gamma" (the steeper the angle, the higher the gamma and the greater the film's contrast).

The gamma of a film can be controlled by several variables, such as development time, developer type, freshness of the developer, rate of agitation during development, and type of light source used to expose the film.

Film manufacturers provide sensitometric curves for each of their films. Figure B.8a illustrates the curve of Kodak's Ortho 3, an extremely high-contrast film. This curve reveals that a very slight change in exposure will provide a rapid jump in film density. This characteristic is ideal for printing production because the film will record sharp, clean lines between image and nonimage areas of the original copy.

It is interesting to observe the sensitometric curve of a duplicating film, such as Kodak's 2574 (figure B.8b). A duplicating film is designed to produce either duplicate film negatives from original negatives or duplicate film positives from original positives by contact printing. Duplicating film can also produce film positives from opaque positive originals on a process camera. Figure B.8b shows a curve that increases from right to left instead of from left to right as a normal film negative does. This corresponds to the duplicating characteristics of the material.

Film Speed. **Film speed** is the third main variable that can be used to class light-sensitive materials. Each film or plate material requires a different amount of light to cause a chemical change in the silver halide emulsion. Emulsions that require little light are called "fast" and those that require much light are called "slow." Because there are so many different materials, each requiring a different amount of light, the concept of "fast versus slow" becomes meaningless. For that reason, an "exposure index" is assigned to each film by the manufacturer. The ASA system (developed by the American Standards Association, now called the American National Standards Institute) applies a number scale to relative film speed—the higher the number, the faster the film. For example, a film with an ASA rating of 25 will require twice as much light to create the same image as does a film rated at ASA 50. Exposure index is assigned as a function of the type of light source used to expose the film. Table B.2 lists the ASA ratings assigned to Kodak's Ortho 3 for several lighting conditions.

It is important to understand that color sensitivity, contrast, and film speed are unrelated variables that cannot be directly compared. It is possible to identify films that exhibit any combination of the three characteristics.

Key Terms for Appendix B

carbon arcs
mercury vapor
pulsed xenon
metal halide
actinic output
color temperature
color sensitivity
wedge spectrogram
blue-sensitive
orthochromatic
panchromatic
contrast
characteristic curve
film speed

Appendix C

Exposure Calibration of a Halftone Computer

Main Test

Make a single main exposure of a 24-step reflection density guide (gray scale) at same size reproduction (100%) by using a halftone contact screen (figure C.1). Use a lens opening that is two f/stops smaller than the largest opening. Try an exposure of 30 seconds if two 1500-watt 5000° Kelvin lamps are used at 48 inches. Develop the negative according to the manufacturer's recommendations, keeping all steps absolutely consistent.

Examine the negative. The largest dot (highlight) should fall between the 0.0 and 0.30 density of the gray scale. If the highlight does not appear within this range, change the camera exposure and produce another negative. Repeat the procedure until the required position is reached.

Make a note of the density of the gray scale step that holds the largest highlight dot on the negative (that is, from the original gray scale). Then examine the shadow end and note the density that carries the smallest reproducible shadow dot. Obtain the basic density range (BDR) of the screen by subtracting the highlight density from the shadow density.

Flash Test

Next expose a second sheet of film through the same halftone screen but use a special flashing lamp. Cover about a quarter of the film with an opaque sheet of paper (such as cardboard). Expose the open area for 5 seconds. Then, without moving the film or screen, shift the opaque paper so that it covers only half the sheet and expose for another 5

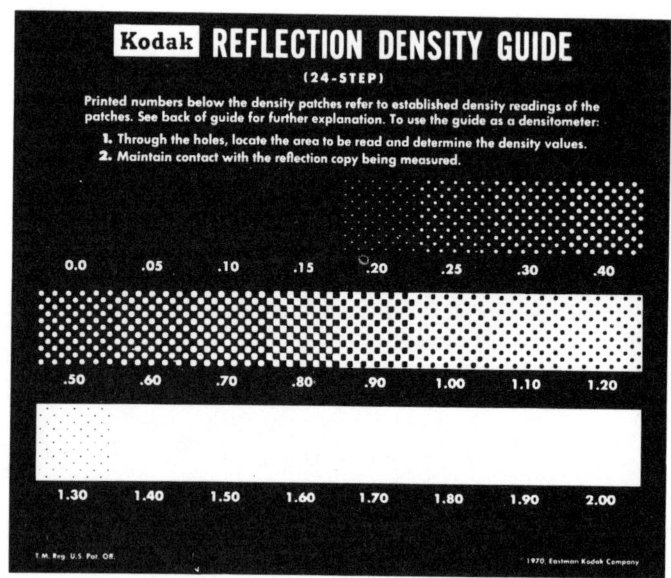

C.1. Twenty-four-step reflection density guide The main exposure test shows a range from .20 to 1.20, or a basic screen density range of 1.00 with a 30-second exposure. Courtesy of Eastman Kodak Company.

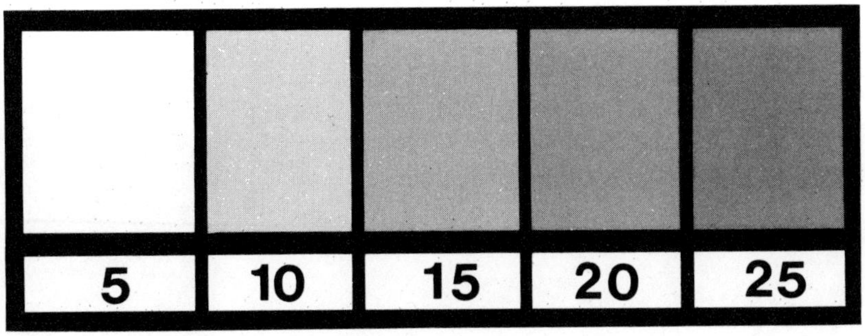

Figure C.2. Flash exposure test The flash exposure test shows that the smallest reproducible dot was obtained at 10 seconds.

seconds. Now the first quarter of the film has received 10 seconds of light and the second quarter has received 5 seconds. Repeat this procedure, exposing the third and fourth quarters until a step pattern has been formed from four sections with 5-, 10-, 15-, and 20-second exposures, respectively (figure C.2). Again process the negative according to the manufacturer's recommendations, keeping all steps absolutely consistent.

Examine the negative for the smallest reproducible dot. Because you are viewing a negative, you will be looking for a small, dense area. The open area around it is the actual dot. If an acceptable dot has not been produced, duplicate the previous technique while moving from 20 seconds to 40 seconds (or decrease the amount of filtration in the flashing lamp).

The smallest printable dot is obtained with a flash exposure of 10 to 25 seconds. Anything less becomes nonreproducible. The time that was used to produce this dot becomes the basic flash exposure time.

Bump Test

If your halftone computer (such as Kodak's Q–15) can be calibrated for a bump or no-screen exposure, place a small sheet of film on the filmboard and attach a contact screen. (If a bump calibration is not possible, move on to the next section.) Be sure to use the same halftone screen for all tests. Return the original 24-step gray scale to the camera copy-board and expose the film through the lens by using the main exposure time that was determined to give the best highlight dot. Then remove the halftone screen, but be careful not to shift the film. Close the camera back and again expose the film through the lens. Use an exposure time that is 5% of the first or main exposure when the screen was used (use 10% if it was a gray positive halftone screen). Five or 10% of a main exposure can be set on modern, electronic, integrated type of timers. If your timer is without light integrator, use the main exposure but cover the lens with a 1.30 neutral density filter (5% ımp) or a 1.00 neutral density filter (10% ımp). Process the resulting negative with nsistent development.

Examine the resulting negative for the nallest highlight dot and measure the density of that step on the original gray scale. Compare that density with the highlight density for the negative made with only a main exposure. The difference between these two numbers is called the "highlight shift." It is a result of the 5% (or 10%) no-screen exposure.

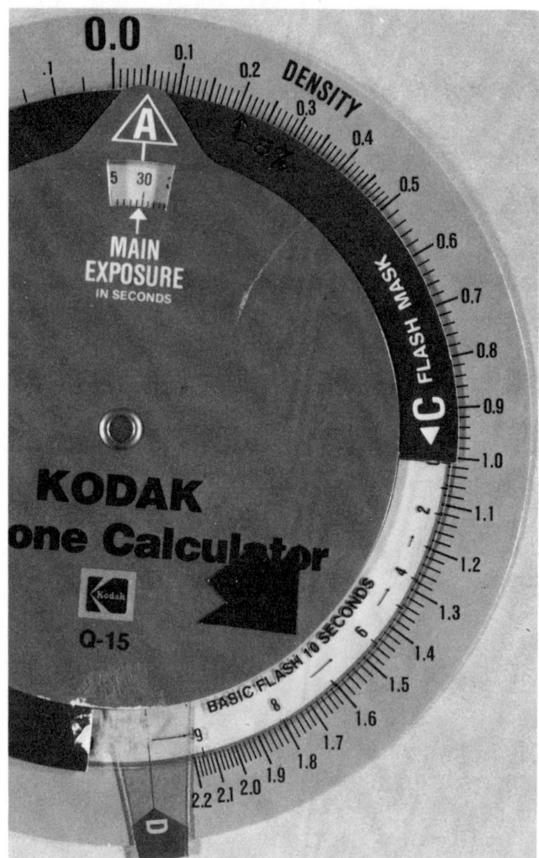

Figure C.3. Step 1: Setting the basic flash dial
Courtesy of Eastman Kodak Company.

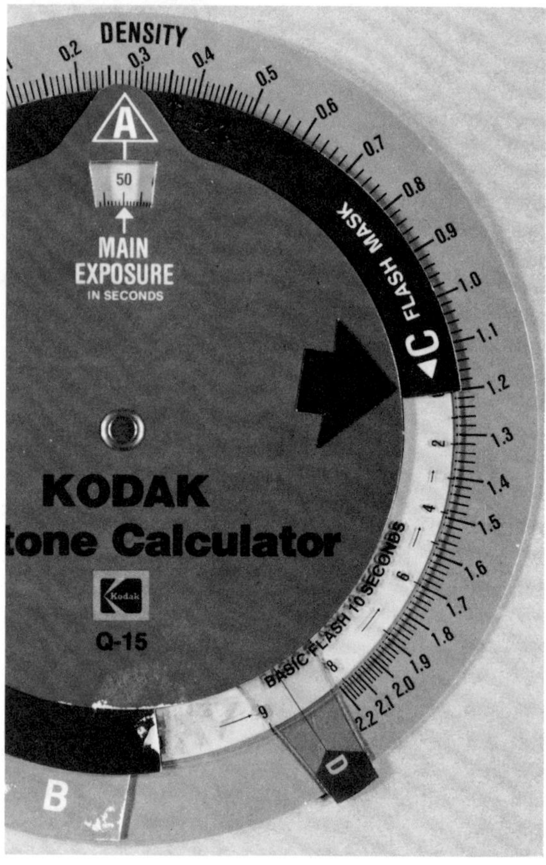

Figure C.4. Step 2: Identifying the density that produced a printable shadow dot
Courtesy of Eastman Kodak Company.

Halftone Computer Adjustment

The final step in halftone calibration is to apply the test information to some device that will generalize and be able to predict exposures for all future halftones. There are several devices that can be used. Each adjusts or applies the information in a different manner. For the Kodak Halftone Negative Computer, Q–15, the procedure is as follows:

Step 1. Rotate the basic flash (clear) dial until the flash exposure time, determined from your flash exposure test (figure C.2, 10 seconds), is centered in the slot of the red flash mask labeled *C* (figure C.3).

Step 2. Set "0" of the basic flash mask *C* opposite the shadow density that produced an acceptable dot (see figure C.1, density step 1.20) from the main exposure test (figure C.4).

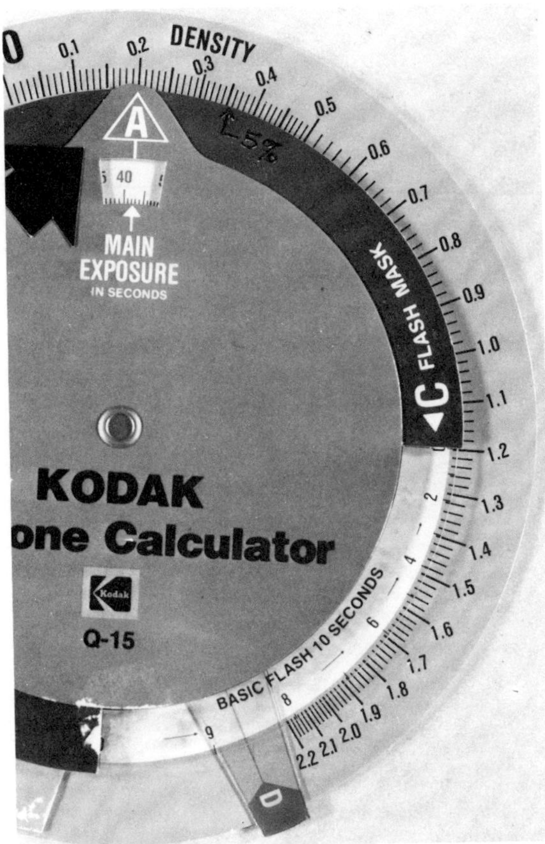

Figure C.5. Step 3: Identifying the density that produced a printable highlight dot

Courtesy of Eastman Kodak Company.

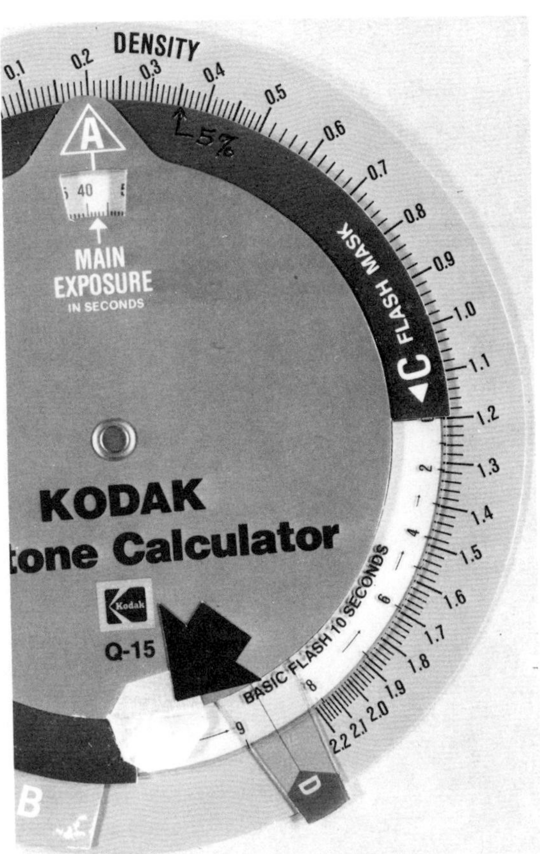

Figure C.6. Step 4: Fastening the main exposure, flash mask, and basic flash dials to lock in the basic data

Courtesy of Eastman Kodak Company.

Step 3. Rotate the top dial and point *A* to the density step that produced an acceptable highlight dot (see figure C.1, density .20) from the main exposure test (figure C.5).

Step 4. Fasten the three wheels together with a piece of tape as illustrated in figure C.6. The three wheels are: (1) the green, main exposure wheel labeled *A*, (2) the flash mask wheel labeled *C*, and (3) the clear, basic flash dial.

Step 5. With all dials in the above positions, rotate tab *B* (controls main exposure time) until the proper main exposure (see figure C.1, 30 seconds) appears in the window opposite *A* (figure C.7). Secure tab *B* to the yellow base with tape (figure C.7).

The Q–15 Kodak Halftone Calculator is now calibrated to produce main and flash halftone exposures.

Figure C.7. Step 5: Placing the proper main exposure time in Window *A* Secure tab ***B*** **to the computer's base**

Courtesy of Eastman Kodak Company.

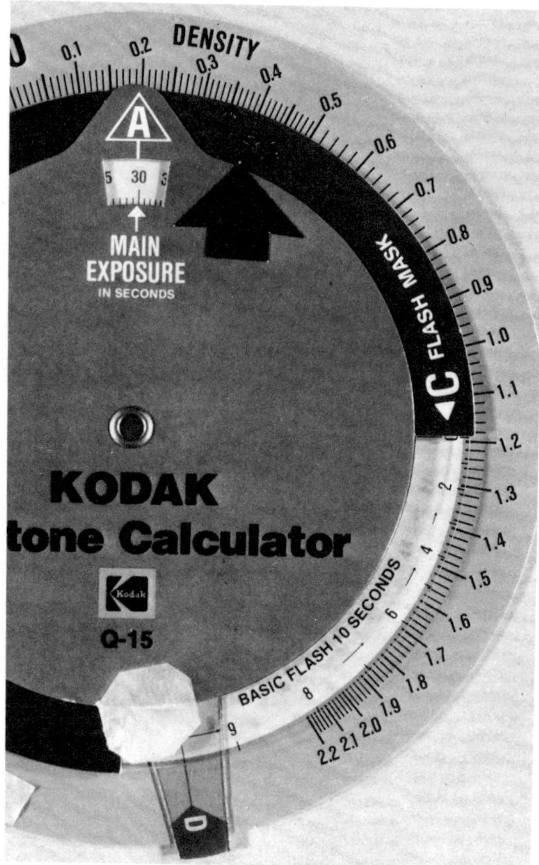

Figure C.8. Identifying the density step that produced a printable dot from a 5% bump

Courtesy of Eastman Kodak Company.

To calibrate for a bump or no-screen exposure, refer to the bump test negative and select the density step that produced a printable highlight dot (adding a 5% bump to our test negative produced a printable dot in density step .35). With the dials positioned to the calibrated settings, place a mark on the red flash mask *C* dial opposite this density step (figure C.8). To calibrate for other bump percentages, it is necessary to first make a test negative and repeat the above procedure. The calculator is now calibrated for determining bump exposures. Refer to chapter 7 for details on operation.

Appendix D

How to Use Basic Resources in the Graphic Arts to Locate Technical Information

There are many times when the student, manager, or technician needs to locate information about some aspect of the graphic arts but is at a loss as to how to find it. Perhaps a student has been assigned a research paper and needs to locate everything that has been published on a specific topic. A manager might want to read about a new system of production flow. The shop foreman might be having problems with some process and is trying to learn more about alternative approaches. Whatever the reason, locating information is a common problem, and unfortunately most people don't know how to solve it. The purpose of this appendix is to outline the procedures and resources available to help you find that information.

To begin any search, you need to get an idea of how much information is available on the subject. To do this, you need to have a quick overview. Any basic printing text (such as this one) can give you a summary of what is known in the field. Use the index to locate your topic in the book and then skim it for information. Then examine the bibliography for other basic works on the subject.

Another way to find an overview of a subject is to use one of the encyclopedia-like books on printing. *The Lithographers Manual*, published by the Graphic Arts Technical Foundation, is one example. It is brought up to date every five or six years and is a very technical treatment of every area of lithography. Use the index to find your information.

A more comprehensive approach is *The Printing Industry: An Introduction to Its Many Branches, Processes and Products* by Victor Strauss. It has sections on all phases of printing and is less technical than *The Lithographers Manual*. To date, only the first edition, published in 1969, is available. For each chapter a list of books is included for more detailed study.

If you find there are additional books that cover your area of concern, the next problem is to locate them. Many printers have them in their personal libraries. Almost any large library should have them as well. Some possibilities might be the library of a college or community college, a technical institute with a program in printing, the library of a large printing company, or a public library in a large city. Many small libraries can borrow books from larger ones, so if you can't find exactly what you are looking for, ask a librarian.

You may have enough information from the additional books you found in such sources as *The Printing Industry*. If you want more information, look in the card catalog in a library. Card catalogs can be difficult to use. One reason is that the word you think describes your topic might not be the word the cataloger used. Most large libraries use the same subject headings as the Library of Congress in Washington, D.C. Here are some useful headings from that system:

- Printing (used for general books about the whole industry)
- Printing, practical (used for books that are about technical aspects)
- Lithography (used for books concerned primarily with lithography for artists)

- Offset Printing (used for books that are about technical aspects of industrial lithography)
- Screen Process Printing (used for books that are about technical aspects of industrial screen printing)
- Serigraphy (used for books about screen printing for artists)

You might also find information under:

- Advertising
  layout and
  typography
- Book Industries and Trade
- Color Printing
- Color Separation
- Chromolithography
- Electrostatic Printing
- Flexography
- Handpress
- Intaglio Printing
- Linotype
- Map Printing
- Newspaper Layout and Typography
- Paper—Printing Properties
- Photolithography
- Printing Industry
- Printing on Plastics
- Proofreading
- Stereotyping
- Type and Type Founding
- Typesetting

If at any time you're having trouble finding what you need, be sure to ask a librarian for help. That's what librarians are there for!

There are over two hundred magazines concerned with printing in one form or another. Printing shops or schools may receive many of them. Sitting down and thumbing through many issues of magazines, however, is not an efficient way to obtain information. Indexes can be helpful. An index is a list of all the articles in a number of different magazines or journals. All the titles of articles that relate to the same subject are grouped together, with the name of the publication, date, and page number included for each one. Most indexes are compiled so that by looking in one book you will find everything under a subject heading that was published in a single year. The *Business Periodicals Index* indexes *Graphic Arts Monthly* and *Inland Printer/American Lithographer* (as well as a few other magazines concerned with publishing) and can lead you quickly to some technical information.

Graphic arts abstracting services are probably the best sources of technical information. An abstracting service tries to keep up with all the literature in a certain field. It indexes articles so you can find them and gives a summary (called an abstract) of the article so you can tell whether the article will actually be helpful to you.

Graphic Arts Literature Abstracts is published by the Graphic Arts Research Center (Rochester Institute of Technology, 1 Lomb Memorial Drive, Rochester, NY 14623). This service abstracts international as well as American sources and is a guide to and summary of current research. The Graphic Arts Technical Foundation (4615 Forbes Avenue, Pittsburgh, PA 15213) publishes *Graphic Arts Abstracts,* which abstracts both books and articles.

Figure D.1 shows a sample entry from *Graphic Arts Abstracts* that was found under the subject heading of "Stripping—Image Assembly." There is a great deal of information here. The title of the article is "Alternative Ways from Mechanical Paste-up to

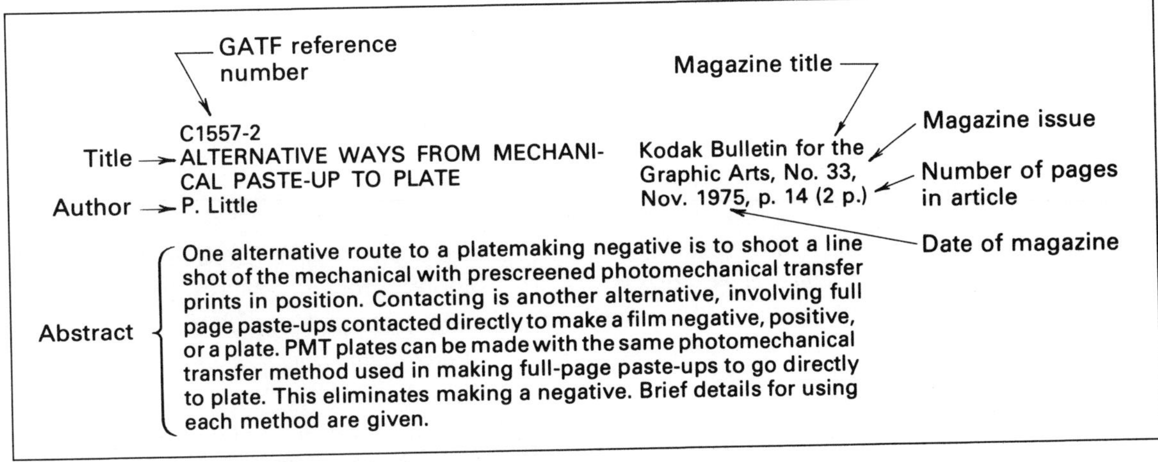

Figure D.1 A sample entry from *Graphic Arts Literature Abstracts*
(Courtesy of Graphic Arts Technical Foundation.)

Plate." It was written by P. Little. You can find the article on page 14 of the November 1975 issue of the *Kodak Bulletin for the Graphic Arts,* Number 33. The article is two pages long. Also included is a short paragraph that describes the scope and content of the material. The number "C1557–2" is a GATF reference number. If you cannot locate the publication, *Graphic Arts Abstracts* will send you a photocopy if you provide the reference number. *Graphic Arts Literature Abstracts* provides similar information and service.

In addition to using these publications as an index to find information, you can keep up with what is currently happening in the printing field by regularly reading the summaries and then reading the complete articles if you have time. The only difficulty with these abstracting services is the cost. Because they are highly specialized, only very large libraries or libraries that cater to the printing industry will have them.

Selected Bibliography

Advances in Printing Science and Technology. Vol. 1: *Printing Inks and Color;* Vol. 3: *Halftone Printing;* Vol. 4: *Paper;* Vol. 5: *Inks, Plates and Print Quality;* and Vol. 6: *Recent Developments.* Elmsford, N.Y.: Pergamon, 1964–1975.

Arnold, C. *Ink on Paper 2.* New York: Harper and Row, 1972.

Arnold, G. *Creative Lithography and How to Do It.* New York: Dover, 1941.

Bairey, E.H. *Fundamentals of Silk-Screen Process.* New York: Drake, 1970.

Biegeleisen, J.I. *Screen Printing.* New York: Watson-Guptil, 1971.

———. *The Complete Book of Silk Screen Printing.* New York: Dover, 1963.

———, and Cohen, J.A. *Silk Screen Techniques.* New York: Dover, 1958.

Birkner, H. *Screen Printing.* New York: Sterling, 1971.

Carlsen, E. *Graphic Arts.* Peoria, Ill.: Chas. A Bennett, 1965.

Carter, T.F., and Goodrich, L.C. *The Invention of Printing in China and Its Spread Westward,* 2nd ed. New York: The Ronald Press Company, 1925.

Caza, M. *Silk Screen Printing.* New York: Van Nostrand Reinhold, 1974.

Chambers, H.T. *Management of Small Offset Print Departments.* Boston: Cahners, 1969.

Cleeton, G.U., and Pitkin, C.W. *General Printing.* Bloomington, Ill.: McKnight, 1953.

Cogoli, J.E. *Photo-offset Fundamentals,* 4th ed. Bloomington, Ill.: McKnight, 1979.

Cumming, R.F., and Killick, W.E. *Single Color Lithographic Machine Operating.* Elmsford, N.Y.: Pergamon, 1969.

Davis, A. *Graphics: Design into Production.* Belmont, Calif.: Pitman, 1974.

Dennis, E.A., and Jenkins, J.J. *Comprehensive Graphic Arts.* Indianapolis: Howard W. Sams, 1974.

Eisenberg, J., and Kafka, F.J. *Silk Screen Printing.* Bloomington, Ill.: McKnight, 1957.

Eliot, B. *Silk-Screen Printing.* New York: Oxford University Press, 1971.

Gilson, T. *How to Screen Print on Cylindrical and Contoured Surfaces.* Cincinnati: Signs of the Times, 1970.

Goudy, F.W. *Alphabet and Elements of Lettering.* New York: Dover, 1922.

Gravure Technical Guide. New York: Gravure Technical Association, 1975.

Halpern, B.R. *Color Stripping.* Pittsburgh: Graphic Arts Technical Foundation, 1955.

———. *Tone and Color Composition.* Pittsburgh: Graphic Arts Technical Foundation, 1956.

———. *Offset Stripping—Black and White.* Pittsburgh: Graphic Arts Technical Foundation, 1958

Jaffee, E. *Halftone Photography for Offset Lithography.* Pittsburgh: Graphic Arts Technical Foundation, 1960.

Kagy, F.D. *Graphic Arts,* 2nd ed. South Holland, Ill.: Goodheart-Wilcox, 1979.

Karch, R.R. *Graphic Arts Procedures,* 4th ed. Chicago: American Technical Society, 1970.

Kosloff, A. *Mitography.* Beverly Hills, Calif.: Bruce, 1952.

———. *Ceramic Screen Printing.* Cincinnati: Signs of the Times, 1962.

———. *Screen Printing Electronic Circuits.* Cincinnati: Signs of the Times, 1968.

———. *Screen Printing Techniques.* Cincinnati: Signs of the Times, 1972.

Lasky, J. *Proofreading and Copy Preparation.* New York: Agathon, 1941.

Latimer, H.C. *Advertising Production Planning and Copy Preparation for Offset Printing,* 3rd ed. Norwalk, Conn.: Five Mile River Press, 1974.

The Lithographer's Manual, 4th ed. Pittsburgh: Graphic Arts Technical Foundation, 1979.

McMurtrie, D.C. *Book: The Story of Printing and Bookmaking,* 3rd ed. New York: Oxford University Press, 1943.

Marsh, R. *Silk Screen Printing.* New York: St. Martin's Press, 1974.

Moran, J. *Printing Presses: History and Development from the 15th Century to Modern Times.* Berkeley: University of California Press, 1973.

New York Times. *Style Book for Writers and Editors.* New York: McGraw-Hill, 1962.

Noemer, E.F. *The Handbook of Modern Halftone Photography.* Demarest, N.J.: Perfect Graphic Arts, 1965.

Polk, R.W., and Polk, E.W. *The Practice of Printing.* Peoria, Ill.: Chas. A. Bennett, 1964.

Raines, G. *How to Design, Produce and Use Business Forms.* Philadelphia: North American Publishing, 1972.

Reed, R.F. *Instruments for Quality Control.* Pittsburgh: Graphic Arts Technical Foundation, 1963.

———. *Offset Lithographic Platemaking.* Pittsburgh: Graphic Arts Technical Foundation, 1967.

Reinfeld, G. *Opportunities in Graphic Communications—The Printing Industry.* Louisville, Ky.: Vocational Guidance Manuals, 1971.

Rogers, J.R. *Linotype Instruction Book.* Brooklyn, N.Y.: Mergenthaler Linotype Company, 1925.

Roy, R.H. *Management of Printing Production.* Washington, D.C.: Printing Industries of America, 1953.

Senefelder, A. *A Complete Course of Lithography.* Reprint of 1819 edition. New York: DaCapo Press, 1968.

Shapiro, C., ed. *The Lithographers Manual,* 5th ed. Pittsburgh: Graphic Arts Technical Foundation, 1974.

Shokler, H. *Artists Manual for Silk Screen Print Making.* New York: Tudor, 1960.

Silver, G.A. *Printing Estimating.* Chicago: American Technical Society, 1970.

Southworth, M. *Color Separation Techniques.* Philadelphia: North American Publishing Company, 1974.

Spence, W.P., and Vequist, D.G. *Graphic Reproduction.* Peoria, Ill.: Chas. A. Bennett, 1980.

Strauss, V. *The Printing Industry.* New York: Bowker, 1967.

———. *Graphic Arts Management.* New York: Bowker, 1973.

Thomas, I. *The History of Printing in America.* Reprint of 1810 edition. New York: Weathervane Books, 1975.

Turnbull, A.T. *The Graphics of Communication: Typography, Layout, Design.* New York: Holt, Rinehart and Winston, 1975.

Zahn, B. *Screen Process Methods of Reproduction.* New York: Drake, 1970.

Glossary

Accordion fold. Several folds made parallel to each other.

Acetate sheet. Clear (or frosted) stable-base plastic material commonly used for overlays in paste-up.

Actinic light. Any light that exposes light-sensitive emulsions.

Actinic output. Energy that activates or hardens light-sensitive coatings; consists of shorter wave lengths of visible spectrum.

Additive colors. Colors that make up white light; red, blue, and green are the additive primary colors.

Additive plate. Presensitized lithographic plate on which ink-receptive coating must be added to exposed area during processing.

Additives. Compounds that control such ink characteristics as tack, workability, and drying time.

Adhesive binding. Fastening together of printed sheets or signatures with glue.

Agitation. Flow of solution back and forth over film during chemical processing.

Antihalation dye. Dye that is generally coated on back of most transparent-based film to absorb light that passes through emulsion and base during exposure.

Aperture. Opening through which light passes in the lens of a camera.

Ascender. Any portion of a letter that extends above the x-height.

Asphaltum. Tar-like material used as an acid resist in gravure printing.

Assembling. Finishing operations that bring together all elements of a printing job into final form; common operations are gathering, collating, and inserting.

Back-lighted copyboard. Equipment in some process cameras for photographing transparent copy; light is projected through the back of the copyboard and the lens to the new film.

Balance. Equilibrium of the visual images on a sheet.

Ballard shell process. Special technique used by many gravure publication printers for easy removal of copper layer after cylinder has been printed.

Basic density range (BDR). Range of detail produced from halftone screen by main exposure.

Basic exposure. Camera aperture and shutter speed combination that will produce a quality film image of normal line copy with standardized chemical processing.

Basic sheet size. Basis from which all paper weights are determined by the manufacturer; differs for each of the four paper classifications: book paper (25″ × 38″), writing paper (17″ × 22″), cover paper (20″ × 26″), and Bristol paper (22½″ × 28¼″).

Basis weight. Weight in pounds of one ream (500 sheets) of the basic sheet size of a particular paper type.

Baumé. Density scale used by Antoine Baumé, a French chemist, in graduating his hydrometers.

Bimetal plate. Plate manufactured with two dissimilar metals; one forms the ink-receptive image, and the other the solution-receptive area.

Blanket cylinder. Part of a rotary press that transfers the image from the plate cylinder to the press sheet.

Bleed. Extension of a printing design over the edge of a sheet.

Blueline flat. Special flat prepared as part of one multiflat registration system; carries all important detail, including register marks.

Blueprint. Inexpensive photomechanical proofing material; is exposed through the flat on a platemaker, developed in water, fixed in photographic hypo, and then washed to remove fixer stains.

Blue-sensitive material. Photographic material that reacts to the blue part of a white-light exposure.

Body-height. Distance from the base line to the top of a lowercase letter x in a given font; varies depending on alphabet design; also known as x-height.

Bone folder. Most common type of hand-folding device; consists of a long, narrow blade of bone or plastic.

Book paper. Most common type of paper found in the printing industry; available in a wide range of grades and noted for easy printability.

Bridge. Surface of a gravure cylinder between wells.

Bristol paper. Stiff, heavy material used for business cards, programs, file folders, inexpensive booklet covers, and the like.

Brownline. Inexpensive photomechanical proofing material; is exposed through the flat on a platemaker, developed in water, fixed in photographic hypo, and then washed in water to remove fixer stains; the longer the exposure, the more intense the brownline image.

Buckle folder. Paper-folding machine that operates by forcing a sheet between two rollers and causing it to curve.

Bump exposure. No-screen image exposure made through the lens; used to change contrast by compressing the screen range.

Burner film. Piece of transparent film that allows full passage of light to the cylinder when preparing a gravure mask.

Burnisher. Tool used to apply pressure to a small surface; usually has a long handle and a hard, smooth ball or point.

Cab. Special film mask used in gravure printing; is punched and marked to be used as a guide for stripping negatives prior to making a gravure cylinder.

Calendering. Paper-making process that passes paper between rollers to smooth or polish the paper surface.

California job case. Most popular case for holding foundry type; contains all characters in a single drawer.

Camera-ready copy. Finished paste-up used to create the images of the final job.

Cameron press. Web-fed printing machine used in book production; prints from rubber plates imposed on a flexible belt; designed to rapidly mass-produce an entire book.

Carbon arcs. Rods whose electromagnetic emission is heavy in blue and violet light; were commonly used as a light source for the graphic arts industry.

Carbon printing. Process of transferring the positive image to the cylinder mask in conventional gravure.

Carbon tissue. Gelatin-based material coated on a paper backing and used in gravure printing.

Carousel carrier. Multicolor screen printing equipment that holds individual screen frames, one for each color; rotates around a central axis and sequentially moves each screen into position over object to be printed.

Casebound cover. Rigid cover generally associated with high-quality bookbinding.

Center lines. Lines drawn on a paste-up in light-blue pencil to represent the center of each dimension of the illustration board.

Chain gripper delivery. Press delivery unit technique in which sheets are pulled onto the delivery stack by a mechanical system.

Characteristic curve. Visual interpretation of a light-sensitive material's exposure/density relationship.

Chase. Metal frame used to hold forms during relief plate making or printing.

Chaser method. Method of arranging furniture around a relief form when it is not a standard dimension.

Checking for lift. Procedure that checks all elements within a locked chase; determines whether they are tightly fixed in position and will not move or fall out during handling or printing.

Clip art. Art supplied in camera-ready form; copyright given with purchase; available from a number of companies that specialize in providing the service to printers.

Closed shop. Shop that requires craftspeople to join a union to maintain employment.

Coated paper. Paper with an added layer of pigment bonded to the original paper fiber surface to smooth out the rough texture.

Cold type composition. Preparation of any printing form intended to be reproduced photographically.

Collating. Finishing operation in which individual printed sheets are assembled into the correct sequence.

Collodion. Viscous solution of cellulose nitrates and ether and alcohol used as a coating for photographic plates.

Colloid. Any substance in a certain state of fine division.

Color sensitivity. Chemical change response in a particular silver halide emulsion to an area of the visible electromagnetic spectrum.

Color temperature. Measure of the sum color effect of the visible light emitted by any source.

Combing wheel. Type of sheet separator.

Commercial printing. Type of printing in which nearly any sort of printing job is accepted.

Common edge. Method of multiflat registration in which two edges of each flat are positioned in line with each other; if edges are lined up with corresponding edges of the plate, all images should be in correct position.

Complementary flats. Two or more flats

stripped so that each can be exposed singly to a plate but still have each image appear in correct position on final printed sheet.

Composing stick. Instrument in which foundry type is assembled in lines for printing.

Composition. Process of assembling symbols (whether letters or drawings) in the position defined on the rough layout during image design.

Comprehensive. Artist's rendering that attempts to duplicate appearance of final product.

Contact printing. Process of exposing a sheet of light-sensitive material by passing light through a previously prepared piece of film.

Continuous-sheet-feeding system. Technique on a press that adds sheets to the feeder system without stopping the press in the middle of a run.

Continuous-tone photograph. Image created from many different tones or shades and reproduced through photography.

Continuous-tone photography. Process of recording images of differing density on pieces of film; continuous-tone negatives show varying shades of gray or different hues of color.

Contrast. Noticeable difference between adjacent parts in tone and color.

Control strip. Piece of film used in automatic film processing to gauge the activity level of solutions in the machine; several times a day the photographer sends a preexposed control strip through the machine and then examines the processed piece to determine whether machine adjustments need to be made.

Conventional gravure. Method of preparing gravure cylinders that delivers well openings of exactly the same opening size.

Copy. Words to be included on a rough layout; final paste-up; or, in some situations, final press sheet.

Copyboard. Part of a process camera that opens to hold material to be photographed (the copy) during exposure.

Copy density range (CDR). Difference between the lightest highlight and the darkest shadow of a photograph or continuous-tone copy.

Counter. In gravure printing, angle between the doctor blade and the cylinder; in relief printing, sunken area just below the printing surface of foundry type.

Counting keyboard. Operator-controlled keyboard that requires end-of-line decisions as copy is being typed.

Cover paper. Relatively thick paper commonly used for outside covers of brochures or pamphlets.

Crash. Gauze-like material that is sometimes embedded in the perfect binding adhesive to increase strength.

Creasing. Process of crushing paper grain with a hardened steel strip to create a straight line for folding.

CRT (cathode ray tube) character generation. Third-generation typesetting system that generates images by utilizing a computer coupled with a cathode ray tube.

Ctn weight. Weight in pounds of one carton (ctn) of paper.

Cutting layout. Drawing that shows how a pile of paper is to be cut by the paper cutter.

Cylinder line. Area of a printing plate that

marks the portion used to clamp the plate to the plate cylinder; always marked on the flat before stripping pieces of film.

Dampening sleeves. Thin fiber tubes that, when dry, are slightly larger in diameter than the water form roller; when moistened, they shrink to form a seamless cover.

Dark printer. One of the halftones used to make a duotone; usually printed with the use of black or another dark color; often contains the lower middle tones to shadow detail of the continuous-tone original.

Darkroom camera. Type of process camera designed to be used under the safelights of a darkroom; can be either vertical or horizontal.

Dead form. Any form that has been printed and is waiting to be remelted or distributed (if hot type).

Decalcomania. Process of transferring designs from a specially printed substrate to another surface; products are sometimes called decals.

Deep-etch plate. Offset plate with the emulsion bonded into the base metal.

Delivery. Unit on a printing press that moves the printed sheet from the printing unit to a pile or roll.

Demon letters. In foundry type composition, lowercase *p, d, q,* and *b.*

Densitometry. Measurement of transmitted or reflected light with precision instruments and the expression of these measurements in numbers.

Density. Ability of a photographic image to absorb or transmit light.

Depreciation. Financial technique of spreading the cost of major purchases, such as equipment or a building, over several years.

Descender. Any portion of a letter that extends below the base line.

Design. Process of creating images and page layouts for printing production.

Developer. Chemical bath used to make the image on a light-sensitive emulsion visible and useful to the printer; some developers are used in the darkroom to process line film; others are used in proofing, plate making, stencil preparation in screen printing, and some areas of masking in gravure.

Developer adjacency effect. Underdevelopment caused by chemical exhaustion of small, lightly exposed areas when surrounded by large, heavily exposed areas.

Diagonal line method. Technique to determine size changes of copy.

Diaphragm. Device that adjusts the aperture, or opening size, in the camera lens.

Diazo. Light-sensitive material developed by exposing to ammonia fumes; also, a material used in one of the proofing processes.

Die cutting. Finished technique used to cut paper to shape.

Diffusion-etch process. Process used in gravure printing to transfer an image to a gravure cylinder; involves the preparation of a photomechanical mask that is applied to the clean cylinder; acid is used to eat through the varying depths of the mask into the cylinder metal.

Diffusion transfer. Photographic process

that produces quality opaque positives from positive originals.

Direct image nonphotographic plate. Short-run surface plate designed to accept images placed onto its surface with a special crayon, pencil, pen, typewriter ribbon, and the like.

Direct image photographic plate. Short- to medium-run surface plate exposed and processed in a special camera and processor unit; used mainly in quick print area of printing industry.

Direct/indirect process. Method of photographic screen printing stencil preparation in which stencil emulsion is applied to clean screen from precoated base sheet; when dry, base is removed and stencil is exposed and developed directly on fabric; see also **Photographic stencils.**

Direct process. Method of photographic screen printing stencil preparation in which stencil emulsion is applied wet to screen fabric, dried, and then exposed and developed; see also **Photographic stencils.**

Direct screen color separation. Color separation method that produces a color-separated halftone negative in a single step.

Direct transfer. Process used in gravure printing to transfer an image to a gravure cylinder by applying a light-sensitive mask to the clean cylinder; light is passed through a halftone positive as it moves in contact with the rotating cylinder; acid is used to eat through the varying depths of the mask into the cylinder metal after the mask has been developed.

Dominance. Design characteristic that describes the most visually striking portion of a design.

Dot area meter. Transmission or reflection densitometer designed to display actual dot sizes.

Dot etching. Chemical process used to change dot sizes on halftone negatives and positives.

Dot-for-dot registration. Process of passing a sheet through the press twice and fitting halftone dots over each other on the second pass.

Double dot black duotone. Reproduction of a continuous-tone original made by printing two halftones, both with black ink; its purpose, when compared with a halftone, is to improve quality in tone reproduction.

Drafting board. Hard, flat surface with at least one perfectly straight edge that is used to hold the board during paste-up.

Dressing the press. Process of placing standard packing on the platen of a press.

Drying time. Time it takes for something to dry or for liquid ink to harden.

Dry offset. Printing process that combines relief and offset technology; in dry offset, a right-reading relief plate prints onto an intermediate blanket cylinder and produces a wrong-reading image, and the wrong-reading image is then transferred to paper as a right-reading image.

Dry transfer. Cold type method of producing camera-ready images in which pressure-sensitive material carries a carbon-based image on a special transparent sheet; the image is transferred to the paste-up by rubbing the face of the sheet.

Ductor rollers. Any press roller that moves ink or water from the fountain to the distribution rollers.

Dummy. Blank sheet of paper folded in the same manner as the final job and marked with page numbers and heads; when unfolded, can be used to show page and copy positions during paste-up or imposition.

Duotone. Reproduction of a continuous-tone image that consists of two halftones printed in register and that adds color and quality to the image.

Duplicate plates. Relief plates made from a (master) form that was not intended to be used as a printing surface.

Duplicator. Any offset lithographic machine that makes copies and can feed a maximum sheet size of 11 by 17 inches.

Dynamic imbalance. Defect in the cylinder balance on a press such that the cylinder differs in density or balance from one end to the other.

Electric-eye mark. Mark added to the gravure cylinder as an image to be read by special electronic eyes to monitor registration.

Electromechanical engraving. Method of producing a relief plate by actually cutting an image into a material with a device that is electrically controlled.

Electromechanical process. Technique used in gravure printing to place an image on a gravure cylinder by cutting into the metal surface of the cylinder with a diamond stylus.

Electroplating. Process of transferring very small bits (called ions) of one type of metal to another type of metal.

Electrostatic assist. Licensed device (by the Gravure Research Association) that pulls ink from the cylinder wells in gravure printing by using an electronic charge.

Electrostatic transfer plate. Transfer plate produced by electrical charges that cause a resin powder to form on the image area; the powder is then fused and forms the ink-receptive area of the plate.

Electrotypes. High-quality duplicate relief plates made by producing a mold from an original form; the final printing plate, which is made from silver and copper or nickel, is then produced in the mold by an electrochemical exchange.

Embossing. Finishing operation that produces a relief image by pressing paper between special dies.

Em quad. Basic unit of type composition; physical size varies with the size of type being set (for 12-point type, an em quad measures 12 points by 12 points; for 36-point type, it measures 36 points by 36 points).

Emulsified. Condition in which something has become paste-like from contact with a highly acidic substance.

Emulsion. Coating over a base material that carries the light-sensitive chemicals in photography; emulsion in mechanical masking film and hand-cut stencil material is not light-sensitive.

En quad. Unit of type composition whose physical size varies with the size of type being set; two en quads placed together equal the size of the em quad for that size of type.

End sheets. The two inside sheets that hold the casebound cover to the body of the book.

Equivalent weight. Weight, in points, of one ream of regular size paper; see **Regular sizes.**

Evaporation. Conversion that occurs when a liquid combines with oxygen in the air and passes from the solution as a vapor.

Exacto knife. Commercial product with interchangeable blades.

Excess density. Density difference after the basic density range of the screen is subtracted from the copy density range (CDR).

Fake color. One-color reproduction printed on a colored sheet.

Fake duotone. Halftone printed over a block of colored tint or a solid block of color.

Feathering. Tendency of ink on a rough, porous surface to spread out.

Feeding. Action of a unit on a printing press that moves paper (or some other substrate) from a pile or roll to the registration unit.

Fillet. Internal curve that is part of a character in alphabet design.

Filmboard. Part of a process camera that opens to hold the film during exposure; a vacuum base usually holds the film firmly in place.

Film speed. Number assigned to light-sensitive materials that indicates sensitivity to light; large numbers (like 400) indicate high sensitivity; low numbers (like 6 or 12) indicate low sensitivity.

Final layout. See **Mechanical.**

Finish. Texture of paper.

Finishing. Operations performed after the job has left the press; common operations are cutting, folding, binding, and packaging.

Fit. Relationship of images both to the paper and, if multicolors, to each other; often confused with the term *registration,* which refers to position of the sheet.

Fixing bath. Acid solution that removes all unexposed emulsion in film processing; is the third step in the process and follows the developer and stop-bath; also called fixer.

Flare. Exposure problem caused by uncontrolled reflection of stray light passing through the camera's lens.

Flash exposure. Nonimage exposure made on the film through a halftone screen; regulates detail in the shadow area.

Flat. Assembled masking sheet with attached pieces of film; is the product of the stripping operation.

Flat bed cylinder press. Press designed so that the sheet rolls into contact with the typeform as a cylinder moves across the press.

Flat color. Ink the printer purchases or mixes to order for a specific job.

Flexography. Primarily a relief package printing method based on a combination of rubber plates, solvent-evaporating inks, and web printing.

Floppy disk. Small magnetic record used to capture keystrokes by recording electrical impulses; major advantage is instant data storage and retrieval.

Focal length. Distance from center of lens to filmboard when lens is focused at infinity.

Focusing. Process of adjusting the lens so reflected light from the object or copy will be sharp and clear on the film.

Fold lines. Lines drawn on a paste-up in light-blue pencil that represent where the final job is to be folded; small black lines are sometimes drawn at the edge of the sheet to be printed and used as guides for the bindery.

Font. Collection of all the characters of the alphabet of one size and series.

Form. Grouping of symbols, letters, numbers, and spaces that make up a job or a complete segment of a job (such as one page set to be printed in a book).

Formal balance. Design characteristic in

which images of identical weight are placed on each side of an invisible center line.

Form rollers. Any press rollers that actually contact the plate.

Fountain. Unit that holds a pool of ink and controls the amount of ink passed to the inking system on a press.

Four-color process printing. Technique using cyan, magenta, yellow, and black process inks to reproduce images as they would appear in a color photograph.

Franklin Printing Catalog. Privately published pricing guide for printers to use to determine average costs for nearly all operations or products.

French fold. Traditional paper fold made by first creasing and folding a sheet along its length and then making a second fold at a right angle to the first, across the width.

Frisket. Sheet of paper placed between two grippers to hold a press sheet while an impression is made; the form prints through an opening made in the frisket.

f/stop system. Mathematically based way of measuring aperture size in the lens of a camera; f/stop numbers predict the amount of light that will pass through any lens; moving from one f/stop number to another always either doubles the amount of light or halves it.

Furniture. Any line-spacing material that is thicker or larger than 24 points; used primarily in relief printing.

Furniture-within-furniture technique. Method of arranging furniture around a relief form when the form is of a standard furniture dimension.

Galley. Sheet-metal tray used to store hot type.

Galley camera. Type of process camera used in a normally lighted room; film is carried to the camera in a light-tight case, the exposure is made, and the case is carried to the darkroom for processing.

Galley proof. Proof taken from a hot type form on a device called a galley proof press.

Gathering. Finishing operation that involves assembling signatures by placing one next to the other.

Gauge pins. Mechanical fingers that hold sheets in position on the tympan of a platen press.

Glaze. Buildup on rubber rollers or blanket that prevents proper adhesion and distribution of ink.

Grain. Mechanical or chemical process of roughing a plate's surface; ensures quality emulsion adhesion and aids in holding solution in the nonimage area during the press run.

Grain long. Condition in which the majority of paper fibers run parallel to the long dimension of the sheet.

Grain short. Condition in which the majority of paper fibers run parallel to the short dimension of the sheet.

Graphic images. Images formed from lines.

Gravity delivery. Process in which sheets fall into press delivery stack simply by falling into place.

Gravure. Industrial intaglio printing in which an image is transferred from a sunken surface.

Gravure Technical Association. Professional organization that provides consultative assistance, technical materials, and a variety of services to the gravure industry.

Gravure well. Sunken portion of a gravure cylinder that holds ink during printing.

Gray scale. Continuous-tone picture of shades of gray used by graphic arts photographers to gauge exposure and development during chemical processing;

also known as step tablet or step wedge.

Grippers. Mechanical fingers that pull a sheet through the printing unit of a press.

Gripper margin. Area of paper held by mechanical fingers that pull sheet through printing unit of press.

Guillotine cutter. Device used to trim paper sheets; has a long-handled knife hinged to a large preprinted board, which can be used to accurately measure the size of each cut.

Halftone photography. Process of breaking continuous-tone images into high-contrast dots of varying shapes and sizes so they can be reproduced on a printing press.

Hand-cut stencil. Screen printing stencil prepared by manually removing the printing image areas from base or support material.

Hanger sheets. Major part of the packing on a platen press.

Hardening. Stage in ink drying when vehicle has completely solidified on paper surface and will not transfer.

Headstop. Mechanical gate that stops the paper on the registration unit of a press just before the gripper fingers pull the sheet through the printing unit.

Hickey. Defect on the press sheet caused by small particles of ink or paper attached to the plate or blanket.

Highlight area. Lighter parts of a continuous-tone image or its halftone reproduction.

Holding lines. Small red or black marks made on a paste-up to serve as guides for mounting halftone negatives in the stripping operation; are carried as an image on the film and are covered prior to plate making.

Horizontal process camera. Type of darkroom camera that has a long, stationary bed; film end is usually in the darkroom, and lights and lens protrude through a wall into a normally lighted room.

Hot type composition. Preparation of any printing form used to transfer multiple images from a raised surface; examples include Linotype, Ludlow type, foundry type, and wooden type.

Hypo. Fixing bath of sodium thiosulfate.

Illustration board. Smooth, thick paper material used in paste-up to hold all job elements.

Image assembly. Second step in the printing process; involves bringing all pieces of a job into final form as it will appear on the product delivered to the customer.

Image carrier preparation. Fourth step in the printing process; involves photographically recording the image to be reproduced on an image carrier (or plate).

Image conversion. Third step in the printing process; involves creating a transparent film image of a job from the image assembly step.

Image design. First step in the printing process; involves conceptual creation of a job and approval by the customer.

Image guidelines. Lines used in paste-up to position artwork and composition on illustration board; are drawn in light-blue pencil and are not reproduced as a film image.

Image transfer. Fifth step in the printing process; involves transfer of the image onto the final job material (often paper).

Imposing stone. Metal surface on which letterpress forms are arranged and locked into a chase or metal frame.

Imposition. Placement of images in position so they will be in desired locations on the final printed sheet.

Impression. Single sheet of paper passed through a printing press; is measured by one rotation of the plate cylinder.

Impression cylinder. Part of a rotary press that presses the press sheet against the blanket cylinder.

Incident light. Light that illuminates, strikes, or falls on a surface.

India ink. Special type of very black ink used for high-quality layout.

Indirect process. Method of photographic screen printing stencil preparation in which stencil is exposed and developed on a support base and then mounted on the screen; see also **Photographic stencils.**

Indirect relief. Process that involves transferring ink from a relief form to an immediate rubber-covered cylinder and then onto the paper; often called dry offset printing.

Indirect screen color separation. Color separation method that produces a continuous-tone separation negative; requires additional steps to produce color-separated halftone negatives.

Informal balance. Design characteristic in which images are placed on a page so that their visual weight balances on each side of an invisible center line.

Ink proofs. Press sheets printed on special proof presses, using the ink and paper of the final job; are extremely expensive and usually reserved only for high-quality or long-run jobs.

Ink train. Area from ink fountain to ink form rollers.

Ink viscosity. Measure of resistance to flow.

In-plant printing. Any operation that is owned by and serves the needs of a single company or corporation.

Inserting. Finishing operation that involves placing one signature within another.

Instant image proof. Proofing material that creates an image when exposed to light and does not require special equipment or chemicals.

Intaglio printing. Transferring an image from a sunken surface.

Job estimate. Document submitted to printing customers that specifies the cost of producing a particular job.

Job schedule. Schedule prepared for each printing job as it passes through each production step; shows how long each step should take and the order of movement through the shop.

Job scheduling and production control. Section of most printing companies that directs the movement of every printing job through the plant.

Justification. Technique of setting straight composition in which the first and last letters of each line of type fall in vertical columns.

Knife folder. Paper-folding machine that operates by means of a thin knife blade that forces a sheet of paper between two rotating rollers.

Laser cutting. Process used in gravure printing to transfer an image to a gravure cylinder by means of a laser that cuts small wells into a plastic surface on the cylinder; the finished plastic surface is then chrome plated.

Latent image. Invisible change made in film emulsion by exposure to light; development makes latent image visible to the human eye.

Lateral hard-dot process. Type of well design used in gravure printing in which a cylinder is exposed by using two separate film positives: continuous-tone and halftone.

Lateral reverse. Changing of a right-reading sheet of film to a wrong-reading one.

Lead. Thin line-spacing material used in hot type composition; is lower than type high and is generally 2 points thick.

Lead edge. Portion of a sheet that first enters the printing press; for sheet-fed automatic presses, the gripper margin is the lead edge.

Lens. Element of a camera through which light passes and is focused onto the film.

Letterpress. Process that prints from a raised or relief surface.

Lever cutter. Hand-operated guillotine paper cutter.

Ligature. Two or more connected letters on the same type body.

Light integrator. Means of controlling film exposure by measuring the quantity of light that passes through the lens with a photoelectric cell.

Light printer. One of the halftones used to make a duotone; is usually printed with a light-colored ink and often contains the highlight to upper-middle tones of the continuous-tone original.

Light table. Special device with a frosted glass surface and a light that projects up through the glass for viewing and working with film negatives and positives.

Line photography. Process of recording high-contrast images on pieces of film; line negatives are either clear in the image areas or solid black in the nonimage areas.

Line work. Any image made only from lines, such as type and clear inked drawings.

Linen tester. Magnifying glass used for visual inspection.

Lithography. Transfer of an image from a flat surface by chemistry.

Live form. Any form waiting to be printed.

Lockup. Process of holding a relief form in a frame or chase.

Logo. Unique design created to cause visual recognition of a product, service, or company.

Logotype. Two or more letters not connected but still cast on the same type body in relief printing.

Lowercase. Letters in the alphabet that are not capitals.

Magnetic tape. Tape that stores keystrokes by recording electrical impulses; is a faster and more practical method of information storage than paper tape.

Main exposure. Image exposure made through the lens and a halftone screen; records detail from the highlights or white parts of a photograph to the upper-middle tones; also called a highlight or detail exposure.

Make-ready. All preparation from mounting the image carrier (plate, cylinder, typeform, stencil) on the press to obtaining an acceptable image on the press sheet.

Mask. Any material that blocks the passage of light; is used in paste-up, stripping, and plate making; is generally cut by hand and positioned over an image; photomechanical masks used in color separation are produced in the darkroom.

Masking. Continuous-tone photographic image that is used mainly to correct color and compress tonal range of a color original in process color photography.

Masking sheets. Special pieces of paper or

plastic that block the passage of actinic light; are most commonly used in the stripping operation.

Master flat. In multiflat registration, the flat with the most detail.

Master plate. In gravure printing, a frame with register pins that hold the film positives in correct printing position during exposure to the cylinder masking material.

Mechanical. Board holding all elements of composition and artwork that meet job specifications and are of sufficient quality to be photographically reproduced; also called a paste-up, final layout, or camera-ready copy.

Mechanical line-up table. Special piece of equipment used in the stripping operation; comes equipped with roller carriages, micrometer adjustments, and attachments for ruling or scribing parallel or perpendicular lines.

Medium. Channel of communication; mass media are radio, television, newspapers, and magazines.

Mercury vapor. Popular light source for the graphic arts industry that operates when current passes through a mercury gas in a quartz envelope; a mercury vapor lamp emits massive peaks in the blue-violet and ultraviolet regions of the visible spectrum.

Metal halide. Recent development in light sources for the graphic arts; a metal halide lamp is a mercury lamp with a metal halide additive and is rich in blue-violet emissions.

Middle tone area. Intermediate tones between highlights and shadows.

Moiré pattern. Undesirable image produced when two different or randomly positioned screen patterns (or dots) are overprinted.

Molleton covers. Thin cloth tubes that slip over water form rollers.

Monofilament screens. Fabrics made from threads composed of a single fiber strand, such as nylon.

Multifilament screens. Fabrics made from threads composed of many different fibers, such as silk.

M weight. Weight of 1,000 sheets of paper rather than of a ream (500).

Mylar sheet. Clear (or frosted) stable-base plastic material commonly used for overlays in paste-up.

Negative-acting plate. Plate formulated to produce a positive image from a flat containing negatives.

Newage gauge. Gauge used to test hardness of copper.

News case. Container formerly used to store foundry type; upper case held capital letters, and lower case held small characters.

Nib width. Area of contact between impression roller and plate (or image) cylinder on any rotary press.

Noncounting keyboard. Keyboard that can capture operator keystrokes without end-of-line decisions.

Nonstandard cut. In paper cutting, manipulation of positions and order of cuts to gain an additional sheet; always produces press sheets with different grain direction.

Occasional typeface. One of the six type styles; includes all typefaces that do not fit one of the other five styles; also known as novelty, decorative, and other typeface.

OCR (optical character recognition) system. Optical scanning device that converts, stores, and/or outputs composition from special typewritten information.

Off-contact printing. Screen printing in which screen and stencil are slightly raised away from printing material; stencil touches stock only while squeegee passes over screen.

Offset. Press design in which an image is transferred from a plate to a rubber blanket that moves the image to the press sheet; offset principle allows plates to be right reading and generally gives a better-quality image than do direct transfers.

Offset lithographic press. Any machine that can feed sheets larger than 11 inches by 17 inches.

Offset paper. Paper intended to be used on an offset lithographic press; surface is generally smooth and somewhat resistant to moisture.

On-contact printing. Screen printing in which screen and stencil contact material throughout ink transfer.

Opaque. Liquid used to "paint out" pinholes on film negatives; also used as adjective meaning not transparent or translucent under normal viewing.

Opaque color proofs. Proofs used to check multicolor jobs by adhering, exposing, and developing each successive color emulsion on a special solid-base sheet.

Open shop. Shop that does not require craftspeople to join a union to maintain employment.

Optical center. Point on a sheet that the human eye looks to first and perceives as the center; is slightly above true, or mathematical, center.

Orthochromatic. Condition in which photographic materials are sensitive to all wave lengths of the visible spectrum other than red.

Oscillating distribution rollers. Press rollers in ink and water systems that cause distribution by both rotation and movement back and forth parallel to other rollers.

Overcoating. Protective coating placed on most transparent-based film to protect film emulsion from grease and dirt.

Overhead. Cost of operating a business without considering cost of materials or labor; typically includes cost of maintaining work space and equipment depreciation.

Overlay. Sheet of packing added under tympan sheet during make-ready; composed of built-up and cut-out areas to increase or decrease pressure on final press sheet.

Overlay sheet. Sheet often used in paste-up to carry images for a second color; clear or frosted plastic overlay sheet is hinged over the first color and carries artwork and composition for the second.

Oxidation. Process of combining with oxygen; in aerial oxidation, a solution or ink combines with oxygen in the air to evaporate.

Package printing. Printing service that prepares containers for consumer products; is one of three main subdivisions of gravure printing.

Packing. On hand-fed platen presses, material used to control overall impression; top packing sheet holds gauge pins that receive press sheet during image transfer.

Padding. Simplest form of adhesive binding and an inexpensive way of gluing together individual sheets to form notepads.

Panchromatic. Condition in which photographic materials are sensitive to all visible wavelengths of light plus some invisible wavelengths.

Pantone Matching System (PMS). Widely accepted method for specifying and mixing colors from a numbering system listed in a swatch book.

Paper lines. Lines drawn on paste-up board to show final size of printed piece after it is trimmed; are measured from center lines and are usually drawn in light-blue pencil.

Paper tape. Continuous band of paper (about 1″ wide) that stores keystrokes when punched; punched holes can then be read by other machines to output characters.

Paste-up. See **Mechanical.**

Patent binding. See **Perfect binding.**

Penetration. Drying of ink by absorption into substrate (usually paper).

Perfect binding. Common adhesive binding technique to glue together signatures into a book, usually a paperback; also known as patent binding.

Perfecting press. Press that prints on both sides of the stock (paper) as it passes through the press.

Perforating. Finishing operation in which slits are cut into stock so a portion can be torn away.

Photoelectric densitometer. Instrument that produces density readings by means of a cell or vacuum tube whose electrical properties are modified by the action of light.

Photoengraving. Relief form made by photochemical process; after being exposed through laterally reversed negative, nonimage portion of plate is acid etched, allowing image area to stand out in relief.

Photographic stencils. Screen printing stencils produced by use of a thick, light-sensitive, gelatin-based emulsion that is exposed and developed either on a supporting film or directly on the screen itself; the three types include direct, indirect, and direct/indirect stencils.

Photomechanical proofs. Proofs that use light-sensitive emulsions to check image position and quality of stripped flats; are usually exposed through the flat on a standard plate-making device.

Photopolymer plates. Plates formed by bonding a light-reactive polymer plastic to a film or metal base; polymer emulsion is hardened upon ultraviolet exposure; and unexposed areas are washed away, leaving image area in relief.

Photostat. Photographic copy of a portion of a paste-up; images are sometimes enlarged or reduced and then positioned on the board as a photostat; also called "stat."

Phototypesetting. Cold type composition process that creates images by projecting light through a negative and a lens and from mirrors onto light-sensitive material.

pH scale. Measure of acidity of a liquid; numeric scale is from 0 (very acid) to 14 (very alkaline, or a base); midpoint, 7, is considered neutral.

Pica. Unit of measurement used by printers to measure linear dimensions; 6 picas equal (approximately) 1 inch; 1 pica is divided into 12 points.

Picking. Offset press problem identified by small particles of paper torn from each press sheet and fed back into the inking system.

Pigment. Dry particles that give color to printing ink.

Pilefeeding. Method of stacking paper in feeder end of press and then operating press so that individual sheets are moved from top of pile to registration unit.

Pinholes. Small openings in film emulsion

that pass light; are caused by dust in the air during camera exposure, a dirty copyboard, or, sometimes, aciditic action in the fixing bath; must be painted out with opaque in the stripping operation.

Plate cylinder. Part of a rotary press that holds the printing form or plate.

Platemaker. Any machine with an intensive light source and some system to hold the flat against the printing plate; light source is used to expose the film image on the plate; most platemakers use a vacuum board with a glass cover to hold the flat and plate.

Plate-making sink. Area used to hand-process printing plates; usually has a hard, flat surface to hold the plate and a water source to rinse the plate.

Platen press. Traditional design used almost exclusively for relief printing; type form is locked in place and moves into contact with a hard, flat surface (called a platen) that holds the paper.

Plates. Thin, flexible aluminum sheets for lithographic printing; can be purchased uncoated and then sensitized at the printing plant or obtained presensitized and ready for exposure and processing; specific characteristics may vary depending on end use.

Plating bath. Solution used for electroplating.

Point. Unit of measurement used by printers to measure type size and leading (space between lines); 12 points equal 1 pica; 72 points equal 1 inch.

Polymerization. Chemical process for drying expoxy inks.

Positive-acting plate. Plate formulated to produce a positive image from a flat containing positives.

Posterization. High-contrast reproduction of a continuous-tone image; usually consists of two, three, or four tones and is reproduced in one, two, or three colors.

Preprinted paste-up sheets. Sheets commonly prepared for jobs of a common size and layout specifications; are printed with blue lines to help paste-up artist position composition and artwork.

Prepunched tab strips. Strips of film punched with holes and used to hold flat in place over pins attached to light table.

Pressboard. Hard, heavy sheet used as packing material when dressing a platen press.

Prewipe blade. Blade sometimes used in gravure printing to skim exess ink from cylinder.

Primary plates. Relief plates intended to be used as printing surfaces and capable of producing duplicate plates.

Printing. Permanent, graphic, visual communication medium; includes all the ideas, methods, and devices used to manipulate or reproduce graphic visual messages.

Printing processes. Relief, intaglio, screen, and lithographic printing.

Process camera. Large device used by graphic arts photographers to record film images; can enlarge or reduce images from the copy's original size and can be used to expose all types of film.

Process color. Use of ink with a translucent base that allows for creation of many colors by overprinting only four (cyan, magenta, yellow, and black).

Process color photography. Photographic reproduction of color originals by manipulation of light, filters, film, and chemistry.

Proof. Sample print of a job yet to be printed.

Proofing. Process of testing final stripped images from flat on inexpensive photosensitive material to check image position and quality.

Proportion. Design characteristic concerned with size relationships of both sheet size and image placement.

Proportionally spaced composition. Composition made up of characters that occupy horizontal space in proportion to their size.

Proportion scale. Device used to determine percentage of enlargement or reduction for piece of copy.

Publication printing. One of the three main subdivisions of gravure printing.

Publishing. Category of printing services that prepare and distribute materials such as books, magazines, and newspapers.

Pulsed xenon. Recently developed light source for the graphic arts; xenon lamps are made by filling quartz tubing with low-pressure xenon gas; output is similar to sunlight.

Punch-and-register pin. Method of multiflat registration in which holes are punched in the tail of the flat or in strips of scrap film taped to the flat; the punched holes fit over metal pins taped to light table surface and cause the flat to fall in correct position.

Quading out. Filling a line of type with spacing material after all characters have been set in a composing stick.

Quick printing. Printing operation characterized by rapid service, small organizational size, and limited format of printed product.

Quoins. Metal devices that hold or lock relief forms into chase.

Ream. Five hundred sheets of paper.

Reflectance. Measure of ability of a surface or material to reflect light.

Reflection densitometer. Meter that measures light reflected from a surface.

Register marks. Targets applied to the pasteup board and used in stripping, plate making, and on the press to ensure that multicolor images fit together in perfect register.

Registration. Unit on a printing press that ensures that sheets are held in the same position each time an impression is made.

Reglets. Thin pieces of wood used to fill small spaces and protect larger furniture from quoin damage during lockup.

Regular sizes. Sizes other than basic sheet size in which paper is commonly cut and stocked by paper suppliers.

Related industries. Category of printing services that includes raw material manufacturers (ink, paper, plates, chemicals), manufacturers of equipment, and suppliers that distribute goods or services to printers.

Relief printing. Transferring an image from a raised surface.

Reproduction proof. Proof taken from hot type composition and of such a quality that it can be photographically reproduced.

Resist. Material that will block or retard the action of some chemical.

Retouching pencil. Special pencil used by retouch artists to add detail or rapair continuous-tone images.

Reverse. Technique of creating an image by use of an open area in the midst of another ink image.

Right-angle fold. Any fold that is at a 90° angle from one or more other folds.

Right reading. Visual organization of copy

(or film) from left to right so that it can be read normally; see **Wrong reading.**

Rollup. Technique used to cover an area on a gravure cylinder for re-etching.

Roman. One of the six type styles; is characterized by variation in stroke and by use of serifs.

Rotary press. Press formed from two cylinders, one holding the typeform and the other acting as an impression cylinder to push the stock against the form; as the cylinders rotate, a sheet is inserted so an image will be placed on the piece.

Rotating distribution rollers. Press rollers in ink and water systems that cause distribution by rolling against each other; see **Oscillating distribution rollers.**

Rotogravure. Printing by the gravure process from a round cylinder.

Rough layout. Detailed expansion of thumbnail sketch that carries all necessary printing information to enable any printer to produce final reproduction.

Rubber cement. Semipermanent adhesive sometimes used to attach artwork or composition to paste-up board.

Ruler. Measuring device used to transfer linear dimensions; is available in both English and metric units.

Saddle binding. Technique of fastening together one or more signatures along folded or backbone edge of unit.

Safelight. Fixture used in the darkroom to allow the photographer to see, but not expose, film; color and intensity of safelight vary with type of film used.

Sans serif. One of the six type styles; is characterized by vertical letter stress, uniform strokes, and absence of serifs.

Scoring. Finishing operation that creases paper so it can be easily folded.

Screen mesh count. Measure of the number of openings per unit measure.

Screen printing. Transferring an image by allowing ink to pass through an opening or stencil.

Screen ruling. Number of dots per inch produced by a halftone screen or a screen tint.

Screen tint. Solid line screen capable of producing evenly spaced dots and of representing tone values of 3% to 97% in various line rulings.

Script. One of the six type styles; is characterized by a design that attempts to duplicate feeling of free-form handwriting.

Scumming. Offset press condition in which nonimage areas of the plate accept ink.

Self-covers. Covers produced from the same material as the body of the book.

Sensitivity guide. Transparent gray scale often stripped into a flat to be used as a means of gauging plate exposure; also used in one method of direct color separation.

Sensitometer. An instrument that exposes a step tablet or gray scale onto light-sensitive materials.

Series. Variations within a family of type; common series are bold, extra bold, condensed, thin, expanded, and italic.

Serif. One of three variables in alphabet design; refers to small strokes that project out from top or bottom of main character strokes.

Set. Ability of ink to stick to paper; properly set ink can be handled without smearing.

Set-off. Transfer of excess ink from one sheet to another when press is overinked.

Set width. Distance across nick or belly side of foundry type.

Shadow area. Darker parts of a continuous-tone image or its halftone reproduction.

Shaft. Center support of a press cylinder.

Sheet-fed press. Press that prints on individual pieces of paper rather than on paper from a roll.

Sheet off. Process of removing excess ink from ink rollers by carefully hand rolling a sheet of paper through the ink system and then removing it.

Sheet separators. Elements used in the press feeder unit to ensure that only one sheet is fed into the registration unit at a time.

Sheetwise imposition. Arrangement in which a single printing plate is used to print on one side of a sheet to produce one printed product with each pass through the press.

Shore durometer. Device to measure rubber hardness in units called durometers; the lower the rating, the softer the rubber.

Short-stop. See **Stop-bath.**

Shutter. Mechanism that controls the passage of light through the lens by opening and closing the aperture.

Shutter speed. Length of time the lens allows light to pass to the film; is adjusted by use of a shutter.

Side binding. Technique of fastening together pages or signatures by passing the fastening device through the pile at a right angle to the page surface.

Signature imposition. Process of passing a single sheet through the press and then folding and trimming it to form a portion of a book or magazine.

Single-edge razor blade. Tool used to cut and trim materials during paste-up.

Slipsnake. Fine, abrasive stone or hard rubber eraser used to remove images from plates.

Slug. Thick line-spacing material used in hot type composition; is lower than type high and is generally 6 points thick.

Slur. Condition in which an image is inconsistent in density and appears to be unsharp or blurred; is usually caused by platen press roller condition or adjustment.

Snap fitters and dowels. Method of multiflat registration in which adhesive dowels are attached to the light table surface; plastic snap fitters that fit over the dowels are stripped into the tail of the flat; exact image position can be controlled, since the flats will always fall in the same position on the dowels.

Soft covers. Book covers made from paper or paper fiber material with greater substance than that used for the body of the book but much less substance than binder's board.

Special purpose printing. Printing operation that accepts orders for only one type of product, such as forms work, legal printing, or labels.

Specialty printing. One of the three main subdivisions of gravure printing.

Spectral highlight. White portion of a photograph with no detail, such as the bright, shiney reflection from a metal object.

Spoilage allowance. Extra sheets delivered to the press to allow for inevitable waste and to ensure that required number of products are delivered to the customer.

Spot plater. Machine used to build up the metal in small areas on a gravure cylinder.

Square serif. One of the six type styles; is characterized by uniform strokes and serif shapes without fillets or rounds.

Squeegee. Device used to force ink through the stencil opening in screen printing; also used in plate making.

Stable-base jig. Exposed piece of stable-base film containing register marks, with a density between 0.7 and 1.0; used as a carrier for color transparencies during color separation process.

Stable-base sheet. Sheet that will not change size with changes in temperature.

Staging. Process of covering bare metal in gravure printing.

Staging solution. Solution used as a resist in the etching process; prevents dots or tones from being etched.

Stain. Black liquid used by retouch artists to add detail on continuous-tone images.

Standing form. Form that is never destroyed, melted down, or distributed so that it can at some time be reprinted.

Stat. See **Photostat.**

Static eliminator. Piece of copper tinsel mounted in delivery system to remove static electric charge that makes it difficult to stack individual sheets of paper.

Static imbalance. Defect in cylinder balance on a press that occurs when a cylinder is not perfectly round or has different densities within a cross section.

Stencil. Type of mask that passes ink in the image areas and blocks ink passage in nonimage areas.

Step-and-repeat plate making. Method of making identical multiple plate images on a single printing plate with one master negative; special machines move the negative to the required position, expose it, and then move it to the next location.

Step tablet. See **Gray scale.**

Step wedge. See **Gray scale.**

Stereotyping. Process of producing a duplicate relief plate by casting molten metal into a mold (or mat) made from an original lockup.

Stone proof. Proof taken from a form in hot type composition without the use of a machine.

Stop-bath. Slightly acidic solution used to halt development in film processing; is sometimes called the short-stop.

Straight composition. Composition in which the first and last letters of each line of type line up in vertical columns; also known as justified composition.

Stream feeder. Press element that overlaps sheets on the registration table; allows registration unit to operate at a slower rate than the printing unit and gives better image fit.

Stress. One of three variables in alphabet design; refers to distribution of visual "heaviness" or "slant" of the character.

Strike-on composition. Cold type method of producing images by striking a carrier sheet with a raised character through an ink or carbon ribbon.

Stripping. Process of assembling all pieces of film containing images that will be carried on the same printing plate and securing them on a masking sheet that will hold them in their appropriate printing positions during the plate-making process.

Stroke. One of three variables in alphabet design; refers to thickness of lines that actually form each character.

Subjective balance. Design characteristic in which images are placed on white space in such a way as to create a feeling of stability.

Substance weight. Weight in pounds of one ream of the basic sheet size (17″ × 22″) of one particular type of writing paper.

Substrate. Any base material used in printing processes to receive an image transferred from a printing plate; common substrates are paper, foil, fabric, and plastic sheet.

Subtractive plate. Presensitized lithographic plate with ink-receptive coating applied by the manufacturer; nonimage area is removed during processing.

Subtractive primary colors. Colors formed when any two additive primary colors of light are mixed; subtractive colors are yellow, magenta, and cyan; yellow is the additive mixture of red and green light; magenta is the additive mixture of red and blue light; cyan is the additive mixture of blue and green light.

Successive-sheet-feeding system. Most common form of press-feeding system; feeder unit picks up one sheet each time the printing unit prints one impression.

Sucker foot. Element used in the press feeder unit to pick up individual sheets and place them into the registration unit.

Surprint. Technique of printing one image over another.

Tack. Characteristic of ink that allows it to stick to the substrate (usually paper).

Technology. Any concept (or group of concepts) that extends or amplifies the ability to meet a human need.

Text. One of the six type styles; is characterized by a design that attempts to recreate the feeling of medieval scribes.

Thermoplastic. Condition in which a material is capable of being heated and re-

Thermosetting. Condition in which a material is not capable of being reformed after hardening and curing.

Three-cylinder principle. Most common configuration for most offset lithographic presses; the three cylinders are plate, blanket, and impression.

Thumbnail sketch. Small, quick pencil renderings that show size relationships of type, line drawings, and white space as the first step in the design process.

Tinting. Offset press problem identified by slight discoloration over entire nonimage area, almost like a sprayed mist.

Tones. Values of white, black, or color.

Tool. Extension of human abilities.

Tooth. Roughening of the threads of monofilament screen fabrics to increase the stencil's ability to hold on to the fabric; is applied prior to mounting a stencil.

Trade shop. Printing operation that provides services only to other printers.

Transfer lithographic plate. Plate formed from a light-sensitive coating on an intermediate carrier; after exposure, an image is transferred from the intermediate carrier to the printing plate.

Transmission densitometer. Meter that measures light passing through a material.

Transmittance. Measure of the ability of a material to pass light.

Transparent-based image. Any image carried on a base that passes light; transparent-based sheets can be seen through.

Transparent color proofs. Proofs used to check multicolor jobs; each color is carried on a transparent plastic sheet, and all sheets are positioned over each other to give the illusion of the final multicolor job.

Trapping. Ability of one ink to cover another.

Triangle. Instrument used to draw right-angle lines with a T-square; is also available in a variety of angles, such as 30°, 45°, and 60°.

Trim lines. Lines often added to a paste-up in black india ink so they will reproduce on the final job; are used to guide paper cutter in trimming the paper pile.

T-square. Instrument used to draw parallel lines.

Tusche. Lithographic drawing or painting material of the same nature as lithographic ink.

Tusche-and-glue. Artist's method of preparing a screen printing stencil by drawing directly on the screen fabric with lithographic tusche and then blocking out nonimage areas with a water-based glue material.

Two-cylinder principle. Offset lithographic duplicator configuration that combines the plate and impression functions to form a main cylinder with twice the circumference of a separate blanket cylinder.

Tympan sheet. Top oil-treated packing sheet that holds the gauge pins; often referred to as a drawsheet.

Typeface. Alphabet design used in a printing job.

Type family. Unique combination of stroke, stress, and serif created and named by a typographer; is generally made up of many different series.

Type high. Distance from the face to the feet of hot type; for English-speaking countries, type high is 0.918 inch.

Type-high gauge. Device that measures 0.918, or type high, is used to accurately adjust relief press form rollers to evenly touch the form.

Type specifications. Directions written on rough layout that informs compositor about alphabet style, series, size, and amount of leading or space between lines.

Type style. Grouping of alphabet designs; the six main type styles are roman, sans serif, square serif, text, script, and occasional.

Typographer. Craftsperson who designs typefaces.

Uncoated paper. Paper is made up merely of raw interlocking paper fibers; see **Coated paper.**

Underlay. Piece of tissue or paper pasted under the form in areas light in impression.

Unity. Design characteristic concerned with how all elements of a job fit together as a whole.

Uppercase. Capital letters in the alphabet.

Vehicle. Fluid that carries ink pigment and causes printing ink to adhere to paper or some other substrate.

Velox. Prescreened halftone print used to mount on a paste-up board; looks like a regular photographic print but has been broken into small dots for reproduction.

Vertical process camera. Type of darkroom camera that is contained entirely in the darkroom; is a self-contained unit that takes up little space because the filmboard, lens, and copyboard are parallel to each other in a vertical line.

Vignetted screen pattern. Pattern made up of gradually tapering density and found in halftone screens; produces the variety of dots found in a typical halftone reproduction.

Viscosity. See **Ink viscosity.**

Visual densitometer. Instrument that helps the operator to measure density by visual comparison.

Wax coater. Device used to place a thin layer of wax over the back of a piece of artwork or composition so that the copy can be repositioned any number of times.

Web-fed press. Press that prints on a roll of paper.

Wedge spectrogram. Visual representation of a film's reaction to light across the visible spectrum.

Wet-on-wet printing. Printing of one color directly over another without waiting for the ink to dry.

Window. Clear, open area on a piece of film created on the paste-up by mounting a sheet of black or red material in the desired location.

Wipe-on metal plate. Surface, pregrained metal plate coated at the printing plant with a diazo type of emulsion.

Work-and-tumble imposition. Printing on both sides of a sheet, with the tail becoming the lead edge for the second color by turning the pile for the second pass through the press.

Work-and-turn imposition. Printing on both sides of a sheet, with the same lead edge for both passes through the press.

Work order. Production control device that carries all information about a particular printing job as it passes through each step of manufacturing.

Writing paper. High-quality paper originally associated with correspondence and record keeping; is considered the finest classification of paper, except for some specialty items.

Wrong reading. Backwards visual organization of copy (or film) from right to left; see **Right reading.**

x-height. Distance from the base line to the top of a lowercase letter x in a given font; varies depending on the particular design; also known as body-height.

Zeroing. Setting or calibrating a densitometer to a known value.

Index